H.Freudenberger

The Economic Development of Continental Europe
1780–1870

68–70 Sum –

Some other works by the same authors

S. B. Saul

The Myth of the Great Depression in England
(Macmillan, 1969)
Studies in British Overseas Trade
(Liverpool University Press, 1960)
Technological Change: The United States and Britain in the Nineteenth Century
(editor) (Methuen, 1970)
Social Theory and Economic Change (editor with Tom Burns)
(Tavistock, 1967)

A. S. Milward

The Economic Effects of the World Wars on Britain
(Macmillan, 1970)
The New Order and the French Economy
(Clarendon Press, 1970)
The Fascist Economy in Norway
(Clarendon Press, 1972)
The German Economy at War
(Athlone Press, 1965)

The Economic Development of Continental Europe

1780–1870

BY
ALAN S. MILWARD
AND S. B. SAUL

LONDON. GEORGE ALLEN & UNWIN LTD
RUSKIN HOUSE   MUSEUM STREET

First published in 1973

Vol 1   ISBN 0 04 330229 7 hardback
         ISBN 0 04 330230 0 paperback

Printed in Great Britain
in 10 point Times Roman type
by Unwin Brothers Limited
Old Woking, Surrey

Preface

We began to write this book together because we had both taught the subject for many years and thought that there was a real need for a textbook in English setting out and analysing in some detail the work that has been done on the modern economic history of continental Europe. We knew that we could not claim to be experts in all the fields we had to cover but we felt that this would be more than offset by the opportunity to compare experiences within Europe and to offer a consistent approach to our problems.

We omitted Britain deliberately, although we have not assumed that the reader has a prior knowledge of British, or of any other, economic history. We felt that with so many texts available on the economic history of that country there was very little we could hope to add and that we would rather use our space on problems and areas where the literature was much sparser. There was another reason for omitting Britain. No one who teaches the economic history of continental Europe can fail to notice how most of the available material in English is written from an English, or an American, point of view. The economic history of continental European countries often appears in a perspective in which the significant features are those which differ from the history of Britain or the United States. We hope that by putting the economic development of the Continent itself in the forefront of the picture the perspective will be less distorted.

As we got into the work our interest and excitement developed and the book steadily lengthened. Yet we were reluctant to cut back because we found so much that is not easily available to students. Eventually it became obvious that we had written more than a single volume, although we have to admit that no entirely logical division of the subject matter has been achieved. In the main the present work relates to Western Europe to 1870, though the single chapter on Scandinavia goes up to 1914. In our later volume will be found all our work on Eastern and Southern Europe, as well as the conclusion of the studies of France and Germany. The more general chapters are spread between the two in their appropriate order. Originally we started with a chapter setting out our general ideas on the nature of growth and development. We then decided that it would be much more logical to re-write this altogether, to place our ideas in the context of the detailed studies of particular regions and, inevitably, to make it the conclusion of our work.

The book started as a textbook and that is what it remains. It is not a work of research, though sometimes we have had to look long and hard for our secondary sources, and for that reason we have deliberately avoided a great apparatus of footnotes. Since the book is designed specifically for English-speaking students we have referred only to a few important books of general significance in other languages in our reading lists, though we have tried to indicate where further references to works in foreign languages can be found.

All our measurements are metric. We give a table of exchange rates for currencies for periods where these were stable enough for comparisons to be meaningful. Except where in everyday usage there is an English name for a foreign town or region we use the contemporary name and if the modern name is different we put it in brackets afterwards. Our motive in deciding to use the contemporary rather than the modern name is no more than the practical one that so many states and provinces have disappeared and have no exact modern equivalent. To decide such a question either way is to offend linguistic nationalism and political sentiments. We hope our decision will be taken as a purely pragmatic one; it certainly has no other significance for us.

We were fortunate that a combination of circumstances, including a Ford Fellowship for one of us, brought us together for a year in Stanford University. We were even more fortunate in the development of our co-operation. At first we viewed the work as two separate contributions joined together in one volume and divided the work between ourselves accordingly. In the event, we criticised each other's drafts so thoroughly, discussed the issues so frequently and interfered so helpfully in each other's work that this is a joint book in a far truer sense than we ever intended. Well-cherished prejudices and interesting, but unlikely, theories have had to be given up in the face of the historical evidence which such a book accumulates. The starting point of each chapter, however, was that one of us was responsible for collecting the material and producing the final version. In this volume Milward did this for Chapters 1, 4, 5, 6 and 7 and Saul for Chapters 2, 3 and 8.

So many people help, very often quite unconsciously, in producing a book of this kind that it is not really possible to mention them all. The students of the University of Edinburgh, of the University of East Anglia, and of Stanford University, with whom so many of these ideas have been discussed so often have played a big part in its formulation. In addition to them we would particularly like to thank Professor M. Abramovitz, Bill Albert, Professor Paul David,

Professor Scott M. Eddie, Professor M. W. Flinn, Joe Harrison, Professor T. C. Smout, Claudine Milward and Sheila Saul. Irene Brooks, Moira McIntyre and Mrs S. Simpson gave us excellent and indispensable secretarial help. The maps were drawn by Barbara Morris and we would like to thank her for her help and cooperation.

Contents

Contents of An Economic History of Continental Europe, 1850–1914

Maps

Table of Measurements

hectare	2·471 acres
metric ton	2204 lb
kilometre	0·621 miles
kilogram	2·204 lb
hectolitre	22·0 imperial gallons (liquid measure)
	2·75 imperial bushels (cereal measure)
Russian pood	36 lb
verst	0·66 miles
dessiatine	2·7 acres
tchetvert	5·77 imperial bushels

Ton is used throughout to mean metric ton. 1 quintal = 100 kg,

m = million
km = kilometre
ha = hectare

Exchange Rates against Sterling, 1913

The following is a list of rates applying in 1913. In Sweden, Denmark, Holland, Germany, Belgium and France these rates had been stable for the previous forty years. The other rates had varied from time to time.

Norway krone ⎫	
Denmark krone ⎬	18
Sweden krona ⎭	
Russia ruble	9·55
Germany mark	20
Holland gulden	12
France ⎫	
Belgium ⎬ francs	25
Switzerland ⎭	
Spain peseta	25
Italy lira	25
Austria krone ⎫	24
Hungary korona ⎭	
Bulgaria lew	25
Serbia dinar	25
Romania leu	25

Introduction

Although the title of our book is as straightforward as it could be it is perhaps still capable of raising wrong expectations. It is only fair to say what exactly we are trying to explain and expound. Our ultimate purpose is to help to explain the changes in European society over the last two hundred years. A society based on agriculture has been replaced by one based on industry and commerce, and in the process society has become wealthier and acquired a completely new set of institutions, of ideas and of capital equipment. Its levels both of production and of consumption are far higher and this has, in the main, been the result, not of harder work, but of a different organisation of economic activity.

This is, or should be, the underlying theme of all modern history. And in presenting it as our own main theme we are only doing what the first scholars to use the phrase 'economic history' also did. They were discontented with the existing state of historical studies because they felt that the subjects which historians concerned themselves with at that time, and also the way in which those subjects were handled, meant that history was no longer adequately explaining the changes that had taken place in society. By extending the range of historical studies to include the problems of economic existence, of production and of consumption, and by using the theoretical framework of economics, economic historians hoped to provide a fuller explanation of what had happened. Although our book deals in detail with several very specialised topics it does so in order to throw more light on the problem of social change, of the evolution of one type of society from another.

For that reason it begins with a description of European society in the eighteenth century and of its modes of production. Our starting-point has to be an arbitrary one because we are concerned with the problem of change, and modern European society was always changing rapidly. By taking the society of eighteenth-century Europe, 'the old régime' as French writers called it after the French Revolution, as our starting-point, we are able to deal with most of the more important developments in economic life in the subsequent period. But even in the mid-eighteenth century some western European countries had already experienced substantial economic development and social change and some of the explanations of what happened after the mid-eighteenth century are only to be found by studying an earlier period. Our book had to begin somewhere and where the explanations for what happened lie in the period before our beginning we hope we have indicated this. Any study of the period after 1780 can only show how important to western Europe the earlier period was. For example, the crude calculations of relative levels of income in different countries in the past which are possible indicate that at the end of the eighteenth century countries like France, Belgium and Germany had levels of per capita income about one-third higher than Japan in 1920 and over twice as high as China in 1935. For this to be so these western European countries must already have gone some way along the path of economic development before our starting-point. The process of economic development is a very long run one and often needs a long historical explanation.

But the starting-point we have chosen has also been chosen by other scholars because it is the starting-point of the changes in the British economy and in British society known as 'The Industrial Revolution', a phenomenon often seen as the very basis of the modern European world. We are not writing about Britain, but the particular changes there which have been called 'The Industrial Revolution' had such an enormous impact on other European countries that they do mark a turning-point in European history generally. By changing the scope of production they seem to have increased the speed of social change, and their impact on continental Europe was as significant in this respect as in Britain. The coincidence in time between these changes and the social and political changes spreading from the events of the French Revolution finally persuaded us that we must begin our analysis with a study of the European economy immediately before these two events did speed up the process of change.

But while it tries to explain this general phenomenon of economic and social change this book is particularly and closely concerned with one aspect of this: the way in which economic development took place, the forces that contributed to it, the obstacles that impeded it, and the reasons why economic development occurred in different parts of Europe at different times and at different speeds. We are in fact writing particularly about two things, economic development and economic growth. Economic development is a concept very familiar to the present day. The development of the available resources in any society, of labour, capital and raw materials, and their deployment in a more productive way we see as the very basis of change in modern society. For that reason we would claim that the study of economic development explains more of the changes in the countries we are considering than the study of any other single phenomenon. The concept of economic growth is a more limited one and for that very reason harder to define.

dev. + growth differentiated

For most purposes economic growth may be defined as a sustained increase in income per head of the population. But for most of our period in most of the places we cover there was a marked increase in population and where this increasing population was maintained at the same income level as earlier that might well be considered by some as economic growth also. We have not used economic growth to include that particular state, but it may be as well to bear in mind that population growth almost always went with increases in per capita incomes in our period. These two questions are by no means independent and we have considered the links between them in Chapter 2. Economic growth might also be defined as a sustained increase in the output of material goods per head. As a historical fact it has usually involved not merely the output of a greater quantity of material goods per head but also an increase in their range and type. In order to achieve economic growth sweeping structural changes are usually necessary in an economy. Only for relatively short periods and in very uncommon circumstances is economic growth possible by only intensifying the existing pattern of economic activity. In Denmark the process of economic growth depended more on the intensification of agricultural activity than in most other European economies but the section dealing with Denmark in Chapter 8 shows that growth there was not long confined to this process of intensification. Like economic development, economic growth necessarily requires and produces social change on a vast scale.

Economic growth is sometimes discussed as though it were an increase in economic welfare per head if welfare is defined as those services and goods normally exchanged for money, including, of course, leisure. But we have sought deliberately to avoid all value judgments on whether or not economic growth or economic development are in themselves good or bad. We are concerned with explaining why and how they occurred. In any case economic growth involves very considerable changes in what we may call the quality of life. It follows that output per head may increase when it bears no relationship to welfare and, as a corollary, welfare may be increased by things which are not provided for money. Furthermore it is possible, and there are historical examples in our period, for welfare in this sense to be improved without any change in output. It can simply be redistributed, as it was in the French Revolution.

Economic growth is much more susceptible to precise measurements than economic development. But although we have considered it as an objective phenomenon which we want to explain we have not considered it simply and entirely as the sum of certain measurable economic factors. For example the relationship between the capital stock in a country and its annual output can be calculated within a reasonable level of accuracy after 1870 for several of the countries with which we deal. So also can the amount of capital theoretically required to produce a given increase in national output. There is a close and fixed relationship between this proportion and the amount of its net income that a country invests and the annual rate of growth of output. But in reality increasing investment proportions did not in fact result in a proportionate increase in the rate of growth. Partly this was because developing countries needed to be provided with social overhead capital, transport systems, post offices and so on. Partly it was because the machinery developed in the early period of industrialisation saved labour while using more capital for each given quantity of output. Labour could be combined with capital in different proportions and in each of the societies we deal with the judicious entrepreneur would combine them in different proportions because the balance of economic factors was different in each of these societies. It is needless to elaborate further. In spite of the apparent mathematical simplicity of these relationships their real historical relationship was determined by the complex interaction of a variety of factors. These other factors, like the stock of capital, although they too can sometimes be measured with considerable accuracy, have meaning only within the full context of the social and economic environment in which they are employed, and, however precisely defined, economic growth also refers ultimately to the wider process of economic and social change. To put the matter more simply an essential element in economic growth is that it be sustained over time. Over that time the factors which we use to define it are themselves altered in meaning by the process of change.

By concentrating our efforts on why and how economic development and economic growth took place in continental Europe we have given little attention to some other subjects which usually occupy more space in textbooks of economic history. We do not wish to suggest by this that they are not important, only that they are less relevant to our theme. The study of economic history can be divided into two general areas. The first is the question of how much and why nations' incomes have changed over time; the second is the question of the uses to which these resources have been put. The first is concerned with production; the second with consumption. Our main concern in this book has been with the first. Consequently there is relatively little in this book about labour history, the history of trade unions, or the history of social and welfare legislation.

It is not possible to make this divorce between production and consumption absolute because the changes in consumption which are brought about by changes in production themselves often cause further changes in production. The most obvious structural change in economies in the process of development is a shift in the emphasis of production from the agricultural sector of the economy to the manufacturing sector, so that the process of development has come to be almost synonymous with the process of industrialisation. Agriculture provided about one half of the net national income of France between 1825 and 1835 and about one-third between 1908 and 1910. The increased number of non-agricultural workers and, usually, of urban dwellers which resulted from similar developments in many countries raised the internal demand for foodstuffs. As incomes grow the rise in demand for manufactured goods and services is likely to be proportionately greater than that for foodstuffs, but there will be some increase in demand for food. This demand on the agricultural sector was usually made more noticeable in our period by the fact that population was also increasing in numbers at the same time as its employment was changing. A poor response to this demand from the agricultural sector would either raise food prices and increase the costs of industrial development or lead to imports of foodstuffs and a possible worsening of the international terms of trade, that is to say that import prices would rise relative to export prices. The success with which these consumption problems were solved affected the degree to which further changes in production could take place. Furthermore manufacturing industry usually proved more capable of improving its productivity than agriculture and the rewards to those employed in it were often higher. There were inherent forces in the process of economic development which redistributed income within society and the extent of further changes in production was fundamentally affected by this redistribution.

Indeed the question of the distribution of income seems to us to be a topic of central importance even in a book slanted, as this one is, towards the history of production. Unfortunately it is also the most neglected topic in economic history. The fact that it is so neglected has hampered us at every turn and if we have little to say on this subject we are faithfully but unwillingly reflecting the silence of our precursors. Further research in this direction would confirm or rebut many of the more tentative arguments advanced in this book.

So much for the general approach of the book and the reasons for the balance of its contents. There are two other assumptions we have made to which it is only fair to draw attention.

One was that a national framework was, for most of the topics we are dealing with, more appropriate than an international one. Before 1914 most European countries still had highly individual political and social systems and their economic development was very much determined by these particularities. The 'international economy' was still in an embryonic stage before the First World War. Where we have discussed movements of population, of capital and of technology and where we have discussed the mechanisms of international trade or of political events of an international scope such as the French Revolution and the Continental System, we have done so in an international context. Otherwise, our assumption was that the nation state had such a great influence on economic development that our book still had to be built on a skeleton of national economic histories.

The second was that no particular theory of economic development would be wide enough to marshall suitably all the historical evidence which we wished to assemble. It may be that so pragmatic an approach will offend some readers, but it was also part of our desire to remain as neutral as possible and to try to explain, historically, what had occurred. The assumptions contained in our arguments and explanations are drawn from different theories of development, and the more the evidence from different countries accumulated the more we felt we were right to be so eclectic. However, we are not trying to dodge conclusions where they follow from the evidence, they are presented in the concluding chapter of Volume 2. The reader who wishes to become more familiar with the theories of development which have been advanced will find them more fully referred to in that chapter.

Finally, why end our work in 1914? Mainly because the dimensions in which development can be discussed are different after the First World War. Before that event the framework of economic development was what we now call 'capitalist'. After the Russian Revolution there was another and very different possible framework for development which came to have a great influence on developing countries, not least in Europe itself. Before the Russian Revolution there is a certain unity. The leaders of the Russian Revolution based their historical theories on the history of economic development elsewhere in Europe and deliberately sought to bring about a type of economic development of which the end result would be a new and better society. Possibly the least important result of this was to cause us to end our book where we did. The First World War also marks a rapid development towards a stage when the workings of the international economy become at least as important to the development of many of the countries we are considering as their own national economies. In this sense too it begins a different period needing to be written about in a different way. We think the period we have chosen does have a certain unity and we hope it will prove a suitable one to illuminate our themes.

Chapter 1

The European Economy in the late Eighteenth Century

EUROPE AND THE INDUSTRIAL REVOLUTION IN GREAT BRITAIN

An increase in the volume of production in the British Isles, sustained with few interruptions throughout the eighteenth century, increased much more rapidly in the last few decades of that century. Changes in the organisation and techniques of production, which had already been developing for a long time, burst into greater prominence in an efflorescence of technological invention, and the widespread social and economic changes which came as a consequence produced the expression 'Industrial Revolution'.

The description of these events as a 'revolution' is justified on every ground because the technological changes, especially the discovery of new techniques of manufacture in the metal and textile

Map 1. Europe in 1780

industries, changed the whole structure of social organisation and the patterns of life and thought of eighteenth-century Britain. A new society emerged whose social structure was determined by the mechanics of industrial production rather than by those of agriculture. If our attention is confined merely to the technological changes themselves, the concept of an industrial 'revolution' in the 1780s becomes only a British phenomenon. The astonishing occurrence of a number of inventions in a short space of time and the rapid concentration of capital and labour in factories, which occurred partly as one consequence of these inventions, give even the merely technological aspects of these changes a revolutionary aspect in Britain because of the speed with which they took place. These innovations were adopted more slowly in most parts of the continent of Europe so that the concept of an industrial 'revolution' at the end of the eighteenth century in this narrower sense has no great relevance outside the field of British history. But all the first and greatest analysts of these events, Smith, Ricardo, Saint-Simon, Engels and Marx, set out to analyse, not a series of changes in industrial techniques as such, but the quite new economic basis which these changes created for human society. In this wider sense the industrial revolution was a European phenomenon from the outset. From the continent, what had taken place in late eighteenth-century Britain was seen, and correctly seen, as profoundly revolutionary, threatening the very foundations of social organisation. The developments in manufacturing industry transformed the economic position of Britain in relation to the European lands and by changing the balance of economic power, changed also the balance of political power. At the same time these events in Britain posed profound social questions to European society. To some, they were a fearful menace to a much-valued social position and way of life, to others a way of improving their income and to many a wonderful new hope for the overturning of a society they detested.

It is only in the light of these fears and hopes of social revolution that the Industrial Revolution in continental Europe can fully be understood. The enormous increase in productive capacity in Britain demanded, if only for reasons of political power, a similar response on the continent. From the very start therefore, the economic developments in Britain seemed certain to spread to mainland Europe and their coming was anticipated with different feelings by different parties. British society was transformed by internal forces, but the first industrial revolution could only happen once. Continental societies were transformed by events coming from *outside*, captured by forces which their leading groups could often not help but regard as enemy forces.

'The Industrial Revolution' should not be confounded either with 'industrialisation' or with 'economic growth'. Both of these last were possible in the eighteenth-century European society without revolutionary implications. They were in fact typical of the more developed nations. Both could and did take place in perfect harmony with the social arrangements and political structures of many European states, whereas the industrial revolution, an altogether larger phenomenon, implied nothing less than the destruction of the old social and political order. The growth of industrial output and an increase in the number of people employed in manufacturing industry, which together might be defined as 'industrialisation' and, also, in so far as it can be measured for that period, the stricter conception of 'economic growth' had both been marked features of eighteenth-century Europe.

The output of the French cotton cloth manufacturing industry, or at least its consumption of raw cotton, seems to have grown at an annual average rate of 3·8 per cent before 1788, and so did the output of the coal mining sector. Although the data for constructing such a series for agricultural output are especially unreliable, present work suggests that there was a growth of 60 per cent in final agricultural output in France between 1701–1710 and between 1781–1790. Perhaps such an estimate is too high, although it should be borne in mind that the more fragmentary evidence about the growth of agricultural output in Germany over the same period also indicates a striking increase in production. The population figures for the early eighteenth century are not precise either but on the whole it does not seem unreasonable to accept that the overall rate of growth of the French economy in the eighteenth century was about, or slightly above, 1 per cent per annum. It was, therefore, growing at about the same rate as, or perhaps slightly faster than, the British economy.

It is not yet possible to impute rates of growth to other European economies in that period. However, it was a period of economic recovery from the disastrous famines and murderous wars of the previous century, and in almost all economies a noticeable increase in agricultural output and a noticeable increase in the output of some industries is to be remarked. The expansion of the agricultural frontier in Germany, particularly in Prussia, into lands often deserted as a result of war in the first part of the seventeenth century, and in Russia into lands never previously ploughed, led to an increase in the amount of bread grains (rye and wheat) produced. Towards the end of the century, the volume of these grains traded internationally seems to have increased although the totals remained very small. Stettin (Szczecin) and Odessa developed as ports for grain export. Similarly, Naples developed as a port for the export of olive oil from Calabria, where the olive trees began their relentless march over the countryside as peasant farmers began to produce for northern European markets and for Marseilles soap works. Examples from industry are not hard to find; the output of pig iron in Russia increased from 110,000 tons in 1718 to over 163,000 tons in 1800, while there was at the same time an increase in the output of handicraft goods. In Valencia and Catalonia, the development of the cotton and silk manufacturing industries after 1750 awoke Spain from its long industrial stagnation and made it once again, in mid-eighteenth-century terms, into an industrial power while establishing the modern economic supremacy of Catalonia over Castile. These are but a few of the many examples which might lead us to suspect that measurable economic growth was also taking place elsewhere in Europe, although only in certain restricted regions. That growth was reflected in the great increase of international trade, both between European countries and between Europe and its many colonies. The last half of the eighteenth century witnessed a remarkable increase in the diversity of goods traded and in the number of economies participating in these trades.

The study of economic history in Britain has always focussed attention on the problem of why the industrial revolution occurred there. Obviously it is not part of this book to try to answer that question. But clearly such a question also has implications for continental society since its answer, by identifying important economic differences between Britain and the continental economies, might suggest much about the economic history of mainland Europe. It is, however, only one method, and not an especially important one, of approaching the economic history of the mainland. It is unfortunately, an approach which has dominated most British economic history writing about other European societies, a fact which has meant that their economic history has been constantly measured against a British yardstick: Britain has been seen as the norm for economic development in this period and all other societies as aberrations. Most theoretical models of growth or development were derived until very recently at no very great distance from the objective historical experience of the industrial revolution in Britain. It is possible that such an approach, leaving aside the distorted view of the history of the mainland which it necessarily presents, is also misleading about internal developments in Britain for it tends to exaggerate the differences between eighteenth-century Britain and many other European societies. Neither socially nor economically was eighteenth-century Britain strikingly different from *all* other European countries. And it was for that reason that the industrial revolution there immediately aroused so much interest elsewhere in Europe.

It has often been suggested that the industrial revolution in Britain was the consequence of a process of continued industrialisation in the eighteenth century, that it was an acceleration of industrialisation to such a speed that it became a qualitatively different process. But most recent research into the French economy in the eighteenth century has demonstrated that the increase in industrial output per head in the eighteenth century was probably faster than that in Britain. It has become, as a consequence, much less easy to explain the occurrence in Britain, in the last quarter of the eighteenth century of the new phenomenon of industrial revolution. The spread of industrial handicrafts, particularly the manufacture of cloth, and the development of the iron industry, to both of which scholars drew attention as the origins of the industrial revolution in Britain, were equally marked in eighteenth-century France. Nor were they lacking in many other European economies. If this general explanation no longer seems valid, this is more true of the more detailed and specific explanations frequently offered. Usually these take the form of isolating one particular factor in the British economy in the eighteenth century lacking in other European economies or, to put it another way, of finding the precise advantage of the British economy over the least disadvantaged of all the mainland economies.

For example, a factor frequently so isolated is the price of coal. The technological changes in the British industrial revolution depended on a ready supply of cheap coal. Mass production in the textile industries was accompanied by the utilisation of a new and much more powerful source of energy, James Watt's improved steam engine. The changes in the technique of iron manufacture hinged on the process of smelting iron ore by the use of coke, a product of coal. That coal was more widely available in Britain and at a cheaper price than on the mainland, has caused most scholars to consider this as a particular British advantage. Certainly the greater price of coal on the mainland was a factor of considerable importance in explaining why new manufacturing techniques were adopted more slowly there. But it should be remembered that coal was a very costly material to transport and that its relative cheapness was a regional effect in Britain as well as on the continent. It was cheap at the pit-head and its price increased sharply with the distance it was transported. In some parts of Europe it either was or could have been as cheap, and in those parts of continental Europe where it was not mined there were always possibilities of substitution except in the process of refining pig iron. In France, for example, the mass-production of textiles was based in many areas on the development of new methods of using water power.

Another specific advantage of the British economy is often said to have been the ready access to water transport. In an age when carriage by land was very expensive and slow, access to rivers or the sea drastically reduced the costs of carriage of raw materials. Obviously, many areas of France, Germany, or Spain were much further from navigable water than it was possible to be in Britain. Similarly, the development of a crude system of handling money and providing credit in eighteenth-century Britain has been noted and it has also been pointed out that in eighteenth-century France, for example, credit was difficult to obtain on any but the most swingeing terms. The great development of foreign trade in eighteenth-century Britain has also been used to explain the source of profit for investment and also the development of a market for manufactured goods and it has been justly pointed out that this development was much less marked in other eighteenth-century economies, in Germany and Russia for example.

[Ins.!]

The most frequent of such attempts to isolate a particular factor which may have caused the industrial revolution to take place in Britain has been the demonstration that British agriculture was differently organised from that of mainland Europe. The existence of a relatively restricted group of large landowners who let their land to tenant farmers many of whom were men of some wealth and standing and who in their turn employed a large force of paid labourers to cultivate the land was a phenomenon restricted almost entirely to Britain. Elsewhere in Europe the land was more usually cultivated either by the peasantry whose farms were small, but whose rights over the land could amount to something close to full ownership, or by a labour force whose labour was to some degree customary and compulsory and not so dependent on the wage contract as in Britain. It is usually supposed that the peasantry had 'disappeared' in eighteenth-century Britain because economic progress had proceeded further there and the organisation of agriculture which had ensued was a better base for future economic development than the more 'archaic' societies existing on the continent.

All these attempts to isolate single factors which can explain the fact that the first industrial revolution occurred where it did and also the attempts to build general models of economic development which incorporate a revolutionary experience akin to that in Britain tend to break down before the enormous diversity of the continental economies. The more their history in the eighteenth century is considered, the greater appears the difficulty of finding one single factor in the British economy not present in some continental economies. The possibility remains, of course, of explaining the occurrence of the industrial revolution in Britain as the result of a unique concentration of economic advantages not exactly possessed by any other economy. But this argument is too tautological to be of much value. It should also be remembered that interest in the first industrial revolution has been such that research has concentrated very heavily on it so that we know far more about the British economy in the eighteenth century than about other economies. And because this particular approach has dictated a particular path of research, we know far more about the disadvantages of continental economies compared to Britain than about their advantages. One example of this will suffice, that of the United Provinces. No country had such easy access to cheap water transport, its financial and commercial experience and techniques were more advanced than in Britain, the per capita value of its overseas trade was much greater, its social structure more flexible and its agriculture, although differently organised, as efficient and progressive as that of Britain, it was an exporter of capital. It had, however, no easily-minable reserves of coal. Is it possible to impute to this one lack the fact that the Netherlands did not undergo the experience of the industrial revolution when all the immediately surrounding areas did so? It should be remembered that even by 1914, when many countries with no worthwhile coal reserves had industrialised the Netherlands still remained a relatively unindustrialised land. The price of coal is too small a matter to be made the deciding factor in the occurrence and timing of nineteenth-century European industrialisation.

The more that is discovered about the history of economic development in Europe, the harder it becomes to define the precise economic differences between Britain and other eighteenth-century economies. Nevertheless, the impression remains, and quite justifiably, that in some way Britain was a more developed economy in the late eighteenth century. Consequently, economic historians have proposed another general explanation of the industrial revolution there, that it was the result of attaining a particular level of economic development. Britain, as it were, was 'ripe' for the industrial revolution; the continental economies were not. This 'ripeness' was constituted by a level of development in industry, agriculture and trade and a level of sophistication in economic and social arrangements which, although partly to be found in many continental economies, was nowhere wholly to be found to the same degree. Since the conjunction of economic factors which constituted this 'ripeness' has not been identified with any great degree of

B

convincingness, economic historians have tended recently to explain it as a social rather than an economic state. They have isolated those particular social factors which seemed to them to be especially responsible for the growth of capitalist industrial enterprise and come to the conclusion that there was a greater stock of those qualities in Europe in the eighteenth century than elsewhere in the world, and a greater stock of them in Britain than anywhere else in Europe. For example, the industrial revolution is often now interpreted as being the result of the will to break the fetters of traditional society, a triumph of the emancipated individual exercising his will to work hard and to make money and in so doing to transform existing social and economic arrangements. It is this type of approach which has caused greater emphasis to be placed on the role of the heroic entrepreneur or on the degree of 'freedom' in enterprise, whereas the older approach tended to confine itself to matter-of-fact issues about production costs and factor endowment.

Social explorations of this kind leave much room for the personal prejudices of the explorer to intrude, especially at the stage of deciding which social and ethical attitudes are particularly useful for capitalist development. In any case entrepreneurs required different qualities according to the fabric of the national society within which they operated. The precise personal qualities required for success in business in Germany were not the same as in Britain or France because the relationship of government and business was different there. British society has been described as more 'open', freer, more enterprising, and less prejudiced against industry and trade than that of other European countries. At the same time industrial activity in eighteenth-century Britain has been held to have taken place in a less restrictive legislative framework, less hampered by the interference of government and freer to exercise those peculiar virtues which are claimed to go with the successful development of capitalism. Research has already shown that one, at least, of the supposedly hide-bound societies, France, proved as capable of growth as Britain in the eighteenth century. These social explanations, however, would freely allow the possibility of economic growth in traditional economies but seek to distinguish between the capacities of different societies to break the mould in which they were set and to accept that wider phenomenon, the industrial revolution.

The vision, still, apparently, often seen, of eighteenth-century Britain as having any of these qualities to a worthwhile extent is surely a mirage. Neither does Britain seem to have been a more 'open' and 'free' society than that of Sweden, Denmark, the United Provinces, Switzerland and some Italian states. In all those areas, the social barriers to moving upwards through the class structure into its higher positions were weaker than in Britain and such may also have been the case in France, however legally distinct the status of nobility there. Since it is generally true that the industrial revolution was not the work of noblemen but of bourgeois groups, often of relatively low status, the question must really be one of how far such groups could drive their economic and social ambitions through the obstacles set in their path by the traditional aspects of old regime society. Even in this light it is difficult to see Britain as a country where the bourgeoisie had greater power, even locally, than in the United Provinces or in Switzerland. Certain mercantile or manufacturing towns in countries where the juridical scaffolding of old regime society was very tightly preserved were in fact governed and controlled with respect to their local activities entirely by the powerful bourgeois groups in the town. Such was the case in France with Dunkirk or Elbeuf, an important centre of the wool manufacture. No doubt such would have been the case with the Royal Free Boroughs of Hungary had there been any comparable manufacturing or mercantile activity to speak of there. The origins of the controlling nobility of Italian cities like Venice or Milan were bourgeois at no great distance. Cities like Geneva, Zürich and Amsterdam were seats of bourgeois economic and political power which still served to stimulate the envy and emulation of the bourgeoisie even of rich and developing mercantile cities such as Liverpool or Nantes.

That the mercantilistic methods of industrial regulation which confined production within a tight set of rules governing location, quality and quantity decayed earlier in Britain than elsewhere is certainly responsible for the relative degree of freedom from central or local government control enjoyed by British manufacturers. But the arguments which link this freedom to the industrial revolution there are not always so convincing. For one thing the degree of freedom is sometimes exaggerated. It was most to be observed in the cotton industry. But that industry was likewise relatively free from controls in other European economies. Secondly, the early origins of the industrial revolution lie in the concentration of rural textile manufacturing industries into single large enterprises and everywhere in Europe such rural domestic activities had been successfully fostered by private capital in the eighteenth century and were tending to grow at the expense of the older more controlled activities in the same way and following the same paths as in Britain. Such rural industrial activities, as we shall see, were the most salient feature of eighteenth-century industrialisation, as salient in France and many parts of the Low Countries as in Britain. Thirdly, after

1750, the tide of administrative opinion in many countries was all towards destroying the privileges and powers of the older corporate manufacturing industries and the guilds which managed and controlled them. The local actions of French *intendants* in the second half of the eighteenth century were concerned continually with attacks on monopolies and privileges. It was one of them, Turgot, who transferred his activities to the national level when he became Minister of Finance and used central legislation to make trade and industry freer. His actions had parallels in many states. Between 1784 and 1787 the great reforming Emperor Joseph II attacked the privileges of corporative industry in its most ancient seat of power, the Austrian Netherlands. The influence of liberal and physiocratic thought permeated central administration very quickly.

The reason why it did so suggests a fourth caution against stressing too strongly the differences in industrial freedom between Britain and the continent. Governments reversed their mercantilistic policies of import substitution by the establishment of privileged 'manufactures' in favour of policies of relative freedom of industry and development of agriculture with such remarkable alacrity because their ultimate aim was national economic power. When the physiocrats suggested that import substitution had failed precisely because its result was a manufacturing sector where production costs were too high to compete and that this could be remedied by the free development of the agricultural sector and those industries more closely connected with it, governments were quite ready to try this alternative road to economic strength, the more so as the history of the privileged 'manufactures' in the face of the newer, freer, rural industries was not a happy one in the eighteenth century. It may therefore be put forward as a general hypothesis that where central government was *most* powerful after 1750 the guilds and corporations were weakest. The striking example of this is the contrast between France and the Austrian Netherlands. In the seventeenth century the central government in France had more or less successfully imposed the royal will on guilds and corporations in order to tighten control over them. In the eighteenth century, by relaxing that control, it was able to weaken them. For however much the aim of the corporation itself might have been to restrict production and access to the craft in the interests of its members such was never the aim of the government, whose policy was always devoted to greater and better output. In Belgium, where there had been no centralisation in the seventeenth century the guilds had retained great powers. Consequently the attacks on their powers by the Austrian government after 1780, which were conceived entirely in the interests of economic development through freedom, were construed as an attack on local freedoms and constitutional liberties. Interference by the central government was often to promote liberty of manufacture and economic development.

Finally, it should be said that there were an infinite number of useful and helpful acts by eighteenth-century governments. Even before 1750 when the trend was still towards regulation and control the regulations could be applied with great knowledge, flexibility and subtlety. They were so applied in Dauphiné in France, for example, where the *intendants* often preserved local industries against the jealousies of neighbouring Lyons. Whether tightening mercantilistic controls or loosening them, eighteenth-century governments played a significant part in encouraging industrial activity and although there are many cases where their actions seem to have been harmful, especially when their rules prevented textile producers from responding quickly enough to changes in fashion on the market, there are just as many cases where they were indubitably useful.

The main reason for the greater involvement of government with industry in some areas of the continent, or for the greater control of restrictive guilds in others, was the fact that industrial manufacture was less developed there. Nothing destroyed the power of the guilds so quickly as the growth of industry outside the area of their control, which often coincided with the town walls. What weakened the guilds of the Austrian Netherlands most in the eighteenth century, was the growth of manufacture there and the multiplicity of competing privileges and exclusive monopolies claimed by the producers to the point of complete unenforceability. In this case freedom of manufacture was often the result of an excess of regulations. The growth of rural manufactures in eighteenth century France was one reason why the government withdrew its support from the guilds which sought to restrict these newer activities. Where governments maintained strict controls and supported the guilds and close corporations to the hilt, this was normally because industrial development was so feeble that there seemed no other reasonable choice of policy. Thus, the restrictive attitude of the Russian government was quite realistic for it did, beyond question, encourage the growth of a considerable iron industry in eighteenth-century Russia which could scarcely have been created without the privileges accorded to the enterpreneurs. Consequently, rather than being a cause of the greater level of economic development in eighteenth-century Britain, the early decay of the guilds and lack of government regulation of industry were more likely its results.

On the whole, therefore, looking at the problem with a view to identifying social differences, has been no more successful than the attempt to find economic differences. In both cases there has been a certain lack of historical perspective. It has never been very clearly demonstrated which particular ethical qualities and social attitudes were universally valuable for the many different types of economic development which have occurred in Europe since the eighteenth century. Such approaches have shifted discussion away from establishing the precise economic and social advantages which made some economies more developed than others into a vague territory of not very sustaining cultural gleanings. In general, it will be found that where social differences existed between eighteenth-century societies, they were themselves the result of a long process of economic change rather than its cause.

That process was very long indeed. If other European economies were less developed than that of Britain in the late eighteenth century, that is to be explained not in terms of what happened in the eighteenth century, but in terms of what happened over several centuries. It is the whole process of historical development over that time that accounts for the 'ripeness' of the British economy rather than the rate of development in the eighteenth century itself. The possibility of industrialisation in the mainland economies of Europe did not depend on the extent to which they possessed or did not possess particular factors present in the British economy but on their total economy and society as moulded by many centuries of historical development. To measure them against the yardstick of the British economy is to miss many aspects which were frequently vitally important in determining their future economic history.

Let us therefore now shift our perspective to a pan-European one. Previous centuries of development determined that the industrial revolution happened, not in Europe's wealthiest, most populous, most powerful and most productive country, France, but in an island off its shores. The development gap between Britain and France was, however, very small and in the eighteenth century it was getting smaller. But what are we to say of the development gap between France and Romania, a country only 1,000 miles distant whose national consciousness was little more than a historic memory and whose economy justified in every respect the description 'primitive'. The differences in level of economic development between continental countries in the late eighteenth century were quite as wide as those between contemporary western Europe and an economy like that of contemporary Madagascar. It is this single fact, more than any other, which must surely lead us to reject interpretations culled from the observed history of Britain, the United States or Russia and to emphasise that there had already, by 1770, been an enormous variety of European economic experience and that the capacity to develop of the various European states should be judged in terms of the economy and society of those states, the more so as it was so much to be conditioned in the nineteenth century by their centuries of previous history. To explain these differences in development merely in terms of the presence or absence of factors which caused the industrial revolution in Britain, or the presence or absence of factors responsible for the successful growth of the economy of the United States, is hopelessly unhistorical, because it does not cover a sufficient period of time to fully explain such wide differences. Explanations must be couched more nearly in terms of the whole historical experience of European societies before 1770.

This is not to deny in any way the usefulness of development models as an approach to the problem of eighteenth-century development, but merely to suggest that a certain level of historical sophistication is necessary in their construction. As more research is done into the early periods of history of the less-studied European economies, a better perspective will no doubt emerge and, with it, more convincing models of development. At the moment, one of the saddest comments about the state of economic history studies is the extraordinary lack of explanations for the emergence of such great differences in the level of economic development in Europe. There is still great scope for research here. France and certain other West European countries in the late eighteenth century already had a more sophisticated economic apparatus than many contemporary undeveloped countries. They were in fact, in the present sense of the word, not undeveloped at all. They had efficient and knowledgeable civil services; some had well-developed internal waterways for transport; France had a comprehensive and well-maintained road network; all exhibited proofs of long-sustained capital accumulation. The visitor to eighteenth-century France or the United Provinces would have seen much more fixed capital in those countries than the visitor to most contemporary African or Asian countries. In eastern Europe most countries exhibited, often in the most exaggerated way, all the familiar features of the undeveloped economy, penury on every hand, no dwellings, machines or even roads worthy of the names, often no administration worthy of the name.

We propose to examine the continental economies and societies at the time of the industrial revolution in Britain. In this way their particular capacities to meet the new and difficult circumstances presented by developments in Britain may emerge. At the same time, the variety and complexity of their social and economic patterns may serve as a warning against theories of development constructed from the evidence of one or two countries while at the same time helping us to define in a narrower field the particular advantages which the developed societies had over the undeveloped.

These advantages were social advantages, although not in the sense in which historians have recently used this concept. Rather they were differences in social structure which had already been created in continental Europe by the late eighteenth century. These differences related to the differences in the economies of the various European states and their previous development. The long process of European economic and historical development had produced differences in the structure of society by the late eighteenth century of which the differences which existed between Britain and the mainland were part and parcel. Britain, for example, much more closely resembled France in its economic and social structure than France resembled Romania. An examination of the economic and social structures of the European economies at the time when the agricultural basis which had for so long formed European society was being transformed into an industrial basis by the industrial revolution in Britain will show how complex and diverse the pattern of economic development in continental Europe already was by the close of the eighteenth century and how the occurrence of the industrial revolution in Britain, an occurrence which was the occasion of so many fears and hopes in other European societies, was but a part of this diversity.

THE AGRICULTURAL BASE OF SOCIETY

Outside the borders of a very small number of city-states, the economy of Europe under the old regime was almost entirely based on agriculture. In every country the land accounted for the greatest part of the available productive capital. The share of the population dependent on agriculture for its income was very high. In France before the Revolution it was about 90 per cent and certainly not less than that in any other major country. The institutions of society were appropriate to this agricultural base, not designed to further social change, as are some modern institutions, but rather to preserve society in its existing framework, to get the land cultivated, to bring in the harvest, to divide its yield and to continue the governance of the state, often on a very local level. Industrial activity, other than that which arose from the agricultural sector of the economy and was carried on in conjunction with it, and commercial activity, other than the grain trade, existed only as small islands of economic difference in a sea of agricultural effort. Such islands may seem in retrospect very important for the future, but at the close of the eighteenth century the pattern of economic activity was dominated by the land and its yield.

A failure of the harvest or a period of consecutive poor harvests could produce not only a prolonged economic depression but an enormous increase in deaths in the population. Although human existence was less immediately connected to the success or failure of the crops than it had been in the previous century, all the evidence shows that this emancipation had not proceeded very far. In no large country on the continent was the economy so diversified as in France, yet even there a sharp rise in the price of bread grain as in 1758–9 and 1767–8 could produce a corresponding rise in the death rate. Figure 1 shows the intimate connection between high grain prices in one area of France and the incidence of high death rates. It also shows that the connection was less immediate than it had been in 1693–4 and 1709–10. The improvement in the situation may be attributed to better farming practices and to improvements in transport which allowed for the relief of epidemics but it was still true in the eighteenth century that a harvest catastrophe, such as occurred in 1789, could so reduce consumers' expenditures on manufactures as to produce a severe industrial depression and an economic and political crisis so violent as to destroy the whole social framework of the old régime. The French Revolution was in the profoundest economic, as well as political, sense the crisis of the old régime. It had its roots in the failure of the eighteenth-century economy to solve adequately the problems of agricultural production and to distribute equitably the yield from that production, problems so severe that their solution in France required the construction of a society based on quite different premises. To that extent the 'Great Revolution', as it came to be called, was as much the result of the economic developments in the eighteenth century as was the Industrial Revolution, which also destroyed the fabric of the old régime. But, like the Industrial Revolution again, the effect of the French Revolution on other countries, although very profound, was often only a demonstration effect. It destroyed the apparent moral certainties on which old régime society was based but in only a small area of western Europe did it destroy that society itself. Elsewhere those forms of social organisation which existed with great similarity all over Europe in the eighteenth century survived well into the next century and influenced very strongly the pattern and type of economic development.

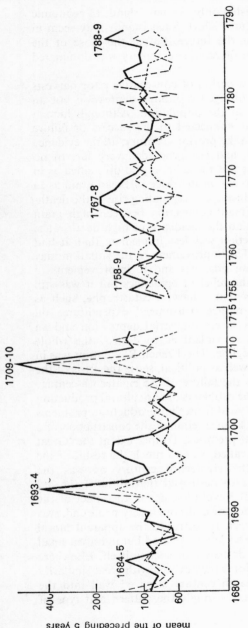

Fig 1.   The incidence of Famine in East-Central France, 1680–1790

The solid line on the graph is the percentage of the price of wheat at Rozoy in the department of Seine et Marne near Meaux in relation to the median price of the five preceding harvest years. The dotted line is the percentage of deaths at Dijon in relation to conceptions over the harvest year in which the prices are measured, and the dashed line is a similar index for the region of Gien. The two population indices are thus compared with a measurement of percentage price increases. Notice how those harvest years with steep price increases correspond with a high incidence of death, particularly in the terrible famines of 1693–4 and 1709–10. That correspondence becomes less marked in the second half of the eighteenth century. The absolute dependence of the population on bread in the earlier period may be less absolute in the later (although high prices still produce more deaths) or farming techniques may be improving to provide for the increase in population throughout the century so that the deaths in bad years are less. *Source*: J. Meuvret, 'Les crises de subsistances et la démographie de la France d'Ancien Régime', *Population*, 1946.

THE NOBILITY

The ownership of land, and thus of the greatest part of the available capital, was concentrated very heavily in the hands of a small class, the nobility. In Hungary 60 per cent of the land was owned by the nobility, in Poland 78 per cent. These were probably the two highest proportions. In Sweden the proportion was relatively low. The precise definition of the word 'nobility' causes much trouble for historians and caused even more trouble for eighteenth-century governments. Nevertheless the fact is that such a class with certain common characteristics and certain common legal privileges did exist throughout Europe. To be noble was not necessarily to own land; there were many landless nobles in Italy and many in Hungary and Poland holding no more than a mere plot. Nor was it necessary to possess a patent of nobility to hold land; there were non-noble freeholders everywhere. A very high proportion of the land, however, was considered to belong to the *fief* or *seigniory* of a noble family. In all those areas, therefore, where the actual cultivators and hereditary possessors of farms were not noble, only a small proportion were held in the modern sense of a 'freeholding'. The ultimate right of possession, the *dominium directum*, as distinct from the right of user, was associated with the fief of a noble family. In western Europe these juridical arrangements were descended from the feudal system of the early medieval period and the land, as a consequence, had become enmeshed in a complicated network of land law, payments and dues as the original feudal fiefs had become inextricably mixed and subdivided with the rise and decay of families. In eastern Europe the juridical connection of the nobility with landholding was of much more recent origin and so were the legal privileges which accompanied it. As a consequence the pattern of landholding was both simpler and cruder.

The nobility did not often recognise or acknowledge its own homogeneity. One cause of this was the diversity of its origins. In France the centralising policies of the royal government had led it in earlier periods to rely on a corpus of administrators whose origins were non-noble. Over time, and as a result of service in the highest offices of state, such families could attain the very highest noble ranks. Such was the case for example with the descendants of the great seventeenth-century finance minister Colbert. Likewise the corporations of lawyers who administered justice in the thirty-one sovereign courts, among them the local *parlements*, which still claimed and exercised the right of sanctioning royal decrees, had developed into a separate caste of interlocking families in many of which the high legal offices were almost hereditary. Both these groups of nobles were looked down on by families of more ancient lineage, although such families were often much poorer. Such distinctions prevented the legal nobility, the *noblesse de robe*, from marrying into the most ancient rural families, and by the formal genealogical rules governing presentation at the court, the families ennobled over the preceding three-and-a-half centuries were theoretically excluded. It was, of course, the business of genealogists to adjust these matters, within certain rules, for money. In fact in the eighteenth century the distinction between the non-legal nobility, the *noblesse d'épée* and the *noblesse de robe* became less and less observed. The nobility, influenced by background economic conditions which increased its income and its economic and political power, came in many countries, but particularly in France and Russia, to evolve a much more conscious and coherent view of its own special position in the state, to assert its powers both against the central government and against the poorer rural classes. In France the *noblesse d'épée* came to depend increasingly on the legal knowledge and constitutional and political powers of the *noblesse de robe* which became in many respects the spokesman for the cause of the nobility in general.

There were comparable differences in income and status between persons entitled to call themselves noble in other lands. The lesser nobility of Poland (*drobná szlachta*), were clearly distinguished from the great nobles by their smaller estates and wealth. In Hungary, where the privileges accruing to one of noble blood were perhaps greater than anywhere else, families clung to their titles when as poor as any peasant cultivator. In the same country the normal size of a great noble's *latifundium* was at least 10,000 hectares. Many families were endowed with more than one such estate. The Estherházy family were probably the greatest private landowners in Europe, owning about 3,500,000 hectares. In Castile existed noble families who were at the very bottom of the income scale, surviving on charity.

Not only were there differences between noble status within countries, but also between countries. The concept of nobility in Russia was a fairly recent invention, part of the process of westernisation. In Sweden, alone among eighteenth-century states, the questions of who was a noble and why were asked with their full intent. There the nobility was both less powerful in relation to other social classes and to the royal government and also more open to penetration by men of merit or wealth. In 1740 only 16 per cent of Swedish noble families could trace their lineage back as far as the average French noble dynasty. By the third generation after ennoblement 84 per cent of the Swedish noble family inheritances had either been interrupted or had survived intact only through the marriage of a daughter. Nor were there any common privileges which the nobility could universally claim. The most common was the right to trial before their peers, but the power of the government could often curtail this right. From the standpoint of future economic development the most important privilege was the exemption from taxation. The very existence of such a right made it worth while for governments to concede patents of nobility only after the greatest care. In France, whose government was a much more complicated and sophisticated machine than elsewhere, the central power had infringed this right of the nobility and was able to claim from them small sums in taxation. In Spain only the grandees were exempt; the lesser noble, the *hidalgo*, had to pay. In Russia and in Prussia the fiscal privilege was granted only on condition of fulfilment of duties to the state.

These differences were related to the relative strength or weakness of the central government over time. Although, therefore, sharp differences of income, status, habit, manner and power differentiated the nobility, it still tended to define itself as a class in its long struggle against centralised and often despotic royal government. As economic circumstances in the eighteenth century operated in its favour, it pressed harder for its own political independence, an independence usually expressed in terms of the defence of ancient constitutional liberties. From the ranks of the French nobility emerged theorists of the nobility's racial and class origins and its future destiny, Boulainvilliers and Montesquieu, who were to have an important influence in many other lands. Thus, despite all differences, the nobility in times of political and economic crisis functioned as a coherent class with particular interests; and, in the eighteenth century, this tendency was strengthened rather than weakened.

It is well to remember in how small a group such great economic power was vested. All attempts to measure the exact proportion of the nobility to the rest of the population provide variable answers, partly because our information about the size of the total population is none too accurate, but more so because they depend on a prior definition of nobility. The actual estate of nobility embraced 8,918 people in Sweden in 1760, or 0·5 per cent of the population. The class of 'equal to nobility', however, was larger than that of the nobility. Even defined in this larger way, the nobles were still only about one per cent of the population. In Finland the nobility were 0·4 per cent of the total population. Outside the Scandinavian countries the nobles were numerically more significant. In Poland they accounted for between two and five per cent of the population. Both there and in Hungary, low income in no way implied a declension into the commonalty, and the proportion of nobles was consequently the higher. In Hungary it is variously estimated at between 4·8 per cent and 6·7 per cent. One reason for the variation is the great difference which existed between the various Hungarian territories. In the parts of Croatia and Slavonia which formed the Military Frontier, there were no noble landlords; in those lands most recently recovered from Turkish domination, the nobility were less than 2 per cent of the population; in Transylvania, they were 4·4 per cent. The seat of power of the Magyar nobles was the great plains of the Danube and the Tisza, that is to say, the best available agricultural area. About one-half that group constituted the greatest landholders in Europe; the members of the other half were practically landless.

In France, the variation between localities was much less marked. In most areas, the nobility defined in its widest sense, constituted about 2 per cent of the population. The royal declaration of 1695, establishing the *capitation* tax on all sections of the population, divided it into twenty-two separate sections according to the ability to pay and nobility of various categories appear in each of the first fifteen sections. Nevertheless, the variations in wealth between regions seem to have been much less marked than elsewhere. In Spain, the nobility were 4·4 per cent of the population, in Russia less than 1·5 per cent.

SYSTEMS OF LAND MANAGEMENT

To say that the ownership of the land was vested in such small groups is not to say that they always played a part in its cultivation or even its management. Because agricultural production was the foundation of society, it was the system under which the land was cultivated which lay at the heart of eighteenth century economic development. The apparent similarity of the class structures of European countries disguised extreme differences in the control over the most vital aspect of the economies of those countries. Two questions are involved. Under what system and by whom was the land actually cultivated?

In most areas of western Europe, the lord had certain rights over the peasant's output, rights which derived from the mediaeval institutions of serfdom and lordship. The lord had received a parcel of land as a fief from the crown. The serfs had been either subjected to compulsory labour by the lord or had bound themselves to such services in return for protection. Their legal attachment was to the quality of his lordship, he was their *seigneur*. Beyond the duties of labouring for given periods of time on the *seigneur's* estate, the serfs were also restricted in their personal movements, in their economic activities, and in their freedom to dispose of their own goods and children. In many areas of western Europe, these arrangements had almost entirely disappeared but the serfs had 'commuted' their physical and personal obligations for cash payments. There were three ways in which this had taken place. Temporary economic conditions, such as a shortage of labour, might have strengthened the serf's bargaining position, or the lord himself might have preferred liquid capital to labour, or the central government might have intervened. Suffice it to say that the state of serfdom had become uncommon, but in its gradual disappearance it had left the *seigneur* the right to cream off a considerable sum in money payments from the peasants' production.

– in France

France was the country in which the deficiencies of the system led to a successful peasant revolution and, for that reason the questions of who farmed the land and how the output was distributed have been most investigated there. The land law derived its concepts from the mediaeval institutions, the 'feudal system', and spoke still in feudal terms. But 'commutation' of labour services had taken place at an early date and the institution of serfdom had almost entirely disappeared. Even where serfs survived in very small numbers they were not bound to the noble fief and were as free before the law as any other non-noble. In its origins the feudal institution of serfdom had been a method for getting the land cultivated by binding the labourers to the noble estate, by compelling them to a certain quantity of unpaid labour and by controlling the disposition of their children. The decay of this institution had coincided chronologically with the decision of the nobles to let out their estates in separate farms. The proportion of the land cultivated by peasant farmers in France was already high in the eighteenth century. They were not freeholders in the modern sense of the term, for 'commutation' had left them with large financial obligations to the *seigneur* which acknowledged the origins of their title to the land. Such payments were customary rather than fixed like a modern rent by supply and demand. The peasants, however, did not owe physical obligations to the *seigneur*; their labour was their own. The proportion of the land actually cultivated by this emerging peasantry was very different from region to region. In the Limousin it was as high as 50 per cent. There, the nobility retained under its direct ownership only 15 per cent of the land; in Dauphiné their share was lower, 12 per cent. In Burgundy, 35 per cent of the land was in noble hands, and in the Orléannais 40 per cent.

Where land had passed out of noble hands, it was not always on long leases to the peasantry. In many areas of France, the bourgeoisie had invested in land and had acquired about 16 per cent of the total land surface. Only in the Austrian Netherlands and the United Provinces could a similar phenomenon be observed. The clergy, 1·8 per cent of the French population, owned between 6 and 10 per cent of the landed property. Land not held by nobles, clergy or bourgeois and not leased to peasants was either royal land or common land. In effect, therefore, the pattern of landholding and cultivation in France was varied and diversified. Peasant holdings existed side by side with great noble domains. The domains themselves were often cultivated by peasants on leases of varying time spans, and it is perfectly possible to discern in eighteenth-century France the beginnings of the peasant proprietary economy which still dominates the French agricultural sector. The essential difference lay in the noble's ancient legal rights over the output of the peasant farm.

The noble might choose to cultivate his domain directly, residing there and employing the poorer peasants as labour. Or he might let it to the peasants and live on his rent-roll. Or he might adopt an intermediate position and cultivate his domain by means of sharecropping contracts in which he provided the capital stock and equipment while the cultivator provided the labour, the basis of the contract being the sharing-out between both parties of the harvest's yield. Whatever system he adopted, his goal was the same, money income, for if he cultivated the domain himself his income came from sales of the harvest in nearby markets. Beyond the boundaries of the domain, peasant farming was the usual practice; but the feudal dues still had to be paid, even though to all intents and purposes the farm was hereditary in the peasant family.

Nobles holding fiefs had certain rights of justice within that fief. On the maintenance of such rights depended a number of highly vexatious and invidious payments from the peasant. The lord might have the right to hunt and fish over the land, to keep pigeons and rabbits, to levy road tolls, to maintain a mill, oven or wine-press which the peasants on the fief must use, and even to monopolise the sales of wine over a given period. These rights were usually referred to as the *banalités*. In the eighteenth century they were

increasingly 'commuted' in return for money payments from the
peasant as liquid capital became more important to the *seigneur*
than the exercise of petty local privileges and commercial monopolies. Nevertheless the basis of these payments was the direct
threat that the *seigneur* would resurrect his rights and insist on them
in a legal process in which he could hardly lose, since it would be
tried by his fellow landlords. In fact, the *noblesse de robe* in general
took a much more commercial view of these arrangements than the
noblesse d'épée, and it was in their domains in particular that these
ancient laws were applied to the last degree for a commercial
purpose for which they had been in no sense devised. Although each
single payment could be very small, the sum total over the peasant's
working lifespan represented no small inroad into his potential
surplus. In the Toulouse area the loss was 11 per cent of the peasant's
gross income.

The *banalités* were rights of lordship, appertaining to the position
of the *seigneur*; other rights appertained to the fief and could be
claimed by any holder of it whether he were noble or not. They
also had long been commuted into money payments of different
kinds. The main one was the *cens*, an annual payment in either
cash or kind often fixed by law for very long periods and distinguished only by its legal origins from an annual rent. Other
payments were designed to acknowledge that ultimate ownership
of the land lay elsewhere, the *lods* and the *ventes*, dues payable
whenever the land was bequeathed or sold. These last payments were
very variable both in their size and in their frequency of occurrence.

Any estimation of what the peasant lost out of his annual income
to the *seigneur* as a result of the exercise of these dues has to be a
regional one. Where arable farming was most profitable and where
the grain trade was most active, the *seigneur* was most interested in
acquiring liquid capital, partly to meet his wage bill where he cultivated his own domain and partly because, being more commercially-
minded, he required greater sums either for consumption or
investment. In the region of Toulouse, where the nobility lived a
life of active farming and exported the wheat grown on their
domains by way of the Canal du Midi either to the local urban
markets or further afield into the Mediterranean, and where they
used the various legal devices open to them without hesitation and
with few scruples, the payments from the peasant were increasingly
used by lords as a way of forcing the peasant to sell part of his
land back to the domain. This 'reconstitution of the domain', a
process much more noticeable elsewhere in Europe, was eloquent
testimony to the revived attractiveness in the eighteenth century of
investment in land. It could not proceed too far in France for two

reasons. In the first place, the fiefs were often not continuous areas but widely-scattered ones linked together only by legal title, leaving the noble little alternative but to live from rents. In the second place, the main cash nexus or nexus in kind which existed between the *seigneur* and peasant was irrevocable. Only with the greatest difficulty could the *cens* be increased, in itself a main cause for the burden of the *banalités* to be increased, but, after payment of the *seigneur*'s dues, the peasant had full control over the disposal or testamentary disposition of his land. This stood in contrast to many other societies, Prussia for example, where the transfer of land between classes was almost impossible and where, as a consequence, the land-market scarcely existed. In this light, it is reasonable to regard the French peasants as tenants, if tenancy be defined as the existence of a firm cash nexus. The *seigneur* could not easily get more land except by purchase, and increases in his wealth or income had to come either from larger money payments from his tenantry or from the better exploitation of his own domain.

The financial dues owed by the peasant to the *seigneur* were by no means the only claim on his output. The French government and army were complicated and expensive. The nobility were exempt from the older taxes which brought in the larger part of the revenue. The main burden of a highly regressive tax system therefore fell on the peasantry. It was they who paid the chief tax, the *taille*, a tax on personal income. In the main part of France, the *pays d'état*, the *taille* could amount to a third of the peasant's income. In peripheral areas and in a large area of the south it was much lower. In addition to the *taille*, the peasant shouldered the burden of the indirect taxes. The most oppressive was the *gabelle*, a tax levied by the government on the consumption of salt of whose manufacture and distribution it had a monopoly. Having satisfied these obligations, the peasant still had his tithes to the church, nominally one-tenth of his produce but usually considerably lower. The tithe, however, was almost invariably collected in kind so that in a period of rising prices like the eighteenth century it did not in any way diminish as a burden. In the Toulouse area the loss to the peasant because of *taille* was 14 per cent of his gross income. But Toulouse was an area of low *taille*, in general the proportion of the peasant's output creamed off by the *seigneurs*, the state and the church was between 30 and 40 per cent.

The peasant's economic position depended on the size of his holding. In order to survive over many generations the peasant family needed a substantial area of land. The general law of inheritance tended to mitigate against this by inducing subdivision of the holding to provide for all the male heirs, although in legal practice it was often possible to avoid this eventuality. There was in every region of France a substantial proportion of landless rural dwellers and also of peasants whose holdings were too small for them to survive without eking out their farming income by other means, one of which was to sell their labour to the larger landholders whether peasant, bourgeois or *seigneur*. This was the distinction between the *laboureur*, the peasant with sufficient land to plough and thus to participate in the profitable production of grain, and the *manouvrier*, whose land was small and who as a consequence had to sell his labour and thus share much less in the profits of the expansion of arable farming. In general the proportions of the *manouvrier*'s holding to that of the *laboureur* were greater where more of the total land was in the hands of the peasantry as a group. In the Limousin the *laboureur*'s holding was about four times greater than that of the *manouvrier*; in the Laônnais it was about nine times greater. The capacity of the *laboureur* to meet the increasing payments demanded from him rose with rising grain prices; the burden on the *manouvrier* increased as much while his economic position was less fortunate. In such economic circumstances the desire of the peasant to free himself from having to pay the feudal dues was the greatest force behind the peasant revolution of 1789, and the length of time which the revolutionary governments took to satisfy his demands completely kept the fires of rural discontent burning until 1793.

laboureur
manouvrier
(Poorer)

Where the *seigneur* neither cultivated the domain himself nor collected the dues from the peasants farming it, he cultivated it under the system of *métayage* (share-cropping). It was once commonly argued that the *métayer* represented a kind of half-way house along the path of progress, more advanced than a serf, but not so advanced as a peasant paying *cens*. To take such a view of things was quite to misunderstand the power of the noble landlord. Only at very brief and rare moments in the past had the lower rural orders ever been able to influence the system by which the land was cultivated. The essential decisions had been taken by the landlord, except where the central government had intervened. That is to say that all over Europe the landlord made his own entrepreneurial decisions on the most appropriate method of cultivating his lands. The decision was made within the framework of customary law, a law always much modified by the lord's own manorial justice. But the major constraint on his entrepreneurial decisions was the central government's own policy which might for various military, social or economic reasons be aimed at protecting the poorer rural groups. It is in this light, as the result of a particular entrepreneurial decision by the *seigneur* rather than as the result of the march of progress, that the position of the *métayer* should be viewed.

métayer

Contracts for *métayage* were most common in the southwest of France. Elsewhere in Europe, they were most frequently met with in Italy. A typical region was one area of Poitou, the Gâtine poitevine. There, three-quarters of the land was cultivated under such contracts. Usually the *seigneur* provided the farm with all its equipment to the cultivator on the basis of a profit-sharing agreement on the next harvest. The tenure therefore was annually renewable and the cultivator effectively no more than a labourer with a temporary right of user over a certain amount of fixed capital. This was a state of misery for the *métayer*, totally excluded from the possibility of improving his contract or improving his yield, but an excellent arrangement for the *seigneur*, much more profitable and flexible than the fixed *cens*. Its origins lay in the increasing poverty of the peasant farmers in the sixteenth century. They had been reduced to a state where the lords had been able to reconstruct the small holdings of the *cens* payers into large enclosed farms, reordering the countryside and the social order in their own interests. It should be noted that in such a system, enclosure was not a step to improved farming methods; under such tenures, investment was discouraged and the land farmed in the interests of the shortest possible run profit.

The entrepreneurial decisions of the *seigneur* were more determined by market considerations in France than in many other European lands because there was a more active grain market there. The fundamental distinction between *laboureur* and *manouvrier* was a distinction between bread grain producers and bread buyers. Bread was the staple article of diet and as the population increased so did bread prices show a long run secular upwards trend. The advantage therefore lay with the bread grain producer and the *seigneur* had every incentive to cultivate his estate for the active and buoyant grain market. For the lower orders the economic objective was to get hold of enough land to plough, otherwise rising grain prices tended to worsen their position. The amount of debt among the French peasantry in the eighteenth century rose as peasants were often constrained by the economic situation to take land on highly unfavourable terms. Against this background the *seigneurs* pursued their own decisions which, although seemingly easier to effect, were still conditioned by price movements.

debt increased

The long-run secular price rise for arable products was interrupted in 1778. The years from 1780 to 1787 were, comparatively, years of low prices. The result was that those larger peasants who had managed to meet their obligations without falling into debt were now placed in a much worse position. Their investment decisions, as those of all others in the countryside, had become attuned to

1780–7 lo prices

constantly rising food prices. The way to prosper was to get more land and debt acquired in land purchase was no serious affair in the long run, given the economic trend. Although the price fall in 1778 was only the start of a short intercyclical contraction in a long-run secular upswing, it caused a sudden deterioration in the position of those rural groups who had best been able to share in the expansion. The *manouvrier*'s position was theoretically improved by the lower prices for he was a consumer and not a producer of bread. But the reaction of the nobles to the contraction was to make a much more earnest attempt to increase their income from feudal dues. The upward price movement began again in 1788 and was immediately accentuated by the failure of the harvest of that year, causing bread prices to rise to levels not known since the famine years of the early eighteenth century. In so far as the short period of lower prices had eased the burden on the *manouvrier*, its benefit was quite eliminated by so sudden and so violent an upward movement. The rural economy was too impoverished to survive such shocks. It broke apart in a more formidable version of the peasant revolts which had so frequently menaced it before. On this occasion the peasant revolt coincided with a deep political crisis, itself partly due to the difficulties of sustaining the government on so narrow a tax basis. The resulting Revolution was sustained until agricultural society was reorganised in a new mould. In retrospect, this reorganisation although often no more than a series of political concessions wrung by the peasantry from reluctant governments, can be seen to have sounded the death knell of the old régime throughout Europe, for the deficiencies of eighteenth-century French society were repeated everywhere else in their more general aspects. But there were also extremely important differences of detail everywhere.

The pattern of rural society in other countries varied very much both in relation to the system of cultivation and the disposal of the surplus. Since the arrangements in France had such profound consequences for the old régime and their re-ordering so profound an effect on our modern world, it will be readily understood that the type of society which existed in other lands was also of vital significance to their future development. It should be said that our knowledge is often much less than it is in the case of France, for less research has been done.

– in Germany

It has become a convention of historical descriptions of Germany to distinguish between the eastern parts of the German area in which the more usual pattern of cultivation was that of large noble estates cultivated by serfs (*Gutsherrschaft*) and the peasant economy which prevailed west of the river Elbe (*Grundherrschaft*). This distinction is insufficiently precise, because it fails to distinguish between the many different kinds of peasant tenure in the west. In addition, there were areas east of the Elbe where the preponderance of noble estates was much less.

The situation was most analogous to that in France in Baden and Württemberg, in south-western Germany. There the peasantry occupied holdings which were being increasingly subdivided. The peasantry owed no obligations to the lord's estate beyond the payment of the feudal dues and, as in France, the lord's income was in cash. The burden of these feudal payments in Württemberg may have been lower than in France, and the proportion of freehold land, 10 per cent, higher. In Hohenlohe the payments equivalent to the *cens* were only 2·4 per cent of the peasant's output. But the tithe (*Zehnt*) was much higher, sometimes 25 per cent. When the royal domain in Hohenlohe was divided into individual farms in the eighteenth century the dues paid by farmers amounted to 32·4 per cent of their net profit on arable land. The states of north-west and central Germany had evolved a similar system of peasant tenure but a more active policy of intervention by the government to protect the tenantry had led, especially in the north-west, to hereditary holdings of a larger size. In these areas, rather than a continuing process of land subdivision, a landless class had developed, working for larger tenants and on the noble domains. Hanover, for military reasons, had followed the policy of peasant protection further than all other states and had restricted both its own claims and those of the lord on the peasants' output. The legal framework protecting the substantial peasant holding, the *Meierhofverfassung*, served as a model for other lands where the government pinned its faith in such a policy to encourage economic development. Outside the Hanoverian boundaries, peasant holdings also tended to be large, although in some neighbouring areas there were still serfs bound to labour on the domains. In these areas, the rural proletariat was much more in evidence than in the south-west, because restrictions on the sub-division of peasant holdings in order to maintain a minimum unit of land use necessarily, in an age of rising population, created a larger landless class.

In Hesse, the domain was usually farmed by leasing for long periods and the leases tended to become hereditary. In Thuringia and Saxony peasants held their lands for feudal dues in cash and the size of holding, thanks to protection by the government, was larger than in the south-west, although smaller than in Hanover.

In south Germany, primogeniture was the normal rule of inheritance, so that in the Alpine lands and in Bavaria the largest peasant holdings were to be found. But this was of less significance for the future development of Bavaria, because less of the land was actually in peasant hands. The greatest Bavarian landholder was the church, holding over half the land in many areas and everywhere being a greater landholder than the nobility. The ruler himself held 13·6 per cent as his domain, leaving only 4 per cent as unencumbered peasant land.

Eastward of the Elbe, the noble estate was still most usually cultivated by serfs. It was believed for a long time by historians that the general prevalence of serfdom in eastern Europe and its relative rarity in the west were evidences that the west had advanced further along the path of economic progress. The most potent dissolvent of serfdom was thought, not unreasonably, to have been money. The greater involvement of the feudal economy of western Europe in trade was thought to have increased the range of goods available and to have induced the lord to substitute cash payments by his serfs for labour obligations. This was contrasted with the widespread practice of serfdom in eastern Europe where, it was argued, 'the money economy' had not yet dissolved the feudal ties.

Unfortunately for this view, many large noble estates in eastern Germany were actively engaged in producing grain for the market, often quite distant. From the ports of Danzig (Gdansk), Elbing (Elblag) and Königsberg (Kaliningrad) 300,000 tons of grain a year were shipped to western markets at the end of the century. The great size of the noble estates in those areas provided the opportunity to exercise economies of scale unrealisable by the peasant cultivator. In addition, the institution of serfdom gave the lord a ready supply of free labour, an advantage which enabled him to overcome high transport costs. Over most of eastern Europe, however, the great estates were not cultivated for this purpose. In Hungary, the transport problems were so severe that the product of the estate could often not be marketed, and both there and in Russia the estate could function as an almost self-sufficient unit. But in Pomerania, in Mecklenburg and in northern Poland, where grain could be shipped down the Oder or the Vistula to Baltic ports and thence to grain-deficiency areas, the institution of serfdom coincided with a high degree of involvement of the noble landlords in a commercial economy.

Even more unfortunately for the earlier concept that the decay of serfdom was a function of economic progress was the fact that, at the very period when the compulsory labour services were most rapidly disappearing in the west, they were being imposed for the first time in the east. In fact, eastern serfdom was not the last vestige of a historic feudal system, it was a comparatively recent development; and, although it closely resembled its western European medieval precursor, it was not exactly the same. The two types of serfdom were sometimes distinguished in Germany, where they both existed, by separate words, *Leibeigenschaft* and *Erbuntertanigkeit*. The feudal servitude of western Europe had involved subjection to the fact of the lord's lordship, to the legal quality of his person, *Leibeigenschaft*. *Erbuntertanigkeit*, the concept which was more common in the east, involved subjection to the land. As the frontier of arable farming had been pushed further eastward in Europe, the colonising process had been accompanied by institutional arrangements which tied the cultivators to the land. In many areas colonised by German settlers, whole villages had been bound in this way. Slav villages would often have a worse legal status, and this status tended to spread westward into more purely German areas. The *Erbuntertan* remained, however, a full legal person, belonging to the estate and not to its possessor. He is best considered as a part of that estate's capital equipment, a tool for cultivating the land when little other technology than human hands was available.

The practical difference between *Leibeigenschaft* and *Erbuntertanigkeit* became blurred in the eighteenth century. The Imperial decrees abolishing serfdom in Bohemia and Austria spoke of *Leibeigenschaft*, although the word was quite new there. In Germany attributes of both conditions could be legally identified in the same person both in the east and the west. In Russia the serf lost his legal entity and was left entirely in the hands of the noble for matters of justice. Certainly the two institutions were strikingly alike in their incidence. The *Erbuntertan*, like the western serf, was liable to compulsory, unpaid labour on the lord's estate for a number of days in the year. His children might not leave the estate, nor marry without the permission of the lord. He himself was subject to all manner of restrictions on his economic activity. If his labour services were fixed at the discretion of the lord, from the serf's point of view his social and economic position was much the same whatever the legal origins of his status. And, economically, the net result to the lord of the two systems was much the same also. *Erbuntertanigkeit* in fact provided one advantage for the lord of particular value: it bound the children of the *Erbuntertan* to labour in the manorial economy in the lord's household as servants at a much lower wage than free labour could have claimed (*Gesindedienst*). But to all policies of land reform in the eighteenth century, the difference was crucial. To abolish serfdom in the west, as the French government was repeatedly called on to do, was in most areas to sweep away a number of constraints on the full manhood of the human being, which had come already to be thought of as regrettable. Although it might have important economic effects, particularly where it removed restrictions on the right of movement, it was essentially a juridical statement. But in the east, to abolish serfdom in this sense was economically meaningless, not merely because the personal status of the *Erbuntertan* was less degrading in eighteenth-century eyes, but because it involved no less than the abolition of the total economic fabric. It implied a complete restructuring of the whole economy.

The rough correspondence between the area of *Erbuntertanigkeit* in Germany and that of *Gutsherrschaft* shows how closely bound they were. It was seen at its most rigid in the central and eastern territories of Prussia, where it was used by the government as the basis of the whole social and military order. The Prussian nobility became a legally impenetrable cast, administering their estates and, in return for the full gamut of fiscal and juridical privileges, officering the army whose regiments they recruited themselves on their own estates. Under Frederick II bourgeois encroachments on noble land were ended and with royal encouragement the nobility used the device of the entail (*Fideikommiss*) to prevent their estates from being broken up through the normal incidences of family history by bequeathing them through two generations during their own lifetime. The entail was widely used by the nobility everywhere, but nowhere were there so few legal restrictions on its deployment as in Prussia. While noble estates in Sweden were being broken up by government policy, while a peasant society was emerging in France and in many parts of western Germany, the manorial economy of the great estate was being developed in Prussia into the fundamental social and administrative unit of the country.

The amount of land in the noble estates of many parts of Prussia was very much increased in the eighteenth century, not least because the process of settlement and colonisation in these areas was still a continuing one. At the end of the reign of Frederick II almost one-third of the cultivators were recent settlers. The area of *Gutsland* doubled in Brandenburg during the century and increased threefold in Pomerania. In East Prussia this expansion was sometimes at the expense of the smaller cultivators. The nobles cultivated their estates for a growing external market. The farms of the serfs were little more than the plots which the time left to them permitted them to cultivate. The noble estate was the basis of local administration and of army administration, the noble both entrepreneur and recruiting officer and, because the biggest food market was the army, the final arbiter of the price of the serf's produce. The regular periods of military duty in most years of his working life, the liability to provide fodder and grazing for military horses, the high military taxes to sustain so proportionately high an army not only tended to reduce the peasant cultivator's interest in improving his yield but annulled many of the advantages of security of tenure which the rigid divisions of society carried with it. Henning's calculations show that an East Prussian peasant's dues were much less in terms of real produce than those of a peasant in the western districts around Paderborn, but that better yields per unit of land-holding in the west made the effective burden there less.[1] The military basis of Prussian society meant that the development of *Gutsherrschaft* in the eighteenth century was arrested by the control and interference of the government. In Mecklenburg where the government had much less power than in Prussia the peasant holdings were suppressed and incorporated into the noble's domain throughout the century. Here, as in Prussia, the western concepts of serfdom, *Leibeigenschaft*, were assimilated into the law and allowed the noble to claim more effectively a number of minor dues which he had previously claimed only with difficulty and he became a greater and greater consumer of the services of his peasants and serfs. In Mecklenburg as in Brandenburg the labour service (*Frondienst*) owed varied between three and six days per week but it was much less rigorously controlled. Although the ducal govern-ment permitted the redemption of labour services on its own domains this practice never spread to the noble estates. The number of peasant holdings may have been reduced by 60 per cent between 1729 and 1794. The motive behind this reconstitution of the domain was the profit accruing to the lord from grain exports. The possi-bility was provided by extending the burden of dues on the serfs so that they could not maintain their plots as economic units and, faced with a hostile land law, lost their hold on them. Mager's calculations based on Klüver's early survey estimate that the burden of dues, taxes and food purchase on the serf was between 75 and 80 per cent of the gross return on his unit of land if he is assumed to have spent one-twelfth of his gross return on food.[2] Without knowing the serf's expenditure on other necessaries as a proportion of his gross return it is not possible to estimate his true net return but it is clear that in normal circumstances he was operating close to or at a deficit. The result of this was to create a 'landless prole-

[1] F. W. Henning, *Dienste und Abgaben der Bauern im achtzehnten Jahrhundert* (Stuttgart, 1969).

[2] F. Mager, *Geschichte des Bauerntums und der Bodenkultur im Lande Mecklen-burg* (Berlin, 1955); H. H. Klüver, *Beschreibung des Hertzogthums Mecklenburg und dazu gehörigen Länder und Oerter* (Hamburg 1737–42).

tariat' larger than elsewhere, rigorously bound to the estate by law and economic necessity.

– in Spain

The division between the systems of *Gutsherrschaft* and *Grund-herrschaft* in Germany corresponded very roughly to the division in land tenure practices between western and eastern Europe. Although such practices were much modified by governmental power or local custom, as a general rule in all those areas of western Europe which had been a part of feudal society land law still derived from that society and land holding had evolved on lines comparable to those in France. Where feudal society had not existed, in areas which had been occupied by non-Christian invaders from other societies and subsequently reconquered, the system of land-holding was based on a more 'colonial' pattern, land-law having been devised to encourage settlement and ploughing of the land.

This division was therefore also present in Spain. In Galicia most of the peasant farms were cultivated on hereditary leases as in France and the peasant had even acquired the right of sub-letting. In most areas of northern Spain the distribution of the peasant population between those whose main income was derived from selling their labour and those whose income came from selling their produce seems to have been very similar to that in France. The landless or almost landless labourers (*jornaleros*) were less than 25 per cent of the total population in Galicia and Asturias; in the Basque provinces, where peasant right was even better established, they seem to have been quite rare. In Aragon, Valencia and Catalonia, the lord still retained and farmed large parts of his domain and the demand for wage labour appears to have increased the proportion of wage labour in rural society. Nevertheless in all those areas and in Castile, where the lord was usually less interested in the direct cultivation of his own domain, which was let on very long leases, the distribution of the output was on much the same lines as in France, although as yet we know too little to be more precise. In southern Spain, however, the nobility lived almost entirely off rent-rolls accruing from large estates reconquered from the Moors and settled. Nobility and wage-workers alike lived in the towns and the landless workers, about five-sixths of the population in Seville, journeyed out each day to cultivate the fields. In the main arable areas of Portugal, hereditary leases accounted for 28 per cent of the land. Where such leases had not developed, the nobility, as in south-western France and in Italy, had developed a system akin to *métayage* which enabled them to redivide the output annually.

– in the Netherlands

In the Low Countries, the 'commutation' of feudal labour services had produced as many local differences of tenure as in the western areas of Germany. As a general rule the proportion of land held by the nobility was relatively low; in the Prince-Bishopric of Liége it was 25 per cent while 46 per cent of the land was held by the peasantry. The Austrian government in 1755 had permitted all payers of feudal dues whether in cash or kind on royal domains to redeem their obligations by a cash payment. But these reforms were of much greater significance in the Austrian Crown Lands than in the relatively remote dependency of the Austrian Netherlands, for there feudal dues had already frequently fallen into disuse and could not easily be revived by the nobility in the eighteenth century. In Flanders, feudal payments were rare and in Liége the bishops no longer collected *taille*. Budgets show that in fact in Liége, a larger peasant farmer might retain up to 50 per cent of the return on a typical year's operations. He was much better off than his French cousin across the border. Both the Austrian Netherlands and the United Provinces, like many areas of eastern and northern Germany, had considerable stretches of land which were converted into arable land in the eighteenth century and this played a major part in changing the pattern of land tenure. For example, the larger peasants of Drenthe and Groningen bore a superficial resemblance to the *Meier* of the neighbouring German Münsterland, but in fact the Groningen peasantry alone had similarly well-established but essentially feudal tenures. Drenthe had been colonised in the eighteenth century and the peasant leases usually stipulated that a third of the yield should go to the land-owner. In Overyssel, feudal services lasted into the first quarter of the nineteenth century.

– in Scandinavia

In Denmark government policy was derived from what had happened in Hanover and 'peasant protection' had a high priority. Serfdom was abolished in 1788 although the act of abolition was more the end of a process of internal agricultural reform rather than the beginning.[3] In Sweden and Norway most land had been

3 See chapter 8.

settled comparatively recently but the system was quite different from that of *Gutsherrschaft*. Peasant right had become almost absolute. In Norway the *odel* tenures allowed the peasant the right to regain land whose possession he had lost. In Sweden, even where the *dominium directum* still lay in the hands of the noble, it was quite common for the peasant cultivator to pay no feudal dues. Tenancies on royal estates were redeemed into freeholds, the crown taking as tax what it had previously taken in feudal payments. The poverty of the Swedish peasantry cannot therefore be attributed to the social system to the same extent as elsewhere in Europe. The supply of land was plentiful, the cultivator could retain a higher proportion of his output and his labour was his own. In such a society there was much greater scope for technological improvements in farming to produce higher incomes by improving yields, and since so much of the land was cultivated by peasants rather than nobles the tendency might be for higher incomes to produce a more favourable ratio of investment to consumption. The contrast with Mecklenburg, separated only by a narrow sea from Sweden is absolute and indicates once again how explanations of the differing course of economic development in Europe lead us back well before the eighteenth century.

– in the Habsburg Empire

It was in the Habsburg Empire that the problem of the deployment of the peasant's output was most seriously tackled by the government. In part the government's actions were just one aspect of an attempt to centralise and unify the administration of a collection of different territories with widely varying histories and constitutional relationships to the Imperial government, in part they were 'peasant protection' for the same military motives as in German states, but they were also, certainly after 1780, during the reign of Joseph II, a conscious attempt to further the development of the country by the explicit encouragement of agricultural investment. The desired aim, running like a constant thread through the various twists and turns of government policy, was to create a peasant proprietor class with sufficient income and security of tenure and to provide a relatively liberal economic framework within which it could operate. To achieve this, the whole nexus of relationships between government, nobility and serfs had to be revalued. Hungary was unquestionably that part of the Empire where the serf retained the smallest part of his output and was least well protected. The ancient privileges of the Hungarian nobility established by the Convention of Szatmar prevented the Imperial power from really being effective there and the nobility were less troubled by the power of the government in Vienna. The greatest scope for intervention lay in Bohemia and Moravia and it is there that we can best see the fundamental nature of these problems for eighteenth-century society.

After the final defeat of the Hussite forces in 1620 the Czech lands of the Austrian crown had been settled with a new nobility, mostly German, and the Czech cultivators had been subjected to a brutal serfdom. The Imperial government tried to modify this brutality in is own interests in the eighteenth century. In 1738 labour services (*robota*) were restricted to three days a week except in harvest periods. In 1751, a general edict which applied also to Bohemia and Moravia forbade further incorporation of serf land into the domain. Although such legislation was not easy to enforce the seriousness of the government's intention to change affairs in Bohemia was demonstrated when Prince Mansfeld was deprived of his estates in 1768 for violating the laws. In 1770 forced domestic service was abolished together with the marriage fee to the lord for the marriage of the serf's children. At the same time all commercial privileges of the lord over the serf which might block the establishment of a true market price for the serf's produce were abolished. The urgency of the problem was revealed by the Bohemian famine of 1772 in which it is estimated that one-tenth of the peasant population died. The consequence was the *Robotpatent* of 1775. The amount of labour service due to the lord was regulated in ratio to the size of the serf's holding; landless serfs were liable for only thirteen days unpaid manual labour a year and the total of labour due increased in accordance with the amount of land held. But where the labour service due was less than the maximum of three days a week, the lord could insist on wage labour up to that level. The length of the day and the distance to be travelled to work were both controlled.

Such measures, although alienating the nobility, had only a crude incidence on the peasant for there was a tremendous variety of landholding in Bohemia. The 'full peasant' might hold up to 60 acres, the lesser serfs merely a garden. The lord's domain was usually farmed by the peasants on short-term leases, the rest of the estate offered little more security of tenure to those who could not maintain their obligations. The work of eliminating these differences began on the royal estates under the direction of Franz Anton von Raab and it was hoped that what was done here would spread to the noble estates as standard practice. The 'Raab system' consisted of making a new cadastral survey of the domain, dividing the serf plots into more equal areas at the expense of the domain lands and establishing a fixed scale for the 'commutation' of servile dues. This was not unlike the procedure which the nobility of Denmark were persuaded at the same time was commercially advantageous to them, but the obstacle to this persuasion in Bohemia was that the reforms, which were clearly a pilot scheme for noble estates, implied an increase in the tax burden on the nobility. For it was the ultimate intention of the government to raise its revenue from a uniform land-tax as this seemed the only way in which the same amount of government revenue could be raised if the peasant was to retain more of his output. The Austrian government was trying to arrive at the state of affairs which existed in Sweden but on the basis of a wholly different recent historical experience and, in trying to shift the tax burden from the peasant to the nobility, was trying to win for the peasant what he only won in France as the result of the Great Revolution.

It is hardly surprising that the effort should have failed. In 1782 the task began of completely abolishing *robota* throughout Bohemia and Moravia by extending the 'Raab system' to all estates. Many of the early attempts at regulation broke down because inaccurate accounting of the previous decade's operations on the estate led to an unfair reallocation of land and because many of the early leases were too short-term to offer any greater security than the previous serf tenures. The intention was that the peasant should retain 70 per cent of his gross income, the remaining 30 per cent to be paid in the proportion of $12\frac{2}{9}$ per cent to the state and $17\frac{7}{9}$ per cent to the lord and the church. Had this been everywhere achieved, it would have meant a considerable drop in the share of the peasant's output going to the lord while increasing the state's revenue and maintaining it constant, not at the expense of the peasant, but of the lord's income. Between 1749 and 1763, the state had taken 42 per cent of the peasant's gross income. These reforms would apply only to the wealthier peasantry because if the noble were to be left with his domain, there would be insufficient land to create an economic farming unit for every peasant on the estate. But poor peasantry would benefit from the previous regulation of *robota* and the consequent increase in the demand for wage labour.

The 'Raab system' together with budgets for settlers on new lands in Austria give us some insight into the size of peasant holding necessary to conduct profitable operations. Budgets for Prussian settlers on the new estates of Pardubitz with 5 hectares of highly fertile land each show an annual income of 139 florins and outgoings of 148 florins. Those with 15 hectares of land, however, were relatively prosperous. The 'Raab system' normally awarded at the start 5·5 hectares but this was found insufficient. We may therefore

Raab system : ÷ ld ; strong peasantry.

suppose that on averagely fertile land under the reformed system, about 10 hectares of land per peasant household was necessary if the aims of government policy were to be achieved and the peasant to retain a sufficient surplus to sustain a higher level of investment. In the Austrian Netherlands the Abbé Mann advocated 12·5 hectares as the size of the ideal peasant farm and with all due allowance made for variations in farming practice and soil fertility, this would seem a good yardstick against which to measure the size of peasant holdings elsewhere.

In fact the whole Austrian experiment was brought to a halt by violent revolt in 1789 and the Austrian crown lands remained for some time frozen in a curious state which, although it was not serfdom, which had been formally abolished in 1781, retained the structure of a serf society closely regulated by the government. Tebeldi's calculations for the 1840s estimated that the economic position of the Austrian peasant was still far worse than that which policy had aimed at sixty years before.[4] By that time, when, it should be remembered, peasant holdings had shrunk due to increasing sub-division to cope with rising population, the average German and Slav peasant in the Empire was retaining only 30 per cent of his income plus 14 per cent which went to servicing debts; the lord was taking 24 per cent and taxation 13 per cent. His situation had scarcely improved from the eighteenth century when estimates show he was retaining about 27 per cent of his gross income and it was no better than that of the French peasant before the revolution.

Yet something survived of this great period of agricultural reform. The general decree of 1781 abolished all the personal incidences of serfdom (*Leibeigenschaft*) and this, taken with decrees regulating the burden of labour services, provided effective maxima for such services in many areas of the Empire creating an active labour market and much more personal mobility, even though after 1798 'commutation' of labour services became very difficult to achieve. Labour services were regulated in Austrian Silesia in 1771, in Lower Austria (where they were fixed at two days a week) in 1772, in Styria and Carinthia (three days a week) in 1778, in Carniola in 1782 and in Galicia in 1786. The general decree of 1781 abolished compulsory domestic labour and all *banalités*. The result was ironical. Where Joseph II had hoped to produce a stable peasant freeholding society, what emerged was a society where the larger peasant was sufficiently emancipated to profit from the wage labour of the less emancipated. Rigid restrictions on social and labour mobility, like those prevailing in Prussia, were relaxed to the point where economic development and social change could prevent the Emperor's peasant dream from

4 A. Tebeldi, *Die Geldangelegenheiten Österreichs* (Leipzig, 1847), p. 217.

ever becoming a reality. Nor was the consequence in the long run the failure of the country to develop economically, for Bohemia became one of the earliest of European areas to industrialise.

In Hungary the opposition to Joseph II's policies was most formidable and they had little effect there. Hopes of success would in any case have been more slender, not only because of the great power of the Hungarian nobility, but also because of the high degree of landlessness amongst the peasantry. About one-third of the land was peasant land in Croatia and about one-quarter in Hungary proper, a smaller proportion than elsewhere in the Empire. Labour services were, on the average, 104 days a year. In Slavonia, and the Banat about half of their number was usually commuted, but in Hungary proper very little. The great noble estates of the arable plains relied heavily on labour services but their economy was very different from the *Gutsherrschaft* of Mecklenburg. Transport over featureless dusty tracks which turned into quagmires in winter was too discouraging. There were scarcely any roads even to the river ports and the economy of a great Magyar estate remained patriarchal, self-sufficient and isolated; grain surpluses in a good year were stored for consumption in a bad year because there was no market to which they could be shipped. Here the subjection of the peasantry did not increase in the eighteenth century through the commercial activities of the lords, as was common elsewhere unless the government intervened. It was merely a part of the fixed and unchanging order of things, an order which paid little regard to the outside world.

– in Poland and Russia

The agricultural economy of Poland was more externally oriented for she had been an exporter of rye since the seventeenth century. Measurements of the income accruing to Polish noble landlords in the eighteenth century show that, although it rose, the increase did not come from the increasing grain market so much as from a secondary commercial activity, distilling, of which they had a monopoly. On those noble farms leased from the royal domain, distilling was responsible for 40 per cent of the income by the 1780s. As a part of the noble's total income the peasant's contribution was diminishing. But that is merely to measure his money contribution, for distilling depended not only on deliveries in kind from the serfs but on their labour too. Nevertheless the peasant retained his land and no significant landless group developed as it had in Mecklenburg. The same was true for the whole Baltic area.

C

But there the resemblance ends, for the average size of the holding of a crown peasant in Poland was about 11 hectares, whereas in Lithuania the average peasant holding was 18·5 hectares and in Latvia 25 hectares. The concepts of *Leibeigenschaft* had made little headway in Poland, the serf was an *Erbuntertan*, the lord's claim on his surplus was therefore the forced labour which the peasant owed to the dominical farm and the payment in kind which he occasionally made. The burden of these dues was about 20 per cent of the peasant's gross annual return.

In Russia and in Poland alike where the importance of the serf consisted in his labour dues, the wealth of the noble could most accurately be computed by counting the number of his serfs for there was no other item of capital equipment on the estate which approached them in total value. Although the value of an individual horse in such a system was greater than that of a man, its demands were just as great, its flexibility as a tool less and its replacement period shorter. There were 3,404,700 serfs in Poland in 1791 on noble estates, 9,997,625 in 1795 in Russia. The average holding of serfs per noble in Russia in that year was 51·8. In 1777 32 per cent of the nobles held less than ten serfs and 30·7 per cent between ten and thirty serfs. In that year 4·1 per cent of the Russian nobility owned over 500 serfs each. The inequality of serf holding was thus extremely wide and it was almost certainly wider in Poland where a considerable number of the lesser gentry owned two serfs or less.

Like the Polish nobility the Russian nobility were also becoming grain exporters. It was the argument of the earliest historians of Russian agriculture that this trade, taken in conjunction with a much greater internal trade, led to an increasing level of monetisation in the economy of the noble estate. It was accordingly argued that the system of farming the estate by forced labour dues (*barshchina*) was giving way before a more advanced economic system, that of cultivating the estate on leases to the serfs (*obrok*). Recent research has drawn attention to the existence in many areas of a combination of *barshchina* and *obrok* where some peasants on the estate owed labour services and others made money payments. Such 'mixed dues' presented no problem to earlier scholars for they assumed that any element of monetisation was a sign of progress and so counted mixed dues as *obrok*. This was to see developments in Russia with western eyes for although the Russian nobility might ape the French nobility in dress and manner and although this in itself necessarily increased their consumption and their demand for liquid capital, their commercial opportunities were very much more circumscribed.

Over such vast distances and in so backward an economy trade moved very sluggishly and the Russian estate was as self-sufficient as the Hungarian. If 'mixed dues' are not counted as *obrok*, the relative proportion of estates cultivated by pure *obrok* or by pure *barshchina* does not change in favour of *obrok* in the eighteenth century. What actually happens is that the number of estates cultivated by a mixture of the two systems increases. The explanation for this may lie in the changing status of the nobility itself. It received its privileges as a noble class from Tsar Peter I in the early eighteenth century in return for being bound, like the Prussian nobility, to state service. Such service could take the noble far from his estate, as indeed could many other events in so huge a land. Where the lord was absent the most feasible system of cultivation was *obrok*, *barshchina* demanded constant supervision and enforcement of the labour services. As the Imperial government weakened, the nobility escaped from its obligations until the Tsarina Catherine II freed them formally from such service in 1762. Although public employment remained the livelihood of many Russian families, a movement back to the estate began in the 1770s, briefly interrupted by Pugachev's revolt from 1772 to 1774. As nobles returned to their estates they found it more convenient to consume a higher proportion of their serfs' labour and introduced elements of *barshchina* into what had been formerly *obrok* systems thus bringing about an increase in the proportion of 'mixed dues'. The nobles' objective was an adequate balance of liquid capital and labour services rather than merely an increase in liquid capital. Nothing could better make the point again that where the central government did not intervene the contract between the peasant and the noble was formulated simply by the entrepreneurial decision of the noble. Nor did increasing commercialisation and increasing trade result in a slackening of the ties of serfdom; in Russia, as in Mecklenburg and Poland it strengthened those ties. Russia was the extreme version of a society where the central government abandoned the peasants entirely to the nobles, but the economic developments inside the estate were only an extreme version of the economic pressure which the French nobleman brought to bear on his feudal tenants.

This could be further exemplified by the introduction of serfdom into the areas of 'New Russia', those lands on the Black Sea conquered from the Turks in the last third of the eighteenth century. At first these lands were declared open to settlers from Poland and Germany but forbidden to Russian serfs in order not to disturb the manorial economy of the country within its old frontiers. The number of settlers arriving was very small and in 1796 serfdom was extended into New Russia and the Caucasus although it did not embrace the earlier foreign settlers there. Furthermore it can also be shown that where arable farming was most intensive, serfs were a greater proportion of the total male population. They formed 60 to 70 per cent of the male population of some of the black-earth provinces, whereas they formed only 49 per cent of the male population of the whole country. At the end of the eighteenth century, Ukrainian homesteaders in the lands captured from Poland were also subjected to serfdom. Even the much discussed land reform plan of Count Sievers in Livonia which aimed to create a hereditary peasant society, as in north Germany, and which was refused by the Tsar, would still have retained serfdom as a part of that society. There is every indication that serfdom was increasing its hold in Russia and that where the lord could demand more labour services he did do so.

– in Romania

One final example will confirm this trend, that of Romania. The peasants were first tied to the land in Wallachia at the very end of the sixteenth century and there as elsewhere in eastern Europe it was a device for getting the newly acquired lands settled and culti-vated. In fact the Wallachian Decree of 1595 was derived from Hungarian practice in the recently settled Transylvanian province. The dues in Wallachia were very light, twelve days work a year, compared to the six days a week of Mecklenburg or the five days a week of Russia. In the eighteenth century, legal changes supported by the Phanariot rulers of the Romanian lands who wished to settle even greater areas introduced the concepts of feudal dues and serfdom in a much more comprehensive way and all witnesses agree that the condition of the Romanian peasantry deteriorated sharply in that period. In 1770, Alexander Yppsilanti fixed the burden on the peasants at one-tenth of their gross income. On the very eve of the French Revolution therefore, Romanian society was just being formed in the very economic mould that in France the revolution would destroy.

Conclusion

Let us sum up the conclusions that derive from this survey:

1. The structure of the agrarian sector of the economy was very different from one European state to another and within states regional differences could be just as great.

2. These differences were not confined to the methods of farming the land but involved profound differences in the social system and the economy, for, just as agriculture was the basis of the economy, so was the pattern of land tenure and land ownership the basis of society.

3. Although everywhere the level of agricultural productivity was very low, there were considerable differences in productivity which were not merely the result of differences in the soil or climate but reflected a higher level of investment or greater degree of knowledge on the part of the cultivators. The wheat yield for a given quantity of seed in the Netherlands was over twice that common in Germany, that in Germany greater than the most fertile areas of Russia.

4. The higher level of agriculture in some regions was a function of the differences in the social system in so far as some systems permitted greater savings or encouraged a higher level of investment through greater internal demand. Therefore those systems which had already developed a higher level of savings or investment were also better constituted for development in the future so long as that development was based on the agricultural sector.

5. It is not easy to see which types of societies were best constituted for such growth. In every case the arrangements of land tenure derived from the historical past and this past still dominated economic arrangements. The payments made for the use of the land were not rent in the modern sense. They were representative of a much wider set of factors than supply and demand and their level fixed by custom, by history and by the whole social system. In some areas, however, a peasant society had emerged with a guaranteed title to the land. In these areas the proportion of the output of the peasant farm which the peasant could retain varied enormously. The surplus which he lost went to government, to the nobility or to the church. In every case it could still theoretically be used for investment but the likelihood was much greater if it went to the nobility. Therefore the systems where the nobility were able to cream off the biggest share of the peasant's output were theoretically just as well constituted for development as those where the peasant was best established. Similarly, those areas with an overwhelming preponderance of very big noble estates also had many theoretical advantages for development. It all depended on what the noble or the peasant did with the money.

6. Patterns of consumption varied widely between the nobility of different countries. The Russian nobility, imitating their western peers, were notorious for the lavishness of their consumption. The greater the isolation of the estate, the less the noble's incentive

to market crops for cash and the greater the tendency to a pattern of consumption dictated by the extent to which the estate was able to sustain itself autarkically. Few nobles anywhere had any real system of cost accounting and hence their decisions between consumption and investment were arbitrary ones or governed by national custom. That was also true of the peasantry amongst whom national custom was more marked than amongst their superiors and for whom local custom was even more important. But as we have seen peasant consumption was very low everywhere compared to that of the nobles.

7. There is no evidence that the growing external and internal trade in the eighteenth century operated in a uniform way on these various societies. It did not necessarily encourage the noble to transform labour services into money payments and was not responsible for 'the decay of serfdom'. The effect of access to a market was different on each society and was also a function of the way that society was organised. For example, in some societies, greater access to markets, either foreign or domestic, led to an increase in labour services because the nobility were able to impose this on their serfs. Thus the tendency in eighteenth-century Europe was for these differences in social and economic organisation to grow rather than diminish. Where the government did not intervene, the decisions dictating the social pattern were all essentially entrepreneurial decisions by the noble on the best use of labour and liquid funds.

8. If the question of future growth is considered from the point of view of investment in commerce and industry rather than in agriculture, these differences of social structure were still vitally important. They were partly responsible for the varied pattern of capital holdings in different societies and for the differing attitudes to industrial development which prevailed there. Not only that, the differences in land tenure were responsible for the extent to which any potential industrial labour force was bound to the land by law (as in Russia) or by the protection of the government (as in Hanover) or by the fact that land was widely available on reasonable terms (as in Sweden). Alternatively they were responsible for the existence in other areas of a large poor group bound to the land only by the fact that no better employment existed (as in France or Württemberg). Where this agricultural proletariat was most developed, it could still be bound to the land by law as well as by lack of opportunity (as in Mecklenburg or Hungary). The possibilities, it may be said, were infinite, but in every case the existing social system at the end of the eighteenth century had a profound effect on the pattern and type of future development.

FARMING METHODS AND AGRICULTURAL IMPROVEMENT

It is now necessary to look at the question, what did the noble or the peasant do with the surplus. Did he save it, invest it or consume it? The background conditions for agricultural investment were *shld be* extraordinarily favourable; a rising population meant a rising demand *qualified* for food, particularly for bread, and this was reflected especially *to incl.* after 1750, in rising prices. The rise in the price of grains may be *higher incom* seen from Figure 2. Grain was almost everywhere the most important

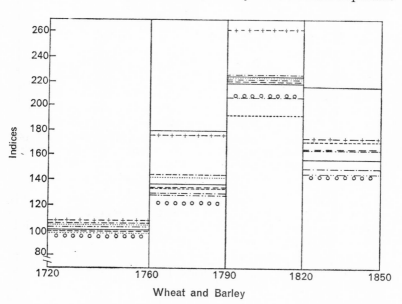

Fig. 2. Indices of cereal prices, 1721–1850. (The period 1721–45 = 100) (*Source*: B. H. Slicher van Bath, *The Agrarian History of Western Europe*, London, 1963, p. 230.)

—··——··——··— Friesland
○ ○ ○ ○ ○ ○ ○ ○ ○ Zealand
— —— —— —— — England
— — — — — — — — France
—·——·——·——·— N. Italy

———————————— Strasbourg
—·—··—··—··—··— Berlin
-+-+-+-+-+-+-+-+ Denmark
▬▬▬▬▬▬▬▬▬ Friesland
.... Groningen

product of the land. 53 per cent of the cash value of the net output of Prussian farms in 1800 was accounted for by grain, only 24 per cent by animal products; in most areas of Germany today these proportions would be reversed. As shown in Table 1 Toutain's figures for the growth of French agricultural output in the eighteenth century show a proportionately greater increase in animal output but the value of that animal production was very small compared to that of arable output. Their reliability for the period 1701–10 is very doubtful indeed but the likelihood is that the figures for that decade are overstatements.

Table 1. *The increase of agricultural output in eighteenth-century France*

Period	Cereals		Meat		Wine
	Value (000 current francs)	*Quantity (00,000 kilograms)*	*Value (000 current francs)*	*Quantity (000 tons)*	*Quantity (000 hecto-litres)*
1701–10	826	59·1	73	160	33·5
1751–60	716	61·5	88	227	27·3
1771–80	1,179	75·6	148	316	29·8
1781–90	1,369	85·3	257	459	24·5

Source: J.-C. Toutain, 'Le produit de l'agriculture française de 1700 à 1958. Estimation du produit au dix-huitième siècle', *Cahiers de l'Institut de Science Économique Appliquée*, no. 115, July 1961.

In Germany the rise of grain prices was clearly greater than that of the prices of animal products. Grain prices in Schleswig-Holstein doubled between 1731–40 and 1791–1800, the prices of animal products increased by only 50 per cent. The increase in grain prices was also greater than the increase in the price of industrial crops such as flax or silk. Figure 2 shows how the prices of wheat and barley continued to increase in Europe for all those places where we have sufficient information until the end of the Napoleonic Wars. The phenomenon was not a local one. The situation reproduced in Table 2 based on records of the estates of Count Schaff-

Table 2. *Index of prices of goods produced and of wages on the Schaffgotsch Estates in Prussian Silesia*

Period	Grain	Commercial Crops	Wages
1711–50	100	100	100
1751–90	117	110	111
1791–1810	157	125	121

Source: W. Abel, *Geschichte der deutschen Landwirtschaft* (Stuttgart, 1962).

gotsch in Silesia must have been generally valid for many parts of Europe.

In all those areas where arable farming was not greatly disadvantaged by the climate, bread grains were the principal cash crop. Ploughing up required a high initial capital investment and the kind of agricultural improvements encouraged by the eighteenth-century economy placed a premium on such investment.

However, the level of investment was only to a small extent a function of the level of demand as expressed in rising prices, it was far more a function of the total social system. Many of the social systems which seemed to be best organised for response to rising prices did not really respond, whereas others, in which the economic conditions seemed less promising, did. In Russia where there were huge areas of fertile virgin land to be cultivated, the degree of agricultural improvement was quite negligible. Of course, investment there took the form of bringing new lands into cultivation. But so it did everywhere in eighteenth-century Europe where this was possible and in many areas this process was accompanied by distinct increases in productivity whereas in Russia this was less noticeable. Certain kinds of improvement could take place within certain societies without demanding any changes in the social framework. Other types of improvement required nothing less than the reconstruction of rural society. The reasons why this was so were mostly concerned with the communal nature of farming.

Over large areas of Europe the system of farming the land had developed around the practice of leaving some part of the total stock of land available to the village or community fallow for a certain period in order to restore its fertility. Outside the Mediterranean area and the northern forest zone, where arable farming was less developed, the typical system was for the village to have at its disposal a certain number of common fields, most usually three, in which all the inhabitants had a greater or lesser share. The shares were held in the form of strips, often not contiguous, divided by earthern baulks or ditches. The fields themselves were rotated according to a commonly-agreed pattern. In a three-field system, for example, one field would lie fallow one year in every three. Where the land was less fertile five-, six-, and even seven-field systems were devised with the principal cash crop, which was almost always a bread grain (rye or wheat) being cultivated every fifth, sixth or seventh year instead of every third year. In some areas it was common practice to rotate the strips themselves among all the members of the village so that each would have his turn on the best land in each field. This practice was growing in the more densely populated areas of Russia and seems to have been a response to population growth. This was the highest level of communality and was unusual; in most areas the strips had become fixed.

Even though fixed, the strips were not private property. Just as the concept of freehold land was uncommon legally, so did village custom impose the most rigorous conformity to communal practice even on the cultivator least encumbered by the ties of thralldom, serfdom, or feudality. The village communally decided on the dates of ploughing, sowing and reaping. The crops to be cultivated were decided by what had been found most practicable over time. Every member of the village was therefore caught up in an agricultural routine sanctioned by history and imposing on all the unchanging rhythm of the communal agricultural year. In many villages in France and the Austrian Netherlands it was the time-honoured custom on a certain day of the autumn to throw open the stubble fields to the communal herd in order to supplement the resources of the village common on which the herd had to live for the rest of the year. This custom, *vaine pâture*, served, together with the fact that every cultivator in the common fields was at the mercy of the level of cultivation practised by his neighbour, to discourage any experimentation with crops or farming methods. It emphasised more than any other the fact that the concept of private property was still in its infancy.

The development of such a concept was ardently opposed by the poorer members of the village community. The village in most areas was surrounded by extensive areas of woodland or heathland which for many purposes was regarded as communal property. To the poorer inhabitants, it served as pasture for their animals and as a source of food, fuel, and building materials. The various rights which they had over the village commons represented a considerable part of their total wealth. Their livelihood was thus intricately involved with the communal practices of the village. Those villagers who had enough strips to make it worth their while to collect them together into a single land unit large enough to plough and sow with grain had every advantage in emancipating themselves from the routine of the common fields. In France, peasants who could benefit in this way were numerous enough for local administrators to induce the government to permit enclosure of individual farms within the village community in certain areas. Such actions were directly harmful to those whose strips were too small to be worth converting into a private enclosed holding and they were able to put up a determined resistance to enclosure.

The animals of the village were usually kept in common, so that improvement of the stock by selective breeding was virtually as impossible as attempting different methods of arable farming. In fact there was a very close correspondence between the output of the arable strips and the quantity of animals, for no other fertiliser than animal manure was used and the fertility of the ploughland depended on the amount of manure available. Any increase in arable farming on the same area of land in order to respond to the increased demand for bread grain was difficult without an increase in the animal stock. Where new land was not available, an increase in the animal stock could only occur at the expense of the arable land. It is easy to slip into the argument that because of these immutable facts of nature there was no way in which eighteenth-century farming could respond to rising prices except by the destruction of the communal system. Such an argument is a false statement of the position for it implies that communality was simply an institution to be changed. It was not. It was the very basis of the farming economy and rural life. To most of its members, higher prices were not an opportunity for dynamic response, but a threat to their existence. The basic problem posed by population growth was that of keeping the greater population alive. When no other sectors of the economy had any great importance, the communal system of agriculture did keep the population alive. Although there were great famines in the late eighteenth century, in Bohemia in 1772, in France in 1789–90, they were less frequent and less disastrous than in the previous century. That, in itself, is an indication that the communal farming system did improve in spite of the apparent impossibility of changing the relationship between arable and animal farming in favour of arable.

The weakness of the communal system of agriculture lay in its potential inability to respond satisfactorily to a *continuing* population increase. The evidence from the eighteenth century is that it could respond adequately up to a certain point. There was no absolute contrast between a survival system of farming based on communal methods and a system of farming for profit based on private property. Both systems could be used, and were used, either for mere survival or for farming for profit. The level of efficiency of the communal farming system was in general in most areas very low and if opportunities for profit presented themselves the system could be improved without too great difficulty in order to respond to these opportunities. The growth of population in the eighteenth century was therefore a decisive stimulus to the improvement of the communal farming system. If the population were to continue to grow however, the ability of the communal farming system to respond to such pressures was not infinite. Certain important innovations in farming methods were not realistically applicable within the communal framework and the continued growth of population would eventually demand the adoption of every possible innovation unless another population disaster were to occur. The improvements in productive methods in eighteenth-century agriculture can be divided into those which could be and were adopted within the framework of the communal farming system and those which in the long run really demanded the dissolution of the communal system into one of private property in order to be effective.

Improvement within the existing communal system could take place in four directions. In the first place, there was still plenty of uncultivated land available in some parts of Europe which could be taken into cultivation by the increment to the human population in those areas. This process could also be helped by minor technological improvements in drainage. In the second place, the increasing knowledge of other lands outside Europe made new crops available, crops which were not indigenous to Europe but could be successfully cultivated there to relieve the apparent impasse. Thirdly, it was possible to devise new methods of crop rotation, using European crops, which could provide extra food for the cattle or eliminate or reduce the quantity of land which had to be left fallow. Fourthly, it was possible to disseminate the knowledge of all such improvements more rapidly and extensively and to help the small cultivator to introduce them. The improvement in agricultural output in the eighteenth century was mainly the result of these four processes.

Even in a relatively densely-populated country such as France, there were still regions which could be taken into cultivation in the eighteenth century; the cultivated area of Brittany was extended by one-tenth in response to population growth. Between 1766 and 1780, requests for the reclamation of 400,000 hectares of land were received by the French government. Much reclamation was a function of improved drainage techniques, for example, the building of new polders in the Groningen marshes, the extension of arable cultivation over the Campine (Kempen) heathlands in the Austrian Netherlands, the draining of the wild Danube heaths in Bavaria. It could also be the result of deliberate decisions by the government on a change of land use. For example after 1759 the Spanish government encouraged the ploughing of lands in Castile by withdrawing grazing privileges from the Mesta, the corporate guild of sheep-farmers who produced one of Spain's best-established export commodities, fine wool. Everywhere where new farms could be carved out or arable land extended, the pressure of population growth encouraged this tendency.

But the most striking example of the extension of the cultivable area was the more productive use of the common and waste lands within the village economy over an extensive area of northern Europe. This was achieved by the introduction into the communal open-field village of the system of exploitation known as *Koppelwirtschaft*. This system involved the removal of the distinctions between common fields, peasant fields and wasteland or commons, laying out the whole village land in a fairly evenly-divided number of areas and, usually, joining together the strips into units. These rationalised areas were all involved in a regular process of rotation so that within the space of time covered by the rotation all land would be involved in the system of cultivation. Not only was more land cultivated but the tiresome disputes over rights of user which prevailed in the open fields were partly eliminated. The aim of the system was to combine pasture and arable land in a better combination by avoiding the rigid distinctions between them. In Mecklenburg, *Koppelwirtschaft* served as a method of extending the arable area, in Schleswig-Holstein where the climate was wetter it served as a method of increasing the animal herds.

This rationalisation of the village farming system spread over the whole area from the Netherlands along the littoral of the North Sea and the Baltic to the borders of Poland and created a more or less contiguous area in which, although the social systems remained different, many of the disadvantages of open field strip farming were removed. The origins of these reforms, however, were very different in different areas. They spread into northern Germany from Scandinavia. The Field Consolidation Act of 1749 in Sweden permitted consolidation of the strips in the open fields if agreement could be reached between all the village cultivators and this consolidation was often the prelude to enclosure of the land. In Denmark, a series of agricultural commissions after 1757 established regional enclosure laws and in 1768, were replaced by the General Land Use Department which furthered both enclosure and rationalisation within the old system. The driving force there was the government which was able to convince noble cultivators of the benefits of a prosperous tenantry and the reforms were well established before the abolition of serfdom in 1788. The rationalisation movement spread from Denmark southwards into the Duchies of Schleswig and Holstein which were governed by the Danish crown. There, the pressure for reform clearly came from the peasantry, both the free peasants of the North Sea marshes and the serfs on the eastern coasts. Only in 1766 did an official land reallocation act for Schleswig support the peasants' activities in joining their strips together. As in Denmark, the process went ahead together with that of enclosure of a village. The Land Commission for Schleswig-Holstein began its work in 1771, serfdom was abolished in 1805. From there the movement spread into the small territory of Lauenburg. Lauenburg belonged to Hanover which had established one of the firmest of peasant protection policies and whose ruler, King George III of Britain was a noted agricultural reformer. Here too, the demand for redistribution came from the peasantry who hoped to acquire more land as their neighbours in Holstein had done, but both the state and the nobility developed a fiscal interest in developing improved peasant cultivation. The labour services were eliminated from the start and *Koppelwirtschaft* carried out on an individual basis. The movement began in 1771 on the royal domain and after 1801 on noble estates; there was no general enclosure law until 1824. From there, the movement spread into Mecklenburg at the close of the eighteenth century although there were experiments on the estates of Oberlandrat von der Lühe as early as 1700. Here, of course, the initiative had come entirely from the nobility and the movement took the form of further incorporation of peasant land into noble ownership. Serfdom was abolished in Mecklenburg in 1820 but the act of abolition made little difference to the real economic relationship which had been developed.

Westwards of Schleswig-Holstein lay territories more anciently settled where the pattern of land tenure had become too complicated to be simplified in this way. But both Hanover and Brunswick had played the leading role in defending peasant tenures and carrying out cadastral reforms in favour of the peasant. In the Austrian Netherlands, the process of dividing up the common land proceeded apace; there were general orders to this effect for Hainaut in 1757, for the Brabant Campine (Kempen) in 1772 and for Namur in 1774. The result was an area from the Channel to Mecklenburg and throughout southern Scandinavia in which the margin of cultivation was extended, by 20 per cent in Schleswig-Holstein, and in which the level of agricultural productivity was increased. South of this area these changes failed to take effect; the 1768 laws on enclosure of commons in Upper and Lower Austria had little effect.

The new crops which European farming adopted from other areas of the globe were, with one notable exception, cash crops. Maize (Indian corn), tobacco and sunflowers were all grown for the market in areas where they could be successfully cultivated. In parts of Languedoc, French cultivators began to plant maize in order to reduce the incidence of fallowing the land from alternate years to one year in three. In southern areas of Russia and in Bessarabia, maize was a frequently seen crop by 1800. Tobacco was cultivated in the Austrian Netherlands after 1776 and became a crop of some importance in the Ukraine. The sunflower was adopted especially in Bulgaria. Although rice was an older crop in Europe, the extension of its cultivation in the Po valley reflected the same trends. But by far the most important of these new crops was not a cash crop, the potato. The potato was capable of providing a far higher calorific intake from a small plot of land than any bread grain and was therefore particularly cultivated where population pressure and the inheritance system together had created extreme sub-division of the land. It became a valuable addition to the food supply in Norway where the peasant holdings were very small and where the climate favoured the potato over other crops. In Flanders, where sub-division had also reduced the size of farms, the potato covered about one-tenth of the cultivated area and was perhaps more common in the Ardennes. In the Baltic areas of Germany it spread as a field crop after 1750 but not to the same extent as in the Low Countries. In Poland it was cultivated only in the west, in Austria hardly at all and in Russia only by German colonists.

The new methods of crop rotation which developed were all methods for lessening the amount of fallow land. By the planting of root vegetables, turnips in particular, or by the sowing of clover or beans, the nitrogenous elements could be restored to the soil while it still produced a crop which could on some occasions be used as fodder. The Norfolk rotation, the best known of these systems, involved the use of turnips. Although such changes of routine were difficult in the open fields, they were not impossible and throughout the Low Countries clover and turnips were cultivated whether the fields were enclosed or not, although the tendency was for these developments to accompany and encourage the enclosure movement among the peasantry. Such innovations also brought with them improvement in the methods of ploughing, sowing and threshing all of which no doubt were responsible for the higher yields of agriculture in the Low Countries.

How far greater dissemination of agricultural knowledge took place is difficult to determine. Superficially, royal and noble landlords everywhere displayed an extraordinarily high degree of interest in agricultural techniques. George III of England was known as 'Farmer George' and the Emperor Joseph II set his imperial hand to the plough to encourage his peasants. The French queen, Marie-Antoinette, playing at milkmaids in the grounds of Versailles, was likewise a distant reflection of the importance and respectability of agriculture. Societies for the dissemination of agricultural knowledge sprang up everywhere. The first regional agricultural society in the United Provinces was founded in 1752; in 1764 the Academia de Agricultura was formed in Lerida in Spain and the Kärnter Ackerbaugesellschaft in Carinthia. All such societies indicated the awareness of the regional nobility that economic conditions were in their favour but many of their discussions remained on a fashionably theoretical basis inhibited by lack of real desire for change or simply lack of real agricultural knowledge. At the end of the century, the Free Economic Society of St Petersburg debated and declined a proposition to teach five serfs out of a hundred on the estates of its members to read – but not to write. The Hungarian Experimental Economic Institute founded in 1780 was closed down after the French Revolution.

Of greater importance was the practical knowledge acquired by pioneers of agricultural change on their own estates, for such knowledge could be compiled in handbooks and made more widely available. One of the best sources of such information was that provided by the handbooks used to instruct the agricultural administration of Prussia. In a country where, in some regions, a third of the land belonged to the crown and where a substantial part of the royal revenue depended on the efficiency with which it was cultivated, it was hardly surprising that a trained core of land managers should have been created. The 'Agricultural Handbook' of Johann Beckmann became established as a teaching manual in the early eighteenth century. By the mid-century, the so-called 'cameralist' administrators were being taught a subject in the University of Halle which could fairly be described as agricultural economics, rather than the mere mechanics of pig-breeding. This happy combination of practice and theory was unique to Prussia. It produced by the last decade of the century the works of Albrecht von Thaer, the greatest of all the propagandists of better agricultural methods.

In France, the interest in improved farming methods was quite high among the nobility, for many of them had more practical experience of such matters than their peers in other lands besides having the capital to invest. The Marquis de Turbilly organised his lands in Anjou into a model estate in 1737 and awarded 'medals of merit' to his tenantry. The first writing to have an impact comparable to that of the cameralist school in Prussia was Duhamel du Monceau's translation and elaboration of the works of the English reformer Tull in 1750. Henry Patullo's *Essay on the Improvement of Land* in 1765, was the first work to describe properly the new methods of crop rotation practised in England and Flanders. Duhamel's work deservedly achieved considerable renown and was translated into Polish by the Polish agricultural reformer Piotr Switkowski, an ardent propagandist of crop rotations. In the Austrian Netherlands, the Abbé Mann also publicised and elaborated these practical developments. In Hungary, Count Antal Amadé reorganised his estates and Samuel Tessedik and Gergely Berzecviczy both published works on agriculture of some value. In the last decade of the century

D. M. Poltoratskii began his agricultural reforms in Kaluga province in Russia.

OBSTACLES TO IMPROVEMENT

But changes of any kind were adopted only slowly and the capacity for the agricultural base to improve its productivity merely by greater knowledge was very limited. Arthur Young's account of French agriculture in 1789 shows how isolated reformed estates and modern practice were forty years after Duhamel's book. South of a line from Luxembourg to the Atlantic coast just south of the Loire estuary, scarcely any improvement at all had taken place. Even in 1840, the yield of wheat per hectare in the French department of Nord was 20·7 hectolitres whereas in the more southerly departments of Lot-et-Garonne and Var it was respectively 9·4 and 9·5 hectolitres. The knowledge of technological improvements could only spread into France from the north, not the south, and the pattern suggests that its spread was very slow. Differences in yield of almost exactly the same order were observable between the Netherlands and Russia. The use of the scythe for reaping in the Baltic provinces of Russia never spread to the southern areas where the sickle remained the only reaping tool. The agriculture of southern Spain showed no improvement at all.

It has been argued that the areas where yields were highest were all areas of denser population and that agricultural improvement was thus a function of population increase when the supply of uncultivated land was no longer very large. In Sweden, yields were certainly much lower than in the Low Countries in spite of all the land reforms; extra output could be achieved by cutting a new farm. But the subsequent experience of many eastern European societies in the nineteenth century suggests that this is too simple a view of the situation. High yields were a function of a wide range of social factors as well as of the pressure of the population on land resources. Each of the types of innovation we have been discussing was especially applicable to a certain kind of social framework and impracticable in others. For example, the cultivation of completely new crops such as the sunflower or potato was often a response to differences in the structure of landholding or the type of land tenure practised, neither of which were determined entirely by population density although it did have some effect on their evolution. The potato was adopted most rapidly as a peasant crop in north-western Europe, the sunflower in Bulgaria. Contracts for *métayage* in France commonly stipulated that there should be no change in the types of crop grown and similarly restrictive clauses were imposed by the church on church lands in order to safeguard its tithe. Everywhere the existence of open fields and communal farming was an obstacle to better practice but a significant difference of attitude can be remarked between the peasants of Denmark or Holstein and those of Austria or France. These differences in response were usually attributed by government to the existence of a regular market and government efforts were increasingly directed towards the removal of internal barriers to the marketing of foodstuffs. Restrictions on the internal movements of grain were relaxed in 1769 in the Austrian Netherlands and finally abolished in 1774 in France. The intention of the Austrian government was to establish a peasantry with free access to a market and to let the forces of supply and demand do the rest.

But what happened when there was no market? In those areas where none of these types of innovation could be seen, their lack was to be attributed to the deficiencies of the social structure and the economy alike. The incomes of Polish and Russian nobles were not spent on agricultural investment but on consumption and therefore went mainly to increase the imports of these two lands. The existence of serfdom in so absolute a form in Russia pushed all entrepreneurial decisions by the nobleman in favour of increasing his income not towards more productive agricultural methods but towards a more ruthless exploitation of his serfs. Such exploitation was a form of capital depreciation for the stock of serfs was in many cases the greatest capital asset of an estate. What was occurring in Russia may well have been disinvestment rather than investment. 'Some people point out the wealth of certain nobles', Komarov wrote in 1814, 'but the answer to that is easy: the sole source of their wealth, whatever kind of domain they have, is derived essentially from the number of their serfs and, in general, from the great extent of their domains and the profits which they take from them, profits whose sole object is to insure the subsistance of the landowner and his family.'[5]

Nowhere are the social obstacles to innovation better demonstrated than in the failure to adopt the one innovation which would indisputably effect a long-term change in the basic problem of the relationship of arable farming to animal farming rather than merely provide a short-term alleviation of the pressure on food supply. This was the development of artificial meadows (leys). By sowing the land with grass mixtures it was possible to produce high quality pasture in the period when the land had formerly lain fallow and at the same time achieve all the results which the fallowing process had achieved.

[5] M. Confino, *Domaines et seigneurs en Russie vers la fin du dix-huitième siècle* (Paris, 1963), p. 141.

Such an innovation could permanently alter the relationship between cattle and grain but, more than all others it demanded enclosure and placed a high premium on the concept of private property. Where a custom such as *vaine pâture* prevailed temporary fences could be erected at certain periods of the year to protect the crops but those crops once gathered, the fences were broken down and the herd turned on to the fields to pasture. No one in such a system would invest in the creation of artificial grassland to feed his neighbours' cattle. To adopt ley-farming was to opt out of the whole social system. It is not surprising therefore that the French government at first permitted enclosure only in those areas such as Champagne where there was a much smaller emphasis on arable farming. Only in those areas where *Koppelwirtschaft* developed, and in the Austrian Netherlands and Flanders where enclosure of commons was encouraged, was the enclosure of the open fields commonly undertaken. Those French writers who advocated enclosures in France, on the English model, usually did so not so much to make an economic statement about agricultural improvement as to mount a political attack on the social system of their country. When faced therefore, with the possibility of a much more throughgoing reform, neither the French economy nor society was able to accept its social and economic implications. How much less, therefore, were such long-term changes possible in Austria, Spain or Russia.

In all these areas the noble's own interest lay only in introducing reforms which did not threaten the social system of which he was the chief beneficiary. Nor was this true merely of eastern Europe. The noble was not an entrepreneur in the sense which modern economic theory has attributed to that word. In the last resort his position depended on maintaining the existing system; any reform, such as ley farming, which more directly threatened that system, would have to be repudiated. That was the ultimate limit to the level of agricultural investment and where almost all available capital and labour was in the noble's hands, as in Russia, it was a highly effective one. Within its existing social framework, eighteenth-century society was not capable of a sufficient degree of long-term change to cope with the rising population nor the growing financial demands of state and nobility. The French Revolution was a reflection of these profound economic difficulties and a search for a new solution.

THE INDUSTRIAL SECTOR

We have already seen that some of the states we have been considering were richer in terms of per capita incomes than many present underdeveloped countries. The extreme inequality of the distribution of the available income meant the existence everywhere of a small market for expensive consumer goods, jewellery, watches, glassware, furniture, porcelain and luxury clothing. The existence everywhere of armed forces also meant a market for military and naval equipment, gunpowder, firearms, rope and heavy iron equipment such as cannon or anchors. Indeed, it was dangerous for even a small state to be without a cannon foundry or a source of clothing for its soldiers. Everywhere, naval dockyards and arsenals were the biggest and most highly-organised factories for they produced much the most impressive piece of eighteenth-century technology, the wooden ship loaded with cannon. On the possession of such mighty weapons, the acquisition of territory and therefore sources of produce and alternative markets outside the European continent depended. The remaining market was that of the household and clothing purchases of the population as a whole.

– Artisanal industries

The manufacturing activities of the eighteenth-century economy may be classified according to whether they fitted this traditional mould or not. We shall look first at those that did and then at one of the most striking developments of the eighteenth-century economy, the growth of rural industries, usually textile industries, with quite different forms of industrial organisation and a different relationship to the government from the older industries. Economic historians have unanimously seen in this process of rural industrialisation the source of subsequent large-scale industrialisation because the rural textile industries were among the first to undergo the technological transformations of the Industrial Revolution. To understand their development in perspective however, it is important first to look at the older industrial activities.

Most governments had encouraged the development of such industries very energetically until about 1750, not only for reasons of defence and self-preservation, but because they associated economic strength, which they thought of as a static position attainable by good government and careful administration, with an adequate volume of industry. The circumstances of the agricultural economy after 1750, increasingly led governments to favour agriculture as the source of economic strength and to regard its improvement as the best, or only, means of raising incomes. Such a view, encouraged by the theories of the physiocratic economists, was partly based on lessons learned from practical experience. In general the 'manufactures' which were established and encouraged everywhere by mercantilist governments, with subsidies and monopoly rights did not do well. It was not a wholly false assumption that this was because no sufficient market for them could exist until agricultural investment had raised agricultural incomes to a higher level. But there were many other reasons for their failure.

These were well exemplified in Bavaria, where the government made persistent attempts to introduce 'manufactures'. With the exception of the old-established glass manufacture, the average life of such manufactures was thirty-six years. The industrial activity of the whole country embraced mining, salt-manufacture, iron smelting and forging, minting of coin, printing, candlemaking, paper manufacture, spice milling, dyeing, grain milling and brewing together with the luxury industries which all German courts hoped to establish for revenue reasons. No new establishment approached the older glass industry in size and some impression of the feebleness of the total industrial sector may be gained from the fact that the total employment in the glass industry (by no means all of it full-time employment) was 1,300, in the textile manufactures about the same and in the pottery manufactures about 780. Firms with more than thirty employees were rare. The population of Bavaria in 1770 was 1,284,000. If we estimate the size of the available labour force at 850,000 the percentage of those employed in that year in the manufactures was 0·12 per cent. Such manufactures were closely supervised and regulated by the government on the grounds that certain theoretical advantages would accrue, as, for example, the more efficient use of raw materials and capital by better organisation, by bulk purchase and sales and by the better training of the workforce, or that the quality of the final product would be firmly regulated, an important matter bearing in mind the luxury market at which the product was aimed. But such advantages could not compensate for the restricted nature of the market. In Bavaria, it was restricted almost completely to the city of Munich and all the manufactures were urban except the glass manufacture, whose location was determined by its raw material source. The glass industry was also the only one to export after 1750. In general, the circumstances of the founding of such manufactures were such that their nature was revealed after a short period of operation as uneconomic. Their costs of production and of marketing were too high and the sources of raw material supply often dried up. But the main reason for their failure was the violent changes of fashion in the markets on which they depended. A sudden shift of taste could bankrupt a porcelain works.

The efforts of the Bavarian government to industrialise were therefore almost a total failure. Hardly any of the manufactures survived after 1833. All that can be said in their favour is that a tiny part of the labour force was trained and some marginal improvements in techniques occurred (in the grinding of optical lenses for example). Such was the picture almost everywhere. The total value of the production of manufactures in Bavaria was only about 30 per cent of the value of the quite unorganised handicraft output of the peasants, such as wooden toys and metal objects. If coal mining be considered as a rural handicraft, which it effectively was in Bavaria, the ratio of the value of output would be only 1 to 6.

The deficiencies of the market were probably as marked in Bavaria as anywhere in western Europe, but Bavaria's access to foreign markets was no more restricted. The essential defects of organisation and structure of the Bavarian enterprises were very typical of similar enterprises elsewhere even though in other areas, the volume of output and employment created by such manufactures was greater. The Archbishopric of Osnabrück with 120,000 inhabitants persisted throughout the century in the introduction of luxury manufactures such as porcelain in the hope of achieving a favourable trade balance. In volume and value of output the most important industry there remained, however, the coarse linen cloth made by the peasantry. The Prussian government introduced and sustained similar manufactures; the Wegely cloth works in Berlin employed spinners throughout Pomerania, but the most important single industry, once again, was the weaving of coarse linens in the countryside.

At the height of the period of liberal agricultural reform in the Habsburg Empire the government still pursued a policy of industrialisation along these lines behind a high tariff barrier. The first Viennese paper manufacture created by the government in 1732 employed 19 people in 1758. The biggest glass works employed 40 people at the most. The biggest manufacture was the Linz woollen manufacture, employing over 1,000 in the central buildings where the cloth was produced and on an average about 30,000 part-time spinners in the countryside. There was no enterprise on such a scale in Berlin or elsewhere in Germany. The famous Waldstein woollen mill produced in fact only about 1 per cent of the total woollen cloths made throughout the Empire, although, typically of such enterprises, its products were exceedingly fine and of far greater individual value than peasant productions. The manufactures in Bohemia produced about 5 per cent of the total woollen cloth output of the province. The glass industry of Bohemia employed 1,423 people in 1,792. Where urban markets were smaller, in the Alpine areas and the eastern provinces, industrial activity of this kind scarcely existed at all. The total employment in full-time industry in Carniola in 1792 was 800.

The greatest centre of industrial activities of this kind had always been the Low Countries. The decline of the traditional cloth and handicraft industries of the Austrian Netherlands impressed visitors forcibly. 'This country which in former times possessed the most ingenious artisans of every description,' William Fawkener reported to a Committee of the English Privy Council in 1791, 'has not advanced one step in manufactures for more than a century while the neighbouring nations have at the same time been making such rapid strides. The only manufactures that now flourish in these Netherlands are linen and laces.'[6] Fawkener was impressed, like other observers, with the relative technological stagnation of the older cloth industries. Nevertheless, the total employment offered by the corporate industries of the Flemish towns remained much higher than elsewhere except in Paris and they showed considerable responsiveness to new developments. The output of printed cloths in Antwerp rose from 1,094 pieces in 1754 to 62,650 pieces in 1770. Such towns retained many advantages over the rural cloth manufacturing areas. Their control lay in the hands of a well-established and powerful corporate guild which, however resistant it was to new forms of industrial organisation, had a wide network of trading connections and a great fund of practical business knowledge, all too often lacking in the German and Austrian state officials who controlled the manufactures there. Their political and financial independence was much higher. Above all such towns had a pool of skilled labour quite lacking in the contryside where the quality of the labour and of the finished product was very low. It is quite possible to argue that the guild-controlled industries of towns such as Ghent, Antwerp, Ypres or Bruges, after the determined efforts of their Austrian rulers to make the guild structure more flexible and responsive to changing conditions, would have shown a great revival under the spur of industrial developments across the Channel and in France. The experiment was never tried because the occupation of the Netherlands under the French Revolution destroyed the power of the guilds much more effectively than the Emperor had been able to do. Northwards, in the United Provinces, however, the decline of the older industries and the guilds was manifest. The famous cloth-manufacturing town of Leyden saw its output more than halved in the century and its corporate and financial power correspondingly diminished.

[6] H. Pavelka, 'Englands Wirtschaftsbeziehungen zu den Habsburgischen Niederländen im achtzehnten Jahrhundert' in *Mélanges offerts à G. Jacquemyns* (Brussels, 1968).

The attack on the guild privileges in Spain was often for the purpose of setting up similar monopolistic agencies more closely controlled by the government. The royal silk manufactory at Talavera de la Reina, was built and operated by Frenchmen from Lyons under government protection. The Guadalajara wool manufactory kept its accounts in Dutch for thirty years. The government's main effort was concentrated in the Castilian heartlands, a decision which made much political sense but very little economic sense. To carry raw cotton to Avila in central Spain over a road system that scarcely existed and when robbery was so prevalent that goods had often to be carried in armed convoys was to impose production costs on the manufactory so high that its market must inevitably be very circumscribed. Most of the Castilian manufactories were planned as integrated firms which, in the circumstances of the eighteenth-century economy, might well have led not to economies of scale but to diseconomies. Elsewhere the dispersal of the manufacturing process reduced costs. In this respect the Spanish enterprises repeated in their creation a problem which lay at the heart of such attempts at industrialisation elsewhere. Urban labour was more costly, much more costly, than rural labour. Rural labour was part-time, ignorant and clumsy. It was incapable of producing goods of the quality desired on the luxury markets that existed. But the competition on those markets was ruthless and the markets very small, the secret of maintaining a hold on them was to be located in the right place, to reduce costs to a minimum and to introduce new products.

If this could be done, sustained industrial activity was possible. This may be seen in two cases, those of Lyons and Paris, the two greatest manufacturing cities of continental Europe. In a period when the manufacture of silken cloth proved to be frequently an economic failure whether attempted in Austria, Spain or Antwerp, the large city of Lyons devoted itself almost entirely to that activity. The unit of production was no more than five people usually working in a garret. The organisation of production was rigidly mercantilist. The trade was managed and the capital provided by the great merchants of the city who financed the sale of the finished article throughout Europe, the Near East and America. The city itself was one of the largest of European cities apart from the great administrative capitals and its merchants had long controlled the trade in luxury goods into Switzerland and down the Rhône Valley to the Mediterranean and Levant. As in the manufacturing towns of the Netherlands, the labour was highly skilled and often the jobs it performed were almost hereditary in the family. Although having every disadvantage of such archaic organisation, the industry prospered by the merciless exploitation of the labour force by the city merchants. 'The sedentary life of these individuals', a contemporary government reporter wrote, 'the quality and, sometimes, the insufficiency of their food, often their excessive work, reduce them to a most feeble complexion. The children of this class of men, born to weak fathers, come into the world for the most part unhealthy and rickety. From the cradle they are taught only how to handle silk and then how to work it and they are without strength or ability for any other occupation.'[7] Their average working day was eighteen hours long. The conditions of existence of artisan workers in Paris were no better and their numbers were far greater. Although almost entirely lacking in 'factories' in the modern sense, it was already the greatest industrial city of continental Europe. The advantage of Paris as a centre of manufacture was the great size of the city and the concentration of wealthy people in its environs. Large areas of the city were devoted to artisan production in small workshops, 350,000 of its inhabitants were employed in such places in 1791, by far the greatest single concentration of industrial workers. Unlike those of Lyons a high proportion of the goods made in Paris were sold in the city itself.

– Iron Manufacture

One industry above all had a peculiar significance for national defence and was thus the focus of government efforts to industrialise: the manufacture of iron. The industry had a dual aspect everywhere. Partly it was a rural activity practised on the estate where the resources were available. The pig iron so made was sold to ironmasters who forged it into numerous household and agricultural articles. But its other aspect was that of a necessary military prop. The production of pig iron for cannon usually took on a larger scale and the producers specialised in this particular market where the insistence on high quality was very marked. Pig iron for general purposes was produced almost everywhere where there were resources of iron ore and wood for the manufacture of the charcoal with which the ore was smelted. It was especially important in the economies of three countries, Sweden, Russia and France, but Sweden, by virtue of turning out a much better quality product, was able to specialise particularly in the production of pig iron for cannon founding.

The total output of pig iron in Sweden was approximately 50,000 tons yearly. In the last quarter of the century, important

[7] L. Trénard, 'La crise sociale lyonnaise à la veille de la Révolution' in *Revue d'histoire moderne et contemporaine*, vol. 2, 1955.

technological changes in the British iron industry, particularly the introduction of coke-smelting and the puddling process, operated to increase British output, but until that time Russian and Swedish producers dominated the British market. Even after the invention of the puddling process the quality of Swedish iron continued to keep it in very high demand as the basis for wrought iron. The changes in the manufacturing process in Britain were thus a more potent threat to iron producers in Russia and France. Nowhere were there such handicaps to effective competition by using the new British methods as in Russia. The total make of iron there in 1800 was 160,120 tons. The industry was located in the Ural mountains, a thousand miles from the main Russian centres of consumption and still further from the export markets on which it depended to absorb about one half of the total production. Over 300,000 people were employed in labouring, more usually on a casual or part-time basis, for the furnaces, forges and transport companies. It could frequently take two years to get the pig iron to St Petersburg (Leningrad) by river transport and it is an intriguing question how, in such apparently hopeless circumstances, the industry could have prospered and grown to such a size. One answer seems to be that the state of economic backwardness may in fact carry with it certain competitive advantages. In Russia, for example, it was possible to provide the entrepreneurs of the iron industry with serf labour, bound to the works on the same terms as their fellows to the land. Although such labour was very uncooperative, it was still cheaper than the labour used by ironmasters in other countries and compensated to some extent for the higher transport costs. But the comparative advantages of the Russian iron industry were soon eliminated by developments elsewhere.

The process of smelting iron ore with coke rather than with charcoal and the development of the puddling process gave rise to a type of iron-manufacturing industry where capital equipment and productive capacity were both far greater.[1] Big coke blast-furnaces began to appear instead of the small charcoal furnaces on which production had previously been based. In France where the iron industry had developed very considerably in the eighteenth century, the conflict between the old and the new technology developed before the end of the century. The history of the adaptation of the new technology will concern us in later chapters. The traditional technology already supported a large industry whose basic unit of production was the small charcoal-fired blast-furnace, usually operated as part of the lord's domain. Total output in 1796 was 132,000 tons. The demand for iron for naval guns and for military

[1] See pages 197–200.

purposes was very fluctuating. In times of war, the market showed tremendous expansion followed by general collapse in peacetime and this volatility, together with the difficulty of meeting the high specifications set by the naval ordnance board, discouraged all but the larger iron forges from competing in this market. In spite of her large iron production therefore, in 1770 France satisfied about one-twentieth of her own demand for naval iron. The main market for iron goods was agriculture, followed by domestic equipment. Consequently, the main determinant of the volume of output was a highly imperfect multitude of local markets throughout France, because French iron, unlike that of Russia or Sweden, was very rarely exported. The size of the French population therefore accounted for the fact that even at the end of the century, despite the great technological changes in Britain, British iron output was still less than in France. Even in 1830, ploughs still accounted for between one-fifth and one-third of the total iron output in France. In so far as there was a national market for iron, it was limited to a few major producing places and a few major commercial centres such as Bordeaux and Lyons. But the local markets were very restricted and many iron-producing regions sold their products far and wide outside their own areas through an intricate network of minor commercial intermediaries. Brittany, being more isolated than other regions, had the highest proportion of its sales on the local market, about two-thirds. The technology of the charcoal blast-furnaces was well adapted to such imperfect marketing arrangements, the furnace could readily be closed down and re-opened as the market conditions changed.

This was not the case with the new technology. Blast-furnaces which smelted iron ore by means of coke were much more substantial pieces of capital equipment. The coke-smelting process was first achieved in France in 1769 by Gabriel Jars after an exhaustive study of methods elsewhere which was financed by the government. He had twice visited England and once visited Germany under their auspices. But the process was really established by Marchant de la Houlière who visited England in 1775 and brought back William Wilkinson to France. The government's motive was to use the new techniques to produce a higher proportion of its own naval cannon and Wilkinson's main experiments in the forging process were at the royal cannon foundry of Indret near Nantes in the Loire valley. In 1785, fifty years after Abraham Darby's discovery of the process in England, the first successful coke-smelt was achieved in the new blast-furnaces built at Le Creusot by the ironmaster Ignace de Wendel, who had also visited England, Styria and Carinthia under government auspices. The government's motives were of the most traditional kind and the Le Creusot iron furnaces were in one sense no more than a modern 'manufacture' of the kind which so repeatedly failed in Germany or Spain. But to view them in that light would be to ignore the immense difference in scale and scope of the technology involved, for with their establishment a new world of industrial and social organisation crossed the Channel from England to France. The output of iron in France by that time had increased by more than three and a half times since 1738, but with the establishment of the Le Creusot works the processes of industrial development and economic growth were overtaken by the Industrial Revolution.

Elsewhere in Europe, the iron industry remained confined to the older processes. From the hilly areas of the Rhineland, German pig iron was transported into the neighbouring northern areas and manufactured into finished products in small towns such as Solingen, Hagen and Iserlohn. Nuremberg and Fürth were comparable centres of wrought iron production in South Germany and local supplies of iron ore in Styria had given rise to a similar but smaller manufacturing industry there. In the countryside around Liége, Charleroi and Namur in the Austrian Netherlands, the manufacture of iron articles was a well-established domestic activity and economic historians have seen it as the beginning of industrialisation in those areas. At the end of the century, however, it employed less people than the older-established corporately-controlled urban textile industries of that area. The only comparable developments to those at Le Creusot were on the borders of Prussian Silesia where Frederick II induced William Wilkinson to develop a cannon foundry using coke-smelted pig iron, in order to protect his newly acquired provinces. Seen in retrospect, this was also the origins of the industrialisation of Upper Silesia, again indicating that, given the right choice of industrial process and location, such heavily protected and subsidised and traditionally-organised ventures could be highly successful.

– Coal Mining

Both in Silesia and Le Creusot, an important factor in establishing the new process was the availability of a coal which could be successfully converted into coke. Only in certain local areas was coal a familiar product; it was not used as domestic fuel in Paris until the last third of the century and nowhere was it so heavily consumed as in Britain. Its main use was in industrial processes such as soap-boiling, glass-making and brewing and for firing steam engines used to pump mines. It was most mined in the coalfield stretching from northern France into the Austrian Netherlands. On the Netherlands side of the frontier it had long been mined, but in 1767, there were still only twelve Newcomen steam engines working there. Perhaps as a response to the sharply-increasing price of wood after 1760, noble families on each side of the frontier began to develop coal mines around Anzin on the French side of the frontier. The Compagnie d'Anzin which controlled the mining rights to the whole area, was formed in 1767. In 1789, it employed 4,000 workmen and twelve steam engines and by that date, French coal output was probably more than 500,000 tons whereas in the earlier part of the century it has been about 75,000 tons.

– Domestic industries

Coal-mining is more logically seen as a new industry rather than a traditional mercantilist manufacture. Its growth depended on the development of quite new markets. But it remained very small compared to other industries which could be placed in the same category. It is to the growth of these industries that we must now turn. Paradoxically, in spite of the very few successes which government policies of industrialisation achieved and the noticeable decay of many old-established industries, the eighteenth century was a period of marked industrialisation. The industrialisation that took place was of a quite different kind from that which most governments had sought to establish. Its most general aspect everywhere was the part-time employment of the rural labour force in manufacturing activities carried on in their own homes. The goods they made were seldom produced either for the luxury or the defence market. An overwhelming proportion of them was cheaper textiles intended either for consumption by the less wealthy consumers of the urban market, by the rural population itself or by inhabitants of distant foreign lands. Their labour was casual and not highly-skilled. The industries were loosely-organised on a variety of different patterns, but in almost every case were largely independent either of government capital or of government control. Such regulations as were passed to control them, and they were frequent, were seldom effective because of the widely-scattered nature of the activities to which they applied. It is impossible not to be struck by the extraordinary growth of spinning and weaving in the countryside of many European areas. In some areas the manufacture of iron products, toys or watches developed in the same way, but textiles, whether of linen, wool or the newfangled cotton were the typical rural product. The technological transformations which initiated the Industrial Revolution in Britain, were heavily concentrated in these rural textile industries and their development on the continent may therefore be seen as the true precursor of the Industrial Revolution there rather than the older 'manufactures'. But setting on one side the developments of the Industrial Revolution itself and looking at the matter simply from the point of view of employment in industrial activities whether those industries were 'revolutionised' or not it would still be true to say that the most industrial landscapes in late eighteenth-century Europe, for all their lack of chimneys, were the country areas around Lille, Rouen, Barcelona, Zürich, Basel and Geneva.

Such industries usually developed in the teeth of the opposition of the old-established urban textile industries. Legislation in France in 1762 confined the powers of the guild to the area of the town itself and removed most institutional restraints on rural industry. Unfortunately, recent research into the development of rural industry has not provided a very clear answer as to why it did develop. Was there a rise in incomes in some western European areas such that the consumption of cloth was increased and the new market captured by rural producers? Or was there merely a shift of production from town to countryside? Or were the rural industries more an aspect of the pressure of population on the available resources? With increasing sub-division of farms and the increasing price of bread, the poorer members of the rural community, roughly the equivalent of those with no, or too little, land, would be driven into non-agricultural forms of production to eke out their incomes. The evidence that most strongly supports this view is a general coincidence between density of population, poor quality of land and extent of rural industry, but this general coincidence is by no means universal. It has been also argued that the main force for the development of rural textile industries was the desire of entrepreneurs to escape from the control of the guild and to employ cheaper labour. This would not account for those areas where the peasant owned his own stock of raw materials and fixed capital and sold the final product to itinerant buyers. It may be remarked that if the explanation which derives from increasing population and pressure on agricultural incomes is the more powerful one, the ease with which the rural producer could carry out his activities was greatly improved by the entrepreneurial activities of the urban merchants who in various ways provided the credit for his operations. It was also improved by the fact that eighteenth-century warfare was much less devastating to the rural economy than in the previous century. In the Austrian Netherlands there were no military campaigns between 1748 and 1792, where previously armies had scarcely ever ceased marching. Whatever the immediate reason for such industrial growth, rural producers captured much of the textile market previously held by urban manufacturers and provided the larger part of the textiles exported to new foreign and colonial markets. Peasant producers in remote and isolated rural Europe were thus linked to other continents in a long and complicated chain of trade and finance.

The one area of rural France where textile industries were conspicuously absent was the countryside around Paris. In northern and western France, they were widespread but more important in certain areas than others and differently organised. In Poitou, rural weavers seem typically to have produced single orders for urban bourgeois clients. In Brittany and in the woollen-cloth area around Sedan, the products were sold in local market places. In the Vendée and in some parts of Picardy the products were sold to itinerant merchants who had no other stake in the business. But the most typical organisation everywhere was that in which the controlling figure was the _fabricant_, the putter-out. He it was who provided the liquid capital to finance the manufacture by giving credit to the weavers and spinners and who collected the woven cloth for dyeing and finishing. Sometimes he controlled the dyeing and finishing operations also, sometimes he provided the raw material on which the spinners worked, sometimes he owned the weavers' looms and rented them to their operators. The putter-out was usually an urban merchant and the last stages of manufacture were invariably carried out in towns. The cloth manufacturers of Abbeville, in the Somme valley, provided work for twenty-five villages in the area in 1789; the final products were exported to North America and the West Indies. The putter-out Goudard employed 6,000 spinners and weavers in Languedoc in 1770; Brandes employed 2,100 in the Orléannais of whom 1,800 were spinners. The town of Elbeuf in Normandy, which had never been controlled by guilds, employed 15,000 in wool manufacture, of whom 10,000 were in the Norman countryside. Here the putter-out owned the raw material and controlled the whole process.

The international connections of these remote areas reveal the importance both of colonies and of intra-European trade in opening new markets. In western France one area, Bas Maine, specialised in fine quality linens rather than the usual coarse linen clothing. Its products were concentrated by the putter-out at the town of Laval and sold in markets all over the world, frequently in South America. The coarser linens of Haute Maine, Perche and Vendômois were collected by putters-out from all over the area and sold on the domestic market, especially in Paris, but a certain quantity every year was shipped to the West Indies for negroes. The wool provided for the spinners of high-grade woollen yarn around Sedan was imported from Spain. The flax used to spin linen yarn in the area around Lille was imported from Flanders. Silken cloths began to be made in Dauphiné in the eighteenth century for shipment to Geneva and for ultimate sale in Switzerland or Germany. Linen cloths made here were shipped to Beaucaire often for ultimate sale in Spain, Turkey or the Near East. After 1750 the bigger putters-out there began to pursue foreign orders directly, one firm of glove makers in Dauphiné had direct accounts with clients in New York, Santo Domingo, Moscow, Amsterdam and Naples. As textile manufacturers began to produce cotton and linen mixtures and then to make cloth purely of cotton, the international connections became more extensive. Cotton was an exotic raw material which could not be cultivated at all in France. It was imported from Santo Domingo, Turkey, The Levant and Cayenne and, increasingly, from North America, destinations to which the final manufactured cloth would not infrequently return. The most important of the textile manufacturing areas from the standpoint of quantity of production were Normandy and Picardy. Normandy became increasingly concerned with cotton manufacture partly because the development of Le Havre as an important trans-Atlantic port made that town the principal cotton market for France. Dauphiné merchants frequently crossed the whole country to obtain their raw cotton there and sell their cloth. In the Austrian Netherlands the small town of Verviers and the Vesdre valley developed into an important woollen manufacturing area. Wool was imported from Spain, Germany, Poland, Luxembourg, France, Saxony, Bohemia and Portugal, soap and olive oil were also imported from France. The raw wool trade was financed by Dutch merchants.

In all these respects the evolution of the French textile industries in the eighteenth century closely resembled that of the British textile industries. The expansion of a rural handicraft into a major industry organised by urban capitalists, the replacement in the countryside of agricultural work by industrial work as the main source of income, the continued improvement in the machinery used and the expansion of total output which all preceded the Industrial Revolution in Britain, all took place equally in France. There were differences. The concentration on cotton cloth was much less in France than in Britain, silken, woollen and linen goods remained important products. But the organisation of the textile industry and its markets followed similar patterns. It is noticeable, however, that the technological improvements of the earlier period of the eighteenth century which preceded the major innovations of the mule-jenny and the water-frame, almost all originated in Britain. This did not mean that France was deprived of technological knowledge. British laws forbidding the export of skilled labour and of machinery were not effective barriers in time of peace to the desire of French manufacturers and of the French government to keep pace. Consequently, technological innovations in Britain spread very quickly across the Channel. John Holker, an English political refugee, was responsible for introducing a number of English innovations, the spinning-jenny among them. John Kay, the inventor of the flying-shuttle lived in France for some time and sold his invention there. When the Lancashire cotton manufacturer Milne introduced both the water-frame and the mule-jenny into France between 1779 and 1785, the new factory technology of cotton spinning was born there. Already, in the 1780s, the concentration of capital and labour into mechanised factories was duplicating developments in Britain and beginning the transformation of the rural industries into urban activities once more.

But one major difference persisted throughout the century between the French and British textile industries, the smaller size of total output in France. It was this factor more than any other which caused the French textile industry to be less innovative. The greater output of the British industry was related to its larger markets. In both countries the proportion of total output exported was remarkably high, but the enormous colonial and naval expansion of Britain in the eighteenth century provided a larger colonial market for cotton cloth than France had and it was in the cotton industry that the major mechanical innovations occurred. Technological innovation in both cotton and iron manufacture in France came through conscious adaptation of British methods and often through the migration of British manufacturers and workmen. Already, French industry had developed a symbiotic relationship with that of Britain which could be rudely and dangerously broken by the frequent wars of the eighteenth century. In the French textile industries the speed of technological copying was such that it can hardly be argued that, given a continued mobility of labour and knowledge, France would have suffered unduly. Most of the British innovations in the textile manufacture were adapted in France in considerably less than a decade and in silk and linen manufacture the innovations sometimes originated in France. But the level of industrial output per head in Britain was greater than in France although its rate of growth may well have been higher in France in the eighteenth century as a whole. This greater level of industrial output was a reflection of the greater market beyond Britain's shores. The repeated naval wars of

D

the eighteenth century all played their part in holding back the French textile industry for two reasons. Firstly, it was impossible to export goods with such ease when ports were blockaded and the seas were busy with hostile warships. Secondly, in all wars except the war of American Independence, France lost overseas territories to Britain. French foreign trade in the eighteenth century was extremely buoyant but the biggest trade booms came on the conclusion of peace treaties; the wars themselves were very damaging. What limited their harmful effect on France was the relative shortness of their duration. When in 1793 war broke out between France and Britain which was to last, with less than one year's peace, until 1814, the symbiotic relationship between French and British industry was to be drastically broken. Not only was France to be deprived for a much longer time of the opportunity of overseas market expansion on which technological innovation depended but also of the chance of importing the knowledge of such innovations from Britain.

The difficulties of industrialisation in the eighteenth-century economy are brought out very clearly by the effect that the situation of being in second place had on the French economy in spite of its many advantages and its long-sustained growth. Not only was the industrial sector forced into dependence on British technology, however ready it was to innovate, by the greater size of the British market but it was also forced into specialisation in different products which in themselves were less capable of leading to an expansion of output than the British products.

The development of larger markets for textiles depended on producing a simpler, cheaper, more standardised good. The technological innovations in the British cotton and wool industries were designed precisely to do this, they all went in the direction of cost-reduction. British manufacturers therefore established a decisive position in that part of the textile market that was most expanding and most expandable by further cost-reducing innovations. The French manufacturers were obliged to compete by differentiating their product from the British product. Because of the technological gap that existed in cost-reducing innovations they could not differentiate by making cheaper materials but only by a certain insistence on quality and style, attributes about which their rivals could afford to care less, and they therefore were forced into that part of the market which was less capable of expansion. It was a position in which they already found themselves in the mid-eighteenth century and they were never able to escape. After 1760 the wool manufacturers of Elbeuf deliberately lowered the quality of their product to compete with British producers. Elsewhere fine taffetas and high quality linens were replaced by muslins, percales, and cotton velvets, but the replacement was always designed for a more expensive market than the fustians and cottons made in Britain.

The nearer in time we come to the French Revolution, the more does a certain simplification of manners and dress become apparent in European society, a consequence not merely of the intellectual influence of the literature of the enlightenment, but of the improved status and greater self-assertiveness of bourgeois society. As bourgeois society began to impose its tastes and its habits on the more privileged classes the market for costly products, the market at which most of the mercantilist manufactures of the eighteenth century had been aimed, began to lose importance and the domestic market for simpler and less costly goods to expand. The effect of this was particularly marked on the textile industries. Thus, changes in the habits of domestic consumers coincided with the effect on the textile industries of European overseas expansion. The effect of these changes was to provide a great stimulus to textile manufacture in the French countryside. But at the same time Britain was more favoured by these changes than France. Just as Britain's colonial expansion was more remarkable than that of France, so was the imposition of bourgeois tastes on consumers more noticeable than in France. The advantage of the British textile industry over that of France was therefore related to a certain extent to the overall difference in society. This is not to say that the British nobility were less powerful or less prominent in society than their French counter-parts *vis-à-vis* the bourgeois groups. The imposition of bourgeois tastes was not a matter of social habit; it did not reflect a more 'open' a more 'democratic' or a more 'socially mobile' society; it reflected differences in the distribution of income and in the spending power of consumers. These differences were related to fundamental differences in taxation in the two countries. The French government raised more money by central taxation than the British government and because nobles were so lightly taxed, the burden fell more heavily on bourgeois groups and reduced the level of their con-sumer expenditure. Furthermore, all accounts of eighteenth-century France agree that the peasantry were noticeably poorer than their English counterparts, they had less clothing, ate less food and in some areas went barefoot or had no windows in their dwellings. This difference again was related to the heavy burden of taxation which fell on them; in those areas where the *taille* was lower the living standard of the peasantry was higher. One of the most important factors in accounting for the differences in the French and British textile industries in the eighteenth century is the difference in the distribution of income within society after taxation.

It was this factor together with the greater overseas market which mainly accounted both for the greater size of total output of all textiles in Britain and for the fact that a greater proportion of total output consisted of the simpler cotton cloths. Imports of raw cotton into France at the end of the century were about 5,000 tons, into Britain over 8,100 tons. And it was these factors, the greater output and particularly the greater output of cotton cloth in Britain which in their turn gave rise to the important innovations of the last quarter of the eighteenth century. Unfortunately, economic historians have shown little interest in these important questions of income distribution, often preferring to explain the difference between British and French society in the eighteenth century by more nebulous concepts such as the lack in France of a 'spirit of enterprise'.

If the French textile industry had considerable disadvantages when compared to that in Britain it threatened in its turn, both by its size and its modernity, rural textile industries elsewhere which had also grown in the eighteenth century but to a smaller size than in France. Most areas of northern and northwest Germany had well-established rural linen industries. Since the late Middle Ages linen and cotton mixtures had been made there. In the mid-eighteenth century, pure cottons began to be made in Augsburg in south Germany and from there their manufacture spread into the countryside of Silesia and into the borders of the Netherlands and the Rhineland. In Schleswig-Holstein the manufacture of linen cloths was much more common on the northern heath lands and in the marsh lands; in all the better arable areas of the duchies there was little industrial activity. In Russia peasant handicraft industries were less common in the fertile black-earth region than elsewhere. They were most common, however, where noble landlords had allowed whole villages to desert agriculture for industry in order to get greater income from their serfs as Count Sheremetiev had done with the village of Ivanovo. In Switzerland, Zürich, Winterthur, and Geneva, all became important urban centres of rural textile trades and all had developed the manufacture of cottons by the end of the century. From Lausanne to the Black Forest into Swabia and southwards to the foot of the Saint Gothard pass, cotton manufacture was the standby and in some cases the chief activity of rural households. In most of that area the land is relatively infertile. In western Switzerland watch making was also a dispersed rural industry run on exactly the same lines. The same trade was pursued in the German Black Forest but in a much more primitive way; in Switzerland division of labour had been carried much further and the watch-movements were usually made by the urban putter-out. In the Habsburg Empire until the rapid development of cotton spinning in Bohemia in the 1790s linen, wool and cotton production were customarily only a winter occupation of the rural dwellers although an increasing one. The typical rural handicraft industry of the Liége area was iron work. In Lombardy it was the spinning and weaving of silk. All these nascent industrial developments were more important to the countries in which they were situated than the older urban industries or royal 'manufactures', but all, with the exception of those in Switzerland, were much less well equipped to withstand competition from British mass-production than French industry was.

The sources of capital for these rural industrial activities were much more varied than those of the older mercantilist manufactures. In the latter case the government had always been either the provider of capital, or had provided guarantees against capital losses to private individuals establishing industries, or had provided monopoly rights or other privileges. This kind of cooperation between government and private capitalists was responsible for the foundation of Le Creusot and other developments in eighteenth-century France; de Wendel was a friend of the Minister of Finance, Calonne, and the participants in the company were the great financial officers of the state. Many shares were retained as royal shares to give the government some control. In most German states the share capital for new manufactures was also subscribed either by the court itself or by the state officials and financiers. Sometimes the government support came in a less direct but no less potent form. The French state had reserved to itself the right to dispose of all mining rights on its territory in 1744. It was therefore able to assign monopoly control over a large part of the northern coalfield to the Désandrouin family when the Compagnie d'Anzin was formed. In Russia the state could conscript labour for industry.

The rural industries usually required far less initial capital investment. A spinning wheel was relatively cheap. Even its improved version, the jenny, cost only the earnings of a French textile worker over four months to purchase in 1790. A loom was more costly and it is no doubt for that reason that where fixed capital was provided by the putter-out it usually took the form of a loom rented by the year to the weaver. Much of the capital equipment needed could be purchased by reinvesting the proceeds of the enterprise but this did not solve the problem of financing the marketing of the goods. The relatively small amounts of capital needed seem to have been very readily obtained. When the merchants of Lyons refused to provide capital for rural industries in Dauphiné because of the fear of rival production the capital was obtained from Switzerland. Some of the capital used in developing the coalfield in the north of France came from the Low Countries. The finishing and marketing of Bohemian linens was financed by German merchant houses in Nuremberg and by wealthy Silesian merchants. The iron industry of the Rhenish provinces was financed by banking houses in Cologne. The Vienna banking house of Fries invested heavily in the attempts to establish cotton manufactures in Lower Austria in 1786.

There was a capital market in Paris, in Amsterdam, in Geneva and in certain German towns, particularly Frankfurt-am-Main. Its connection with industry was however very slight, mainly because the industries which developed in the eighteenth century did not frequently need to have recourse to it. The French government used bankers to make payments abroad, for subsidies to other governments, for buying military supplies such as cannon, or for buying grain in times of dearth. Such bankers were very international figures. A closely-knit network of Swiss and Huguenot protestant financiers carried out such international services for the French government. One of them, Baron Necker, became Minister of Finance for five years. Some of the first directors of the Bank of France, founded in 1800, came from this circle. Their counterparts were the merchant houses of Amsterdam and Frankfurt-am-Main or the Greppi bank of Milan, all of whom had business which was essentially international. The bigger part of the Paris capital market was made up of 'financiers' rather than bankers, men whose business was essentially domestic and revolved around the lease ('farm') of the national taxes. The organisation for tax collection and the revenue of the taxes themselves were jointly regarded as a piece of royal property to be leased to the highest bidder. Temporary associations of financiers would bid for the right to farm the taxes and the crown would thus obtain its revenue in advance and leave the business of subsequently collecting the taxes to the successful bidders. The strength of the tax farmers' position was that they supplied the treasury with a steady stream of long and short term credits and this combined with their revenue collecting activities gave them a most powerful inside position in manipulating government funds. Given their position it is not surprising that the General Tax Farmers should have become the primary investors in government long-term debt and subsequently could not be got rid of even when they became a more or less self-perpetuating body. By the very nature of their business these financiers directed investment into secure government funds with low interest rates rather than into more risky industrial, commercial or agricultural activities. It would appear therefore that although the capital market was more highly organised in France than elsewhere this had little or no effect on the greater development of rural industry there.

It is not very convincing to argue that the relatively greater strength of rural domestic industry in France was due to a more favourable institutional framework. After all, if whole manufacturing villages could arise in Russia, where serfdom was more absolute than anywhere, and could even be encouraged by noble landlords, the advantages of free rural institutions such as existed in Switzerland must at the very least be regarded as not proven. France was a more densely populated country than most others in Europe and this, combined with the law of inheritance which provided more generously for younger sons than it did in many other lands, might have led to a greater subdivision of the farms. This, in its turn, might have led a greater part of the population to supplement its income from the land from other sources. But how then is the similar evolution of the textile industries in Britain, which was much less densely populated and where the law of inheritance was far less favourable to younger sons, to be explained? Or, indeed, the same process in Switzerland where the tax burdens on the peasants were less than elsewhere and the standard of comfort apparently higher? There do not seem to be any particular geographical advantages which single out France, Britain and Switzerland. Textile industries everywhere required flowing water for washing and dyeing and at the end of the century for operating the machinery, but that was available almost everywhere. It is impossible to believe that nearness to resources mattered much when the raw material whose use was developing so rapidly, cotton, came from so far. It appears that capital already moved across frontiers and, perhaps more important at the time, so did capitalists. We are driven once again into the explanation that, whatever the origins and causes of rural industrialisation, its extent was largely determined by market factors.

The most remarkable demonstration of this was the growth of the rural cotton industry in Catalonia. Until the middle of the century the Spanish government had persisted in reserving the trade of its vast Empire to joint-stock companies with monopoly privileges. The goods they exported were to be produced by equally privileged manufactures. The relative failure of these industrial enterprises meant that while most trade with the Spanish colonies was in goods smuggled in from other countries many industrial developments in Spain were discouraged or even absolutely prohibited. The gradual dissolution of this rigid monopoly structure took place on two fronts. Firstly, the privileges awarded to royal manufactures in Castile were gradually curtailed and the restrictions on rural industry removed. Secondly, the monopoly privileges of the trading companies were also dismantled until trade with the

Empire was made available to all Spanish areas in 1778. These developments coincided with the development of the rural cotton industry in Catalonia. Only in the 1780s were Catalonian merchants allowed to own an unrestricted number of looms. Even so, water-frames were in use there almost as early as in France. Arthur Young on his travels found the whole area more prosperous than any part of France and all observers testify to the modernity and prosperity of the industry. The share of goods of Spanish origin in the total imports of the Spanish colonies rose from about one-eighth in 1700 to over one-half in 1789. Given a satisfactory export market, the transformation of the rural textile industries into a more mechanised and centralised industry could take place quickly. It was the existence of the export market which removed some of the limitations which the low incomes and the inequality of their distribution placed on the domestic market for textiles. The proportion of textile manu-factures exported from eighteenth-century France was much higher than the ratio of exports to output in other industries. In its turn foreign trade raised the level of domestic incomes and was often not subject to the same ultimate institutional and social limitations as was the attempt to raise the level of domestic income by agri-cultural investment. It is therefore with some remarks about the extent and pattern of foreign trade that we must conclude.

TRADE AND MARKETS

The mid-eighteenth century was one of the most remarkable periods of trade expansion in modern history, in spite of the severe setbacks caused by the naval wars between France and Britain. It also represented a notable break with the pattern of trade which had existed in Europe since the sixteenth century. Until the inauguration of a longer period of peace by the Treaty of Utrecht in 1713 the greater part of European trade moved within European seas. After that treaty the expansion of trade between Europe and other continents became ever more important and that trade grew much more rapidly than trade within the confines of Europe. By the mid-eighteenth century this inter-continental trade had acquired what seemed an irresistible momentum such that even the most effective of naval blockades could only restrain it temporarily. The demand for manufactures in the colonies of European powers became more constant and in return the prices of 'colonial wares' in European markets fell to the point where their consumption became wide-spread. The value of world trade appears on the evidence of the crude calculations that are possible to have increased by between one-third and one-quarter between 1740 and 1780 and trade carried in European vessels probably accounted for about 75 per cent of the total value of world trade.

[handwritten margin notes: 1740-80, world trade, 25-33%]

It is true that by present-day standards the quantity of goods traded was very small. But it should also be remembered that the composition of the world's capital stock was also very different. A larger proportion of the non-agrarian capital was not fixed capital but circulating capital. When European traders first explored more distant markets they had few manufactured goods which they could place in them, but when they did succeed in opening a regular trade the returns on the capital invested could be very high. The importance of the new trades was that they attracted capital investment more readily than other forms of enterprise, both because of the potential profit and also because the original investment was seldom com-mitted for a longer period than three years. Normally the investor regarded each 'venture' as a separate undertaking to be wound up on its conclusion and the profits of the voyage to be distributed among the various participants. But by attracting the capital in this way overseas trade was ultimately widening the market for the very limited range of manufactured goods produced in Europe and providing a basis for an increase in production which the domestic market would often not have provided.

The centre of this investment activity was the armed merchant vessel capable of long and dangerous voyages and because it could carry an armament of iron cannon, able to quell and subordinate by its superior fire-power most non-European nations. Such sailing vessels were the triumph of eighteenth-century European technology and the floating epitome of European civilisation. Their labour force was larger, their management and their machinery more complicated than that of most manufactures. Between their wooden walls lived almost every stratum of European society. Behind the muzzles of their guns took place the emigration of European peoples with their commercial and technological knowledge, their intellectual ideas and their diseases, and behind the same guns the spread of European commerce to other continents developed. The greater European powers were thus intimately engaged in a battle for trade at the same time as they battled for political power and influence elsewhere in the globe.

Although European trade seems to have been so large a part of world trade it was very unequally shared between the various European states. In the 1780s about 40 per cent of the total tonnage of European merchant shipping sailed under the flag of the United Kingdom or France. The only other two countries with large merchant fleets were the United Provinces and Denmark (including Norway). Some European powers scarcely participated under their own flag in this sea-borne trade. The merchant fleets of Prussia, Russia and the Habsburg Empire were insignificant, their combined tonnage only the equivalent of that of the Kingdom of the Two Sicilies. The extraordinary importance of Britain and France is emphasised by the relative decline of the trading activities of the United Provinces. The war with Britain between 1780 and 1783 had a disastrous result on the trade both of the United Provinces and France. But it is noticeable that whereas French trade recovered with redoubled vigour after 1783 that of the United Provinces did not. Amsterdam remained a great centre of commercial power controlling much trade that was no longer carried in its ships. Trade retained an overwhelming importance in the economy of the United Provinces. But the growing exclusion from the more important colonial markets may well have had serious repercussions on the internal development of the United Provinces for there were few changes in industrial activity to be noted there at the close of the eighteenth century.

In contrast, the advantages of expansion in colonial markets are revealed in the case of Denmark, a country of similar size. The Danish Asiatic Company founded in 1732 developed so flourishing an entrepôt trade at Copenhagen that it came to dominate the life of the city in the way the great trading companies of Holland had earlier dominated the life of Amsterdam. The growth of calico printing and sugar refining in Denmark were direct consequences of this trade, for the calicoes were destined for export to the East Indies. The Danish island of St Thomas became the greatest entrepôt and transhipment point in the West Indies.

In fact the great value of colonial trade was in the way in which it led to entrepôt trading activities. The redistribution of 'colonial' goods to other European ports from the great colonial trading ports of Liverpool, Bristol, Bordeaux, Nantes, Amsterdam and Copenhagen established trading routes and commercial connections which would later serve for the export of domestic industrial products also. The great rise in the participation of ships from Hamburg and Bremen in colonial commerce began in the 1770s and was an extension of their earlier participation in the redistribution of products originally imported into Bordeaux and Amsterdam.

The development of such mercantile activity was not simply the result of enterprise and initiative, it depended on having something to sell. It was not the creation of a market, but the extension of a market, for in most cases the products sold in such distant lands were either the same as, or very similar to, the products sold at home. In 1783, five ships of the newly-created Austrian East Indian Trading Company visited China. Two years later, the Company had to be wound up. Similar ventures promoted by the Russian government were no more successful; enterprise was not enough.

The development of industry in certain areas of Europe is obviously related to the phenomenon usually described as 'imperialism'. But, because of the great differences in the level of economic development in Europe itself, it is not very useful to apply the word 'imperialism' merely to the commercial relations between European and non-European states. The pattern of trade within Europe was frequently 'imperialistic' in the same sense. The more developed European areas also had 'colonial' areas in Europe which served as sources of primary products and as markets in the same way as West Indian or East Indian islands. However, the poorer European areas were less responsive as markets than those areas of North and South America and of the Antilles to which people of European stock had already begun to emigrate. The whole German area reflected the differing levels of economic development within it. In the Habsburg Empire the Austrian lands had a 'colonial' relationship with Hungary in spite of the tariff barrier which separated them. In 1782 61·5 per cent of Hungarian imports by value consisted of manufactured or semi-manufactured goods; 34·5 per cent of Hungarian exports were raw materials, 35·5 per cent foodstuffs and drinks and 27 per cent animals. Over one half of all Hungarian exports went to Austria and 27 per cent of all imports came from there.

Such dependence of the poorer areas on the richer was expressed not merely by the direction in which goods were traded but also by the dependence of the poorer countries on foreign commercial capital and skills. When the Spanish government operated its own closed trading system to its colonial territories a high proportion of the goods exported there were produced outside Spain and when the system was demolished that was still the case, although less so. Economically, the town of Cadiz seemed to have retained its monopoly of the American trade for it was from there that the great argosies still sailed and there that the financiers collected the capital for each venture. The reality was different, for not only were the goods foreign but much of the capital too. Merchants in French ports subscribed to the capital stock of the Cadiz trading voyages and Swiss capital seems also to have contributed. In 1773 30 per cent of the share capital of the Danish Asiatic Company was foreign-owned. Portugal, for all the size of the merchant fleet, pursued a commercial policy strictly inhibited by that of Britain. Embargoes and high tariffs on Spanish manufactures reflected British pressure in Lisbon. In 1796 Britain supplied 96 per cent by value of Portuguese woollen imports, 47 per cent of foodstuff imports and 38 per cent of metal imports. In the same year 59 per cent of the value of exports originating in Portugal went to Britain and 22 per cent of the products originating in Brazil. 'Broadly viewed' says Furtado, 'the Portuguese–Brazilian economy of the eighteenth century resembles an affiliation – and a basic one at that – with the most rapidly growing economic system of the time: the British. The so-called gold cycle might be considered as a more or less integrated system, within which Portugal played the role of a mere supply station'.[1]

One of the most marked aspects of eighteenth-century trade was the dominance of the greater colonial powers with their large mercantile fleets. It should be borne in mind that for the German states overland trade was of far greater importance than for other European countries, so that Table 3 which shows the size of

Table 3. *Approximate size of European merchant fleets in the 1780s*

Country	Total Tonnage	Number of Ships	Average Tonnage per Ship
United Kingdom	881,963	n.a.	n.a.
France	729,340	5,268	138
Holland	397,709	1,871	213
Denmark and Norway	386,020	3,601	107
Sweden	169,279	1,224	138
Spain	149,460	1,202	124
Kingdom of the Two Sicilies	132,220	1,047	126
Hanseatic Towns	101,347	467	217
Portugal	84,843	300	283
Habsburg Empire	84,090	1,141	74
Venice	60,332	418	144
Genoa	42,130	643	66
Ragusa (Dubrovnik)	40,749	163	250
Russia	39,394	523	75
Danzig (Gdansk)	28,857	77	375
Prussia	21,497	99	217
Total of European fleet	3,372,029		

Source: R. Romano, 'Per una valutazione della flotta mercantile europea alla fine del secolo xviii' in *Studi in Onore di Amintore Fanfani*, vol. V. (Milan, 1962). The figures are collected from the reports of French consuls. Details of smaller fleets are omitted.

[1] C. Furtado, *The Economic Growth of Brazil* (Berkeley, 1963), p. 37.

merchant fleets will inevitably give a false impression of the volume of German foreign trade. In spite of this reservation and in spite of the size of the Italian and Swedish merchant fleets it is difficult to resist the conclusion that ownership of colonies was a powerful aid to the process of market expansion. The most consistently dynamic sector of foreign trade throughout the century was the trade in 'colonial goods', sugar, coffee, tea, spices, rum, cotton and tobacco which were brought into the ports of the colonial powers and then re-exported to those European powers without colonies. The return freights to the colonies were very varied, but textiles and slaves remained in high demand always. All colonial powers developed in this way a valuable entrepôt trade. Throughout the century this was the most significant factor in the overall increase in the value and volume of foreign trade.

In general the balance of this colonial trade was usually in favour of the colonies. The value of the trade from the French West Indian islands to France in the 1780s was about 185,000,000 livres; their imports from France only 78,000,000 livres plus the value of the slaves. The two greatest participants in this trade were the towns of Bordeaux and Nantes. Over 300 ships a year in the 1780s sailed from Bordeaux to the West Indies and 150 from Nantes. In both cases the West India trade was the basis of an important intra-European trade in redistributing the imports. In fact the Bordeaux merchants themselves concentrated their activities on the trans-Atlantic trade and left a lot of the ensuing intra-European trade to foreigners. Between 1773 and 1788 45 per cent of the colonial imports into France came into Bordeaux and 20 per cent of French exports to the West Indies left from there. The trade was violently interrupted by the American War of Independence but recovered immediately after 1783 and rose to still greater heights. With it rose the number of foreign ships sailing to other European ports, particularly Amsterdam and Hamburg, from where the colonial goods were further redistributed throughout the Netherlands and Germany. There was also a small but significantly increasing number of ships leaving for the Prussian port of Stettin (Szczecin) and for Russia. Cotton was also re-exported to Liverpool. Underlying the whole structure was a steady local trade in wines to the United Kingdom and to Ireland.

If the proportion of vessels of various nationalities visiting the port of Bordeaux in this period is compared over time it can be seen that the growth in the number of Dutch ships was less than the increase in the number of those of other nationalities. The same phenomenon has been observed in other ports. Of the colonial goods passing through the Sound into the Baltic Sea between 1731 and 1740, 60 per cent were re-exports from Dutch ports; between 1761 and 1770, only 20 per cent. This decline was not evident in the quantity of grain carried through the Sound. Dutch merchants were retaining their hold on the less dynamic part of the Baltic trade but losing it on the more dynamic sector. The value of Dutch trade with the East and West Indies at the end of the century was only one-third the value of the trade with Europe and it is difficult to resist the conclusion that in the eighteenth century the United Provinces were being ousted from the trade which had built up so large a fleet. The subsequent revolution and the occupation of the country by the French led to the loss of many of the Dutch colonies to the British and the disappearance of the Netherlands as a power in Asiatic trade. The importance of trade in the Dutch economy still remained overwhelming and the wealth of the country must have been a reflection of its previous trading power, no matter how that power was eclipsed after 1750.

The commercial domination of some European areas by others was also reflected in their social structure. In Russia, and elsewhere in eastern Europe, except in Bulgaria, there was no trading bourgeoisie. Trade was handled by foreign middlemen. The commerce of the Balkans with the Habsburg Empire for example was controlled by Turkish merchants. Such a state of affairs implied serious consequences for the future economic and social development of these areas. Everywhere in the eighteenth century the position of merchant was compounded with that of banker. The large amounts of capital which the merchant handled, the knowledge of foreign matters and of money which he acquired, the relatively high ratio of circulating to fixed capital, all made his function of banker a natural extension of his mercantile activities. The annual value of the trade of some of the Bohemian cloth merchants was five times the average yield of a fief. To be deprived of the advantages to economic development of the wealth, knowledge and experience of a mercantile bourgeoisie was to be placed at a grave disadvantage.

It is therefore all the more interesting that in the eighteenth century some areas whose trade had been almost entirely carried on by outsiders should have begun themselves to participate ever more actively in international trade while other areas failed to do so with any success. Against the relative failure of Prussia and the Habsburg Empire to develop their mercantile marine should be set the growing emancipation of the Baltic ports and the Hanseatic towns from foreign domination. The growth of the trade of Hamburg and Bremen at the expense of that of the United Provinces was remarkable after 1760. After 1765 the ports in the Gulf of Bothnia were allowed to trade directly rather than through the harbours of

Stockholm or Åbo (Turku). By 1800 the volume of shipping trading between Sweden and Finland and between both these countries and the rest of the world was twice what it had been in 1730. One reason was the rapid growth in exports of pitch and tar, essential raw materials for other maritime powers, another was the growth in salt herring exports after 1758. The development of the merchant fleet of Naples after 1760 was very rapid and the French were gradually forced out of the oil trade from Naples to Marseilles. Such a development indicated the economic emancipation of the whole kingdom for so low were incomes there that there was little demand for French products and the oil trade produced a favourable trade balance for the Two Sicilies. Why the Marseilles soap-boilers should have imported oil from Naples when it was so common a product everywhere is not so easily explained unless it be attributed to the rapid spread of olive trees in the area which may have lowered the price by comparison with other Mediterranean regions. The rise of Naples was accompanied by the rise of Trieste. Trieste was primarily a port for the export of German and Austrian manufactures to the Levant and for the import of raw cotton from the same area. It also served as an entrepôt port for fruits brought by Calabrian vessels from Naples.

Against these examples of successful emancipation can be set equally numerous examples of decline. The decline of Danzig (Gdansk) after 1772 was really a feature of the growing political pressures brought by the Prussian government on Poland and the trade was mostly transferred to the port of Stettin (Szczecin). But the port in most notable decline, Venice, could hardly attribute its failure to such simple causes. In spite of monopoly privileges and export incentives the industries within the city declined. Restrictive trading rules discouraged other Italian states from using the harbour and diverted the entrepôt trade from the south to Trieste. The town of Amalfi, once a centre of east–west trade with more than 50,000 inhabitants, became a poor town with less than 3,000.

The advantage of foreign trade was not that it was a good thing in itself but that it extended the market for industry. There are numerous examples in the eighteenth century of towns developing an extensive trade with very little impact on their industrial or social structure. Ancona was deliberately fostered as the port of the Roman states in rivalry to Venice but its success as a free port did not stimulate the stagnant Roman economy in any way. Examples of previous histories of this kind were particularly numerous in Italy. Whether an increasing volume of trade or an increasing export of primary produce stimulated the rest of the economy depended on many factors, its impact was much less direct and obvious on poorer areas than on those countries such as France which were already developed.

OBSTACLES TO TRADE

The obstacles to trade were still very great, especially to overland trade. They could be overcome in favourable circumstances. The deepening of the Ghent–Bruges canal made the ports of Ghent and Antwerp accessible to ships entering the Austrian Netherlands at Ostend, road building such as the construction of the Louvain–Aachen road enabled these goods to be carried eastwards more cheaply, lower tariffs on transit trade to Germany than in the neighbouring United Provinces combined with the foregoing to concentrate the transit trade from Britain to internal German markets through the southern rather than the northern Netherlands. Germany itself, however, was criss-crossed with national tariffs, river tolls and road tolls. There were internal tariffs between the separate territories of Prussia. Over the same area there was an equal confusion of currencies, Austria and south Germany traded in silver gulden, Prussia, Saxony, and Brunswick in silver talers, Rhineland states, Hesse and Württemberg used French coinage. In Russia there were no roads, only wide dusty areas in summer and impenetrable bogs in spring and autumn. In 1815 400,000 people were employed in haulage on the River Volga. Ural pig iron took two years to reach St Petersburg (Leningrad).

In more developed areas there was great urgency to remedy this state of affairs. The United Provinces had 2,850 kilometres of road, including a complete east–west road, almost all of which were built in the eighteenth century. Baron Stein built roads for the transport of Westphalian yarn to the spinners of Wuppertal and for the transport of grain to the hill valleys of the Sauerland. In 1784, a canal for small ships from the North Sea to the Baltic was built through Schleswig-Holstein, the precursor of the Kiel canal. Prussia joined the rivers Elbe and Oder by the Plauen and Finow canals and the Oder to the Vistula by the Bromberger canal. In France the canals from the Loire to the Sâone and the Sâone to the Seine were begun. The Sâone–Loire canal was a factor in choosing the site of the Le Creusot works. The canal de Briare provided a waterway from the Loire to Paris and thus enabled ironmasters in the Nivernais to ship their goods to Le Havre without the difficult and tiresome navigation of the lower Loire. After 1750 the upper

Scheldt was canalised and coal traffic moved by boat after 1782 between Cambrai and Valenciennes. In Poland the Oginski canal from the Dnieper to the Niemen was completed and the Royal Canal from the Dnieper to the Vistula was built. In Spain the Ebro was canalised as far as Tudela and the Spanish government embarked on a huge and uncompleted project to link Castille by canal to the Bay of Biscay.

None of these developments should mask the fact that to travel from Castille into Asturias or Galicia was still only possible on foot or by mule. Even where, as in France, there were good roads and an organised system of public carriage journeys were very slow, five days from Paris to Lyons by *diligence* in 1776 and three days from Paris to Lille. In such conditions overland trade moved only when the economic circumstances were very favourable. Maritime trade was the more important and in the eighteenth century it became increasingly important. In the Mediterranean outbreaks of piracy could force trade from the Balkans to pass by land and this maintained the position of Leipzig as a great inland fair. But the other great fairs such as Frankfurt-am-Main, Beaucaire and Pest declined in relative importance. The consequence was that both participation in and distribution of the benefits of the increasing trade were very unequally divided in Europe. Where countries had already found themselves underdeveloped compared to their neighbours, the pattern of trade tended often to reaffirm their relative backwardness. Its advantages were to be reaped only by states whose economic or social circumstances were able to respond to the opportunities presented. No more than in agriculture or in industry was there an easy route to economic development in commerce.

CONCLUSION

What can be said is that where internal economic and social development had created a structure in which industrial development was possible and, perhaps, necessary, the existence of an overseas market was vital to completing the transition from a domestic textile industry to a centralised, mechanised, textile industry. But before this effect could be produced a long path of industrial and social change had to have already been covered. It is an obvious fact, but an often forgotten one, that there were many different stages of economic development to be observed in late eighteenth-century Europe. The explanations of why this should have been so are still the task of economic historians dealing with an earlier period than that covered by this book. But it was these differences of development which were to dominate the economic history of Europe after 1750 and remain its most salient feature. It was the existence of such differences that made both industrialisation and economic growth particularly difficult to achieve.

The remarkable developments in the economy of France in the eighteenth century should not blind us to the difficulty with which they were achieved nor to the economic consequences of being only the second nation to industrialise. The history of all other European economies show how extraordinarily difficult the problem was. Neither in agriculture, nor in industry nor in trade was there a clear path to economic development which could be pursued by the diligent and determined government. Every economy had certain severe disadvantages and a few particular opportunities. The social changes which had taken place in France and the greater complexity of the French economy appeared to provide an infinitely more satisfactory base for the continued development of the country than the relatively stagnant and limited society and economy of Russia. But the fact that the specific technological changes associated with the Industrial Revolution occurred first in Britain showed both at the time and in the future how little it could avail an economy to have developed as successfully as France. How immeasurably more deterring therefore were the obstacles to the economic development of other European societies!

Fundamentally, the problem of development was a social one; not one of social attitudes, but rather of the extent to which previous economic history had changed the social structure of the different nations. To seize the slender opportunities for development was to bring about a violent disruption of the social structure. To cope with this disruption it had already to have achieved a certain flexibility. But to begin by reforming the social structure would not necessarily produce any significant measure of development in return for disturbing the social framework which was the basis of the eighteenth-century state and government. Development could not be engineered in this mechanical way, although where the government was endowed with more absolute powers and was less inhibited in its actions by the social structure, as in the Russia of Peter the Great, it had been possible to force through violent economic and social changes for a brief period. In spite, therefore, of the relatively high levels of income of certain of the European countries in the late eighteenth century, their economic future did not necessarily appear a particularly cheerful one. And for those with lower incomes and less developed economies the outlook was dark.

SUGGESTED READING

There is a good short analytical description of eighteenth-century European society in the first chapter of E. J. HOBSBAWM, *The Age of Revolution 1789–1848* (London, 1962). For France alone there is a more comprehensive but now rather out-of-date description in H. SÉE, *Economic and Social Conditions in France during the Eighteenth Century* (New York, 1927). Equally out-of-date and only very occasionally touching on economic history, but still a good read, is W. H. BRUFORD, *Germany in the Eighteenth-Century: The Social Background of the Literary Revival* (Cambridge, 1935). An interesting experiment which has never been followed up is the comparative study by several different authors, A. GOODWIN (ed.), *The European Nobility in the Eighteenth Century* (London, 1953). The editor's own essay on the Prussian nobility and that of M. ROBERTS on the Swedish nobility are particularly interesting. There is a very specialised work on the French nobility, R. FORSTER, *The Nobility of Toulouse in the Eighteenth Century. A Social and Economic Study* (Baltimore, 1960). A work of a more general nature is F. L. FORD, *Robe and Sword: The Regrouping of the French Aristocracy after Louis XIV* (Cambridge, Mass., 1953). E. G. BARBER, *The Bourgeoisie in Eighteenth-Century France* (Princeton, 1955) is an attempt to analyse a historical situation with the help of sociological concepts. K. J. KERNER, *Bohemia in the Eighteenth Century* (New York, 1932) is a more discursive work.

The financial difficulties of the eighteenth-century French state are analysed in two works of thorough research which aim to make a contribution to the continuing and narrowly detailed study of the financial crisis of the eighteenth-century French state, G. T. MATTHEWS, *The Royal General Farms in Eighteenth-Century France* (New York, 1958) and J. F. BOSHER, *French Finances 1770–1795: From Business to Bureaucracy* (Cambridge, 1970). They may be read in conjunction with D. DAKIN, *Turgot and the Ancien Régime in France* (London, 1939).

The connection between state finance and social organisation is well illustrated in W. E. WRIGHT, *Serf, Seigneur and Sovereign: Agrarian Reform in Eighteenth-Century Bohemia* (Minneapolis, 1966), but there is little other work in English on eighteenth-century European agriculture. B. H. SLICHER VAN BATH, *The Agrarian History of Western Europe A.D. 500–1850* (London, 1963) is only able to deal very fleetingly with one century, but its conclusions are set out in a separate article, 'Eighteenth-century agriculture on the continent of Europe: evolution or revolution' in *Agricultural History*, vol. 43, 1969. A. J. BOURDE, *The Influence of England on the French Agronomes 1750–89* (Cambridge, 1953) discusses the ideas of eighteenth-century agricultural reformers in France and R. FORSTER, 'Obstacles to agricultural growth in eighteenth-century France' in *American Historical Review*, vol. 65, 1970, comes to some common sense conclusions about why they were usually not implemented. A much-quoted classic of eighteenth-century British materialism and philistinism, A. YOUNG, *Travels in France* (London, 1792) is still easily available in several editions in spite of being so much about turnips and clover.

As far as eighteenth-century industry and trade are concerned there is practically nothing written in English. W. O. HENDERSON, *Studies in the Economic Policy of Frederick the Great* (London, 1963) deals with Prussia in a relentlessly factual way. His article in a similar vein 'The genesis of the industrial revolution in France and Germany in the eighteenth century' in *Kyklos*, vol. 9, 1956, has proved a useful introduction to the subject for some time. Also by the same author is 'The Anglo-French Commercial Treaty of 1786' in *Economic History Review*, vol. 10, 1957. P. CHORLEY, *Oil, Silk and Enlightenment: Economic Problems in Eighteenth-Century Naples* (Naples, 1965) deals with an unusual subject. So does the rather limited J. C. LA FORCE JR, *The Development of the Spanish Textile Industry 1750–1800* (Berkeley, 1965). One small example of mercantilist manufacture is discussed in H. FREUDENBERGER, 'The woollen goods industry of the Hapsburg monarchy in the eighteenth century' in *Journal of Economic History*, vol. 20, 1960. Two articles deal with the relationship between monetary policy and mercantilism, R. V. EAGLY, 'Monetary policy and politics in mid-eighteenth-century Sweden' in *Journal of Economic History*, vol. 29, 1969, and E. J. HAMILTON, 'War and inflation in Spain, 1780–1800' in *Quarterly Journal of Economics*, vol. 59, 1944.

As far as these more detailed subjects are concerned it is impossible to pursue the subject further without reading in other languages. There are two studies of French eighteenth-century agriculture which in their scholarliness, their understanding of economics and history and their warm and genuine humanity are an example to all historians and an encouragement to all readers. One is the fine essay by M. BLOCH, *La Lutte pour l'individualisme agraire dans la France du dix-huitième siècle* (Paris, 1930). The other is a large and excellent book, C.-E. LABROUSSE, *La Crise de l'économie française à la fin de l'Ancien Régime et au début de la Révolution* (Paris, 1944). For Germany there is W. ABEL, *Geschichte der deutschen Landwirtschaft vom frühen Mittelalter bis zum neunzehnten Jahrhundert* (Stuttgart, 1962), which is vol. 2 of G. FRANZ (ed.) *Deutsche Agrargeschichte*. On eighteenth-century industry the literature has become for the most part very specialised. The last good general survey for France was E. TARLÉ, *L'industrie dans les campagnes en France à la fin de l'Ancien Régime* (Paris, 1910), valuable for its approach but now made rather out-of-date by much specialised research into particular regions and industries. In Germany the specialisation at least is only regional and an example of its output is R. FORBERGER, *Die Manufaktur in Sachsen vom Ende des sechszehnten bis zum Anfang des neunzehnten Jahrhunderts* (Berlin, 1958). There is an interesting specialised work on eighteenth-century banking, H. LÜTHY, *La banque protestante en France, de la révocation de l'Édit de Nantes à la Révolution*, vol. 2 (Paris, 1961). An attempt to assess all aspects of economic life together at the end of the eighteenth century in Germany is made by several authors with varying success in F. LÜTGE (ed.), *Die wirtschaftliche Situation in Deutschland und Österreich um die Wende vom achtzehnten bis zum neunzehnten Jahrhundert. Berichte über die erste Arbeitstagung der Gesellschaft für Sozial- und Wirtschaftsgeschichte in Mainz 1963* (Stuttgart, 1964). An excellent article by F. CROUZET, 'Croissances comparées de l'Angleterre et de la France au dix-huitième siècle' in *Annales*, vol. 21, 1966, has more ideas and handles a wider theme than most books.

There are no research journals which deal particularly with eighteenth-century economic history and research is published in almost all the journals cited in our later reading suggestions. The French journal, *Annales*, tends to attract articles dealing with society as a whole viewed from an economic standpoint and its book reviews are often organised around general themes rather than published separately.

Chapter 2

Population Growth and Migration

THE SETTING

In 1800 the population of Europe and Asiatic Russia was probably something like 190 million. Extremely inadequate statistics lead us to believe that it had been about 145 million in 1750: if it was of this order of magnitude, that would mean a rate of growth per decade for the second half of the eighteenth century of under 6 per cent. Over the next two half-century periods this rate of growth was to accelerate to 7·4 per cent and 9·1 per cent per decade, the absolute level of population being about 275 million in 1850 and 425 million in 1900. The permanent emigration overseas of something like 40 million people meant that the natural increase of population, particularly in the second half of the century, was considerably higher however. These events were by no means unique: in the eighteenth century the rate of growth in Europe matched that in

Asia simply on account of the very high growth rates achieved in Russia and other parts of eastern Europe. But in the nineteenth century population in Europe grew considerably faster than in the rest of the world except for those areas of recent settlement being populated by European emigrants. All the same, it is important to remember that the events we are discussing in this chapter have a wider framework of reference outside Europe. When we come to the difficult question of why population growth began to accelerate in the eighteenth century it may be that we ought to look for some worldwide causes. Possibly improved communications and the consequent greater contact of peoples throughout the globe had in the long run resulted in the development of greater natural resistance to disease. Possibly this had brought higher death rates initially in the sixteenth and seventeenth centuries until the resistance began to show itself in the eighteenth. But this is pure speculation: there is no evidence for it, just a phenomenon to be explained. Here we shall have to confine ourselves to what is known about Europe.

It is considerably easier to understand the process of population growth in nineteenth-century than in eighteenth-century Europe, partly because the statistics are better and partly because in the later period the links with economic change become more straightforward. But an assessment of the causes and effects of eighteenth-century changes is absolutely crucial to our understanding of the nature of European society at that time and to our analysis of the forces which were to lead to the staggering economic changes of the next century. Growth was certainly irregular and probably not great before the 1740s. The opening of the century saw death stalking

Table 4. *Population of some European countries in the eighteenth century (millions)*

	1750	1800		% Annual Rate of Growth
Sweden	1·78	2·35		0·6
Finland	0·42	0·83		1·4
Norway	0·59	0·88		0·8
Sicily	1·3	1·7		0·6
Spain	7·4	10·4	(1787)	0·9
Netherlands	1·9	2·1		0·2
Austria	1·4	1·9	(1790)	0·8

Source: *Cambridge Economic History of Europe*, Vol. IV (Cambridge, 1967) pp. 63–7.

all Europe as a result of war and the diseases that it spread and of some particularly bad spells of weather. The Great Northern War (1699–1721) had most serious effects on the population of Sweden and Finland. Then in 1709–10, for example, a summer of torrential rain was followed by a winter of such intense cold that in Flanders the wine is said to have frozen in the glasses, weather which in varying degrees was repeated in many other parts of Europe. Plague appeared in north and central Europe in 1708–11 and moved briefly but devastatingly into southern France from Marseilles in 1720–1, never to appear in western Europe again. Recovery from these disasters was followed by more years of bad weather and epidemics in the 1740s, but then more continuous growth set in and the results can be seen in Table 4. Some of the figures are very rough and they take no account of boundary changes and migration but they give some idea of the kind of growth that we must try to explain. Before doing that, however, we must make a more general assessment of the causes and consequences of population growth.

THEORY OF POPULATION GROWTH

Whatever may be the precise relationship between population growth and economic growth, the nineteenth-century experience certainly provides a most complex series of patterns. Sweden had a low population growth and high growth of per capita product: Italy low population growth and low income growth: the United States high population and high income growth: Russia high population and low income: Holland high population and moderate income growth. Every possible combination seems to have been present. Could the relationship be a random one therefore? The answer is most definitely no. It varied according to particular circumstances and to whether the causal effects were moving most powerfully from population to economic change or vice versa.

Improvements in economic conditions may affect population directly by lowering the death rate. This may result from an improvement to food supplies created by more efficient agricultural output and transport, thereby increasing resistance to disease and eliminating local famines, or from a distinct improvement in environmental factors such as personal cleanliness, better sanitation, more adequate clothing. It may come from better housing, though in the initial stages the urbanisation which normally accompanied economic growth might raise the death rate on account of the worse squalor this created. A rise in income or in employment prospects might also raise the birth rate over the short run at least by inducing earlier marriage. This may result from farm holdings becoming more easily available, or from the relative growth of those occupations where higher fertility was the norm. For example, coal miners usually had larger families than farmers: if the number of miners increased relative to that of farmers then the birth rate would automatically rise without the need for any change in the fertility of either of those two groups. Birth rates and death rates interact. Larger numbers of children surviving may lead couples to control their families so that there are fewer to survive: marriages may become less prone to end through the premature death of one partner and so be more fertile. However, birth and death rates are in themselves inadequate indicators of the causes of population change. Both are much affected by changes in the age distribution. The *age dist.* more very young and very old there are in proportion to total population the higher will be the death rate: the more women there are aged between 15–45 the higher the birth rate. The birth rate is also influenced by the proportion of women marrying, the age at which they are married, the degree of illegitimacy and, as we have just mentioned, the frequency of widowhood.

But ignoring these complications, in the previous paragraph we have looked at the interaction of births and deaths as if population were an entirely negative factor. Population is assumed to build up to the level of resources available and to decline if for any reason these resources are reduced. In such circumstances the standard of living of the mass of people remains unchanged over time, hovering always near the subsistence level. This is the situation envisaged by *Malth.* Thomas Malthus: he felt that population was always tending to *Probl.* grow at a faster rate than the resources available and that it was perforce held back by war, famine and disease. The rise of population of itself did not tend to force up the level of resources. Undoubtedly such a Malthusian situation obtained in many of the lower income parts of Europe in the eighteenth and nineteenth centuries. How soon these areas in the east and south came to face an 'overpopulation crisis' depended largely upon how much land there was to expand into. In the eighteenth century many of these areas were very sparsely populated, but by the end of the nineteenth this way of escape was no longer available and we can read most terrifying accounts of living conditions in the Ukraine and Galicia, for example, where these problems were at their worst. It has been argued that any gradual increase of economic resources was normally offset in this way by a rising population. Nevertheless there is a physical limit to the speed at which any population can grow. Suppose that resources could expand over a period of time at a markedly faster rate than this population limit. Then the average income would rise and so create the conditions for continued investment, for further increases in income and possibly for changes in cultural attitudes to family size which would destroy the barrier that population growth appeared to set to long term economic growth. But what precisely was this barrier, this self-sustaining backwardness of a growing population deprived of any long term growth in average incomes? The key lies in the emphasis on a 'gradual' rise in resources. Productivity may be limited by an inelastic supply of natural resources, especially land, a problem which is intensified if climate, tradition or technology inhibits any change in the pattern of land usage. Alternatively the decline in mortality, sometimes combined with a rise in births following upon a slow growth of resources, may increase the burden of dependency; that is to say these trends may increase more than proportionally the young and the old who contribute nothing to total output. This may have the effect of actually reducing the level of savings available to the population, and so cutting off completely the extra investment necessary to achieve a faster rate of growth.

This, then is the barrier. But as we have said, the physical limit to the rate of growth of any population lies far below actually experienced long term rates of economic growth. So, in the right circumstances it has been possible to break through the barrier and in nineteenth-century Europe this was less difficult than it is today since many major killing diseases – tuberculosis and cholera, for example – remained to restrict the rate of population growth, and their impact was worsened by the relatively high level of mortality in the rapidly growing towns. Eventually the decline in mortality was followed by the beginning of a marked fall in fertility which further held back the growth of population. Above all, European countries were able to siphon off much of their surplus populations through an unparalleled degree of internal and external migration, though it was unfortunate that it was not physically easy to emigrate from some of the areas worst hit by population problems because of their geographical remoteness.

By and large the population barrier was not a serious handicap to nineteenth century industrialisation except in those areas of the east and south and, for that matter, Ireland, which experienced low incomes and a cultural pattern giving high fertility and very high rates of population growth and where the obstacles to economic change – in rural areas above all – were very severe. There, incomes grew all too slowly and population all too quickly. Indeed, in some areas of south-eastern Europe per capita income very probably declined. But once the barrier was broken, what would the impact of population then be? The argument now takes a Keynesian form: the increase in demand from rising numbers enjoying rising incomes gives a continued boost to further investment, and so to further economic growth. This may arise partly because the growing size of the market offers ever greater economies of scale. It may be *induces* that an expanding market makes businessmen more venturesome in their investment policies, for they can always hope that the market will catch up with them if they create excess capacity. It builds up a 'climate' of optimism. Fast growth also gives more opportunity for the installation of the most up-to-date technologies, whereas with stagnation this may occur only when old equipment comes to be replaced. An alternative explanation assumes that demand is adequate and suggests that the rise in population is most beneficial in offering unlimited supplies of cheap labour for industry. This enables the fruits of investment to be channelled largely towards the profit makers who will tend to save heavily and provide the wherewithal for further investment and further growth.

In part both population and income rose because of their association with technological change. Technology gave greater control over health and production. Technology extended the limits set by natural resources in many fields: international trade made each country less reliant on its own specific range of natural resources. More often than not it was less resources than institutions and the receptivity of society to change which proved to be the real Malthusian barrier. We do not have to bother overmuch with the absence of coal in Denmark, for example. The meaningful contrast is between the strangulating effect of the village community in Russia and the greater ability of Danish society to break with the past in many different respects. But stress on technology takes us to an alternative view of the relationship between population and economic growth. If we can assume that there was no shortage of investment opportunities, that these were provided sufficiently by technological change, then a slower population growth might mean that less capital was required for widening the stock and more was available to introduce new techniques. Such a point of view explains in part why the slowing down of population growth in the twentieth century has not reversed the trends in economic expansion of the previous hundred years.

Those are the theoretical relationships. We must remember that economic growth was never solely the result of population growth, and often connected with it at all. Equally population change could arise from entirely non-economic factors such as changes in climate, the incidence of wars and of particular diseases. But we must return to the eighteenth century to see how far these possible relationships applied to the real Europe of that time. Our main question here must be: was there a self adjusting mechanism by which population adapted its rate of growth to the capacity of the economy to support it at some conventional standard of living, or was population change the result of certain exogenous forces and if so what effect did this have upon the development of different economies? The first approach would lead us to look above all for changes in the birth rate and the factors influencing it. The non-economic external forces are more likely to have had most influence on the level of mortality.

EIGHTEENTH-CENTURY POPULATION GROWTH IN EUROPE

One thing we must stress right away is the wide range of demographic experience in Europe. In the last three decades of the century the population of Finland was growing at a rate of 1·3 per cent per annum, comparable only with that of Russia. In England and Wales and in Prussia growth was just under 1 per cent per annum in the last decade of the eighteenth century; in Scandinavia it was 0·6 per cent and possibly much the same for all the German principalities together; in France and Austria it was more like 0·4 per cent. The birth rate in Russia around 1800 was over 43 per thousand, and in some rural areas and small towns in Hungary it reached 50 per thousand. In Württemberg it was 40; in Bohemia, Moravia and Slovakia together 35, and in Scandinavia between 31 and 33, though in Finland it was 41. Great differences in the expectation of life at birth are recorded too. In Spain it was 26–27 years: in France 29: 34–5 years in Sweden, Denmark and Finland. In Norway it was over 38 years, yet in Russia it was still only 28 in the late 1870s. These are crude measures based on inaccurate statistics but they point unerringly to different cultural patterns and to potentially serious problems in some areas. The very high rates of growth in the east and north east could only be maintained without disaster so long as colonisation of new land or migration to new areas was possible. Already the authorities in southern and south-western Germany were taking action to restrict marriages unless a man could prove his ability to care for his family, and the number of beggars was beginning to rise alarmingly.

The basic mechanism behind these variations is all-important. The age and extent of marriage probably was the most important single form of demographic control available in societies where there was only a modest degree of control over conception within marriage. We can see how powerful was the effect of changes in marriage patterns from some calculations made by Ohlin.[1] The rate of population growth in Sweden at the end of the eighteenth century was 0·53 per cent per annum. Had 95 per cent of the women married instead of the 91 per cent who actually did, it would have been 0·66 per cent. If the average age of women at marriage had been five years younger than it was, growth would have been 2 per cent per annum. In the east and south-east of Europe marriage was early and almost universal. Fertility was high as the figures in the last paragraph show, and population built up inevitably to the capacity of the economy to sustain it. A study of three Hungarian villages has shown that between 1770 and 1800 over half of the brides were under 20 and a quarter were between 20 and 24 years old. Not surprisingly the birth rate stood at 52 per thousand. But in the west there had developed a pattern of much later and less universal marriage. In Sweden the average age of brides was 26 at the end of the century: in the rural areas around Paris it was 25 and in Brittany it was higher: in Amsterdam in 1776 only a third of the brides were under 25. A study of Rovsø in Jutland found that at the end of the eighteenth century the age of first marriage was as high as 31·6 for men (34·5 for all marriages) and 27·6 for women (30·3 for all marriages). The effects of early marriage were partially offset by younger couples tending to have more widely spaced births and infant deaths were more common in large families but the contrast east and west of a line running roughly from St Petersburg (Leningrad) to Trieste still remains a sharp one. In the west, therefore, some control over population growth was being exercised: the birth rate was being held down and this may have helped in a modest way to raise incomes, savings, investment and productivity. Subsistence crises were never far away, but the possibility of achieving some material advance in living standards was there too and in the more developed regions in the eighteenth century shortages were increasingly mitigated by a greater ability to hold stocks of food and to trade. The reasons behind the western marriage patterns are not fully understood but a major factor was certainly the existence of the nuclear family as the basic social unit. Marriage implied the setting up of an independent household and was therefore deferred until a man was in a position to undertake this role. Over time such

[1] G. Ohlin, *The Positive and Preventive Check*, unpublished Harvard PhD. thesis, 1955.

deferment had got embodied in local customs or even in local law. In societies where an extended family group was the social unit a young newly married couple could more easily be absorbed and there was no virtue in delay. Of course, this difference in social structure had an impact far beyond population, especially in affecting the incentive to invest for future returns, but the existence of such a preventive check to population growth, helping to maintain a standard of living distinctly above the subsistence level, explains in some degree why western Europe was better placed than most areas to seize the opportunities offered by new industrial and agricultural technologies. Even so, we must be careful not to be too dogmatic over this. To some degree the types of family customs were devices for managing the capital stock and the differences that existed were related to the availability of extra land. No doubt there were lags before these social arrangements adjusted to the reality of the economy but the existence of the extended family usually meant that in the recent past more land had been available to plough as family size increased. In eighteenth-century Spain we have good evidence of the effect of land policies on population growth – though this did not necessarily in this instance express itself through family customs too. In Asturias, Galicia and Valencia where the means for establishing new household were not restricted, population doubled but Estremadura with its many huge estates remained sparsely populated and the whole century saw a rise of only 50 per cent.

It would be quite plausible to argue that the rise in population in western Europe in the eighteenth century was due to a fall in the age of marriage as improved economic circumstances released some of these limitations. This would indicate a close link between economic and population change, the causal effect running initially from the former to the latter. But for it to be true we need to present not only supporting demographic evidence but also to indicate what substantial economic changes took place. In fact there seems to be no clear evidence that the rise in population was due to a rise in the birth rate resulting from a fall in the age of marriage. Things may have been different in England where distinct economic change was taking place: in countries such as Finland where there were considerable opportunities for clearing land and for using new techniques a fall in the marriage rate contributed to the remarkable rate of natural increase. But for most parts of Europe we must look to other explanations.

SWEDEN AND FRANCE IN THE EIGHTEENTH CENTURY

We can best solve our problem by examining more closely two areas which have received particular attention from demographers – Sweden and France.

The sequence of events in Sweden is reasonably well established. After bad years at the beginning of the century, population grew quickly from 1720 to 1735, rising by at least 15 per cent. During the next decade, however, it actually fell slightly. Thereafter it began to rise again, interrupted by famines or by war and famine in 1772–3, 1783–5, 1790 and 1800 but growing at a particularly rapid rate in the 1750s and 1760s. The burst of growth in those two decades in part reflected the large excess of births of a quarter century before and was to be continued into the 1790s, 1820s and 1850s. The older interpretation of all these events was a Malthusian one – that after the disasters of the early years of the century, population built up to the limits of subsistence again, overexpanded and brought about the setbacks of 1735–45. More recent research gives a different emphasis. The expansion from 1720 in part resulted from the weeding out of weaker elements in society during the earlier disasters and from some reaction to previously delayed marriages or, and probably more important, to delayed conceptions, but in the main it arose from largely autonomous factors – a milder climate, better harvests, absence of wars and major epidemics. In 1736 came a change. Epidemics of influenza and typhus were reported in Denmark and Northern Germany as well as in Sweden. The first major smallpox outbreak in Sweden occurred in Malmö that same year – all experts agree that smallpox became really serious in Europe only in the eighteenth century. Crop failures followed, weakening resistance to these diseases rather than raising the death rate greatly in themselves. Starving men and women might also turn to eating offal, bark and grass and suffer disease as a result. The impact of natural catastrophes varied with the nature of the rural economy: the more diversified, the less likely that it would be absolutely devasted. It was workers dependent on rural industry who were usually worst off. They were buyers rather than sellers of food and high prices tended to hit them just at a time when demand for their own output collapsed. The death rate in Norway reached 69 per thousand in 1742, yet in parts of northern Sweden rates as high as 100 per thousand have been found for that period. Soldiers returning from the Swedish-Russian war of 1741–3 spread disease further. War also had the effect of reducing food supplies because of the requisitions made by the military. However, in the late 1740s the climate improved again, the epidemics receded and so the cyclical boom in births arrived at a peculiarly favourable time.

The stress is therefore on fortuitous events which were by no means confined to Sweden. The normal incidence of death was not necessarily much reduced: elimination of the periodic crises could well have set up a train of events leading to sustained population growth. But if all this was true we need to know why this expansion was not checked eventually. In Sweden, as well as in other places, there seem to have been two main reasons. In the first place the growth of numbers brought a significant response from farmers. The higher prices of foodstuffs and the ready supply of cheap labour led to improvements in crops and rotations, expansion of the cultivated area and development of new interests such as dairying, none of which required much investment. Secondly, after about 1765 the age of marriage in Sweden began to move upwards. 'Moral restraint', in Malthus's words, was coming in again to stem the pace of growth, not necessarily because population was pressing on resources but for a variety of reasons, linked with landholding and the maintenance of new, higher standards of living. In this sense the fall of the birth rate in the late nineteenth century represented no very new phenomenon. Nor was the eighteenth-century control of births achieved solely through variation of marriage patterns. For some countries there is evidence of the use of birth control within marriage to the same end. This was apparent in those parts of Spain, for example, where the opportunities for improving agricultural output were limited, and by 1860 Spain had the lowest rate of fertility in Europe. But elsewhere certainly the more positive check of famine began to appear again – in Russia, parts of Prussia and in Ireland.

Towards the very end of the century there were signs of a change in the pattern of events in Scandinavia. The population of Denmark had grown only slowly until the last quarter of the eighteenth century but then it began to accelerate rapidly. Probably this was brought about mainly by a rise in the marriage rate and in fertility associated with the extensive agrarian reforms of those years, later intensified by the high level of food prices obtaining during the Napoleonic Wars. The same can be said of Skåne, Sweden's most advanced agricultural area and the part of the country closest to Denmark. Economic change was now positively inducing population growth rather than simply permitting autonomous population growth to continue.

In France it is generally agreed that population was falling from 1690 to 1720 and then remained stationary for two decades. The reasons are much the same as those suggested for Sweden. Then population began to grow: it was about 19 million in 1700 but after the famine of 1709 fell to more like 17 million. By 1891 it was approximately 26 million. Changes in frontiers confuse the situation to some extent. One authority puts total French growth from 1755 to 1776 at 0·8 per cent per annum, but at only 0·5 per cent when allowing for these changes. About one million more people were brought under French rule by extensions of the frontiers: the population of Lorraine at the end of the eighteenth century was 835,000 and of Corsica 124,000. The rate of population growth in France by that time was low compared with most other European countries but already in the previous century France had become the most densely populated territory in Europe. There was a distinctly lower level of mortality in this second half of the century: not a falling level but a lower stable level due to the absence of the calamities of earlier years – plague, famine, wars – though the years 1779–84 saw another demographic catastrophe as a consequence of successive harvest failures. Every calculation shows a declining trend in infant mortality though there were large variations from year to year and from region to region. It still remained high, nevertheless – 200–250 per thousand – as did the incidence of death among all children. Only 60 per cent of those born alive reached their fifteenth birthday.

There is little sign of changes in fertility in response to greater economic opportunities. The evidence is fragmentary and is derived from the intensive work of French demographers into the history of particular villages. From this we get a fascinating account of French rural life at least for the region centred on Paris. Peasants married late – 25 for women and 27–8 for men: few remained unmarried. If both partners survived to remain married for twenty years on average they had six children, but many marriages were broken by death and the average number was only four. Rarely in these rural areas were there many illegitimate births, though young unmarried women went to Paris to have their babies, and recent research has brought to light a high level of illegitimacy in the village of Meulan near Paris from girls normally resident in the city. Figures of conceptions in all regions show that they were at a peak at the end of spring and at their lowest level in early autumn. Taking average conceptions over the years as 100, in eighteenth-century Paris they were 113 in May and 92 in September; in Brittany and Anjou they were 130 in May, 137 in July, 84 in October and 71 in November. The explanation is not certain: it may be due to physiological rhythms or to diet variations.

Yet we must note the variations from these patterns. The upper classes married much earlier – at 18 for men and 21 for women in

E

the second half of the eighteenth century – but a high proportion remained unmarried. There is clear evidence of birth control among these groups too – a good indication always being the age of the mother at the birth of her last child. Studies of the peasantry in Brittany suggested a very high fecundity of women and no evidence at all of the birth control that the peasantry elsewhere may well have been applying by the end of the eighteenth century. But there was a high death rate too and no strong indication of any population growth at all over the century. In Paris there was no excess of births over deaths between 1750 and 1790, for despite the high number of foundlings, the birth rate was lower than in rural areas and mortality high. But all over Europe the older administrative centres gained little in population. Antwerp, Bruges, Ghent and Malines in Flanders had failed to reach the levels of a century before by 1794. In Holland Amsterdam was much the same though the booming port of Rotterdam had grown fast. Milan and Venice were both stable over the century and the population of Rome rose from 142,000 to only 163,000. Cologne, Leipzig, Munich, Frankfurt, Nuremberg grew slowly too. In all those cities the death rates were relatively high, though not all of them had the low birth rates found in Paris. The rural pattern varied too: in parts of the Netherlands, in Alsace, in Bradenburg–Prussia population growth markedly slackened after about 1760. For this there were often special local factors, of course: in the province of Overyssel in the Netherlands, for example, the textile industry got into difficulties and the temporary prosperity derived from peat digging came to an end. Yet in the lands along the coast south from The Hague where a more intensive form of agricultural production was being developed, population increased much more readily. These variations are complex and difficult to explain, but they are of special interest because we shall see later that a major factor in nineteenth-century history was the movement of people between regions – from one cultural pattern to another and from one form of population behaviour to another.

But despite all the complexities, the most acceptable explanations for the growth of population in most parts of Europe are to be found in non-economic factors – the reduced virulence of epidemics, the relative absence of wars, and in the northern regions at least, favourable changes in the climate. Except for the 1740s and 1780s after 1720 the winters were considerably milder than had been usual and the effect on crops was highly beneficial. These forces went far to eliminate the crises which had been experienced in earlier years and brought about a lower average level of mortality. Very little of this reduction in the death rate can be attributed to medical improvements. Some scholars believe that inoculation was more effective against smallpox than was once thought to have been the case, but in France anyway, the rigid intellectual medical world was too hostile to allow such experiments. Nor were there very widespread environmental improvements – in food, clothing, sanitation – which derived from economic change. Here and there economic opportunities – above all improvements in agricultural techniques – seem to have brought a fall in the age at marriage and a rise in fertility but it was sporadic and largely confined to the last years of the century. But though agricultural improvements in the west eased some of the social pressures of this surge of population, as one contemporary French demographer, Louis Henry, has pointed out, population increases of this magnitude in countries not actively industrialising often meant that extra people could only stay where they were or add to the urban population as extra artisans, servants, or people with little or nothing to do. Such developments are of considerable importance to an interpretation of the political upheavals of the end of the century, and the consequences of differences in population experience between regions and classes may have been far-reaching.

EUROPE IN THE NINETEENTH CENTURY

In most countries the rates of natural population growth in the nineteenth century became much greater than they had been in the eighteenth. Some achieved the highest growth rates in the early decades – see Table 5. These rates were then maintained for the rest of the century though the absolute increases in population were much modified by emigration. This was true of Norway, of Sweden and of England and Wales. The majority of countries experienced an acceleration in their rates of growth after the middle of the century and it was then that emigration became so vital in releasing this great pressure of numbers. The huge differences in the absolute levels of growth that were noted for the eighteenth century remained. In the 1820s Norway, Finland and Great Britain had the highest rates, Sweden, Germany and Russia came next, Denmark, Holland, Austria, Italy were about the European average and France and Spain experienced the slowest growth. By the end of the period Poland, Russia and above all Bulgaria were leading: Holland, Romania, Denmark, Finland and Serbia were not far behind: Belgium and Spain were among the slowest and France stood uniquely with an almost stable population.

Table 5. *Nineteenth-century European population change*

| | | | | | (*per 000 inhabitants*) | | *Actual population (millions)* |
| | Excess of births over deaths | | | | *Birth rate* | *Death rate* | |
	1841–60	*1861–70*	*1871–90*	*1901–10*	*1901–10*		*1910*
Sweden	10·8	11·2	12·2	10·9	25·8	14·9	5·5
Norway	14·2	12·9	13·8	13·3	27·5	14·2	2·4
Denmark	11·0	10·8	12·7	14·5	28·7	14·2	2·7
Finland	9·6	2·2	14·4	13·2	31·2	18·0	3·1
Netherlands	7·3	10·4	12·6	15·3	30·5	15·2	5·9
Belgium	7·0	7·6	9·7	9·7	26·2	16·5	7·4
Germany	9·2	10·3	11·8	14·3	33·0	18·7	64·9
Austria ⎱	5·1	—	7·5	11·4	34·7	23·3	28·6
Hungary ⎰				11·3	37·0	25·7	20·9
France	3·2	2·7	1·8	1·2	20·6	19·4	39·5
Italy	6·2	—	8·9	11·1	32·7	21·6	34·4
Spain	—	—	—	9·2	34·4	25·2	19·6
Bulgaria	—	—	—	18·2	41·4	23·2	4·3
Russia	11·6	13·2	14·2	16·4	46·4	30·0	165·1
Romania	—	—	—	16·2	40·2	26·0	7·0

MORTALITY

After the Napoleonic Wars the forces which had brought down the general level of mortality in the previous century continued to operate, though the crisis years saw striking if only temporary rises in death rates associated with food shortages. But other factors came to play a part too. One of the most important of these was the rapid extension of the area devoted to the growing of potatoes in northern and western Europe and parts of Germany in particular. In Sweden the ratio of land under potatoes to that under grain was 1 : 100 in 1800 and 1 : 15 in 1830 and by 1835 the crop was large enough to feed one fifth of the population of Norway. The precise manner in which the growing of potatoes affected population growth is a matter of some controversy. Given the link between food short-ages and the death rate it probably lowered mortality by providing a higher and more stable level of nutrition until, of course, the failure of the potato crop itself in the 1840s. It may have raised fertility by allowing couples to marry earlier as a result of reclamation or sub-division of farms, it being possible to maintain a family on a much smaller acreage under potatoes than under grains. However, there is no evidence of this from the Scandinavian statistics: indeed all the Norwegian measures of fertility show a remarkable stability between 1750 and 1840, though we should remember that with falling mortality even the stability of fertility is significant. It has been suggested from the experience of pre-industrial Norway that an important role was played by the decline in the force of epidemics which permitted a rise of population and that this may in turn have generated increased production of foodstuffs. In countries such as Sweden and Denmark the spread of the potato was a response partially to the reclamation and cultivation of new land and partially to the greater freedom in land use provided by land reform. In most countries, however, the growing of potatoes was not a response to a buoyant agricultural situation at all but a temporary palliative to a seriously worsening agricultural crisis. Nevertheless, in western Europe it offered a breathing space: the Malthusian check on population growth was put aside and industrialisation and urbanisation were under way before the 'new nutritional space', as Dovring puts it, was taken up.[2]

A second major influence on mortality was Jenner's discovery of vaccination against smallpox in 1789, intensified some would say, by a fortuitous decline in the virulence of the disease itself. Where vaccination was introduced the fall in mortality was dramatic but it was some considerable time before the protection was made available in the remoter parts of Europe. Significant advances in the treatment of other diseases had to wait until the second half of the century and in the 1830s there arrived a new and particularly virulent disease, cholera, which killed a half of those affected and attacked all classes of society alike. But it came at a time of active scientific study: by the 1860s there was a working knowledge of the mode of its transmission and two decades later the specific causative organism had been identified. In 1870 Pasteur established the microbial origin of infectious diseases; in the 1880s Koch identified the tubercle bacillus. Although these discoveries were not directly linked to economic change, they emerged from societies devoting attention to rational scientific experimentation. Above all the use of these new discoveries was, not surprisingly, most pronounced in the richest countries. But economic growth had a more direct effect on mortality by raising standards of nutrition, as well as through the discovery and transmission of medical knowledge. In the long run, too, greater wealth made possible investment in urban sanitation and in more adequate housing, thereby bringing down sharply the levels of mortality in urban areas, though certainly in the first instance the evils of unregulated urbanisation increased rather than reduced

2 *Cambridge Economic History of Europe*, vol. VI (Cambridge, 1967) p. 634.

mortality. The worst effects of urbanisation were to be found in those cities like Warsaw which were overwhelmed by a flood of immigrants from over-populated rural areas and lacked the resources to overcome their difficulties until well into the twentieth century. At the root of the improvements in mortality enjoyed by the more advanced countries lay the greater resources available for investment, the higher real wages, the better and more regular food supply, the improved transport facilities. Mechanisation itself eventually led to better working conditions if only because machines took over the most arduous, dangerous and debilitating tasks. Nevertheless, there remained a sharp distinction between the incidence of death in rural and urban areas. In Denmark, for example, females born in 1840–4 had an expectation of life at birth of 48·2 years in rural districts and 40·1 in Copenhagen: for 1880–4 the comparative figures were 54·7 and 47·2 years.

It is therefore not difficult to understand why the fall in mortality was so continuous and so widespread. Table 5 shows that it came most quickly and was most marked in countries with a modernised and flexible agricultural structure in easy contact with the medical discoveries of the west, free from the worst evils of early urbanisation. Eventually, the fall in the effects of some major diseases and the reduction of food shortages through improvements in transport brought the decline in mortality to almost every part of the Continent in the second half of the century. Only in those regions of the Balkans and in Russia where the natural increase pressed so heavily upon an inflexible agricultural structure as to bring about a continuous series of devastating famines, was the gain small. Even in Russia the death rate fell very sharply from 36 per thousand in 1891–5 to 27 in 1911–13 and, though part of this improvement was due to changes in age composition, there was undoubtedly a significant real lowering of mortality too. Table 6 conveys some idea of the differential effects of mortality changes throughout the continent.

One curious feature of the pattern of mortality all over Europe was the behaviour of infant mortality – death in the first year. Apart from the mortality of those over 40, this was the last of the indicators to fall and yet when it came at the very end of the century, the decline was amazingly rapid. In Bohemia, Moravia and Slovakia, for example, the rate stayed at about 250 per 1000 (1 child in 4 dying in the first year after birth) throughout the century, began to fall around 1895 and by 1914 was 179. In Prussia it was rising during the last half of the century up to 204 per 1000 in 1899–1901 but by 1909–11 was down to 177. In The Netherlands it was 204 per 1000 in 1870–9 and only 130 in 1900–9. An important feature of the low mortality rates in Scandinavia was the fact that infant mortality

Table 6. *Expectation of life at birth of males, 1840–1910*

	1840	1880	1910
Denmark	42·6	46·1	55·4
Norway	43	48·5	55·2
Sweden	41·4	46·8	55·7
Finland		38·2	46·5
France	38·9	41·1	53·9
Netherlands	33·7	40·7	48·4
Germany		36·3	47·2
Italy		34·3	46·1
Switzerland		41·4	50·6
Austria		31 (1870–80)	40·6 (1906–10)
Russia			31 (1895)
England and Wales	40·2	42·4	51·2

Source: H. Hart and H. Hertz, 'Expectation of life as an index of social progress', *American Sociological Review*, 1944.

was falling at a much earlier time than elsewhere in Europe. In Sweden it was 176 per thousand in 1816–20, lower than the rate in Prussia a century later: it was 144 in 1856–60, 97 in 1896–1900 and down to 72 in 1910–14. At the turn of the century when infant mortality stood at under 100 in Norway it was 264 in Bavaria and 273 in Saxony. Differences in the absolute levels of infant mortality reflect above all relative levels of material well-being and were lowest in Scandinavia where average real incomes were high and the evils of urbanisation less serious than in Britain, for example. Regional and occupational differences may also have reflected different weaning cultures. It is not altogether surprising that infant mortality lagged behind the fall in the general death rate, for recent evidence has shown that improved health in mothers has to operate for a generation or so before it reflects itself in the health of an infant. After 1900 the statistics did in fact begin to show a significant fall in deaths from what were known as wasting and developmental diseases which were mostly affected by the mother's health. Since the baby is dependent on its mother for food, the improvements in diet and public health of the nineteenth century made little direct difference to infant mortality. In fact it has been suggested that the switch from breast to bottle feeding worsened infant mortality because of the poor hygienic practices followed in handling milk and preparing the bottles. But it is hard to explain why infant mortality began to decline so rapidly throughout the continent around the turn of the century. The improvement came most markedly through the post-neonatal mortality rate (end of first month to end of first year) where social and environmental factors began to be the dominant factors. It was achieved most by control of bronchitis and pneumonia and, above all, summer diarrhoea. Why it should come about in countries whose living standards, sanitation practices and patterns of medical care and of child rearing varied so considerably is not yet known.

FERTILITY

Turning now to fertility, the basic question is why did it stay so high for so long as the figures in Table 5 show, given the long term effects on total population of reduced mortality? In Norway and Sweden, for example, the birth rate was by no means high by European standards, given the preventive checks we have been discussing, but to the 1860s there was no downward trend, and with very low death rates, produced the fastest overall rates of population growth in Europe. In the east, where the cultural pattern already had resulted in high birth rates, the trend was for them to rise still higher. Even allowing for the weakness of the birth rate as a measure, it is significant that in Russia it rose from around 42 per thousand in 1800–30 to over 50 in the second half of the century. The net reproduction rate, measuring the number of female children which will be born to every newly born girl before she dies, stood at 1·96 in the Ukraine in 1896–7, meaning that the population would about double in a generation. The only parallel to this level of fertility in the west was to be found in some mining areas, in Munster in Germany for example. In Bulgaria, where population was growing faster than anywhere else in Europe at the end of the century, the birth rate was a little lower at 41 per thousand but that country enjoyed a much more moderate death rate than Russia, possibly because of less pressure on land. In Germany as a whole the birth rate seems to have risen to the 1870s and outside the big cities little evidence has been found of birth control. In Denmark, marital fertility was higher in rural areas than in the capital for all generations born since 1815, suggesting a considerable difference in degrees of birth control. Clear evidence for birth control has been found for the mid-nineteenth-century Netherlands from the sharp differences in fertility which appear between various provinces when adjustment has been made for differences in age structure and marriage rates. Provinces such as Friesland and Drenthe show birth rates well below the average. It was a deliberate decision not to outgrow subsistence and an *ad hoc* control depending on child mortality. If a child died, control might be relaxed to produce another. As infant mortality fell so control became permanent. It may well have been the case everywhere that the high infant mortality rates prevailing helped maintain the birth rate for much of the century.

We can only offer some broad ideas on the generally well maintained level of fertility. Clearly urbanisation raised the opportunities for earlier marriage, though there were considerable differences in the degree to which these were seized: in Germany in 1895 46 per cent of all coal miners between the ages of 20 and 30 were married but only 31 per cent of metal workers. In the east the cultural pattern favouring early marriage persisted and in some instances institutional arrangements, like the redistribution of land carried out periodically in Russian villages, put a premium on fertility and the wretched poverty made another child no great burden, possibly, even, a comfort. In 1900–2 the annual marriage rate per thousand persons unmarried over the age of 15 was 87·3 in Bulgaria, 73·1 in Hungary, 35·3 in Sweden and 41·9 in Norway. Generally, it was the persistence of old cultural behaviour patterns that kept up fertility over the long run rather than economic changes. It is striking how in Russia, for example, the four Baltic provinces had a pattern of relatively low marriage rates in 1900 which seemed derived from those in neighbouring Scandinavia. The further one moved from this area, the higher the rate became. It seems a clear example of a very gradual diffusion of western nuptiality patterns and disintegration of the old Russian village traditions. But economic change did play an important direct role as we have seen, by increasing the relative shares in total populations of those groups, such as miners, with the highest fertility rates. Furthermore, insofar as the swelling population was absorbed by industrial development, population increase was a response to economic change or it would have been checked by emigration or lower birth rate.

POPULATION IN NINETEENTH-CENTURY FRANCE

But the most unusual demographic pattern in Europe was that in France, paralleled to some degree only by events in Spain. French population growth in the nineteenth century was much the slowest in Europe, so much so that in 1907 and 1911 there was an actual excess of deaths over births. Again, uniquely in Europe, immigration matched emigration, taking the period 1851–1911 as a whole. The death rate was not very different from that elsewhere in western Europe though to be sure it did fall more slowly than almost any other in the last three decades of the period. But it was the existence of the low and steadily falling birth rate that so distinguished France from all other countries and left her missing out one whole stage of the normal demographic transition – where mortality falls fast with the birth rate stable. The net reproduction rate was already low at 1·1 after the Napoleonic Wars. It fluctuated between that level and 0·95 during the century but by the First World War had settled at the lower level. This compared with figures like 1·4 for Sweden, Germany and Italy.[3] The French marriage rate was not low nor did French men and women marry at unduly late ages. In 1906–10 the mean age of newly married women was 25·3 in France: in most other western countries it was between 26 and 27. The percentage of French women single at ages 45–9 in 1900 was 12: in Belgium it was 17, in Sweden 19, in Germany 10. Only in eastern Europe was it significantly lower, 4 per cent in Hungary, 5 per cent in Russia (ages 40–9) and 1 per cent in Bulgaria. The low level of fertility was clearly the result of extensive use of birth control within marriage. There were large differences between departments: in 1910–12 the net reproduction rate was 0·62 in the Seine (Paris) and 1·35 in Finisterre and Morbihan in the north west. But in general the main distinguishing feature was the low rates which existed in the bulk of rural areas. Fertility was already low and falling prior to 1850 and these areas became relatively more and more important to the French demographic pattern as the century wore on, compared with similar areas in Germany, say, where industrialisation was more pronounced.

We shall discuss in more detail in a later chapter the effects of this unusual demographic pattern on the growth of the French economy. Here we simply search for an explanation of the slow growth of population itself. To some degree this is a false distinction to make, for whatever the initial causes of either, it seems likely that the slow rate of economic change and the persistence of the traditional agricultural pattern of life acted as a brake on fertility. To this must be added the point that for a largely agricultural country the population of France was already high in relation to land area by the standards of the time in 1800 and undoubtedly this was to have a

[3] In Sweden fertility was much lower than in Germany and Italy but the lower mortality enabled more girls to survive to the age of child bearing. A rate of 1 means that the population is simply replacing itself over time: 1·4 means that in a generation it will grow by 40 per cent.

significant impact of rural behaviour over the next hundred years. A more general explanation is often offered in terms of the laws of inheritance of the *Code Napoléon*, under which an estate had to be divided among all the children. The contrast is made with the English system of primogeniture whereby in cases of intestacy only the eldest had a claim. This was exceptional but in general more could be willed to a single heir in most parts of Germany than in France, Russia, The Netherlands, Belgium and the Rhine provinces. Bohemia and Silesia were of the single heir pattern as were parts of Moravia but other parts of that area and nearby Slovakia and Galicia were on the divided inheritance pattern. It was not always an unchanging system, as we shall see. In Sweden, for example, the rising value of land in the nineteenth century brought about successful agitation against division. The argument is that in the west anyway, divided inheritance inhibited population growth because of the fear of breaking up the family farm into ever smaller parts especially in a country already heavily populated and with little land available for reclamation. It has been argued that divided inheritance offered the possibility of early marriage but also an incentive to restrict families within marriage – the typical French rural pattern. Single inheritance allowed the eldest to marry early and breed without restraint but the younger children might well find their marriage delayed. The net effect of each pattern would therefore be hard to determine. The real difference is that the single heir system encouraged the younger children to leave the land and move to the towns where this was possible. The pattern of behaviour could be a complex one. In Holland, for example, one son was typically designated as sole heir and on marriage his bride lived with him under his parents' roof though there was apparently very little economic incentive for him to marry early as he still had no control over the family activities. His brothers and sisters should have left but often they remained as unmarried members of the household, virtually as servants. When new opportunities came up, however, these hangers-on rushed out to set up their own houses. So in the last quarter of the nineteenth century with the use of artificial fertilisers on the sandy soils of the east and south, it became possible to divide up family farms into viable smaller units and the old inheritance pattern faded away just as it had done earlier in the more fertile clay soil areas. Whatever the force of all these arguments for western Europe, it is apparent that in the east the restraints on fertility inherent in the divided heirs system failed to operate. Consequently one encounters a high population growth and constant subdivision of the land which had disastrous consequences.

THE DECLINE OF FERTILITY

The last major feature of nineteenth-century population developments in western and northern Europe at least, came in the last
quarter when fertility began to fall off quite sharply. Fundamentally
there was nothing new in this, for many of these societies had already
been operating preventive checks to population growth through the
age of marriage and also by some form of birth control. It was the
change in degree of control that was so striking. In all countries
birth control played the major role but in some it was accompanied
by a rise in the marriage age too. In Sweden the birth rate was about
30 per thousand in the 1870s and 23·5 in 1911–13: in Germany it
fell from 39 to 28 over those years: in Switzerland from 31 to 23·6.
In the relatively industrialised regions of Bohemia and Moravia
further east it was 39 in 1870 and 26 in 1914. The effects of birth
control are very apparent from some Danish statistics: of the
generation of mothers born in 1840–4 (and therefore bearing children
from about 1860 to 1890) 40 per cent of their children were born
before the mother reached the age of 30. Yet for the 1880–4 generation of mothers 55 per cent of the children were born before that
age. There was in fact a steady fall in the age of marriage for women
in Denmark over these generations and a fall in the proportion
widowed, though these factors which would tend to raise fertility
were offset to some degree by a rise in the proportion of women
remaining single to the age of 50 – from 12 per cent to 16 per cent.
This was a change brought about largely by the emigration of men
far in excess of that by women.

Though it is possible that new requirements over the education of
children and restrictions on child labour may have lengthened the
period before a child could begin to contribute to a family's income
and so have offered some incentive to limit the number of children,
this was hardly a major factor. It may be that with the fall in infant
mortality, children ceased, in a sense, to be so unimportant and with
increased consideration for their welfare came a decline in the birth
rate, something associated too with higher educational levels, though,
to be sure, infant mortality declined only slowly prior to 1900.
Economic change also brought with it new ways of spending money –
on goods, on holidays, on health, on education. Not only did this
affect the well-to-do, but gradually it permeated down through the
income scale. In the richer countries one social group after another
found its incomes rising and with it the possibility for the first time
of spending in these new ways, and, above all perhaps, of aping the
consumption habits of those just above in the social scale. Reducing

the size of family was one way of achieving these new-found aspirations. In those countries where incomes were failing to rise the fall in fertility was slight: similarly in the more developed countries it was amongst the poorest, those least likely to be able to move into new spending habits that the decline was least noticed. For all that we must not ignore the fact that about this time new, cheap and effective rubber contraceptives began to be marketed which were far more acceptable to many than the clumsy artificial devices available earlier and the usual natural methods.

Another interesting aspect of this phenomenon was that it was accompanied by a decline in illegitimate fertility too. From the middle of the eighteenth century there was a great secular rise in illegitimate births all over Europe reaching a peak around 1880: in Sweden, for example, the rate rose threefold between 1750 and 1880. The reasons are not entirely clear: the change may well have been linked with the social disorganisation which accompanied the economic changes of the time and with changes in social values. The huge differences to be observed in the illegitimacy rates between one country and another also pose great problems of interpretation. In 1876–80 illegitimate births per 10,000 total births were 1,018 in Sweden, 1,014 in Denmark, 903 in Germany, 838 in Norway, 791 in Belgium, 776 in France, 489 in Switzerland and 318 in Holland. Common law marriages were particularly widespread in Eastern Europe: in Carinthia for example, in 1880 45 per cent of all women were single at the end of childbearing yet south of the Danube the cultural patterns created some of the lowest illegitimacy rates in Europe. There were great differences within countries too: illegitimacy was especially high in the northern provinces of Portugal for example, and it may be that this was because economic circumstances and a sex structure distorted by the heavy emigration of males forcibly excluded a lot of the female population from marriage. Certainly the proportion of women single at ages 50–54 in 1900 was as high as 30 per cent in some of these provinces compared to 10 per cent further south. However this may be, the illegitimacy rate then began to fall along with marital fertility though not equally over all age groups. In several countries it rose very quickly in the 15–19 age group and fell very sharply for those over 25. We must presume that there was a fall in the mean age of pre-marital intercourse among girls and that they were the group least likely to be informed on the new methods of contraception. The improvements in control techniques had its major impact on illegitimate births to older women who were more likely to be better informed. It is hard to believe that arguments related to the standards of living and to social aspirations are relevant to changes in illegitimacy.

Coming at a time of steeply falling death rates, this change in fertility did not greatly slow down the growth of population in the more advanced countries and since it was least felt in the more backward areas, did very little to halt the headlong rush of population expansion there. Although, as we argued at the beginning of this chapter, nineteenth-century population growth gave a considerable boost to those countries already in the process of economic change, in areas less favoured by natural resources, and hindered by institutional barriers to change, the consequences of high rates of growth were extremely serious. Furthermore, in a country such as Italy, though population never grew rapidly, any acceleration was dangerous, for the density of population was dangerously high by mid-century – in the sixteenth and seventeenth centuries Italy had been the most densely populated country in Europe. In Holland, too, where the birth rate dropped only slowly after the 1870s ($36 \cdot 2$ per thousand in that decade and $30 \cdot 9$ in 1900–9) the density of population moved up from 80 per square kilometre in 1830 to 110 in 1870 and 180 in 1910, much the highest in Europe for a largely agricultural country.[4] In addition, the changes in the pattern and organisation of farming which were a feature of development throughout Europe, even if they did not reduce the demand for labour, offered little possibility of absorbing the rise in the labour supply. At some time in the nineteenth century, therefore, almost every country was faced with serious problems of poverty and unemployment arising from these changes. It was fortunate indeed that circumstances were uniquely favourable for the partial resolution of these problems through migration both within and without Europe. It is to this phenomenon that we now turn.

MIGRATION

The motives that impelled millions of Europeans to uproot themselves and their families were many and varied. To be able to emigrate there were two prime requirements: first a man must have freedom to move, and second, he must possess the means to exercise this right if he so wished. This second point was a crucial one: it meant that those most in need were rarely the first to go and it was ironical, though not entirely fortuitous, that those most in need – in the east and the south – lived furthest away from the most desirable points of emigration. The straight subsidisation of migrants was

[4] In Belgium it was 259 per square kilometre and in England and Wales 239.

undertaken only on a very minor scale: the reduction of transport costs and the remittances sent back by relations who had already migrated, were very much more important in encouraging the flow. Even so, millions went with barely enough to see them through the journey and were destitute and open to every kind of exploitation when they reached their destinations. Some borrowed their fares from employers or intermediaries and were even more open to abuse as a result.

But if few moved positively in search of democracy, freedom to go was an important matter. It required first of all the abolition of institutions such as serfdom which bound a man to a lord. Such bondage did not necessarily prevent a man from migrating seasonally or for longer periods where his obligations to his lord were satisfied in money rather than in labour terms, but for movement out of the country its complete removal was essential. Sometimes even this was not enough: in Russia after the ending of serfdom the peasant was still enmeshed in his obligations to the village commune, something which did not finally disappear until just before 1914. Then there were legal restrictions on movement. In the west this was mainly an eighteenth-century matter but in many German states absolute prohibition lasted until the 1820s and migration was frowned upon until after 1848. In Austria an ordinance of 1784 treated emigration as normally forbidden and a law of 1832 was milder only by referring to an emigrant as one who 'departs' rather than as one who 'absconds' In 1867 movement became free, apart from the need to satisfy obligations for military service. Emigration from the Balkans was helped by the Russo-Turkish war of 1877 which released many areas from Turkish restrictions. When they did let people go, governments did little to protect the emigrants beyond requiring licenses for agents of shipping and railway companies and controlling certain contract labour practices. The Hungarian government tried to institute a more rigid control system in 1909 and gave the Cunard Company the exclusive right to carry Hungarians from Fiume (Rijeka) to New York. But Cunard could not cope with the rush and had to direct many to the north German ports where they could avoid the government regulations. But here and there emigration had its effect in stimulating interest in social, economic and political reform in the hope of stemming the tide. People do not drain away as they did in Norway, for example, without bringing about some rethinking over the whole quality of life in the home country.

The key question is one of motive, for emigration was rarely accomplished without anguish and hardship and the benefits were most often reaped only by the succeeding generations. Some went because the economic situation at home was hopeless, some because the chance of getting land somewhere offered greater opportunities to them and their families. Some sought new opportunities, some went to avoid change. Some were escaping from their families, or from restrictive laws and customs bearing on marriage. Some wanted to escape military service, some disliked taxes and the insolence of officials. Some went overseas in search of greater political and religious freedom but they were very much in the minority. If he migrated permanently to the United States the immigrant enjoyed his political rights but he did not go to seek them and as for religion, one writer has neatly commented that 'the prospect of earthly ease was a stronger stimulus than that of heavenly bliss'.[5] But the astonishingly small number of immigrants who took out citizenship in Argentina and Brazil before 1914 shows that for many political rights counted for nothing. Some were influenced by local and temporary factors such as bad harvests and fluctuations in business activity. Some were paid to go: some went for the adventure. At time it became almost a fever, an irrational frenzy. The decline in the fare helped: from Continental ports it was around $20 in the 1880s but competition at times got it to half that level. The increasing tide of literature about prospects and the letters sent back by earlier migrants were important, not so much from the point of view of motive, but as sources of knowledge on the basis of which the decisions to go were taken. By 1900 something like half of the immigrants into the United States went on prepaid tickets with their fares paid by relatives already in America. Girls from Galicia, for example, went into domestic service in the United States while their fiancés were in the army, sending them their tickets for the crossing when their military service had ended. An Ellis Island survey of 1909–10 found that 58 per cent of Jews were helped to migrate by remittances, 36 per cent of German immigrants, 27 per cent Swedes and a lower proportion of Italians, Slovaks and Poles. Indentured work – getting a free passage in return for binding oneself to work for a specific employer for a given term – was prohibited by law in the United States in 1884 but the practice still went on. The ethnic solidarity of Scandinavians prevented such exploitation of their compatriots but it was common right until 1914 for immigrants from southern and eastern Europe.

Basically, both inter- and intra-continental migration derived from the demographic and industrial revolutions in Europe. The pressure of population on limited land resources and the subdivision of land holdings that this brought in its train, were the most important individual causes of European migration. But the effects of population growth were sometimes more sophisticated than that. The

[5] M. A. Jones, *American Migration* (London, 1960), p. 98.

cyclical movements in the birth rate reaching peaks in the 1820s, 1840s, 1860s, 1880s, were certainly of real significance in bringing about the waves of migration of 1844–54, 1878–88 and 1898–1907 as those born during the birth peaks reached maturity and the most popular age for migration.

Economic change played its part firstly by undermining the ways of life of certain groups. There were the craftsmen, independent shopkeepers, small farmers and cottagers who suffered from the greater sophistication and liberalisation of economic life. The rising price of land encouraged the very small farmer, hit by divided inheritance, to sell out, as it prevented him from buying his way out of his troubles. The opening of new areas of production and lowering of transport costs put more pressure on European farmers after 1870. Nowhere was this problem more keenly felt than in Italy where it was accompanied by a fall in exports of oranges and lemons as American home production rose, and a prohibitive French tariff on Italian wines. The growth of industry in certain parts of Europe helped resolve those problems, by attracting immigrant labour direct from the worst hit areas, by encouraging intensive farming near the great urban centres, and by creating a labour shortage in some rural areas which was resolved by immigrants from other countries. Furthermore, European demand for imports created labour shortages in many regions overseas, thereby inducing workers from Europe to migrate. Eventually, new forms of employment helped to stem the flow of emigrants altogether in countries such as Germany and Sweden by raising real wages, improving the quality of urban life and making possible the provision of social welfare services.

Those who argue that the pull from the United States was the main force governing migration seem to have little understanding of the basic forces in European history. Certainly the precise moment of departure might be determined by conditions overseas, partly by raising a man's expectations and encouraging him finally to cut his ties with his homeland, and also through the greater ability of former emigrants to send money home in good times. But concentration on the United States ignores the volume of migration that eventually came about, all in response to purely European conditions. The selection of migrants was in no sense random as the pull thesis seems to imply. It is difficult, too, to explain the sharp differences to be found in the intensity of out migration among populations at similar poverty levels and equally free to move. Some took militant action to improve their lot, others for a variety of complex motives accepted the situation in a mood of resignation and moved on.

By far the bulk of Europeans migrating overseas went to the United States, but those that went to South America, particularly to Argentina and Brazil, were relatively very important to those countries. Before 1900, when more Italians went to Brazil than to the United States, they comprised two-thirds of the immigrants there and Italians also made up 70 per cent of all those emigrating from Europe to Argentina. In the generation after 1895 one-eighth of the whole population of Argentina was Italian and in 1910 one-third of the inhabitants of the Brazilian State of São Paulo were of Italian origin. Altogether from 1821 to 1924 55m Europeans emigrated from Europe including 19m from the British Isles, but they were only part of a complex pattern of people moving from their homes in Europe, whether permanently or seasonally. It was a pattern carrying Polish peasants to and from East German estates, Appalachian coalmines and Silesian and Westphalian steelworks. Italian hotel workers moved between Lausanne, Nice and Rio, and Russian peasants moved permanently into Siberia and in droves every summer to the harvests in the southern steppe. Nor was it simply a nineteenth century movement. In the previous century Frederick the Great colonised broad stretches of his eastern provinces and there was an immense movement of people from Central Russia south into the Ukraine, to the new Russian steppes, to the Crimea and to the south east. In 1815 Russia had a population of about 45m and of these almost 15m lived in regions newly acquired in the previous century. Possibly 4–5m of these were migrants. There was a great movement too, into the empty lands of the Balkans. Dissenting congregations of Germans and Swiss, and many thousands of the Palatinate Germans found their way to the American colonies in the 1720s and 1730s and several thousand mercenaries, used by the British in the War of Independence, stayed on. Some migrated from their homelands in Europe to colonial islands and outposts but their numbers were small. Within Europe the great arteries of the Rhine and Danube were already well used by migrants seeking seasonal occupations. Men moved seasonally and for longer periods from the mountainous regions – the Pyrenees, Alps, Massif Central, Ardennes, Dolomites. Peasants from the Ardennes would walk as far as Hungary; the Pyrenees were emptied as men moved into Spain or to Bordeaux as labourers. From the Massif Central migrants travelled seasonally to the Midi for the grape harvest whilst others went further afield, working in the towns or moving around as pedlars, perhaps staying away from home for years at a time.

– *Migration from Germany*

After the end of the Napoleonic Wars the hard weather of 1816–17, together with the economic dislocation created by new boundaries and tariffs, brought about the first significant wave of migration from Europe, and families from the Upper Rhine began to jam the ports of the Netherlands. Perhaps 20,000 Germans crossed the Atlantic and at this time, too, significant numbers of families from Württemberg were encouraged to trek to Southern Russia where the Tsar offered them land and supplies and exemption from military service. During the next decade the movement to America was slight, but considerable numbers of Eastern Germans were now persuaded by Russian emissaries to migrate into the new Kingdom of Poland. Some were farmers: some were weavers and artisans who had lost their markets after the high Russian tariff of 1822 and crossed to enjoy the benefits of tariff protection themselves. A trickle of 7–10,000 colonists and mercenaries moved to Brazil in the 1820s too. So far, it had been a very limited emigration, an escape from poor prices and bad harvests and also the beginnings of that movement of small farmers who were being gradually squeezed by the growing population and the pressures of reform in agricultural techniques and institutions.

Growing activity in the United States, the hard winter of 1829–30 and the revolutions of 1830 all helped to revive the flow again. Revolutions affected migration, less for political reasons than through the indirect consequences of disrupted trade, the cutting-off of credit, and the raising of taxes. The continuing emigration of the 1830s and 1840s, largely from Rhineland areas, was a carefully planned movement of families. They read gazetteers, maps, papers, letters: small farmers were joined now by lower middle class people, feeling themselves ill at ease in a changing economy and experiencing competition from overseas producers too. The Dutch ports went out of fashion, for the fares were high and sailings irregular, since no important return freights came back into Rotterdam. Le Havre took in cotton from the American South and emigrants trekked to that port in covered wagon style until Le Havre became at times almost a German town. Bremen developed as a centre for the import of tobacco and by the mid-1840s was rivalling Le Havre in the emigrants' favours. The Bremen authorities offered migrants free and controlled accommodation in the town to win a return cargo for the tobacco ships which might otherwise have gone to Hamburg. Migrants were the foundation of the port's prosperity and conditions were always better there than elsewhere because the Free State authorities were well aware of their importance. Hamburg's bulk trade was with England and so the migrants went from there to Hull, then overland by canal barge, and set sail from Liverpool, making this the cheapest as well as the most varied route.

Until the 1860s overseas emigration from Europe was largely confined to the upper Rhine valley and the Celtic areas of Britain and rather more than 1½m Germans left their homeland. In the following three decades it was the Scandinavians, Prussians, Saxons, Bohemians, Italians who emigrated most of all. Thereafter the years from 1890 to 1914 were to be dominated by movement from the Baltic, Eastern Europe and the Mediterranean – Italians, Spaniards, Finns, Latvians, Poles, Russians, Hungarians and Greeks. Table 7 gives the general pattern of the flow. There were, however, certain major surges, the first coming between 1847 and 1854, the second in the 1880s and the third lasting from 1909 to 1914.

Failure of the potato harvest sparked off the first great wave in the late 1840s, though events in continental Europe, bad as they were, did not compare in severity with those in Ireland where dependency on this one crop was much greater. During the years of revolution, 1848 to 1850, emigration fell away.

Table 7. *Average Annual Overseas Migration from Europe 1846–1910.*

	Europe	Germany	Sweden, Norway, Denmark	France, Switzerland, Netherlands, Belgium	Italy	Austria, Hungary	Russia	Spain, Portugal	Balkans
	(000s)	(000s)	(000s)	(000s)	(000s)	(000s)	(000s)	(000s)	
1846–50	257	36·5	4	14	0·2	1·6	0·1	0·4	?
1851–60	539	124	11	25	5	6·2	0·4	12	
1861–70	566	127	49	21	27	8	0·9	18	
1871–80	629	125	45	24	52	22	12	39	
1881–90	1,399	269	119	57	198	87	63	161	2
1891–1900	1,218	105	70	26	316	145	128	211	7
1901–10	2,476	55	98	32	723	468	355	283	71

Source: D. Kirk, *Europe's Population in the Inter-War Years* (Geneva, 1946), p. 279 and W. F. Willcox, *International Migrations*, vol. II passim (New York, 1931).

Partly this was because land values fell and it became easier to buy or more unwise to sell. Transport was disturbed and the harvests improved. Though no doubt a few of those most disenchanted departed, revolution, far from encouraging people to go, seems to have held them back; it is significant that emigration from Britain continued at a high rate over those years. But then came another great flow as the basic forces of land fragmentation and industrial change began to override all other considerations once again. Baden, Württemberg and the Palatinate actually lost population but it was now a very widespread movement. The westerner was being squeezed as the economy developed, the easterner dispossessed as a result of population growth and institutional changes in agriculture. Of course California gold had some effect: Germans, Swedes, Danes, Bohemians – even Frenchmen – succumbed to that lure.

Emigration from Germany resumed quickly after the Civil War, and reached its peak in 1872–3. Then followed a series of lean years on both sides of the Atlantic when migration was low, only to boom again to reach the highest ever point for German migration in the 1880s. Now harvests had little part to play: it was a flight from agriculture, coinciding with peaks in home activity, not with depressions as in earlier times. It was a migration of those who enjoyed no profit in a boom but instead found the effects of economic development penetrating and disrupting village life ever more. Always the greatest number going overseas came from the west and from the north. Many left the eastern regions but even at the peak of the 1880s only a half of these went overseas; the rest moved mainly to Berlin and the Ruhr.

Table 8 indicates the complicated nature of German migration, though inevitably it fails to show the considerable flows of migration within each area, particularly in the west. Because of the importance of Berlin, mid Germany was a net receiving area from the 1870s, as the pace of overseas emigration slackened and the flow of people

Table 8. *German Migration Patterns, 1843–1910.*

(1910 area but excluding Alsace-Lorraine)

	Total	W. Germany	Mid Germany	E. Germany
	(000s)	(000s)	(000s)	(000s)
1843–52	−624	−593	−3	−28
1852–61	−682	−536	−102	−44
1862–71	−932	−508	−23	−401
1872–81	−604	−180	+92	−516
1881–90	−1,240	−413	+249	−1,077
1891–1900	−329	+253	+254	−836
1901–10	−85	+316	+371	−772

Source: International Economic Association, *The Economics of International Migration* (London, 1958), p. 212.

Note: W. Germany = roughly current West Germany

Mid Germany = roughly current East Germany and Berlin

E. Germany = eastern provinces of Germany now part of Poland

(+) = Net immigration; (−) = emigration

from east to west within Germany continued. The great mobility of Germans at this time is shown by the fact that in 1907 only a half of the population were living in their place of birth and 15 per cent had moved considerable distances over state or provincial lines. By this time there were 2 million east Germans in Berlin-Brandenburg and over 800,000 in Rhineland Westphalia. Complaints of labour shortage in the east began to mount in the 1880s with the enactment of laws cancelling the permits of some 40,000 non-German residents in the German Polish provinces and cutting off seasonal migration. This coincided with a shift towards a more labour intensive form of agriculture in that area, especially the growing of sugar beet and other root crops. It has been calculated that on a 60-hectare estate under the old three-field system 573 man days and 139 woman days of work were required. The more complex Norfolk rotation required 567 man days and 1,048 woman days and a rotation with sugar beet 774 man days and 2,405 woman days. Above all it was seasonal labour that was demanded, for this new development coincided with the wider use of threshing machines which reduced the amount of winter labour required. To this was added the great loss of local labour to the west as industrial demand surged forward after 1886. Between 1895 and 1907 nearly 900,000 workers were lost in German agriculture through migration of all kinds. In Saxony there was a loss of $15\frac{1}{2}$ per cent of the workforce, in Mecklenburg $10\frac{1}{2}$ per cent, in East Prussia and Brandenburg over 9 per cent, though it was a migration out of agriculture in the west just as much as in the east. From 1890 onwards the ban on migrating labour was gradually relaxed though strict control and registration were exercised. In 1911–12 730,000 alien migrating workers received passes to cross the German eastern and south-eastern frontiers, four-fifths of them coming from Russian Poland and almost all the rest from Austrian Galicia. Many stayed for eight or nine months, getting some industrial work before and after the agricultural season, but all were compelled to leave Germany by 20 December when their passes expired. The nature of these shifts of population in the eastern frontier region caused much alarm for military reasons but attempts to settle German colonists there met with no success. Men from the west would not go to farm such infertile land and the big estate owners objected to any erosion of their supply of cheap labour. There were other types of seasonal workers too, above all building workers from Italy working mostly in Prussia and Alsace-Lorraine. A Catholic Congress Report of 1912 listed the seasonal workers in Germany as 380,000 Russian Poles, 200,000 Austrian Poles, 150,000 Italians, 90,000 Ruthenians, 60,000 Belgians and Dutch, 50,000 Austrian Germans, 30,000 Hungarians, a total of almost one million, such was the call of a rapidly developing country surrounded by others in the main less fortunately placed.

– Migration from eastern Europe

Poland was one of the areas of Europe worst hit by the acceleration of population growth and the economy offered only very limited alternative occupations to its people. The very high rate of natural increase for the whole area – 17 per thousand in 1906–10 – can be compared with that of countries given in Table 5. In Austrian Poland the rate of growth was less frightening than in Russia, but there was a desperate problem of sub-division of land. In 1902 two-thirds of all holdings were under 5 hectares and, in addition, local peasant industries were facing ever more severe competition from the factory products of Silesia and Lower Austria as a result of recent improvements in communications. Emigration from the area rose sharply after the mid-1890s. First the majority went to Brazil, but then they turned to the United States, though Ukrainians from East Galicia preferred Canada for the most part. To 1914 about a million people emigrated from that part of Poland. In Russian Poland the emancipation of 1807 had made no provision for land for the former serfs: a century later landless labourers formed a sixth of the village populations and a half of the emigrants. In addition a further sixth had holdings of less than two hectares. Internal migration brought the population of Warsaw soaring from 175,000 in 1860 to 730,000 in 1900, creating some of the worst slums on the Continent. At Lodz, the cotton textile centre, population rose from 28,000 to 325,000 over the same years.

In 1900, too, three-quarters of the world's Jews lived in eastern Europe. There were perhaps 800,000 in Austrian Poland, 260,000 in Romania where anti-semitism was particularly severe, but over 5 million in Russia, virtually all of them living in the Hebrew Pale, an area of Russian Poland established in 1832 to which the Jews were confined. Movement was strictly controlled, as was the right to own property in rural areas. Concentration of Jews in the towns, the narrow petty trading and craft basis of much of Jewish economic life in Russia, together with high rates of natural population increase, led inevitably to pauperisation. In addition, after the assassination of Tsar Alexander II in 1887, a series of pogroms resulted in considerable loss of life and property. But restrictions against Jews were being lifted in most other parts of Europe, and with the United States beckoning too, a huge emigration got under way. From 1860 to 1900 some 400–500,000 Jews entered the United

States and in the next fourteen years another $1\frac{1}{2}$ million. Jewish colonies were established in Canada, Argentina and elsewhere in South America and by 1914 there were possibly some 50,000 Jews in Palestine. Moreover, for these people the rate of repatriation was extremely low. In addition, large numbers spread into the great cities of Europe and Jews quickly came to play a major role in the industrial and commercial development of certain countries. Nowhere was this more the case than in Hungary. There they came to dominate middle class life, partly because of their own skills and initiative, partly because there were no other groups in that society which could produce such a class of people when it was needed. The doctors, lawyers and teachers of Hungary were approximately 70 per cent of Jewish origin by 1910: they were less significant as industrial entrepreneurs if only because Germans joined in there too. The Magyar nobles did not object because there was no possibility that they would surrender their political grasp and consequently there was less anti-Semitism in Hungary before 1914 than elsewhere in eastern Europe and this naturally intensified the migration. But despite greater hostility there was a heavy movement into German and Austrian cities after 1890. In 1910, for example, over a half of the 'professional' graduates coming out of the University of Vienna were Jewish. It was a migration of great economic and social significance at the time and one which was to have tragic consequences a generation later.

Large scale seasonal migration was a feature of many parts of the Austro-Hungarian Empire. This was typical of regions governed by divided inheritance laws, with small farms, distant from urban markets and so precluded by this – and sometimes by the climate – from indulging in the type of intensive farming practiced by small peasants in south-western Germany, for example. Just prior to 1914 possibly 400,000 peasants moved every year for seasonal work from the Empire into Germany – Poles, Galicians, Hungarians – almost a half taking some employment in industry and a small number passing through to seek work in Sweden and Denmark. Around 1914 some 12,000 Polish seasonal workers were helping with the sugar beet harvest on the Danish islands. In Hungary internal seasonal migration was also very extensive as peasants from the poorer regions on the fringes of the kingdom moved to bring in the harvest for the Magyar landowners on the central plains. Many Hungarians emigrated over the border to live in Graz and Vienna: a few moved permanently to Germany and to France. Not until the 1870s did the numbers leaving the Hungarian Empire for overseas rise significantly: over the previous two decades there was plenty of work on railways and canals and on river improvement schemes.

Indeed to the 1850s, many Germans were still moving into Hungary as they had done for a century, filling up lands that had been depopulated by the wars with Turkey. But railway building came almost to a halt for a decade after 1873. The estate owners responded to the worldwide fall in grain prices by cost-cutting actions, concentrating on mechanising the most labour intensive operations, threshing and harvesting. From 1886 to 1890 legal emigration averaged 22,000 annually: from 1901 to 1914 as population pressure reached its peak, the exodus rose to 110,000 per year. The rate of migration was highest from those areas where subdivision was most rampant – Slovakia for example – though in absolute terms Magyar peasants formed the largest group. Emigration from Galicia was even heavier in relative terms than that from Hungary; here too subdivision was most acute. From 1891–1900 265,281 people emigrated from that area for longer than a season: from 1901 to 1910 it rose to 488,416. The overwhelming majority of emigrants left for the United States: in 1903 100,000 went and in 1907 almost twice that number, the biggest long term migration from one country to another in a single year for the whole period. A few went to Canada: some tried their luck in South America, lured by the promises of Italian steamship companies. They found, not the promised land, but the hardest of toil on the coffee plantations and in the unkind climate many died.

– *Russian Population Movements*

Almost all of the emigrants from Russia consisted of what might be called alien peoples. Taking the years 1899 to 1913, 41 per cent were Jews, 29 per cent Poles, 9 per cent Lithuanians, 7 per cent Finns, 6 per cent Germans and only 7 per cent Russians, these last moving mostly to Canada. Jewish and Polish migration we have already discussed. The rate of migration from Finland was one of the highest in Europe. In 1900 two-fifths of the farms were under three hectares and there were large numbers of landless labourers too. An expansion of population far less restrained than that in Sweden, crashed against resources from the 1860s onwards and in addition the switch to dairy farming and growing displacement of crops by grass reduced the demand for labour markedly after 1890.

On the other hand, over the century to 1914 some $2\frac{1}{2}$ million Germans and Austrians (not Poles) migrated into Russia, most of all during the three decades after 1860. Over a million Persians, Chinese and Turks entered too after 1890. Many Persians migrated annually as common labourers and perhaps 20–30 per cent of the labour on the Baku oilfields was Persian. Some two million passes were issued annually for seasonal migration from the central regions of European Russia to the Black Sea steppes, but the most remarkable and concentrated of the Russian migrations was the movement into Siberia, second in magnitude only to the Atlantic migration, though, as we have seen, there was a great movement southwards from the central regions which began in the eighteenth century and continued through the first half of the nineteenth. In general the Siberian migration was brought about by population changes, by poverty, by land tenure conditions, by changes in the legal status of peasants, by improvements in communications, and it resulted in the creation of a new society with a higher level of prosperity and greater degree of social flexibility than the migrant had enjoyed in European Russia.

Exile to Siberia began to become a significant form of punishment in the mid-seventeenth century and the numbers sent there grew rapidly from the time of Peter the Great onwards. How many were forced to go is not known, possibly 1,000–2,000 per annum in the eighteenth century, though some escaped and some were killed by Siberian peasants who disliked the intruders and blamed them for all their ills. Many went voluntarily, fleeing from serfdom, military service, prison, creditors, but by the end of the eighteenth century the population of this vast land was only about 710,000 though of these 80 per cent were of European Russian origin. For most of the nineteenth century further development was slow: true, under Count Kiselev the government provided for the establishment of peasants around Tomsk and Tobolsk, but only 320,000 were officially affected between 1831 and 1866.

The pace of migration quickened after serf emancipation in 1861, but still the numbers remained small. The peasant needed permission to leave his commune and help to overcome the awful hazards of distance and climate and hostility when he arrived. By 1885 the Urals Railways had got as far as Tjumen, some 400 km east of the Urals, and from there Tomsk, 1,200 km. further east as the crow flies, could be reached by the Tobol and Ob rivers – a voyage of two or three weeks – so that the whole journey from the Volga to Tomsk could now be done without walking, and a peasant could leave for Siberia and get there in time for work that same season. Among the migrants of the 1880s the major factors sending them were inadequacy of land, impoverishment of the soil, poor location. Few went for political or idealistic reasons: they moved only when their backs were to the wall, and in Siberia the peasant could hope for little better than the pursuit of a form of subsistence farming to satisfy his basic needs. Essentially it was still a defensive migration.

A series of events then led to a tremendous outburst. First there were the disastrous famines of 1891–2 and of 1898: then to the continuing pressure of population on the land was added during the 1890s the onerous tax burdens imposed by Count de Witte to finance his programme of modernisation. The first section of the Trans-Siberian Railway from Cheliabinsk, just east of the Urals, to Omsk was opened in 1895 and Cheliabinsk became the migrant entrepôt centre for both those going and those returning. From a village of 7,000 inhabitants in 1893, by 1916 it was a city of 71,000 people. From 1906 onwards the Stolypin reforms released the peasant from his bondage to the local community. Along with this reform, the colonisation of Siberia was now felt by more and more officials to be the guarantee of Russia's future and so the budget for migration rose. In 1907 it was 13 million roubles, or four times the 1900–4 average: in 1912 it had doubled again. The money was available for loans, for medical aid, bridges, roads, water communications, to establish agricultural supply stations, to help newcomers to cover the costs of dividing up of farm lots. The Tsar ceded crown lands in the east; the town of Novosibirsk was created and the crown supervised the installation of $\frac{1}{4}$ million peasants in the region. From 1890 to 1904 some 1,400,000 emigrated and in the next decade a tremendous burst of something like 3 million. The percentage who returned was small too – an average of only about 10 per cent for 1896–1909, though it could be as much as 46 per cent in a year of very bad harvest such as 1911.

Most of the emigrants made for a very limited area, a land of monotonous plain and fertile soil very similar to the Black Earth region of European Russia, bounded to the north by forest, to the south by arid steppe land. Beginning some 200 km beyond the Urals it stretched along the 55° parallel for 2,000 km varying in width from 600 to 200 km. Within that area it was Altai province with Novosibirsk as its centre and Tomsk that took most people – almost 40 per cent of the total between 1885 and 1914. The region to the north of the 55° line was particularly favoured for there the trees provided wood for construction, for fuel and for artisan work. Beyond the Yenisey river the terrain became difficult and few migrants were to be found until the Amur river was reached in the far east. The Black Earth and Steppe zones of European Russia regularly provided 60 per cent of the migrants but sizeable numbers moved from the western provinces of White Russia (13 per cent of the whole), a cold, forested land whose peasants were well adapted to the colonisation of Siberia's forest regions to the north of the Black Earth belt. The Moscow industrial region, the areas to the north and west, the Caucasus, the Grand Duchy of Warsaw, hardly participated at all.

We shall say more of the consequences of this colonisation later, but basically from being in 1800 almost entirely a European country, a century later Russia had become a truly Eurasiatic power with over a fifth of her population living outside Europe. The authorities never allowed serfdom to take root in Siberia – indeed the fact that it was an area without seigneurial rights had long disinclined nobles and government officials to try to open it up. The worst evils of land speculation were avoided too, but huge problems were created all the same. Most serious of all was the fact that colonisation seemed merely to transfer the problems and evils of agriculture in European Russia to Siberia. Already in some areas land was becoming short, fallow was reduced, cutting of trees encouraged erosion. The ignorance of the peasants, the shortage of capital, their unwillingness to move elsewhere, especially to the forested areas, fastened on the area a monoculture which threatened to ruin the new lands. Here and there migration seemed to release the spirit of adventure and to lead to concentration on new products, helped by the building of the railway and the ending of the Cheliabinsk tariff which had been levied on all imports into European Russia from the east. The export of butter, above all from the Tobolsk area, was the most remarkable of these changes, and by 1914 it was estimated that about half of the meat sold in the markets of St Petersburg (Leningrad) and Moscow came from Siberia. But such progress cannot conceal the essentially primitive nature of the Siberian economy. Nothing was more different than the colonisation of the United States with its international and diversified nature. The Siberian migration was a national, subsistence, defensive migration contrasting sharply with the speculative, offensive character of the crossing of the American continent.

– Scandinavian Population Movements

In Scandinavia the pattern of migration was less complex. There was an important element of internal migration responding to changes in the pattern of growth at home. In Sweden, for example, there was much migration of threshers, navvies, beet pickers, peat diggers, building labourers. Women worked in gardens, carded, threshed, rowed on the waters around Stockholm. Above all there was a large movement of seasonal workers into the great timber forests of the north. In the summer the cows were sent to the hill pastures and the women and children of small farmers migrated north to tend them while the men stayed to cultivate land in the valleys. In winter the position was reversed: the men moved to work in the forests and the women lived in the valleys where they had taken the cattle. All the same, overseas emigration completely dominated the demographic history of the nineteenth century. Overwhelmingly the emigrants went to the United States though there was some migration between the Scandinavian countries themselves and a movement of Swedes to other parts of Europe.

Until 1860 the rate of emigration was well below that of Europe as a whole but, precipitated at first by the poor harvests of the next decade, the last significantly to affect population trends in the west, the rate moved well above average in all the Scandinavian countries, most in Norway, least in Denmark. The highest migration rates for each were 401 per 100,000 in Denmark in 1886–90, 759 in Sweden at the same period, and 1,105 in Norway in 1881–5. In Sweden the pace distinctly slackened around the turn of the century as more rapid industrialisation attracted the rural surplus internally to a growing extent.

With the lowest death rates in Europe, emigration from Scandinavia was hardly the result of dire necessity. True, the numbers of landless labourers and poor cottagers began to build up in all three countries, but emigration became significant well before anything approaching the rural crises of eastern Europe had been experienced. The early movement from Norway and Sweden was probably linked with resentment at the power of the established Lutheran church, though often such people needed the further blow of economic recession to cause them to take up their roots entirely. These emigrants usually went with their families never to return. By the end of the century more commonly it was single young men who emigrated, one in three returning home. In general emigration came more from a craving for material betterment than from actual physical need. The cultural pattern of marriage helped to keep the population above subsistence level: the economy did not necessarily provide for any marked material advancement, however. In Sweden a primogeniture system fixed land ownership in the hands of 200,000 peasant proprietors and 9,000 nobles and gentry – numbers which did not greatly change over time. So outside the gentry there was a rigid and often bitterly hated class system ranging from the strong peasant aristocrat to the landless labourer. The agricultural population was most numerous in the southern and western counties, and it was from these that the bulk of emigrants came – from Alvsborg, Skaraborg, Kalmar, Jönköping, Malmöhus. The first three of these actually suffered a net loss of population between 1880 and 1910. The proportionate loss was highest where the soil was least fertile and the markets distant. Cottars and agricultural labourers formed the bulk of emigrants. Many servants left the rich farms of Skåne: girls who usually worked in the fields with the men began to feel that domestic service in the United States would be more pleasant and profitable. The potato crop in the south, for example, was typically harvested by women in gangs of twenty or thirty, kneeling in rows and scraping for the tubers with their fingers. Such a disagreeable form of exploitation made the pain of leaving home all the easier to bear. The agricultural crisis of the 1880s hit hard at places such as Dalsland and Värmland which had abandoned diversified farming to concentrate on oats and where many farms had been bought on mortgage at a high price. Värmland was the worst hit of all: in the 1880s 40,000 of a population of 268,000 left and about 30,000 went overseas. Then there was the influence of the lumber companies. As one peasant put it 'The corporations control the market for our forest products. They prevent us from using the rivers to float our timber. They out-vote us in communal circles. They control even our rights to market our own property. Therefore one peasant after another has become discouraged and has sold his estate rather than live under these conditions.'[6] Others became indebted to the companies for unpaid rent and were forced to work for them to pay off their debt. No wonder their children got away as quickly as possible. Nevertheless, to 1900 Norrland was looked upon as a second America as lumbering and iron mining increased. Peasant owners might leave the forest areas but labourers moved in, anxious for work.

In Denmark this upward social grouping played a vital role. There too were men who felt they had a right to a living from the land and if it was taken from them they would rather emigrate. Also when North Schleswig was conquered by Prussia in 1864 young men avoided military service wholesale by migrating to Denmark and to the United States. From 1870 to 1901 the loss from emigration in the province exceeded the natural growth of population. Religious factors played a larger part than in many other countries too. Revivalism found fertile ground in Denmark, the Mormon faith above all. Except for England and Scotland more went to Utah from Denmark than from any other country in Europe, though of course their share in total emigration was very small. In general the proportion of men in the total emigration was high. At the height of Danish emigration in the 1880s the annual net flow of males averaged $51 \cdot 1$ per 10,000 of total male population: for females the rate was $20 \cdot 2$. From 1910–14 the average male rate was $31 \cdot 9$ compared with only $4 \cdot 6$ for women. Women also formed a high proportion of the immigrants into Denmark – mainly Swedes coming as servants – and consequently the sex balance in the country

6 F. E. Janson, *The Background of Swedish Immigration 1840–1930* (Chicago, 1931), p. 329.

became noticeably distorted. In Denmark as elsewhere emigration became a highly organised business. American railway companies, working closely with the shipping lines, were very active. There were 10–15 agencies for shipping companies in Denmark by 1890 and they employed over a thousand sub-agents all over the country – tradesmen, merchants, innkeepers. One result of their work was the fact that 75 per cent of all direct emigrants from Copenhagen travelled on tickets made out to some definite settlement or destination. Inevitably this network was sensitive to economic conditions in the United States and it is arguable that emigration from Scandinavia was more responsive to the pull from the other side of the Atlantic than anywhere else in Europe, given the motives for moving and the highly organised nature of the trade.

From 1865 to 1914 600,000 people left Norway, almost all going to the United States. This was a bigger proportion of the total population than in any other country of Europe except for Ireland, and, after 1890, Italy. Just under two-thirds of the natural increase was lost over the half century. There had been some emigration in the eighteenth century and before: Dutch shippers liked Norwegian seamen and many sailed on Dutch vessels. Some then stayed on in Holland, some went to London, some manned ships for Peter the Great in Russia, but perhaps most went to settle in the Dutch colonies in the east. The tradition continued into the nineteenth century: over 4,000 Norwegian seamen deserted from their ships between 1856 and 1865, 11,000 in the 1870s and 19,500 in the following decade. As for the mainstream of migration, there were small beginnings before the Civil War, enough to build up gradually a fund of knowledge about the United States. Some ships left direct for the American West Coast during the gold rush days. The outburst after 1865 coincided in part with the swings in population growth. The 1850s saw the largest absolute increase of population in Norwegian history and this bulge came onto the labour market twenty years later. In 1879 there were 71,000 males aged 18–22 compared with 61,000 ten years before, for example. So strong did the outflow become that for a few years in the 1880s the population actually fell.

Obviously swings in birth and death rates cannot account for a movement of this size. It was largely a rural movement caused by the twin pressures of overall population growth and a slowly changing internal economy. Industrialisation and modernisation of agricultural techniques went forward more slowly than in Sweden and Denmark. In Norway there was a relatively rigid system of primogeniture whereby the maintenance of younger brothers and sisters as well as parents was normally accepted as the responsibility of the eldest son when he took over the family property. These brothers and sisters sometimes received a cottager's plot on the farm and sometimes they became farm servants. In the coastal areas, where fishing was the main source of income, farms were sometimes divided among all the children and this led to continuous fragmentation of holdings. Indeed, subdivision became a very severe problem in Norway. But in an economy where the supply of land was inelastic and the manufacturing sector stagnant, the younger brothers and sisters were almost doomed to a life of rural poverty. In mountain and fjord areas cottagers and servants were treated very much like members of the master's own family, and in such an egalitarian system the younger brothers and sisters would not wish to become the eldest's inferiors and it was from such areas that migration was most pronounced. Internal migration varied from place to place and from time to time but in general it developed slowly, and consequently emigration not only reached very high levels, but also persisted after 1900 when in Sweden it was distinctly slackening. What had started as a family movement became more and more an emigration of young males who had grown up with the United States before their eyes and who moved at the earliest possible moment. From being an escape from limited economic opportunities, it became a tradition, and as time went on men began to move more from non-rural areas, including professional men who sought to escape from their typically large families – a trend which came as a great surprise and was bitterly resented as being almost a form of treason. Social unrest and tension slackened as the cottagers declined from 25 to 3 per cent of the population. Possibly this skimming off of the surplus together with the rise of industrial opportunities helped to bring about a rise in real wages after 1860, though the gap between rural and industrial wage levels hardly narrowed at all.

– *Migration from Italy, Portugal and Spain*

The census of 1871 showed that already by that year there were some 270,000 Italians registered as living in foreign countries – some 155,000 in Europe and 86,000 in South America. Thereafter the numbers of emigrants rose steadily: an average of 135,000 left their homeland each year from 1876 to 1886, 270,000 during 1886–1900 and 625,000 from 1900 to 1913. The peak was reached during the years 1896 to 1905 when 860,000 people left each year: over the next five years 650,000 left annually, but of all these about 400,000 and 250,000 respectively emigrated to other parts of Europe and approximately 80 per cent of such emigrants eventually returned home. The proportion of those returning home to those newly emigrating to the American continent rose steadily too from 20 per cent in 1887–91 to 68 per cent in 1907–11. In the last decade before the First World War some 300–400,000 emigrants were returning to Italy annually. The main feature of both Italian and Slav migration was that it was predominantly male, contained a high proportion of illiterates and was for the most part not permanent.

The reasons are not hard to find. It is obviously absurd to stress the pull of the United States as the major factor in the movement of people who were so desperately anxious to get back home again. The fall of cereal and other agricultural prices which brought a crisis to farmers throughout Europe in the 1880s came upon Italy just as the population was exploding. Government action through tariff protection was slow and inadequate and the decade following 1885 was one of the blackest in Italian history. To this must be added the extreme misery found among the peasants of southern Italy. Soil erosion, malaria, high taxes played some part and the state demonstrated a total lack of interest in the plight of the area. Above all there was acute fragmentation of the peasant holdings in the deep south and intense exploitation of labourers and sharecroppers on the large estates further to the north and in Sicily. The hilly districts, the poorest and some of the most populous areas, were the first main sources of the movement: then it spread slowly to the coastal regions and after 1900 came a great outpouring from Sicily. Such people were an easy prey for the 'padroni' in the eastern cities of the United States who hired out workers in huge bands and charged them large commissions, having already advanced passage money for the journey across the Atlantic. It was from the south, from Abruzzi, Molise and southwards, that the great bulk of the emigrants to the United States came, though it was not until after 1900 that these formed the majority of all emigrants. Before that date more people migrated from the north, from the Alpine regions above all, and these went above all to Europe and to South America. The province of Veneto regularly lost 2 per cent of its population every year, sometimes over 3 per cent, though the numbers returning home at the end of the working season were always high. Relatively few emigrants came from the central regions – Tuscany, the Marches, Latium, Umbria. One estimate is that from 1876 to 1900 over 500,000 southern Italians left for the United States compared with only 73,000 from the north but 440,000 northerners left for Argentina alone compared with 230,000 from the south. Between 1901 and 1913 the balance shifted and 1,700,000 southern Italians left for the United States and 328,000 for Argentina compared with 347,000 and 316,000

F

respectively from the north. But these figures take no account of emigration to Europe nor to other parts of South America.

In 1911 there were over 400,000 Italians in France, working in mines and quarries, in agriculture and in construction gangs. The largest bloc was to be found in Marseilles, but just before 1914 the great burst of activity at the Briey iron ore mines in Lorraine drew large numbers. Workers from the French countryside in the main held aloof from ore mining and few miners moved from the coalfields; consequently by 1913 65 per cent of the workers at Briey were Italian, 15 per cent other nationalities and only one-fifth were Frenchmen. There were 47,000 Italians there in 1913 and Briey with its booming growth and varied population was more like a mining town of the American west than anything else. Italians also formed just under 4 per cent of all mining and smelting workers in Germany in 1907. Sometimes they were deliberately moved about as strike breakers and earned the title of the 'Chinese of Europe' for their lack of solidarity with the labour groups around them. They might well have been called the Irish too, for they were widely engaged in constructional work of all kinds – on the great Swiss tunnels, on rebuilding the fortifications of Metz and Cologne after 1871, on railways in Greece, Serbia, Bulgaria, Romania – even in Russia. Only in Norway were they defeated by climatic conditions. An important element too were the skilled tradesmen going to Switzerland, France and Germany. Friuli in the Dolomites was one of the greatest sources of such emigration. Boys were trained there from an early age to go and work at a special craft in a foreign land – in the glass industry in Lyons for example. The special contribution of Italian emigrants to the industrialisation of Europe was out of all proportion to their numbers.

It was in South America that the Italian played his most striking role, but emigration from Spain and Portugal was very important too. Table 9 offers one recent estimate of immigration into Argentina; these statistics vary according to the mode of calculation and the allowance made for returning migrants, but the general pattern remains the same. The basic fact is that a country of 1,800,000 inhabitants in 1869 received 2,500,000 permanent European inhabitants in under fifty years. The flow reached a peak of 220,000 in 1889; in 1905 the 100,000 mark was passed again and stayed above that level to the First World War, exceeding 200,000 in 1910 and 1912. Most of the emigrants from Italy before 1870 were men who had little stake in the land; many were induced to move by agents who at one time were receiving $5 for every immigrant secured for Argentina. Thereafter it seems that many northern Italians, though rendered poor by the inability of their land to sustain a growing

Table 9. *Shares in gross immigration into Argentina,*
1857–1910

	1857–80	per cent 1881–1900	1901–10
Italy	63·1	61·7	45·1
Spain	16·0	19·5	37·0
France	9·6	8·0	1·9
Russia	0·2	1·5	4·8
Total (000) gross	440·5	1,489·0	1,764·1
net	172·8	957·6	1,120·6

Source: Carlos F. Diaz Alejandro, *Essays in the Economic History of
the Argentinian Republic* (New Haven, 1970), p. 23.

population, were nevertheless not in a state of abject misery and
went to Argentina positively to be farmers. Also at least a third of
those going before 1900 were craftsmen – masons, carpenters,
gardeners, sailors. Those from the south went more out of sheer
destitution, and were willing to take any job available and one in
four settled in the city of Buenos Aires itself.

The most remarkable figures in this migratory movement were the
seasonal migrants, known as the *'golondrinas'* or 'swallows'. With
the seasons in the northern and southern hemispheres reversed, it
was possible for such men to work two harvests every year. Italians
entered Argentina at the end of the year, sometimes as many as
30,000 of them, though the average of seasonal immigration from
all sources was 100,000 between 1900 and 1910. They lived cheaply,
slept out of doors and went home with savings well above the wage
for a year's work as a farm labourer back home. Some did it for
nearly twenty successive years. Opera stars got two seasons in the
same way – two winters – and many a modest Italian company
enjoyed the bonus of a tour in South America.

In Brazil the big flow of emigrants came after the abolition of
slavery in 1888, though in earlier years there had been a trickle of
German and other farmers seeking to establish replicas of European
valleys in a far-off land. Conditions proved so difficult that in the
1850s many German States banned emigration to Brazil. In 1870
the Brazilian government agreed to pay the travel costs of immigrants going to the coffee plantations and the owners undertook to
pay their expenses during the first year and to give land to grow
food. This made possible the first large inflow of labour and soon it
was to coincide with chronic depression in Italy. More than two-

thirds of the Italians going to Brazil after 1884 arrived before 1902 when the Italian government began to discourage the flow on account of the conditions on board the emigrant ships. It barred emigration to Argentina for the same reason later. However, they were replaced by Portuguese, attracted to Brazil by ties of language and culture and by Spaniards whose emigration patterns were considerably more widespread. The overall pattern of gross Brazilian immigration is given in Table 10. Portuguese immigrants came from the districts of the interior north of the Tagus river where extreme fragmentation of land holdings had been experienced. Further south the pull of Lisbon and the demand for labour on the large estates kept immigration low and pulled in workers from other areas. Net emigration from Portugal from 1886 to 1911 totalled about 380,000 and at its peak after 1900 the loss was equivalent to about 30 per cent of the natural increase of population.

Table 10. *Immigration into Brazil, 1884–1913*

	Portugal	Italy	Spain	Germany	Russia
1884–93	170,621	510,533	103,116	22,778	40,589
1894–03	157,542	537,784	93,770	6,698	2,886
1904–13	384,672	196,521	224,672	33,859	48,100

Source: R. E. Poppino, *Brazil* (New York, 1968), p. 193.

Early in the nineteenth century restrictions were placed on emigration from Spain but they proved impossible to enforce in the long run. By 1881 some 74,000 Spaniards had emigrated to Argentina, 29,000 to the United States and less than 9,000 to Brazil. In 1882, the first year accurate statistics were kept, 72,000 people emigrated but in many years the figure rose above 100,000 and in 1912 reached a peak of 257,000. Very few left for the United States; a maximum of 4,766 went to Mexico in 1907 but 1,250,000 emigrated to Cuba between 1882 and 1923. As we have seen, large numbers went to Argentina and Brazil and many moved to work elsewhere in Europe, especially in France. Spaniards did not take much part in the harvest work in South America but there were Spanish golondrinas all the same, as all work fluctuated with the harvest. Railways needed more men, agricultural products required processing, the sprawling cities called for more skilled and unskilled workers to build and service their facilities. In the main the Spaniards emigrated from the peripheral regions – the Canaries, Asturias, from around Santander and Barcelona and from the Basque region. Most of all they came from Galicia in the extreme north west whence men had regularly left for seasonal work in Castile in the eighteenth century and which still supplied labour to that province and even to Portugal throughout the nineteenth century. Another important source of migrants prior to the 1890s was south-eastern Spain whence they journeyed as contract labour to Algeria, especially to Oran. There they were frequently savagely exploited and from time to time suffered badly at the hands of outlaws. But of more than 4 million Spaniards emigrating between 1882 and 1923, 3,300,000 returned home. The pattern was very similar to that from Italy and not surprisingly a high proportion of all emigrants were male.

– Population movements in France and Switzerland

France was never a country which experienced heavy emigration. In the seventeenth century the Huguenots fled from persecution but the authorities always found it difficult to persuade Frenchmen to go out to their North American colonies. In the nineteenth century the tradition continued and emigration was far smaller than that from nearly all other countries. All the same, it was by no means non-existent and derived from those factors which combined to bring about an extensive internal migration. The influence of rural poverty is demonstrated by the fact that the bulk of emigrants came from the Midi, from the mountainous departments of the Pyrenees and of the Alps, the basins of the Garonne and Rhône rivers, and the eastern frontier departments. To the general factors causing rural distress can be added the more specific influence of the fall of agricultural prices in the 1880s, intensified by the ruin of many vineyards through phylloxera disease. Many vine growers moved out to take up the occupation again in North Africa and South America. The North American colonies naturally attracted a large proportion of the emigrants from the south, though peasants from the Pyrenees were particularly prone to go to South America along with so many Spaniards from Northern Spain. Even so, at its height of 45,000 emigrants per annum during the 1880s and again after 1900, the movement was low in proportion to total population, compared with that experienced by most other European countries. Low population growth was clearly one factor and Frenchmen apparently did not feel the same urge to look to the opportunities offered by the United States as did Scandinavian peasants, for example. Possibly the role of divided inheritance laws in preserving a stake in the land for most peasants played some part too. Furthermore, after 1850 industrialisation went forward rapidly enough in

France to bring about a marked redistribution of population internally. So much so that France enjoyed a sizeable immigration from surrounding countries. Some of it was seasonal – in 1904 some 40,000 Belgians entered to work in the fields of the northern departments and around Paris and some 10–20,000 Spaniards were picking grapes in the south, figures which were probably below the normal level. The extent of net permanent immigration into France is hard to determine because of changes in the naturalisation laws, but Bunle put it at 1,300,000 between 1851 and 1911.[7] This compares with the same author's estimate of total French emigration over those years of 2 million. Allowing for emigrants returning home, there was probably no great difference between the two movements.

The natural increase of the population of Switzerland in the nineteenth century, like that of Belgium, was modest but emigration reached considerable heights around 1850 and again as a result of the rural distress of the 1880s. Between 1850 and 1888 a natural increase of population of just over 700,000 was reduced to 525,000 by emigration, mostly to the United States. For several centuries, though, Switzerland had experienced a very special kind of emigration in the form of her mercenary soldiers. It has been estimated that from the fifteenth to the eighteenth centuries 2 million Swiss soldiers served in foreign lands and altogether 1 million were killed – or about a half of the natural increase of population. Even for the period 1800–50 of roughly 100,000 emigrants, one half was accounted for by losses of mercenaries in the Napoleonic campaigns. After 1890, however, there was a marked change in the pattern of population movement linked with the rapid industrialisation of the Swiss economy and paralleling similar experiences in France and western Germany. Though from 1888 to 1914 another 125,000 Swiss emigrated, 300,000 aliens went to live in Switzerland. Almost a third of the increase of population in those years came in this way – the highest proportion in Europe for the time. Most of them were Germans and Italians: the former were typically craftsmen or domestic workers and the latter as usual were heavily engaged in the construction and mining industries.

– The Consequences of Emigration

In general terms what were the consequences for Europe of this enormous movement of peoples? Certainly almost every political, social and economic problem was conditioned by it in some way in

[7] W. F. Willcox, *International Migrations* (New York, 1931), vol. II, chap. VIII.

those countries where migration was significant. The movement of labour within Europe, either seasonally or permanently, increased its productivity, raised European income as a whole, and swelled the volume of its trade. Whether for the receiving areas the stimulus arose more from the incomes of the newcomers or from the opportunity they offered of holding down wages, and boosting the rate of profit and, possibly, of investment, is hard to say.

For the losing areas emigration, whether intra- or inter-continental, had mixed results. By eliminating redundant labour and disguised unemployment, by checking the subdivision of holdings, it contributed to a more efficient pattern of farming, encouraged the introduction of machinery and new crops and, by raising farm incomes, helped stimulate the economy as a whole. For countries such as Norway, Italy and Germany, the emigrant trade gave a considerable impetus to the growth of certain ports – Bremen, Hamburg, Oslo, Genoa, Naples – and to the local shipping industries. Table 11 shows for example how 'Continental' third class passengers moved to the United States in 1913. 'Continental' was the word used by the Shipping Conference for central and east European passengers – not British or Scandinavians or Italians, Greek and others from the south. Third class passengers were almost all emigrants.

Table 11. *'Continental' third class passengers carried to the United States and Canada, 1913*

From British ports:	101,300
From continental ports	
Fiume (Rijeka)	38,900
Rotterdam	114,800
Antwerp	71,200
Trieste	25,000
Le Havre	69,300
Hamburg	147,700
Bremen	195,600
Libau (Liepãja)	31,700

Source: British Parliamentary Papers, *Shipping and Shipbuilding Industries after the War* (1918), vol. XIII, App. II.

The passengers from British ports transhipped through Libau (Liepãja), Bremen and Hamburg, most being brought from the first port to avoid the German frontier control stations which forced emigrants to go by German lines. The Austro-American Line operating from Trieste and the Canada NLVD line from Rotterdam were controlled by the two German lines – Hamburg America and North German Lloyd – who also had a quarter share in the Holland America Company.The Belgian Red Star Line sailing from Antwerp and the American Line from Southampton were owned by International Mercantile Marine of New Jersey. The international emigrant trade had become very big business indeed.

With the migrants went increased exports of local products – fruit, wine, oil, garlic, cheeses, macaroni from Italy, for example – though insofar as the mass of emigrants went to the United States the impact of emigration on trade was small. Trade links were most effectively established in this way with non-industrialised countries and this benefited Britain far more than other European countries. Although emigrants all took out with them some capital, large remittances back home soon came vastly to outweigh this loss. We know nothing of the size of intra-European remittances; but a careful study has suggested that in 1907 almost $220 million was sent back to Continental Europe from the United States. Italy received $70 million, Austria-Hungary $65 million, Norway and Sweden $25 million, Russia the same and Germany $15 million. As we shall see in a later chapter, these were significant contributions to the current balances of all these countries with the exception perhaps, of Germany, where its relative role was certainly much less.

But there was one very serious disadvantage: the migrants were mostly young people. Having shouldered the burden of rearing them, the mother country lost its sons and daughters just as they became producers. In countries suffering from serious agricultural over population such a loss was not serious, for the marginal product of these men was probably near zero anyway. But in countries where this was not the case – in Scandinavia – it was a different matter. To give one example, in Sweden in the 1880s the working population rose by only 0.6 per cent. If, however, we add to this those aged 15–64 who emigrated, the actual growth of workers would have been 14.2 per cent.[8] Taking the continent as a whole and including the United Kingdom over the whole country, one-tenth of the average population emigrated and perhaps one quarter of the labour force.

Above all we should remember that for many of those concerned emigration was an occasion for immense grief, breaking up families, severing deeply loved cultural ties. They left overwhelmingly because they were forced to do so, not because they wanted to move. That in the end future generations may have benefited from the move very greatly in an economic sense makes no difference to the tragedy experienced by the generation that went.

[8] E. H. Phelps Brown, *A Century of Pay* (London, 1968), pp. 89–90.

SUGGESTED READING

The literature is so immense that only the barest selection can be made. Articles are to be found in every academic journal – some of the best in the *Scandinavian Economic History Review*. The most important specialist journals are *Population Studies* and the French journal *Population*. A special issue of the journal *Daedalus* (Spring 1968) was devoted to the history of population growth and a selection of some of the most important journal articles will be found in D. V. GLASS and D. E. C. EVERSLEY, *Population in History* (London, 1965). There are a large number of general works; among the most helpful are C. CIPOLLA, *The Economic History of World Population* (London, 1962), E. WRIGLEY, *Population and History* (London, 1969), M. REINHARD, A. ARMENGAUD and J. DUPÄQUIER, *Histoire générale de la population mondiale* (Paris, 1968) and A. ARMENGAUD's *Population in Europe 1700–1914* (London, 1970). *The Cambridge Economic History of Europe* contains important chapters on population – in vol. IV (Cambridge, 1967) by HELLEINER and in vol. VI (Cambridge, 1965) by GLASS and GREBENIK. A particularly interesting general article is H. J. HABAKKUK, 'Population problems and European economic development in the late eighteenth and nineteenth centuries', *American Economic Review: Papers and Proceedings* (1963).

As for works dealing with population growth and its effects in a general way, one can make only the slightest of selections. The sections dealing with the matter in S. KUZNETS, *Modern Economic Growth* (New Haven, 1966) are most impressive as is his essay 'Population and economic growth' in the *Proceedings of the American Philosophical Society*, June 1967. THE UNITED NATIONS' *Determinants and Consequences of Population Trends* (1953) is a classic. A. J. COALE and E. M. HOOVER, *Population Growth and Economic Development in Low Income Countries* (Princeton, 1958) is also rewarding. See too the chapter in W. W. ROSTOW (ed.) *The Economics of Take-off into Self-Sustained Growth* (London, 1953) by LEIBENSTEIN and the subsequent discussion.

Turning to studies of particular countries there is P. C. MATTHIESSEN, *Some Aspects of the Demographic Transition in Denmark* (Copenhagen, 1970); M. LIVI BACCI, *A Century of Portuguese Fertility* (Princeton, 1971); K. R. MAYER, *The Population of Switzerland* (New York, 1952); M. DRAKE, *Population and Society in Norway 1735–1865*, (Cambridge, 1969) and the chapter on population by W. W. EASON in C. E. BLACK, *The Transformation of Russian Society* (Cambridge, Mass., 1960). E. A. WRIGLEY, *Industrial Growth and Population Change* (Cambridge, 1961) discusses north-western Europe.

French demographers have produced such outstanding work and pioneered techniques so effectively that every effort should be made to study the literature in that language. A general work is J. C. TOUTAIN, *La Population de la France de 1700 à 1959* (Paris, 1963). Specialist works are P. GOUBERT, *Beauvais et le Beauvaisis de 1600 à 1730* (Paris, 1960), E. GAUTIER and L. HENRY, *La population de Crulai, paroisse normande* (Paris, 1958) and the latter's *Anciennes familles genevoises* (Paris, 1956).

Bohemia, Moravia and Slovakia are discussed by P. HORSKA in 'L'état actuel de recherches sur l'évolution de la population dans les pays tchèques aux XVIIIième et XIXième siècles' Société de Démographie Historique, *Annales de Démographie Historique* (1967).

A great deal of work has been done on migration, though most of it looks at the question from the point of view of the assimilation of migrants into American society whether north or south. The European aspect is less well covered. The basic facts on international migration were set out in two volumes by I. FERENCZI and W. F. WILLCOX, *International Migrations* (New York, 1929–31) and though the figures have had to be revised in detail since then it remains a standard work. More specifically concerned with the timing of migration are H. JEROME, *Migration and Business Cycles* (New York, 1926), B. THOMAS, *Migration and Economic Growth* (London, 1954). There is also an important article on the subject by R. EASTERLIN, 'Influences on European overseas emigration before World War I' in *Economic Development and Cultural Change* (1961), though rather biased towards the 'pull' argument as indeed is much American writing. FRANK THISTLETHWAITE covers new aspects of migration from the European point of view in an article 'Migration from Europe overseas in the nineteenth and twentieth centuries' reprinted in H. MÖLLER, *Population Movements in Modern European History* (New York, 1964). The best general books on migration from Europe to the U.S.A. are M. L. HANSEN, *The Atlantic Migration* (Cambridge, Mass., 1940) a classic study but not strong on the European background and more recently P. TAYLOR, *The Distant Magnet* (London, 1972), a well-written scholarly work with much to say about the forces bringing about emigration.

As for works dealing with particular countries, the following contain important material on the European background and in many respects contribute much to our general understanding of the development of those countries. M. WALKER *Germany and the Emigration 1816–1885* (Cambridge, Mass., 1964); R. F. FOERSTER, *The Italian Emigration of our Times* (Cambridge, Mass., 1919); T. C. BLEGEN, *Norwegian Migration to America 1825–1860* (Northfield, Minn., 1931); F. E. JANSON, *The Background of Swedish Emigration 1840–1930* (New York, 1970); D. S. THOMAS, *Social and Economic Aspects of Swedish Population Movements* (New York, 1941): M. WISCHNITZER, *To Dwell in Safety. The Story of Jewish Migration since 1800* (Philadelphia, 1948.)

Information on internal migration has to be derived from study of general works on the countries concerned. For the Russian migration to Siberia see D. W. TREADGOLD, *The Great Siberian Migration* (Princeton, 1957) but a far more comprehensive study is F. X. COQUIN, *La Sibérie* (Paris, 1969).

Chapter 3

Technological Change

There is little doubt that technological change has been a major force in promoting economic growth over the last two centuries. Just how important is a matter for debate. Some economists have argued that it has been far more significant than simply the increased employment of capital and labour. Evidence is mounting to suggest that this is an exaggerated view and that we ought to maintain the emphasis that earlier analysts gave to variables such as the ratio of savings to national income. But however that may be, technology has clearly played a most important role in many aspects of growth – not just in raising incomes but in changing the location and size of industry, in altering the role of different raw materials, in changing social patterns of work, in altering for good and ill the quality of life itself. As for capital we must, at least, stress the importance of determining the amount of technological advance incorporated when any investment is made. Technology embraces in these contexts a wide range of activities. It may mean a new process of manufacture or a new final product. In some circumstances it can better be described as 'know-how' – the ability to organise and operate plant within the existing range of technological knowledge. It involves all those supplementary benefits accruing from the expansion of centres of industrial activities known as external economies. It includes the economies reaped from increases in the scale of activity and the greater efficiency derived from the process of learning a job by doing it again and again. It relates, too, to the quality of the workforce at all levels.

THE THEORY OF TECHNOLOGICAL CHANGE

For analytical purposes distinctions must be drawn between the invention of a new process and the invention of a new product and between the first exploitation of an idea and its subsequent diffusion to other producers. Strictly, too, we ought to differentiate between a shift of technology within the present range of knowledge, that is to say, adjustment of the combination of factors used in a known process according to the dictates of the relative prices of those factors, and the finding of a new technology so that land, labour, capital and materials are combined in a different way altogether. Theoretically this is a most important distinction to make but in practice it is one not easy to recognise, since both types of changes often occur together. An innovation may be labour-saving, using more capital in relation to labour, or it may be the opposite, or more rarely it may be neutral and save both in the same proportions. It may save skilled labour at the expense of using relatively more unskilled labour. It may save on materials or use more material but save labour. A variety of possibilities exists.

Many of the early innovations of the industrial revolution appear to have been labour-saving but by no means all of them. The speeding up of textile machinery was capital-saving: the steam engine required less capital than the water wheel for a given output of power and improvements in the steam engine concentrated on saving fuel. Some of the process developments of the late years of the nineteenth century, requiring the use of hydro-electric power, were extremely capital intensive but in general, as the century wore on, more and more innovations saved on both factors though to different degrees in each case.

A major element in the substitution of capital for labour has been the cheapening of capital goods relative to wages as a result of technological progress in the capital goods industries but in general evidence as to the bias of inventions is hard to come by. One might think that most effort would be put into saving that factor that loomed highest in total costs but we lack real evidence to prove that this has regularly been the case. One problem is that capital-saving innovation often consists of relatively minor improvements such as changes in the layout and operating speeds of machinery, which easily go unnoticed but which may be so numerous as to be more important in total than the single spectacular labour-saving developments. We must also make a distinction between an industry and the economy; railways, for instance, were capital intensive in themselves but the reduction in the time taken to transport goods allowed business men so to reduce stocks that railways brought down the capital : output ratio of the economy as a whole in spectacular fashion.

The need for innovation may arise from steeply rising marginal costs; up to a point a technology may be perfectly adequate but it may not be able to stretch to meet new demands at all. The hand spinning and weaving processes left the merchant at the mercy of the peasant's work routine at a time when the possibilities of growth of the market seemed unusually encouraging. So he was attracted to the machine because it broke an organisational barrier. Another example of this can be seen in the carting industry in Spain which served well enough for most of the eighteenth century but then began to suffer a severe crisis. Demand for carting rose because population was growing and also because this led to a need to increase grain imports. Carters depended on grazing sites along the roads and on winter pasturage for their horses but it was the rise of population itself which led to the enclosure of these lands. So the cost of transport rose sharply, putting an absolute stop to growth until the bottleneck was broken. Many local industrialists everywhere faced the same situation in an era of poor transport if they wished to increase output beyond the limits set by the size of the local labour force.

A more significant question in the context of nineteenth-century European experience is the relevance of a technology developed in one country to the industrial and social conditions obtaining in others. A new process may be developed to save a factor short in one region but not in another. The reluctance to adopt coke smelting for iron on the continent, initially anyway, was not due to inertia but was a proper reaction to the fact that it was an expensive process producing poorer iron than that made with charcoal and only worth while when the supply of wood, or the labour to process the wood, was very expensive to come by. From the first steam engines made on the continent far surpassed those made in Britain with respect to fuel economy because of the relative prices of coal in the two areas. French locomotives tended to have high first cost because they were designed to save fuel more than the British or German. A French driver got a fuel saving bonus too – unthinkable in Germany where he simply had to get there on time. A process may call for special patterns of industrial organisation and for skills not always available. Thus, new textile technologies such as ring spinning and the Northrop automatic loom were, for technical reasons, not easy to accommodate in an industry where cotton spinning and weaving were carried on in separate establishments. New products such as artificial dyes and pharmaceuticals required high skill in research and development, while machine-tool making called for a rare degree of skill from the operatives. A product may require peculiar market conditions present in one place but not in another. The mass production techniques which emerged in the United States after 1850 were relevant only where there was a mass demand for a homogeneous product. It was therefore simple to introduce mass production of sewing machines into Europe, but much more difficult with the motor car. The new electro-chemical processes of the early twentieth century could only be undertaken where power was very cheap, that is to say in those regions – Norway, Switzerland, the French and Italian Alps – where hydroelectric power could be generated.

More difficult problems arise from differences in labour supply. It is often argued that American technology was determined in large measure by the fact that labour was relatively expensive. Whether this induced Americans to substitute capital for labour in existing processes or gave a labour-saving bias to the new technologies, the problem arises as to the relevance of techniques developed in countries where labour is relatively expensive to countries where labour is cheap and capital is the scarce factor.

This is an issue that concerns developmental economists today. Is it not sensible, they argue, for undeveloped countries to adjust their technologies to save the scarce factor, capital, and employ more of the abundant factor, labour? The counter-argument to this is that for the country as a whole the aim should be to maximise output per head, to make the most effective use of the scarce capital by using advanced techniques and not to waste it in small applications here and there. Certainly to do this would give less employment but maximising the rate of return to capital provides for the most rapid growth of jobs in other sectors of the economy. Any objection that this approach would fail to raise the wage level and therefore the level of internal demand could be overcome, it is argued, where a government is prepared to provide the main stimulus to demand, though *sustained* growth must inevitably depend on long run trends in internal purchasing power. The difficulties arising out of such a situation will be seen when we study Russian development after 1890.

The history of technology in the nineteenth century suggests that in general innovators in all countries tended to adopt the most modern techniques in the capital goods and durable consumer goods industries with only minor modifications. Blast-furnace practice, for example, by 1914 was more capital intensive in Germany than in Britain and more so in Russia than in Germany; the pattern followed the timing of expansion and therefore the availability of the latest technology, not the relative levels of labour costs. Sewing machines were made on the same kind of capital equipment in New York, Glasgow and Moscow. It was in Hungary with its ample supply of labour that highly capital intensive techniques were devised for grain milling.

The explanation is complex. For technical reasons there were serious limits to the degree to which adjustment could take place. It seems likely that there was not, as theory assumes, an unlimited range of opportunities for substituting labour for capital. Sometimes the technical choices were all bunched at the capital intensive end, as in steel, with only minor adjustments possible in the handling of the metal but not in its actual processing. For the manufacture of interchangeable parts there was often no alternative machine technique, so exacting were the standards of accuracy required, though more or less workers might be used to tend the machinery according to the price and skill of labour. On occasion the techniques available were either very capital intensive or very labour intensive and a huge shift in the relative cost of labour would be necessary to make it worthwhile to change from one to the other. Norwegian fishermen continued to rely on small coastal fishing boats for their cod and herring catches and exported the fish dried and salted to low income markets. The really profitable trade was to sell fresh frozen fish to high income countries but this required bigger vessels to fish as far away as Newfoundland, and investment in quick freezing plants. There was no half-way house.

Other constraints might arise from the fact that the machine-making industry was the last to emerge in the more slowly developing countries of the east and therefore they had to buy what was available in the west or go without. What was offered tended to be based on western practice. Furthermore, in so far as new industries in those countries were managed by westerners, they not unnaturally chose the techniques they understood best. But it would be wrong to think that the transfer was based on ignorance or inertia or fixity of technology. There is much evidence that the heavy use of capital involved in using modern techniques was more than offset by the low cost of labour operating the plant. The argument that this low cost reflected low productivity is rarely true; it reflected more labour's inability to reap the rewards of its productivity. It is significant that those American manufactures which were competitive in Europe before 1914 were either new products or products which reaped great economies from the scale of operation made possible in the protected home market. In a wide range of industrial activities American manufacturers were unable to compensate for the higher cost of labour by the use of labour-saving methods and were not competitive internationally. More specifically an American observer noted in 1907 that the Singer sewing machine plant at Podolsk near Moscow, using American methods, had costs well below those of the parent in New York. Another report put American costs of making relatively coarse cotton yarn as 20 per cent above those in a good Russian factory. The most modern plant was not only in many instances the sole available, but it offered substantial competitive advantages; that it was made yet more profitable by some modifications to allow greater use of labour at each machine, does not alter the fact that the most modern machines were employed.

This kind of modification was possible and desirable in many instances and produced what are known as intermediate technologies. If the iron- and steel-making furnaces were the most modern available, far more labour was used in handling the material as it moved through the plant. So output per furnace in Russia was far more impressive than output per man. Another means of saving on capital was to buy second-hand machinery. It was rarely possible to buy old steel plant, but it was open to a manufacturer to buy used machine tools and textile machines, though to be sure the best manufacturers in the less developed countries rarely did so. It was probably more a means of saving on initial outlay than of maximising profitability. The use of second-hand equipment was probably most common in shipping. Table 12 shows the striking differences in practice in Europe in this respect.

Table 12. *Steam vessels added to national fleets in 1914*

	Tonnage Added (000 net tons)	Percentage New Vessels
United Kingdom	955	97
Germany	387	85
France	137	61
Italy	137	12
Norway	152	59
Sweden	66	62

Source: British Parliamentary Papers, *Shipping and Shipbuilding Industries after the War* (1918), vol. xiii, p. 56.

Probably more than any others the textile industries lent themselves to modification according to factor costs and skills. It was relatively easy to vary the number of machines any worker tended and to alter their speed. Spinning much the same types of yarn, just before 1914 the number of operatives per thousand spindles

operatives/1000 spindles

was 9 in Italy and Silesia, 6 in France on average, 3·5 in Westphalia and possibly 2·5 in the United Kingdom. In the 1890s for spinning good quality yarn it was estimated that spindles in Alsace ran 25 per cent slower than those in Lancashire but the Alsace workers also had more breakages and were slower at repairs, so that their spindles operated only for 80 per cent of the time theoretically possible, compared with 95 per cent in England. The situation could be complex, however: the Russian cotton industry ran its spindles faster than the German and used at least twice the labour to tend the broken yarns. Possibly the Lancashire engineers there had their own special prejudices. Looms varied in speed too: for weaving plain cotton goods 80–85 cm wide, in England the looms were typically running at 240 picks a minute in 1890 compared with 190–200 in Switzerland and 150–160 in Alsace. In Italy female workers were so slow at piecing the ends that almost 40 per cent of the time worked was lost in this way.

speed of mach'g

It has been suggested that one reason why undeveloped countries adopted the latest technology was that labour, in the sense of a stable, reliable disciplined labour force, was still very scarce in such countries; not expensive in terms of wages but very hard to come by. It is not altogether clear how true this was for the simple type of repetition work carried on in textile mills or in operating the more modern automatic machine tools. In the Podolsk Singer plant it was thought that the firm benefited from a labour force which was quite happy to carry out the same routine task day in day out all year long. Certainly, there was a shortage of the best type of skilled labour for some tasks in industry in many countries. This arose partly because its productivity was already very high in some of the traditional craft trades, and so there was much to be said for using such skill to the best advantage by employing the most up to date technology in new industries. But in the higher income countries of the west at least, there was a rich supply of labour in the craft trades and in local joinery shops or jobbing works where repair of metal equipment was normally carried out and we should be careful not to attribute too many of the difficulties of industrialisation to labour difficulties. The cost of capital has to be considered with some care too. Oftentimes it was not cost but sheer unavailability at any price that limited investment.

But now to return to some of our original questions about technological change – its nature and its diffusion. To some extent inventions have always been directed towards overcoming certain bottlenecks or shortages in the production process, either of labour or of materials. In part, therefore, change has been biased towards areas where demand was immediate and the prospective costs of production reasonable. But there may be a long gap between the time when the potential is realised and the breakthrough is made. Coke smelting of iron, for example, would have been worth while for at least a century before it was actually achieved and even then it was some seventy years before it was used on any scale and with any success outside Britain. Equally there are many discoveries of pure science which were only put to commercial use after a considerable delay; electricity is the most obvious. One cannot generalise on any of these matters, for on the other hand the difficulties of mining down to the rich coal beds of the Ruhr were quickly overcome when the demand for coal became really pressing. There is a tendency for inventions to come in clusters simply because they are inter-dependent. The development of new machine techniques during the industrial revolution called for improvement in power production, in machine tools, in metal manufacture, in instrumentation, in lubrication. Later in the nineteenth century techniques in industries such as chemicals, electrical engineering and automatic machine-tool making were similarly inter-dependent and it is possible that countries such as Belgium, which because of their early start in industrialisation concentrated on the standard steel processes, coal mining and textiles, failed for this reason to benefit in a wide sense from the second round of innovations. At any one time some industries have more leverage than others and lead to a more than normal spread of technical knowledge so their absence may have far-reaching consequences.

Another version of this process is the concept of learning whereby the installation of capital equipment itself provides the vehicle for learning in the economy, as well as within the industry itself. These external benefits to the growth of industry provide the most powerful argument for tariff protection through the building up of 'infant industries' as a means of promoting the acquisition of skills and technical knowledge beneficial to industry as a whole. On the other hand it is argued that one feature of technological change is that industries that have once seen rapid progress come to a stage where further advance of a similar order of importance becomes more and more unlikely. Textile manfuacture and the steam locomotive, for example, developed very rapidly but towards the end of the nineteenth century saw only minor further gains and steel has never since enjoyed anything like the shattering reduction of costs brought by the Bessemer and Siemens processes. This is as important a matter to the countries concentrating on those industries as the fact that late comers may emerge to compete with them. On the other hand an industry created on the basis of a new scientific principle – the steam engine or electric power, for example – may well come into production very quickly, even though manufacturing techniques are poor and crude, simply because it is possible to charge a high price. In such an industry for a time the potential for technical change may be very high and the possibilities of exploiting the economies of scale may be considerable too.

Up to the middle of the nineteenth century it is arguable that technological progress in Europe owed relatively little to pure science or, indeed, to flashes of inspiration. In the main it came from enquiry and resourcefulness on the part of practical men. Experiment and patient trial and error there was in plenty but luck too. Bessemer discovered his steel process when looking for a cheaper way of making iron; Perkin discovered aniline mauve dye when trying to synthesise quinine. True there was a considerable increase of interest in science throughout the seventeenth and eighteenth centuries and this had its impact on industrial developments but it was methodology, measurement and systematic experimentation that was important rather than theory. Of course there were exceptions. To give one example, the manufacture of soap was an entirely hit or miss process in the eighteenth century. In 1780 Berthollet, who converted Scheele's scientific ideas on chlorine bleaching into a viable industrial process, published his theoretical ideas on soap-making. Thirty years later Chevreul placed the technique on a sure qualitative basis and his work remained for long the corner stone of scientific soap making. For the first time manufacturers had a real insight into the events they were trying to control. As an official appointed by the French government to supervise the dyeing industry, Berthollet did much to advance both theory and practice in that industry too though he never involved himself in the industrial application of any of his discoveries – unlike Chevreul who did so and failed. In many processes the initial ideas had to be followed by much trial and error experimentation to make them industrially worth while. Contemporaries took the view that this was the British *forte*; continental men of science were the more imaginative and though the industrial revolution, in a technical sense, was essentially a British process, the European contribution was a significant one – in bleaching and dyeing, in soap, paper and glass making, in hydraulics and in agricultural improvements too. It was in machine-making that the British were supreme, though even there French engineers such as Jacques de Vaucanson pioneered important developments in machine-tools in the second half of the eighteenth century, though their full development and exploitation eventually came elsewhere.

However all that might be, in the second half of the nineteenth century scientific experimentation became more and more important, most of all in the chemical industry but in metallurgical and mechanical fields too. If the technical discoveries of the industrial revolution were a response in the main to long felt needs, now more and more innovation derived from attempts to apply scientific discoveries to economic ends. Invention was now fostering need. One must not exaggerate the break. Perhaps the Gilchrist Thomas process for using phosphoric ore in steel making was the last really major triumph of the practical amateur, but engineers, albeit scientifically untrained, continued to make those steady improvements to industrial machinery which have always been the very essence of technological change. The great new ideas are best known, but an enormous amount of credit is due to those largely anonymous men who transformed the first crude steam engines, mules and electric motors into ever more efficient and economical tools of industry.

Technology itself resulted in certain biases which were of supreme importance in the overall process of growth. Nearly all the new technology of the nineteenth century promoted the concentration of industry through reductions in transport costs, by substituting coal for wood and developing technologies with heavy fuel needs, by creating technologies where the economies of scale were large and by the emergence of external economies in the form of benefits offered by one industry to allied processes, and finally through the creation of social overhead capital of many kinds. Only with the arrival of petrol-driven lorries, new fuels and refrigeration was the trend towards concentration reversed towards the end of the nineteenth century. In the eighteenth and early nineteenth centuries industry by and large needed less fixed capital than working capital to cover the gap between buying materials and paying wages, and selling the product. Yet by 1900 there were many industries faced with very large overhead costs indeed and this called for new types of corporate enterprise, new management techniques and new financial organisations and controls. So the joint-stock company, the investment bank, the techniques of accountancy and of scientific management were themselves a response to the demands of new technologies. But of course there was no sudden or complete change. The private company did not become outdated overnight. Some of the most successful firms in Europe remained private and many German joint-stock companies were managed as if they were private firms.

Turning to the diffusion of technology, we have already discussed the influence of relative factor prices. The conditions for adopting a new technology were different if it was required as extra capacity, from those relevant if it was to replace existing plant. In the former case the total costs of the new had to be less than those of the old method. In the latter case the total costs of the new had to be less than the variable costs of the old, for the fixed costs of the old had to be carried whatever happened. It was by no means always profitable for a firm to replace its old equipment by new; this might mean that its costs would be higher than those of its competitors but that was a penalty of an earlier start. Of course the greater the increase in demand the easier it was to bring in new technologies. In this sense growth became a cumulative process.

But apart from considerations of this kind diffusion would depend on knowledge, on the extent of the expected gains and on the degree of certainty of that gain. Sometimes a new technology completely crushed the old everywhere. The Hall-Hérault process for the manufacture of aluminium, developed during the late 1880s reduced costs over the older methods immediately by something like 75 per cent and there was no survival for the out of date under such conditions. More often, however, the effect of a new process was initially to stimulate efforts to reduce costs in the old.

It is a matter for some dispute how important it has been to initiate technological change. The pioneering process might be laborious, expensive and ultimately fruitless. There were advantages to be gained from waiting, from avoiding the initial difficulties, from gathering more experience of costs and markets. If the process worked well, of course, the innovator could establish his market position and reap monopoly profits and hope to retain his lead by further development. The German chemical manufacturers are often and rightly regarded as pioneers of research and development *par excellence*, prepared to invest heavily and to wait years for the returns to come home. Yet they were also excellent at searching out and buying up the ideas of others. It was often the ideal solution for the big man to let smaller firms experiment and to take over the process and the know-how when the time for expansion arrived. Most private manufacturers in the smaller countries had no such options. They could not hope to match the German excellence in production engineering and solid product merit; for them it was the striking and the new if they were to advance at all.

THE TRANSFER OF TECHNOLOGY

Knowledge of technologies and the ability to master them was invariably a major problem. Various types of transfer were employed. Individual firms might use the same basic techniques to manufacture a variety of products. Out of this type of organisation arose the large general engineering firms so typical of every country right to 1914 – Cockerills in Belgium, Borsig in Germany, Burmeisters in Denmark. They were by no means necessarily backward technologically simply because they did not specialise. Alternatively the same basic technology might be passed on between, as well as within, firms and applied to one product after another, as interchangeable techniques were used for guns, sewing machines, watches, bicycles and motor cars the processes depending on essentially the same kinds of machine-tool techniques. As the century wore on there was a great increase in the volume of technical literature being made available but the direct transfer of skills through men which was the dominant form of transfer at the beginning of the nineteenth century was never wholly dispensed with.

Initially almost all the movement was from England. There were entrepreneurs and managers, people like John Holker who in the eighteenth century managed the Royal Cotton Factory at Rouen and supervised a whole group of mills in Normandy. There was Aaron Manby with his workshops at Charenton and Le Creusot, exercising a profound influence on French engineering in general. Few had greater influence than the Cockerills of Bury who created a modern wool textile industry in Belgium and then went on to build the great ironworks at Seraing, the finest on the continent in the first half of the nineteenth century. Another was John Hughes, founder of the steel industry in the Donbas area of Russia. Then there were skilled men who installed machinery and instructed in its use. Such was William Wilkinson who erected a new royal cannon foundry in France near Nantes, advised on the erection of blast-furnaces at Le Creusot and then went on to do similar work in Silesia. There was Richard Roberts, inventor of the self-acting mule who stayed in Alsace for two years, planning requirements and arranging for delivery of machinery. After the Napoleonic Wars relatively few industrialists left Britain; now it was the heyday of the immigrant workers, mostly skilled men who either carried out the critical processes themselves – puddling, for example – or exercised supervision, that most vital of functions in a workshop. They were a common feature of the industrial scene in western Europe early in the century and were still widely dispersed in Russian factories, in cotton mills above all, at the end of the period. By and large such men were regarded as a necessary evil. They were expensive, difficult to handle and, worst of all, often not good at their work. Why should they be? The place for a first class puddler was in South Wales and for a weaver in Lancashire. If he was in France he might be regarded with some awe but back home he probably

couldn't hold his job. Georges Dufaud, ironmaster from the Nivernais, wrote of this from London in June 1823: 'Wales and especially
Cyfarthfa have and keep the best puddlers in the world. An ordinary
and careless puddler is not employed and unfortunately it is the
rejects who come to us.'[1]

Along with this exodus went a procession of industrialists,
economists and engineers, pouring into Britain when the short
period of peace intervened during the war period, but above all
making the journey after 1815, seeking whatever Britain had to
offer. Their welcome varied and sometimes perhaps with good
reason. It was not a one way movement, however. James Watt's
partner, Matthew Boulton, recruited many foreign skilled workers.
For engravers he went to Vienna and to Sweden, though the best
known workers at Soho were a Fleming and a Frenchman. In fact
a number of French workers, skilled at luxury metal trades were
tempted to take employment with Birmingham firms.

Finally, a method of diffusion that grew in importance very
markedly in the last quarter of the nineteenth century was the
establishment of branch plants in other countries. In part it was
motivated by a desire to avoid tariffs. In the chemical industry
above all there was a powerful incentive to hold on to new processes
and to seek patent protection overseas. Solvay, for example,
developed his process for making soda by setting up plants all
over Europe. Curiously enough, the parent plant in Belgium was not
well located for raw materials – salt had to come from France,
for example. So the original factory still only employed 500 men
in 1914 but in France two works employed 2,500, in five German
works there were 5,000 men, 600 at a plant in Spain. In Austria –
Hungary there were works in Galicia, the Salzkammergut, in
Bohemia, Bosnia and Transylvania and there were 2,500 workers
in three Russian factories. In the dyestuff industry by 1904 there
were six German and two Swiss companies manufacturing in
France, whereas only one major plant was French owned. It was
much the same in Britain; of five big plants two were German
and one Swiss. By 1896 the Nobel explosives empire included
seven factories in Norway and Sweden, twenty-three in Germany,
six in Austria Hungary, seven in France, ten in Spain, three in
Belgium, the same in Italy and in Russia, eight in Britain as well as
plants in Portugal, Switzerland and Greece. In Italy the electrical
industry was particularly international in character with the American Thomson Houston company, the German Siemens Halske,
and Swiss Brown Boveri all owning major plants there. In textiles

[1] G. Thuillier, *Georges Dufaud et les origines du grand capitalisme dans la
métallurgie en Nivernais au dix-neuvième siècle* (Paris, 1959), p. 225.

the Scottish manufacturers of sewing thread, J and P Coates had factories in Germany, Bohemia, Hungary, Russia and Spain. In the heavy industries local firms in the less developed countries not infrequently formed an association with more experienced manufacturers. Thus in Italy Ansaldo went into association with Schneider of Le Creusot to manufacture munitions and to compete with Terni who were allied with Vickers. In this way technology was transferred but control was retained in what were considered to be essential defence industries.

Of particular interest are the origins of what has come to be known in more recent times as the 'American challenge'. American companies set up establishments in Europe for a variety of reasons – to avoid tariffs, to take advantage of low labour costs, to come closer in touch with the special needs of the market, to provide better servicing facilities. The earliest American investment of this kind may well have been the establishment of Tiffany's store in Paris in 1850 but the rapid growth of this kind of investment had to wait for almost another fifty years. The electrical manufacturers were among the first to take the initiative. Westinghouse began operations in Europe with a small shop making their patent brakes in Paris in 1879, built more brake works in Germany and Russia in the 1890s and then directed their continental electrical engineering operations through Société Anonyme Westinghouse in Paris. The Thomson Houston company had a plant in France too and International Western Electric, a subsidiary of American Telephone and Telegraph, itself had subsidiaries in France, Belgium, Italy, Norway, Spain and Russia by 1914. International Harvester had big plants in Sweden, France and Germany and a particularly heavy investment in Russia, where by 1913 the Moscow factory employed 3,000 men making mowers, reapers, binders, and gas and oil engines. Standard Oil of New Jersey had subsidiary companies in Holland, Germany, Denmark, Romania, Belgium, Italy and Austria. These were only the major examples and a great deal of American investment is hard to detect, as branches were incorporated under local names. Certainly the American invasion of Europe had progressed much less than the invasion of Britain but it had become a significant element in the diffusion of new products in Europe by 1914.

The ability of one country in this way more easily to make use of technologies developed elsewhere was highly advantageous. No country could expect to establish on its own a competitive advantage in a wide range of industrial activities, especially with initial investment outlays and sometimes research and development becoming more necessary and ever more costly. By the setting up of branch plants not only products but also production methods were more readily transferred. It could be argued that branch plant operation would mean that all new ideas would continue to be derived from the parent but in fact this rarely proved to be the case. Either the offspring developed an independence of its own or the appearance of new products and new production techniques stimulated the search for new ideas in all countries concerned. Often it was the most modern sectors of industry which were introduced by foreigners – electro-chemical and metallurgical industries in Norway, ore mining in Northern Sweden, steel in Russia, electrical engineering in Hungary. Yet it was not always so; shipbuilding, for example, usually grew from local roots in the smaller and greater industrial countries – in the Netherlands, Denmark, Norway and Italy for example. But in all these countries there were long traditions of shipbuilding and a continuous process of development in technology. Sharp discontinuities normally required imported techniques.

But now we must turn from these general remarks about the growth of technology and study in some detail events in particular industries so that our later discussion of the role of such changes in the development of individual countries will be more readily understood.

THE DEVELOPMENT OF TECHNOLOGY

– Coal

Coal was to a considerable degree the key to nineteenth-century industrial growth. It was the source of fuel for stationary steam engines and for locomotives and steamships and played an essential role in the manufacturing process for several metals and minerals, but above all for iron. Water power continued to be used throughout the century and still by 1900 many of the largest textile mills in Germany for example were so powered. Pneumatic power was applied to a variety of hand tools and at the end of the century hydro-electric plants came into use for generating electricity. Fuel oil and petroleum were growing in importance but all these other fuels were very marginal. Coal was king. Being bulky and heavy in relation to its value, transport costs were an important element in the final cost of coal and in most countries a major contribution of railways came through its carriage. In Russia in 1913, for example, 22 per cent of all railway freight traffic by weight was coal. In the great coalfield of north western Europe, covering the Ruhr, Belgium, Luxembourg and France pithead prices varied widely; Belgian coal at the end of the nineteenth century could be half as expensive again as Ruhr coal. But not much coal moved from cheap to dear areas because of the weight of these transport costs. Even so, from an economic point of view progress in the industry derived more from the reduction of such costs and from the opening up of new mines than from any striking developments in coal-mining technology. Early mining consisted simply of shallow pits sunk into out-cropping measures. The Belgian fields were the best known and best developed in eighteenth-century Europe. The seams outcropped onto valley sides and could easily be worked from horizontal galleries. But as demand grew it was necessary to sink deeper shafts and to install pumping machinery to remove the flood water. The first Newcomen steam engine in Europe for this purpose was installed at Jemeppe sur Meuse in 1720. In 1790 the maximum depth of the Belgian mines did not exceed 220 metres; by 1838 the deepest was 437 metres and by 1866 there were a number of 700–900 metres and one of 1,965 metres. But mining at this depth brought other problems. The use of steam to raise coal from the pit bottom was first introduced in Hainaut in 1807. Later iron wire replaced rope for haulage and such wire was being made in Germany by the mid-1830s. Metal cages running in guide rails replaced hanging baskets and the shafts were strengthened with a revetment of iron. The Davy lamp (1816) and improvements by Meuseler in Belgium and Marsaut in France helped overcome the problem of identifying firedamp and as early as 1823 its use was made obligatory in French mines most open to this danger. Greater ventilation struck at the gas itself. Fire placed under one of two shafts gave satisfaction in Britain but not in Belgium where the mines were deeper, the galleries lower and the gas concentration often more intense. Various types of ventilator fans were introduced; that of Théophile Guibral was for many years found almost universally throughout Europe. Underground the horse gave way to stationary engines for haulage in the main road-ways and at the face ponies replaced boys.

Above all it was geological factors which determined how effec-tively these new methods could be employed. None of them could fully resolve the basic physical difficulties of the Belgian mines, for example. Seams grew narrower and more irregular; roofs needed more timbering, the coal more washing. Belgian coal mining was thus coming to the point of diminishing returns just as the fields in the Ruhr and the Pas de Calais were being opened up. At first Ruhr coal was easy to get but the seams sloped downwards and as mining moved northwards the shafts became progressively deeper. Even there despite the large size of mining unit which averaged over 800 men per pit at the end of the century, labour productivity began to fall. It did the same in many parts of Europe, though the absolute levels of output per head varied greatly as Table 13 shows. Productivity in Upper Silesia and Poland in 1913

Table 13. *Annual output per man employed in the coal industry, 1874–1913.*

| | Metric tons | | | |
	U.K.	*France*	*Belgium*	*Germany*
1874/8	270	154	135	209
1894/8	287	208	174	262
1909/13	257	195	159	256

Source: British Parliamentary Papers, *Royal Commission on the Coal Industry* (1926), Vol. 1, p. 127.

was even higher than that in Britain and the Ruhr. The natural conditions there were the best in Europe, rich in workable seams, often very thick, fairly free of faults, only moderately inclined and with little trouble from gas. More detailed figures give us the relative position of the main fields in Europe in 1913 – this time in tons per manshift. At the head was Upper Silesia ($1 \cdot 131$), Poland ($1 \cdot 125$) and the U.K. ($1 \cdot 016$). Then came the Czech fields ($0 \cdot 955$) and the Ruhr ($0 \cdot 93$), the small Dutch field ($0 \cdot 807$), the Saar ($0 \cdot 79$), France ($0 \cdot 69$) and finally Belgium ($0 \cdot 53$).[2]

The industry remained very labour intensive and productivity dependent upon natural conditions. Size of operation and the length of shifts were responsible for some differences but the possibilities of substituting capital for labour were very limited except at the pithead. There one might find an array of plant for loading, conveying, sorting and washing coal, though even so female labour, with little alternative work available, was widely used for this work. Pneumatic boring machines were introduced in the late 1850s but machine cutting had to await the coming of cheap steel for the cutters and a cheap, safe form of power. Compressed air was safe but there were big transmission losses from compressor to machine. The availability of electric power brought improvements in underground haulage but prior to 1914 had not much affected the getting of coal in Europe. In 1913 8 per cent of coal output was cut by machine in Britain, 10 per cent in Belgium, 2 per cent in the Ruhr compared with 51 per cent in the United States. It was still basically a pick and shovel industry, fundamentally different from most others in that the technological transfer from other industries was minimal so far as the coal face was concerned. Like house building, the industrial revolution to a major degree passed it by.

Given these very limited advances in technology, it is not surprising that labour productivity fell, for remarkable increases in output were

[2] *British Parliamentary Papers, Report of the Technical Advisory Committee on Coal Mining* (1944–5), Vol. IV, p. 141.

Table 14. *Annual average output of coal (including lignite) in Europe 1830–1913.*

	Austria-Hungary	France	Metric tons Germany	Russia	Belgium
1830–4	0·15	2·0	1·9	—	2·4
1870–4	7·2	15·4	41·4	1·0	14·7
1890–4	19·9	26·3	94·0	7·1	19·9
1910–13	33·5	39·9	247·5	30·2	24·8

Source: B. R. Mitchell, Statistical Appendix, *Fontana Economic History of Europe* (London, 1971), vol. 4, p. 37; N. T. Gross, 'Economic growth and consumption of coal in Austria and Hungary', *Journal of Economic History* vol. xxxi., (1971).

called for by the insatiable demands of industrial growth, as shown in Table 14. Inevitably the trend of coal prices remained above that of most other industrial inputs, for miners were by no means the lowest paid of industrial workers at the end of the nineteenth century. Almost everywhere coal miners were the hardest part of the labour force to recruit. The job was unpleasant and very dangerous and the mines were frequently located in rural areas. Though centres of industry developed near coal resources, the opening up of the coalfields inevitably took the mines and their villages some distance from the urban centres.

– Textiles

In most countries of Europe industrialisation flowed first through the textile industries, above all through cotton manufacture. The reasons for the predominance of textiles are not too hard to find. There was a ready market at home; skilled labour formed a relatively low proportion of total labour requirements; the initial investment could be quite modest; the technology was capable of considerable adjustment according to the qualities of labour available. In any case, so great were the cost advantages of most of the new machines developed, for the most part in England, that they could not be ignored with impunity for long.

Although there was a long history of improvements in textile technology, the eighteenth century saw the beginning of a series of innovations which permitted vast increases in output, improvements in quality and quality control, and reductions in cost which far surpassed anything that had gone before. Most of these machines were initially designed for use by the newly growing cotton industry.

The reasons for this are partly that the technology was most easily applied to that fibre, partly that demand for cottons was most elastic and partly because it was a new industry lacking in established traditions. The raw material, the labour and the quality of the product were more firmly controlled by entrepreneurs in cotton than in other textiles, possibly because cotton was imported. So the capitalists could respond particularly rapidly to market changes. Before the machine age cotton would be opened, cleaned and carded, that is to say disentangled, by hand into a loose roll. It was then drawn out and slightly twisted on a spindle into a 'roving' and then spun into yarn by much the same technique. The new machine technology in spinning involved two new concepts. The first was to apply rollers to the manipulation of the yarn; it was first developed in England by Wyatt and Paul in the 1730s but more effectively by Richard Arkwright with his water frame (1769) which required the external power of a horse or water and produced a strong well twisted yarn for hosiery and cotton warp. The second idea, seen first in Hargreaves' spinning jenny (1765) though similar machines were being developed in Belgium at the same time, was to mount the spindles on a moveable carriage to reproduce the essential features of the drawing out of the yarn in hand spinning but to permit several spindles – eight initially – to be worked at once. With the jenny the operator turned the spindles by a wheel set to his right hand and moved the carriage with the left. It produced a fine but weak yarn suitable for weft. The mule (1779) combined the rollers of the frame with a moveable carriage technique of the jenny. Its chief merit was to allow considerable variations in the relationship of the speed of operation of the spindles and that of the rollers and moving carriage so permitting the spinning of every type of yarn. The machine was also capable of much refinement over time. Crompton's first mule was a clumsy wooden affair with twelve spindles; by 1795 it was a cast iron device and 180 spindles were already to be found. By 1830 there were machines of 300 spindles and by 1914 as many as 1,200. The speed of operation was accelerated too, though this could be varied to fit in with the skills of the operatives. The self-acting mule developed by Richard Roberts in the late 1820s brought all the complicated operations under power, for to that time several, including reversing the spindles to 'back off' the yarn, were done by hand. It was the self-actor which brought great economies of large scale operations to spinning.

In general, the gains in cost were large, the yarns were more regular in quality and finer yarn could be spun than ever before. Very fine yarn, for example, fell to one quarter of its previous price in Britain between the mid-1780s and the end of the century though prices in general were rising over those years. The price tended to stabilise at about half of the 1800 level three decades later, though by this time to the new spinning techniques had been added various types of cylindrical machines providing continuous carding, drawing and roving prior to spinning. Carding was a process for disentangling, straightening out and interlacing fibres: before the machine age it was carried out with a wire toothed board held in each hand. By 1785 Arkwright had developed a continuous carding machine, using a cylinder covered with card teeth from which the cotton was removed by a comb. A later development was to make spinning continuous with carding instead of the can of roving having to be carried from one machine to another. This machine was the work of J. C. Bodmer, a Swiss who lived for many years in Lancashire, though it was more used on the continent than in Britain. New techniques emerged for opening the cotton and in the United States the cotton gin was developed to remove the seeds from the cotton mechanically, so bringing down the cost of the raw material. For the manufacturer fixed costs were not all that high. A new 180 spindle mule cost £38 in Britain in 1795 but second-hand machines were available to experimenters on the continent. Nor was there need for large or purpose-built mills in the early days. A steam engine was another matter. The cheapest around 1800 cost about £500 but this would drive over 2,000 spindles and the beginner would hardly want to start on such a scale. But there were already second-hand engines and in any case water wheels were far more widely used on the continent and could be fully installed for half the horse power cost of a steam engine though above a certain number of spindles the wheel usually required a supplementary steam engine. The steam engine also guaranteed continuous production better than a water wheel. The first jenny entered France in 1773: the first mechanical spinning mill was set up in 1778. Mechanical spinning was first seen in Prussia in 1791, in Russia in 1793 and in Switzerland in 1794. The appearance of the mule led to a decline in the frame but after the Napoleonic Wars demand moved towards coarse strong yarn and the frame returned in an improved form known as the throstle. The basic difference was that the frame/throstle machines drew the roving out and then twisted whereas the jenny/mule types did both simultaneously in imitation of hand spinning. The mule was essentially an intermittent process and the throstle continuous. The self actor was adopted in Europe rather more slowly than other machines; it was relatively expensive and most useful where labour costs were highest. It was not used for cotton in Alsace until 1852 and in Germany not until the 1860s.

For wool spinning it arrived in Alsace in 1838 but was not adopted until the 1850s: in Germany it was first used in 1859. In general worsted spinning was mechanised earlier than woollen partly because the parallel wool fibres of worsteds were more akin to the cotton fibres for which the machines were originally designed and because raw material costs were higher in woollens. This made the saving of labour costs less urgent in that branch of the industry.

Hand weaving consists basically of sending a shuttle holding the weft, or cross threads, through the warp, or lengthways threads and driving the weft threads closely together to form an even cloth. The alternate warp threads are raised and lowered by healds operated by foot treadles, forming a passage or 'shed' for the shuttle. The suspended lathe provides a bed along which the shuttle runs and also enables the weaver to beat together the weft threads. John Kay's flying shuttle, brought to France from England in 1747, speeded up the process by enabling the weaver to throw the shuttle entirely with one hand and swing the lathe with the other. It was the disequilibrium in supply that this helped to create that encouraged the search for faster spinning methods though the flying shuttle was not used in worsted manufacture because of yarn defects until mill spun yarn arrived. These spinning advances in turn created a bottleneck in weaving which proved technically much more difficult to overcome. Cartwright's power loom of 1787 was only the first of numerous efforts at a solution of the problems of coordinating the basic movements of healds, shuttle and lathe and driving them from one source of power as well as arranging for the loom to stop if the thread broke. Until the end of the Napoleonic Wars it was no more than novelty. A variety of machines were then turned out by men such as Horrocks, Roberts and Hattersley in Britain, Heilmann, Koechlin and Magnan in France, Schönherr in Germany, to mention only the most famous.

In Belgium the absence of a tariff on imported yarn and the concentration of production on goods at the lower end of the quality range encouraged producers to shift more quickly to mechanical weaving than elsewhere but in most countries hand weaving lingered on in cotton and even more in wool and linen for a surprising length of time. In the Zollverein in 1861 there were 6,250 power looms in woollen and worsted mills as against 21,000 hand looms in such mills and 67,000 in cottages and small workshops. In all Germany there were 125,000 hand looms and 57,000 power looms in cotton manufacture at that date and 200,000 hand and 80,000 power looms in the same industry in France in 1866. In Russia in 1910 still some 15 per cent of factory-made cotton yarn was sold to the kustarny hand loom weavers and this takes no account of the yarn produced by home workers themselves. Why did the hand method survive so long? In part it was a technical question; power weaving of cotton did not become seriously competitive with the hand loom even in Britain until the 1830s and in the Yorkshire wool textile industry it was little used at all before 1840. In woollens the cost advantage was even less than in worsteds and cottons, for the variety of finished products precluded the long runs so suited to power weaving. The initial cost of power looms was high and the machine called for immediate reorganisation of work but above all the delay must be attributed to the fact that hand weaving was part of a whole social system. Income earned in hand weaving was but one element of a much broader pattern of economic activity and landlord/tenant or master/serf relationships. Where the cost reduction achieved by mechanical methods was quick and drastic as in spinning, the domestic industry was shattered despite the social ties; where it was less dramatic, as in weaving, the old methods survived much longer. In fact it is more correct to say that the range of factors influencing the adoption of power weaving caused it to be unusually regional in its impact. The hand loom disappeared far more quickly in Alsace and Bavaria than in most other parts of France and Germany for example. It went quickly in Belgium too – except in linens where the pressure to mechanise was less – because the social system had already geared itself in the previous century to adjust to the conflicting demands of agriculture and domestic industry.

These changes in spinning, weaving and the preparatory stages were accompanied by improvements in the finishing techniques. By the end of the eighteenth century roller printing of cloth over wood and copper blocks had come into use and it is significant that two of the major cotton manufacturing centres in Europe – Alsace and Ivanovo near Moscow, were initially centres for calico printing and there the mechanisation of this process went hand in hand with the adoption of other new technologies. There were, too, very important changes in chemical technology which lowered the costs of cleaning, dyeing and bleaching. Different fibres called for special machines. Wool for worsted spinning needs combing rather than carding in order to lay fibres as straight as possible. This proved difficult to mechanise and the problem was not satisfactorily resolved until in 1845 Josué Heilmann of Mulhouse produced a machine which could also be used in the manufacture of fine cotton yarn. In importance it ranks with the greatest textile inventions. It cut costs, made possible the use of short fibres for worsteds and combined with the use of cheap cotton warps, gave a new life to the worsted industry. Likewise it helped boost fine cotton spinning. In the last years of the eighteenth century the water frame was

modified to spin flax but the machine was not a success and in
1810 in France Philippe de Girard presented a solution whereby
the fibre was passed into a very alkaline solution before spinning
and he lived long enough to see it bring mechanisation of flax spinning to many parts of Europe. In 1832 he also developed a machine
for 'heckling' flax, basically the same process as combing.

The weaving of patterns called for different sets of warp threads
to be raised at intervals rather than the straightforward lifting of
alternate threads in plain weaving. This laborious process was
usually carried out by a draw boy who inevitably much slowed the
whole operation. Many attempts were made in France to mechanise
the technique for silk weaving and the Jacquard loom which came
at the end of the eighteenth century was the final synthesis of these
experiments, enabling all the operations of pattern weaving to be
worked from the loom by one man. It was quickly adopted in silk
because the benefits were large and obvious. In 1788 there were
14,800 looms in Lyons of which about 100 were types developed by
precursors of Jacquard. By 1833 there were 32,000 looms of which
20,000 were of the Jacquard type. As with many machines this
too, proved difficult to adapt for other fibres but by the 1820s they
were being used in Switzerland for weaving fancy cottons and in the
next decade for patterned worsted cloths.

The second half of the nineteenth century brought a mass of
improvements in all branches of textile technology, few very radical
but all cumulating into striking reductions of cost and improvements
in product. At the bottom end of the spectrum, for example, came the
growth of the shoddy industry as machines and chemical processes
made possible increased utilisation of waste. Rag wool came to
provide more and more of the materials used in the woollen industry,
though not the worsted, and the process contributed heavily to
making woollen cloth more competitive in price throughout Europe.
Automatic feed mechanisms were developed for many processes,
including carding. Rotary machines replaced the old fulling stocks
in the most important finishing process for woollen cloth.

But the most important innovation in the second half of the
nineteenth century was the improvement in the continuous spinning
techniques of the throstle brought about by the introduction of ring
spinning. The throstle was much more popular for cotton on the
continent than in Britain because it was used for spinning coarse
yarn which was more important for the cotton industry there. On
the other hand, the mule was preferred for worsted spinning in
France, and this enabled that industry to specialise in producing
fine cloths. Ring spinning originated in the United States in 1828
but was little used until the 1870s, by which time it had been much

G

ring sp f. coarse yarn

improved. Ring spinning with its high degree of twist was not suitable for producing fine yarn but it was adopted rapidly in those European countries concentrating on coarse yarn. Industries growing late in the nineteenth century used a particularly high proportion of rings as Table 15 shows – Italy, Sweden, Norway and Denmark,

Table 15. *The cotton spinning industry in Europe in 1912–13*

	Spindles 000	% Mule		Spindles 000	% Mule
U.K.	55,653	81·0	France	7,400	54·0
Germany	11,186	46·0	Russia	7,668	43·0
Poland	1,322	33·0	Italy	4,600	25·0
Austria	4,909	51·0	Spain	2,000	40·0
Belgium	1,492	33·0	Switzerland	1,398	82·0
Netherlands	479	41·0	Sweden	534	27·0
Portugal	480	27·0	Denmark	90	16·0
Norway	75	28·0			

Source: J. A. Todd, *The Cotton World* (London, 1927), p. 169

for example. Switzerland, with a much greater emphasis on fine spinning maintained the mule to the same extent as Britain and so did the Nord region of France. In most of Germany the bulk of spinning was for counts up to 50 and so rings were popular but in Saxony, where the demand was for soft spun hosiery yarns, the mules were predominant. (Count is a measure of the quality of yarn: the higher the count the finer the yarn; 50 is of medium quality.) The important thing to note is that retention of an older form of technology in no way indicated poor entrepreneurial behaviour. We can see this clearly from an Italian computation made in 1912. The cost per pound of spinning count 16 yarn (very coarse yarn) was 1·02 cents by rings and 1·53 cents by mules or half as much again. At count 40, however, the relative costs were 4·1 cents and 3·54 respectively. It was around count 40 that it was generally felt that ring spinning lost its advantage. Ring spinning was also used for spinning and twisting worsted yarn but only for twisting woollen yarn. Automatic (Northrop) looms, so-called because the supply of weft was continually replenished without stopping the loom, and electric drive were other major changes coming at the turn of the century but by 1914 their impact had not yet been of major significance.

Table 15 shows the enormous dominance of Britain in cotton spinning, a dominance which was paralleled in weaving too. The situation was very different in wool textiles: it is difficult to obtain accurate figures of output, but one estimate puts raw wool retained for home consumption at 492 million lb in Britain in 1902, 457 millions in France, 380 millions in Germany, 132 millions in Austria Hungary and 59 million lb in Italy. An alternative measure is given in Table 16.

Table 16. *Capacity in the Wool Spinning Industry in 1913*

| | 000 spindles | | |
	Worsted yarn	Woollen yarn	Both
France	2,366	712	
Germany (excl. Alsace)	2,364	n.a.	
Italy	378	521	
Russia			1,500

Source: Committee on Industry and Trade, *Survey of Industries* (London, 1928), part III, pp. 242–56.

There were interesting contrasts in the structure of the cotton industry throughout Europe. The Italian industry, for example, followed the British and Swiss pattern with considerable differentiation of function between plants. In 1912 60 plants did both spinning and weaving, 56 only spun and 225 only wove. The patterns may have had something to do with the strong influence of Swiss managers and superintendents and with direct Swiss investment. In Alsace in 1912 32 firms spun only, 94 wove only and 41 did both; in the Nord and Normandy integration was even less pronounced. This pattern of organisation hardly supports the view that it was the timing of innovation that determined the structure of the industry, that when both spinning and weaving could be mechanised together, both were put together. In fact in Britain and in other countries the trend towards integration came before 1850 and faded thereafter as firms strove for more specialised production. However, the Russian industry was highly integrated, despite the powerful English influence. Some of the plants were very large by any standards. The Krenholm mill at Narva near St Petersburg (Leningrad) was one of the biggest in the world, employing 12,000 workers with 475,000 spindles and 3,670 looms just before 1914. There were two other mills containing over 200,000 spindles. One reason for such integration and large size of mill in Russia was that output consisted mainly of long runs of coarse standardised cloth. Furthermore the need for the factory owners to create social overhead capital around the mills to the extent of creating whole villages with schools, churches and so forth encouraged a structure whereby the whole family could be employed and the full economies of scale reaped.

For every 100 roubles spent on building and equipping cotton mills it was estimated that 40–50 roubles were not infrequently spent on facilities outside the mill proper. The most important cotton mill in Germany before 1914 was the Augsburg Mechanische Baumwoll Spinnerei und Weberei with 127,000 spindles, nearly 3,000 looms and employing 3,000 workers.

But if the production of textiles was widely spread, output of the necessary machinery was highly concentrated. All but the most specialised of spinning machinery was a monopoly of a few British makers. Large firms produced standardised machines, utilising highly skilled labour with techniques that were difficult to adapt to simpler mass production methods, dominating the markets of the less developed nations such as India and China and offering overwhelming competition which tariffs as high as 50 per cent could not defeat. It was the outstanding nineteenth century case of a skill-intensive monopoly. Such firms saw no point in manufacturing overseas, though they set much store by their servicing facilities. Even in Alsace where there was a distinguished tradition of machine making, four fifths of the spinning machinery was English in 1912. Loom making was less completely dominated by the British; firms were smaller and demand both at home and overseas more subject to special whims and fancies. The Swiss were strong competitors here in some markets. In Italy in 1895, for example, four fifths of the spinning machinery was of British origin and the rest Swiss; but only three eighths of the power looms were British, half Swiss and the rest Italian. Possibly even more significant was the fact that half the steam engines were Swiss, three-eighths Italian from Tosi of Legnano and Neville of Venice and only about one eighth from Britain. But more of that side of the engineering industry later. Dyeing and finishing machinery was exported from Germany and Germany concentrated too on stocking, glove and lace machinery. Consequently, although British dominance was remarkably high, the demand for textile machinery throughout the world was so great that German exports of special types of machinery formed one of the largest groups in her exports of all types of machinery in 1913 – 116 m gold marks out of a total of 938 m for non-electric machinery. British exports were about four times as great, Swiss about a fifth the size of the German.

– Iron and Steel

If the textile industries were those first and most widely affected by the industrial revolution, it was the iron and steel industries that really set their stamp upon it. An industry hitherto functioning on a small scale, widely dispersed in rural areas, came to be concentrated in huge plants in a few favoured locations throughout the continent. By 1900 the greatest area of production covered the Ruhr, French Lorraine, Luxembourg and Belgium. Next in importance was the largely foreign-owned industry in the Russian Donbas and then there were older but still important industries in German Silesia, in Bohemia and in the Ural Mountains. Elsewhere there were centres old and new, grimly hanging on in competition with these major producers, either turning out specialities or enjoying substantial protection and subsidy. Such were the steel firms in Sweden, in Central France, in the Austrian alpine region, in Hungary and in Italy.

The main factors underlying these changes were two, technological advances affecting the utilisation of raw material and the fact that these and other technological changes put an immense premium on large scale production. The economies of scale were not by any means highly significant for every industry affected by technological change in the nineteenth century but for iron and steel they were vital in two critical ways. Once it became technically possible, it also became progressively more economic to concentrate the various stages of iron and steel manufacture and fabrication in one location, thereby saving costs of transport, utilising the by-products of one operation in another, above all gas, but most of all saving fuel by minimising the extent of reheating of the metal between one process and the next. Secondly, after the discovery of new methods of steel making, the optimal size of plant units – blast furnace, steel furnace, rolling mills – became ever higher, whereas before they had been restricted to a marked degree by the physical power of individual workers. The overall effect of these successive advances was a striking reduction over time in the prices of iron and steel. The Bessemer and subsequent steel making processes were particularly remarkable in their long run consequences; so rapid was the fall in price that a material which had hitherto been made only in very small amounts for special purposes, now competed with iron in every area of use and, despite further reduction in the cost of production of iron, had widely eliminated it by 1914.

The manufacture of iron and steel takes place in a series of stages. The process begins in the blast furnace where iron ore is converted into molten iron. The first of the technological advances of the eighteenth century made it possible to use coke for this process rather than charcoal. The new technology was slow to catch on in Europe for a variety of very good reasons and not always by any means because of ignorance or ineptitude. Demand for iron was not expanding rapidly. Coke blast iron was a poorer quality metal; it was not easy to change from one process to the other because existing furnaces were too small and the blast too weak. Above all the coke smelting process did not of itself significantly reduce costs over the charcoal process where charcoal was still easily available. In France, therefore, where coal deposits were widely scattered and distant from the ore, the advantages of coke smelting were negligible. What it did do was to ease the situation created by the high cost of charcoal in Britain and so cut back the profitable export of iron to Britain from Sweden and Russia. It was only when it became possible to use mineral fuel for subsequent stages of production and so to establish integrated plants on the coalfields that the use of charcoal disappeared quickly. After 1850 charcoal smelting rapidly gave way to coke in France and Prussia; in places where coal was expensive it lasted much longer. In Italy charcoal smelting began to disappear with the imposition of tariff protection in the 1880s; in Sweden it remained universal right to 1914. By the second half of the nineteenth century, however, improvements in blast-furnace technique, above all the use of a hot blast, and increases in size of furnace, had made coke smelting much the more economic process. Inevitably the constant improvements in fuel economy, first in iron and then in steel manufacture, made it more and more desirable to locate the industry for proximity to ore supplies rather than to the fuel.

Iron from the blast-furnace may be poured into moulds and such cast iron is put to use where strength is required and its brittle qualities are no great disadvantage. It was widely employed as the support for all types of machinery, for example. Cast iron cannot be shaped in any other way, however, and the bulk of the output of the blast furnace was cast in the form of rough 'pigs' and then subjected to further refining to remove most of the remaining carbon to produce wrought iron which would then be squeezed, hammered or cut into whatever shapes were required. In the eighteenth century the making of wrought iron involved a long and costly process of heating and beating in charcoal fires. In 1784 Henry Cort achieved one of the most dramatic cost-reducing triumphs of the industrial revolution through his puddling and rolling process, whereby the pig was decarburised in a reverbatory furnace where coke could be used, since fuel and metal did not come into direct contact with each other. Instead of being hammered, the metal was put through a series of rotating rollers which not only completed the refining process but also produced iron in standardised crude shapes. Cort's invention was followed by a whole succession of improvements, saving fuel, ore and labour but the puddling furnace itself resisted such change. It was limited in size to the physical ability of the puddler to use his puddling iron to stir, divide and remove the molten iron. He became the true aristocrat of the industrial revolution for his strength and his skill, but above all because his function was resistant to technological change. Attempts to mechanise the process achieved a small measure of success on the other side of the Atlantic but the problem was eventually resolved in an entirely different way. Significantly enough, in stumbling on a technique which would eventually replace iron by steel, Sir Henry Bessemer was really seeking to make iron without a puddler. Some steel was also made by the puddling process by shortening the burn and leaving a higher carbon content in the metal. Krupps did this, and so did makers in Carinthia and the Harz mountains, but the metal was of poor quality and the process never more than a technical curiosity.

Coke refining was quickly taken up because the cost advantage was very marked, the quality of coal was less important than for coke smelting and the plant easier and cheaper to construct. So on the continent, as in the United States, coke refining came before coke smelting though their invention and use in Britain came in reverse order. In 1821 puddling was introduced in Belgium; in the same decade it came to Aachen and the Saar and coal was shipped up the Rhine to the works of the Siegerland for the purpose. In 1827 149 puddling furnaces in France produced 40,000 tons of iron. In 1830 it came to Vitkovice in Galicia, in 1835 to Upper Silesia. But the full solution of integrated coke smelting and refining was an expensive undertaking and for a time a mix of new and old technologies resulted. In any case poor transport allowed the small man to retain his local market. In 1830, for example, in France coke-smelted pig formed only 9 per cent of total output but coke-refined wrought iron was already a third of total output. So puddlers imported their iron from small local smelters or, if conveniently located, from Britain. But the market prospects for wrought iron began to develop quickly as it was required for constructional purposes, especially for bridges, for iron plates, for industrial machinery and, above all, for iron rails. Rails, and to some extent plates, could only be made on a big scale and so more and more integrated plants began to emerge. This process was given a significant boost in certain places by the fortunate existence of black band ore where iron ore and coal were found together in the same formations – in the Ruhr for example. Even though this ore usually ran out quickly, the initial impetus to growth was all-important.

The Bessemer process of steel making, discovered in 1857, was astonishingly simple; air was blown through the molten iron in a 'converter', rapid decarburisation followed and steel, which is in effect iron with a somewhat higher carbon content, was produced in about twenty minutes. Since no heat was applied, iron was ideally used direct from the blast-furnace and it rapidly became apparent that the process was suitable for use only with haematite ore which had a low phosphorus content, ore which was much less widely available in Europe than the high phosphorus 'minette' ore. The first plants in Europe were set up in Sweden and France experimentally in 1858. In Germany Krupp erected a Bessemer plant at Essen in 1862; in Austria a small converter was built in Styria in 1863 and a larger plant at Vitkovice in 1866. The speed of diffusion is impressive, though the supply of the right kind of iron remained a problem and for a time both Belgium and the Ruhr imported pig from Britain for the purpose.

Almost immediately an alternative 'open hearth' process became available. The essential characteristic of this technique was the regenerative principle, whereby waste gas from the blast furnace or gas from low grade coal was used to heat a honeycomb of bricks and these in turn superheated air and gas fuel which combined in the furnace to heat metal in a shallow oblong box of heat resisting material – the hearth. The principle was first developed in Britain by Sir William Siemens and shortly after, in 1864, Pierre and Émil Martin succeeded in making steel by adding scrap to the molten metal in their small works at Sireuil in Charente in France. Two years later they made an agreement with Siemens which laid the foundation for the subsequent development of the Siemens–Martin process. It was used more widely in Britain than elsewhere; in 1913 79 per cent of steel was made in that manner there, compared with 40 per cent in Germany, 34 per cent in France and none in Belgium. The Bessemer process was cheaper, though the metal was more approximate in quality. Such steel was produced in very large plants and was particularly well suited to steel rail making. The Siemens–Martin produced a more homogeneous steel, closer to specification, best for custom work in which the British industry specialised. The ability to use scrap metal and the high efficiency of relatively small furnaces made the Siemens process a godsend to small producers and to countries deficient in coal. A steel-using firm such as Burmeisters in Denmark could now economically use scrap to produce some of their own steel plates. Italy too, found it very valuable and it made possible the location of plants near the markets instead of on the coast – at Milan for example. In 1913 there were 67 open hearth furnaces in Italy and only two Bessemer converters, together turning out some 850,000 tons of steel.

There remained the question of using the ample supplies of

phosphoric ore. Some attempt was made to leach ores to reduce the phosphoric content – at the Vitkovice works in Galicia for example – but with little success, though the ore so produced was good enough for making puddled iron. The problem was finally resolved by the Gilchrist Thomas process of 1878. Limestone was added to the molten metal to combine with the phosphorus; it was removed in the form of a slag which was subsequently pulverised and used for fertiliser. The furnaces were lined with dolomite bricks to prevent the slag from eating away at the usual 'acid' silicon bricks. Steel made from this ore was known as 'basic' steel as opposed to 'acid' steel made from non-phosphoric ore. The new technique was seized on within months, for it made possible exploitation of the deposits of minette ore in German and French Lorraine and, after 1890, the rich ores of northern Sweden.

Not every raw material problem was satisfactorily resolved in this way, however. In Galicia, for example, the difficulty was that the rather poor ore had not sufficient phosphorus content to be used by the basic process but too much for the acid. The solution, evolved at Vitkovice, was to devise a duplex process; molten metal was placed in an acid furnace and then transferred to a basic lined furnace. It sounds simple but there were immense problems to be solved, for the pig changed its chemical content during the transfer and it was always difficult to synchronise the work of two types of furnace. The duplex process was employed on a small scale in Britain, in the United States, Canada and Japan but not elsewhere in Europe.

After 1900 the availability of cheap power from hydroelectric stations made possible some small advances in the smelting of steel in electric furnaces. The quality of such steels was very high, since the impurities inevitably introduced when coke is used as a fuel were reduced to a minimum and the technique was attractive to countries deficient in coal. Even so, the demand for so expensive a material was not great and the whole technique was still in its infancy in 1914. In 1908 there were seven electric furnaces in Germany, five in Austria and the same number in France, four in Italy, three in Sweden, two in Switzerland and one in Luxembourg and Spain. In 1912 German output of electric steel was 74,000 tons compared with her total steel output of over 18m tons.

Along with these basic advances in production methods went improved techniques of handling, use of more powerful and complex rolling equipment and the development of electric drive, though as was the case with cotton mills to 1914 the latter was by no means invariably the least expensive technique. Two advances deserve special mention. One was the increase in blast furnace size; the average German furnace produced 5,000 tons a year in 1870; by

1895 it was some 27,500 tons and in 1910 49,000 tons, two thirds above the average British furnace. In Westphalia the average was more like 60,000 tons; in the Russian Donbas the average in 1912 was about 50,000 tons, though for all Russia it was only a little over a half that level. The second advance was improvement in coke oven practice and here the continental producers were clearly in the lead. In 1861 the Belgian, Évence Copée, pushed up the coke yield greatly by his invention of the coke retort oven which was improved and marketed by the German firm of Otto and Co. The Pernolet oven was devised in France in 1862 for the recovery of the by-products of coking; five years later came the Carvés oven, producing high temperature tar as well as coke. From 1880 to 1900 by-product ovens improved rapidly and became more widely used. The production of tar by that method was one of the foundations of the German organic chemical industry. Blast-furnace gas engines were pioneered by Cockerills in Belgium and far more rapidly adopted on the continent than in Britain, partly at least because of differences in fuel costs.

Integration of steel plants may be defined in a variety of ways. It may mean integration forwards into structural and mechanical engineering or backwards into the ownership of coal and ore mines. Table 17 gives details of integration of a more restricted kind – in

Table 17. *Integrated steel plants in 1913*

	No. of plants	% share of regional output
Ruhr	14	84
Saar	4	88
Belgium	15	97
Nord and Pas de Calais	5	81
German Lorraine	5	64
French Lorraine	10	72

Source: N. J. G. Pounds and W. Parker, *Coal and Steel in Western Europe* (London, 1957), p. 305.

steel making itself from the blast-furnace to the production of bars, rails, strip, etc. and shows how significant this had become in north western Europe by 1913. Only in Luxembourg/Lorraine was there any marked absence of integration, largely because there was considerable specialisation on the production of pig iron in that area for export to other steel producing centres – notably to the Ruhr.

Not all countries shared equally in these advances. In general the

German industry led the way in adoption of new technologies, in size of plant, in integration though not, to any marked degree, in the development of new ideas. The reasons for this leading role will be discussed elsewhere in this book. Certainly an important change came over steel technology after 1880. Before that time discoveries had been largely empirical; thereafter they resulted more from chemical research and the work of trained metallurgists. It is possible that the high quality of German technical education was particularly helpful in these circumstances. Yet the argument is less convincing than it is for the German superiority in chemicals. France had its Écoles Superieures des Mines in Paris and St Étienne. Furthermore knowledge of new processes was readily available in excellent journals such as *Stahl und Eisen* and *Annales des Mines* and few attempts were made to stifle progress by patent action. In any case, after 1895 the French industry showed a remarkable resilience in this as in many other sectors. Like the British steelmakers, the Belgian industry seemed to lose some of its *élan* in the years before 1914. It was the first to adopt puddling on the continent and the last to stop; the penalties of an early start seem to have been very severe. Yet in Russia the newly created steel industry of the Donbas derived much of its knowledge of the latest technologies from Belgian industrialists. It is a point which would hardly justify reference to general entrepreneurial weakness among this group. Not all the new developments originated with the major producers. It was during the second half of the nineteenth century that the Austrian steel industry began to establish that reputation for technical ingenuity and inventiveness that it has never lost. In part it derived from the need to overcome a poor resource endowment; in part it came too from institutions of such excellence as the Montanische Hochschule at Leoben. It was an Austrian, Franz Koller, who in 1885 invented the first of the alloy steels – tungsten steel – which were eventually to be used for metal cutting, allowing machine-tools to be run at faster speeds than ever before.

The reduction of the cost of iron and then of steel were crucially important for the whole process of industrialisation in the nineteenth century, so all-pervasive was the influence of the metal. Through its use in machine making, constructional work, for rails, for ships and locomotives, for weapons of war, it had a tremendous expansionary effect. From 1880 to 1914 European steel output grew at some 4 per cent per annum and in only eight years did output drop at all. Only from 1882 to 1886 did it fall for more than one year at a time. In an industry where scale effects were considerable, growth of this order tended to become cumulative because of its own contribution to the reduction of costs.

If the German industry led the way in size of output by the end of the period – see generally Table 18 – and in rates of growth at least to 1900, in the following years rates of growth at least com-

Table 18. *Annual average production of crude steel, 1880–1913*

	Metric tons				
	1880–4	1910–13		1880–4	1910–13
Germany	0·1	16·2	Luxembourg	n.a.	1·3
France	0·5	4·1	Sweden	0·2	0·6
Italy	0·2	1·0	Austria–Hungary	0·1	2·5
Belgium	0·2	2·3	Russia	0·2	4·2
U.K.	1·9	6·9			

Source: B. Mitchell, Statistical Appendix, *Fontana Economic History of Europe* (London, 1971), vol. 4; C. Prêcheur, *La Lorraine sidérurgique* (Paris, 1959).

parable to the German were to be witnessed in many parts of Europe and it was in Russia just as much as in Germany that the largest plants most approximate to those in the United States were to be found. Modern or not, the Russian industry required very stiff tariff protection, as well as heavy subsidies. Russian costs were higher and the distance from the big markets of St Petersburg (Leningrad) and Moscow added more to costs than, say, the transport of steel by water from the Ruhr. Russian steelmasters enjoyed low raw material costs because of the high grade ore used, but they suffered severely from high coal prices compared with western steelmakers – this almost certainly more than poor utilisation of coal. There seems to have been little difference in labour costs per unit of output between east and west but in any case such costs were too small a part of total costs to make much difference.

The Italian steel industry also enjoyed the indirect benefit of subsidies though the level of tariff protection was not high by European standards and was particularly modest for imported pig iron. In fact the Italian industry depended upon a complex supply of materials. In 1913 she imported 222,000 tons of pig compared with home production of 432,000 tons and also imported 326,000 tons of scrap. There was in this a logical element of specialisation. Italy avoided to some degree that area of production where mineral fuel costs were relatively high and unavoidable – smelting – but concentrated more on using cold imported material in open hearth furnaces located near the sources of demand. Other factors dictated the use of this technique too; the Martin furnace was better for making the steel plates needed for shipbuilding and the minimum economic size of furnace was perhaps one fifth of that of a Bessemer converter. For a relatively small industry, scattered by historical locations and market needs, the choice was obvious. Total output in 1913 was modest but the misallocation of resources through developing this industry alleged by some writers is not very apparent given the degree of specialisation and the low tariff level. Similar specialisation was to be found elsewhere, of course. On the ore fields in Luxemburg, for example, twice as much pig was produced as finished steel in 1913.

All too often the steel industry is considered solely in terms of the great concentrations in the Ruhr and the Donbas. For the bulk trades this is true enough, but the technology was flexible enough to admit a wide range of other suppliers. Italy and Luxembourg specialised and adapted, as we have seen. Sweden supplied charcoal steel right to 1914; Styria also leaned more and more towards high quality manufacture. The Danes used scrap to turn out their highly specialised forgings: so much so that 7·5 per cent of the steel forgings used by British shipbuilders in 1914 came from Denmark. The Dutch even began making steel just before 1914 using a second-hand Bessemer converter, though admittedly this was a somewhat unusual occurrence.

– Engineering

Innovation and growth in iron and steel went hand in hand with developments in the prime using industry, engineering. The modern era in engineering opened with the new textile machines and the steam engine. The steam engine was developed almost entirely in Britain during the eighteenth century, first as a pump and subsequently to power machinery. James Watt's engine of the 1780s called for vast improvements in machining techniques and metallurgy before his concept became an engineering and commercial reality, though we do well to remember that experimental engines were successfully made on the continent at much the same time without attempting the level of sophistication achieved in Matthew Boulton's foundry in Soho, Birmingham. Textile machinery moved slowly from wood to iron construction and from water to steam power and the demands on machine tool makers became more acute as the machines grew in size, complexity and accuracy. Until the middle of the nineteenth century the British were unrivalled in machine tool making with their lathes for cutting revolving pieces of metal, planers and shapers for machining flat surfaces, boring machines for making cylinders and the gauges to ensure the desired accuracy. Along with these went machines such as Nasmyth's steam hammer, the epitome of power and delicacy, for precise forging of pieces of metal, large and small.

Isolated examples can be found of the use of steam power on the mainland of Europe before 1800 and steam engines were being built in France and Belgium in 1815. But it was only after that date that the real development got under way. Even more than in England, this growth of steam power was linked with mining and metallurgy rather than with textiles, initially at least. For pumping in mines, for powering rollers, for providing sufficient blast for iron smelting there was not the same alternative as there was between water and steam for textile machinery. Soon after the end of the Napoleonic Wars more and more independent builders began to emerge. Some, such as Egells who set up his machine shop in Berlin in 1821 and Harkort who began manufacture at Wetter in Westphalia two years earlier, had experience in British works. They imported and then copied British tools. The German, Franz Dinnendahl, described the problems of a pioneer steam engine maker of this time.

'It was impossible to find a smith who was capable of making an ordinary vice, never mind forge parts for machines, or do a piece of boring. I was obliged to do my own forging without ever having learned the job. However, I succeeded in forging with my own hands all the machine and even the boiler.'

The absence of someone skilled in forging plates explained the fragility and imperfections of his boiler and some of the parts of the engine such as the cylinders and pipes and pumps left much to be desired too. Nevertheless it worked, and Dinnendahl never had the advantage of a stay in Britain. It was Jacques-Constantin Périer at the Chaillot foundry who created the first great French mechanical engineering works, in fact the Soho of France. Not all of his first steam engine (1779) was locally made, for some of its more complicated parts were supplied by Boulton and Watt. But when he visited the works in 1786 Watt did not conceal his admiration and described Périer's steam engines as being 'excessively well' made. The more famous foundry at Le Creusot (1785) obtained many of its first engines and tools from Chaillot. After 1815 the manufacture of steam engines in France began to expand rapidly. Textile machinery makers such as Risler, Dixon, Schlumberger and Koechlin were very much to the fore as were general engineering shops such as those of Cavé, Hallette, Manby and, of course, Le Creusot. Many of these graduated later to locomotive building. Within a short space of time independent improvements in design began to emerge especially directed towards fuel economy, so much so that by the time of the Paris International Exhibition of 1862, British steam engines were being derided in comparison. It was the French too with their widely scattered coal resources, who led the way in improving the technology of water power. Fourneyron's machine of 1827, for example, is generally recognised as opening the modern era of practical water turbines. From the first his machine had the characteristics of a motor created for industrial use, and in 1843, ten years after the publication of his design, 129 factories had been created or enlarged using his turbines – in France, Germany, Austria, Italy, Poland and even one in Mexico. This was only one of a succession of French contributions of this kind in the first two-thirds of the nineteenth century: Koechlin, for example, built turbines to a new patent and at the Paris Exhibition of 1855 it was apparent that the French had created something of a monopoly in this field of technology.

Several of the major steam engine builders began as textile manufacturers, set up shops to repair machinery and engines and gradually changed over to concentrate upon their mechanical engineering work, though it was some considerable time before there was any considerable specialisation *within* these engineering shops. Escher Wyss and Sulzer in Switzerland and Cockerill in Belgium followed this path, for example. Koechlin and Schlumberger in Alsace followed the same course, though remaining textile spinners for a longer time too. By the late 1830s their reputation had grown to the stage that they were making copies of English self-acting mules for sale in Normandy and in foreign countries, even though these machines were not required in their local market for almost another decade.

In many countries the early engineering workshops became veritable training grounds for later engineers. In London the works of Maudslay and John Penn performed this role above all others. In Berlin there was the Egells iron foundry where many, including August Borsig who was soon to be running the largest mechanical engineering works on the continent, received their early training. It was the practical knowledge and experience of the industrialists themselves, of the managers and of the chief technical men that was the key to the growth of the industry from the supply side at least. Contrary to what is sometimes asserted, the skill required of the ordinary worker was no rare commodity, outside the machine-tool maker's shop. Even before the arrival of automatic tools the new machine tools of the industrial revolution eliminated the need for the highest manual skills. In any case reservoirs of skill quickly built up – in local jobbing shops, in local repair works for agricultural machinery, in local craft industries, in shipyards. Royal armaments factories and similar royal establishments were one of the biggest sources of such skills: almost every German state had one such institution and this gave Germany a real advantage in the development of machine construction. All this was intensified by the arrival of railways and iron ships with their need for ever larger repair and maintenance facilities. Skill was less important than factory discipline for any but the most specialised techniques.

But among the entrepreneurs there was no substitute for experience. Whether or not they went to technical schools, on the continent as in Britain most engineers were trained in the works of other engineers. Some like Gottlieb Daimler worked in Britain; sons frequently followed their fathers. The value of a very thorough understanding of a highly technical business clearly outweighed in many eminent examples the disadvantages of nepotism. Albert followed August Borsig, Heinrich followed Johann Jacob Sulzer, Charles Brown of Brown Boveri followed the same calling as C. E. L. Brown and there were many others.

The career of Brown, known as the father of Swiss mechanical engineering, is a fine example of the power of experience to transform a whole sector of industry. Discovered working at Maudslays, in 1851 he was persuaded to move to the Sulzer works at Winterthur. There Brown designed the epoch making steam engine – the *Ventilmaschine* – which swept through Europe, being quickly recognised as a far more efficient steam engine than the American Corliss valve engine which to then held the field. This discovery made Sulzers into one of the great engineering works of the continent. Brown was the engineer and Sulzer the entrepreneur. Later they pioneered together the application of superheated steam in engines. In 1871 Brown left Sulzers to manage the Winterthur locomotive works for thirteen years. His son, at the age of 23 was made director of the electrical department of the Oerlikon works, to that time just a small foundry, and there he pioneered long distance transmission of electric power. Eventually in 1891 he founded Brown Boveri and under his father's advice took up the manufacture of the steam turbine recently developed in Britain by Sir Charles Parsons and it was this which made this firm into one of the great names in European engineering within a decade. Such was the role of genius and experience. Without introducing factors of this kind the growth of machine building in Switzerland remains a great puzzle, for the range of home demand for machinery was in fact very limited indeed.

From the demand side no greater impetus to growth came to engineers than from the coming of the railway. Coach and wagon manufacture offered very few serious technical problems and gave considerable opportunities for benefiting from economies of batch production. There was a great deal of woodworking involved and wheels and axles could be bought out if necessary. So within a short time most countries, large or small, were providing their own rolling stock. Locomotive manufacture offered more serious problems but such were the market opportunities in the larger countries anyway that local manufacture quickly developed. But a sharp contrast between locomotives and rolling stock was apparent in the less advanced countries. Before 1878, for example, the Piedmont railways bought 6,947 carriages overseas and had 9,859 manufactured in Italy but of the 641 locomotives purchased only 39 were locally made to that time.

In France and Germany imports were dispensed with very quickly. Despite a slow start at railway construction in France, already in 1834 there were three firms in Alsace, including Koechlin, able to make locomotives, as well as the Hallette works at Arras and Le Creusot. In 1842 there were 146 locomotives in France of which 88 were English, but the role of the foreign made was declining rapidly and by 1854 French locomotive output was already running at some 500 per annum. It is noteworthy that for all France's alleged industrial retardation French makers were quickly numbered among Europe's major exporters, though they were helped by French investment in foreign railways. Of those 602 engines imported into Italy, for example, 372 came from France, mainly from the Koechlin works in Alsace. In Germany the same sequence is apparent. In 1842 of 245 locomotives in all the states 38 were German made: by 1851 there were 1,084 locomotives, 679 locally made. In Russia too very special efforts were made to promote the industry and by 1865 two fifths of the 660 locomotives in use had been locally made. Locomotive making began normally either in big metallurgical establishments such as Le Creusot and Cockerills, or in machine shops such as Borsig, Egells or Schwarzkopff in Berlin or Cavé in Paris. Koechlin followed the other classic engineering route – cotton spinners, textile machinery, locomotives. Initial orders from local lines encouraged a considerable dispersion of the industry quite apart from the large number of servicing workshops required. This was particularly true of the German states. The first German locomotive was made in Dresden: Borsig in Berlin made his first in 1841 as did Kessler in Karlsruhe and Maffei in Munich. Henschel in Cassel began construction in 1845, Egestorff in Hanover and Hartmann in Chemnitz (Karl Marx Stadt) in 1846 as well as Clett in Nuremberg who was soon to be a major force in bringing about the general development of engineering in Bavaria. By the end of the century the number of works had been reduced to about twenty, but several had reached massive size, employing up to 5,000 men on locomotive making alone.

In Vienna the State Locomotive Works employed 1,500 men and produced 140 locomotives at that date and the Budapest works were half as big again. In Russia the Kolomna works were turning out about 250 locomotives a year and at Sormovo near Nijni Novgorod was a works second only to Kolomna which had been set up by an American syndicate and the entire stock of machinery sent out from the United States. The smaller countries were by now well to the fore too. Sweden had exported her first locomotive as early as 1880. In Switzerland the Winterthur works made its 2,000th engine in 1909 and a high proportion had been exported. In Italy the Breda works had 2,000 men on making engines for home railways, using wheels and axles imported from Germany. In Belgium there were four well-known works, including the largest producing 200 engines a year. In Holland the Nederlandsche works had been established deliberately to reduce the virtual monopoly over supply hitherto held by the Manchester firm, Beyer Peacock, and even in Denmark a small manufacture was carried on at Århus and of course most coaches and wagons were made locally.

So emerged the largest area of engineering in Europe. Some were specialists; others such as Borsig, Cockerill, Carel, the Kolomna works had other and sometimes more important interests. Given expert chief designers, the technology was not difficult to achieve, though it was easier to substitute for imports than to win export orders. Tariffs, subsidies and conditions embodied in railway loan contracts all helped local builders. Possibly a more important factor in their favour was the fact that economies of scale were more often than not nullified by the European tradition of ordering to design. Only rarely were European engineers prepared to accept standard models and engines were invariably subjected to much costly finishing and detail. The practice went to extremes with French engineers but it was common for a locomotive to be carefully filed down by hand after completion and subjected to as many as twelve applications of paint and varnish.

There is no need here to analyse in detail the general economic impact of railways, or indeed of canals, as this forms an important part of our discussion of individual countries. The iron and later the steel industries benefited as engineering did. The huge investment required gave a marked boost to growth and since the capital market for railway and canal shares was often a very compartmentalised one and attractive to overseas investors, it did not necessarily draw funds heavily from the rest of the economy. The unusually large pool of unskilled labour required in construction rendered labour supply problems minimal. The effect of the reduction of transport costs has been a matter of some controversy of recent times. As Table 19

Table 19. *Typical costs of freight transport in Germany, 1800–1900*

	1800	Tons/km in pfennigs 1850	1875	1900
By main road	40	?	27	25
Railways	—	10	6·7	3·7
Rivers and canals	4	—	1·3	1
Sea	—	—	0·32	0·25

Source: S. N. Prokopowitz, *L'industrialisation des pays agricoles* (Neuchâtel, 1946), p. 112.

suggests, costs by water transport were considerably below those on rail but rail offered speed, flexibility and regularity, immensely important advantages in the land-locked areas of Europe where water traffic was much affected by the severe winters and where few natural waterways offered effective east-west links. Sometimes, too, the flow of the stream might move against the natural movement of the bulk traffic. This was so with the Danube. It was cheaper to take grain down river to the Black Sea, ship it to a northern port and carry it into central Germany by rail than to carry it by barge slowly upstream.

The last quarter of the nineteenth century saw far reaching innovations in engineering in Europe which came to establish a whole new set of comparative advantages and above all to offer great opportunities to newly developed and small countries. These industries owed little to British tools and traditions; much of their impetus derived from within Europe itself, though in manufacturing techniques they leaned heavily on the use of machine-tools created in the United States from the middle of the century onwards. These tools – milling machines, turret lathes, grinders – made it possible for unskilled workers to produce relatively small parts in large numbers with a high degree of accuracy, parts capable of being assembled into a final product without further hand fitting. The technique was first applied to the manufacture of guns, then to sewing machines, watches, agricultural machines, some electrical machinery, office machines, bicycles and, finally, to motor cars. The key to the successful imitation of these American technologies was the existence – or creation – of a large homogeneous demand, the development of

the relevant marketing techniques and the prefection of organisational reform within the factory. Even unhampered by the longer
industrial traditions of Britain, the adjustment was not easy. Sewing
machines made their way through being manufactured and serviced
in Europe by American firms; office machinery was largely imported
to 1914. On the other hand, the Swiss watch makers, taken by
surprise by American competition responded quickly and effectively;
the bicycle found better markets in Europe than across the Atlantic
once the American tools had been brought in to make them.

American-type farm machinery such as mowers, binders, reapers
was either imported or manufactured locally by branches of American
firms. For example, in 1907 in France 16,000 binders, 55,000 mowers
and 10,000 reapers were sold but of these only 600 binders, 200
reapers and 10,000 mowers were made locally. The rest came from
the United States and Canada. Ploughs were typically made locally
to fit real or imagined special requirements, though at Leipzig
Rudolph Sak's works were the largest in the world concentrating on
plough making and aggressive selling techniques gave him huge
markets in Russia and in Austria–Hungary. It was on the Hungarian
plain more than anywhere else that the massive application of
machine techniques to agriculture took place. Besides American
harvest machinery there was extensive use of steam threshers,
formerly imported from Britain but by the end of the century made
in Hungary in British-owned factories. There were, too, more
steam ploughs in Hungary than anywhere else in Europe, though
they were heavily used in the sugar beet district of Magdeburg in
Germany too.

Possibly the most spectacular development in Hungary was the
new technique of roller milling, developed in the 1840s. Grain was
passed through pairs of spirally fluted iron rollers, followed by
pairs of plain rollers. Huge milling establishments were set up as
well as foundries to make the rollers which were soon being exported
to all parts of Europe. This link with agricultural and general
engineering was an important factor in bringing industrialisation to
largely agricultural regions. By 1914 one of the greatest engineering
works in Europe was that of Ganz in Budapest. In the second half
of the nineteenth century they became well known as makers of
these cast iron rollers, exporting them even to the United States.
They also manufactured steam ploughs and railway equipment.
Later with the help of German capital they developed into one of
the foremost manufacturers of electrical equipment in Europe. Yet
this was not an unexpected isolated success. Establishments of this
kind were to be found in other places too, not so large perhaps but
following a similar pattern. In Sweden, for example, Bolinders

began a brilliant engineering record from the manufacture of steam saws and engines for the lumber industry. Swedish railway equipment was manufactured from the 1870s by existing firms that had grown up on agricultural demand. De Laval in Sweden and Burmeister in Denmark were eventually to go far beyond the initial spurts they enjoyed from making cream separators, though admittedly the latter already had a reputation in shipbuilding too by 1870.

Russian agricultural techniques were more backward than those in the west but the very size of the market encouraged the emergence of a large machinery industry there too before 1914. There was a German plant at Kharkov making threshers, seeders, hand rakes and reapers; another at Odessa making 120,000 ploughs a year with yet a third in Moscow operating at the same level of output. Then there was the great International Harvester plant already mentioned. There was a locally-owned centre of the agricultural machinery industry in the Berdiansk area of Southern Russia where machine techniques were in widest use. By 1913 there were altogether 800 factories in Russia employing 39,000 men on agricultural machine making, not including local peasant industries. The importance of all this for engineering in general in that country need hardly be stressed. Recent though it may have been, to think of such manufacture as unimportant by 1914 would be a most serious error.

Machine-tool making was the most highly skilled of all the engineering trades and it was dominated by German makers. In the heavy class of tool required by shipyards and railway workshops the Germans were almost on a par with the finest British makers but in making the newer lighter machine-tools originating across the Atlantic, they were well ahead. Ludwig Loewe in Berlin and the Reinecker and Wanderer works in Chemnitz produced machines of a quality and on a scale that was not matched elsewhere in Europe. In Berlin too the American Niles Company had set up a very modern factory. Inevitably German engineering firms benefited from close contact with such outstanding works which were centres for the diffusion of the latest ideas on machining, lubrication, and the organisation of machine work. In Belgium and France where machine-tool makers developed only slowly along these lines after 1870, the engineering industry as a whole suffered as a consequence.

– Power Engineering

The most significant new industrial development of the last quarter of the nineteenth century was related to power, to the use of new forms of power and to the manufacture of engines to produce that power. The basic principles of electricity were established earlier in the century but for some time they were only applied to the electric telegraph. It was Gramme, a Belgian living in Paris, who in 1870 made the first dynamo of practical dimensions capable of producing a truly continuous current. Its success was immediate and for a time France led the world in electric arc lighting for streets and for lighthouses. But the inefficiency of the generating devices and the absence of an effective system of power distribution remained a major handicap. Then in 1880 came the incandescent lamp and with it a great stimulus to central generation and distribution. Lighting was followed by electric traction but here Europe followed the United States only slowly, largely because local authorities had only recently invested in alternative forms of transport. Finally came electric motors for driving machines and with them a major revolution in industrial practice and location. Once long distance transmission became possible, industries were released from bondage to coal or water for their power sources. Individual electric drive gave greater freedom for factory layout over that allowed by the driving of machines by belts run from central shafting. Portable electric tools and the ability to derive power from a central station gave new life to the small workshop too.

Two giant German firms led the way in these events – Siemens Halske and the Allgemeine Elektrizitäts-Gesellschaft (A.E.G.) – much helped by their contacts with investment banks, for the providers of capital for electrification schemes were in a strong position to nominate the suppliers of the necessary equipment. France, like Britain, was slow to develop an independent industry of her own, relying heavily on American investment, but other countries in Europe were more active. Two sizeable companies operated from an early date in Sweden, helped by contacts with banks and by the absence of local coal which made electric power more than usually promising. At Eindhoven in The Netherlands Gerard Philips in 1891 established an incandescent lamp factory. Between 1895 and 1916 output rose from 100,000 to nearly 6·5 million lamps per annum and by the latter date over 3,000 workers were being employed in the plant. In Switzerland existing engineering traditions spilled over into electrical engineering in the way we have described. It was with Oerlikon that Brown accomplished the path-breaking Lauffen–Frankfurt transmission of power over a long distance (115 miles) at high voltage and it was he who produced one of the first consistently successful electric motors for industry, demonstrated for the first time at the Frankfurt Exhibition in 1891. Three years later Brown Boveri achieved a major triumph in winning the contract for the Frankfurt Municipal Power Station. The

German industry was wedded to continuous current machinery and opposed the alternating current machinery that Brown had been developing. Now the outsider had gained the critical contract. The enormous success enjoyed by Brown Boveri with the Parsons steam turbine too derived largely from the much improved generator which was linked to it.

The Parsons turbine was one of the most impressive products of the electric age. Parsons realised that there was urgent need for an engine to drive dynamos directly and that this was unlikely to be achieved by the traditional steam engine because of its reciprocal action. In fact so great was the speed of his turbine, patented in 1884, that he had to devise a new high speed generator for it, which in many ways was as remarkable as the turbine itself. Licences for manufacture were granted to many firms throughout Europe. Already in 1882 De Laval had developed a small turbine because he too had found difficulty in getting a motor capable of producing the high speeds needed for working his cream separators. The speeds were, even so, well below those of the Parsons engine and it only was suitable for small power but it fulfilled the need admirably. Turbines competing with the Parsons soon appeared. One was the French Rateau engine (1896): another was the simple Zoelly turbine built by Escher Wyss in Switzerland but the most effective was the Curtis turbine which was made on licence from the American patentee in many European countries. This final fling of steam was a product of only the best engineering firms in Europe, so exacting were the requirements. It is a testimony to the speed and quality of engineering skill built up on the continent that they were manufactured in such widely scattered centres.

In Hungary the Ganz company led the way in electrical engineering. The German A.E.G. had an interest in the firm to be sure, but it was the enterprise of certain brilliant engineers that made its reputation. Budapest was one of the first cities in Europe with an electric tram system and in the mid-1880s it was Ganz engineers who developed a commercially practical transformer system which permitted the wide use of alternating current. At the turn of the century it was their engineers again who startled the industry with a brilliantly original tender for the extension of the London Underground. Elsewhere in the Empire it was the Austrian Welsbach company which introduced the Osram lamp in 1906. By 1913 the Russian industry was large enough to be building a half of all the machinery being introduced in the country though in part this was due to the existence of some very large foreign owned plants – Swedish Ericsson employed 2,700 workers on telephone equipment in 1916 and Siemens Halske had over 2,000 men employed in Russia too.

It is not difficult to understand why the industry emerged from so many offshoots. Right to 1914 many developments were very much the province of gifted engineers who may or may not have enjoyed a rigorous scientific training. In a new industry of this kind there was no reason why ideas should be concentrated; indeed, with the shift away from traditional engineering there was every reason to expect them to be dispersed. The coming of hydroelectric power in any case gave a particularly strong boost in areas deficient in coal resources – Switzerland, Italy, Sweden and Norway, southern France. Of course success was most easily achieved where there were reservoirs of skill available but evidently these were well scattered over the continent. As in chemicals high standards of performance and frequent innovation weighed as heavily with the market as price. And although scale of production and rich sources of finance were powerful allies, they were not everything. The Germans might produce the standard solidly made competitively priced equipment; the Swiss and Hungarians offered these other qualities.

It is not nearly so clear why France and Germany were so much to the fore in the development of the internal combustion engine. The advantages of a form of power which could be operated intermittently were obvious but the first engines, which used gas, had the disadvantage of immobility arising from their source of fuel. The first practical gas engine was produced by the French engineer Étienne Lenoir in 1859 but it was the German Otto engine, first developed in the late 1860s, but manufactured from 1872 by the newly formed Gasmotoren Fabrik Deutz A.G., which really swept the market. Small oil engines were produced from the 1880s onwards and came to be used widely for pumping purposes, for powering small boats and for driving electric generators before central station supply became available. But then came two epoch-making inventions.

One, still utilising oil as fuel, was the diesel engine. Diesel, at one time an apprentice with Sulzer, developed his engine first with the help of Krupps and the Augsburg Maschinenfabrik A.G. and by 1895 was ready to dispose of the rights throughout the world. One great engineering name after another vied for the prize, and land diesels were soon in wide use. It was first used as a marine engine in 1902–3 fitted to a French canal barge. Sulzer fitted a diesel to a Swiss lake cargo ship in 1904 and the first motor tankship was built in a Volga shipyard the same year. Diesels built in Sweden were used for paraffin barges on the Baku–St Petersburg (Leningrad) water route with such success that Nobels soon converted their entire fleet. In 1902 an Amsterdam firm, Nederlandsche Fabriek van Werktuigen en Spoorweg-Material, got a diesel licence, and within six years had put diesels into two former steamer clippers and the Werkspoor family of engines became some of the most successful of all marine diesels. But the real breakthrough in ocean shipping came from Denmark where between 1907 and 1912 the East Asiatic Company took delivery of sixteen vessels, replacing all but one of its fleet and among these were several powered by diesels. By 1913 there were essentially eight types of sea-going marine diesels made in seven countries on the continent, yet not a single British engineer had produced his own design of marine diesel. It was a European triumph indeed, for the United States had had little to contribute either. Enterprise, engineering skill of a high order and for some makers at least, shipbuilding traditions of real distinction and, we should not forget, the daring of the shipping companies and the oil tanker owners who were prepared to support these ventures, all played their part.

The second invention was the petrol engine. Gas and oil engines had all run at slow speeds and it was Daimler, once chief engineer with Gasmotoren Deutz, who realised the potentialities of a small, light, high speed motor, capable of developing power by reason of its high speed rotation. At much the same time, Karl Benz, who also had experience with gas engines, was building his first motor vehicle in Mannheim with an engine using petrol but running at very low speed. It was not surprising that these new concepts should spring out of experience of the gas engine. Because he clung too nearly to the old and was unwilling to modify his ideas, Benz was the less successful of the two. By the end of the century the public was turning away from his very reliable but terribly slow motor cars. The first engines to be installed in cars for sale commercially were manufactured to the Daimler patents in Paris by the firm of Panhard and Levassor, formerly makers of woodworking machinery. Panhard and Levassor had already been making petrol engines under the Daimler patents. Daimler himself was not greatly interested in cars initially and had applied his engines to several uses, more particularly to power river and harbour launches. The first Panhard with a Daimler engine was preceded by a Peugeot with a similar engine mounted in the rear and purchased from Panhard. The new technology was adopted with great enthusiasm in France and by the end of the decade there were a dozen or so car makers there, and output had reached 2,000 cars, far in excess of that in any other country in Europe or in the United States. The origins of the French makers were varied; Bouton was a mechanic, Renault a student, Bollée and Peugeot small industrialists, Delahaye made agricultural machinery, de Dion was an aristocrat as was Bugatti in Italy. The De Dietrich firm was a much older Alsace firm which had found itself on the wrong side of the frontier in 1871 and shifted to Lunéville to make railway wagons. If any pattern emerged at all over the whole of Europe there was some preponderance of firms that had originally been carriage makers or producers of bicycles and allied engineering products. Opel in Germany began as a sewing machine manufacturer in 1862. Laurin and Clement (later part of Skoda) in Bohemia were bicycle makers, Darracq in France made sewing machines and bicycles, Minerva in Belgium made motor bicycles, Fiat in Italy, ball bearings. The motor car itself, after all, was the culmination of a long history of technological improvements – the differential gear enabling the wheels to go at different speeds around a curve came from steam vehicles, the manufacture of ball bearings was boosted by the cycle boom, the suspension was inherited from carriage makers.

Enthusiasm for the new vehicle was immense; in Austria besides Laurin and Clement, major firms included Daimler, Fiat and Reichenberger, the last with a total output in 1911 as large as 1,000 cars. Italy entered the industry rather slowly but in 1907 in Turin alone there were 32 manufacturers and in Milan another 15. The largest makers at that time were Isotta Fraschini with 700 employees and Fiat with 800, and in Naples Pirelli had a huge works employing 5,000 men making tyres as well as a range of other products. It was Dunlop's pneumatic tyre, introduced to the continent by Michelin in 1895, that in fact converted the car from a dangerous toy to a serious means of transport. By 1913 Fiat was producing 4,500 cars annually making it one of the biggest such firms in Europe: in that year they were surpassed by Peugeot with 5,000 and Renault with 4,700. Five Russian makers have been identified for the pre-1917 period. The Baltic engineering works in Moscow produced some 300 cars in 1912 and another works at Riga the same number in 1913–14 but all these works were of very recent origin. The smaller countries were less heavily involved – seven makers are known to have existed in The Netherlands before the war, six in Sweden, five in Denmark all in Copenhagen, and four in Spain. The small size of the local markets and the difficulty small assemblers experienced in obtaining major components from abroad, possibly helped to inhibit their development. The contrast is Belgium with its much deeper tradition of heavy engineering, where 63 firms, some of considerable size, have been identified.

It was the French industry that dominated the pre-war scene with an output of 45,000 cars in 1913 compared with about 20,000 in Germany and less than 10,000 in Italy. Why this should have been so is not clear. Since 1870 the French had shown much interest in developing some kind of mechanical vehicle to replace the horse –

witness the work of Bollée and Serpollet with steam carriages. Possibly French engineering traditions were well fitted to the manufacture of the quality bespoke car that was typical of the industry to 1914. It was in the manufacture of engines that the French excelled to such a degree that they almost monopolised the supply of power plants for aircraft until war came in 1914. Size of the home market could hardly be considered a vital factor, for a considerable proportion of French output was exported. For example 200,000 cars were made between 1909 and 1913 alone, yet total car registration in France in 1913 was only 125,000 compared with 208,000 in Britain and 93,000 in Germany. Up to a point the French succeeded because in the relatively easy market conditions before 1914 they eschewed too rapid innovation either in models or production techniques or in prices. But this is not to say that the French were not to the fore when major technological improvements were concerned. In cars as in aircraft the power : weight ratio is the critical factor. Ford attacked it by lightness of parts. Renault chose a technical approach through major improvement of the clutch and gearbox, a solution making for better performance rather than for lower cost, however. It is strange that the German car industry led by Benz, Opel, Daimler, Adler, had such an undistinguished record. The temporary eclipse of Benz may have been important, for the industry was beginning to expand quite rapidly when it was cut short by the First World War. It is something which requires more study, for the backwardness continued right through the inter-war period.

The spread of the motor car through Europe was due in part to the fascination of the invention and to its obvious superiority over other forms of local transport if it worked properly, and this was perhaps an optimistic age. Being basically an assembly process, entry was relatively easy. Parts could be bought on credit and the customer paid part of the price in advance. Prior to mass production the fixed capital commitment was relatively low and the penalties for small output not great. Inevitably there were many casualties but the process led not to the collapse of the industry but to a constant spread of interest and, through the competitive process, to the emergence by 1914 of a limited number of firms that were to dominate the industry for many years to come. As long as there were local foundries available, some imported machine-tools and possibly a ready supply of engines the industry could begin, if not necessarily flourish almost anywhere. By 1914, however, it was beginning to concentrate in engineering centres such as Paris and Turin because of the need to be near supplies of components if manufacture on a large scale was contemplated. The motor car was important for itself, for creating in some countries already by 1914 almost the largest of their engineering industries but perhaps above all for the way in which it brought new tools and production techniques to Europe. It was at Billancourt, for example, after a strike at the Renault works that F. W. Taylor's techniques of scientific management were first brought to bear in France. The logical extension of these techniques to full mass production had not come to Europe by 1914; the car remained an expensive perquisite of the well-to-do but the foundations were well and truly laid in many countries. Engineering was now so very obviously not confined to the favoured few.

– Shipbuilding

Power and metallurgy played a vital role in another field of technology – shipbuilding. The main developments of the nineteenth century are well known. Paddle steamers were used on rivers as early as 1807 though not regularly on ocean crossings for another two decades. Screw propulsion came in the 1840s and the active development of iron ships began at that time too. The first sea-going vessel to be fitted with compound expansion engines was launched in 1854. Compounding means the use of the expansive power of steam at different pressures in two or more cylinders, the object being to achieve economies of fuel consumption. The idea was not new but because of the high pressures involved it could not be taken up until improvements were made in boiler construction. Indeed, the iron screw steamer had to face many problems of coaling, boiler and engine safety, of propellor shafting and of hull fouling before it could be widely adopted. The triple expansion engine, the greatest single improvement in the marine steam engine, was patented in France in 1871 by Benjamin Normand and installed in a vessel two years later. Later in that decade the launching of H.M.S. *Iris* at Pembroke in 1877 marked the beginning of the era of steel ships. These developments in engines and construction were only possible because steel became available in special qualities at much lower prices and they were accompanied by changes in the carrying capacity of ships and in design so as to bring about improvement in the weight/cargo/space relationship.

Until the late 1860s sail remained dominant on most sea routes. Substantial reductions in costs were achieved in the first three-quarters of the nineteenth century less through technological changes, than from the fact that the general growth of world trade offered shippers greater prospects of picking up return cargoes rather than coming back home in ballast, with no payload or spending time idle in ports waiting for cargoes. The iron hull markedly reduced sail costs too. There are those who have argued that sail was responsible for most of the lowering of costs on world routes right to 1900 but this is clearly an erroneous view. Certainly sail continued to carry many of the bulk cargoes on the long distance routes. Steam was less advantageous the longer the voyage and the greater the percentage of carrying capacity that had to go to carrying coal. Buying coal *en route* did not help, as the price of coal in the southern ports inevitably reflected the cost of getting it there. So steam came late on routes such as those from Europe to Australia and to San Francisco. On the other hand, the opening of the Suez Canal in 1869 reduced the voyage to Australia from 10,000 miles to about 6,000 miles. At this stage length steam was immediately competitive and with further technological improvements pushed more and more into the Far East trade too. Traffic clearing German ports became dominated by steam as early as 1873. On intra-European routes sail lost its lead before that date and was insignificant before the end of the 1880s. On inter-continental routes sail lost its lead rather later – after 1880. But a study of German shipping productivity, measured by total port clearings per man employed, shows a rise of 94 per cent between 1873 and 1887 and of this 68 per cent was due to technological changes in steam and only 14·7 per cent to similar changes in sail, most of which came from the pressure of steam competition anyway. Steam had one more great triumph after the triple expansion engine – the adaptation of Parsons' steam turbine to marine work, though its use was confined to naval vessels and to large Atlantic liners. In 1886 the first steam vessel was built with oil tanks; hitherto oil had been carried in barrels or tins on ordinary cargo vessels. By 1900 Lloyd's showed 193 tankers of 637,000 tons deadweight and in 1913 441 tankers of 2,430,000 tons, though in fact the amount of crude oil shipped by water was still quite small and all refined oil was moved in barrels and cans.

Calculations of freight rates on goods shipped from the United States to Europe show the effects of these changes. A deflated index, corrected for general price movements, shows a fall from 100 in 1830 to about 42 from 1865 to 1874. It stays at that level until the next decade and then begins to decline again to 28·3 in 1900–4 and 24·2 by 1910–14. Such were the dramatic consequences of technological change as well as of the more intensive use of ships made possible by the great expansion of world trade. Many other such series could be quoted but an alternative measure is to show the changing share of shipping freight in the delivered cost of goods. The cost of shipping covered over 30 per cent of the price of Baltic fir in London in 1863 and only 14 per cent in 1884; for Black Sea wheat delivered to Liverpool the share was 18 per cent in 1864 and less than half that proportion in 1886.

The transition from sail to steam was not easily achieved; many builders were deficient in steam technology, short of capital, their yards too small. The first iron shipbuilding yard in Germany, the Vulcan in Stettin (Szczecin), dated from 1851; in 1909 it was still the largest private yard and employed about 7,000 workers, much the same as the Schichau yards in Danzig (Gdansk). Size became a major feature of the industry, though a considerable share of the activity took the form of building naval vessels. In 1909 shipbuilding employed 70,000 men in the private yards in Germany and another 20,000 men in three government yards. Table 20 shows the relative position of European shipbuilders in 1913.

Table 20. *European shipbuilding in 1913. Gross tonnage 100 tons upwards*

	Ships	Tons
Austria	17	61,757
Belgium	54	30,181
Denmark	31	40,932
France	89	176,095
Germany	162	465,226
Netherlands	95	104,296
Italy	38	50,356
Norway	74	50,637
Sweden	18	18,524
U.K.	688	1,932,153

Source: Lloyd's Register.

Despite the absence of any but the smallest local steel industry the Dutch industry held fourth place. Plates were imported from Germany, no disadvantage as many British shipyards did likewise; forgings were imported rough and then finished; the quality of engine building was high and Dutch shipyards were responsible for some notable innovations. It was in 1910 that the Nederlandsche yard built the first successful sea-going motor ship, the tanker *Vulcanus* of 1,100 tons. They employed 2,000 men in 1909 and three other Dutch yards employed over 1,500 men. The average size of ship built in Dutch yards was considerably below that in France and Germany but Dutch shipbuilding capacity, measured by size of berths, was much superior to that of any other of the smaller

Table 21. *Capacity of European shipyards in 1914.*
Number of berths by length in feet

	250–400	400–600	600–700	+700
U.K.	175	162	58	185
Belgium	3	5	—	—
Denmark	9	4	—	—
France	19	14	14	9
Germany	69	52	8	11
Netherlands	40	38	6	—
Norway	13	9	—	—
Sweden	11	7	—	—

Source: Committee on Industry and Trade, *Survey of Industries* (London, 1928), part IV, p. 404.

countries in Europe as Table 21 shows. By 1914 vessels of almost 10,000 tons had been constructed there. The Danish yards were small – the largest vessel built by Burmeister was 6,075 tons – and the Danish fleet itself reflected this. In 1914 the average size of its steam fleet, taking ships above 60 tons net, was 800 tons compared with 1,400 tons for Italy and 1,300 for The Netherlands and the proportion capable of averaging more than 12 knots was 12 per cent compared with 28 per cent and 29 per cent for the other two countries. Italy and The Netherlands were involved much more extensively in the ocean liner trade. The Ansaldo yard at Genoa was also geared to building heavy warships and just before 1914 turned out the *Giulio Cesare* of 21,500 tons as well as exporting warships to Argentina of almost 7,000 tons. Burmeisters in Denmark operated in much the same fashion as the Dutch builders, though they made a speciality of forgings, using up to 80 per cent Danish scrap in making the steel, and even exporting the finished product to British yards. At a maximum they employed 3,000 men but shipbuilding was only one of a wide range of activities, too wide a range many thought. In Italy subsidies and rebates on imported materials eased the problems of local builders but still in 1913 under a third of new steam tonnage came from local shipyards – much the same as in Norway. Good yards in the smaller countries could flourish in a highly competitive world, sometimes with an underpinning of local orders, partly because labour costs formed a high proportion of total costs in an industry where the economies of scale in any one yard were not great and where individual, as opposed to batch, building remained the general rule. Yards in northern Europe could get their steel easily enough and the ability to build high performance engines for special purposes was a great asset – something the Danes and Dutch enjoyed and the Norwegians totally lacked.

Such an analysis leads us to discuss in more general terms the role of smaller countries in engineering and allied industries when facing competition from Britain and Germany in particular. The power of Swiss engineering was remarkable, given the need to export a high proportion of all output. A relatively large textile industry had provided a sound basis for engineering through repair and machine building from early in the nineteenth century and the Swiss were able to maintain a specialised export of textile machines throughout the period. The role of certain individuals we have already noted but the really vital element was the ability of the Swiss to concentrate on high quality production and on constant innovation. Sulzer, Oerlikon, Brown Boveri, Escher Wyss all followed this road to success and the chemical manufacturers too. For them there was no question of choosing to follow up the ideas of others; at this the big producers would come out on top every time. In the manufacture of boots and shoes, an industry which remained small scale everywhere in Europe to 1914 despite the growing use of American automatic machinery, the Swiss firm C. F. Bally was the largest in Europe with one factory in Zürich of 2,600 employees and eight smaller works employing another 1,500 men. Innovation here took the form of plant specialisation; the smaller units specialised on heels, inks, webs and so forth while the main factory, though turning out many different kinds of shoes, forged the usual reputation for quality and styling. The output of 66,000 pairs a week was four times the largest in France and 30 per cent above the highest in Germany.

Engineering works could import gears and forgings in the rough state and finish them, in other words, doing the labour intensive part for themselves. Bulk dyes were imported for further processing too. As we have seen, many less developed countries got their footing in world markets through the processing of primary products such as pulp, paper, butter, cheese, chocolate, beet sugar, beer, flour. Norway's failure to carry out much fish processing in her own factories or to advance significantly from pulp to paper making is a good indication of her industrial immaturity. But although the smaller countries had their processing industries and their consumer goods industries with relatively simple techniques and secure local markets, this was not all. Almost everywhere they had more sophisticated industrial sectors which provided real industrial growth points. Small firms had the advantage in that they found it relatively easy to insert themselves into the pattern of world trade in manufactures by carving out special niches not requiring excessively large markets. In some ways too the smaller countries were much favoured by the nature of world trade before 1914. Tariffs were generally very low, and there were many important industries with a high labour content where the advantages of scale production were much less pronounced than they were later to become. Thus it was that the Swiss did so well in making high quality electrical machinery, diesels and turbines, all large articles made in small numbers, using a great deal of skilled labour. The smaller countries made more of an impact with such capital goods rather than with consumer goods where economies of scale tended to be more significant.

It is impossible to discuss any but the major branches of industry in one chapter. Some smaller sectors such as glass making, enjoyed rapid innovation. Belgium emerged as a major world producer of glass after independence in 1830. The industry was concentrated around Charleroi and soon came to depend heavily on overseas markets. Exports of window glass alone rose from 18m kg in 1850–4 to 134m in 1890–4 and 210m in 1910–13. Precisely how this leading position was achieved is difficult to determine: the resource position was favourable but not unduly so. Labour was cheaper than in Britain but the glass blowers were more productive anyway. Inherited skills may be part of the answer but however this may be, the Belgians shrewdly blunted the force of inevitable competition by taking an active part in the formation of international associations which sought to establish levels of output in Europe for various types of glass.

In almost every country there were huge arms works. In the late eighteenth and early nineteenth centuries they provided important reservoirs of skilled labour – Liége is one excellent example. New metals and new machining techniques were often pioneered in such works, partly because the technical requirements were high and partly because cost was not always the key factor. Technological benefits spilled over into civilian industries through improved marine engines, better and safer explosives, new metals and more accurate machining techniques. Subsidised production of arms by a firm such as Ansaldo helped to foster other industrial activities within the same organisation. We do well to remember, though, that a great deal of industrial activity was carried on in small shops for local needs, protected by distance and by culture yet providing important reservoirs of skill when the need arose for something more ambitious. Such works did not determine the overall rate of growth; they were, we might say, part of the scene but even in major industries the number of small plants was striking. In France in 1906 58 per cent

H

of those employed worked in establishments of ten workers or less; in Germany a third were so employed.

– Chemicals

One other manufacturing industry requires our detailed attention, however, the chemical industry. It never employed huge numbers of workers but is of special interest because of the degree of innovation, because of its linkage with other industries such as textiles and electricity and because there appeared earlier than elsewhere the tendency to apply large sums to research in the hope of bringing out new products and new processes.

In the eighteenth and early nineteenth centuries the main industrial chemicals were sulphuric acid and the alkalis, potassium carbonate and sodium carbonate (soda). The manufacturing process for sulphuric acid was simple; ground sulphur was burned in some kind of vessel and the gas absorbed in water. The chief eighteenth-century advance was essentially an engineering one, transforming the scale of operations through the use of huge lead-lined vats. Such were the economies of scale that the price fell from 20p per oz to $1\frac{1}{2}$p per lb in a few decades. At the higher price it was used mainly as a medicine but at the end of the century it was being used to make hydrochloric acid from which chlorine was freed for use as a bleaching agent. Alkalis were needed by a variety of industries but above all by textile finishers for the manufacture of soap to scour and clean the cloth. Both types of alkali were derived at this time from materials in short supply, potassium carbonate from wood ash in a ratio of one part to 600 parts of wood, and soda either from barilla yielded by the saltwort plant grown mainly in Spain or from kelp derived from dried seaweed largely in western Scotland. From the nature of the processes used, all were costly and only economic because the growing demands of the textile industry forced prices up rapidly. Furthermore, the supply of barilla to France was cut off during the Napoleonic wars. These difficulties were resolved in France by Nicholas Leblanc, using simply mineral agents, sulphuric acid and salt. Combined they produced hydrochloric acid and sodium sulphate. The latter was mixed with chalk and heated; the resulting black ash was leached with water and soda obtained by evaporation. The successful commercialisation of this process founded the heavy chemical industry and, indeed, until after mid-century, the alkali industry was synonymous with the chemical industry. It was a revoltingly dirty and smelly process and its heavy use of salt and of fuel fixed its location in one or two favoured spots from the first.

In 1850 output in France was about one-third of that in Britain. The industry first concentrated near Marseilles which had been an old centre of the soap and sulphur industries and where coal, salt and limestone were available. Soon competition developed from more efficient firms such as St Gobain and Kühlmann in the north. The French industry suffered in comparison with the British, partly because of duties imposed on raw materials, but above all because the small-scale plants in the south, poorly located in relation to the consuming industries of the north and east, could in no way compare with the huge concentrated plants of Merseyside and Tyneside. The German industry was yet more backward; the first plant was not opened until 1843 and under the regime of low protection of the 1870s output declined and imports rose to three-quarters of the level of home demand. Here was an industry with economies of scale indeed.

eco's of scale

From the middle of the nineteenth century brimstone gave way to other materials in the manufacture of sulphuric acid, particularly pyrites, which was obtained from Spain and in smaller quantities from Norway. The output of acid soared not only to feed the Leblanc industry but because of the demand for superphosphate as a fertiliser, obtained by treating mineral phosphate rock with acid. The price of acid was held down by this use of alternative materials and also by a major improvement in the manufacturing process in the form of the Gay-Lussac towers introduced at St Gobain in 1835. These were designed to absorb the spent oxides of nitrogen hitherto allowed to escape into the air, though it was some decades before further refinement led to wide use of the process.

But far-reaching changes were at hand. Since the early years of the century it had been obvious from laboratory work that soda could be derived simply by the ammonia soda technique, whereby a brine solution was saturated with ammonia and then with carbon dioxide. The process yielded sodium carbonate and ammonium chloride which could then be treated to recover the ammonia. However, the complexity of the equipment required and the difficulty of recovering the costly ammonia held up commercial exploitation for many decades. These problems were resolved by the Belgian Ernst Solvay during the 1860s and his new technique spread rapidly. The older industry reacted quickly by reducing its material costs, and so long as the Leblanc makers could sell their by-product, bleaching powder, at a good price they could survive. But new pressures came into play once more. Another laboratory technique brought about the decomposition of salt by passing an electric current through a solution, leaving caustic soda and hydrogen on the cathode and chlorine on the anode. Could it be done commercially? It was the

Solvay 1860's

German Leblanc manufacturers at Griesheim who succeeded with the process in the 1890s and by so doing spelt the doom of all other Leblanc makers. In this as in other electro-chemical processes the advent of cheap hydroelectric power was crucial. The new technique had its problems; the joint production of chlorine and soda in fixed proportions made it hard to satisfy the demand for one without over-producing the other – a not uncommon problem in chemical manufacture. The hydrogen was usually burned away but before the war was being used to inflate airships. Even as late as 1898 world output of Leblanc soda was 600,000 tons annually; a few years later it was less than one-tenth of this figure.

Solvay licensed production by his process all over the world. The German industry, unhampered by any significant prior investment in Leblanc techniques, expanded rapidly and production of alkali rose eightfold between 1876 and 1900. In Austria the last plant of a small Leblanc industry closed in 1903 and by that time there was one Solvay works of some size in the Salzkammergut and several small scattered plants satisfying local needs. The French industry suffered more from the Leblanc heritage but even so, by 1903 virtually all Leblanc production had ceased. In Belgium Solvay naturally reigned supreme and in Switzerland the establishment of a Solvay plant in a good location on the German side of the border effectively destroyed the home industry. In many countries – above all in France – the old Leblanc makers found their salvation in the manufacture of superphosphate and after 1900 this replaced the Leblanc process as the main single use for sulphuric acid. In France in 1913 three quarters of the output, in Germany over 50 per cent and in less developed countries, such as Italy and Spain, virtually all acid output was devoted to this use. World output of superphosphate rose from 0·9m metric tons in 1880 to 4·8m in 1900 and 11·2m in 1913. In that last year France and Germany each produced over 2m tons and Italian output surged from 0·33 tons in 1900 to about 1m tons in 1910. Belgium and The Netherlands made several hundred thousand tons each and even Russia 115,000 tons in 1913. It was the simplest of chemical processes, consisting simply of treating the crushed rock, mined in North Africa, with acid. Superphosphate was cheap to make but expensive to transport, so generally production took place in a number of modest sized local factories.

The heavy chemical industry was the triumph of the engineer and the salesman rather than of the chemist. It was also the triumph of the diplomat for after Solvay relatively little emphasis was given to further technological change but far more to organising control over world markets. For innovation we have to look elsewhere and around 1880 this began to emerge in the form of the synthesis of organic products. From it came the production of dyestuffs, pharmaceuticals and perfumes, based far more on pure chemical research than was the case with the older inorganic industry. The two sectors were interlinked because large quantities of inorganics were required for the new processes – sulphuric and nitric acid, chlorine and alkalis – but the roots of growth were different. Essentially for organics these were two; one was the rise of coal gas industries and the other the development of organic chemistry so that compounds could be isolated from tar. An entirely new phase in the history of the chemical industry was at hand.

synthetic dyes

The first synthetic dye, mauve, was isolated by G. F. Perkin in England in 1856, fortuitously because he was looking for a way to synthesise (that is to say, build up from its separate elements) quinine, when he stumbled on this first coal tar dye. In 1859 the bluish red silk dye, fuchsine, named after the fuchsia flower, was produced in the laboratory of the Renard Frères dyeworks in Lyons by heating crude aniline in the presence of tin chloride. Jean Gerber-Keller of Mulhouse replaced the tin chloride by mercuric nitrate but this was held to infringe the Renard patent, as French law protected the end product not the process. So he moved to start manufacture in Basel where he was soon joined by others who felt frustrated by the monopolistic activities of the fuchsine patent holders. For some years the chemical industry seemed happy with these new colours which supplemented rather than replaced natural colourants, until in 1869 Perkin in England and Caro, Graebe and Liebermann in Germany produced alizarin as a result of purposeful research, determining the exact composition of madder and following this by the synthesis of alizarin. In 1870 madder, grown mainly in France, cost 90 German marks a kilogram; a decade later its alizarin equivalent cost 8 marks. Many other dyes soon followed but the most difficult problem proved to be the artificial production of indigo. Synthesis in the laboratory was achieved by Professor Bayer in 1880 but the method was too complex for commercial production. Two German firms, Badische Anilin und Soda Fabrik (B.A.S.F.) and Hoechst took over the rights and pooled their research resources but the Baeyer synthesis never did work out and the companies bought patents for two indigo syntheses discovered in the Swiss Federal Polytechnic in Zürich. Still immense problems had to be faced but it was B.A.S.F. that in 1897 solved the problem after twenty years of research and an expenditure of some 20m marks. Not for the first time chance played its part, for the breaking of a thermometer during an experiment showed that mercury was the ideal catalyst for their process – the oxidation of naphthalene to phthalic acid. Hoechst followed their own course and used the opportunities offered by cheap hydroelectric power to make cheap chromic acid which they then used for phthalic acid manufacture. As the makers reported 'synthetic indigo was almost snatched out of their hands' such was the demand. In 1895–6 India had exported 187,000 tons of natural indigo and by 1913–14 this was down to only 11,000 tons and the price of the dye had been halved.

This was the first classic case of sustained costly industrial research after a pre-determined goal. The German triumph resulted from a combination of entrepreneurial skill and tenacity, large laboratories well staffed – in 1897 B.A.S.F. had 150 chemists in its employ – and the special talents of these men trained in the famed Technische Hochschulen. Emigrant German chemists were attracted back home from Britain and by 1913 production of dyestuffs in France and in Britain was in the hands of German and Swiss companies. Hoechst, Bayer, the third great German manufacturer and the major Swiss firm, C.I.B.A., all had works in France. They easily got around the ineffective tariff by importing concentrated dyes from the home plants and in France simply diluting and repacking them. The requirement that patents should be worked in France was particularly weak but the lack of protection for processes inhibited that search for more economic methods of production, which was always a great feature of the dye industry. It was in fact only the Swiss makers who managed to hold a place in world dye production at all along with the Germans, a considerable achievement, not least because in 1900 exports provided 93 per cent of the Swiss market. In 1913 German firms and their foreign subsidiaries made about 140,000 tons of dyestuffs (Germany used internally perhaps 20,000 tons), Swiss firms 10,000 tons and the rest of the world's independent makers another 10,000 tons. The Swiss benefited from the financial resources of Basel and from the fact that the city was commercially part of Alsace where the major part of the French cotton industry was to be found. Furthermore her textile exports were of very high quality and needed constant innovation in colours. Dye making got a good start from the French *émigrés* after the fuchsine affair and then came to be concentrated on expensive, technically difficult products, changing output frequently as existing processes became easier to work. The Swiss patent law gave German firms little hope of protecting their processes there but they came to supply from their factories along the Rhine the essential coal tar distillates and intermediate and process chemicals. The Swiss firms had also for long made use of cheaper immigrant German labour and as late as 1911 foreign workers still provided 51 per cent of the employment in the chemical industry, though by that time the Swiss had also begun to make alternative use of this labour by establishing branches

Table 22. *Employment in the Swiss chemical industry in 1913*

C.I.B.A.	2,900 (800)	Geigy	700 (300)
Hoffman	950 (400)	Sandoz	340

Source: F. Haber, *The Chemical Industry 1900–1930* (Oxford, 1970), p. 162.

across the borders in Baden and Alsace. Table 22 shows the size of the main firms in the Swiss industry with the number employed overseas shown in the brackets.

The German industry also made rapid progress in the development and production of drugs, for there were many scientific and engineering links between dyes and pharmaceuticals. Hoechst's drug division was started in 1883; in 1892 Robert Koch entrusted them with the manufacture of tuberculin which eased identification of the disease. Paul Erlich's compound salvarsan, for treatment of syphilis, was first manufactured by them too. In 1906 they began making novocain which became the standard preparation for local anaesthesia. Bayer followed the Swiss example by keeping away from producing many of the bulk dyes but they too developed an extensive range of pharmaceuticals. In 1897 aspirin was launched with an advertising campaign on an unprecedented scale and this was followed by several sedatives of which the barbiturate, veronal, was the most successful. Synthetic perfumes and photochemicals were other specialities followed by the German industry. Bayer, who employed 10,600 workers in 1913, were generally considered to be weak on innovation and engineering techniques but outstanding at commercial development. It was B.A.S.F. with 12,000 workers in one factory in Ludwigshafen on the Rhine which had the greatest research traditions but who in general were less profitable than their nearest rivals, a not uncommon feature of highly technically oriented firms. These two along with Hoechst all made heavy chemicals too but only as raw materials for their own manufacturing processes. Tar came from the Ruhr coke works as well as being directly imported from Britain, France and Belgium.

Both in Switzerland and Germany the dye firms were run by men willing to listen to expert technical advice and to spend money on research. But their success also derived from a keen commercial acumen, from high standards of production engineering and from as sharp an interest in the discoveries of others as in their own researches. The holdings of the large German firms in smaller Swiss and German chemical companies was almost a form of venture capital investment enabling them to keep abreast with new ideas but freeing chemists and businessmen from the possibly too suffocating influence of a large organisation. It is possible that the emphasis on applied science in the German technical schools was more relevant to the needs of these industries than the more theoretical training of the École Polytechnique, though in France such an emphasis on pure theory proved its value in the electro-chemical fields. Yet it is important not to exaggerate the element of research in the German success but to realise that it was a combination of talents and circumstances. One must bear in mind, in addition to those factors just mentioned, that a powerful self-reinforcing interaction of industrial developments got under way there. Coal tar recovery was particularly well carried out in the German coke ovens; the growth of demand for chlorine and nitrates stimulated the inorganic sector; coal tar dyes and explosives developed at much the same time and both needed large amounts of sulphuric and nitric acid. With the discovery of explosives from phenol (lyddite) and toluene (T.N.T.) the links became very close and encouraged the formation of integrated concerns.

The final achievement of organic chemistry before 1914 was the production of artificial silk or rayon. It began when Count Chardonnet started spinning a thick solution of nitrocellulose into fibres by forcing it through fine holes in a metal plate at Besançon in 1892. Like other innovations in chemical engineering, this new industry depended on associated developments elsewhere. The search for filaments for electric lamps helped produce the nitro-cellulose and cuprammonium process and this fused with the emergent chemistry of the wood pulp industry, whereby wood was disintegrated by treatment with acids or alkalis, to create the viscose process which ruled the artificial fibre industry from 1906 onwards. In this as in many other ways technological progress was a cumulative process. Similar interaction may be seen between the contribution of electricity to chemical technology and the role of chemistry in promoting electrical engineering through new types of insulators, lubricants and coatings. More detailed discussion will be given to electro-chemistry in a later chapter when we discuss the growth of Norwegian industry but one of the most remarkable breakthroughs of all came in the manufacture of aluminium. To 1885 it was a metal too expensive to be used for anything but rings, brooches, statuettes and the like. The average price per pound in the early 1850s was over $500. A series of new processes had by the 1870s reduced the price to $10 though the metal was of low purity. Then in 1886 Hérault in France and Hall in the United States simultaneously brought out the electrolytic technique and by the mid-1890s the price had fallen to 30 cents and further still to 20 cents per pound in 1913. So revolutionary was the new method that, unlike what happened in the Leblanc-Solvay contest, the old techniques were shattered overnight. Indeed, much of technological history has to be analysed in terms of the degree of cost reduction achieved. Coke smelting of iron was only slightly superior to charcoal in certain circumstances of raw material supply but puddling killed the older refining processes more drastically. Solvay only gradually established its complete ascendancy over Leblanc; synthetic indigo destroyed the natural dye within a few years. By 1913 world production of aluminium was 68,000 tons of which the United States and Canada produced 28,000 tons, France 14,500 tons, Switzerland 11,260 tons and Germany 800 tons.

The culminating point of innovation in the pre-war chemical industry came just before 1914 when B.A.S.F. successfully developed the Haber-Bosch process for the synthesis of ammonia. It was the result of much intensive research and of the resolution of many complex problems of chemical engineering, for the process involved the continuous use of a large volume of gases at high temperatures and pressures. It called for close liaison between the makers of capital equipment – especially the producers of special steels – and the chemical industry itself and in that sense almost a new industry was created. It required a large volume of output, since the process was highly capital intensive. In a technical sense it represented the summit of pre-war achievements but by the exacting nature of its demands in both an engineering and an economic sense it ushered in a new era for the industry.

By 1914 the European leadership in world chemicals was undisputed. No less than 85 per cent of world exports derived from there and the United States depended entirely on technologies originating there. True, the United States produced 34 per cent of world output; next came Germany with 24 per cent, Britain with 11 per cent and France with 8·5 per cent but these figures give no indication of the qualitative power of European industry. More than any other area this represented the supreme height of pre-war European industrial technology, though to keep our perspective right it must be stressed that nowhere was it a large industry in relation to total output. Even in Germany in 1907 it employed only 1·3 per cent of the workforce and was responsible for $3\frac{1}{2}$ per cent of exports.

– Agriculture

Finally we must briefly discuss agricultural technology for this industry remained by far the greatest employer of labour in Europe throughout the period and even though technology did not advance nearly so quickly as in other sectors, the diffusion of new ideas in agriculture throughout the continent brought marked increases in the productivity both of land and of labour. Furthermore, in the late eighteenth and first part of the nineteenth century great efforts were made to increase the supply of land available by reclamation, using new drainage techniques and at the same time the supply of labour was being transformed to different degrees in different areas by the growth of population, by migration and by the lure of the towns.

Some of these changes in technology were discussed in chapter 1 and as we saw there, modifications of tenurial conditions were an important pre-requisite of technological adjustments. Not only was this necessary to provide the incentive to undertake improvement but to a considerable extent communal farming systems had to disappear to permit individual experiment to flourish. Some qualification to this is necessary because it is now clear that far more variations in the patterns of open field farming existed than was once thought. A three-year rotation, for example, could be extended by fallowing every fourth, fifth or sixth year and instead cultivating pulse or corn on the fallow. But peasants were conservative men; they had no margin to risk the failure of the main crop. On their private garden plots a striking degree of experimentation went on, but in the open fields only tried practices were acceptable. So it remains true that modification of these arrangements was desirable to bring about a rapid change in technology, though the strip system did not necessarily disappear with the communal arrangements. This was something which varied greatly from region to region.

Improvement of agriculture in Europe in the eighteenth century and before took a variety of forms, including consolidation of strips, adoption of new crops and new rotations which in turn depended on improved plant breeding and seed production, reclamation of land and selective breeding of livestock. Subsequent progress to a considerable extent took the form of the elaboration and diffusion of these earlier technologies with the notable addition of new implements and new sources of fertiliser. The innovations in crop rotation which spread from the Netherlands west to Britain and south into Germany in the seventeenth century and then diffused more and more widely, began with the sowing of grass leys on the former fallows. This was followed by the introduction of new fodder crops such as sainfoin and clover and, later, turnips which were all used for winter feed. These technologies had both biological and organisational aspects. They eliminated the fallow, enabled more stock to be kept and to be better fed and increased the supply of natural manure and, indeed, called for its careful accumulation, a major factor for a society without artificial manures. The coming of the fodder crops was far more significant technologically than the grass leys simply because their nitrogen fixing properties raised the productivity of the soil. Essentially these changes led to a more productive form of mixed farming and brought in their train advances in animal breeding, seed selection, sowing techniques and improved preparation of the seed bed. The new rotations gave greater flexibility to farming, making it easier to adjust the balance between animal and grain production according to the relative profitability of these two forms of output. Farming became more complicated; there were more plants to be cultivated and the abolition of the fallow intensified and speeded the rhythm of the farm. The new crops, especially the roots, were labour intensive but they were well suited to the position agriculture found itself facing in Western Europe in the middle years of the nineteenth century. There were still adequate supplies of labour but industrialisation was going forward rapidly enough in urban areas to offer good prices for meat and other animal products. Mixed farming with new rotations depended on these two factors – rising urban incomes and a high density of farm labour. But it is important to remember that various forms of this kind of intensive husbandry were to be found in several parts of Europe by the mid-eighteenth century where market, soil and labour conditions and the whole pattern of society favoured the adoption of advanced farming methods and it was by no means restricted to the landed estates. In Flanders, Brabant, Zealand and Friesland, the Palatinate, Baden, Nassau, in Schleswig-Holstein, near towns such as Würzburg and Augsburg, in the Po Valley and Catalonia would be found examples of longer rotations, fodder crops, convertible husbandry, heavy manuring and the growing of industrial crops such as flax and dye plants.

As time went on many different rotational patterns began to develop according to local needs and circumstances. One Hungarian estate in 1874 had thirty-six different rotations in use, for example. In Sweden and Denmark there emerged very specialised forms of convertible husbandry. The pattern remained for about half the land to be under corn and the rest in artificial grass but the rotation might extend to as many as sixteen courses. In some the grasses were left down for several years at a time and in others root crops were used in connection with dairy husbandry. On the Dutch polders more complex rotations could be found running over twenty years in which grass played a minor part, but simple patterns were infinitely more common. In the 1870s in the Netherlands variations of the Scandinavian alternate husbandry were to be found but in predominantly corn growing areas there would be a rotation such as rape, winter barley, wheat, oats, beans, wheat, oats, clover.

In other areas potatoes and rye would cover two-thirds of the land with the remaining third buckwheat, oats, barley, beans or clover: elsewhere it was one-fifth potatoes, two-fifths clover and two-fifths grass. The variations were manifold.

But the changes came at different rates partly because of the slow transformation of rural institutions. To some extent too the new technology came up against the age old view that the true role of farming was to provide the daily bread and in this sense it was easier to gain acceptance of crops such as maize and potatoes which were for immediate consumption. Maize could only be grown in the Southern regions: it was high yielding but required heavy manuring too. Potatoes were tried initially on peasant plots and were taken up reluctantly at first as the varieties sown had a poor taste. Their cultivation developed most rapidly in the poorer areas as a result – in Ireland, Norway, Southern Germany and the mountain areas of France. Fallow persisted reasonably enough where climates held back the maturing of the crop and where there was no time after the harvest for new sowing – in mountain regions for example. In countries where land was not in short supply and extensive farming was carried on, fallowing was a reasonable way of avoiding the expense of manuring. Much fallowing continued justifiably in dry climates and in any case these southern regions were poorly placed to tap urban markets for animal products. But in temperate Europe the persistence of fallow was rarely justified and its disappearance is a reasonable measure of agricultural progress. In Prussia, for example, fallow declined from 21 per cent of cultivated land in 1800 to 2·5 per cent in 1913. Northern Europe had the supreme advantage over the south that its vast plains, covered by alluvial mud, made excellent grain growing soil. Summer rains allowed the growing of barley, oats and rye sown in the spring and over large areas the grain rotation system permitted two harvests a year. Each summer southern Europe was one harvest behind the north and the climate was better for pasturing there too. Climatically Hungary lay between these extremes and there the area of arable land lying fallow fell from 21·5 per cent in 1870 to only 8·4 per cent in 1910.

But diffusion depended heavily on economic factors and as we have pointed out, the rotations had the great merit of facilitating adjustment to changes in relative prices. This was particularly important in western Europe after 1870 when grain prices dropped as a result of new supplies coming to the market from the east and overseas, whereas the rapid increase of urban incomes maintained the level of prices for animal products. But in the second half of the eighteenth century it had been wheat prices that led the way, though all foodstuffs rose to some degree. Consequently improving farmers sought greater output from their land but looked most kindly on rotations which emphasised grain output. Land prices rose sharply. Among the reasons for this trend a major role must go to the rise in population; there was also an increase in the number of horses which called for more fodder and extra land. The boom, which lasted to the end of the Napoleonic Wars resulted in the spread of new methods of cultivation and also produced a great spurt of reclamation. Polder making began again in the Netherlands, in Schleswig-Holstein the cultivated area rose by 20 per cent; in almost every country in Europe individuals or governments undertook investment outlays of this kind.

The need to maintain the fertility of the soil increased as yields rose. The nitrogen derived from the fodder crops of the new rotations and the manure of the animals being pastured was only part of the answer. Night soil, wood and peat ash, oil cake were all used but about the middle of the nineteenth century the idea of using other fertilisers began slowly to take root. Crushed bones for phosphate and the import of Peruvian guano came first. Chilean saltpetre followed, though it was not used much before 1870. Sugar beet responded well to heavy applications of sulphate of ammonia and this came as a by-product of gas-making plants. Potash salts were mined at Stassfurt in Germany and after 1880 the Gilchrist Thomas process provided an excellent fertiliser in large quantities in the form of the basic slag which was drawn from the furnaces as a residue when smelting phosphoric iron ore. Particularly between 1900 and 1913 there was a very sharp increase in world consumption of fertilisers. The feared shortage of nitrogeneous fertiliser was overcome almost as soon as it was recognised, by a variety of electrolytic processes which made possible the production of a variety of compounds based on the fixation of the nitrogen in the air, though before 1914 the rapid increase in output of nitrogenous fertilisers still came overwhelmingly in the form of Chilean nitrates and sulphate of ammonia recovered from coke ovens. World production of superphosphate rose from $0 \cdot 9$ metric tons in 1880 to $4 \cdot 8$ metric tons in 1900 and $11 \cdot 2$ metric tons in 1913. Output of basic slag rose from $1 \cdot 6$m metric tons in 1900 to 4m metric tons in 1913. Slag and superphosphate, mixed with potash salts, made an ideal fertiliser for sugar beet and other root crops and was much used by Dutch farmers in particular. World consumption of potassium rose from 230,000 tons in 1900 to 1m metric tons in 1913. One other major development was the reclamation of sandy soils for arable farming which was only made possible by the application of artificial and other manures towards the end of the nineteenth century. With the heavy use of green crops and manures it became possible to grow rye on sandy soils in Denmark and North Germany, for example. Such then was the continent-wide revolution in farming practice – and also of course in chemical output – that ushered in the twentieth century.

Even so, the use of artificial fertilisers was very unevenly distributed. Table 23 gives the annual consumption of such fertilisers in kilogrammes per hectare of arable land in a number of European countries. Such figures as are given in the same source for later years suggest that consumption in Hungary and the Balkan countries

Table 23. *Use of artificial fertilisers in Europe from 1910–13*

Kg. per ha. of arable land

Denmark	25	Germany	50
Norway	14	Belgium	69
Sweden	14	Netherlands	164
France	20	Poland	17
Switzerland	15	Italy	14

Source: Cambridge Economic History of Europe vol. VI, (1965), p. 656.

was very low indeed. Insofar as farmers used artificial fertilisers on permanent grassland the figures in the table which are related only to the area of arable land are naturally boosted and this in part accounts for the very high level of consumption shown for the Netherlands. Countries with a high density of animal population of course used a great deal of animal manure. But apart from superphosphates which were widely and cheaply manufactured, the heavy use of other fertilisers was confined to a few intensive farming areas.

So long as supplies of labour posed no serious problems, progress through the use of new farm implements was geared to increasing the output per unit of land through better cultivating practices, to methods for saving crops in poor harvesting conditions, or to producing crops of higher quality. The substitution of scythe for sickle, for example, only gathered force after the 1830s, for it was simply a labour saving technique. Gains in work time of the order of 30 per cent were obtained, more for barley and oats than for bread grains, though the sickle cut lower and was easier to use on uneven land. The adoption of the scythe coincided with the decline of casual labour supplies in the west, as rural craft industries decayed and above all as women workers showed a growing disinclination for such hard labour on the farm with emigration offering a better alternative. By 1900 small tool reaping was to be found commonly only in parts of Portugal, Italy and Spain. The iron plough and seed drilling techniques were the most decisive innovations in machine technology of the eighteenth century and both were intended to increase yields rather than to save labour. The reaping machines which began to appear about the middle of the nineteenth century were certainly labour-saving but were crop saving too. Their adoption depended upon a number of circumstances; field patterns and sizes were crucially important as indeed they were for the iron plough, which was normally drawn by a horse or two and was most effectively used on fields larger than those present in most strip systems. The reaper was the more economical the heavier the crop but in the intensively farmed areas of the west it was less the cost of labour than the small size of plots that hindered its adoption. The progress of mechanical reaping in France and Germany is shown in Table 24. The contrast between France and Germany in the 1890s, however, certainly is a reflection of the large numbers of immigrant workers available on the grain estates of eastern Prussia.

Table 24. *Employment of mechanical reapers and harvesters in France and Germany*

		No.	% of corn area mechanised	Corn area (m. acres)
France	1882	35,000	6·8	2·1
	1892	62,000	11·5	3·7
Germany	1882	20,000	3·6	1·2
	1895	35,000	6·0	2·1

Source: E. L. Jones and S. J. Woolf, *Agrarian Change and Economic Development* (London, 1969), p. 75.

The much more extensive pattern of farming in Hungary and the southern steppes of Russia, for example, led to a greater use of mechanical reaping. The harvest in the Great Hungarian Plain provided 40–60 days work per person annually in the 1860s and only 14–21 days around the turn of the century. Where there were also good supplies of seasonal labour, the joint effect was to allow a greater acreage to be under arable crops and a greater proportion of the harvest to be collected in good time.

Mechanical threshing progressed much faster than reaping. When machines came early in the nineteenth century they certainly saved labour but this was probably not their main function. After all, much threshing was done in the winter months when time was less valuable and it seems likely that their main advantage to the commercial farmer was to save time and so get grain to the market as quickly as possible before the price had gone far along its usual seasonal fall. It also produced grain of a higher and more homogeneous quality which could the better compete with imported grains. But another major reason for the victory of the threshing machine was the absence of such an intermediate technology as existed between sickle and reaper. The flail was also a particularly heavy, cumbersome tool, not very suited to use by casual labour. But in considering the role of labour costs in stimulating invention and innovation in European agriculture, it is significant that potato and beet lifters, potentially the most labour saving of all inventions, made almost no progress before 1914.

New sources of power were of more than marginal importance only to the larger farms, though towards the end of the century small portable oil engines began to give the farmers the flexibility and low first cost that their operations called for. On the other hand the steam plough needed well drained fields. Its use involved much carrying of coal and water and its high first cost meant that it had to be given large stretches of land to keep it working long enough to cover its overheads. On the large estates it was useful if it eliminated temporary hired labour; all such farms had their permanent labour force and if these had nothing else to do during ploughing time, the use of the steam plough was rarely justified.

There was inevitably a considerable interaction between industrial and agricultural technologies. The spread of the iron plough, for example, was dependent in part upon improvement in the supply of iron, for a mere ten English ploughs required a ton of metal and French ploughs even more. At the same time this demand from agriculture and the rise in the numbers of horses with their requirements for shoes and nails were of major importance for the expansion of the iron industry itself. Steam power played a more limited role, for substitute power was often available; most threshing machines were still horse-powered in 1913 for example. It was in the processing industries that the contribution of industrial technology was particularly great – in the new techniques of grain milling by metal rollers, in distilling, in sugar refining, in butter making. Sometimes these gains might be remarkable indeed. In distilling the simple technological innovation of a Berlin engineer, Pistorius, patented in 1817, increased the output capacity of a distillery four fold at a capital cost which could be amortised in a year; within a decade it was being very widely used in eastern Europe. The technique of extracting sugar from beet emerged as a laboratory process in the middle of the eighteenth century, but only began to make continous progress from the 1830s. The rate of technological improvement can be gathered from figures of the percentage weight of sugar yielded from a given weight of beet roots. In Germany in 1836–40 it was 5·7 per cent and in 1899 13 per cent: in Russia the growth was more dramatic from 1·5 per cent in 1830 to 10 per cent in 1898. With this went a much greater size of productive unit – in Russia the average factory output was 51 tons in 1848 and 3,170 tons in 1898 involving, of course, a much higher level of investment. Modern Czech historians see it as the key industry in the process of industrialisation of their country from the 1860s onwards. The area under sugar beet in Bohemia and Moravia jumped from 11,500 hectares in 1859 to 123,000 in 1872. Demand for processing machinery and for steam engines to power them rose rapidly. Several engineering firms in the Prague area emerged to satisfy these needs and were eventually to play a major role in the growth of engineering generally in Bohemia. By the 1890s world beet production was already considerably higher than that of cane sugar and of a world output of 6·5 million tons in 1908–9, 5·2 million tons was produced in Germany, Austria, France and Russia (2 million, 1·3 million, 0·8 million and 1·1 million tons respectively), and for all these countries exports played a significant role in the balance of payments. Another development was the manufacture of margarine. The basic processes were discovered in France during the Napoleonic Wars but were only adapted and made commercially viable by the Jurgens Brothers much later in The Netherlands after 1870. There was no law to protect the French patents in The Netherlands but the main reason why the new industry flourished there lay in the fact that there was a historical continuity between margarine and butter. All through the nineteenth century Dutch merchants had been engaged in organising the collection of supplies of butter from many parts of northern Europe for sale to Britain in particular and now used the same contacts to distribute margarine. Huge amounts of beef tallow were needed to make oleo, the basic oil used in the process, and a network of factories was spread all over Europe from Scotland to Russia to make use of local fat supplies and there were also heavy imports from the United States. This severe limitation on growth was eliminated from about 1906 onwards through the substitution of vegetable oils such as cotton oil, coconut fat and palm-kernel oil but the bottleneck had caused overall growth in Western Europe to be relatively slow. Output in that area was about 100,000 tons in 1875 and 500,000 in 1913. In this last year the turnover was distributed as follows: Germany 210,000 tons, The Netherlands 88,000, U.K. 84,000, Denmark 42,300, Norway 27,400 and Sweden 23,600 tons. It is interesting to note that the two largest Dutch manufacturers Jurgens and van den Burgh built factories in Germany close to the Dutch border to avoid the heavy tariffs imposed in 1879. They later took over other concerns and in 1914 they were responsible for 70 per cent of total output in Germany.

The figures in Table 25 show what great variations in yields existed for various crops throughout Europe. Such calculations have serious deficiencies for analytical purposes as they fail to show the huge regional differences within countries. To some extent they reflect ignorance and poor farming practice, to some extent climatic differences and also relative factor scarcities. Where land was abundant in relation to labour, for example, it was not profitable to cultivate it so intensively and to seek such high yields as where land was relatively more expensive. The contrast between France

Table 25. *Average crop yields from 1909–13*

	Wheat	Rye	000 kg/hectare Barley	Oats	Potatoes
Denmark	33·1	16·8	23·1	18·9	148·3
Belgium	25·3	22·1	27·5	23·7	186·4
Netherlands	23·5	18·1	25·8	20·1	142·9
Germany	21·4	18·2	20·7	19·7	137·0
Austria	13·6	13·8	15·1	12·8	99·3
France	13·2	10·4	13·9	13·0	85·7
Hungary	12·6	11·7	13·3	11·1	79·7
Russia	9·1	8·5	n.a.	n.a.	74·0
Italy	10·5	11·0	8·9	10·6	57·6

Source: Scott M. Eddie, 'Agricultural production and output per worker in Hungary 1870–1913', *Journal of Economic History* (June 1968), p. 213.

and Holland must in part be explained by the fact that grain growing was a much more specialised activity in Holland, whereas in France it took a high proportion of the cultivated area in every department. But the contrast between on the one hand Austria and Italy, for example, and the best countries in the west clearly reflects in considerable measure the differences between good and mediocre farming practice. The contrast between Russian grain yields and those elsewhere is also very striking and to be explained only in small part in terms of objective conditions facing farmers there. Statistics of animal population are given in Table 26. They too must be used with care, for a large figure per head of population might indicate relatively backward nomadic forms of farming. This was the case with sheep in Russia, for example. The Russian figures for horses certainly reflect an over-abundance in relation to the size of peasant holdings. These horses were much used by the army and

Table 26. *Animal Population in Europe from 1909–13*
   (*a. per 000 population; b. per 000 hectares*)

	Cattle		Horses		Pigs		Sheep	
	a	b	a	b	a	b	a	b
Denmark	818	606	194	144	532	394	264	195
Netherlands	346	690	56	112	215	429	152	303
France	365	289	82	65	170	134	415	328
Germany	311	396	70	89	338	430	98	114
Austria	321	324	63	64	225	227	85	86
Russia	270	132	179	88	89	44	331	162

Source: Ibid., p. 214.

military purchases or confiscation caused the peasantry to keep more than strictly agricultural factors warranted.

The intensive rearing of cattle and pigs in Denmark and Holland is very apparent, though in Holland the high density of population much reduces the ratio of animals to people. These figures do not indicate of course the great strides made in the selective breeding of animals for specific purposes. Improvements in animals went by stages, and was much encouraged by the greater ability offered by new fodder crops to keep animals alive over the winter. Often areas would be known for breeding stock of above average quality and a first step would be to buy such stock to raise standards generally. Flanders bought Dutch cows: Poitou supplied beef cows to Brittany; Provence got some of its best sheep from Auvergne. A more elaborate action was the import of animals from more distant parts – sometimes as a result of government intervention. The spread of Spanish merino sheep to many parts of Europe in the eighteenth century is the outstanding example of this type of development. In 1747 Frederick the Great of Prussia imported Spanish merino rams but some years before a small flock had been imported into Sweden with official support and by 1763 there were 65,000 pure merinos in Sweden and 23,000 merino crossbreeds. Much more far reaching was the process of systematised selection and creation of new breeds. The need was obvious: Arthur Young found that in the Southern Alps the weight of adult sheep was 30 or so kilograms; today this is the weight of a 4–5 months' old lamb. Selective breeding began seriously in Britain in the eighteentu century, though at first it rested on experience and intuition rather than upon any scientific principles. But not only did this new development require major changes in control over land use, it also called for greater size of land holdings to increase the size of the herd and higher crop yields to maintain it. Not surprisingly this kind of investment was limited only to the most sophisticated of agricultural producers throughout the whole nineteenth century. Nevertheless in Hungary, for example, the native breed – primarily a draft animal – was more and more replaced by western European types of beef and dairy cattle. In 1869 the former type provided 90 per cent of the cattle population: in 1911 only 30 per cent.

The diffusion of agricultural technology followed a range of paths. Agricultural societies published journals and papers that were more and more widely read. In some countries co-operatives, either for producing, marketing, buying, finance or a combination of those, played a significant part. Sometimes there were effective government advisory services. Individual propagandists stumped around pressing their views. But above all there were the landlords or more often their stewards, who spread new ideas to their tenants and at least in Scandinavia and parts of Germany insisted on certain cropping and rotation practices through their leases. It was the small owner, free from this kind of influence, who was often least affected by technological change.

CONCLUSION

We have made this long survey of technological change partly because of its intrinsic importance in the process of development and also as a frame of reference for subsequent discussion of such development in individual countries. Inevitably we have concentrated upon the major inventions and innovations but we must stress yet again those small adjustments to techniques which went forward continuously – the changing of machine speeds, the improvements in quality, economy in materials, changes in factory layout and so forth. In total their contribution to technological change must have far exceeded that of the better known break-throughs.

But above all the process of technological change was the result of a complex interaction of forces. We can illustrate this by one final example. Several writers have commented upon the causes and effects of the growth of rural industry in Europe in the eighteenth century. There is evidence that in some parts of the continent, Flanders and Switzerland for example, the rise of agricultural productivity and the increase in inter-regional competition in agriculture forced those farmers in less fertile areas to develop rural industries as a substitute form of activity. Not all farmers responded to the pressure of competition in this way and it calls for a close study of individual societies to decide why they differed in this respect. Possibly it was easier where the tight and inflexible arrangements of the three-field system were not present; possibly too it was linked with market opportunities. Whatever the reason, some responded very positively. Eventually they were to face competition again, now from more advanced industries, using the new machines of the industrial revolution. Again some failed to survive but many responded effectively because the very process of creation of rural industry had formed the environment in which it was most likely to take place. Rural industry built up a stock of skilled labour and of experienced entrepreneurs with the will and ability to adjust yet again to changed conditions. Technological change in agriculture therefore, brought about a shift into industry and conditions which were conducive to continuous response and to further technological change. The whole economic development of many regions of Europe has to be seen as taking place under the pressure of a series of technological changes of this varied nature.

Technological change brought new goods and new qualities of goods; it played a great part in raising incomes. It is significant that one major problem of nineteenth-century society, the housing of the mass of people, was much worsened by the fact that very little technological change came about in the actual construction of houses. It remained a very labour intensive process and with real wages generally rising after the middle of the century, and sites getting progressively more expensive in urban areas, housing costs tended to rise markedly in relation to all other costs. Inevitably technology brought with it great problems in the form of the industrial conurbations and new conditions of work, though it is important to avoid romanticising what was in fact the grinding poverty and squalor of most eighteenth-century rural life. Some technologies, those in chemicals above all, caused such problems of pollution that governments intervened at an early stage to enforce some control. Elsewhere – in Sweden, for example – governments took action to regulate the depletion of forest resources. In general, however, the environment was left to look after itself.

SUGGESTED READING

The literature on technology is very scattered and in many cases highly specialised. A great deal of interest will be found in books dealing in a general way with the economic development of particular countries. Unfortunately the history of technological change itself is rarely written with any real appreciation of the economic factors involved. The economic books in turn devote little time to history. The literature in English on the economics of technology is extensive and of high quality. E. MANSFIELD, *The Economics of Technological Change* (London, 1969), J. SCHMOOKLER, *Invention and Economic Growth* (Cambridge, Mass., 1966) and W. E. G. SALTER, *Productivity and Technical Change* (Cambridge, 1960) are probably the most relevant in the context of this chapter. The chapter by A. K. SEN, 'Choice of techniques of production' in a book edited by K. BERRILL, *Economic Development with special reference to East Asia* (New York, 1964) is also valuable. In a more specialised area there is EDITH PENROSE, *The Economics of the International Patent System* (Baltimore, 1951) and also a series of interesting essays in E. A. G. ROBINSON, (ed.), *The Economic Consequences of the Size of Nations* (London, 1960).

In *The Unbound Prometheus* (Cambridge, 1969) DAVID LANDES discusses very brilliantly the development of industrial technology in Western Europe in the nineteenth century and this is the one indispensable book for students of this topic. This work first appeared in the *Cambridge Economic History of Europe*, vol. VI (1965) and there an extensive bibliography will be found. See too in that same work the article by R. PORTAL, 'The industrialisation of Russia'. *The Oxford History of Technology*, volumes IV and V edited by CHARLES SINGER and others is a very detailed study of technical change itself but is uneven in quality and absurdly biased towards British inventions. Much better from a European perspective is M. DAUMAS, *Histoire générale des techniques* (Paris, 1962–) though to date only the first three volumes, running up to 1850, have been published. The first two, lying outside our period, have appeared in an English translation. There is much of value too in A. P. USHER, *A History of Mechanical Inventions* (revd. ed., Cambridge, Mass., 1954). W. O. HENDERSON, *Britain and Industrial Europe* (Liverpool, 1954) discusses the transfer of technology across the Channel. R. CAMERON, *France and the Economic Development of Europe* (Princeton, 1961) provides some material on intra-European transfers and JOHN P. MCKAY, *Pioneers for Profit* (Chicago, 1970) is a good detailed account of foreign direct investment in Russia. F. A. SOUTHARD, *American Industry in Europe* (Boston, 1931) is helpful factually too.

As for particular sectors, the chemical industry is perhaps covered most thoroughly in L. F. HABER's two books *The Chemical Industry during the Nineteenth Century* (Oxford, 1958) and *The Chemical Industry 1900–1930* (Oxford, 1971); in P. HOHENBERG, *Chemicals in Western Europe 1850–1914* (Chicago, 1967) and J. J. BEER, *The Emergence of the German Dye Industry* (Urbana, 1959). Material relevant to continental

Europe will also be found in W. J. READER, *Imperial Chemical Industries; a History* (Oxford, 1970). E. A. WRIGLEY, *Industrial Growth and Population Change* (Cambridge, 1961) tells something of the coal industry in north-west Europe, and the coal and steel industries are discussed with varying degrees of economic sophistication by N. J. G. POUNDS in *The Ruhr* (London, 1952) and *The Upper Silesian Industrial Region* (Bloomington, 1958) and by POUNDS and W. N. PARKER in *Coal and Steel in Western Europe* (London, 1957) .The student may also wish to consult J. VIAL *L'Industrialisation de la sidérurgie française 1814–64* (Paris, 1967) and articles in the periodical *Revue d'histoire de la sidérurgie*. For Russia see R. PORTAL, *L'Oural au XVIIIᵉ siècle* (Paris, 1950).

For the textile industries there is no worthwhile modern source in English. A contemporary work of interest is G. VON SCHULZE GAEVERNITZ, *The Cotton Trade in England and on the Continent* (London, 1895) but here it is essential to consult books such as F. X. VAN HOUTTE *L'Évolution de l'industrie textile en Belgique et dans le monde de 1800 à 1939* (Louvain, 1956) and H. BLUMBERG, *Die deutsche Textilindustrie in der industriellen Revolution*, (Berlin, 1965). The literature on engineering is virtually non-existent apart from histories of particular firms. A useful account of the development of the internal combustion engine industry is to be found in E. DIESEL and others, *From Engines to Autos* (Chicago, 1960). There is a variety of books for car enthusiasts on the early pioneers such as Renault, Peugeot, and Porsche, but a more serious work is J. ICKX, *Ainsi naquit l'automobile* (2 volumes, Lausanne, 1961). H. MOTTEK, H. BLUMBERG, H. WUTZMER and W. BECKER, *Studien zur Geschichte der industriellen Revolution in Deutschland* (Berlin, 1960) is an excellent source for all technical change in German industry. Where they are available the student could with advantage consult the very interesting series of reports on overseas industries issued by the United States Bureau of Manufacturers as a *Special Agents Series* from 1907 onwards.

As for agriculture there is much to be learned from B. H. SLICHER VAN BATH, *The Agrarian History of Western Europe, 500–1850* (London, 1963). There is much of interest too in FOLK DOVRING's article, 'The transforma-tion of European agriculture' in volume VI, part II of the *Cambridge Economic History of Europe* (Cambridge, 1965) and in his book *Land and Labour in Europe 1900–1950* (The Hague, 1956). See too D. WARRINER, *The Economics of Peasant Farming* (London, 1939) and E. L. JONES and S. J. WOOLF, *Agricultural Change and Economic Development* (London, 1969). F. B. ARTZ, *The Development of Technical Education in France 1500–1850* (Cambridge, Mass., 1966) and P. N. MUSGRAVE, *Technical Change, the Labour Force and Education* (Oxford, 1967) make some contribution to this important subject.

Chapter 4

The French Revolution and the Continental System

THE FRENCH REVOLUTION AND THE INDUSTRIAL REVOLUTION

It is often argued that the most powerful dissolvent of the eighteenth-century economic structure was the tremendous social change which accompanied industrialisation. Everywhere states were forced either to industrialise or to lapse into a position of economic weakness and military helplessness. Such an argument would suggest that it was the events of the industrial revolution in Britain which changed the structure of eighteenth-century European society by making industralisation necessary. The industrial revolution, because it had to be accepted, and, because, once accepted, it had an irresistible dynamic of its own, eliminated the many barriers to economic development which eighteenth-century society presented.

It is certainly true that observers in mainland Europe noticed that the rapid developments in industry in late eighteenth-century Britain

Map 2. France during the Revolution

implied certain shifts in economic and political power. In particular they placed considerable wealth in the hands of certain bourgeois groups, and this was beginning to be reflected, although only just beginning to be reflected, in the structure of British society. Such observers also pointed to the relative strength and power of bourgeois groups in the richer mainland societies, such as France and the United Provinces, as compared to their tiny numbers and absolute political insignificance in poorer societies such as Prussia or Russia, and assumed that the startling economic changes in Britain would, if they spread to the mainland, weaken the relative economic strength of the nobility everywhere, if only by reducing the proportion of the available capital stock which they controlled. In this sense no doubt, in the long run, the industrial revolution was a powerful dissolvent of eighteenth-century society and did, by its own momentum, eliminate some of the institutional barriers to economic development which were present in that society.

Such an argument, however, is a dreadful simplification of history. To accept it as any more than a proposition about a *general tendency* of economic and social development in the nineteenth century would be a serious error. For it in no way accounts for the varying degrees of receptivity to industrial developments of different societies. To put the matter another way, certain European states which seemed, economically, to be ideally equipped for accepting the technology of the industrial revolution did not accept it for a long time, and one of the most frequent reasons for this lag in development was that their societies were incapable of assimilating such changes. The mere fact that the industrial revolution had happened outside their borders did not automatically predispose them to accept it themselves. Occasionally it had quite the opposite effect.

A much more powerful dissolvent of the society of the old régime was the series of political events in France between 1789 and 1815, the French Revolution, the counter-revolution and the reign, both as king and emperor, of Napoleon Bonaparte. The process of increasing industrialisation did gradually change the social structure of the agrarian economies of eighteenth-century Europe; but the French Revolution struck violently and suddenly at this structure and destroyed its moral justification in a way that no gradual process of economic change could ever have done. The French Revolution could not succeed in creating a new form of society to replace the old, for it did nothing to change the economic base of society. But it did create a society in which such economic changes were much easier.

Between 1789 and 1815 France experienced a successful bourgeois political revolution against the power of king and noble, a violent and prolonged peasant revolution, a series of governments and constitutions very different from anything seen before, a long political debate about the present and future state of mankind in which almost every view of the human condition subsequently to be raised in the nineteenth century was given a preliminary airing, a bitter civil war, the rule of a military usurper sanctioned by no ancient right of blood or inheritance, and twenty-one years of warfare more costly and on a more massive scale than any eighteenth-century wars. Not only was this France's experience, but that of all neighbouring mainland Europe as well. The French Revolution in order to defend its very existence sent its armies to all neighbouring states, where rulers were deposed, noblemen driven from their estates, constitutions drawn up, legal codes written and all the political assumptions of the French Revolution embodied in the creation of what it was hoped would be a new society in the whole of Europe. Finally Napoleon attempted a political and economic reconstruction of the whole European continent which carried the principles of the French Revolution into societies where it had not yet penetrated. Although in 1815 Napoleon was crushed by military defeat and everywhere, even in France itself, kings returned and king and nobles together tried to reconstruct the society of the eighteenth century, it no longer had any real support accruing to it on the basis of its moral justification or its traditional nature. After a Corsican army officer had become king and emperor through his own huge abilities no one could forget that a peasant revolution and a bourgeois political revolution in France had succeeded. Both in the changes which it effected in France and outside the borders of France, and in the subsequent example which it held before mens' eyes that extraordinary changes could be brought about by revolution, the French Revolution was the determining force of European history in the nineteenth century. The economic development of all European states was profoundly affected by it and took place under its shadow.

In the first place the French Revolution was caused by the economic difficulties which beset the society of the old régime. Although the immediate and proximate causes of the Revolution were peculiar to France, especially the financial crisis of the government, the underlying causes were generally present in almost all European societies because they were causes inherent in the nature of the old régime. The French Revolution was, in one aspect, an attempt to find an answer to the economic difficulties of eighteenth-century society generally. Even the specific financial crisis which provided the occasion for the political revolution in France had its

to raise
revenues

roots in the structure of eighteenth-century society, for it was accentuated by the difficulty of raising central government revenues when taxation was not levied on the noble classes, a difficulty which was also present in most other societies.

In the second place the success of the revolution itself served as a threat and an encouragement to other societies. Because the old régime had been seen to be destroyed in one country, the organisation of society and of the agrarian economy in all other states was threatened by the successes of the French peasants and of the French bourgeoisie. The revolutionary politicians between 1789 and 1794, whatever their position on matters of detail, professed political beliefs based on the liberation of the human spirit and on the removal of all impediments to man's full exercise of his personal capacities. Even their successors and Napoleon Bonaparte accepted many of these premises, for they were the only thing that could sanction their power. Such a plan of action won much support from bourgeois groups in other societies who gave support to similar revolutions because they felt their liberty of personal action circumscribed by aristocratic and traditional forms of government. It also fell with peculiar aptness on the ears of the rural classes elsewhere. It was a direct challenge to the whole concept of serfdom, henceforward increasingly seen as morally degrading and spiritually crippling. Furthermore, as industrial economies developed, analysts of this development came to see it also as restricting the human capacities in the same way as the old régime had done. In particular the new and growing class of industrial workers soon came to be thought of as being victims of the new society as the serfs had been victims of the old. From the views of Robespierre or Danton, who abhorred the condition of serfdom on moral grounds, to those of Marx or Engels, who abhorred the condition of proletarian on similar grounds, was but a short step. Indeed such views were fully formulated by Marx already in the 1840s. Ideologically, the Russian Revolution of 1917 was in direct descent from the French Revolution, and its economic origins had many points of similarity. The French Revolution established an equation in men's minds between revolution and human liberation which survived throughout the nineteenth century and is still a powerful force today.

The French Revolution was the first successful peasant revolution of modern times. As such it also provided an example which was to have great relevance for the rural population of other societies. The one group whose gains in the Revolution were not taken away from them in 1815 with the restoration of the king was the peasantry. The bourgeois republicans, all but the richest and most powerful of their members, were not again to control French politics until

1848, the nobles never regained the rights they had had before the Revolution even though they regained most of their lands, the restored dynasty lasted only fifteen years. But the peasants, who were united in only one thing, their hatred of the *seigneurs*, achieved their every aim, the removal of all surviving 'feudal' payments to the *seigneur* or to the church and the right to enjoy their land in full freehold tenure. Although they were already much nearer to this state of affairs than the peasantry in most other parts of Europe in the late eighteenth century, the fact that it had been achieved was of extraordinary significance in all other societies. After 1815 the French peasantry survived as an example, not a particularly literate or enlightened one, to the poorer rural classes of all other lands. That example was to be copied many times in the future, and it is not yet exhausted.

From its beginnings, therefore, the French Revolution was an event of European significance rather than merely French significance. It was responsible for the destruction of one society and the creation of another. The barriers which eighteenth-century society had opposed to social change were weakened everywhere because the justification for their existence was no longer so clear. Because these barriers, as we have seen, were often proper to the natural development of a society based on an almost wholly agrarian economy, as eighteenth-century society was, their weakening impeded the efficiency with which that economy functioned. After 1789 nobility in other European lands enforced the sanctions which were part of the agrarian system in an atmosphere of increasing unease and tried to develop methods of cultivating the land which did not seem so to depend on brutality. By weakening the capacity of the agrarian economies to function the French Revolution increased their receptivity to the economic and social changes associated with industralisation.

But at the same time as it did so it called into existence everywhere a fierce agrarian conservatism which took the form of a determined opposition to industrialisation. Industrialisation was seen as encouraging a change in the balance of social power by weakening the position of the nobility *vis-à-vis* the bourgeoisie and thus as a force furthering the type of political development associated with the French republican government. For political reasons it was resisted by some sectors of the population everywhere at all costs. Thus the very idea of economic development came to be associated with particular forms of political organisation. This association also was the result of the French Revolution. The fervour with which proposals for economic development were either advocated or rejected in the nineteenth century owed its strength to the connection forged in mens' minds between economic development and desirable, or undesirable, political and social change.

It is not simply on the ideological and the exemplary levels that the French Revolution was a European rather than a French event, however. French armies occupied at various times, the Austrian Netherlands, Liége, the United Provinces, the states of northern and western Germany, Savoy, Piedmont, Genoa, Tuscany, Lombardy, the Austrian provinces, Venezia, the Dalmatian coast, Switzerland, Spain and Poland. To a greater or less degree, they imposed the revolutionary settlement in France on these territories too. The Austrian Netherlands, Liége, the left bank of the Rhine, Piedmont and, for a shorter time, other areas of northern Italy were actually annexed to the French Empire and participated in its government and constitution. After 1806 Napoleon attempted to reorganise Europe both politically and economically to the exclusion of Britain – the 'continental system'. This expression is sometimes used to indicate no more than the series of customs measures which Napoleon took to keep out British commerce from the mainland of Europe, a mere tactical device. But this is to fail to grasp the enormous scope of Napoleon's plans which were in effect to construct on the basis of the economy of the whole of Europe an economy in France that would be the equal of the British economy.

For the whole period 1789–1815, therefore, the history of the French economy is part and parcel of that of the economy of almost the whole of Europe. Such a historical experience was quite unique to France and suggests that there is only a limited value in comparisons between economic development there and in Britain in the same period. Even after 1815, this experience was still to play its part in French economic history, in the revolution of 1830, in the revolution of 1848, in the history of the Paris commune, and, more importantly, in the social structure which it bequeathed to France which was quite distinct for a long time from that of other states. The relationships between the French Revolution and economic life were extremely complicated. So were the relationships between the French economy and other European economies in this period, and of this second subject much less is known, although such relationships were more important than in subsequent periods.

This is the more unfortunate as it was in the period of the French Revolution that the vital organisational changes, the concentration of labour and capital together with the introduction of new mechanical methods of production which were essential to the industrial revolution first took firm root in France and elsewhere. Within the terms of our definition of 'industrial revolution' in Chapter 1 such a revolution took place in France between 1770 and 1815. A word of caution is necessary here. So small was the growth of total physical output over that period compared to its extraordinary growth in Britain that if we define 'industrial revolution' in terms of a sudden rapid rise in the output of manufactured goods and use previous events in Britain as a means of measuring how great that increase ought to be, we would not categorise these years in France as being a period of 'industrial revolution' there. But if the importance of the 'industrial revolution' lies in the fact that it was a revolution, a revolution in economic and social organisation, its beginnings in France can be unhesitatingly placed in this period.

It is necessary to be very clear about definitions of 'industrial revolution' in this case. Economic historians have always disagreed on when the industrial revolution occurred in France, because they have disagreed on the nature of the phenomenon they were looking for. Some have even held that there was no industrial revolution in France at all, because the changes associated with the growth of industrial society there were so long drawn-out compared to their sudden and violent nature in Britain and, later in the nineteenth century, in other countries such as Germany or Russia. But the changes which *did* take place in French industry and in French society were so like those which had previously characterised the British economy that most economic historians, reasonably enough, have agreed that France did indeed have an industrial revolution and have tried to define it temporally. Some, Dunham for instance, place it between 1815 and 1848.[1] Others have tried to place it as late as the 1850s.

The tendency to relegate the industrial revolution in France to a later period in the nineteenth century has been partly the result of not clearly defining the concept of 'industrial revolution'. If, instead of looking for such an organisational and social phenomenon, we look rather for a period of time when the rate of growth of the economy is suddenly much increased and for the economic phenomena which many have argued are related to such an increase (higher ratios of investment to consumption for example), the only such period that can be discovered in France is that of the 1850s. To set aside the concept of the 'industrial revolution', therefore, and to use a supposedly more scientific one such as 'the take-off into self-sustained growth', would demand placing this 'take-off' in mid-nineteenth-century France. It is very difficult to argue, however, that the economic phenomena of the 1850s in France have much in common with the 'take-off' in Britain in the late eighteenth

[1] In his book, A. L. Dunham, *The Industrial Revolution in France, 1815–1849* (New York, 1955).

century and early nineteenth century. There seems to exist a happy coincidence between the 'industrial revolution' in many countries and the 'take-off' there; they happened at more or less the same time. This is not so in France, where no apparent coincidence exists between the introduction of new methods of mass production and industrial organisation and unusually high growth rates. The only coincidence that does exist is that the second railway boom of the 1850s seems to have its effect in the high rate of growth that can be measured in that decade.

Before that time, however, French textile industries and, in particular, the cotton goods industry had not only undergone a complete transformation but had registered enormous increases in production so that by 1848 their output was far beyond the scope of anything dreamed of by eighteenth-century statesmen. By that date also the French iron industry had developed the technology of a new age, big blast-furnaces and rolling-mills, which produced a similar, although less marked, rise in output. In the 1840s the first railway boom saw the completion of many of the most important lines of the railway network. By the 1850s therefore, France already had much of the apparatus of an industrial society. Whether or not the concept of an 'industrial revolution' is thought to have any meaning, the vital changes in the French economy took place before the 1850s, and the first of them, particularly those in the cotton goods industry, took place before 1815.

The early history of the industrial revolution in France was thus inextricably mixed with events in the whole of continental Europe. It was a much less isolated and clear-cut phenomenon than the first industrial revolution and this is one reason why the pattern of growth of the French economy after the start of the industrial revolution was significantly different from that recorded earlier in Britain. The industrial revolution in France began in a period of exceptional political uncertainty and extreme and violent economic disturbance.

THE ECONOMIC CAUSES OF THE FRENCH REVOLUTION

The economic origin of the French Revolution was the general shift of economic forces in eighteenth-century agriculture to favour the larger noble landowners. The long-run rising trend in the price of bread grains, caused by the rise in population, favoured those whose units of landholding were sufficiently large to farm them for a cash crop whose price was well-sustained. Such a movement provided a reassuring background to the economic operations of most noble landowners because it greatly increased the potential value of the capital stock which they held. Where the noble directly exploited the land himself by means of serfdom, this potentially increased value could be converted into an actual increase in value by a resolute enforcement of all the legal and customary sanctions at the noble's command. This we have already seen happening in many of the areas of northern Germany east of the River Elbe. But in France, where the system of noble exploitation of the estate had for long been to lease it out to peasant cultivators and where those leases had become extremely difficult to alter or revoke, the noble's chances of capitalising on the upward trend in grain prices depended on the extent to which he could increase the sums of money paid to him by the peasants in recognisance of his 'feudal' superiority.

The general theme of French noble landowners' activity in the eighteenth century is their attempt to compensate for the fact that so large a part of the land was cultivated by peasants on secure tenures by applying a wide range of financial pressures on that peasantry. This they were able to do by virtue of their local power as judges, the *noblesse de robe* increasingly became spokesmen and defenders of the cause of the nobility as a whole and their legal judgments on matters of land law and feudal tenure during the century slowly eroded the peasantry's defences against noble pressures. Indeed, the *noblesse de robe* because of their legal knowledge and power were usually considered more grasping as landlords than the more ancient *noblesse d'épée*. The quit-rents (*cens*) paid for the leases could often not be increased because they had become customary payments or could only be increased at infrequent intervals. Noble landlords, therefore, resorted to every device which their status as *seigneur* still accorded them. Minor dues (*banalités*),[2] many of which had been falling into disuse and in some cases had actually fallen into disuse, were revived and claimed to their full extent.

Such developments, although they rested on ancient laws and privileges and although argued in law courts in an archaic language and sometimes decided on archaic legal prejudices, were in fact symptomatic of the relatively high level of development of the French economy. It was the good internal means of transport and relatively high level of specialisation of function in the countryside which gave France an active grain market, both locally and for exports to Spain and Italy. It was the existence of this grain market

[2] See Chapter 1.

which determined the fact that French landlords were more interested in the commercial exploitation of their estates than were their peers in most other parts of Europe. One of the most active local grain trades in France was that along the Canal du Midi from the Toulouse area both to the Bay of Biscay and the Mediterranean. Cash from grain sales was an important part of the income of nobles in that area. Those peasants everywhere whose unit of landholding was big enough to allow them to participate in the trade benefited in much the same way. Everything depended on having a sufficiently large unit, and, in order to keep their holding, the more substantial peasants were obliged to bow to the legal pressures and financial demands of the noble landlords. The tenacity with which 'feudal' right was defended in the eighteenth century was thus for a purpose which was in most respects thoroughly commercial rather than feudal.

For most peasants the financial burden of keeping land or acquiring land increased as the potential gains from the land also increased. By virtue of its legal and social position the French nobility was able to mop up a lot of the increased profit on farming operations; in their case, ultimate ownership of the land was made to compensate financially through feudal law for the fact that only with the greatest difficulty could they extend the physical area which they themselves exploited directly. A brief depression in bread grain prices and a drop in wine prices in 1770 fell in such circumstances with peculiar force on those peasants who were being forced to make such high payments to maintain their land holdings. The fall in prices only exacerbated the nobility's demands for cash because their own profits from grain sales diminished. It in no way weakened their grip on the land for their capital reserves were ample to tide them through so brief a contraction. For those peasants who were not selling a cash crop, the *manouvriers*, the fall in food prices brought only relief. Their relief, however, was short-lived, for in 1788 the underlying upward trend of prices reasserted itself. The harvest of 1788 was a disaster, one of the worst of the century, so that by spring 1789 prices were higher than they had been since the great famines at the beginning of the century. The poorer peasantry were submerged in the most acute distress and some were forced to leave the countryside for towns. The cumulative effect of these price movements was thus to weaken over a comparatively short period both richer and poorer peasants. The only class able to ride out the storm was the nobility. The great distress of 1789 sharpened to the point of fury the peasants' desire to get rid of the claims on their income which the nobles' feudal rights represented.

The dreadful harvest of 1788 also coincided with a severe political crisis whose origins were the nobility's wish to translate its increasing economic power into political power. They seized on the acute financial problems of the royal government as a lever by which they could hoist themselves into power. The shortage of revenue of the central government was partly a function of the narrowness of the tax base. The amount of tax which could be raised from noble assets or income was insignificant, and it was this factor also which gave the *seigneurs* a great economic advantage over other land owners during the period of sharp price fluctuations. Several schemes had been proposed by the government in the eighteenth century to remedy this state of affairs. It was the scheme proposed by the Minister of Finances, Calonne, in 1786, which brought matters to an open conflict and precipitated an attempt by the nobility to control the monarchy.

The crux of Calonne's proposals was an attempt to replace the one direct tax which fell on all the population, the *vingtième*, by a general land tax, which, once approved, would not need further sanctioning by the *parlements*. Although, when the *vingtième* was levied, the nobles also paid, the method of assessment was such that they paid a very much smaller proportion of their income than did the unprivileged classes. Not only was this the case, but the *vingtième* could only be levied after prior approval by the *parlements*. A permanent tax on land would bear much more heavily on the nobility and it would also secure to the central government some part of the increased value of land in the eighteenth century. Furthermore, in levying the tax no distinction between noble and non-noble land would be made so that the new taxation proposals were also construed as an initial attack on the whole structure of noble privilege. It appeared that land ownership and not ancient lineage was to become the basis of rural society for the tax would be assessed by local assemblies of all landowners.

The fierce political opposition which these proposals aroused has to be seen against the background of other eighteenth-century societies. Frequently where the nobility had been subjected firmly to the control of the central government they had been given extensive privileges in return. In France the ancient place as the defenders of the constitution against absolutism which they believed themselves to occupy was being threatened at the same time as the most important of their privileges and the bases of their economic power. Their opposition led them to demand the recall of France's ancient constitutional assembly, the Estates-General of the realm. When the government bowed to pressure and agreed to summon this body, which had not met since the seventeenth century, the bourgeoisie, who formed the Third Estate, proved even more tenacious in their constitutional demands and in addition to be thoroughly hostile to the whole concept of noble privilege.

The long constitutional struggle which began between king, nobility and bourgeoisie and which touched at many points on the reorganisation of eighteenth-century society was turned into a violent revolution by the hunger and misery of the weeks when the harvest of 1788 no longer sufficed and before that of 1789 could be gathered. The price of bread, especially in Paris, reduced consumer spending on manufactured products. The workshop industries, of which Paris was the greatest European centre, saw their production fall steeply in 1789 and unemployment joined to hunger provided a political weapon for those bourgeois groups excluded from the staid deliberations of the self-constituted National Assembly. The debates on the reconstruction of society coincided with the most vivid evidence of its injustice.

It was in these circumstances, independently of the political riots in Paris, that the peasants themselves revolted against the system. It was this revolt and the length of time it was sustained and the determination with which it was pursued that forced the series of constitutional assemblies in Paris, often much against their will, to dismantle the whole apparatus of feudal law. There were serious riots in July 1789 in Normandy, Alsace, the Mâconnais and Franche-Comté. The object of these riots was usually the noble château where the feudal charters on which the *seigneur*'s claims were based were destroyed. Peasant riots, a common event in the eighteenth century, were made more serious because of the hunger in the countryside and were given a political objective by the debates in Paris and the other municipalities.

The first step in dismantling feudal law was taken by the National Assembly on 4 August 1789. The deputies in an orgy of recrimination against each others' privileges, in an idealistic effort to reform the structure of society, and in an attempt to introduce some uniform rationality into the legal system, renounced in some cases and abolished in others certain categories of feudal privilege. When this bout of legislation came to be codified the preamble to the law began boldly, 'the National Assembly destroys in entirety the feudal system'. In reality, what was done was far from meeting the wishes of the peasantry. The legislation was not ratified by the king until October and was immediately repudiated by him in his communications to foreign governments. Furthermore, in codifying the legislation the Assembly drew a distinction between feudal dues and payments attached to the person of the feudal superior, which were thought to have been imposed at some time in the past by main force, and dues and payments for the ownership or use of land, held to be the result of an implicit legal contract and representing a legitimate form of property. Only the former category was abolished without compensation or payment. The only dues from which the peasants were universally liberated were such *banalités* as payments to the *seigneur* not to exercise his hunting rights over their crops or to feed pigeons on them. Dues associated with land transfer or inheritance, entry fees and the other large payments were still liable for payment. Nor did the peasant gain from the abolition of tithe in 1790 for it could now be added to the 'rent' of the land.

By February 1790 the rural violence had become a major revolt in Britanny, in Lorraine and in the central and south-western provinces. But it was a combination of urban rioting with the constant demands of the peasantry that really brought the old régime to an end in rural France. The revolt of the lesser bourgeoisie and artisans against both monarch and Assembly in August 1792 led to the flight of over half the deputies and to the emigration of a significant number of nobles. The National Assembly, transformed into the Convention, introduced universal male suffrage. Its decree of 25 August abolished all feudal payments to *seigneurs* unless the *seigneur* could establish his claim legally on some other basis than that he had previously executed it for forty years. At the same time measures were taken to sell the lands of those noblemen who had fled.

In July 1793 a new law ordered the destruction of all feudal title deeds. By doing so it completed the removal of feudal payments by abolishing them even in those cases where, under the law of August 1792, the *seigneur* had still been able to produce his original feudal charter allowing him to claim the dues. Even at this stage the Convention, fearful of the fundamental rights of property which they wished to safeguard on every hand, tried to limit the abolition of dues to contracts which were feudal in nature. Because of the activities of eighteenth-century landlords in seeking to improve their position by reviving feudal law and adding it even to contracts which had been for the most part straightforward leases the distinction proved too fine to make in the political circumstances. In February 1794 it was swept away too. The land legislation of that month remained the fundamental law of the land throughout the nineteenth century even after the restoration of the French monarchy. Under the terms of these successive laws the French peasantry was turned into a peasant freeholding class with firm rights of tenure in the land and free of the financial burdens which it had previously borne.

THE ECONOMIC CONSEQUENCES OF THE FRENCH REVOLUTION

Such important changes in the economic position of the greater part of the rural community must be counted both for France and Europe as of the greatest consequence. They finally amounted to the destruction of the old régime in France and they began its destruction everywhere, although in eastern Europe only at a long remove.

The creation of a class of peasant proprietors with vested property rights for which they had fought so hard was the most obvious consequence of the Revolution. The rural code issued by the Constituent Assembly gave the landowner the free disposition of his land. He could enclose it if he wished and in so doing could limit the old practice of *vaine pâture*, the pasturing of the common herd on the stubble fields after the harvest, which had been so formidable a barrier to enclosure everywhere. The full liberty of the grain trade was confirmed. This settlement which embodied the clearest principles of physiocratic and liberal economics has, however, been frequently considered to have had a retarding effect on the development of the French economy. Theoretically the peasant should have had a greater proportion of his income available to him either for investment or consumption, in many cases one-third more. But most small peasant farms continued to be farmed in the traditional way and the movement to agricultural improvement of the late eighteenth century did not noticeably accelerate in the early nineteenth century. Throughout the period of the Revolution and the Empire government policy showed much interest in encouraging agricultural improvement. But in the most important area, the reduction of the amount of fallow land either by the development of artificial meadows or by the introduction of crop rotations including root crops, there was little change. The immediate consequences of the Revolution on the land may even have been a slowing down of the pace of agricultural improvement.

The land settlement did nothing to change the physical lay-out of the fields or villages. Indeed by establishing the property rights of the peasants it prevented any such drastic changes in land organisation and use as were enforced from above in Denmark or in the enclosure movement in Britain. The intermingled strips in the open fields remained, frequently unhedged and unditched. The small size of the total land holding of the individual peasant and its divided nature often meant that in spite of his increased income he was discouraged from undertaking the relatively high capital investment necessary to radically alter his farming methods. Before 1815 the government tried by example and exhortation to encourage such changes; after 1815 no attempts at improving the level of education and knowledge in the countryside were seriously undertaken apart from a brief flicker of interest in the 1848 revolution. The survival of the old farming system meant also the survival of many of the communal practices which had prevailed under the old régime. In fact the peasant revolt had in many areas been a revolt to retain those communal practices on which the activities of the landlords had increasingly infringed in the eighteenth century. Thus, for example, the reoccupation of common lands which had been incorporated into the domain in the previous period was a frequent occurrence in the revolutionary period. It was on the common rights that the poorer members of the community depended to supplement their incomes. The peasantry, while eager to liberate their land from the payment of dues, by no means all accepted the view of individual property rights which the bourgeois revolutionaries themselves subscribed to. The practice of *vaine pâture* seems to have continued in many villages in the early nineteenth century although it stood for a conception of property very different from that embodied in the revolutionary land settlement.

All this is to paint a rather gloomy view of the results of the Revolution in this respect. It is a view which is certainly justified by the later history of French agriculture. It remained backward and unresponsive to change and among the reasons for this state of affairs the historical and institutional ones weigh heavily. But it is much less frequently pointed out that the Revolution brought about a sharp upward shift in the income of many peasants. Accounts of their standard of comfort in the 1820s suggest a definite improvement over their level of the last years of the old régime. It is very possible that this improvement provided the stimulus to consumption on the domestic market which allowed the French cotton goods industry to expand in a period when the exports which had been so high a proportion of its output in the eighteenth century became impossible because of war and blockade. There are no indications that the output of consumer goods industries in France suffered any long-term disruption by the loss of so many rich markets, although the growth of their output may not have been so high as it would otherwise have been. Here, the French countryside must have compensated for the loss of Haiti, and for that the Revolution must be responsible. In spite of the doubtful benefits which they conferred on French agriculture the changes in the status of the peasantry conferred one real benefit on French industry at a time when such an incentive was particularly valuable.

Combined with these changes in income distribution were changes in land ownership brought about by the confiscation of church lands and the confiscation of the estates of nobles who fled the country to fight with the Revolution's enemies. From this redistribution of land the peasants were not the main beneficiaries, who were rather those bourgeois with sufficient income or credit to purchase the confiscated lands when they were put on sale. The sales of such land were very successful even in areas where anti-revolutionary sentiment was strong. The Catholic sentiments of the inhabitants of the department of Nord did not prevent them acquiring two-thirds of the available 'national lands' by the end of 1793. One reason for this success was that the lands were sometimes sold relatively cheaply. The most usual method of sale was by auction in quite large lots, lots usually too large for the peasant to purchase. The bourgeois supporters of the Revolution were able to acquire unencumbered land and to acquire it by means of the depreciating paper money issued by the government. In December 1794, when the real fall in the value of the paper currency began, many instalments of payments for national lands were still to be paid. Only in September 1793 was a serious attempt made to allow the poorer rural classes to secure these new lands by means of small loans. It was ineffective and short-lived.

The biggest loser in this redistribution of land was the church, which lost all. In some areas it had previously held up to 20 per cent of the available stock. The nobility lost less and was subsequently able, under Napoleon, and later, when the restored monarchical government voted money to it to allow it to repurchase estates, to regain part of what it had lost. In the Nord its share of the available land fell from 21 per cent in 1789 to about 13 per cent in 1804. That was an area where the noble share of the land had already been lower than elsewhere in 1789. Unfortunately we have few studies for more representative areas. In the same area the peasants' share of the land rose over the same period from about 30 per cent to about 62 per cent. There too the peasants' share was already very high before the Revolution. The bourgeois' share rose from about 16 per cent to about 28 per cent. Considering the small number of bourgeois the increase in the size of their individual holdings was obviously important. Studies of the sale of national lands elsewhere suggest that the proportion of the available stock sold to peasant buyers was higher in the Nord. In the neighbourhood of Versailles and of Mantes they seem to have got hold of only about 13 per cent of the new land. Redistribution of land cannot be said to have greatly added to the peasants' income or possibilities of action.

One process it did continue was the elimination of differences in income and status between noble and bourgeois. It has been argued that because most wealth was in the form of land or buildings and because most investment went into those real estate channels there was no essential difference of economic function in eighteenth-century France between noble and bourgeois. In Toulouse, between 1789 and 1799, 80 per cent of the wealth bequeathed was immobilised in such assets whether bequeathed by noble or bourgeois. But it should be remarked also that the average noble fortune over that period in Toulouse was 239,222 francs; the average size of a bourgeois fortune 22,205 francs. The difference between the bourgeoisie and those below them was also tenfold, but, evidently, the gap between bourgeois and noble was greater because of the absolute amounts involved. In closing such a gap the events of the Revolution could have made little difference, but the elimination of all noble privileges and the very elimination of the legal distinctions appertaining to the rank itself combined with the increase in the landholdings of the bourgeoisie went some way towards this. The later history of formerly noble fortunes in the nineteenth century is not known but the social and political role, at least, of the great landed estate became considerably less important in France than it was in most other European societies.

The Revolution's insistence on individual rights had important consequences in the industrial sector also. The National Assembly on the night of 4 August 1789 when so many privileges were renounced also abrogated the privileges of the guilds. This was confirmed by the Le Chapelier resolution of 1791 prohibiting all forms of association by capital or labour and so ending the long history of the guilds and of the privileged royal manufactures in France. The corporate charters under which the 'manufactures' of the previous century had operated were annulled. The Declaration of the Rights of Man in 1793 affirmed the principle of economic liberty. The *formal* destruction of the corporate system and the *formal* establishment of liberty of enterprise also proved an example to liberal reformers in other lands. The battle for a similar declaration became an important theme of the history of many German states in the next fifty years.

It would be unfair to leave the impression that the legacy of the Revolution to the rest of Europe consisted only in the establishment of the principle of individual property rights, which lay at the heart of liberal philosophy, and in the memory of a successful peasant revolution. As we have seen those two themes of the Revolution had, in any case, not been in complete harmony with each other and they were certainly not to prove so in the future in other societies. The Revolution was a more complicated event than this. Two other economic legacies were also bequeathed. One was the dream of a just and humane 'republic' embodied in the degrees of the Committee of Public Safety. The other was the idea of a rational, efficient, centralised society, free of the multitudinous traditional obstacles of the old régime to proper administration, the barnacles with which history had encrusted the ship of state.

When in the winter of 1793–4 the young republic found itself at war with the other great European powers it discovered that its liberal economic principles were not entirely compatible with the need to organise a war economy and to deal at the same time with its many internal enemies. Riots caused by political discontent and by the high price of bread put the legislators in the position of sharing their power with the Paris artisans. The policies that emerged in this period were intended to defend the new state and keep the support of the populace. The legislators bowed to outside pressure and initiated a period of controlled prices which seemed to hark back to the social policies of the mercantilist royal governments of the past. The fixing both of wages and prices, although it had a long tradition, was also, in this case, inspired by a certain ideal of social justice. This ideal inspired the first schemes of free medical treatment for the elderly, for nursing mothers and for widows, the education acts which established free and compulsory primary education, and the abolition of slavery, afterwards reintroduced by Napoleon. All these measures were later to be associated with the Revolution just as the abolition of noble privilege had been.

For those societies which were to be occupied by French armies it was the centralising and nationalising aspect of the Revolution which was to have a more direct effect, for this aspect was central to the policies of French occupation governments elsewhere whereas many of the other aspects of the Revolution were only exportable with more caution and difficulty. The old provinces of France with their many different relationships to the central government were divided into a rational system of local government units of more uniform sizes. The same reform of local government structures was introduced in all those territories annexed in Napoleon's campaigns. The legal systems of the country, both civil and criminal, were simplified and codified in a marvellously sustained effort which embodied the liberal principles of the Revolution.

These law codes were also to be introduced into annexed territories. The 'Civil Code', for example, remained the law after 1815 on the left bank of the Rhine and created a sharp distinction between commercial practice and law there and in the rest of Germany. A uniform set of metric weights and measures replaced the many regional standards which had formerly served. The metric system also was used in conquered territories after its adoption in France and came gradually to be adopted elsewhere in the nineteenth century. This drive to rationalisation also eliminated the internal tolls and tariff barriers in the French economy and brought to fruition the work of reformers like Turgot in turning the domestic market into a large free trade area. The customs barrier was removed between the different categories of provinces and set on the frontiers of France. The privileges of the old free ports were ended. As a part of that reform the inequalities in taxation between the different provinces were removed.

THE CONTINENTAL SYSTEM

It was only in that one particular, however, that the republican governments continued the commercial policy of the last years of the old régime. The royal government had earlier sought to stimulate industrial development by lowering the tariff on the import of manufactures. The keystone of their policy had been the commercial treaty with Britain in 1786 which provided for reductions of customs dues by each party. The treaty was designed to end the bitter commercial warfare between the two countries which had lasted without respite for over a century. The fall in industrial production in France in 1788 was blamed on the treaty, the cotton goods manufacturers especially claiming that they had been exposed to competition with an industry in a far more advanced state of mechanisation. There is no doubting the unpopularity of the treaty among the members of the Assembly and in the country as a whole. The period of commercial peace with Britain was to last only seven years, the republic revived the warfare of the earlier period and reverted to a protectionist and mercantilist policy. Napoleon's 'continental system' was a more systematic expression of this, a logical development in wartime of a policy which had governed Franco-British commercial relations on each side for all but the briefest of periods since 1688.

The 1786 trade treaty with Britain was renounced in 1793 and later in the same year a Navigation Act limited the import of goods into France to French ships or to ships of the country of origin unless vessel and goods were covered by the issue of a specific licence. A law of 1796 excluded all British goods. In 1798 the colonial trade was entirely reserved to France, although, because of French naval inferiority in the war and the capture of French colonies by enemy forces, such an act was not very effective. The barrier of tariffs and prohibitions was not a strategic device, it was the expression of protectionist sentiment of a democratic assembly. The first increases in tariffs were not aimed against the British but against the woollen manufacturers of the Duchy of Berg in 1791. As the war pursued its course and French military successes on land were countered by naval defeats and the loss of colonies in other continents, proposals began to be considered for excluding British manufactures from the mainland entirely and reserving that market to French industry. Between 1792 and 1800 the official share of France and the Low Countries, which were controlled by French arms, in British exports dropped only from 15 per cent of the total exports by value to 12 per cent. As for most of the eighteenth century the main trade route between the two countries was smuggling, which not only made the official statistics of doubtful value but greatly diminished the value of protection.

Once Napoleon's extraordinary career of conquest had begun there seemed a greater practical possibility of enforcing a protective system which would extend over most of the European market. The origins of this system, the 'continental system', lay in the French Revolution rather than in specific changes of policy by Napoleon himself. Its effects on the development of the French economy have been much argued. It was partly an automatic response to the loss of the colonial trade in wartime, partly a policy of economic warfare against Britain and partly a plan for the development and encouragement of French industry. But at its heart lay the policy of protecting the French market itself against all comers, friend or foe. French protectionism clashed with any wider European revolutionary aspirations and, taking a large view of the continental system, it is fair to categorise it as an attempt to reserve the whole of Europe for French manufactured goods while using it as the prime source of supply of raw materials to France. Once the major European manufacturer, Britain, was excluded from the market such a development was implicit in the situation. But French legislation, in those cases where there was a well-established manufacturing sector outside the new frontiers of France, as on the right bank of the Rhine in the Siegerland and Sauerland, made it explicit. Manufacturers in other countries were often not at all reluctant to be protected against their British competitors. It was a different matter with the trade in colonial goods, tea, sugar, coffee and cocoa. The naval warfare eliminated France from this trade in which she had played so large a part, leaving Britain and certain neutrals, such as the United States, as the only possible suppliers. French decrees against neutrals and the policy of commercial warfare with Britain required the prohibition of a large part of these colonial goods also. This destroyed most of the support outside France for these protective measures making them appear, what in large part they were, an extended measure of protection to the French economy alone.

The continental system was a complicated diplomatic, political and economic construction whose beginning and end is not easy to define. But it may be said to have been erected finally in 1806 after the defeat of Prussia. In that year the French tariff was increased again and the import of cotton manufactures prohibited. This was followed in the same year by the issuing of the Berlin Decrees. All British goods were now excluded from those areas of the continent controlled by, or in alliance with, France and so were a number of other goods deemed to be British whatever their origin. The Decrees were the extension of the French protective system to give French industry a larger market and were also a continuation of the commercial warfare with Britain. They were supplemented, after the inclusion of Russia and Turkey in the continental system through alliances, by the Milan Decrees of 1807. But the continental system was not just a protective device. It also had positive aspects. On the political side it was an attempt at a confederation of states bound together by a common social system based on the new French Civil Code. On the economic side it was a positive system for the encouragement of industrial development in France. Protective tariffs were only one aspect of this encouragement. The system also provided new mechanisms for the creation and stimulation of industry, aids to industrial research, and rules for the regulation of industrial activities. In those areas of industry where the Assembly had proclaimed complete liberty Napoleon introduced the same positive mercantilism that informed his views on trade and created a new framework of industrial administration which replaced the old corporate system.

Before its collapse in the war against Russia the continental system underwent one important modification. The Berlin Decrees had increased the amount of smuggling because some of the colonial goods prohibited, sugar for instance, had, in the eighteenth century, become staples of daily existence rather than luxuries. In 1810 colonial goods were admitted on payment of a very high duty. This change made the barrier against British manufactured goods all the more effective and also brought a higher income to the French treasury. The system as a whole was an uncompromising acceptance of France's changed situation, and an attempt to replace that important source of eighteenth-century development, extra-European trade, carried on only with difficulty between 1793 and

1805 and after 1805 scarcely carried on at all, with a different source for development, the whole continent of Europe. How did the French economy fare during this period of revolution, warfare and reorientation? What effect did the abrupt break with the pattern of eighteenth-century trade and development have on the size and structure of French industry?

THE DEVELOPMENT OF FRENCH INDUSTRY

The industrial revolution in France began before the outbreak of the French Revolution and pursued its course during the ensuing disturbances. The period between 1789 and 1815 cannot therefore be said to have impeded economic development except in a relative sense. In an absolute sense, at certain times the changes of policy provided a stimulus for particular industries and encouraged developments of great value for the future. Once the problem is seen as one of relative economic development the conclusion to be drawn must be a different one. The gap in the volume of industrial output and in the level of technological development between France and her major competitor, Britain, which seems to have been closing in the eighteenth century, widened. The growth in total output between 1789 and 1815 was much less in France than in Britain. The continuing technological innovation on which the growth of industrial output so much depended proceeded in this period at a much slower pace in France than in Britain. Indeed, the rate of technological innovation in the industries which had been most responsible for eighteenth-century economic development slowed down in France while it accelerated in Britain. It may be, that although the process of the industrial revolution already begun was consummated in these years, the development of the French economy was not as rapid as it would have otherwise been. In that sense the Revolution and its consequences were an impediment to the growth of the French economy in this period.

The disturbance of the Revolution created uneasy business conditions and the economy does not seem to have recovered very well from the disasters of 1788–9 before it was plunged into the further slump of 1796. Real recovery only came with the nineteenth century and that was interrupted by the business crises of 1808 and 1810–11. These crises were partly provoked by changes in political conditions and in the political outlook and the political situation seems to have made them more severe than they might otherwise have been.

But even if these movements are regarded as normal business cycles and not to be blamed more than other such cyclical movements or political events the Revolution certainly imposed other difficulties of its own making on the French economy.

In an age when the diffusion of scientific and technological information was a less organised business than it now is the rate of technological innovation depended on keeping in very close cultural contact with those societies where innovation was most advanced. In the kind of technological innovation that was responsible for the development of mass-productive techniques in the textile and metallurgical industries this was even more important. The vital innovations in those industries in the later eighteenth century were frequently not, strictly speaking, scientific innovations, but innovations of different production techniques. Some minor detail of machinery, some small change in the process of production, would be much more significant than a major theoretical discovery. There was no satisfactory alternative to visiting the workshop or factory where the best available technique was practised and to seeing how it was done. As far as French industry in the eighteenth century was concerned the technological gap between its own production techniques and the more advanced ones in Britain had always been present. But the readiness of French entrepreneurs to borrow techniques had meant that innovation in Britain quickly passed across the channel to France. The advantage to the discoverer of a new manufacturing process was therefore very short-lived. This symbiosis of the two economies was rudely shattered by the war after 1793. Technological copying was still possible in wartime, although it was difficult, costly and sometimes dangerous, but it was not possible to the degree necessary to maintain the narrow gap between the two economies, for the narrowness of that gap depended on frequent visits by French manufacturers to those works in Britain where techniques were more advanced. In wartime this was not feasible. It is remarkable how many French manufacturers visited Britain in the one brief period of peace between 1793 and 1814. The number leaving for Britain in 1814 and 1815 seems to have been even larger, a measure of how much wider the technological gap had become and how much worse France's competitive position was in 1815 than it had been in 1793.

The loss of extra-European markets was obviously a severe problem but by 1801 it had been overcome by the development of the domestic market and of other European markets. The simplicity of revolutionary fashions, for example, placed great emphasis on the production of finer muslins to which French cotton manufacturers seem to have been able to respond with alacrity. Similarly, the success of the famous woollen goods manufacturer, Ternaux, after 1805 was due to his skill in imitating 'cashmere' shawls and popularising them in a wider market. Changes in markets were part and parcel of the cloth industry, the penalty of producing a consumer good so susceptible to changes in fashion. The changes in markets after 1793 were an exaggeration of the normal process, but they did not create insuperable difficulties. The difficulties of keeping abreast of the latest machines were insuperable, there was no adequate source of information outside Britain.

In other industries the loss of extra-European trade was a much worse handicap. Some, such as sugar-refining, had depended on a raw material provided in large part through the colonial trade. The sugar refiners of the great colonial ports, Bordeaux and Nantes, fell on evil days after 1793. It was in the west and south-west of France that the reorientation of French trade had the most drastic effects. The thriving trans-Atlantic commerce of these areas came to a standstill. The industrial activities in the countryside of Gascony, Poitou, Aquitaine and Maine which had depended on trans-Atlantic exports had disappeared by 1815 leaving the inland regions purely agricultural areas. Those areas of the French countryside where domestic industry continued to thrive and where it developed into a more mechanised factory industry were in the northern and eastern regions. One factor in this development was the general eastward reorientation of foreign trade and the concentration on the domestic market. The industrial axis of France titled north-eastwards towards the Rhine and the Channel.

– the Cotton Industry

The difficulty in the supply of raw materials applied with particular force to the French cotton industry. Even by 1812, after much experiment with growing raw cotton in Europe and some success in Italy, European cotton, including Turkish cotton, still only accounted for 12 per cent of France's total consumption. The price of raw cotton in Paris or Ghent was more than twice as high as in London between 1806 and 1814. Not only was this the case but cotton coming from the Levant sold for half the price in Leipzig that it fetched in Paris or Ghent. Yet the cotton goods industry developed more successfully than most other French industries and did so while textile industries based on indigenous raw materials did far less well. The French cotton goods industry passed beyond the stage of domestic industry between 1780 and 1792 with the intro-duction of mule-jennies and water frames. By 1815 it was organised as a concentrated factory industry. The use of steam-power to drive the machinery was much less frequent than in Britain, but Périer had built his first steam engines before 1792 and in some factories steam power was already used in the same way as in Britain.

The movement towards concentrated factory production of cotton goods in France did not begin with the mechanisation of spinning, the first stage of production, but with the last stage of production, the printing and dyeing of the grey cloth. The patterns and styles used were copies of those of cloths previously imported from the far east, hence the name of the finished articles, 'indiennes'. Cloth printing required a much greater investment of capital than the simple machines used in domestic spinning or weaving. A lot of land was needed for bleaching, a big building for dyeing, costly tools and scarce raw materials for printing and within the works a systematic division of labour and organisation of production. The entrepreneur frequently came to control the distribution of raw materials to the rural spinners and weavers and to organise their output to fit the rhythm of output in the printing works. The concentration of the industry therefore took place from the top downwards and the greater mechanisation of the first stages in the production process was often organised and even financed by the entrepreneur controlling the finishing end of the business. From the start of this process of concentration cotton goods were more of a luxury in France than they were in eighteenth-century Britain, their sales were on a more restricted and a higher-income market.

The printing of cotton cloth was prohibited in France until 1785 by the opposition of the guilds to the newer textile. Before 1760, however, it spread from Switzerland into the republic of Mulhouse, on the French border and annexed to France in 1798. Some of the firms later to be important in all sections of the Alsatian cotton goods industry, Koechlin, Dollfuss-Mieg and Hartmann, began to print *indiennes* in Mulhouse after 1746. In doing so they distributed the spinning and weaving in the neighbouring French countryside. That Alsace was later to become an important centre of the French cotton industry is certainly to be explained in terms of its proximity to Switzerland where cotton printing had already become established in the eighteenth century. The significance of technological knowledge is well demonstrated here for Alsace was an inland area and until the many tolls on the river Rhine were removed in the nineteenth century its supply of raw cotton came from Atlantic and Channel ports. The transport cost of raw cotton from Le Havre or Bordeaux to Alsace was usually 10 to 15 per cent above its transport cost to Paris, Normandy, or Picardy. In addition Alsace was not near to any great centres of consumption.

The independence of Mulhouse and its proximity to a more highly-developed cotton goods industry and to the manufacturing and financial centres of Basel and Geneva where there was available capital overcame the other locational disadvantages. The municipal government of Mulhouse provided substantial fiscal privileges to entrepreneurs settling there. The first printing works there were exempted from all customs and excise taxes in 1747 and in subsequent years paid only small fixed sums. After the enterprise was established a fixed percentage of the profit was paid in taxation rather than the fluctuating demands of customs and excise payments. Outside the boundaries of Mulhouse the province of Alsace had never been completely incorporated into the French tariff system, it retained lower customs duties and special privileges for the transit trade to Switzerland. This permitted close links between the cotton goods industry in Switzerland, Mulhouse and Alsace. Unprinted cloths could be imported free of customs into Mulhouse and Alsace. The capital for the early printing works in Mulhouse usually came from Basel. Both Mulhouse and Alsace had certain other advantages, a plentiful supply of clean water and relatively cheap wood for fuel, but these advantages they shared with other areas. After the lifting of the prohibition on cotton printing in France both Mulhouse and Alsace remained important centres of the industry.

After 1760 printing works were developed elsewhere but the first entrepreneurs and many of the skilled workmen were Swiss. By 1793 there were thirty-eight such works in Rouen, and Paris, Lyons and Ghent had become centres of the same activity. The best known is that of Christophe-Phillipe Oberkampf at Jouy-en-Josas on the outskirts of Paris. He it was who was the first to use metal cylinders for printing instead of the slower process on the printing table. His first workers were all Swiss. There were fifteen printing works in Mulhouse in 1768. In 1785 the government completely reversed its earlier policy and prohibited the import of printed cloths from abroad except from Switzerland.

The successful development of printed cottons and the way in which they sustained their hold on the market was responsible for many rural spinners and weavers abandoning the traditional linen and woollen fibres for cotton, to meet the increased demand for spun cotton yarn and for cotton cloth. In the town of St Quentin the traditional textile industries declined steadily in importance relatively to the production of cotton cloth. The spinning jenny, which could be used by the domestic spinner, was popularised in the 1770s by the efforts of John Holker, a political refugee from Lancashire who had become Inspector of Manufactures. The first effective machines for carding cotton were introduced under government privilege in 1779 by James Milne, the son of a Manchester cotton goods manufacturer. In 1785 he was given royal privilege to build and introduce Arkwright's water frames. These machines, which could only be used in factories rather than in domestic industry, were constructed in 1787 and Milne and Fairlow, also from Manchester, set up the first mechanised spinning mill, some of the capital being provided by the Duke of Orleans. In 1791 the mill was also equipped with a small steam engine. The yarn produced by these machines had only limited uses and the mill was by no means typical of later developments. The use of mechanical power, whether hydraulic or steam, spread much less quickly than the development of spinning machinery. Nor did most early spinning mills adopt water frames, for in spinning the finer yarns which the market demanded the new mule-jennies were more suitable initially. They seem to have been first used in France in 1789. In 1791 another Englishman, Pickford, signed a contract to build them but by 1801 there were still only a few examples of their use. In the subsequent period they spread rapidly and were the machines principally used by the two biggest manufacturers, Richard-Lenoir and Bauwens.

Mechanised cotton spinning developed in four principal areas at first, in Normandy, in Alsace, in Picardy and in Paris. The earliest developments were in Normandy beginning in the 1790s. The transformation elsewhere took place in the first decade of the next century, especially in the great boom between 1806 and 1808. Both Normandy and Picardy had already been important industrial areas in the eighteenth century and rural industry organised by urban capital had become a steadily greater part of their economy. The attraction of Paris was that it was by far the greatest market for cotton goods and, under the Empire, the greatest area of machine-building. The spinning industry in Normandy remained rather more dispersed than in the Picardy-Flanders region, often to take advantage of the water power in the river valleys. The use of water frames was commoner here than in other regions. In 1792 there was a mill with 2,000 spindles at Fontaine-Guérard in the department of Eure and Frank Morris erected a complete installation of a similar capacity at Gisors in 1795. In spite of the dispersal of the industry Rouen soon became a great centre of production. In more northerly regions this process was more marked. Out of sixty-nine spinning firms in 1815 in the department of Nord fifty-five were in the towns of Lille, Roubaix and Tourcoing. There were forty-four spinning mills in Paris in 1814 with a total of 150,000 spindles. In the same year there were 350,000 spindles in the department of Seine-Inférieure which was only part of the spinning area in Normandy. In Alsace the mechanisation of spinning was much slower. There were five mechanised spinning mills in 1812 in the department of Haut-Rhin. The total output of yarn in Alsace was still only 115 tons in that year; in Nord it was 5,827 tons, in Somme 375 tons; and in Seine-et-Oise, 220 tons. Three-quarters of the yarn spun in Alsace was still being spun on spinning-wheels. The primacy of the Picardy-Flanders region and of Normandy in terms of output became established in the 1790s but during the Empire itself Paris was in some ways the most rapidly-growing industrial centre. There were fifty-two spinning mills there in 1813. The reason for the sudden growth there was not only the existence of the market, for that had been always so, but the claims of the new machinery. Paris was the place where the machine-building industry became first established and the machines were easier and cheaper to obtain there. It had also a plentiful supply of child labour much in demand in the early stages of mechanisation.

But the weight of yarn output is not the most important factor in these developments. If we look at the level of mechanisation in the various areas we can find great differences. The most common form of power in the Paris spinning mills was horses. The first steam engine to be used in the Alsace industry was that in the Dollfuss-Mieg works in 1812. Most of the mule-jennies used by the biggest cotton goods manufacturer, Richard-Lenoir were not driven by power. Of the twenty-one spinning mills in Amiens only two were driven by hydraulic power. Steam-engines were still very little seen in the Nord. On the other hand, in Normandy the use of hydraulic power for spinning was very generally developed and in the use of power coupled with the new machinery the Norman industry was the most developed. In Normandy, even more than in Picardy and Flanders, the new machinery had effectively eliminated by 1815 hand-spinning of cotton which had developed so rapidly in the previous fifty years. The difference with Britain, where by that date there were single works with 100,000 spindles, was very great, however, much greater than it had been before 1789. The price of mule-jennies and of water frames throughout the period was usually three to four times greater in France than in Britain.

The essential mechanical concepts and the first important machines in cotton spinning had become established in France before communication with Britain was cut off. The progress of the industry subsequently was less dependent on that communication. It still suffered from the political events. Its decline in Dauphiné and in some western regions may have been a regional redistribution caused by differing regional advantages as the scope of the industry changed. But in Alsace there was little expansion between 1793 and 1801. Oberkampf sustained heavy losses in 1794–6 when the market was temporarily restricted. The great industrial empires of Richard-Lenoir and of Bauwens collapsed in 1815. The temporary stagnation in Alsace may have been due to the loss of international markets for which a great expansion into the Italian market was not a complete substitute. After 1815 the Italian market was in turn cut off. The early stages of the continental system provided the impetus for the conversion to mechanical spinning. The exports of French cotton cloths increased tenfold between 1807 and 1810; in 1809 the conversion to mechanical spinning slowed down once more and after 1810 hard times persisted to the end of the war. In 1812 Richard-Lenoir tried to convert all his spinning operations, which by that time employed 12,000, into wool spinning. When the tariff on the entry of raw cotton was abolished in 1814 this investment proved a complete write-off. With all these difficulties mechanical cotton spinning became firmly established. Imports of raw cotton rose from an average of 5,000 tons in the years 1789–1802 to 10,800 tons in 1803–4. The number of spindles doubled between 1806 and 1808 reaching the 1,000,000 mark. By that time the average number of spindles per worker had increased in Alsace from the one of the old spinning wheel to twenty.

The cotton goods industry remained largely unmechanised in its intermediate process of weaving. In fact the mechanisation of the other processes proved a great stimulus to domestic cotton weaving. Although stocking frames for producing knitwear and ribbon looms had been automatic for some time the looms on which cotton cloth was woven did not change substantially apart from the spread of the flying-shuttle in the 1780s. The main change was the conversion to weaving calicoes, the finer cloths which the cotton printers required. Parisian and Alsatian firms set up branch organisations in the north, in St Quentin, Cambrai and Arras to secure the weaving of calicoes there. In the Norman Pays de Caux cotton weaving ousted linen weaving before 1815; after 1810 it began to spread into Brittany.

– *Other Textile Industries*

The silk industry had already been using complicated machines in the eighteenth century. The so-called Bolognese mill introduced in the seventeenth century had brought about a higher level of labour productivity than in the spinning of other fibres. The cost of weaving the cloth in the eighteenth century had often been almost half the final cost of the product and numerous inventors, particularly Falcon and Vaucanson, had produced a more mechanised loom than in the cotton industry. The inventions of Joseph-Marie Jacquard, who designed a series of different looms between 1801 and 1810, followed from the experiments of Vaucanson. They culminated in a loom which permitted the automatic weaving of complicated patterns and the principle by which this was achieved was to be applied later in the century to the weaving of other textiles. Although no city suffered more disruption than Lyons in the French Revolution and although the number of looms working there dropped from 16,000 to 3,000 during the Terror, the city, together with its fellow silk manufacturing towns of St Étienne and Firminy was easily able to hold its own during the period as a whole. As far as its raw materials were concerned, the circumstances were opposite to those of the cotton industry. The incorporation of Lombardy into the Empire provided a cheap supply of spun silk and kept the French silk industry well in advance of its German and Swiss rivals. By 1815 there were 10,720 looms active in Lyons.

In the woollen goods industry the rate of mechanisation was slower and the industry more disturbed. Nevertheless, it experienced important changes in organisation. It became organised on a much larger scale and the factories of the large woollen manufacturers of Sedan, Louviers, Elbeuf and Rheims, although they did not use new sources of power, depended on a high degree of supervision and control of a large labour force. William Douglas, greatly encouraged by the imperial government, built wool spinning machinery in Paris in 1806. Another British emigrant, William Cockerill, after a career in Sweden and Germany, began to manufacture more successful machinery of the same type in Verviers in 1800 and after 1807 in Liége. None of this machinery was capable of hydraulic operation and even in Verviers which developed into a great centre of the woollen manufacture far more workers were actually employed outside the factory than inside.

After the occupation of Verviers by France in 1804 the competition from its more mechanised methods of production began to affect the manufacturers of Elbeuf and Louviers. Similar sizes and qualities of cloth from Verviers and Louviers sold in Paris for 39 francs the piece and 50 francs the piece respectively. The difference was not only due to the use of Cockerill's spinning machinery, for studies of its use in Verviers have shown that it reduced the cost of the final product by only between 5 and 7·5 per cent. In general it was much less of a cost reducing innovation than the new cotton spinning machinery; it was also much less universally valuable, for it could not adequately spin combed wool and was mainly confined to carded wool. In spite of these drawbacks it was on such machinery that the growth of Verviers was based for it enabled the area to respond to the demand for wool. The number of looms in the town itself and in the Vesdre valley more than doubled between 1789 and 1812. The response to this competition in France was led by Guillaume-Louis Ternaux, the son of a prominent Sedan manufacturer. Ternaux, who had lived a brief period of the Revolution in exile in Britain, built up a large integrated firm in Sedan of a kind that was copied in other woollen manufacturing towns. He himself opened a factory in Louviers in 1812 which employed 300 workers and was one of the first to use a steam engine. His innovations were mainly concerned with finding and exploiting a market, especially his 'shawls', imitations of fine Indian weaves, which made his fortune after 1805.

The shortage of raw cotton after 1810 tended to favour the production of woollens. But throughout the period the woollen industry suffered from competition from its more mechanised rival, and this made it more vulnerable to the vagaries of the domestic situation. The older woollen manufacturing centres in the south, Mende and Carcassonne, continued their decline. In the Nord the steep decline in the output of combed wool was partly a reflection of the shift to cotton. But where the industry apparently prospered, it also saw great vicissitudes. There were 1,000 looms active in Sedan in 1788, 600 in 1803, 1,500 in 1812. The production of woollen cloth in Rheims fell from 94,615 pieces in 1787 to less than 15,000 in 1800–1. Outside the main centres of production, the industry was as widespread as its raw material and little is known about its levels of output. The official statistics collected by Chaptal indicate that Sedan produced 37,297 pieces in 1812; Louviers, 3,680 (of a larger size); Elbeuf, 21,480; and Carcassonne, 12,000. Rheims was the centre of production of much smaller and finer articles. In terms of employment, the industry in the same year occupied 18,090 at Sedan, 20,000 at Rheims, 9,000 at Carcassonne, and 7,850 at Elbeuf. Whatever allowance is made for numbers employed elsewhere, it is clear that the industry had not developed as a source of employment in the same way as the cotton goods industry. In the latter, assuming a ratio of twenty spindles per employee there must have been 17,500 employed in cotton spinning alone in the department of Seine-Inférieure. The total output of the cotton goods industry was also growing more rapidly.

In the linen goods industry there was practically no mechanisation. The first flax-spinning machinery was patented by Philippe de Girard in 1810, but it does not seem to have been very useful, although its fundamental principles were later the basis of more successful innovations. The material itself was less tractable to mechanical processes than the other textile fibres, part-time peasant labour remained very cheap, and the demand for linen cloth failed to increase. Cotton was the fashion everywhere, much to Napoleon's chagrin. One aspect of the continental system was the attempt to persuade consumers to abandon 'the English cloth' for the traditional French linen. But linen cloth could not be produced in the same patterns as cotton and silk, nor could it be woven so finely except at great expense. The only result of the government's campaign was that de Girard was able to win a large prize for his invention, an invention which eventually visited Austria, Poland, and Britain before it returned to France. The finer linens had depended more on exports than cotton goods before the revolution, nine-tenths of those made in Valenciennes and Cambrai had been exported. The coarser cloths were less affected by the blockades and tariffs. The export of linens from Brittany to the Spanish empire through Cadiz came to a halt. The output of linen in Mayenne fell by two-thirds between 1789 and 1797, roughly the proportion that had previously been exported.

– Machine Building

The sum of these developments in the textile industries, although in every way less dramatic than what had occurred across the Channel, constituted a development which had not as yet affected other countries on the mainland. This will be better seen if the effects of these changes on other industries are examined. The application of machinery on this scale necessitated a machine-building industry in France, and that, in its turn, called into being certain changes in the metallurgical industry. In these sectors too the pace of change was much slower than in Britain, and for this also the long separation from events in Britain was in part responsible. In both these sectors France was further behind in 1815 than she had been in 1793. The changes in the textile industries were also related to certain developments in the chemical industry. There, France does not seem to have suffered in the same way, and Napoleon's active financial encouragement of invention had its greatest rewards.

Steam engines had been much less used for pumping water from mines in France than in Britain. But in the case of the steam engine, as in the case of cotton-spinning machinery, the speed with which technological information passed from Britain to France was remarkable. The brothers Périer in the course of a visit to Britain secured an early model of James Watt's improved version and installed it in their Paris foundries at Chaillot in 1781. In a subsequent visit they secured an arrangement with Watt to produce his engines under licence in their own machine shops, the first of the *Watt's licence* new steam engines to be manufactured on the mainland. The Chaillot foundries kept pace until 1793 with Watt's subsequent improvements; in 1790 they produced their first double-acting steam engine. They were used in flour mills, in water works and in some early cotton-spinning mills, as well as for pumping. By the end of the century, there were three steam engine manufacturers in France. In spite of this alacrity to accept the invention, production was not as large as had been expected. There were still only about 200 steam engines in France in 1810, and during the Revolution the Chaillot machine shops temporarily had to close.

– The Iron Industry

It is in the history of the iron industry that the difficulties and the hesitant nature of the industrial revolution in France are most strikingly observed. A large production had been sustained throughout the eighteenth century in hundreds of scattered manorial furnaces. Only those iron works catering directly to military and naval demand had been organised on a large scale; otherwise, the industry was controlled by noble capital and fed by ore and charcoal from the noble domain. The furnaces mostly worked in periods of slack labour demand, supplying agricultural equipment and domestic utensils. The smelting of ore by the use of coke did not begin until 1785, the puddling process for pig iron was not used at all. *not stagnating*

But it would be quite wrong to convey the impression that the French iron industry was stagnating. The attention paid to developments in Britain was unceasing. There were several attempts at coke-smelting in the 1760s, but the results were often unsatisfactory. After a subsidised journey in Germany and Britain, Gabriel Jars achieved the first successful coke smelt at the de Wendel works at Hayange in Lorraine in 1769. In the next decade the government provided wholehearted encouragement to the industry to adopt new processes. The cannon-foundry at Indret on the Loire used Wilkinson's new cylinder-boring techniques in the hope of making satisfactory domestically-produced cannon, but the regular supply of the right quality of iron was difficult to organise given the structure of the industry. In 1780 the owner of one of the biggest integrated concerns, Ignace de Wendel, contracted with state support to supply the need after he had been paid to visit British ironworks. The outcome was the great Le Creusot ironworks founded with the direct involvement of government capital. The works was built with four modern coke-smelting blast-furnaces designed for an output of 5,000 tons of iron a year. In technical conception it was probably the most advanced works of the time. But like many such bold enterprises its early history was chequered with failure. By 1787 the supplier of the original capital had defected leaving de Wendel to cope with the new works and his own smaller plant at Hayange in Lorraine, which had the only other coke-smelting blast-furnace. The principal difficulty was a metallurgical one, the coke and ore used at Le Creusot did not produce a satisfactory smelt. Indeed, there seemed no coal in France that could be turned satis-factorily into the type of coke which British manufacturers now used. The Hayange works imported its coking coal from the Saarland a few miles over the border where the coke-smelting process had begun to be used occasionally about the same time as Jars's first successful experiments in France.

To overcome these chemical problems required constant practical experimentation with the techniques of production and such experi-mentation was normally based on the evidence derived from practical observation of other works. The important transition to a larger more mass-productive technology which the Le Creusot blast-furnaces proclaimed was something of a sham before 1815. The armies of Napoleon were equipped either with imported iron or with iron produced domestically by the same methods as it had been in the reign of Louis XIV. The government forges at Cosne and the arms manufacturies of Tulle and Maubeuge were untouched by the latest developments. Napoleon's continental policy meant in addition that the naval arsenals, which in all countries were among the largest and most advanced metallurgical works, were sadly neglected. In spite of the great demand for iron occasioned by the war, the iron industry stagnated from Le Creusot's first successful make in 1785 to 1815. The Le Creusot works continued to produce in splended isolation. In that same period, the older technology based on small furnaces and charcoal-smelting disappeared in Britain.

– Other Industries

Where innovations depended less on practical observation of tech-niques and more on theoretical scientific experimentation the war with Britain did not have such disadvantages, so at least develop-ments in the chemical industry during the period would indicate. Cotton printing was an industry closely associated with the chemical industry, the wide range of colours used and the variety of fixing agents all required some chemical knowledge, and the early development of the chemical industry went hand in hand with the finishing processes in the textile industries. Of these the most wasteful in time was bleaching. It was this which meant that the time taken to produce a finished cloth was often two years, for bleaching was an open-air process demanding fine weather for about fifty days for its success. The process was both cheapened and greatly speeded up by Berthollet's process of chlorine bleaching invented in 1785 which reduced the time of the bleaching operation to three to four days. But of even greater significance for the future were the inventions of Nicholas Leblanc with the active patronage and support of the government. When trade with Spain was so interrupted as to cut off the supply of soda, used in the manufacture of soap and glass, Leblanc patented a method of making it from brine and used this method as the basic process of a chemical works on the outskirts of Paris. The Leblanc process was to be the central process in alkali manufacture for over sixty years. The desire to be independent of colonial sugar led to a series of prizes for the distillation of sugar from beet to replace cane sugar. The essential theoretical work was that of a German chemist, Achard, but beet sugar was first produced commercially in 1811 in refineries built with government help in 1810. In 1812 about 1 million francs was made available to create schools which would spread the technique. The total output in 1813 was still only 8,250 tons. When cheap cane sugar was again available, the new industry, and the new crop, disappeared. But they were both to be revived in the 1830s. The production of beet sugar had often been advocated over the preceding sixty years, but it was the continental system which raised the price of cane sugar to the point where what had previously been a laboratory process could become a commercial proposition.

These industrial developments were not responsible for any great increase in coal production in France. Although steam engines were quickly adopted there, they were much less common than in Britain, particularly for providing the power in spinning mills. The fact that the coke-smelting process also played a very limited part in the French iron industry also tended to keep the total quantity of coal mined relatively low. The legal changes of the revolution confirmed the government as the owner of mineral rights and did not disturb the control of the Compagnie d'Anzin over its huge concessions in the northern coal field. The total output of coal in France in 1785 seems to have been about 800,000 tons. The integration of the Belgian provinces into the French economy after 1789 provided the French economy with another source of coal and discouraged any further exploration of the resources of the northern French coal basin. Where the new technology did stimulate an increase in coal consumption it was usually a local phenomenon restricted to those areas near the pit-head where the price of coal was cheaper. The output of the Anzin mining company, by far the greatest part of the output of the whole Nord coalfield, was about 290,000 tons in 1789. By 1818 it had still not regained so high a level of annual output, while the Belgian coalfields far surpassed it.

– Government and Industry

The extent to which the development of French industry in these years was related to the positive encouragement provided by the government has not yet been very thoroughly studied. The period immediately before the revolution was one in which the government actively supported technological modernisation. The introduction of the flying-shuttle, of the mule-jenny and of the coke-smelting process were all furthered by financial encouragement from the government. The revolution changed this pattern of activity, because other things mattered more, and because the destruction of absolutism seemed connected in the minds of the revolutionaries with the introduction of a more *laissez-faire* system. French industry was set free both from government pressures to modernisation and from the pressures of the old corporate system against modernisation. The Revolution also coincided as we have seen with an abrupt break in the process of modernisation and with a decline in output, but too many other factors are involved here for this to be attributable in any way to the change in the government's stance. The recovery of French industry under Napoleon might also be attributable more to the greater stability of the political system and to the great extension of markets brought about by his conquests than to the administrative structures which he devised to fill the gap left by the Revolution's reforms. Nonetheless, those structures were to play an important part in determining the atmosphere in which relations between government and industry in nineteenth-century France were formed. In the larger perspective after 1815 French industry developed in a *laissez-faire* framework, but there were always official administrative connections between the government and entrepreneurs.

The Directory made a large sum of money available for the encouragement of the textile industry in 1797. The next year it organised the first great industrial exhibition, the precursor of many such in nineteenth-century France. The *Conservatoire des Arts et Métiers* had been instituted in 1794 to encourage the dissemination of technological knowledge. Napoleon took up where these efforts left off. There were industrial exhibitions in 1801, 1802, and 1806.

Loans, rewards and medals of achievement were widely distributed. There were public competitions for the invention of wool-combing machinery in 1802, for improved cotton spinning machinery in 1805, and for flax-spinning machinery in 1810. The last produced de Girard's invention. In 1804 Nicholas Appert was rewarded for patenting the first food-preserving and bottling process, the beginning of the modern canning industry. The *Chambres Consultatives*, to provide a link between government and industry were created in 1801. The *Conseil des fabriques et manufactures*, instituted in 1810, provided a large amorphous committee meeting at short intervals. Most of the leading manufacturers served on it including de Wendel, Ternaux, Richard-Lenoir, and Koechlin. Like many of Napoleon's institutions it survived under the Restoration. Such an organisation had one clear effect on economic policy; it was no longer so easy for the government, as it had done under Calonne, to impose tariff reductions on the strength of its own persuasion. The *Conseil des fabriques et manufactures* made its principal demand in 1811 that for more protective duties.

In one other important respect Napoleon effected a lasting reform, in the foundation and regulation of a central bank. After the depreciation of the *assignats*, the paper money of the Revolution, there was no firm financial policy. The Bank of France, founded in 1800, was a consortium of private bankers who filled the gap which had appeared in the handling of the government's own financial affairs since the gradual disintegration during the Revolution of the circle of Swiss bankers who had controlled financial and monetary policy in the closing years of the old régime. The council of the new bank was to be elected by the 200 largest shareholders. The issuing of a new metallic currency, the franc, with a fixed silver value, began in 1802. In addition the Bank of France had the right to issue large-denomination banknotes for the Paris area. Over-issue of these notes in 1805 threatened a further depreciation. The result was that the Bank was subjected to greater control in 1806. The constitution of the Bank was amended to appoint a governor and two deputies responsible to the central government. Dividends could only be paid after consultation with the government treasury. These reforms, which were coupled to the creation of a new system of levying and collecting taxes provided a stable currency and a sound financial system. In doing so they resolved the problem which had been the immediate cause of the downfall of the old régime, besides providing a climate in which industry could recover from the troubles of the Revolution.

– Conclusion

The most important influence on French industry during this period, in spite of the many juridical changes and their sweeping nature, was the changes in marketing possibilities. The problem is more complicated than the assumption that French industry was first cut off from competition by the only more advanced competitor and then set free to dominate other less advanced areas by Napoleon's conquests. The degree of protection against British industry was still only relative. It could constantly be reduced by highly-organised smuggling, not a new method of economic warfare invented for this purpose but the normal trading procedure between the two economies before 1786. It could also be reduced by the financial operations of licensed importers of British and 'colonial' goods into France. Smuggling was simply an extension of mercantilist trading policies for the French government, and where exports could be effected from French-controlled territory to Britain in return for bullion, they were in fact often encouraged by the French government. After the Trianon tariff of 1810 French exporters were often able by operations on the money market with British paper to import a greater value of 'colonial' goods than the value of the goods they had exported beforehand. There were many other ways in which the enormous geographical and financial complications of the continental system were unable to give sufficient protection against an industrial and trading power which had become so powerful. The changes in French industrial output are to be related to particular opportunities which compensated for these drawbacks, the acquisition of northern Italy for example. Such opportunities presented themselves spasmodically and only for short periods of time, the opportunities presenting themselves to British manufacturers were constant and long-term. Trade in large quantities of goods depended on sea transport just as much as it had done in the eighteenth century. Continuing the building of roads and canals, at a slower pace than before the revolution, as Napoleon did, was no substitute for sea-borne traffic, a form of trade which became increasingly difficult for France.

The changes in French industry are such that we can place the beginnings of the industrial revolution in France in the period spanning the French Revolution and the Empire. There was no sudden upward movement in the level of industrial output as there seems to have been in the case of Britain. National aggregate statistics show a long and consistent period of slow development of output and of slow economic growth in France from the early eighteenth century which continues to 1815 and beyond. The economic experience of France when measured in this way was quite different from that of Britain in the first industrial revolution, although the precise nature of the changes which took place in the two economies was remarkably similar. They took place in the same sectors of the same industries and were closely related to each other. The differences which can be observed when the whole economy is considered are, in spite of this, very great. Once the superficial similarities of aggregate statistics are examined for what really happened, it can be seen that the second industrial revolution, that in France, had a very different history from that of the first. We may regard France in 1815 as having travelled some way down the path of becoming a developed, industrial economy, but the economy that was emerging was unlike that which had emerged in Britain and the path it followed to development and industrialisation was also different. Economic history repeats itself no more closely than history because, in each case of economic development, the historical circumstances are different. In the case of France after 1789 they were very different. It will be seen from the subsequent cases of industrial development which we shall examine in this book that these differences did not diminish the problem of industrialising in a world where other industrial powers existed.

THE FRENCH REVOLUTION AND THE CONTINENTAL SYSTEM OUTSIDE FRANCE

The effect on other societies of the reforms of the French Revolution was very much a matter of their level of development in the eighteenth century. In those societies which had shared the French experience of growing foreign trade and industrialisation, the institutional changes which were brought by the Revolution often removed historical obstacles to development which had already come to be seen as no longer justifiable. In more backward societies the changes could have little immediate effect on economic development because the economy itself was not at a sufficiently high level of development to profit from changes which, because of this fact, often seemed remote and abstract from the reality of economic existence. In the Austrian Netherlands, and in Liége, which were occupied after 1793 and ultimately completely absorbed into the French Empire until its destruction in 1814, the history of the period was very like its history in France. The initial impact of the war and the Revolution provoked a severe economic crisis followed by a resumption of

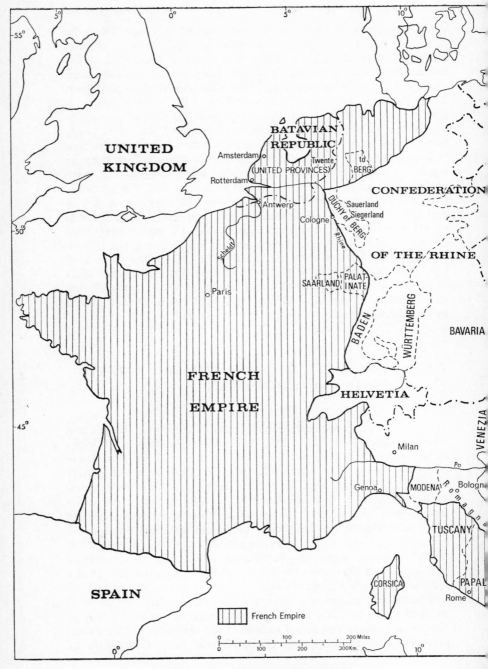

Map 3. The French Empire in 1810

the late eighteenth-century developments there. The recovery was furthered by the institutional changes. The only other comparably industrialised country, Switzerland, had a more varied experience, difficult to assess because of the lack of research on this question. In the unindustrialised areas of Italy, the effect of incorporation into the Empire was of no immediate benefit, more probably it retarded their development. But the institutional changes, even where they did not survive except as a memory, were certainly of importance later in the century. In the German states where wide differences of development already existed, reaction was also very different, but for the areas on the left bank of the Rhine, incorporated into the Empire, these years were a period of great economic change which presaged their later growth into one of the most industrialised areas of Europe, even if the actual developments at the time were less noticeable than those in the southern Netherlands or in Switzerland.

Nowhere was the full gamut of revolutionary experiment and social change experienced as it was in France. First and foremost in all French plans, both of the Directory and Napoleon, was the commercial and economic interest of France. Military occupation by the French was primarily a form of economic exploitation of the occupied territories for the benefit of the French treasury. The ties of political sympathy between the small groups of revolutionaries who created the Helvetic Republic in Switzerland and the Batavian Republic in the United Provinces and the revolutionaries in France did not long survive the reality of a military occupation of this kind. After the creation of the Empire and the final construction of the continental system, the most important question for other economies was whether or not they were inside the French tariff barrier. The system was designed to exclude competitors from the French market and the client states which Napoleon created had less economic favour from the French Empire than their predecessors had had from the monarchy. Those areas inside the French tariff were fully integrated into the new centralised administrative system and the new local government system of France. The revolution imposed on them, however, was not the revolution of the Jacobins or Girondins of 1793 but the codified, systematised, stabilised and essentially 'controlled' revolution of Napoleon. In those respects where the Napoleonic system was the heir both of eighteenth-century enlightenment and of the Revolution, the incorporated areas were endowed with the same legacy. The drive towards national efficiency and the elimination of historical impediments to such an aim led to the removal of internal customs barriers, private privileges and jurisdictions, legal differences and the multiplicity of local divergences of economic practice characteristic of the old régime.

The main instrument of this change was the Civil Code of French law, published in 1804, usually known everywhere, deservedly so, as the *Code Napoléon*. The act of codifying the law of the land, standardising it and making it available to everyone was one of the most remarkable results of the French Revolution. To that extent, Napoleon was himself a revolutionary. Essentially the Code was an attempt to compromise between the legal changes of the Revolution and the subsequent reaction to them; it occupied a middle ground between the society which the Parisian revolutionaries had tried to erect and the old régime. Most historians would agree that it preserved intact the basic ideas of the Revolution, even though it was also a very conservative document. From our point of view its success in effecting such a compromise was of great significance because it became accepted as the blueprint for a society which could replace the society of the eighteenth century without itself being too unstable to survive. The basic principles which it enshrined, equality of all citizens before the law, freedom of conscience, the secularity of the state and the freedom to pursue any occupation were a direct attack on the economic basis of old régime society. They meant, for example, in all areas where the Code was adopted, the gradual destruction of the power of the feudal nobility. Their power had essentially rested on two props, extensive control of land and privilege before the law. The Code contained strict controls on inheritance to provide for division of the land among all heirs and its intention in so doing was to prevent the rise of another landholding aristocracy. There was no provision in the Code for entail, the legal device by which huge estates in some areas, such as Prussia, had been integrally maintained over generations. At the same time the limitations on the concept of full ownership which had prevailed under the old régime were brusquely abolished. Ownership was defined as 'the right of enjoying and disposing of things in the most absolute manner'. Nor could the right of freedom of occupation exist side by side with the privileges of the corporate guilds.

The imposition of the *Code Napoléon* on the Belgian provinces of the Empire finally eliminated the private jurisdictions which had been weakened by the Austrian rulers in the preceding fifty years. It succeeded in breaking the power of the guilds where the Emperor Joseph II had failed in 1783-4. In many ways it represented for the Belgian provinces a continuation and a fulfilment of previous economic changes. It was imposed on the left bank of the Rhine and remained the law there in the nineteenth century when its provisions were either never accepted or were seriously modified elsewhere in Germany. In the United Provinces, in Switzerland, in Italy (where it was put into effect even in the Papal States), and on the Adriatic coast in the Republic of Ragusa (Dubrovnik), it did not survive the French Empire. In Bavaria it was never adopted. In Württemberg it was adopted in a modified way such as to eliminate personal serfdom but not feudal institutional arrangements. In the Kingdom of Poland, which Napoleon recreated from the Polish territories annexed by Prussia in the 1790s and to which he subsequently rejoined Galicia, it was adopted to the extent of breaking the legal tie between the serfs and the land but not to the extent of disrupting the lords' demands on their labour and income. Neither these modifications, nor the rejection of the Code in the restorations of 1815, in any way weakened its character as the basic instrument of the new society. It became the foundation of the legal code of the Kingdom of Italy in 1864 when that kingdom was recreated. It was adopted in its entirety by Romania in the same year.

– in Belgium

The effect of these changes on the Austrian Netherlands and Liége, the area of the future kingdom of Belgium, was complex but on balance beneficial. In spite of the disruption of 1793–4, these areas did not suffer so badly as France from the disturbances. Their foreign trade was mainly coasting trade with neighbouring areas and the transit trade to Germany. Their economy benefited from protection as much as did the French and benefited also from being incorporated into a large market. Before 1793 tariffs had existed, not only between Liége and the other provinces, but between all the other provinces also. Not only were these removed, but also the tariff barriers which separated the whole area from the French market. It is true that these provinces suffered no less than France from the deprivation of technological knowledge which the wars occasioned. But on balance they had less to lose and more to gain from the circumstances of the period than the French economy. The result was the beginnings of the industrial revolution there too. It was the start of a fierce but erratic period of economic development which was shortly to raise Belgium to a level of economic development as high as, and perhaps higher than, that of France itself.

It has already been remarked that to eighteenth-century observers the standard of living of the peasantry of Flanders, Hainaut, Brabant and Liége seemed much higher than that in France. The old régime, partly because it had been more modified by government action and partly because its demands in taxation were less, bore less oppressively on the agricultural sector. Domestic industry was widespread, but in only a few areas had it taken on the aspects of modern capitalist organisation which it had in so many regions of France. The greatest industry was the linen industry of Flanders, usually given as the main source of the peasants' wealth. But, like the French linen industry, it was not so controlled by the central organising figure of the putter-out, nor was it, of course, so susceptible to mechanisation as the other textile industries. The peasant producers normally sold their cloths independently to the merchants of Ghent, Courtrai and Ypres for eventual export to Europe and sometimes, no doubt, to the Spanish and Portuguese colonies. Some estimates rate the number of part-time flax spinners in 1800 in the department of Escaut (Eastern Flanders) as high as 110,000 and the number of linen weavers in Flanders as a whole at the same time as high as 450,000. The woollen industry, although smaller, was much more controlled by the entrepreneurs. Its great centre was the province of Limburg, especially the towns of Verviers and Eupen. What more distinguished the domestic industry of the Belgian provinces from that of France, however, was the development of industries based on iron and of coal-mining. Entrepreneurs in Liége purchased bar-iron and distributed it throughout the countryside to nailers and makers of utensils. Charleroi and its surrounding district were involved in the same activities, but there the bar-iron seems often to have been bought by the household and the product sold independently. The Liége area was also celebrated for the manufacture and assembly of small arms on the same basis. Even rough estimates of the amount of coal mined are difficult to make. Most of the mines were very small, operated by two or three families. Their organisation was very different from that of the large joint-stock companies with extensive mining concessions that operated in the neighbouring French departments. It resembled more that of the German coalmines in the Rhineland. The mine was regarded as the common capital stock of a large number of shareholders each of whom had the right to use the capital stock for a length of time corresponding to the size of his holding. The holding could be as small as 1/192 of the total share. It must be presumed that the small number of larger mines which existed had emancipated themselves from this system, but they were not companies under the central control of the directors as were those in France, and frequently their labour force still had rights in the use of the equipment and in the disposal of profits. The total coal output, however, seems by continental standards to have been high amounting perhaps to 800,000 tons in 1795.

Examples of more modern forms of industrial organisation were not lacking in the late eighteenth century, but they do not seem to have been so numerous or so important individually as they were in France. In certain mines the expense of deeper mining and pumping had required a Newcomen steam engine and even capital investment on this limited scale had usually been beyond the organisational and financial capacities of the older mining companies. Of equal significance for the future was the beginning of cotton-cloth printing in Ghent in the 1770s. As in France, the initial investment in the buildings and equipment was so high that the investors would seek to extend their control over the whole production process and to develop the spinning and weaving of cottons rather than linens in the countryside.

For all these diverse industrial activities open access to the French market was a great stimulus. Capital was not lacking for entrepreneurs to expand production. The sale of the 'national lands' often provided more. In general they were sold in much more corrupt circumstances than in France, and their sale benefited a small group of bourgeois speculators rather than a wide range of population in the middle income groups. Furthermore, the proportion of the available land and buildings owned by the dispossessed church had been much higher than in most parts of France. Two of the first three cotton-spinning factories of the first great Belgian industrialist, Liévin Bauwens, were in former ecclesiastical buildings. The demands of the war economy in France for arms and iron, for coal to refine the iron, and for uniforms could all meet with a ready response in so industrialised an area. In such circumstances the juridical and social changes of the French Revolution removed the main obstacles in the Belgian economy to meeting this suddenly-increased demand.

Whatever doubt attaches to the statistics collected by the imperial government in France, it is clear that the expansion of coal output in these years in the Belgian provinces was much greater than in northern France. By the close of the Empire the coal exports into the former territorial area of France from the Borinage coalfield in the Belgian provinces were roughly the equivalent of the total output of the Anzin mining company and were four times greater than their 1789 level. Between 1802 and 1810 the average output of the Belgian department of Jemeppe alone was about 1 million tons per annum and the combined output of all the Belgian departments was probably about 1,500,000 tons per annum. By 1811 the Ans mine in the Liége basin had over 300 workers. The canal de St Quentin built between 1802 and 1810 joined the River Scheldt to the canal Crozat and permitted much cheaper movement of coal southwards from the Borinage basin. In 1807 construction began on the Mons–Condé canal which would serve the same purpose.

This expansion of coal mining catered to an expanding output in metallurgical industries. In this sector, however, Belgium was handicapped by the inability to develop the coke-smelting process. In the late eighteenth century experiments by Limbourg and by the Abbé Needham had failed to make the process work with Belgian coal and ore. The French government insisted on attempts being made with the new process before it would grant further concessions to industrialists. In 1811 the aptly-named *Société d'Émulation* of Liége offered a prize for the first successful smelt with coke. But all to no avail, the first coke-smelting furnaces were not successfully operated in Belgium until 1827. The demand for more iron had therefore to be met with the traditional technology. The French machine-builder, Périer, started a cannon-foundry at Liége in 1803. The total make of pig iron in the Belgian provinces doubled between 1789 and 1811. In that year of the 143,000 tons produced in the Empire, 37,300 tons were produced in the Belgian provinces. In 1810 Joseph Dony developed a more successful method for obtaining zinc from calamine ore. His discoveries laid the basis of an industry of considerable future importance in the Belgian economy and of the largest company in the European non-ferrous metal industry for many years, La Société de la Vieille Montagne.

As in France proper the difficulties of developing the new iron technology were very much a function of the break in contacts with Britain. In the textile industries this situation seems to have been less inhibiting. In the last decade of the Empire a modern textile industry producing both wollen and cotton goods developed. The town of Ghent, once a European centre of the cloth manufacture, but by the later eighteenth century an insignificant place industrially, developed into a major centre of the cotton-goods industry. The same period saw the development of Verviers and the Vesdre valley into a centre of the woollen cloth industry. The relative decline of textile manufactures in the southern Netherlands had been due in the past to the active trading competition of the United Provinces and to the blockade of the mouth of the River Scheldt which they maintained. When the United Provinces became a French satellite, the Scheldt was opened to trade. Napoleon was responsible for considerable improvements to Antwerp, the biggest port on the river. But the British naval blockade prevented these changes from having much significance before 1815. It was rather the overland trade that developed Belgian cloth exports.

In 1805 the prefect of the department of Escaut wrote in his official report on the cotton goods industry. 'How is it possible to struggle with any hope of success against the manufactures of Bengal, Malabar and Coromandel which have raw materials on the spot and weaving labour for one French sou the day?' It was the last note of an old song. The economic history of Belgium in the next fifty years was to answer his question. In 1799 Liévin Bauwens, a tanner, opened his first cotton spinning workshop in Ghent to cater to the small cotton printing establishments there. His career illustrates perfectly the intermingling of French and Belgian activities in these years. He was a contractor to the French armies in Belgium, a speculator in 'national lands' after the securalisation of the church, his second works was set up in Paris, and he became a favourite in imperial circles such that he too fell from power in 1815. His sisters married other cotton spinners and created a tightly-knit circle of cotton-goods manufacturers in Ghent. The real boom in cotton spinning there came after Bauwens with enormous ingenuity smuggled mule-jennies from Britain, the first to be used in Ghent. The original mule-jennies were copied in workshops and the copies sold to equip other spinning-mills which developed rapidly after 1806. Bauwens himself never moved into the finishing branches of the industry, but in Belgium as in France mechanised spinning was a response to the development of cotton-cloth printing.

One year before Bauwens opened his first spinning-mill the English machine builder William Cockerill was brought to Verviers from Hamburg by industrialists anxious to mechanise. The wool-spinning machinery which he produced there was better than that produced by Douglas in Paris and the Cockerill works became the main continental source of such machinery after 1805. Between 1808 and 1811 21 machine-shops were opened in the Liége-Verviers area. The Cockerill works in Liége itself produced 2,600 machines in 1812. The woollen-cloth industry in the area, far from succumbing to the large French output, was able by its better organisation and mechanisation to produce more cheaply than its rivals and to penetrate deeply into the market of the whole Empire.

– in Switzerland

The only other area of Europe where domestic industry was equally well established and organised in an equally capitalistic way and where the level of incomes in the domestic market seems to have been as high as in the Belgian provinces was Switzerland. But Switzerland was not admitted to the Empire. The formation of the Helvetic Republic only took place after bitter internal disputes which delayed the recovery from the slump of 1793-4. Once formed the Republic found itself discriminated against commercially by its political friends in Paris. Worse than this, its constitution only provoked worse disorders. They were settled by the Act of Mediation in 1803, but only at the expense of returning to a constitution which restored cantonal control over almost every decision at the expense of the rationalisation and standardisation of the Revolution. The provisions of the *Code Napoléon* lasted only five years in most cantons. After 1803 all rural cantons and even Zürich, Basel and Schaffhausen returned to guild control of industry. The Helvetic Republic did not even succeed in removing internal customs barriers, although some steps were taken in 1799 to provide a standard currency for the country. The trade discrimination by France did not diminish; indeed the centralisation and nationalisation of the French state removed such anomalies as the customs position of Alsace and Mulhouse which had benefited Switzerland. The continental system greatly increased the price of raw cotton, a commodity which was in any case difficult to get hold of cheaply in a completely land-locked economy once the route up the Rhine was sealed off by blockade and French customs-inspectors. In addition Geneva, a considerable centre of cotton printing, was annexed to the French Empire.

The vitality of Switzerland's industrial existence was undermined by these events. The cotton spinning industry was mechanised in these years and there was a marked tendency to further concentration in the watch-making industry. In spite of this, the impression remains that Switzerland, which had provided the impetus towards industrialisation in the east of France and also provided some of the capital that made it possible, lost ground in these years. The cotton-printing industry in Geneva was incorporated in the Empire and could no longer get fine calicoes duty free as it had done in the past. The difficulty of spinning fine yarns for the higher-grade cottons produced in Switzerland was increased by the use of cotton from the Levant, not so suitable to the purpose. Domestic cotton spinning seems to have declined in the last decade of the eighteenth century before mechanisation began. Nevertheless the cotton spinning industry was mechanised in the years between 1800 and 1820, roughly comparable to what happened in Belgium and very little later than in France. Marc-Antoine-Samuel Conod, the consul of the Helvetic Republic in Bordeaux, set up the first mechanised spinning mill at St Gallen, in a secularised abbey, with machinery imported from France in 1800. There followed a rapid succession of similar enterprises, Hard at Wülflingen in 1801, Näf at Rapperswil in 1803 and Zellweger at Trogen in 1804. The first spinning-mill not to use imported French machinery was Escher-Wyss at Zürich in 1805, Kaspar Escher developed the first Swiss machine-building shops and after 1810 Escher-Wyss were responsible for equipping further spinning-mills in Zürich and the Aargau. They were followed by Jacob Rieter and Co. in Töss.

In contrast to developments in France the mechanisation of cotton spinning in Switzerland does not seem to have been dependent on cotton printing. Indeed in Geneva and in Basel the manufacture of *indiennes* seems to have almost disappeared between 1798 and 1803. It survived in Neuchâtel (Neuenburg) because of the customs privileges arising out of that canton's special links with Prussia, but it survived only feebly. In 1806 all imports of cotton goods into Italy, other than those manufactured in France were forbidden thus closing the biggest Swiss market. To some extent Switzerland was able to find a substitute in Germany, and Swiss manufacturers began to compete with French cloths on the Leipzig market. But the lead in cotton printing had passed to France. There are even indications that the disruption of the period dried up the ready sources of capital in Switzerland. The capital for the St Gallen works was partly raised in Augsburg.

The corporate bodies which had controlled the watch-making industry in Geneva and the Jura were not restored after 1798. Genevan entrepreneurs began to concentrate the assembly of movements into workshops in the Jura, the Pays de Gex and Savoy. The movement was initiated by the firm of Mégevaud and Trot which moved to Geneva from Besançon in France in 1804. Louis-Benjamin Audemars began to assemble complete watches under one roof in the Pays de Vaud in 1811. But concentration of this kind involved no mechanisation. Technological innovation in watch-manufacturing did not discriminate against domestic manufacturing as it did in the cotton cloth industry, and by 1820 dispersed manufacture by hand seems to have lost little ground.

– in the United Provinces

Countries which had remained relatively unindustrialised in the eighteenth century, such as the United Provinces and Italy, were subjected to fierce competition from French industry against which they were unable to protect themselves, as they had to some extent been able to do against British industry before 1789. In the United Provinces discrimination by the French took the same lines as it had against the Swiss until the last stage of the continental system when the whole area was annexed to France. In fact the Batavian revolutionaries had hoped their new constitution would overturn the rule of the wealthier merchants of Holland whose profits had come mainly from overseas trade and from the stapling, sorting and transhipment trades for which Holland provided such excellent facilities. They would gladly have diverted these profits to investment in agriculture and industry. The irony of their situation was that Dutch industry, which had been in long decline in the eighteenth century, was quite unable to meet the competition. It had relied for a long time on customary markets and practices rather than on any natural advantages and it had the great disadvantage of high labour costs compared to France. Custom had no place in this period in Europe. Even those industries more integrally related to the trading sector, such as shipbuilding, declined. The dissolution of the guilds and the establishment of freedom of occupation had little meaning in such a situation. The domestic spinning and weaving of cotton developed in the Twente region and began to replace linen there. But this was only a feeble and late echo of events elsewhere. The spinning jenny was not introduced until 1796, and no machinery necessitating the transfer from domestic production appeared in the whole period with the exception of a spinning-mill at Amsterdam using water-frames, a venture which was in any case abandoned after 1795.

Meanwhile the Dutch trading activities which had already been declining relatively to those of France in the eighteenth century were severely damaged by the naval blockade. In earlier wars, the French had always depended on Dutch carrying trade, since the United Provinces had been the best-equipped neutral. After 1793 the French government had no intention of supporting a neutral carrying trade by the Batavian Republic. Between 1795 and 1803 Holland's other major rival, Hamburg, was able to benefit because of its commission trade in British merchandise. Dutch merchants were driven to concentrate more on the transit trade. In retrospect the continental system only continued the relative decline of Dutch trade already so noticeable; but it also prevented the growth of any income-producing substitute.

– in Italy

The Treaty of Campoformio in 1797 created the Cisalpine Republic out of Lombardy, Modena and certain papal legations in the north Italian plain. The Treaty of Lunéville in 1801 extended the Republic's area down the Po valley. By 1805, it had become the kingdom of Italy and embraced Venezia also. Eventually it annexed the Papal States. The Ligurian coast and parts of Tuscany and Romagna were incorporated in the Empire. Southern Italy became a client state, the Kingdom of Naples. The constant changes of frontiers, the heavy tributes demanded from the occupied areas, the numerous military campaigns, all operated to the disadvantage of the Italian economy. There was no effective redistribution of the land, although the *Code Napoléon* was introduced in 1810. The annexation of Genoa caused it to be blockaded by the British. Trieste was occupied by the French in 1809 to prevent its use as a smuggling base; the consequence was the collapse of its trade and the flight of its merchants. The Franco-Italian commercial treaty of 1808 reserved the kingdom of Italy as an exclusive French market. French printed cottons flooded the market. Almost every other manufactured good was likewise imported from France.

In fact the economy was so little developed that the juridical and constitutional changes introduced by the French had little meaning. In the provinces of Urbino, Ancona, Macerata and Fermo annexed in 1808, only 13,215 people were listed as exercising the 'liberal professions'. In 1811 in the whole kingdom only 225,440 were listed as 'exercising a craft or some branch of commerce'. 'This country', one of its French *intendants* reported, 'is only agricultural and will always be essentially different from the commercial and industrial countries'.[3] In the Kingdom of Naples there was only one passable carriage road, the road from Naples to Rome. In the north communications were little better. Napoleon's great roadbuilding schemes created routes over the Apennines and began two road networks radiating from Bologna and Milan, but the trade along them in agricultural produce was less significant than their military use. In Lombardy, the principal sign of modern industrialisation that appeared in the eighteenth century, the milling of raw silk, simply provided a source of cheap semi-manufactured materials for the Lyons industrialists. The Italian silk-spinning industry, depending as it did on casual rural labour, was less organised than the French. French commercial policy forbade the export of silk to Switzerland or Germany and concentrated it on Lyons. The silk-weaving industry, occupying about 25,150 workers in a host of small manufacturies was utterly unable to compete with French products. The only industry that could survive the storm was the coarse woollen cloth industry. Its products were made all over Italy and sold on local markets. They were so coarse and so cheap that French manufacturers could not lower their standards or their prices sufficiently to compete. But on the finer markets the French established a greater monopoly than the British had had before 1793, while the Italian economy continued in passive stagnation.

[3] E. Tarlé, *Le blocus continental et le royaume d'Italie* (Paris, 1928), p. 95.

– in Germany

Nowhere was the effect of the French Revolution and the continental system more complex than in Germany. No area of Europe stood to gain more from an abolition of internal tariffs and from a simplification of frontiers. The wide range of industrial activities of the German population and its relatively high level of mechanical skills developed by the local iron manufacturers combined with the relatively high income levels in many areas seemed to offer possibilities of economic development which were mocked by the political state of the country. The changes in the political framework in these years, however, did not reduce the enormous diversity of political practice over the whole area, in many ways they exaggerated it. The Treaty of Lunéville provided for a simplification of the Holy Roman Empire, eliminating the imperial knights and secularising the ecclesiastical states while compensating those who had lost territory when the left bank of the Rhine was incorporated in the French Empire. The remaining large states fought on different sides in the ensuing wars. Prussia was crushed militarily with such effect that the whole social and economic structure of the state was called into question and the most rigid of old régime societies began to borrow from the new society in France. Bavaria, Württemberg and Baden allied themselves with Napoleon. The first two became kingdoms, the last a Grand Duchy. In each of them reform was more muted. The Holy Roman Empire was dissolved in 1806, and on its ruins arose the Confederation of the Rhine, a loose federal organisation which was never subjected even to the degree of centralisation and rationalisation of administration of the Batavian or Helvetic Republics or the kingdom of Italy. From the Palatinate and the Saarland which became a part of France, through Prussia which embarked on a reform programme from above in order to withstand France, to Bavaria which, because of its alliance with France scarcely changed, there was little in common constitutionally, socially or economically.

The area incorporated in the French Empire benefited and responded in much the same way as the Belgian provinces. Demand for iron and coal increased and the introduction of the *Code Napoléon* eliminated many of the organisational barriers in the coal industry to meeting this increased demand. The puddling and rolling processes were introduced at the Dillingen forges in the Saarland in 1805. But the area was too small and too little industrialised for the same changes to be produced there as in the Belgian provinces. The domestic linen industry in this area remained free of the control of putters-out, the sales being made independently in Mönchen-Gladbach and neighbouring markets. Under the Empire many entrepreneurs from Berg on the right bank of the Rhine crossed the river in order to be inside the French tariff barrier and spread the cotton-goods industry which was dominated from the start by the putters-out in these regions.

The most industrialised area of Germany, the Siegerland and Sauerland and the country to the north, although occupied by French armies and subjected to French control was not given free access to the French market. The coal mining industry seems to have been able to expand its sales, partly because of the changes in mining law and partly because the continental system enabled it to export down the Rhine to the Dutch market. The history of the iron industry and of the textile industries in this region suggests another story, that the political events may have retarded the industrial development of the region and, as in France, greatly increased the technological gap *vis-à-vis* British industry.

The great advantages of the coal mining industry in the Ruhr valley were its cheap labour and its proximity to water transport. The mines were very small, but there was a noticeable tendency to increase in size in the high profit years of 1805 to 1809. In fact, the output of coal in Berg probably did not again reach its level of 1812 until 1825. The elimination of British competition also helped in the increase in the output of the iron industry. Before 1800 iron was sold in Frankfurt-am-Main, in Amsterdam or in Hamburg, often for shipment overseas. After 1800 most trade was southwards. For the very highest quality of products the main market was always France. French ironmasters could not compete in quality with their Rhineland rivals and the tools exported from St Étienne were often edged with crucible steel refined in Remscheid. These highly specialised enterprises were usually small-scale and employed few workers. Bigger forges were few and there was nothing at all on the same scale or modernity as the Le Creusot works. The famous Gute Hoffnungs Hütte was created in 1781 and the second of the St Antony forges began operations at Neuessen in 1794, both under the technical direction of the ironmaster Jacobi. They were the first signs of the development of the Ruhr into one of the world's most intensive iron producing centres, but only very remote signs as yet. In 1800 the Gute Hoffnungs Hütte was bought by the Krupp family. In 1803 another name later to be famous in the area emerged when the Haniel brothers, brothers-in-law of Jacobi, bought the share of the Abbess-Princess of Essen in the Gute Hoffnungs Hütte and in the first St Antony forge. The precarious nature of the continental system was however well illustrated by the fact that when the Krupp family lost the Gute Hoffnungs Hütte they began an association for speculating on the fluctuating prices of colonial goods. The early experiments in these larger ironworks reveal the level of technological skill which existed in this region whose metal products were admired everywhere, but in the use of modern technology rather than manufacturing skill the Silesian orefields and those of the Saarland were decidedly more advanced. The advantages of a good technical tradition, however, were excellently demonstrated when Franz Dinnendahl built the first modern German steam engine there in 1803 from a model of a Watt engine. The engine itself was used for pumping in a lead mine. Of the nine steam engines subsequently installed in the same area before 1815 few brought profits to their purchasers and Dinnendahl was still a struggling machine-builder by that date. The first mechanised cotton spinning mill in the same area also appeared at an early date. The Cromford mill at Ratingen was built by Johann Bruegelmann an Elberfeld putter-out in 1784. It had 1600 spindles and used water power to drive the machinery. There were few subsequent examples before 1815 and cotton spinning did not take on the same élan as in Belgium or Switzerland; the history of its complete mechanisation lasted until 1850.

It was more developed in Saxony, a region remote from French influence but equally able to benefit from the absence of British competition. In 1801 two large mechanised spinning-mills were created in Chemnitz (Karl Marx Stadt), one equipped with mule-jennies, the other with water-frames. Their output was intended to satisfy the calico-printers who had set up business in the same area. Cotton printing in Saxony remained backward compared to France, printing by rollers was not introduced until after 1820, but the spinning branch of the industry suffered in no way by comparison with its rivals and remained for many years the most modern part of the German textile industry. The connections between the Saxon cotton industry and the active cotton market in Leipzig remain unexplored, but it may be that in a period when raw cotton supplies came more from the Levant and the East than in the preceding and succeeding periods a centre of the eastward trade like Leipzig had considerable price advantages over more westerly areas.

It remains to say something of the curiously oblique influence of all these events on Prussia. The restructuring of German agrarian society in the nineteenth century will be discussed later, but in the influence which the French Revolution had on the economic policy of so different a society can best be measured in its force for economic change. The Prussian decree of liberty of occupation in 1808, even though it applied only to the textiles and foodstuffs industries, was a revolutionary change in a society where economic functions had been legally defined in the most absolute way and a precise status attached to them. The Edict of Emancipation of 1807, even though enforced only gradually after 1810 by a series of provincial edicts, by declaring the end of serfdom removed one of the main pillars of the whole economy and society. Even though peasant and serf tenures established after 1752 were not recognised, even though freedom could usually only be obtained by surrendering a substantial part of the occupied holding to the lord, the development of any physical or social mobility and of a land market was a remarkable change in a society designed to be static. The restrictions on the guilds introduced in 1811 could be categorised in the same way, however small the change might seem from the viewpoint of Paris or Brussels. The changes in Prussia signified the legal and spiritual impact of the French Revolution throughout Germany. Everywhere feudal law and serfdom were questioned and where they survived as they did in widely varying degree after 1815 the legacy of the Revolution was their continuous erosion in a series of legal reforms.

In a country like Germany, where economic development was not possible without institutional change, such a legacy was all-important. Gustav von Mevissen, the founder of the first German investment bank, came from a family of industrialists in the area administered by the French army. His contacts with France remained close and he was friendly with the group of Saint-Simon's disciples in Paris. His later colleague, Oppenheim, was a friend of the Paris banker Benoit Fould. David Hansemann, to become equally celebrated in banking circles, started his first insurance company at Aachen, in the annexed left bank area, as a copy of the French Compagnie Générale d'Assurances. Ludolf Camphausen, who became Prime Minister of Prussia in the 1848 Revolution, had lived in Paris during the Restoration. He chose as his Minister of Industry and Commerce another Rhineland entrepreneur, August von der Heydt, who had spent his early childhood under French influence in Elberfeld and was later educated at Le Havre in France. When Rhineland entrepreneurs looked abroad they looked westwards to Paris and the triumphant world of the French bourgeoisie. The leaven of the French Revolution worked there, if slowly, with consequences as far-reaching as those in any other country. For Germany the revolutionary legacy, that institutions and society could be changed, was the cardinal factor in economic development in the following fifty years.

SUGGESTED READING

There is an enormous literature on the French Revolution which has probably been the subject of more historical research than any other historical event. Very little of this in any language however has dealt with the economic history of the period. This is particularly noticeable in the absence of modern work on the effects of the continental system on Europe, a subject whose complexity has deterred scholars more than its importance has attracted them.

The way in which historiography has gradually taken account of economic factors in explaining the French Revolution is described in an essay by G. RUDÉ, *Interpretations of the French Revolution*, Historical Association Pamphlets, General Series, No. 47 (London, 1961). His own works have pursued the same path especially *The Crowd in the French Revolution* (Oxford, 1959), which may be supplemented by an article 'The motives of popular insurrections in Paris during the French Revolution' in *Bulletin of the Institute of Historical Research*, vol. 26, 1953. One starting point of this particular line of research is the excellent and very readable G. LEFEBVRE, *The Coming of the French Revolution* (Princeton, 1947), which brings almost up-to-date the ideas and information in an article by H. SÉE, 'The economic and social origins of the French Revolution' in *Economic History Review*, first series, vol. 3, 1931–2. Most of this research is concerned with what may be called the social causes of the French Revolution rather than with its economic effects or with French economic development during the revolutionary period. Its general conclusions are neatly summarised in N. HAMPSON, *A Social History of the French Revolution* (London, 1963). Since that date the general historical approach on which these conclusions are based has been challenged by a new school of argument. This is represented by A. COBBAN, *The Social Interpretation of the French Revolution* (London, 1964) and G. V. TAYLOR 'Noncapitalist wealth and the origins of the French Revolution' in *American Historical Review*, vol. 62, 1967, two works of political argument which appear to be driving the study of the French Revolution away once more from the field of economic history where it benefited so much. There is a general discussion of the impact of the French Revolution on rural society in A. SOBOUL, 'The French rural community in the eighteenth and nineteenth centuries' in *Past and Present*, vol. 10, 1956. R. TILLY, *The Vendée, A Sociological Analysis of the Counterrevolution of 1793* (Cambridge, Mass., 1964) is an attempt to straighten out many of the arguments by forcing them into rather ill-fitting sociological patterns.

On the economic history of the Revolution rather than its social causes there is only S. E. HARRIS, *The Assignats*, Harvard Economic Studies, vol. 33 (Cambridge, Mass., 1930). Modern work on the continental system is even less in evidence being confined to an article by F. CROUZET, 'Wars, blockade and economic change in Europe, 1792–1815' in *Journal of Economic History*, vol. 24, 1964. But there are two older books on the subject, the interesting E. HECKSHER, *The Continental System; An Economic Interpretation* (Oxford, 1922) and F. E. MELVIN, *Napoleon's Navi-*

gation System (New York, 1919). R. J. BARKER, 'The Conseil Général des Manufactures under Napoleon 1810–1814' in *French Historical Studies*, vol. 7, 1969, does not go into the wider economic questions. The impact of the French Revolution abroad cannot adequately be studied in English but there are a few gleanings of economic history in W. M. SIMON, *The Failure of the Prussian Reform Movement 1807–19* (Ithaca, 1955).

In this case it is a less vague procedure to single out a few books in other languages for their importance. C. BALLOT, *L'Introduction du machinisme dans l'industrie française* (Paris, 1923) has been copied from by most authors on the same subject since it appeared. So has E. TARLÉ, *Konti-nental'naja blokada* (Moscow, 1913). A. CHABERT, *Essai sur les mouvements des revenus et de l'activité économique en France de 1798 à 1820* (Paris, 1949) is an early and slightly erratic approach to what is now called 'quantitative' economic history. The literature on the origins of the Revolution should be supplemented by C.-E. LABROUSSE, '1848–1830–1789: comment naissent les révolutions' in *Comité français des sciences historiques, Actes du congrès historique du centenaire de la révolution de 1848* (Paris, 1948).

Two journals specialise in research articles on this period, *Annales historiques de la Révolution française* and *Revue des études napoléoniennes*. They are more useful for their book reviews because research on economic history is just as likely to be published in the journals we mention elsewhere.

Lebrun
Wilson on Neth.

Chapter 5

The Economic Development of France 1815–70

FRANCE IN EUROPE

With the ending of the long and expensive period of warfare in 1815 the economic situation of France was quite transformed from what it had been. The essential change to a different mode of production and therefore to a different society had taken place. But it had taken place partly because of easy access to markets which were by no means so available after 1815. For one thing, after an early experiment with low tariffs immediately after the peace settlement most states quickly found that the survival of their small industrial sectors depended on tariff protection. France herself followed the same pattern and the Restoration government became one of the most protectionist in Europe. The protection was weakened before the 1850s only by the effect of falling prices for manufactured goods and where tariffs were fixed on weight and number rather than on the value of goods falling prices could often increase the tariff's impact. For another thing, although the long period of warfare had furthered these important changes in the French economy it had done so much more in Britain. The cardinal fact for most French producers after 1815 was the existence of an overwhelmingly dominant and powerful industrial producer not only as their nearest neighbour but as a mighty force in all foreign

Map 4. France in the mid-nineteenth century

Departments:

1. Ain; 2. Aisne; 3. Allier;
4. Alpes (Basses); 5. Alpes
(Hautes); 6. Alpes-Maritimes;
7. Ardèche; 8. Ardennes;
9. Ariège; 10. Aube; 11. Aude;
12. Aveyron; 13. Bas Rhin;
14. Belfort; 15. Bouches-du-
Rhône; 16. Calvados; 17. Can-
tal; 18. Charente; 19. Charente-
Inférieure; 20. Cher; 21. Corrèze;
22. Côte-d'Or; 23. Côtes-du-
Nord; 24. Creuse; 25. Dordogne;
26. Doubs; 27. Drôme; 28. Eure;
29. Eure-et-Loire; 30. Finistère;

31. Gard; 32. Garonne (Haute);
33. Gers; 34. Gironde; 35. Golo
(Corsica, not shown); 36. Haut
Rhin; 37. Hérault; 38. Ille-et-
Vilaine; 39. Indre; 40. Indre-et-
Loire; 41. Isère; 42. Jura;
43. Landes; 44. Liamone (Corsica, not shown); 45. Loir-et-
Cher; 46. Loire; 47. Loire
(Haute); 48. Loire-Inférieure;
49. Loiret; 50. Lot; 51. Lot-et-
Garonne; 52. Lozère; 53. Maine-
et-Loire; 54. Manche; 55. Marne;
56. Marne (Haute); 57. Mayenne;
58. Meurthe; 59. Meuse; 60. Morbihan; 61. Moselle; 62. Nièvre;

63. Nord; 64. Oise; 65. Orne;
66. Pas-de-Calais; 67. Puy-de-
Dôme; 68. Pyrénées (Basses);
69. Pyrénées (Hautes); 70. Pyré-
nées-Orientales; 71. Rhône;
72. Saône (Haute); 73. Saône
et Loire; 74. Sarthe; 75. Savoie;
76. Savoie (Haute); 77. Seine;
78. Seine et Marne; 79. Seine et
Oise; 80. Seine-Inférieure; 81.
Sèvres (Deux); 82. Somme;
83. Tarn; 84. Tarn-et-Garonne;
85. Var; 86. Vaucluse; 87.
Vendée; 88. Vienne; 89.
Vienne (Haute); 90. Vosges; 91.
Yonne.

markets and sometimes even in their own heavily-protected domestic market.

Until 1850 in almost every important sector of industrial production Britain was both the biggest producer and also the technically most advanced producer. In some of the most important commodities, the output of coal, of iron, and of cotton yarn for example, British output was greater than the combined output of all those western European lands which had fallen under the influence of the French Revolution. Indeed until 1850 it is quite possible that the gap, both quantitative and technological, between British production and production elsewhere in western Europe was increasing. By that year British pig-iron production was three times as great as that of France, Belgium and Germany combined, her installed steam-power capacity twice as great, her cotton spinning industry over three times as great and even her railway mileage longer. Those measurements of the rate of growth of industrial output which exist also suggest that it grew more slowly in France than in Britain in the period 1815–50. The rate of growth of aggregate industrial product in France in these years seems to have been roughly 2·5 per cent per year whereas it was over 3·5 per cent in Britain. On a *per capita* basis the difference is less because the French population increased much more slowly than that of Britain. Between 1815–17 and 1849–51 raw cotton consumption increased at a mean rate of growth of 4·4 per cent per year in France, at 5·6 per cent in Britain. The mean rate of growth of pig-iron output in France between 1815 and 1847 was 5·4 per cent, for Britain it was about 6 per cent. Therefore probably until the decade 1840–50 the situation of France to Britain was the opposite of what it had been in the eighteenth century. Whereas before 1789 France was closing the gap with Britain, after 1815 that gap was widening. The consequence for France was the persistence for a long time of relative technological backwardness compared to Britain. In most of the more rapidly developing industries British technology was more modern than French. For most of the period, and perhaps as a result of this, British machinery was cheaper than French.

If instead of comparing the volume of principal French and British exports we compare instead their value the result is rather more favourable to France because so many French export goods were of high value. The value of French exports in 1820 was about half that of British exports, although on a *per capita* basis it would be more like one quarter. Between 1820 and 1850 the average annual rate of growth of French exports by value seems to have been marginally higher than that of British exports. Between 1850 and 1875 its rate of growth doubled, to over 5 per cent per year, roughly the same as that of British exports. France was also in the satisfactory position of being able to sustain a net export surplus to both Britain and the United States. This again was the result of specialising in particularly high quality export goods. This export surplus paid in the early nineteenth century for the small import surpluses with other lands occasioned by raw material purchases. In some ways therefore France's international economic situation was rather more favourable than at first glance it appeared. She was already re-established in world export markets by 1820 and the problem was not so much to hold those markets as to find others, whether international or domestic, in the face of the continuing rapid British industrialisation.

Whatever measurements of the rate of growth of French output are used they all agree on one thing, that it grew more rapidly between 1835 and 1850 than between 1815 and 1835. Measurements from individual industries also indicate that the economic gap between Britain and France certainly got wider between 1815 and the 1830s whereas it is not so certain that it continued to widen after that date.

In spite of falling behind relatively France weathered the storm more successfully than any other continental country and the developments which took place there in this period acquired an increasing momentum in the 1830s and 1840s. They were abruptly checked by the revolution of 1848, but then burst out in the 1850s into rates of growth so high that for the first time it could be said that France was 'catching-up' with the world's greatest industrial power. But it is not only on a national scale that 1850 appears as a watershed. For the years 1850–7, which saw so rapid a development of the French economy, also saw a period of even more rapid development in Germany and an investment boom with similar results in almost all west European lands. As far as France alone is concerned the decade of the 1850s represents the ripening of developments of an earlier period, including the long period of economic development in the eighteenth century. For during the entire period the fundamentals of the French economic situation did not change. They were the struggle to develop and industrialise in the shadow of a much more developed power which dominated international markets. In this struggle France was helped by the great advance in development which she had over all other major continental European countries. Ultimately the development of these other lands and especially Germany changed the situation. Although there is a distinct and interesting phenomenon to explain in the 1850s in France, the year 1870, by which time an equally powerful economy, Germany, had emerged on the continent, marks a more satisfactory turning-point.

It is usually said that over the period 1815–70 France exhibits 'slow growth', presumably by comparison with what had occurred in Britain. Such a statement does not have a great deal of meaning. The most obvious event of these years is the successful emergence of a second industrial power in spite of so many difficulties and it is this which needs the most explanation. The circumstances in which French economic development took place by themselves explain much of why economic growth there was 'slower' than in Britain. From the standpoint of economic growth the economic history of France between 1815 and 1870 is unspectacular apart from the period 1852–7. But from the standpoint of economic development it is crucial to the development of the whole European continent. As far as the rest of the continent was concerned France very quickly became a source of innovation, of capital and of entrepreneurs. Because it was in France that the society of the old régime had been most comprehensively overthrown France retained an enormous political importance in Europe, and became also the source of an ever-increasing stream of social and economic thought about the new society. Seen therefore from a continental point of view, the economic development of France which took place so decisively in these years was of enormous importance for every other country. The fact that the measured rates of growth do indicate that the economic and social changes were less rapid than they had been in an earlier period in Britain (and were to be in later periods in other European lands) does not diminish the significance of those changes for all other economies.

But the doubtful assumption that the slow rate of economic growth in nineteenth-century France was a unique phenomenon, or the even more doubtful assumption that it was the central problem of French economic development, have so influenced recent writing on French economic history that much of it has had as its central theme the attempt to explain this phenomenon. These attempts have usually concentrated on finding particular 'weaknesses' within the French economy which could account for the slow growth rate. There will be no attempt to deal with these arguments here in any specific way because the slow rate of growth was a product of France's total economic situation rather than the result of any specific factor. But it is interesting to look briefly at some of the specific factors which have been identified as responsible, because they do form a background to the economic development of France and one which can be constantly perceived.

One factor very frequently isolated in this way is France's alleged deficiency in raw materials. Coal was less available than in Britain or later in Germany and coal which could be converted into a suitable metallurgical coke was particularly hard to find. It has been seen that during the Empire Belgium had already become as important a supplier to French coal consumers as the French mines themselves and this state of affairs continued in the first half of the nineteenth century. Because much of the coal consumed in France had to be transported for quite long distances and some imported, for many, but not all, consumers the price of coal was higher than it was in Britain. Even here it is necessary to be careful because one consequence of this was that the use of water power was more skilfully and cheaply developed in France than Britain. The raw material problems were probably only acute at certain particular points in the development of new industrial techniques. This was particularly the case with the introduction of the coke-smelting process because the coking-coals that were available were seldom near to suitable kinds of iron ore to make the process work. The change from charcoal smelting to coke smelting was therefore less frequently economically justifiable than in Britain. But even for this it will be seen that there were other reasons. To compete on such a scale with Britain by the use of substantially the same technologies meant a high level of coal consumption and at certain moments its high price was a handicap. But it was not always nor even usually an insuperable obstacle. And it should always be remembered that cotton was a raw material which could not be produced at all in France and that the most technically advanced of the centres of French cotton cloth production, Alsace, was the one furthest from the ports where cotton imports arrived.

It is also frequently argued that the society which emerged from the French Revolution was not particularly well constituted for economic growth. There are two ways in which this is said to be true. The establishment of a large class of peasants with an absolute title to the land is often said to have made the recruitment of an industrial proletariat much more difficult. The peasant is said to have generally opposed any schemes of agricultural rationalisation and to have been well content with an economic existence as self-sufficient as possible, selling his labour and buying and selling his produce in the most local of markets and governing his affairs by local traditions. It must be remarked that this was by no means a specifically French aspect of nineteenth century society. In several other areas of Europe the economic arrangements of the old régime were modified by government action, or by peasant revolt, or simply evolved, into rural societies similar to that produced by the French Revolution. If the argument is that French agriculture was held back by the prevalence of small farmers with established tenures and unadventurous policies it would be fair to say that this was true, or even truer, of most other parts of Europe until 1870. In fact the aggregate rate of growth of agricultural product was not noticeably unsatisfactory in France in this period, about 1·2 per cent per annum before 1850, and the agricultural sector showed considerable capacity for change and improvement. Nor is there much evidence that French entrepreneurs had difficulty in getting together a labour force because of the secure land tenures which prevailed. What may be true is that it was more difficult to accustom part-time farmers and smallholders to the dreary discipline and routine of the factory. But that was a difficult job for the entrepreneur in every society and there is no very good evidence that it was more difficult in France than elsewhere on the continent. What is certainly true is that the fierce attachment to individual property rights, which were seldom held in the most efficient pattern, confined the improvements in French farming practice in this period to the sector of larger farms. On small peasant farms, whose land was irregularly distributed about the village, but which represented a permanent family patrimony, technical innovation was very difficult and by 1870 these difficulties were becoming apparent.

Another way in which post-revolutionary society is sometimes said to have held back development is in the established position of the bourgeoisie. Theirs had been the victory, a victory which had cemented the close links between them and the state already forged in the eighteenth century. As a consequence they are claimed to have been less dynamic, less entrepreneurial and generally less interested in industrial and economic activity than is wholly desirable from the standpoint of economic development. Studies such as that of Daumard have shown how large a part of bourgeois income came from property rents, from the interest of state funds and similar safe investments.[1] But it is necessary to be careful about assuming that the French bourgeoisie was not interested in industrial investment. There are no equally competent studies of bourgeois incomes in other countries. And with the coming of the railway and later the joint-stock company there never seems to have been any great difficulty in securing capital from a bourgeoisie which, compared to that of most other continental countries, was rich and numerous. It is also necessary to look very sceptically at the argument that the French bourgeoisie did not provide the necessary entrepreneurial talent. French entrepreneurs, businessmen, engineers and even mechanics were as prevalent in other developing lands as their British equivalents in France.

Furthermore, it is frequently argued that the nature of French society was such as to produce a much higher proportion of

[1] A. Daumard, *La Bourgeoisie parisienne 1815–1848* (Paris, 1963).

relatively small family firms which were not particularly prepared to risk a comfortable existence in the interests of maximising their profits and the existence of such an attitude is then used to explain the slow rate of economic growth. There is evidence that family firms were commoner in France than in countries which developed later. But that could well be because the initial motor in the economic development of France was the textile industry which was dominated by such family firms in all countries in that period because it seldom had to face the problem of having to make a very high initial capital investment. Nor is there any evidence at all that larger non-family firms elsewhere in Europe behaved more dynamically than smaller family firms in France.

Sometimes a different explanation is offered for the supposed sluggishness both of French economic growth and of French economic development, the relatively slow rate of increase of the population. A study of the chapter on population will soon show that there was a very wide variety of experience of population growth in nineteenth-century Europe. But one thing did clearly distinguish the behaviour of the French population from that of other lands, the existence from an early date of a low and steadily falling birth-rate. France missed out one stage of nineteenth century experience that was common to most other countries, the stage where mortality rates fell sharply while the birth-rate still remained high. As a consequence the net reproduction rate there was low in the early nineteenth century and remained low. It is argued that this restricted the size of French markets or, more vaguely, that the failure of the population to grow meant there was no challenge to industrialise nor any general dynamism in the economy. But in the circumstances of nineteenth-century development a more slowly growing population made increases in *per capita* incomes easier to achieve and thus gave France advantages rather than disadvantages in marketing. France was already a densely populated country with a numerous population and the slower rate of growth of population there certainly did not mean there was any labour shortage. It is much more likely that some part of the behaviour of the French population is explained by the type of development that took place rather than itself explaining the pace of that development.

Finally, it is sometimes also argued that the legacy of the old régime caused French consumers and producers to prefer 'luxury' goods such as the finer cottons, silks or wines to the plainer commodities which the new mass-productive methods turned out. In fact, although the old régime and its preferences and tastes were represented in a more thoroughgoing way in France than anywhere else in Europe they were also more comprehensively rejected there.

France was the symbol of the new society as she had been of the old. It makes more sense to look at the level of consumers' incomes in French markets and at the additional markets available to French producers than to attribute the structure of French industry to vague social preferences. French producers sold in the markets in which they *could* sell and these markets were just sufficient to permit the gradual but decisive economic development of the whole country. The qualification is an important one. Because British development left so few export opportunities open to French producers and because those opportunities could often only be seized by specialising in high quality goods rather than in the cheaper ranges which could be produced in greater quantities, French output had to be qualitatively different from that of Britain.

The same statement can be made about this argument as about all the other arguments to do with single factors which have been so briefly cited here; although all have a certain amount of importance they all become less important when the emphasis is shifted from economic growth to the wider issue of economic development. Indeed some of these factors are less explanations of the type of development that took place in France than results of that development. For example, to argue that French development was retarded because industrial producers concentrated on 'luxury' products is to put the cart before the horse. The overall situation of French industry compelled producers to concentrate on such goods if they were to increase their sales and the product mix of French exports represented not a mistaken, but a successful, response to the international economic situation by an entrepreneurial class behaving with sharp business acumen. Even the structure of agrarian society was, properly seen, more the result of the relatively high level of development of the economy than a cause of its retardation in the early nineteenth century. In order to see these arguments in their true perspective it is necessary to study the type of development that did take place and it will be seen how often it was the cause of these particular peculiarities of French society.

THE DEVELOPMENT OF INDUSTRY

In fact economic development followed very closely the lines it had taken before 1815. The textile and iron industries completed their transformation to the new methods of production, although in the case of the iron industry only very falteringly. Means of communication were drastically improved by canal building and by railway construction. And with railway construction methods of raising and deploying much larger sums of capital were developed with important results for the banking system and for investment in general. Other industries gradually adapted to the new mode of production and also to the possibilities opened up by the new techniques of capital management. Meanwhile the economy retained a very large agricultural sector in which the number of people employed did not significantly decrease over the country as a whole before 1870 in spite of the continuing increase in industrial employment and in industrial output. There was a noticeable acceleration in the rate of industrial output between 1850 and 1857. On the other side of the coin the cyclical downturns in the economy, especially when, as in 1848, they were prolonged by violent political events, produced short periods of apparent stagnation. Such fluctuations were often closely related to the development of particular industries or to particular institutional changes, and beneath the apparent gradualness and steadiness of economic development may be seen a long series of severe setbacks and sudden successes all of which indicate how difficult the task of development actually was.

– Textiles

Textile production already played an important role in France's small industrial output in the later eighteenth century. It was responsible for about 20 per cent of the total value, roughly comparable to the proportion contributed by foodstuff industries or by construction and public works. By 1870 its share of the very much larger output was the same, but the conditions in which that output was produced were utterly different. The textile industries in France were the driving force in the industrialisation and development of the country for most of the period 1815–70. The great increase in production and the constant improvements in mechanisation continued the process of economic and social change already begun before the Revolution and spread its effects into other areas of the economy. By 1870 the domestic production of textiles other than silk was becoming a curiosity although there were still struggling hand-loom weavers in the less mechanised of the textile districts.

The cotton industry retained the lead in this process of mechanisation. Cottons also became the most important of the textiles produced when considered merely from the point of view of quantity. By 1850 there were 4,500,000 cotton spindles, almost entirely mechanised, probably about the same number as in the whole of the rest of the continent. After 1815 the spread of cotton cloth manufacture into the countryside at the expense of the more traditional fabrics was very rapid. The cheaper labour available in rural areas attracted putters-out away from the older textile towns and in Picardy, Flanders and Brittany cotton spinning, whether domestic or mechanised, and weaving completely replaced linen and wool. In 1815 the Pays de Caux in Normandy was still a famous region for the older domestic industries, fifteen years later there were about 20,000 cotton looms at work there, two-thirds of them controlled by putters-out from the town of Yvetot. South of the Loire the manufacture of woollens and silks was more able to survive this onslaught. But the only region in the north not to succumb was, curiously enough, Artois. The cotton industry, which had developed there during the Empire, collapsed after 1815 and linen cloth dominated the area by 1840. The best explanation seems to be that the quality of the flax was higher there than elsewhere and this combined with a ready supply of labour familiar with handling the raw material, which still dominated the scene in the neighbouring Belgian provinces of Flanders, gave linen producers there a chance to keep their share of a shrinking market.

The average annual consumption of raw cotton rose from 19,000 tons in the period 1815–24 to 86,000 tons in the period 1865–74. Gradually the United States came to provide almost the whole of the supply although in the early period the Mediterranean and Brazil were still important sources. This pattern of trade was of course violently interrupted by the American Civil War. As the source of supply shifted ever more to America Le Havre became the great cotton port. The cost of raw cotton was as a consequence much lower in Normandy than in Mulhouse. Even in 1850 it took over twenty days for the cotton to be convoyed from Le Havre to that town. In the early period it was carried in convoys of huge covered wagons across the whole of the country. The opening of the Rhône–Rhine canal in 1832 reduced the cost but did not speed up the journey. Only the railway could end Alsace's isolation and the first load of cotton did not arrive there from Le Havre by rail until 1852. Throughout the whole period, however, Alsace was always the most advanced and mechanised region, the area from which technological innovation spread to the other cotton manufacturing areas.

This can be explained by the prominent role of export production in the Alsatian cotton cloth industry. In this region, more than the other cotton textile areas of France, the country's difficult international economic situation was reflected. The total value of all French cotton cloth exports was only about one tenth of those from

Britain in the period 1827–9 and by 1844–5 only about one-fifteenth. In other continental countries where there was a cotton cloth industry exporting its products in small quantities, in Germany and Switzerland for example, wages were lower than in France thus making any possibility of effective competition in non-mass-produced articles very small. France therefore had to compete with Britain in goods produced by mechanised methods and at the same time specialise in the better quality goods, for an emphasis on quality was the only way France could retain part of the international market. The consequence was that total cotton cloth exports were limited by high prices and had less capacity for growth than British cotton cloth exports. Whereas by the middle of the century British cotton cloth exports were usually nearly two-thirds of total output, in France exports represented about one-fifth. These were the forces which shaped the cotton cloth industry in Alsace, specialisation in high quality goods, highly mechanised production, constant technical innovation and successful competition on the international market in the one way in which that was possible. Total production was never so great as in Normandy, which had much better access to the raw material. But most Norman cottons were sold in the heavily-protected domestic market or in the equally protected colonial market in Algeria, the biggest receiver of French cotton cloth exports. Alsatian exports went rather to other European countries and especially to Britain for re-export across the Atlantic and this export trade was the main business of some of the more modern manufacturers.

Part of the success of the Alsatian manufacturers can be explained by the same factor that had helped them before the Revolution, easier access to capital. Another part may be attributed to the existence of a coherent group of entrepreneurs acting in concert to promote and defend their own interests. Certainly both explanations are important because in the type of competition in which Alsace was engaged technical innovation was vitally important and it required capital and initiative to achieve. But more measurable economic factors also can be taken into consideration. In the early stages the Vosges mountains provided an excellent source of cheap water power. By 1835 this advantage was of little use as the spinning mills had become so big that they either had to be driven wholly by steam engines or have steam engines to supplement the hydraulic machinery. Hand-spinning had disappeared by 1825 and ten years later the average number of spindles per firm was about 12,500. In Mulhouse itself it was 19,000. The most modern firms in Rouen in Normandy, by contrast, had only 3,500 spindles. It might seem that in converting to steam power Alsace was badly disadvantaged. The cost of coal in Mulhouse was four times its price in the British cotton capital Manchester. The coal had to come from the Le Creusot and Blanzy basins. Its arrivals were irregular and on occasions agents of the larger cotton firms would fight outside the boundaries of Mulhouse to bribe the coal carriers in order to get a supply from the smaller coalfield of Ronchamps. The situation was eased in the 1830s by the Rhône–Rhine canal, and the building of the Marne–Rhine canal between 1838 and 1853 enabled coals from the Saarland to come by water. On the other hand land in Alsace was cheaper than in Britain and the costs of construction seem also to have been cheaper. Although the worker in an Alsatian spinning-mill looked after only half the spindles of his British equivalent he worked fifteen hours a week more and earned only about half the salary. Furthermore the high cost of coal induced a great deal of technical expertise in designing the machinery so that coal consumption was considerably less than in Britain for the equivalent output of cloth. Even so British coal, like cotton, was cheaper in Normandy than French coal in Alsace and, although the main development of the northern French coalfield came only in the 1840s coals were even cheaper to manufacturers in Picardy and Flanders. Nevertheless by 1836 over half the motive power in Alsatian cotton spinning was steam power. The biggest industrial enterprises on the European mainland, apart from the Cockerill metallurgical works in Belgium, were cotton mills in Alsace, the Naegely works at Mulhouse which had 83,000 spindles in 1839, the Hartmann works at Munster which had 50,000 spindles in 1834, and the Schlumberger works at Guebwiller which had 37,500 spindles in 1827. Such developments were not confined to spinning. After 1840 hand-loom weavers were employed in Alsace only for the very finest cottons, whereas elsewhere they were still increasing in number.

The average speed of a cotton spindle in Alsace increased from 3,000 turns a minute in 1828 to 6,000 turns in 1856. The annual output of a cotton spindle spinning an equivalent thread more than doubled between 1815 and 1835 and then increased by a further 50 per cent by 1845. Great improvements in productivity were also achieved by the introduction of mechanical looms although the improvements were much less imposing. The first mechanical looms to be widely used performed less than 100 actions a minute, those in use by 1872 performed 150. Mechanical looms made in Britain were bought by Alsatian constructors after 1820 and much of the work of perfecting them was carried out in Alsace by constructors such as Jourdain, Risler and Dixon, and, in particular, Josué Heilman. It was Heilman who later designed the first really effective wool-combing machines. Isaac Koechlin built a new works in 1826 equipped with 240 Heilman looms. By 1840 when mechanical looms were as yet hardly used in other regions they outnumbered hand looms in Alsace. By 1870 hand-loom weaving in Alsace was almost extinct. After 1834 the total number of looms declined as the output of woven cloth increased. The number of spindles continued to increase until 1871 although total output of yarn rose relatively more. Self-acting machinery first appeared in the region in 1838 but until the 1850s was adopted only slowly.

One factor underlying these long-run improvements in productivity, and one which applied to all the other cotton textile regions as well as to Alsace, was the concentration of activity under one roof. Although the mechanical loom did not bring such startling productivity gains as mechanical spinning it brought one major improvement in the rhythm of the production process – it ended the seasonal nature of most weaving operations. When domestic weaving prevailed the yarn was usually distributed to the weavers in greatest quantities during the summer imposing strong constraints on the rhythm of yarn production. The weavers finished their cloths in greatest quantities in the winter. Half of the annual production of the firm of Méquillet-Noblot in 1821 took place in the four months November to February. The public did most of its buying in the spring. The entrepreneur therefore needed a considerable stock of working capital to help him overcome the long periods when he had to hold stocks of either yarn or cloth. With mechanical looms concentrated under one roof there was a more regular demand for yarn. There was also a much better control over final quality.

Until the mid-1830s printed cottons, *indiennes*, continued to provide the basis for this remarkable expansion. The maximum number of cloths printed was reached in 1834 although there was no real decline until the 1840s. In 1839 14,000 people were employed in the printing processes alone. The consequence was that the firms were usually large enterprises integrating most aspects of production. Firms like Gros-Roman or Dollfuss-Mieg who specialised in high quality printing also had several large spinning and weaving mills. By 1847 the level of employment in printing had fallen to the level of the 1820s as public taste began to change to other cloths. Manufacturers had to develop other cotton fabrics to replace the *indiennes* in the 1840s and as they did so the other branches of the industry began to reassert themselves over the finishing processes.

This was only one aspect of something that was a perpetual feature in the history of the textile manufacture, an extraordinary susceptibility to the state of the market and to fashion. All textile industries were directly dependent on the level of spendable income in the consumer market. It behoved a cotton manufacturer to keep

a weather eye on the crops growing in the fields and let their condition determine his activities, for any increase in food prices reduced
cotton cloth sales. The slumps of 1822, 1825, 1830–1, 1837 and 1846 *sharp*
were all associated with high food prices and in each case the cotton
industry suffered heavy unemployment and numerous bankruptcies.
In 1847 8,000 of the 21,000 working in the textile industries of
Roubaix were unemployed and almost the same proportion of those
employed in Lille. In both cases the incidence of unemployment was
highest amongst the cotton workers. The industry was as susceptible
to changes in fashion as to cyclical movements in the economy.
Within any one region the number of local changes of fortune was
very high. The industrial development of the towns of Calais and
St Quentin in the northern region would serve as an example. In
1816 English entrepreneurs brought the tulle bobbin to Calais and
it became the most important centre of lace manufacture. From
Calais the mechanised production of tulle spread to Douai and
St Quentin and when, in 1828, the price of lace fell so low as to put
the industry in danger the technical developments which rescued
the industry took place in St Quentin not Calais. St Quentin then
became as much the capital of the finer cotton manufacture in the
north as Rouen of the coarser cloths. In a similar way the concentration of weaving activities and the use of steam engines caused the
cotton manufacture to leave the higher valleys of the Vosges
mountains and to descend to the lower plains of Alsace.

In spite of so many local shifts it is still fair to categorise the other
main cotton regions, Normandy and the North, as being less
advanced throughout the period than Alsace. Normandy was the
region with the most workers and the largest output. For the first
fifty years of the century there were usually twice as many spindles
at work there as in Alsace. But the most modern methods made
their way there only slowly. Water power was widely available.
Entrepreneurs concentrated their activities in the valleys of the
Seine, the Eure, the Andelle and the Risle. The buildings were often
converted mills and the nobles who had previously owned them
contributed capital to their conversion to these new uses. This
dependence on regular water power is emphasised by the decline of
the town of Yvetot which was not in the valleys. In 1847 water
power was still preponderant in the Norman industry. Most of the
yarn was consumed locally and the finished cloths were confined to
the domestic market and to Algeria. In 1860 hand-loom weaving
was still a very typical feature.

The northern region remained in a similar position until the more
extensive coal mining activities of the 1840s began to give it a
decisive advantage. Indeed in the early period it was held back by the

L

relative lack of water power. There were thirty spinning mills in Amiens in 1834 but few were mechanised beyond the stage of animal power. As coal became cheaper the cotton textile industry in the north became more localised and much more advanced. The Motte–Bossut works built in 1843 was the first in France to be completely equipped with self-actors. One great influence on the mechanisation of the cotton industry in the north was the great mechanical improvements made in the other textile industries with which it co-existed in the region. There were less than half a million spindles in the region before 1850; by 1860 there were over a million. The other branches of the industry were less developed there and the yarn was usually sold for finishing elsewhere.

Mechanisation in the other textile industries set more difficult problems than in the cotton industry. The only exception was with wool spinning, already transformed during the Empire. Mechanical looms were much slower to be adapted to wool than to cotton. The technical difficulties of mechanical flax spinning proved so great as to put the linen industry at a decisive disadvantage by the side of the cotton industry. The silk industry remained in an almost completely artisanal stage of production until 1875. All three of these industries however made a substantial contribution to French economic development after 1815. After 1830 woollens became a more valuable export than cottons while the silk industry kept its European predominance throughout the period easily holding its place in the domestic and international markets. The value of its exports in the 1820s was almost half that of the other textiles combined. The growth of woollen exports in the 1830s reduced its importance but in 1845 silk exports were still twice the value of cottons and linens combined.

The larger centres of woollen cloth production which had developed earlier, Louviers, Sedan and Elbeuf, were still responsible for about 30 per cent of the national production in the 1830s, although woollen manufacture was widely scattered throughout the country. The consumption of wool is difficult to estimate. The domestic wool clip seems to have been about 40,000 tons annually for most of the century. The increase in consumption was provided for by increased imports of raw wool which had reached about 40,000 tons per year in the 1860s. The main source of raw wool was Britain although a large proportion of the wool must have originally had some other origin. The consumption of wool in Sedan increased threefold between 1811 and 1834. The first steam engines were applied to wool spinning in 1817 in the small Norman town of Elbeuf and by 1830 twenty were in operation there. There were about 20,000 workers employed there and in the surrounding countryside in the 1820s and about 11,000 in Sedan. These towns not only set the pace in modernisation but also in styles and fashions. The southern wool manufacturing areas sustained themselves only with difficulty by producing inferior versions of the cloths made in the north. They kept their local markets but gradually lost their export markets to their more modern competitors. In some cases they declined into preparing fleeces and carded wool for other manufacturing areas. But even in the more advanced areas mechanical weaving was introduced only slowly. The spinning plant, although mechanised, was smaller than in cotton. In Rheims in 1850 the spinning mills averaged between 5,000 and 6,000 spindles. An innovation which had a more immediate impact than the mechanical loom was the mechanical combing machine which made ordinary wools usable for finer goods and also broke a tighter bottleneck in labour. Although more limited than in cotton the degree of mechanisation was sufficient to bring down the price of the finished cloth throughout the period. Part of this no doubt can be attributed to the falling price of the raw material. In fact the insistence on high quality goods diminished as the industry's output grew. Between 1820 and 1840 cheaper cloths such as unions, mixtures with cotton, and shoddy were introduced from Britain. They were first produced in Normandy and by the mid-century had spread to Sedan. The localisation of the industry should not hide the fact that the main market for fashions was Paris, which was also the seat of many of the entrepreneurs.

The American Civil War disrupted supplies of raw cotton causing a considerable shift to woollen cloths and this seems mainly to have expressed itself in a demand for combed woollen cloth, worsted. The number of wool spindles in the northern region rose from 360,000 in 1860 to 900,000 in 1867, many of them in the town of Roubaix. Easy access to coal led to the almost universal use of steam power in this area. In the smaller towns, however, the hand-loom weaver continued to produce the higher quality goods still very much in demand on export markets. There were as many hand-looms as power looms in Rheims and its surrounding area in 1860 and the countryside of Artois was still full of woollen weavers. In fact the coarser cloths never had any great export success against British competition. Where cloths produced in factories were exported they were more usually the finer worsteds. The two principal export markets were always Britain and the United States although for most of the period about 15 per cent of the exports went to Belgium. The proportion of exports was higher than in the cotton industry and for all the limitations on its mechanisation it took its place by the side of the cotton industry as a prime force for economic development.

The same cannot be said of the silk and linen industries in spite of the great value of silk exports. There seem to have been no power looms for silk weaving until 1843 and thirty years later in Lyons, the great centre of the silk industry, there were 60,000 power looms and 110,000 hand looms. Mechanisation was confined to the application of water power to twisting the threads into yarn, 'throwing'. But the lack of mechanisation did not mean that the industry was a domestic industry in the sense that the other textile industries had once been. Far from it. It continued, as it had already been in the eighteenth century, a highly capitalistic industry with the domestic workers packed together in the city of Lyons tightly controlled by the entrepreneurs and working full-time in the industry. One reason for the capitalistic nature of the industry was the great value of the raw material. Trading and speculating in stocks of silk sometimes brought greater profit to the entrepreneur than the manufacturing process. As a consequence there were many barriers to a closer integration of the different stages of manufacture and a fierce attachment to the operations of the small firm, a state of affairs which was not particularly conducive to mechanisation. The organisation of the trade and the methods of production hardly changed between 1815 and 1870.

Yet it could be argued that this was the great strength of the industry. Silk cloth remained a luxury product until the mid-century and the small highly competitive firms were extremely sensitive to changes in fashion on the market. Those changes in fashion were dictated by Paris and closely followed by the Lyons entrepreneurs. They were dictated by Paris for the international market also. The biggest share of exports was always taken by Britain and, especially after the removal of all British tariffs on French silks in 1860, the industry secured an important hold on the British market. It was therefore a product peculiarly suitable to France's international economic situation. The only period when sales faltered was before 1827 at the height of the vogue for printed cottons, although in the 1850s as tastes moved towards cheaper cloths, sometimes mixtures of silk with other fabrics, the industry showed its inherent resistance to change and witnessed a period of stagnation from which the 1860 Franco-British commercial treaty rescued it. In the 1830s silk preparation and weaving spread beyond the walls of Lyons and an extensive silk-manufacturing zone developed from Villeurbanne to Voiron. Concentration into factories only began in 1875 when the first large silk mills were built.

The production of linen cloth survived the onslaught of cotton only in the northern region of France and even there with difficulty. De Girard's success in inventing flax spinning machinery had no initial impact on France. The many activities concerned with the preparation of flax and the weaving of linen remained rural activities and the finished product tended to have a mainly local importance and to be very little exported. If domestic work became a full-time activity of the peasant rather than a part-time activity it was where cotton replaced linen. De Girard's invention, which was complicated and expensive, was ill-suited to such a rural part-time activity and could only successfully in its first years be taken up by a more mercantilist country where state support was forthcoming. Both he and his invention migrated to Austria in 1815 and thence to Hungary. From there the new technique was taken to Britain in 1824 for the first linen factories and it only returned to France with the efforts made between then and 1830 in Lille to mechanise flax spinning. These efforts were not really successful until 1835 when Scrive imported the machinery for his new spinning mills in pieces from Britain, each piece hidden in a glass retort and sent to a different port. When some were seized by the customs he imported British workmen to make the missing pieces in France. However, by the close of 1836 there were fifteen mechanised linen spinning mills, eight of them in Lille, and French manufacturers were regaining their share of the domestic yarn market and in another decade making inroads into the Belgian market. The machinery which equipped the later mills was made by Schlumberger the Alsatian manufacturer and by a Belgian industrialist in Lille, David van de Weghe.

Linen weaving was still a rural activity in the 1850s although there were already a few workshops with the weavers concentrated under one roof. Concentration was not accompanied by mechanisation until the application of steam power in the 1860s. The incentive for this was, once again, the difficulty of procuring cotton at a reasonable price in those years. The so-called 'cotton famine', which did not in fact severely damage the cotton industry at all, had a greater impact on the linen industry. The number of linen spindles increased from 502,000 in 1860 to 705,000 in 1867 and the same period saw the foundation of the bigger weaving mills. Nevertheless hand-loom weaving still survived extensively in 1870 in towns such as Armentières and Halluin. Improvements to the hand-loom such as the application of the flying shuttle allowed a good hand-loom weaver to equal a mechanical loom in productivity until the 1860s. The total output of linen and hempen cloth rose from 48,400 tons in the decade 1815–24 to 83,400 tons in the decade 1865–74. The domestic crop of flax was estimated at 35,000 tons in 1852 and it certainly grew larger in the 1860s. Nevertheless raw material had to be imported in substantial quantities, about 20,000 tons per year in the 1860s, mainly from Belgium and Russia, to cater for the increase in output which followed mechanisation.

The extent to which textile manufacture was a provincial affair after 1815 is quite remarkable, when, under the Empire, Paris had become the most important centre for the cotton industry at least. Of course sources of water and steam power were not available there and with the eclipse of human and animal power there were good economic reasons for a migration to the provinces. Labour was also dearer in Paris. Of fifty-two textile factories in the city thirty-four had closed by 1829. Yet the city remained an important centre of textile machine production and general engineering and indeed of technical handicrafts of all kinds as well as being the main market and a growing market for all the finer goods.

The entrepreneurs who created the French textile industry were very seldom self-made men. They formed a set of tight family networks in their own regions, family networks which had very little recourse to outside capital. 'We do not live on share capital', wrote the linen spinner Scrive, 'we have no wish to throw to the dogs a name which ranks honourably among those of industrialists.'[2] Even the cotton firm of Thierry-Mieg in Alsace which employed 1,300 in 1850 depended entirely on family capital. The Mulhouse cotton entrepreneurs, many of whom were Protestants, deliberately married their children within their own circle as an instrument of capital manipulation. Proud of their success, resentful of all interference they looked scornfully at other merchants and specially at 'pure' financiers. There were only four joint-stock companies in the cotton industry before 1850. The typical source of fresh investment in the firm was the profits of previous years' operations.

Nevertheless it is easy to allow the attitude of the entrepreneurs to obscure the fact that they did on many occasions need outside help. In the first place the seasonal rhythm of the industry meant there was a great demand for capital at the same moment from all firms. Before 1848 this was met by the activities of local discount merchants who discounted paper in order to provide working capital. The need for such a facility was emphasised in the crash of 1846 when the government was eventually persuaded to found local discount houses (*comptoirs d'escompte*) to tide the manufacturers over their difficulties. In the second place a severe crash could mean that more than working capital was needed from outside. In the crash of 1828 a consortium of Paris bankers provided a 5,000,000 franc loan to the Alsatian cotton manufacturers.

2 J. Lambert-Dansette, *Essai sur les origines et l'évolution d'une bourgeoisie. Quelques familles du patronat textile de Lille-Armentières*, 1789–1914 (Lille, 1954), p. 415.

Schlumberger, who borrowed at the same time from Swiss bankers, made it a working rule afterwards to pay for all the soap, vinegar and candles which he took from his works. Thirdly, only in the very early stages of mechanisation was the cost of the machinery low. The cost of installing a large cotton spinning mill, of about 30,000 spindles, in 1830–5, the kind of mill being built in Alsace, was over one million francs, about 25 to 30 per cent more than the initial cost of the first puddling furnaces of the 1820s. Mechanical combing machinery almost always demanded support from outside capital because of its expense. The mechanisation of the linen industry which took place later than in cotton or wool was certainly only possible through recourse to bank capital although in that case the bankers and industrialists again tended to form a tight circle of a few families in Lille. The cost of the Dickson linen spinning mills founded in 1842 was three and a half times as high per spindle as the cost of a cotton-spinning mill. Furthermore the cost of the raw material was a much higher proportion of the manufacturing cost than was the case with cotton or wool. In 1838 it was 70 per cent of the production costs in the Malo and Dickson works at Dunkirk and in 1849 still 60 per cent. In the silk industry the proportion of raw material costs was even higher. It is obvious that there were normal incidences of business life when the entrepreneurs were not so independent as they sounded and also obvious that there were emergencies when they were not independent at all.

– Iron

Throughout the period 1815–70 France was the largest producer of pig iron on the continent. Output rose from about 200,000 tons annually in the 1820s to an annual average of 1,262,000 tons in the period 1865–9. The situation of the French iron industry, in spite of this great development, was remarkably like that of the French textile industries, for over the same period British output of pig iron which had been very little larger than that of France in 1815 increased until it was four times as great at the end of the period. The charcoal-smelting technique and the small rural blast-furnace were not eliminated by the development of such modern works as Le Creusot. As the demand for pig iron rose the number of charcoal forges increased, only reaching its maximum level in 1837, and the older and newer techniques survived side by side for a long time. This cannot be blamed on a failure to innovate or on an unreasoning attachment to the traditional types of iron. French ironmasters showed an astonishing alertness to technical developments in Britain. Once peace was restored between the two countries they flocked across the Channel to copy the new techniques. The Dufaud

[handwritten margin notes: "1815", "Fr. → GB. to learn tech."]

family, creators of the iron works at Fourchambault in the Loire valley, brought the puddling and rolling processes from Britain in 1815 after visiting British iron works. This first example of the 'English' forge was quickly copied. In 1821 there were already at least nine examples in France. The iron for the forges at Fourchambault was still made by the charcoal process but the Dufauds felt themselves the harbingers of a very immediate future in which the new processes would sweep aside the old. 'Following what has happened in England, and what is also happening in those parts of France which are familiar with English iron, with the exception of some particular and extraordinary pieces of work, cheapness and not the excellence of the quality determines the sale. We cannot hide from ourselves that it will soon be the same with us and we must prepare ourselves to meet this moment.'[3] So wrote Achille Dufaud in 1823. His words find their echo in those of de Wendel transforming the Hayange works in 1820 to the coke-smelting process. 'For several more years the sale of iron foundings is certain; enormous enterprises are being born, canals, steam pumps, railways, water pipes, among other things.'[4]

The interesting thing is that their judgment of the situation was wrong and in some ways it could be said that they were too ready to innovate. The Le Creusot works suffered endless financial and technical difficulties. Its founders went bankrupt in the 1820s and transferred it to two English entrepreneurs, Manby and Wilson, who owned the Charenton iron works in Paris. They in their turn went bankrupt in 1833 and a Paris banker, Alphonse Seillière, installed the Schneider family as managers. In 1840 they were still hoping the same hopes of Dufaud and de Wendel twenty years before and the younger Schneider visiting Britain gave the same advice. 'The great merit of the English and their products is that they make a great many of the same kind of object, as in the workshop from which came three locomotives every month, and nothing else.'[5] This time the moment had indeed arrived and the 1840s were a decade of great success for the operators of large coke-smelting blast-furnaces. But the delay in its arrival requires an economic explanation because in itself it characterises the peculiar nature of French economic development before 1840.

One explanation which is frequently put forward is the high tariff which protected French iron producers from competition from the

---

[3] G. Thuillier, *Georges Dufaud et les débuts du grand capitalisme dans la métallurgie en Nivernais au XIXième siècle* (Paris, 1959), p. 226.

[4] B. Gille, 'Les problèmes techniques de la sidérurgie française au cours du XIXe siècle' in *Revue de l'histoire de la sidérurgie*, II, 1961.

[5] B. Gille, *Recherches sur la formation de la grande entreprise capitaliste, 1815–1848* (Paris, 1959), p. 33.

more modern methods in use in Britain. But this is an argument which must be used with care. Iron was a commodity with a very high transport cost and there were only a few years, such as 1828, when large quantities of British iron could have been sold in France more cheaply than French iron had there been no tariff, and the coke-smelting technique only reduced Belgian prices after 1834. In any case there were in existence in France ironworks which produced by the new 'English' methods and they did not succeed in eliminating the older, allegedly inefficient, methods of production. The percentage of pig iron smelted by coke increased from 13·5 per cent in 1830–4 to only 39·6 per cent in 1845. By that date about 70 per cent of iron refining was done by the use of coal in the 'English' puddling and rolling processes. It was only after that date that the use of coke for smelting was really taken up confidently and charcoal smelting disappeared in the late 1860s. The owners of rural blast-furnaces although they believed strongly in protection believed in it with rather less fervour than the owners of the more modern works. It was the latter that the tariff was really protecting because the charcoal users understood themselves to be squeezing the last profits out of a disappearing technology and also understood that their main problem was one of internal rather than foreign competition. They were well aware that in the long run they could not be competitive.

For the more modern producers the main purpose of the tariff was to protect them against the difference in the price of coal in Britain and France. For those French works using the coke smelting process the cost of the coke was usually over 40 per cent of the total production costs. Wages and, very often, iron ore were a smaller proportion of total cost than in Britain. Charcoal was also an expensive commodity and its increasing cost was a strong motive for conversion to coke smelting. But the element of wages in a charcoal blast-furnace was negligible and, more important, the value of the capital equipment was relatively low and it could be left in disuse for long periods when demand was slack. A coke-smelting blast-furnace needed to be operated all the time to recoup the initial investment. Its full time operation depended on a regular demand for the kind of iron it turned out. In fact entrepreneurs such as Dufaud and de Wendel misjudged this demand which was very faltering before 1845. It was the deficiency of the internal market which retarded the modernisation of the French iron industry rather than the existence of a protective tariff. But to that explanation must be added the explanation that French ironworks did suffer from the high cost of coal, from the fact that coking coal, which was what they needed, was even more costly, and from the fact that the combinations of ore and coal available often produced an unsatisfactory iron. All these raw material difficulties increased the final price and postponed until the middle of the century the arrival of a high enough level of demand for coke-smelted pig and for large mass-produced iron products to enable the newer technology to eliminate the old.

Almost all the modern works were situated on a supply of iron ore and obtained their coal from elsewhere. In the case of integrated works such as Terrenoire in the Ardèche the blast-furnaces would be on the orefield and the forges near to the coal so that a high element of transport costs was involved. The difficulties of Le Creusot were largely caused by chemical problems in the smelting. The Hayange furnaces only functioned on coking coal brought from the Saarland. Many of the other works had to use a substantial admixture of charcoal smelted pig iron to get a satisfactory final product. In Alès bad coke stopped the process in 1834 and it also produced immense difficulties in Decazeville which had been specifically constructed by the Duc de Decazes on its own small coalfield.

In such circumstances the producers of charcoal iron, free of all these difficulties, continued to supply their traditional markets. They made agricultural equipment, scythes, harness and ploughs and also kitchen ware. The owners of 'English' forges hoped to monopolise the sales of large simple castings for constructional work or machinery and until that market was large enough they had no basis to invade the local markets of the charcoal iron producers. What finally set them on their feet was the demand for cheap iron rail in standard lengths. Not until the railway building boom of the 1840s were the sellers of charcoal iron seriously discommoded by the new technology and the hopes of men like Dufaud finally realised. At least 20 per cent of the iron produced in 1830 went into the manufacture of ploughs. After that date textile machinery was increasingly made of iron rather than wood and it was this that sustained the bigger forges in the 1830s. But even in that decade the main market was very local and for very traditional items. The sudden burst of railway building in the next decade, which initially produced a demand for rail too high for the French industry to satisfy, changed the whole nature of the market. Iron rail fell in price by 25 per cent between 1829 and 1845. The railways also produced a great demand for iron bridges, other constructional iron work and of course rolling stock and locomotives. In the 1850s the major iron producers and makers of iron machinery were exporting railroad equipment and metal dredges to excavate the Suez Canal.

The iron industry could not find the same solution to its economic difficulties as the textile industries. In the case of the iron industry to specialise in high quality production would actually have been to forgo the newer technology. Nor would it have been possible to meet the demands from railway builders and machine constructors on the basis of the widely scattered small-scale industry which existed in 1815, even though its products were often of a higher quality. In fact many foreign entrepreneurs migrated into France to bring the new techniques with them and to avoid having to sell their products through the French tariff. Manby and Wilson was founded at Charenton in 1822 by two Englishmen and most of its supervisory staff and skilled workers were British. After 1837 Belgian ironmasters crossed the frontier and transformed the old iron manufacture of Maubeuge into modern works. The 'English' process of refining by coal depended very heavily on the skill of the iron puddler and he himself was in the early stages usually British or Belgian.

The ultimate level of quality was to refine the iron into steel for which before Bessemer's invention only the most expensive processes existed. In France they were the monopoly of a firm which was also of British origin, Jackson at Imphy in the Nièvre. They adopted the Bessemer converter immediately after its invention combining with the Fourchambault works in 1858 to erect a new steel plant. Le Creusot and Hayange soon followed suit. The same metallurgical problems occurred as with the coke-smelting process and the early steel plants had frequently to use imported pig iron. The Siemens-Martin open hearth process resolved these difficulties and was quickly adopted by the works which had begun with Bessemer converters. The responsiveness of the industry to technical change was very high after 1850 and French metallurgists played an important part in advancing the new and cheaper steel-making techniques. The total output of steel in 1869 was only just over 100,000 tons but already the first steel rails had been produced and tested and the technological basis of a large new industry created. Le Creusot employed 10,000 workers, Hayange about 5,000. The main production was now large standardised items often for export. Although in terms of total pig iron output the German iron industry was rapidly catching up with that in France in terms of variety and sophistication of product France was far ahead of any continental rival.

– Coal

It will have become clear in considering the history of the French textile and iron industries that they were placed at a disadvantage by the high cost of coal. French coal reserves were smaller than those of Britain or Germany and many areas of France were a long way from coal supply. This was not necessarily an obstacle to economic development. The nature of economic development in this period was very regional. Certain areas where economic conditions were particularly favourable underwent an intense industrialisation specialising heavily in one industry in which the level of productivity was greatly increased. The cotton industry in Alsace is an example. The techniques of nineteenth-century industrial processes, in which coal increasingly replaced other sources of power, often meant that these particular regional points of intense development were located on coalfields. The department with the highest proportion of its inhabitants employed by industry in 1870 was Nord which was also the department mining the most coal and producing most of the linen cloth and a high proportion of the woollen cloth. But Alsace was not provided with coal at pit-head prices and had to pay high transport costs on all coal except that from the tiny basin of Ronchamps. In certain circumstances the high price of coal could be a handicap to general economic development even though regional specialisation of this kind took place. Three developments in particular drove the economy towards the use of coal, the steam engine, its application to railways, and the production of gas for gas-lighting. Although substitution was possible, as in the high level of development of water power for textile factories in France, a high level of coal consumption was usually a concomitant of a high level of industrialisation before 1870.

The main exploitable French coal reserves were in the northern coalfield which crossed the frontier into Belgium, in the central area around the head waters of the river Loire, and a few scattered basins on the edge of the Massif Central. They were never able to meet the demand for coal in the economy and France became after 1815, and remained, the most important European coal importer. Total annual production increased from 1,100,000 tons in 1820–4 to 12,700,000 tons in 1865–9. Usually production satisfied about 50 to 60 per cent of consumption, which had reached a level of about 20,000,000 tons by the late 1860s. The most important source of coal imports was always Belgium although for Normandy Britain was a more important supplier. In the late 1840s Belgian coal exports to France accounted for about forty per cent of total French consumption, which was roughly equivalent to the proportion they had accounted for during the Empire.

The use of Belgian coal in such quantities testifies to the high cost of mining in northern France in the early nineteenth century because there was a protective tariff against Belgian coal. The tariff was breached by a series of frontier zones in the north where the duties on coal were much lower. This was so as not to penalise manufacturers such as those in the Maubeuge area who had depended entirely on Belgian coal during the Empire. But in the greater part of the northern industrial area Belgian coal paid the full tariff. There were a variety of other ways by which the French market was sheltered from Belgian competition and the geography of some regions of northern France gave a natural protection to French producers which was carefully maintained by canal building policy for some time. The Sambre–Oise canal which allowed Belgian coal from the Charleroi basin access by water to Paris was not completed until 1838 and even then the navigation presented difficulties. When tariffs were liberalised after 1860 the French government nationalised the Scheldt and the St Quentin canals which carried most of the northern French coal to Paris and deliberately offered transport rates below those on the Sambre navigation to preserve the Paris market for French producers. Such devices only served to increase the final cost of coal to French consumers for in 1830 the average price of coal at the pit head in Belgium was half its price in the northern French coalfield.

There was in fact only a sluggish development of mining in northern France until 1834 when a burst of new prospecting began. Until that time the Compagnie d'Anzin pursued a rather conservative policy. Steam engines for pumping were introduced more reluctantly than in Belgium and the eighteenth-century structure of the company scarcely changed. In 1847 when about a quarter of total French coal output came from the north one half of the north's output was still produced by the Anzin company. The companies formed in the previous decade had no great success with their prospecting until 1847 when borings revealed the existence of a deeper westward extension of the coalfield, the Pas de Calais basin. This discovery began a long period of growth of output in which the northern coalfield became the most important. It first mined more coal than the central coalfields in 1863. The main reason for the sluggishness in the north until 1828 was that it was actually easier for coals from the Loire basins to reach Paris by water than coals from the north so that the northern market was the only one available and that was where Belgian competition was strongest. Only with the cutting of the St Quentin canal in 1828 could coal barges gain access to the Oise and thus to the Seine and Paris and from that year the proportion of northern coal used in Paris grew at the expense of central coal. Both central French coal and Belgian coal were usually preferred because of their better quality which also partly accounts for the slowness of expansion in the north.

The extreme importance of cheap carriage for a commodity with so high a unit cost of transport as coal can really be seen in the enormous effort necessary to transport the coal from the central coalfield to Paris. It had first to be taken a short land journey to

Andrézieux on the Loire. The voyage down the Loire was full of problems, not enough water in the river, rapids and shifting sandbanks. At Orléans the barges were transferred to the two narrow canals with high tolls that led through many locks through the Beauce to Paris, the Canal du Loing, and the Canal de Briare. Having finally arrived in Paris the barges were chopped up for firewood. The building of the Canal de St Quentin led to great efforts in turn to improve communications with the centre. These efforts were responsible for the first steam operated railways in France which were coal-carrying lines in the upper Loire. That from Roanne to Andrézieux became the first steam-operated passenger line in 1834. The obstacles in the Loire were circumvented by the Loire lateral canal leading upstream from Digoin. But the journey was too long to compete with northern coal after 1830 and coal from the centre began to depend on southern markets and on the expanding railway system. These markets were quite able to sustain an increasing production. The smaller fields of the Massif Central also increased their output. That of the Alès basin increased from 45,000 tons in 1835 to 415,000 tons in 1845 and coal from there and the central coalfield ousted British coal from Marseilles. Like the northern coalfield the central coalfield was exploited by a few large concerns. Indeed from 1845 until 1854 the central coalfield was controlled by only one concern which was then divided by government action into four separate companies. The smaller basins were often owned by metallurgical firms trying to secure a supply of coal at a constant price. The industry as a whole was not very competitive. It was helped in this by the high cost of carrying coal on long journeys and apart from the competition to sell in Paris each coalfield had a relatively secure regional market on which it could sell at, by international standards, a high price. This regional isolation was not broken down by the railways because they themselves increased the demand for coal so much. But the unresponsiveness of the coal industry is frequently exaggerated. When the demand was there big increases in coal output took place rapidly. The slowness of developments before the mid-1830s is more to be explained, as in the case of the iron industry, by an insufficient demand in the economy.

Engineering

Two factors which go some way to explaining the relative lack of demand are the preference for water power over steam power in the most rapidly developing industry, textile production, and the delay in building a railway network. About half the steam engines used in France in 1835 were used in textile factories and it was only after that date that other markets for steam engines became equally important. There were only 625 steam engines employed in the country in 1830; in 1839 there were 2,450. By 1870 there were 27,088 with a total brake horse power ten times greater than the total in 1839. Before 1835 improvements in hydraulic machinery such as Bourdin's turbine, later perfected by Fourneyron, or Poncelet's improved water wheel, made such machinery easily competitive with steam engines in most areas.

In this early period steam engines provided a considerable part of the market for iron. The other main aspect of machine-building, the production of textile machinery, was not so dependent on iron. In fact the abundance of woodworkers in Paris because of the coach building trade there meant that even in 1840 nine of the twenty biggest machine building shops were still in the capital city. The other great centre of machine-building was Alsace which produced spinning machinery and looms. The biggest manufacturer was Schlumberger who employed 4,000 in 1840 and made the most advanced spinning machinery. But textile machinery production could not compensate for the late development of steam engine and railway locomotive building for it was on these that the iron industry and the coal industry depended for their growth. The reasons for this late development are very complex.

THE DEVELOPMENT OF TRANSPORT AND SERVICES

Transport

One of the great advantages which France had in the early nineteenth century was the existence of an organised and efficient transport system and road network. Most writers describe the roads as carrying little traffic except in the immediate neighbourhood of large cities. But such comparisons, made for the most part with Britain, have no great relevance. In fact in the early nineteenth century almost 200,000 tons of food a year was transported into Paris by road or water and probably over twice that weight of raw materials for Parisian industries. Paris was already the biggest port in the country receiving about 25,000 boats a year either by river or by the canals of St Denis and St Martin. Probably about two-thirds of the total weight of goods carried internally was carried by road rather than by water although wherever possible water was preferred as being cheaper. The governments before 1848 invested large sums in improving the national transport system. Between 1814 and 1846 7,000 kilometres of new main roads were constructed and 22,000 kilometres of departmental roads. Between 1815 and 1848 a further

2,900 kilometres of canals were also built by which time the total length of navigable canal in France was over 4,000 kilometres. There were plans to construct a 'rational' canal system, but those that were finished were usually built because of some immediately profitable freight, particularly coal. The network of canals serving the northern coalfield was extended in 1820 by the building of the Canal de la Sensée, followed by the Canal d'Aire à la Bassée in 1825 and completed by the Canal de St Quentin which finally linked the coalfield to Paris by water. After 1835 canals were built to link the greater rivers such as the Rhine–Rhône canal, and the Marne–Rhine canal. Parallel with this activity went the improvement of river navigations, occasionally by the construction of 'lateral' canals such as that which greatly extended inland the head of navigation on the river Loire.

The first steam-hauled railways comprised the short network around St Étienne and Lyons which began to use steam locomotives in 1832 to reach the navigable water on the Loire. Although they did haul passengers, their success, as that of so many nineteenth-century railways, was based on coal haulage. It provoked a number of other railway-building projects, inspired even more by the success of passenger-carrying railways in Britain. The competing nature of these proposals, and the contrast between the haphazard pattern of construction in Britain and the carefully-planned network being designed by the new state of Belgium, both forced the government to define its attitude to railway construction. It is frequently argued that government hesitation delayed the building of a railway system. This is a reasonable verdict. It was not so much that government thwarted private entrepreneurs who would otherwise have constructed a railway system more rapidly but that it beset railway building with so many safeguards as to delay its full flourishing by a decade. There were, however, other reasons for this delay and government policy was aimed at overcoming them so that in certain circumstances it helped in the completion of lines which might otherwise not have been built.

The attitude of the state to railway construction could not help but be very complicated and it was in no way merely meddlesome and restrictive purely out of traditionalism or timidity. In the first place the government had been very heavily involved for a long time in providing and maintaining a national transport system. It had maintained and improved a national road network since the seventeenth century and after 1815 had devoted a great deal of money to extending the canal system. Napoleon Bonaparte had equipped it with a skilled corps of professional civil engineers responsible for public transport, the Corps des Ponts et Chaussées.

Many of the railway schemes proposed were directly competitive with the canal building projects which were still being undertaken. Nor was it only the government which hesitated between water and rail. The Marne–Rhine canal begun in 1838 received more support from business circles in Paris and Strasbourg than the proposed Paris–Strasbourg railway. In the second place railway construction raised important military and strategic considerations which had not been raised in Britain nor in neutral Belgium. It enormously speeded up the movement of troops and supplies to, and perhaps across, frontiers, something which might equally well benefit an enemy. In the third place it raised very sensitive political issues about political power in the government. The king and his ministers after 1830 were much criticised for their personal financial involvement in the public works projects. Businessmen and contractors politically faithful to the Orléanist monarchy formed a close and not very large corporation exclusive of outsiders of other political persuasions. Permission for contracts to build railways was therefore a burning political issue for the manipulation of railway building policy was a powerful political instrument to be used for and against the government.

Debate on these issues was very eloquent in the 1830s. The state itself never considered seriously owning and building a state railway system. But many railway promoters wanted some measure of state help and encouragement. Some, encouraged by theoreticians of the new society, wanted the state to withdraw from the arena entirely and allow a railway system to emerge purely from the interplay of private interests. But all of these fairly obvious positions were taken up against a background of ideas common to all involved, the necessity of economic development, the necessity to 'catch up' with Britain. This is particularly well shown by the intellectual position taken up by the most ardent group of advocates of a 'national' railway network, the group of bankers and economists of whom Isaac and Émile Péreire, Paulin Talabot and Michel Chevalier were the best known members. They are frequently referred to as 'Saint-Simonians' because of the influence of the philosopher Claude de Saint-Simon on their thinking. But they were primarily men of action. The Péreires were to make and lose a fortune in the most celebrated European bank of the nineteenth century. Talabot was to become briefly the greatest industrialist and financier of his age, and Chevalier's name is commemorated in the Cobden-Chevalier Treaty on tariff reductions between Britain and France in 1860.

Saint-Simon's thought is often quite wrongly described as utopian. He was a liberal philosopher of the eighteenth-century enlightenment who tried to adapt his philosophy to the economic changes taking place in France and Britain in the late eighteenth century. He was among the first to understand that the changes in the mode of production, which in France had also corresponded with the political destruction of the old society, necessarily implied profound changes in the organisation of human society. He sought to identify some rational principles on which this new society could be constructed and identified one of them as the maximisation of its productive capacity. By liberating the productive forces of the new industrial society the needs and aspirations of mankind could ultimately be satisfied. It is easy to see how such a rationale for action appealed to the first generations of French entrepreneurs who felt themselves locked in battle against traditionalism and inertia. But it was not a rationale of a completely *laissez-faire* society. Saint-Simon and his followers, for he was to have many in other developing countries such as the Latin American states where the enlightenment of the eighteenth century had penetrated deeply, considered the state to have an essential role in liberating the productive capacity of industry. Where private initiative could not suffice, the state, in the interests of mankind, must act.

Nothing better fitted this prescription for action than the building of railways. It is difficult now to understand the full measure of the hopes which men placed in railways in this period. They seemed to alter the whole dimensions of time and place. They offered the end of local hunger as grain moved easily over the country, the end of local prejudice, as rural isolation crumbled before such speedy transport, and a whole new possibility of human organisation for action, as people and letters could cover in one day journeys that had previously taken at least a week. Technology had come to the aid of philosophy in abolishing the cruelties and injustices of eighteenth-century society and the heavenly city of the enlightenment took on the form of a railway terminus. It is this which accounts for the religious fervour with which men like the Péreires or Talabot pursued their schemes. Economic development, national pride, the good of mankind and private profit seemed fused in one common interest and only the vacillations of a politically outmoded form of government to stand in the way. These were the years in which schemes to join together all the European capitals were projected and the railway tunnel from France to Britain begun. The more the government vacillated the more the tension between itself and the entrepreneurs grew. This battle of ideas and policy had an extreme effect on shaping the course of French economic history between 1830 and 1860 and the length of railway line constructed over those years varies in accordance with shifts of political power.

The ideas of the Saint-Simonians have been expressed in a more measurable form in modern economic thought through the concept of the 'multiplier' whereby a particular innovation generates further production, employment and income in the economy. Railway building did have many such effects in nineteenth-century economies. Its effects are measurable in France in the high rate of economic growth in the 1850s, the decade when government devoted its greatest effort to the construction of the main-line railway network and to other public works projects. Perroux estimated the average annual rate of growth of national product at 3 per cent in the period 1847–59, a higher rate than for any other decade in the nineteenth century.[6] Since this decade also includes the terrible economic crisis of 1847–52 the measured rate between 1852 and 1857, the period of full concentration on railway building, would certainly be much higher. Subsequent refinements of these calculations do not diminish the significance of this period for the growth of national product. Measurements of the growth of industrial product, however, have indicated that if any period can be singled out as being more significant than the others, a fact which is by no means clear, the period spanning very roughly the years 1835–44 might show a greater percentage rise in industrial product.[7] In a general way it emerges that the economic growth of France in the nineteenth century was speeded up by the period of main-line railway construction. The economic development of France was even more influenced by this period and some economic historians have argued that the 1850s were so crucial as to constitute the true period of the industrial revolution in France. Seen in such a light the struggle over French railway building loses none of the importance it had to contemporaries even if the language in which we now argue about it is less fervent.

One basic problem was that the capital expenditure needed to build a railway system was far greater than the sums which government had previously invested in public works. Outside government the chances of raising the capital depended on two things. It depended on the actual availability of the sums involved, which was both a question of the money being there and of there also being some mechanism for handling it and deploying it in the right place. It also depended on the expectations of businessmen, because

[6] F. Perroux, 'Prises de vue sur la croissance de l'économie française 1780–1950', International Association for Research in Income and Wealth, *Income and Wealth*, series v (London, 1955).

[7] J. Marczewski, 'Some aspects of the Economic Growth of France, 1660–1958', *Economic Development and Cultural Change*, vol. 9, ii, 1961. T. J. Markovitch, L'industrie française de 1789 à 1964, *Histoire quantitative de l'économie française*, AF7, *Cahiers de l'Institut de Science Économique Appliquée* (Paris, 1966).

railway investment only yielded a return when the line had got somewhere and conditions therefore had to be favourable in the future. In fact very few railways were built in the 1830s because a start was made on a large scale only when conditions seemed to be deteriorating in 1837. The government adopted an *ad hoc* policy, while trying to resolve the issues of principle by granting contracts for the construction of some lines which seemed of obvious importance and which did not prejudice any future decisions about the network. But the government did not grant rights of ownership over the lines for long enough periods of time to fully satisfy entrepreneurs that the investment was worth while and in any case investors were deterred by the fact that the government had made no firm statement of intention.

Short lines were built from Mulhouse to Thann, from Alès to Beaucaire, and two competing lines from Paris to Versailles. Contracts were put on offer for a line from Paris to Orléans, for which the government was prepared to guarantee a certain rate of interest, and several plans for lines from Paris to Le Havre, and Paris to the Belgian railway system were canvassed. In 1840 there were about 500 kilometres of track open in France. By the same date the British railway system was more than four times as long and that of a relatively unindustrialised area like Germany about the same length. The only main line in France equivalent in length to those of Britain and Germany was that from Strasbourg to Mulhouse, about 100 kilometres.

After 1841 construction proceeded on the basis of the Legrand plan and the railway law of June 1842 which incorporated it. The government mapped out a main-line system in the form of separate lines radiating from Paris to all the most important towns in the country. The land would be provided by the government although local authorities were supposed to furnish part of the cost of acquisition, a clause which proved impossible to put into practice. The government engineers would construct the road-bed, the bridges, tunnels and cuttings. All the rest, rails, stations and capital equipment was to be provided by private companies. The legislation never functioned except as a framework of ideas within which the government negotiated different terms with each private company. Some lines were eagerly taken up because they went to coalfields or to big centres of population, others were obviously less profitable. The lines to Orléans and to Rouen were finished in 1842. But the government had to provide a subsidy in the same year to complete the track from Rouen to Le Havre. The line to Lille and Brussels was completed in 1846, and that to Calais in 1849. The line to the west did not go beyond Chartres, to the south-west beyond Tours.

The line to Marseilles was open as far as Dijon and again from Avignon to Marseilles. The locomotives for the southern section were floated down the Rhône on barges. Many of the numerous small companies were bankrupt and the government was increasingly called on to provide subsidies. The readiness of investors to subscribe was correlated with the length of time for which the concession was granted. And the average length of time in the period 1842–46 was still only forty-six years. The concession for the line from Montpellier to Nîmes ran for only twelve years. After 1846 the economy moved into a deep depression and railway building ground to a halt. In 1850 Germany had twice the length of track of France and the Belgian system although smaller in length was much denser in relation to the size of the country.

What changed this state of affairs was the seizure of power by Napoleon III. He had himself been influenced in youth and exile by Saint-Simon's ideas and more importantly his reign signified a final break with the monarchist tradition and a return to the 'revolutionary' government of Napoleon I. With Saint-Simon he believed that the key to future human happiness lay in industrialisation and he saw the railway as an essential means to produce industrialisation. The economic crisis of 1847–51 accompanied by high grain prices, falling consumption and violent revolution was all too reminiscent of the crisis which had caused the collapse of the old régime in 1789. Indeed it seemed proof positive that France had not yet escaped from the evils of the cruel society of the past into the promise of the new industrial world. The new emperor used every means possible to encourage railway construction. After 1851 the normal length of concession was ninety-nine years and after 1865 prefects were empowered themselves to grant even better terms to smaller companies building the local lines. The government compelled mergers between the companies and divested itself of the lines which it had been forced to operate. By 1857 six large companies controlled the trunk railways. Credit was made available to the companies on easier terms, particularly by permitting changes in the banking system of which the permission granted to the Péreires to found their new bank, the Crédit Mobilier, as a joint-stock company was symptomatic. The bonds issued by the railway companies were in smaller denominations so that they were more like a modern industrial share. The weaker companies were given a wide range of financial guarantees to complete their lines.

There followed a period of hectic construction. The Paris–Marseilles railway was completed in 1855 and by 1867 when the next economic downturn took place the other planned trunk lines had been for the most part completed. The line to Strasbourg was completed after half the costs of construction had been paid by the government and similar efforts had to be made to push ahead with construction in the more rural west and south-west. Relations between the government and the companies were regularised between 1857 and 1859 by a series of agreements known as the Franqueville conventions. Their main purpose was to get the companies to use the profits from their main lines to pay for the construction of branch lines. The rates of interest on the network constructed after 1859 were guaranteed but if the profits on the pre-1859 lines exceeded a certain percentage they had to be used to further the construction of the post-1859 lines and not distributed to shareholders. The state was entitled to a share of all profits beyond a higher level. As it happened the Northern Railway needed no state help nor did the Paris–Lyons–Mediterranean. The others did and the state found itself heavily involved in branch line finances. The agreements changed the whole nature of railway construction in the French economy. The policy of the government had been to administer a shock to the economy by promoting very rapid railway construction. Between 1852 and 1857 such construction was a highly speculative and often a highly profitable business. After 1859 railway shares took on the nature of a guaranteed investment at a low rate of return, like the government 'rentes', as the less profitable lines were built. The network increased in size more than three times between 1850 and 1860 when there was a net addition of 6,252 kilometres, substantially more than in any other European country including Britain. After 1860 the pace of construction slackened and railway building on an equal and even greater scale began to take place elsewhere.

At the start of railway building the iron industry had some difficulty in meeting the sudden increase in demand. In spite of this a high tariff was still maintained against rail imports from Belgium. Only 3,500 tons of rail were imported between 1835 and 1844 and the initial price paid for rail in France was high. Furthermore the railways were constructed on an impressive scale with few gradients and excellent engineering. All of this was to the long run advantage of the economy, but in the short run it meant that Germany which imported rail at lower prices and built a network to much less exacting engineering standards was able to construct more quickly and more cheaply. It was the same story with locomotives, for the French were reluctant to import British locomotives except where it was absolutely necessary, whereas in many German states British locomotives were imported in parts and assembled and often copied. The first French locomotives were built by Marc Séguin in 1829. He later discovered the tubular boiler, an improvement used universally. Only in the south were British locomotives used widely before the mid-1840s. After that date they were hardly seen anywhere. Many French iron foundries and forges converted to locomotive construction on a large scale. That of Gouin and Co. which became the Société des Batignolles was the best known but there was a wide range of producers. The rolling stock also was produced in France from the outset, mainly by coach building firms such as Desouches in Paris, Bonnefaud in Ivry, and Maucomble in Clermont-Ferrand.

The railway building activities of the 1850s were not the only aspect of the Second Empire's programme of economic development and industrialisation. They were closely connected with the reconstruction of Paris on a vast scale. The Second Empire's efforts in this are still unsurpassed in scale as a combination of town-planning, public works and social engineering. Both in what they destroyed and what they replaced it with they are a perpetual reminder of the unabashed materialism of the government's policy. The construction of the great railway terminals and broad straight boulevards of Paris and the building of a whole new quarter to the north-west has obscured the Second Empire's other public works projects such as harbours and bridges. All had the same aim as the railway-building activity. Indeed without the railways the reconstruction of Paris would have been impossible. When the railway stirred up the remote rural economy of the department of Creuse it was to Paris to build new houses that the labour force migrated. Those emigrating from Burgundy opened wineshops. It was precisely in these years that the markedly regional character of the French economy first began to break down.

– *Capital and Banking*

Both the reconstruction of Paris and the building of railways were based on solutions to the difficulty of providing capital for such immense projects. To understand these solutions it is necessary to look at the history of French banking after 1815. That history is itself of great significance to the whole of European economic development. The European banking system was in most countries very unlike that in Britain. The economic development of most lands took place on the basis of technological developments which were so expensive as to require a high initial capital investment, too expensive to be based on the ploughing back of profits from the firm. The slow development of the French economy meant that, in terms of capital management, it formed a bridge between an economy like Britain, where capital investment in the mechanisation of textile industries could occur slowly over time without recourse to bankers or public loans, and those economies whose development was initially based on costly developments like blast-furnaces or railways. It has been seen that family arrangements and frugality often sufficed for French textile manufacturers to keep their capital equipment up to date, as they had for their British rivals. With railway building it was another matter and the changes in the French capital market and banking system which came as a result ushered in the beginnings of a modern banking system related to economic development all over Europe.

Paris soon became an important money market again after 1815 and attracted private merchant bankers from all over Europe. France had a positive trade balance with Britain and the United States and foreign bankers came to Paris to finance their own countries' deficits with those two powers, making the city an international money market. Until railway building began on a large scale France was a capital exporter. Such exports were mainly to cover loans to foreign governments such as those of Spain and Greece. This together with the management of the French government's own national debt, the 'rentes', and the concomitant business of financing foreign trade was the business of these wealthy family banks. In so far as such banks provided short-term discount which could serve as working capital they did so as a function of their central business – foreign exchange. They did not accept bank deposits and their long-term loans had to be decided on with great circumspection because they were only family businesses and their capital their family fortune. The most powerful of these banks was the Rothschild bank but its business was not essentially different from that of the others and its interests were bound up in co-operating in the same affairs and behaving in the same relatively cautious way. It is a mistake to suppose that there were no contacts between such banks and industry or transport. There were a few and they were important. It is also a mistake to suppose that industrialists wanted more. We have seen that textile manufacturers seldom wanted more than local discount facilities and were antagonistic to bank capital in the form of loans except on rare occasions. Such private banks did have a knowledge of the industrial world and on certain occasions adjudged its activities not too risky to deter speculation. The banker Seillière, related to an Alsace textile manufacturing family, rescued the Le Creusot works in 1836 and installed Schneider as managing director. Jacques Lafitte had investments in printing, gasworks, cotton manufacture, chemicals, glass manufacture and iron works. Delessert had investments in sugar refining and cotton spinning. Such investments provided an obvious source of profit but the constitution of banks of this kind together with the nature of industrial development before the 1830s meant that this source of capital was not much tapped.

Working capital was more frequently provided by local sources than by Paris sources and in towns such as Lille and Mulhouse there was an active discount market. But discount of this kind was costly and inclined to disappear in times of economic crisis. The Bank of France had little connection with this discount market. It had no local branches between 1816 and 1835 and its supervisory interest in charters awarded to other banks was exercised in a highly restrictive way. Certain bankers, among whom Jacques Lafitte was the most prominent, and some industrialists sustained an intermittent campaign against the Bank of France to lower its discount rate and to provide discount on paper which carried less of a guarantee than the high-grade commercial bills which it did discount. But the feeling remained that the Bank should not involve itself with business which was not long-established. While this feeling prevailed the development of branches of the Bank of France in larger provincial cities in the 1830s did not greatly change the situation with regard to discount because the Bank acted only in the remotest way as a prop to the existing local discount agents. After the 1830 revolution the government restored confidence by opening temporary discount banks (*comptoirs d'escompte*) in the provinces. In the economic crisis and revolution of 1848 legislation provided for such banks to re-open and to be a permanent feature. The origins of some later larger banks are to be found in the *comptoirs d'escompte* opened in 1848.

Before 1848 there were sporadic attempts to create banks whose business would be more deliberately geared to providing long-term capital for industry. Émile Péreire had advocated a bank which would keep a commercial portfolio of interest-bearing shares and for which the state, as a gesture to economic development, would provide the initial capital. This was the kind of institution which Lafitte tried to approach in his Caisse Générale pour le Commerce et l'Industrie founded in 1837. In fact it fell some way short of Péreire's ideal. It did not have the same resources in funds as the bank Péreire proposed. Although it was not purely a family bank it was not a joint-stock company able to issue bonds to the public and tap their capital. Like most larger companies founded in France in this period it was a *société en commandite*, a form of association which allowed certain partners to contribute to the capital stock without suffering full legal liability for the company's finances, but did not permit an appeal to the public for more funds by issuing shares. Joint-stock companies required government approval before-hand and in the financial world this was normally only accorded to insurance companies. In fact Lafitte issued interest-bearing notes negotiable for periods up to one month on the deposits placed in his bank and by this device was able to base his operations on control of more capital than that subscribed to the original *société en commandite*. Lafitte had plans to spawn from this bank another bank uniquely constituted to provide industrial capital in which expert scientific opinion would judge the merits of each investment proposition. This second idea came to nothing and the first idea, although in 1838 it had a number of smaller provincial copiers, also collapsed in the crisis of 1848.

These failures are not only attributable to the inadequate con-stitution of the bank. They are also indicative of the narrow scope of industrial investment in these years. Very little long-term capital went to the textile industry which was the most rapidly growing industry. Gasworks, mines and canals were the main outlets. The Rothschild bank contributed to the founding of the Mines de la Grande Combe in the Alès basin in 1836. The banker Casimir Périer was the most active director of the Anzin coal company as well as having investments in machine building. Lafitte organised a consortium of Paris bankers to bid for participation in the four major canals proposed by the government in 1820. When railway building began in earnest the private bankers were very ready to participate, always providing participation did not seriously en-danger them. The idea that the merchant bankers were too con-servative to provide the necessary capital is quite false. But it is true that they did not approach the question with the religious fervour of the Péreires partly because they were already in a safe and very profitable business and partly because the nature of that business led them to distrust such religious fervour. The Rothschild bank showed considerable interest in the Paris–Brussels line after 1835 and participated in the construction of one of the lines to Versailles. But in 1838, fearful of tying down their assets in such long-term investments, they abandoned railway investment temporarily. They returned to the fray in 1842 and were responsible for encouraging other private bankers to participate. They supported Talabot in his vast southern and central railway projects and joined with Belgian bankers to create the Compagnie du Nord in 1845 which controlled the Brussels line and its branches through the northern industrial area. The protestant bankers Bartholony and de Waru participated in the Paris–Orléans line. Lafitte and Rothschild jointly took part in the Paris–Lyons line. Lafitte and Blount were awarded the contract for the line from Amiens to Boulogne. By 1848 the Rothschild bank had about one-fifteenth of the railway shares issued in France and participated in the administration of eight railway companies.

Such bank participation can easily be exaggerated in importance. The bank helped the company to raise capital if it considered the investment worth recommending. Only occasionally did it provide loans in addition to the companies' own original capital stock and such loans were certainly much smaller than the government subsidies in the 1840s. In one special way the banks' international connections were very helpful for it was they who brought in foreign capital from Britain, Belgium and Switzerland by encouraging bankers from those countries to participate. Some estimates have put the proportion of foreign investment in French railway building between 1840 and 1847 as high as one-third of total investment. The British railway contractor Thomas Brassey managed the finances and building operations during the construction of many of the lines in the north. Together with the Manchester firm J. D. Barry he provided half the capital for the Bordeaux–Orléans line. British bankers and contractors even participated in so distant a line as that from Bordeaux to Sète on the Mediterranean. Swiss capital participated in the Alsatian lines and Belgian banks played a big part in the railways connecting Brussels and Paris.

The participation of foreign capital so extensively may not be an indication of the reluctance of French investors so much as an indication of the way in which the private merchant banker operated. His contacts were with the embryonic foreign money markets as much as with the sources of domestic capital. The current of Saint-Simonian thought which had gathered momentum in the previous decades and had even found minor representatives in the private banking world in the Péreire brothers was bound to regard the restricted mechanisms for raising and investing capital an obstacle to the realisation of its hopes for economic development. Certainly Napoleon III whose economic ideas were very much formed by those of Saint-Simon's followers found it so. His policy of economic recovery was also a firm commitment to economic development and he also saw railway building as the basis of development. It was his personal initiative which persuaded the Bank of France to accept a new bank controlled by Isaac and Emile Péreire which would be a joint-stock company and thus be able to raise share capital from the general public. At one stroke the new bank was given an enormous advantage over all the previous private banks, even over the earlier banks of Lafitte. No matter how enormous the private fortune of even a family like the Rothschilds it could not hope to bear comparison with a capital fund which was to be built up by selling shares to the public in relatively small denominations and thereby mobilising the collected savings of France for the purpose of the bank's operations. For such was the size of the Péreires' ideas. They envisaged an organisation which would take the savings of the lesser bourgeoisie out of the hoards where they were kept inactive and immobile, would collect them together in one great pool of capital, and would use that capital for the development of the whole country. The name chosen for the bank, Crédit Mobilier, movable credit, was itself a propaganda statement of these vast ideas. Vast ideas, which provoked the bitter opposition of the established banking community, but which had at the time and have had since a powerful impact on developing countries. For it was the Péreires who first took seriously the idea and tried to put it into practice that capital should be mobilised to actively seek investment in development projects and by reinvesting the proceeds from that investment in further development projects promote the economic development and, as they would have argued, the well-being of the whole world. For such an idea could scarcely be bounded by national frontiers, nor yet by time.

There was an inherent danger in such operations. Investments in economic development were necessarily tied down for a long time in public works and railways. The deposits on which they were based were withdrawable at short notice. Everything depended on sustaining the climate of confidence which development on such a scale should bring. In fact the Crédit Mobilier never functioned on this cosmic scale. In the period of rapid development from 1852 to 1857 it threw itself energetically into railway construction. After 1857 greater caution prevailed as the most profitable trunk lines were already completed in France. Many of them had been completed before 1852 and the Crédit Mobilier was increasingly forced into investment in public works and into competing for foreign loans and business quite similar to that of the earlier banks. Amongst industrial firms only the very largest welcomed contacts with a bank of such scope in which they might well be swallowed up. As the pace of economic development faltered the bank's opportunities got less and in 1867 the Péreires were forced out of its directorate by the Bank of France and the Crédit Mobilier faded from the scene. In retrospect its main contribution in the field of banking activity was to widen the range of interests of the private bankers and introduce them to a much bolder policy of investment. But its greater contribution was in the field of ideas on economic development. It left behind a spate of imitations elsewhere in Europe where the opportunities for such a policy were better and where the most profitable railway lines were still to be built. The Darmstädter Bank founded

in Germany in 1852 had a large measure of capital from the Crédit
Mobilier and to some extent borrowed its ideas. The Austrian
Crédit Mobilier was founded in 1855, the Spanish in 1856 and
similar institutions emerged in Italy and the Netherlands. It is not
known what proportion of the Crédit Mobilier's investments were
placed outside France but it was clearly a high one and that in itself
tends to suggest that French economic development was not slowed
either before or after 1852 by a shortage of capital caused by
deficiencies in the banking system. In the case of the Crédit Mobilier
the banking system was rather jumping the gun than lagging behind.

Although banks which operated like the Crédit Mobilier flourished
in other countries the banks which survived in France were those
which were created after the first flush of enthusiasm for the Crédit
Mobilier had died down. They dealt principally in deposits and the
basis of their business was the very small commission which they
took on the enormous number of petty transactions they conducted.
They are usually called, for this reason, 'deposit banks', and the
Crédit Mobilier, by contrast, an 'investment bank'. The distinction
between the institutions is exaggerated by this nomenclature because
in their origins all these institutions had certain similarities which
distinguished them from the earlier banks. The new deposit banks
borrowed from the Péreires the idea that savings all over the country
could be mobilised into bank deposits, and to this purpose they
devoted a great deal of energy to opening branches in every area.
With the Péreires their directors believed in the concept which they
called 'the democratisation of capital', removing capital transactions
from the world of the Paris private bankers who had, because they
were family firms, dealt only with a narrow circle of wealthy and
trusted customers. Such ideas cannot be taken seriously except as
propaganda. The use of bank deposits and especially the use of
checks for payment was very little developed in nineteenth-century
France and the new banks still only attracted the comfortably-off
to their counters. The investments which they made, like those of
the Crédit Mobilier, were even less 'democratised', because the
safety of such investments, which they saw as the indispensable
requisite for reassuring the public that they would not suffer the
same fate as the Crédit Mobilier, confined them very much to
government loans and similar gilt-edged securities. In fact this
technique was learnt only slowly. All the deposit banks when
founded hoped to take advantage of the rapid economic development which they saw taking place around them. Such were the early
aspirations of, for example, the Crédit Industriel et Commercial,
founded in 1859, the Société de Dépots et de Comptes Courants
founded in 1863, the Crédit Lyonnais founded in the same year and

the Société Générale founded in 1864. All were joint-stock banks like the Crédit Mobilier and all had a much larger nominal capital than the earlier private banks. In their early years they were to be distinguished from the Crédit Mobilier more by the absence of the powerful and dangerous intelligence of the Péreires than by any actual difference in their operations.

The Crédit Lyonnais was founded by a group of Lyons businessmen to respond to their immediate needs for credit. The silk-worm disease which had ravaged French raw silk production in the 1850s had forced the Lyons entrepreneurs into a world-wide search for extra supplies, a search which had greatly increased their credit needs which they felt were ignored by Paris financial circles. In addition the construction of local railways seemed to call for some instrument through which local capital could be directed into them. Furthermore the startling discoveries of chemically manufactured dyestuffs opened a new range of possibilities to the silk industry above all others. The Crédit Lyonnais was particularly associated with financing the production of one such chemical dye – fuchsine. Superimposed on all this was the opportunity which the removal of the British tariff on imports of manufactured silks in 1860 seemed to offer to the city which was still easily the greatest producer of such cloths in the world. The bank emerged as a national deposit bank only very slowly. It lost money in the failure of fuchsine and lost even more money in industrial investments in the financial crash of 1882 when half the deposits were withdrawn by the public in a few weeks. Only in the 1880s did its famous director Henri Germain succeed in emancipating it completely from the influence of Lyons business circles and establishing it as a national bank with headquarters in Paris.

In changing its character in this way he was obliged to constantly avoid all investments which had an element of risk. No doubt the history of the other banks founded at the same time would reveal that success in handling money by a large number of members of the general public likewise depended on pursuing a safe policy. There is thus a curious circularity in the history of French banking in the nineteenth century. Starting from a period when bankers and industrialists eyed each other with great aloofness and suspicion it passed through a period when bankers actively wooed industrialists and finally the suspicions that banking and industry were not good bed-fellows returned. Germain summed it up neatly.

'People have wanted us to look into industrial loans. There are certainly excellent ones, but industrial enterprises, even the best conceived and the best administered, carry risks which we consider incompatible with the indispensable security with which the funds of deposit banks should be employed. We have taken a long time, but the Crédit Lyonnais can find no better example for the employment of its funds than that of the Bank of France.'[8]

This return to the established orthodoxy of the earlier part of the century was not confined to banks but extended also to public finance. The fact that the state speculated on the operations involved in the reconstruction of Paris in a way that was hardly to be distinguished from fraud brought about the funding of the debts of the City of Paris as a regular *rente*. In 1867 a sinking fund was set up to use the revenues from the railway fund and the national forests to reduce the large state debts accumulated by Napoleon III's policies.

But to present the matter in this light is a superficial proceeding. It is true that the most rapid period of economic development in France between 1815 and 1870 coincides with the period when bankers were readiest to provide long-term loans for industrial and public works development. But it does not necessarily follow that the attitude of the banks dictates this rhythm of development. Indeed it may be that the rhythm of development dictated the attitude of the banks. The sources of capital in so complex and developed an economy were many, various and complicated. And the economic development of the country in those years was by no means simply a matter of the provision of capital for transport and industrial undertakings. The foundation of banks like the Crédit Mobilier was based on the justified sentiment that capital accumulation had proceeded for so long in France that there were substantial national savings to be tapped. The history of French industry before 1870 bears this out for it is clear that even by 1870 for *most* entrepreneurs banks were a financial device which smoothed over their problems of maintaining regular supplies of working capital and paying regular wages. Compared to Britain a far higher proportion of the total stock of money was in the form of coinage. Banknotes, commercial paper and other monetary instruments were far less developed. The Bank of France was prepared to discount only a very limited range of commercial paper and usually only at a high discount rate in order to preserve maximum security. The reconstruction of Paris rested basically on the state providing the necessary funds and controlling the speculative operations involved. The Second Empire was beyond question a period of dynamic economic expansion especially in its first years. But part of this is to be attributed to the fact that the government set itself quite deliber-

[8] A. Pose, *La Monnaie et ses institutions* (Paris, 1942), vol. 1, p. 212.

ately to achieve such a result and an even bigger part to the fact that the 1850s were the years of Europe's greatest investment boom of the nineteenth century. The gold discoveries in America and Australia, the industrialisation of Germany, the rapid economic development in the United States, the expansion of European capital and entrepreneurial activity beyond the continent, symbolised in the first attempts at the Suez Canal, all generated an atmosphere of optimism and internationalism. In 1863 freedom of association into joint-stock companies was granted without any application to the Council of State and the use of the industrial share rather than the high-denomination bonds which had characterised the early years of railway building spread the habit of investment down the social scale. The Péreires were the greatest representatives of this epoch but their effect on the development of France itself, as also perhaps the effect of banking institutions in general, has been exaggerated.

THE DEVELOPMENT OF AGRICULTURE

Despite the dramatic events of the Second Empire and their equally dramatic actors it is the continuity of French development which is most noticeable over the whole period. The economy developed along the lines it had already taken before 1815 and new industrial technologies were absorbed into that framework. This was even more true of agriculture than of industry. There the revolutionary land settlement remained the cardinal fact of existence throughout the century. Almost twenty million people, 53 per cent of the population, depended on agriculture for their livelihood between 1855 and 1864. And the basis of rural society was the small peasant landholding, unrationalised, free of all feudal and religious payment, usually unenclosed and usually farmed in the traditional way. Although economic development caused some migration to the towns it was only on a small scale before 1870 and the growth of the towns stimulated the rural economy by providing new and larger markets which the development of better transport brought within reach of parts of the countryside which had previously been very isolated.

Agriculture ceased to provide for the needs of the entire population. There was still a considerable export trade in 1870 including grain exports. But on balance France became a grain importer after 1830 and by 1870 was also a net importer of meat and livestock. After 1816 there was an almost completely protectionist system. Grain imports were only allowed in on a sliding scale of tariffs if the domestic price became too high. In fact between 1821 and 1830 there was only one month in which the tariff was not utterly prohibitive. The tariff was only lowered in 1853. In the 1850s the sliding scale was twice briefly suspended in the face of fierce opposition. Finally in 1860 a system of much lower tariffs was introduced. Its effects lie outside our period, for almost the whole of which French agriculture can be considered as operating in a closed system.

There were still 2,435,000 farms of less than 10 hectares in 1862. There were 636,000 farms between 10 and 40 hectares and 154,000 of over 40 hectares. Very little change in the size and type of ownership had taken place since 1815. The total land area of the farms over 40 hectares was twice that of those under 10 hectares but rural France was nevertheless a peasant society in which the peasants' stake was guaranteed by their success in the Revolution. Those who had fought for full property rights now enjoyed them in full. Those who had relied on the communality of farming continued to do so. Common lands, *vaine pâture*, and collective usages survived long. In the 1848 revolution many enclosures were destroyed and commons reoccupied. The stability of the settlement is shown by the stability of the rural population. Its natural increase was very sluggish in most areas and the increase in the total population came mainly from its increase in the towns and the industrialising areas whose population behaviour was significantly different from that of the countryside even before 1848. Yet if this society was stable it was by no means unresponsive to change. However conservative and traditional in his ways the peasant was still bound to respond to the great changes taking place around him. This can be shown by the increase in the area cultivated and by the changes in crops.

Napoleon's minister Chaptal estimated that there were about 23 million hectares ploughed in 1815. The census of 1852 suggests that the total area under plough was almost 26 million hectares. This seems to tally with much descriptive evidence testifying to the decline in fallow land, wasteland and marshes as the demand for food rose and agricultural methods improved. But the increase in demand for food and the slow improvement in variety of diet went very little way to breaking up the pattern of monoculture which had prevailed in the eighteenth century. The crop which showed the greatest increase in area was wheat. One of the effects of improving diet was to increase the culture of wheat more than that of other grains, but in 1870 France was as much a land of ripening grain fields as in 1815. In the Nivernais workmen would often still stipulate to be paid part of their wages in grain and there was a vast apparatus of legal agreements and contracts based on bread grain. Against this background can be seen a mounting interest in other crops.

M

The quantity of potatoes grown increased about threefold although it suffered a sharp and temporary decline after 1846 with the occurrence of the potato blight. The production of meat doubled and this in itself was obviously a great stimulus to increasing the amount of grassland which also grew steadily after 1835.

Thus far the agricultural economy was able to meet the demands imposed on it. But its response was aided more by changes in other sectors of the economy than by changes in the agricultural sector itself. Of these the improvement in the means of transport was the most significant. The development of market gardening and of the production of early spring vegetables on the backward and remote Breton coast depended on rapid rail transport. So did the development of the milk trade to Paris and other large cities. Not to big cities only, however; butter, which was the basis of cooking in the Nivernais was, for example, usually imported into the area. The coming of the railway could have a strong redistributive effect on agricultural production. This was markedly so with wine. Before the extension of the railway network ordinary wine for current consumption was produced all over the countryside where climatic conditions permitted. Rapid transport allowed specialisation in those areas where climatic and soil conditions were most favourable to large-scale production. The departments of Gard and Hérault began to convert to the monoculture of the vine and the wine they produced was increasingly for the distant Paris market. In fact the agricultural area catering for the needs of each big city was very greatly increased by railway construction.

The most noticeable innovation of this kind was the development of sugar-beet culture. The early successes in refining sugar from beet had very little effect after 1814 when cheaper cane sugar from the West Indies was once more available. By 1830 the output of sugar from native beets was still very low. After that date there was an extraordinarily rapid expansion. By 1840 over 20,000 tons were being produced annually. By the next decade output had doubled. It doubled again in the period 1855-64 and by 1870 was well over 200,000 tons a year making France Europe's largest sugar producer. Such a course of events is proof positive that French agriculture, although it may have had structural and organisational weaknesses, was very responsive to marketing opportunities. In this case the opportunity came because of the nature of the industrial process involved which allowed a very high profit rate in a short time thus permitting in turn a very rapid expansion of refining under its own momentum. Attempts to adjust the tariff against sugar imports in 1835 led only to a clamour from sugar merchants and from the colonies against domestic sugar. As a consequence the refining of

Table 27. Agricultural output in France 1815–70

Period	Wheat	Rye	Barley	Oats	Other grains	Potatoes	Sugar beet	Root crops for fodder	Natural and artificial grass	Flax, hemp	Wine	Milk	Meat	Wool	Silk	Butter, cheese
					000,000 quintals						000,000 hectolitres		000,000 tons			
1815–24	38·79	20·6	10·15	15·51	15·96	25·30	n.a.	n.a.	n.a.	n.a.	37	43	548	n.a.	4·6	113
1825–34	46·34	21·5	10·71	20·56	17·23	42·16	n.a.	n.a.	n.a.	n.a.	40	47	602	58·1	7·9	127
1835–44	52·67	22·3	11·88	25·41	19·12	63·26	16	50	178	2,429	39	58	685	64·3	19·0	153
1845–54	62·25	21·0	12·37	28·81	22·17	49·79	18	50	268	1,837	47	63	823	66·6	18·6	167
1855–64	72·77	18·9	12·93	33·63	20·23	68·77	44	52	313	2,174	48	73	972	60·0	9·8	193
1865–74	74·44	18·5	12·89	33·76	20·46	80·26	77	90	360	1,785	60	74	1,091	47·3	11·8	200

1 quintal = 100 kg.

Source: Cahiers de l'I.S.E.A. Série A.F., No. 2, pp. 13, 14, 15, 16.

domestic sugar was taxed more heavily in 1837 and 1838. The effect of these taxes was to close down many smaller refineries where coal was dearer as in Alsace. But in the north where coal was cheaper and conditions very suitable for beet growing domestic sugar gained rapidly at the expense of colonial sugar. These gains were sustained in the 1850s and 1860s by the adoption of new techniques for beet-sugar refining originating in Bohemia and in Germany, one of the first examples of France borrowing technological processes from less developed lands and a curious one since the French sugar industry was itself so big. The rate of return on the capital investment in a sugar refinery in the 1830s seems to have been proportionately at least 10 per cent higher than that in a textile factory although something should be deducted for the taxes imposed in 1837. The industry needed relatively little help from the money market and its developers seem to have had very little connection with other business circles.

Even though it is quite wrong to regard French agriculture as unresponsive and unchanging in this period the question of who responded and who changed is still very open to debate. Many of these changes could have been produced simply by a change in farming methods by the larger farmers. The most modern grain-growing area in the mid-nineteenth century was the plateau of Beauce which was one of the few areas where large farms prevailed over smaller peasant holdings. Sugar beet was eminently a crop suitable for cultivation on larger land-holdings. This was not true however of green vegetables, potatoes, or wine-grapes, all of which could often be better tended on the peasant farm. The average annual cumulative rate of growth of total agricultural product in real terms was always between 1 per cent and 1·5 per cent between 1825 and 1864, a rate which it does not seem to have achieved in the previous century except for the decade 1771–80. Nor did it again achieve this rate until the twentieth century. It is not completely convincing to explain the sustained contribution of agriculture to the national product simply on the grounds of technical change by the larger farmers. Improving peasant agriculture must have made its contribution also in what was a period of great agricultural prosperity. A considerable part of the decline in fallow land and of the total increase in the cultivated area must be ascribed to this.

Such improvements as there were must have consisted mainly of improvements in day to day farming practice. They cannot be attributed to mechanisation, for most farms were too small for machines to be economical. There were about 11,000 mechanical sowers in use in 1862 and less than 10,000 mechanical reapers and harvesters, one to every 3,000 landholdings. Of course there were improvements in hand tools and particularly in ploughs. Even there research is showing that such minor improvements although they were rapidly adopted north and east of the Loire spread only very slowly into the south and west. Nor can the improvements be attributed to better scientific knowledge. The major scientific discoveries relating to agriculture did not come until after 1840. Pasteur's great discoveries only began in 1856. In any case there was no mechanism for disseminating this knowledge in the rural community. The ordinance of 1816 insisting on each commune providing primary education was never honestly or effectively carried out. In 1839 only 42 per cent of the conscripts in the army could read and those were almost all town dwellers. Male rural inhabitants were generally quite illiterate. The great interest in disseminating agricultural information which had prevailed in the eighteenth century slowly died out as industrial development more and more occupied men's minds. The last survivor of the eighteenth century reformers was Mathieu de Dombasle, inventor of the Dombasle plough, translator of Thaer and Sinclair, and editor of the agricultural journal, *Annales de Roville*. His pupils founded the agricultural schools of Grignon and Grand–Jouan–Rennes. They laboured in vain. There was a flicker of interest during the Second Republic when, in 1848, the Institut National Agronomique was founded. Louis Napoleon's faith in industrial development as the key to economic and social progress caused the Institute to be closed because it was a waste of money. Among the huge sums of money spent on development by the Second Empire very little indeed was spent on drainage, rural education or on providing agricultural credit. One agricultural bank was created, the Crédit Foncier, in 1852. It was a copy of the long-term mortgage banks which had been founded by royal fiat in Prussia and Saxony. Like those banks it existed to provide mortgage credits for large land-owners. It had no impact on peasant agriculture. For some time it was more involved in land speculations in Paris. The Crédit Agricole, founded to supplement it, went bankrupt in 1878 through investing in the Suez Canal. When cheaper rural credit facilities were being provided elsewhere in Europe and when peasants themselves were building up their own cooperative and credit institutions the French peasant, ignored by government, remained individualistic, isolated, illiterate and ignorant. The attitude of government to agricultural resources was the same. Large areas of national forests were transferred from state supervision by the *Code forestier* of 1827. In 1831 100,000 hectares of what remained were sold off quite cheaply. The first laws on forest preservation and on re-afforestation did not come until 1857. By this time the rising demand from industry was being met by timber imports.

In spite of all this the yield of grain crops increased and the weight of animals improved. The yield of winter wheat per hectare increased from 12·45 hectolitres in 1840 to 14·69 in 1862, the yield of sugar beet from 27,300kg to 32,400, while the average weight of a cow increased from 240 kilograms to 324. That it was possible for agriculture to make the contribution it did to the growth of the total economy in the years 1825-64 shows the force which minor changes in the manner of farming could have in an economy where agriculture was still the biggest employer. It also shows how long-run economic development is because however ignorant and isolated the French peasant he had already been for centuries in possession of greater knowledge and better tools than the even more isolated and backward peasantry of central and eastern Europe. The gradual dissemination, far more in the north of the country than in the south, of eighteenth-century ideas on rotations and stock-breeding, continued to improve farming practice in the first half of the nineteenth century. In so far as the Revolutionary land settlement did retard French development its effects were cumulative. As the possibilities of agricultural improvement became greater in scope they became greater than the peasant farmer's capacity to respond and after 1850 the greater contribution was coming from the larger farms. It was the permanence, the immutability, of the settlement that created the problem for its immediate effects were, even from a narrowly economic point of view, more to the good than the bad.

It is also sometimes argued that the nature of peasant agriculture impeded development in industry more than it did in agriculture. So secure was the peasant's tenure that he was unwilling to leave the land for industrial work and when he did so it was sometimes only on a part-time basis. There were certainly great difficulties in getting a labour force in some industries before the 1840s. The main problem was with mines and large iron works because the evolution of the firm was so much less gradual than in textile manufacture. After the mines at La Grande Combe were opened the owners hunted for workmen in Belgium, Burgundy and other mining areas because the local agricultural workers could not be tempted into the mine. The ironworks at Alès combed the Loire valley for ironworkers and found six. How short-range labour migration actually was can be seen from the lists of people working in government arsenals. Such local workmen frequently were attracted back into the agricultural sector at harvest time by higher wages. Many large firms in rural areas attracted a labour force by providing houses or barracks. The Anzin company built 800 houses between 1830 and 1845. The Alès forges provided barracks.

But the recruitment of a labour force was difficult in all countries. The work was dangerous, dirty, monotonous and unpleasant for the most part. And worst of all was the humiliating subjection to the routine and timing imposed by the machine, reinforced by the entrepreneur's desire to 'discipline' his men. One reason why it should theoretically have been more difficult in France than elsewhere was the lower natural rate of increase of the population in the nineteenth century. This, combined with a legal system which encouraged subdivision of the landholding among sons, meant that the proportion of landless younger sons or younger sons with insufficient land to provide an income competitive with that offered by industry was relatively low compared to certain other countries as in Scandinavia. In a general sense this did provide entrepreneurs with a problem which they did not often have to face in countries like Britain or Hungary with a substantial landless class. The wage bid which they had to make to attract labour permanently had to be higher. On the other hand even this general problem cannot really be taken in isolation from other factors as being an obstacle to economic development. Very much the same legal practices existed in Belgium and although the peasant landholdings there were on an average much smaller, thus encouraging the peasant to seek some supplementation of his income from industrial work, a large proportion of industrial workers retained a stake in the land while in full time industrial employment. It may be that the slower growth of French population kept landholdings at a sufficiently larger size in France to prevent such a development on any significant scale. The type of industrial development which did take place in early nineteenth-century France demanded a shift to employment which was usually more unpleasant than agricultural work and more regimented and consequently had to be better paid if the shift were to take place. At the same time the process of development itself offered the possibility of improving agricultural incomes.

Only in 1848 did the spectre of famine stalk the land and it was quickly conjured away. The greater mobility of foodstuffs and of labour played a considerable part here as well as the improvements in production. The physiocrats' programme of free grain movements all over the country had even more force when the grain moved on a dense and efficient railway network. Labour migration also increased with improved transport and this also improved agricultural incomes. In winter labour migrated from the Massif Central to the lower lands of the Nièvre and of Cher. Bretons and Flamands went to cut the wheat harvest in Beauce and the Île de France. But the balance was still precarious enough for certain crops to be terribly damaged by epidemic diseases. The grain disease, oïdium, arrived in 1845 and had covered the whole country by 1854. It was cured by spraying with sulphur, a remedy which would not have been available nor applied in earlier times. The silkworm disease, *pébrine*, which appeared in 1849 was less susceptible to cure. When Pasteur's discoveries showed how it could be overcome in 1865 French silk production had suffered a body blow from which it never recovered. Manufacturers began to import their raw material from China and Japan. The output of raw silk reached its peak with the annual average of 18,600 tons between 1845 and 1854. In the next decade it was only 11,900 tons. By 1870 it had fallen still further. In 1864 the miles of new vineyards which had been opened up in the department of Gard were attacked by another natural disaster, the phylloxera. The disease was not identified and isolated until 1868. Even then its cure was a long and costly business involving the removal of whole vineyards to different sites and their replanting with vines imported from the United States. Wine production reached its peak between 1865 and 1874 with an average annual output of 60,400,000 hectolitres. Within that period came the turning point caused by the phylloxera and in the next decade average output was only 46,000,000 hectolitres a year.

CONCLUSION

Disasters of this kind had a very regional effect. The decline in silk and wine production struck particularly hard at the south. Most evidence suggests that even at the start of the period a clear gap in levels of prosperity and development had emerged between the northern and eastern areas and the less developed south and west. This general difference in prosperity persisted throughout the nineteenth century and seems to have been very much related to the absence of agricultural improvement in the west and south. But the true picture is a much more detailed one in which small areas of development existed side by side with areas where very little changed for a long time. The regional nature of nineteenth-century economic development is better seen in France than in any other economy for the considerable areas of the country with little industrial development and less agricultural improvement did not hold back the development of the national economy. This development took the form of the transformation of certain limited areas where resources in the widest sense were available and where social conditions did not too greatly impede development. While Alsace, the North, some areas on the central coalfields, a few big cities and above all Paris were among the most economically developed areas of the European mainland, the Massif Central, much of the southern littoral and western France existed in a different world of very slowly changing economic and social relationships.

It is this which accounts for the conflicting views which are sometimes expressed about the nature of the mid-century French economy and for the strange contrasts which it presents. And it is these contrasts which have led so many scholars to identify what were obstacles to development in one area as being national obstacles to development. While French entrepreneurs and engineers in the 1850s were designing and building railways all over Europe, peasants in France still reaped by sickle and sowed by hand. When French bankers in the same decade were investing readily and heavily in the economic development of Germany, small manufacturers and farmers in France were still paying swingeing interest rates to borrow money from local lawyers. French textile manufacturers were still timidly copying mechanical methods of production long established in Britain when the entrepreneurs in Paris who sold their wares were beginning a revolution in shopkeeping and retailing that was to set the style for large cities all over the developed world for a hundred years. The origins of this revolution can be traced back to the first big store in Paris which sold ready-to-wear clothes, La Belle Jardinière, opened by Pierre Parissot in 1824. Such ideas came to full fruition when Paris became the terminal point of all the great railway lines. The Bon Marché, opened in the 1850s became the prototype of all the world's great department stores. While extensive government encouragement was still essential to get railways built in the less developed areas of the country French signalling systems, railway equipment and operating methods were being extensively copied all over the continent. Most ironical of all, the ideas underlying financial institutions like the Crédit Mobilier and the Crédit Foncier were eagerly seized on in less developed lands where they were applied to much better purpose.

Many of the explanations for the slowness of French development lose their force when France is placed in a European setting rather than compared with Britain or the United States. The high price of coal, the revolutionary land settlement, the slow growth of population, the difficulty of competing with a similar technology against a greater and more established producer all go to explain both the gradualness and the regionality of French development. But the success of French development also shows that it was by no means necessary to follow the same growth pattern as Britain had done, or Germany was later to do, and undergo an intense period of particularly rapid economic growth. Indeed, in some ways it could fairly be argued that the social changes which were brought about by such rapid growth in other societies and which were themselves necessary to sustain that growth were brought about in France by political change and by revolution.

More than other developed economies France revealed by 1870 the relentless force of historical change in promoting economic development while showing, in spite of the Revolution, over how long a time that historical change must necessarily take place. It was both this process of historical change and the Revolution itself that caused French institutions to be so much copied abroad. Other developing countries felt they could cheat history, or perhaps omit some of it, by borrowing from a land where so much social and economic change had taken place. By lifting institutions from France and incorporating them in their own structure they tried forcibly to modernise their own societies and speed up their own histories. Such attempts were seldom successful because to produce such institutions France had had herself to undergo so violent and profound a revolution. The temptation was still very great and it makes the economic history of France an integral part of that of all other European lands. It was partly responsible for the complicated and manifold financial links which evolved between France and capital borrowers elsewhere in Europe. Already by 1870 as far as mainland Europe was concerned France was becoming the main capital lender. It was even more responsible for the overpowering intellectual and social predominance of France over less developed lands, a predominance which for some, like Spain, Italy or Romania, was to have at several moments a decisive effect on their economic history.

SUGGESTED READING

There are two good modern accounts in English of the economic development of France in this period which should be read in conjunction with this chapter which sometimes disagrees with them on matters which are still the subject of research. Unfortunately both are rather brief. They are C. FOHLEN, *The Industrial Revolution in France 1700–1914*, volume IV, Chapter 3 of *The Fontana Economic History of Europe* (London, 1970) and D. S. LANDES, *The Unbound Prometheus* (Cambridge, 1969). Two older-fashioned accounts are also still valuable, J. H. CLAPHAM, *The*

Economic Development of France and Germany 1815–1914 (Cambridge, 1921) and A. L. DUNHAM, *The Industrial Revolution in France 1815–1848* (New York, 1955). T. KEMP, *Economic Forces in French History* (London, 1971) is a long essay on the political economy of the period which refers to most of the modern work.

On more specialised topics there is A. L. DUNHAM, *The Anglo-French Treaty of Commerce of 1860 and the Progress of the Industrial Revolution in France* (Ann Arbor, 1930). J. A. R. MARRIOTT, *The French Revolution of 1848 in its Economic Aspects*, 2 vols. (London, 1913) is now rather out-of-date. R. CAMERON, *France and the Economic Development of Europe* (Princeton, 1961) is a study of the activities of French banks and bankers outside France. R. CAMERON (ed.) *Essays in French Economic History*, published for The American Economic Association (Homewood, Ill., 1970) is a useful selection of research articles on specialised topics which were originally published in French. There are also some articles on more general themes available in English. Three which have conclusions which are most definitely debatable are S. B. CLOUGH, 'Retardative factors in French economic development in the nineteenth and twentieth centuries' in *Journal of Economic History*, supplement, vol. 3, 1946; R. CAMERON, 'Economic growth and stagnation in France 1815–1914' in *Journal of Modern History*, vol. 30, 1958; and J. MARCZEWSKI, 'Some aspects of the economic growth of France, 1660–1958' in *Economic Development and Cultural Change*, vol. 9, 1961. A different point of view to our own on entrepreneurial qualities in France is elegantly expounded by D. S. LANDES in 'French entrepreneurship and industrial growth in the nineteenth century' in *Journal of Economic History*, vol. 9, 1949. D. H. PINKNEY, 'Money and politics in the rebuilding of Paris, 1860–70' in *Journal of Economic History*, vol. 17, 1957 unravels a complicated subject of some relevance to economic history.

Although the literature in English on this subject, unlike some of the other subjects treated here, certainly extends the argument beyond the confines of our chapter it also has to be pointed out that the literature in French is better and more extensive. A good bibliography of the literature on French industry in this period appears in *The Cambridge Economic History of Europe*, vol. 6, part 1. There are no good general modern economic histories of France but two now very dated works, H. SÉE, *Histoire économique de la France*, 2 vols. (Paris, 1948, 1951) and A. VIALLATE, *L'Activité économique en France de la fin du dix-huitième siècle à nos jours* (Paris, 1937) have their uses. M. LÉVY-LEBOYER, *Les Banques européennes et l'industrialisation internationale dans la première moitié du dix-neuvième siècle* (Paris, 1964) is a work of such enormous reading and research that it almost serves as a general economic history of its period and it has an excellent bibliography. B. GILLE, *Recherches sur la formation de la grande entreprise capitaliste (1815–1848)* (Paris, 1959) and, by the same author, *La Banque et le crédit en France de 1815 à 1848* (Paris, 1959) shed a good deal of light on the period. B. GILLE, *La sidérurgie française au dix-neuvième siècle* (Geneva, 1968) contains some important articles on the iron industry. There are two good books on the textile industry, C. FOHLEN, *L'industrie textile au temps du Second Empire* (Paris, 1956) and R. LÉVY, *Histoire économique de l'industrie cotonnière en Alsace* (Paris, 1912). G. DUVEAU, *La Vie ouvrière en France sous le Second Empire* (Paris, 1946) discusses a subject that we have been forced to neglect.

Research on French economic history is published in a number of specialised periodicals which also contain reviews of the latest books. The most notable of these are *Annales, Revue d'Histoire économique et sociale, Revue d'Histoire moderne et contemporaine* and *Cahiers de l'institut de science économique appliquée* which also includes as it emerges the *Histoire quantitative de l'économie française* prepared by the same Institute. *Revue internationale d'histoire de la banque* in spite of its title also tends to specialise in French economic history. Many local journals also contain good articles and reviews, particularly *Revue du Nord, Annales de Midi, Annales de Normandie* and *Revue d'Alsace*.

Chapter 6

The Economic Development of Germany 1815–70

THE BACKGROUND TO GERMAN ECONOMIC DEVELOPMENT

In the eighteenth century some regions of Germany were amongst the most developed parts of Europe. Not only was this the case but they also had significant advantages for further development. What evidence we have suggests that the western German states were relatively rich countries where per capita incomes were in some cases as high as anywhere in Europe. There was a considerable diversity of manufactures and a plentiful supply of labour already partly employed in industry and practising a wide range of skills from spinning to metal-working. The statistician Dieterici estimated that in the 1820s only about 73 per cent of the population of

73% pop = agr

Germany was dependent on agriculture for a living, a lower proportion than in late nineteenth-century Russia.[1] One-half the value of Prussia's exports in 1828 was manufactured goods, and one-half of those textile goods mostly produced in the framework of domestic industry. Imports of raw materials for the textile industries represented one-quarter of the value of all imports, and raw materials as a whole, one-half the value. Grain accounted for only 8 per cent of all exports. In the western areas and in the north-west, the peasantry was less burdened by feudal dues and by central government taxation than in France and most contemporary observers agree that the standard of living of the west German peasant seemed higher than that of his European counterparts. Many states, including Prussia, maintained a system of free primary education and the level of literacy was certainly higher in Germany than France. But in the more easterly states the evidence suggests a different story, scarcely any development of manufactures and much lower *per capita* incomes than in France and its neighbouring areas. In addition the eastern states had less frequently practised policies of peasant protection and the power of the nobility and the importance of the great landed estate as the basic unit of production were both relatively much greater than in the west and as a consequence the social structure was more rigid. In spite of these great differences which persisted throughout the nineteenth century, and which can hardly be described as regional since they were differences between different German countries, the point must be restated that Germany, like France (where there were also, and still are, great regional differences in income and development), was, in eighteenth-century terms, a relatively developed country.

Not only was this so but its possibilities for future development were all the greater because of its nearness to France and Britain and its close commercial ties to the developed parts of those countries. Access to the new industrial knowledge and to entrepreneurial skills was easy and there was no shortage of British, French or Belgian entrepreneurs ready to export their knowledge to Germany. British and French mechanics were noticeable everywhere in the early nineteenth century. The sons of William Cockerill both built wool-spinning machinery in Prussia. When the first puddling furnaces were built every piece was brought from Belgium or Britain and the puddlers themselves were all foreigners. Nor was there a lack of German entrepreneurs ready to undertake the journey in the other direction; the iron master Friedrich Harkort travelled to Britain in 1818 and brought back a foreman and workers for his

[1] C. F. W. Dieterici, *Der Volkswohlstand im Preussischen Staate* (Berlin, Posen, Bromberg, 1846).

new Witten iron works and there are innumerable similar examples.
Above all Germany was liberally endowed with the one raw material,
coal, on which so much of the new technology depended.

At first sight there seems to be little difficulty in explaining the
industrialisation and development of Germany and a great deal of
difficulty in explaining why that industrialisation began so late.
Until the close of the 1830s the rapid industralisation of France and
Belgium was not matched in Germany and by 1840 even western
Germany was, relatively speaking, a backward area. Only after that
date did developments elsewhere really take root in Germany. When
they did so Germany experienced an industrial revolution much
more rapid and violent than that in France or Britain and began its
transformation into the greatest industrial producer in Europe. The
answer is that side by side with the great advantages which Germany
had existed certain extreme disadvantages which prevented it from
sharing in the industrialisation of its western neighbours. In the
case of Germany in the early nineteenth century therefore we are
often concerned less with explaining why the economy developed
and more concerned with explaining why that development was
delayed.

The problem of development in Germany was one of the removal
of obstacles to development. These obstacles derived from the
history of the country but in spite of this were removable by
administrative action, by political change in the country itself, and
by the pressure of economic and political change in neighbouring
countries. They were easier to change than, for example, low *per
capita* income, absence of literacy or other skills, or shortage of
capital, problems which beset underdeveloped countries today.
Government action and political changes which made little economic
difference in many countries produced extraordinary results in
Germany because the more fundamental economic obstacles to
development were absent from large parts of the country. These
changes may be summarised in two terms, unification and
simplification.

From the signing of the Treaty of Westphalia in 1648 the area
loosely known as Germany had been divided into about 350 separate
jurisdictions, most of them the private jurisdictions of princes and
lords of ancient lineage but some of them the jurisdictions of great
commercial cities, such as Frankfurt-am-Main, Augsburg or
Nuremberg, whose ancient commercial splendour was still not
completely overshadowed by the growth of transatlantic trade.
The precise bounds of Germany were not established, neither were
they later, nor are they now. In this respect Germany differed
fundamentally from France which had been unified into a coherent

why not call them states? Prussia Austr, Sax,

centralised national state at the same time as Germany had been divided among so many private dynasties. In the eyes of most German-speaking peoples the 'backwardness' of their country in the early nineteenth century was the result of this political fragmentation. The drive to develop the country and to emulate events in France and Belgium was also a drive to unify the country politically. The connections between economic and political activity were therefore not only more intimate and more complicated in Germany than in France, they were fundamental to the whole problem of development. Every economic choice implied a profound political choice also. To advocate the development of a road or railway system, of a uniform code of commercial practice, of a common set of weights or measures, in each case was to advocate at the time the destruction of the existing political framework of the country. In such circumstances it is not surprising that Germany never developed a school of economic theory akin to the classical economic theorists in France or Britain who were able to divorce their theoretical speculations from everyday historical or political considerations. For German economists in the nineteenth century all questions of theory and development were seen, necessarily, in a historical context as a part of German history. The development of the economy was an integral part of the creation of a German national state and even of the demarcation of its external frontiers. For Germany was faced with a historical obstacle to development of quite extraordinary size and complexity. Economic development implied economic unification. Political unification implied simplification of the system of government, simplification and unification of the law, of commercial practice, of excise duties, of tolls on rivers and roads, of external tariffs, and even simplification of matters affecting everyone such as the large variety of currencies, weights and measures.

too strong

why?

The drive towards simplification and unification was very much a product of the feeling of economic backwardness which prevailed in early nineteenth-century Germany. It was German economists and politicians who first developed the concept of 'backwardness'. Previously economies had been thought of as either 'strong' or 'weak', states which could be changed. For example, by pursuing a wise economic policy a 'weak' state could become 'strong'. After the industrial revolution in France and Belgium it became more usual in Germany to think of the states of Europe as being strung out in a competitive race to a particular goal in which some were 'advanced' and some including Germany had become 'backward'. Such a conception, which has become part and parcel of economic jargon today, had a most powerful effect in Germany because it harnessed a tremendous driving force of patriotism and nationalism

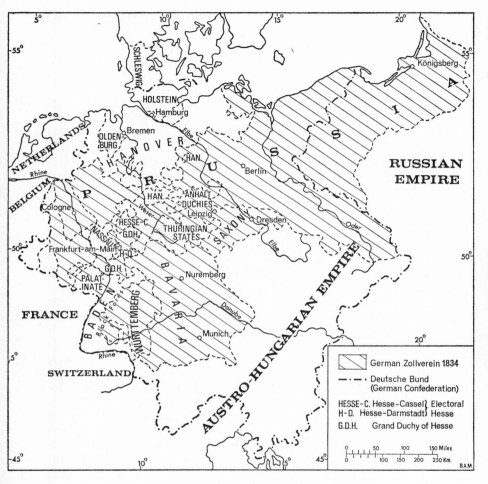

Map 5.   Germany in 1834

to the will to develop and to change the political shape of the country. The economic development of Germany was part and parcel of the creation of a great nation-state in the very centre of the European continent. It was the unification and simplification of the European heartland.

This is more easily understood if the implications for Europe of the construction of a unified railway system in Germany are considered. The railway networks of France and Belgium were peripheral to the continent as a whole. But to construct a railway from Cologne to Frankfurt-an-der-Oder was to open the possibility of a line from Paris to Moscow and to construct a railway from Munich to Flensburg was to open the possibility of connecting Copenhagen with Vienna, Milan and Rome. The building of the German railway system was thus the building of a European railway system. It was the start of the development of the inland economy of Europe as opposed to the western seaboard which had developed in the eighteenth century. It was the beginning of a great unified market in the centre of the continent. It was the re-opening to a relatively unfettered commerce of the ancient overland trade routes, long in decay, to eastern and south-eastern Europe. The economic and political unification of Germany was no less than the transformation of the economic and political existence of the whole continent.

So great a transformation had to be finally a political act or rather a series of political acts. Behind these political acts, no matter how they might be confined to the spheres of diplomacy and war, always lay the relentless drive to emulation and economic development which could alone provide the necessary wealth for military and national safety, and behind the singularly un-capitalistic figures of those Prussian statesmen who created the customs union or of Count Bismarck himself there can be still perceived the same bourgeois pressure to development that activated the more overtly bourgeois governments of France and Belgium. It was in fact the French Revolution itself, in the guise of Napoleon, which first began the simplification of Germany's political structure. In forcing the emperor to proclaim the end of the Holy Roman Empire, Napoleon also brought to an end most of the jurisdictions which descended from that ancient institution including those of the Electors, of the Imperial Knights and some of the Imperial Free Cities. His military allies received a status which they were later allowed to keep and thus arose the kingdoms of Bavaria and Württemberg and the Grand Duchy of Baden. Hanover was likewise transformed into a kingdom although until 1837 its king reigned from London. The ecclesiastical states had their lands secularised and their jurisdiction terminated.

The peace treaties of 1814 and 1815 set up in place of the Holy Roman Empire a so-called Germanic Confederation consisting of thirty-nine sovereign states, including Austria. The Confederation had its own Diet sitting permanently in Frankfurt-am-Main but the Diet was no more empowered to unify the country than the former Imperial Diet and indeed had scarcely any executive authority over the constituent states. Prussia became the biggest state in north Germany, retaining her eastern lands and gaining a large area of the Rhineland and Westphalia, stretching from the Netherlands to Hanover, including many of the regions which were eventually to become the most developed and industrialised in Germany. She also acquired a large part of Saxony and the last remaining Swedish possessions in Pomerania. By contrast the 750,000 inhabitants of Thuringia remained divided amongst nine sovereign rulers. The revolutions of 1848 resulted in the summoning of a national parliament representing all states within the area of the Germanic Confederation including the German provinces of the Habsburg Empire. The parliament was dispersed with the collapse of the revolutions but until 1850 Prussian policy was to create a closer confederation which would exclude the Austrian lands. This was finally abandoned under Austrian pressure and until 1867 the states continued in their separate jurisdictions although these were limited by the growing economic and political strength of Prussia and by the common agreements on tariffs which are discussed below. Finally the situation led to war between Prussia and Austria in 1866 in which Prussia was completely victorious. The outcome of the war was that Prussia annexed Schleswig, Holstein, Hanover, Hesse-Cassel, Nassau and Frankfurt-am-Main, increasing its population by about four millions. The remaining states north of the Main were formed into the North German Confederation with a common representative assembly and a common council in which Prussia's influence, by virtue of the fact that she had five-sixths of the population was preponderant. Prussia also controlled the army and served as the executive arm of the new Confederation. Only Bavaria, Württemberg, Baden and Hesse-Darmstadt remained outside and they participated in the common customs area. This common market was itself represented by a customs parliament. South German armies served with the forces of the North German Confederation in the war against France in 1870. After the victory over France the southern states all entered the Confederation by separate treaties and the Confederation was transformed into the German Empire with the King of Prussia as its Emperor and a set of national representative institutions based on those of the North German Confederation. Austria remained entirely excluded.

The state thus formed was still a federation in which the southern states retained important privileges. Bavaria and Württemberg controlled their own railways, posts and excise duties. Nevertheless it became increasingly centralised and increasingly unitary in form until 1914, apart from Russia the biggest and the most populous state in Europe.

THE ZOLLVEREIN

So much for the process of political unification. The allied process of economic unification took two forms in the early nineteenth century, the creation of the Zollverein, a customs union embracing most of the German states, and the creation of a network of communications. These two processes of course went together for some of the states were so small that the commercial importance of their roads was mainly to join together cities in other states. There were in fact two almost inseparable motives which caused these dynastic states to submit to the pressure of the largest of their number Prussia and create an economic unit which seemed to have little correspondence to the old-fashioned nature of their government and, indeed, in some cases, meant the virtual extinction of any real surviving power for the ruling dynasty. Both motives may be traced back to the events of the French Revolution and the transformation of France into a national and constitutional state.

In the first place the Zollverein was a deliberate attempt to restore the larger markets which the 'continental system' had so briefly created. The destruction of that system in 1814 had meant the collapse of the new trade routes which Napoleon's re-drawing of the map of Europe had created. The continental system had reversed the long relative decline of German industry and in the Rhineland and Saxony had even produced the first stirrings of the German industrial revolution. But after 1815 the restored dynasties everywhere were eager both to protect their manufactures against British and French goods and to use the new forces of nationalism on their own behalf by defining their frontiers more strictly. The French tariff of 1816 sealed off the French market from those Rhineland manufacturers who had depended on it in the previous decade. The Duchy of Berg, now transferred to Prussia, suffered acute distress. Similarly the British Corn Laws of 1815 diminished the possibility of grain exports from Germany to Britain. The union of Holland and Belgium stopped the developing coal output of the

Ruhr because the Dutch market was now supplied from Belgian mines. In the next decade Rhineland coal output seems to have actually declined. The Rhineland states therefore were ready to seek any possibility which would open to them a wider market than that provided by their own consumers.

In the second place there was the desire of Prussia to change its eighteenth-century structure into the structure of a more modern state. Since its territories were not even contiguous the instrument chosen for unification by the Prussian reformers was a national uniform external tariff, applicable to all parts of the state, by the manipulation of which it was hoped to put pressure on all those intervening weaker territories who would be taking their cut from the transit trade between the various parts of Prussia. The wishes of an area like Berg to get into a wider market thus coincided with the wishes of the Prussian government to prevent their prosperous new western territories from leaving the state. Therefore the idea of expansion was implicit in the creation of a uniform Prussian tariff. For unless the intervening territories could be forced or cajoled into a customs union the tariff would not serve its purpose of harmonising the interests of eastern and western Prussia. The Prussian law of 11 June 1816 which abolished all internal tariffs in Prussian territory and the decrees of 1817 which replaced the separate and high tariff barriers of each of the old provinces of Prussia by a uniform and low tariff were not only important acts in the modernisation of the Prussian state but also acts taken in the full consciousness of their significance for the economic future of the whole German area.

The previous local Prussian tariffs had acknowledged the reality of commercial life in a state where each town was a separate local market and the countryside around it was subjected to its commercial domination. The new tariff presupposed the dissolution of these many local markets into one national market. It acknowledged the dissolution of the rigid social stratification of eighteenth-century Prussia. It also presupposed something which had not yet come into being, a national network of communications through which the grain of East Prussia and the coal and textiles of the Rhineland Duchies would both move. In this way policies designed to produce modernisation and administrative reform in order to unify and preserve a traditional absolute monarchy were at the same time policies designed to shape a great new market in the centre of the continent and are, rightly, seen as the beginning of German economic unity.

That economic unity depended more on the political **power and** diplomatic strength of Prussia than on any noticeable harmony of economic interests between the German states. The southern states had strong economic reasons for resisting integration into the Zollverein, their small state-supported 'manufactures' had little chance of competing successfully with the wider and cheaper range of articles produced in Prussia and even less chance of competing with the increasing volume of French and British commodities to which the low Zollverein tariffs permitted entry. Much of the commercial profits of the tiny central states came from the dues which they exacted on the transit trade in British goods imported into northern German ports for distribution in the south of Germany. There was no particular reason why giving up these transit dues would produce any better source of revenue. The northern ports themselves were more interested in free trade with the rest of the world than in the development of the hinterland of Germany. Even in Prussia itself there was strong and justified economic opposition to the Zollverein. The textile manufacturers attracted to Berlin by the demands of the army had no wish to be thrown into competition with the more modern and better equipped cotton cloth industry of Saxony. For all its economic importance therefore the creation of the Zollverein depended more on political pressures than on economic ones and the long story of its successful completion is more meaningfully told by historians of diplomacy than by economic historians. Only the barest outline of this story need be given here.

Until the French tariff of 1822 the central German states showed more interest in a customs union which would align itself with the French market than they did in the Prussian Zollverein. The only successes Prussia achieved were with states that were actually surrounded by Prussian territory. The agreements signed with these enclaves laid down the basic form of the customs union for its duration. The common revenue was divided on the basis of the population of the various states rather than on the volume of goods crossing the borders, which still legally existed for all purposes other than revenue collection. The disappearance of the customs gates meant the gradual merging of the state into Prussia for such states retained an independence of action which was more juridical than actual. Fear of virtual absorption into Prussia, which since the late seventeenth century had had a noticeably more rigid social and administrative system, became a powerful reason for resisting the Zollverein.

Then turning-point came in the years 1826–28. The Anhalt duchies, which lay on each side of the river Elbe and thus depended on the transit trade down that river, were forced by economic pressure into the union and in 1828 the Grand Duchy of Hesse joined the Zollverein by a treaty which allowed it to retain a right of veto on all subsequent treaties. The central states were divided by these events and the way opened for a meaningful agreement with the larger southern kingdoms. From 1828 onwards much of the diplomatic and economic manoeuvring by the independent states was designed to strengthen their hand in future bargaining with the Zollverein, although these manoeuvres also had important economic effects which historians have neglected to study. Bavaria and Württemberg, for example, shared a common customs administration after 1828. In the same year the remaining central states, including Saxony, formed a union whose principal purpose was to ensure a common diplomatic attitude between them in future negotiations. However negative such agreements they also played their part in reducing the obstacles to trade and commerce.

Independent cities such as Frankfurt-am-Main and Bremen hoped to capture the transit trade to the south on a free-trade basis. Such an attitude not only forced the Prussian government to come to terms with the remaining southern and central states but meant that the agreement would be on the basis of much lower tariffs than had previously existed in the southern states. It is interesting to note the weakness of the position of the southern states. Whereas one of the strongest motives for the preservation of the Zollverein was its great and increasing profitability for the smaller members, because of the increase in trade and the way the revenue was distributed, the southern union was much less profitable because of the comparative backwardness of its members. Revenue per head was less than one-half that of the Zollverein and the costs of administration and collection of the tariff were over 40 per cent of the yield. Furthermore, the Palatinate was cut off from the rest of Bavaria by the larger Zollverein and by the union of central states. Accordingly from the moment when the Grand Duchy of Hesse signed its treaty with the Zollverein most pressures combined to reduce the extreme protectionism which had prevailed for so long in central and southern Germany.

An agreement between Prussia and the southern states in 1829 stipulated that the latter would reduce their tariffs to the level of the Prussian tariff by 1832. The central states were thus left at the mercy of Prussian economic policy except where the increasing north-south trade still had to pass through their territories. Electoral Hesse and Hanover, whose stiff opposition to the Zollverein was encouraged by its British ruler, formed the union of the central states into a full customs union in 1830 with a common tariff and a common tax policy. But the enterprise was born to failure when Saxony refused to join and in the same year joined the Zollverein.

In May 1833 the Thuringian states deserted their central partners and also joined the Zollverein. At that point the union was complete in an effective sense for most north-south and east-west trade could now be carried on without tariffs by avoiding the few states which had not joined. Baden did not join until 1835, Frankfurt-am-Main until 1836, Hanover until 1851. The free Hanseatic states retained their separateness until Germany was already a great industrial power, but their tariffs were lower than that of the Zollverein. The long lines of wagons waiting through New Year's Eve 1833 for the toll gates to be thrown open at midnight indicated how important was the collapse of the customs union of the central states. As the year 1834 began and the wagons began to roll forward on their long journeys they rolled forward into a new Germany.

Including the Duchy of Hesse, which had adhered to the Zollverein only by a treaty which it could renounce, the Zollverein in 1831 had embraced roughly 14 million consumers. From 1 January 1834 it included about 23·6 million consumers and stretched from the French frontier to towns which are now in the Soviet Union and from the mouths of the Elbe and the Oder to the Alps. Its extension coincided with the first speculative boom in railway construction and with the great speeding up of trade and communications which the railway implied. Technological change seemed to conspire with diplomacy to make this huge market suddenly even more accessible.

The development of the Zollverein's foreign trade shows how important the extension of the domestic market was. Foreign trade per capita increased from 1834 to 1840 but in the subsequent period of industrialisation the rate of increase slowed almost to stagnation. Although such general calculations cannot really give anything more than a sense of proportion sources suggest that world foreign trade increased by about twice as much in the period 1830–50 as the foreign trade of the Zollverein. The reason for the difference is that the Zollverein took only a very limited share of the trade between European and non-European countries. In this trade the old colonial powers were well-established and the foreign trade of the Zollverein found it easier to make gains in Europe itself. The major increase in foreign trade *per capita* came only after 1854. In that year its value was 55 marks *per capita*, in 1871 it was 132·5 marks. But even then the small increase between 1854 and 1864 is largely accounted for by the incorporation of new areas such as Hanover. The great advance in the value of foreign trade *per capita* came only after 1864, after 25 years of rapid economic development.

TRANSPORT DEVELOPMENT

Before the coming of the railway Prussian road-building policy had been heavily influenced by the political needs of the Zollverein and had been more or less an instrument of diplomatic policy. Although administrators like Stein had great faith in road building and, in the Rhineland, achieved some economic successes with it, it has to be emphasised that Germany had no well-established road network like that of France. After the agreement between Prussia and the southern states work began on the construction of north–south roads with Prussia providing financial aid to some of the smaller states that lay in the way. But the arterial route from the North Sea to Switzerland was to pass through Magdeburg and Nuremberg in order to divert trade into the Zollverein and away from the older route from Bremen through Hanover and Frankfurt-am-Main. Until the coming of the railway travel and trade in Germany remained much more complicated and difficult than in France. The coincident effect of the creation of the Zollverein and the building of the railways was thus even greater. And, of course, the creation of the Zollverein itself eliminated just in time what would have been severe political obstacles to the building of a railway network, the same obstacles which had stood in the way of a proper system of roads.

As the volume of internal trade had increased river transport had partly compensated for the deficiencies of the roads as the number of tolls on the great north–south arteries of the Rhine, the Elbe and the Oder had diminished. The Rhine was by far the most important and Cologne and Mainz were already two of Europe's greatest river ports. The increase in coal traffic down the river to Holland led to the building of the coal port at Ruhrort and although that traffic suffered badly after 1815 other commodities began to move along the river in increasing quantities. The regulation of the major rivers and agreement on their use proceeded very quickly after 1815. But there was relatively little canal building; the Ludwig canal which realised the old dream of linking the Rhine to the Danube was only opened in 1845, when the railway age made it superfluous. By 1850 there were 730 kilometres of canal open to to traffic. The length of navigable river was twice as great and the traffic it carried more important.

Matthias Stinnes began the first regular river services between Cologne and Holland in 1817 by scraping capital together from every possible source, banks, his family, local merchants and so on. In periods of crisis the Prussian government provided him with state transport contracts to keep the line going. Steamships began to be used on these routes as early as 1820. They were particularly valuable in travelling up-river against the fast currents of the Rhine. In 1825 a Dutch steamboat steamed from Rotterdam to Kehl through the Rhine gorges and from that year on the steamship saw a more rapid development on the Rhine than anywhere else in Europe. The Nederlandsche Stoomboot Maatschappij (Netherlands Steamship Company) was founded in 1824 and in 1826 the Preussisch-Rheinische Dampschifffahrtgesellschaft (the Prussian-Rhine Steamship Company) began regular services up-river from Cologne. At first these steamship lines catered as much for passenger traffic as for goods because the handling of goods depended on the development of a system of tugs and lighters in the port of Rotterdam where most of the goods had to be transhipped. As such a system was developed and as the first results of the Navigation Commission of 1831 were seen in the regulation and improvement of the navigation the Rhine and other rivers began to carry a volume of traffic much greater than later in the century. In spite of the early interest in steamships, which were used on the Elbe in 1816 and the Havel in 1817, only on the Rhine were such vessels used regularly before the 1830s. The first boats were built in Dutch yards with English engines; the first German boat was begun in 1830.

Once the railway network began the rivers were quickly reduced to handling only the cheaper bulk freights where speed still did not greatly matter. In 1847 the volume of goods moved on the Rhine from Cologne to Antwerp was only half that moved by rail and on the upper stretches from Mannheim to Basel the figures were much more heavily in favour of rail. The transport of goods up the Neckar and the Ludwig canal to the Danube ceased entirely and only now is the Rhine–Danube canal again to become an effective waterway. Traffic on the Elbe and the Havel in the 1840s was about one-third its volume in the previous decade.

The effect of the railway on Germany was more far-reaching and dramatic than on any other European land. Although it is repeatedly written, and correctly, that the economic effect of railway building in backward countries was in many ways greater than in advanced countries, as far as Germany was concerned the country derived the advantages proper to both stages of development. It did not have the handicaps to railway building of a backward country, capital proved to be readily available, the network was quickly built and a large volume of profitable traffic developed immediately. Of course, without the existence of locomotive and rail manufacturing industries elsewhere the German railways could not have been so quickly built, but after the initial purchases Germany was

sufficiently advanced to develop its own rail and locomotive manufactures very quickly and even to become an important exporter.
On the other hand the same advantages were derived as in an
underdeveloped country, a much more rapid increase in internal
trade than in France, the linking together of raw materials, manufacturing centres and markets which had previously remained
completely separated from each other, and the rapid development
from markets of mainly local significance to a much larger and
more unified market. The railway destroyed social and political
obstacles to development which in France had disappeared long
before the steam locomotive had been invented. The railway came
to Prussia only twenty-five years after the rigid legal distinctions
between social classes which had been the basis of society there had
been removed. It was in fact opposed in many German states on the
grounds that it would be a social leveller which, to a certain extent,
it proved to be. More important than this once it was possible to
travel from Cologne to Hamburg in much less than a day the
political and economic existence of states as small as those in
Thuringia through which a train could pass in an hour seemed far
less rational and no longer so justified by the past. It is meaningless
to separate the creation of the Zollverein from the building of the
railways for both had the same effects, they eliminated the barriers
separating producers and consumers in the one country where those
barriers were the most serious obstacle to economic development.
The skeleton of unified Germany was an iron skeleton. It is in
Germany above all that the significance of the railway for European
economic development in the nineteenth century can be seen, a
significance too wide and too deep to be measured merely in quantitative terms.

The railway was the first force to overcome the obstacles to large
scale capital investment throughout Germany. Local manufacturing
interests in every town eagerly subscribed in order to promote an
extension of demand for their product. The most ardent pioneers of
railway construction were ardent advocates of national unity.
German investors had not had the previous experience with canal
companies and other larger forms of capital manipulation that
French investors had and the railway brought a complete change
of view on investment. Indeed in its importance for future methods of
capital management and in the climate of optimism and of unlimited
future possibilities which it generated the railway had as great an
importance as in its function of improving transport facilities.

Even in more tangible and measurable ways the railway had a
greater importance for Germany. The industrial revolution there
depended in its early stages far less on overseas trade than had the

industrial revolutions in France and Britain. Cotton counted for little and developments in the textile industries were more concerned with the utilisation of domestic raw materials. But basically the very rapid period of development after 1850 depended not on the textile industries but on the utilisation of domestic coal and iron ore resources. The railway reduced the cost of transport of coal in the Ruhr area from 40 pfennigs per ton (by road) in the 1820s to 14 pfennigs per ton (by rail) in 1840 and to 2 pfennigs per ton by 1850. It was a far more cost-reducing innovation than road construction and made coal available at an economic price for a wide range of industrial enterprise. The direct effect of railway construction on the output of both coal and iron was also in its turn very important in the early decades of industrialisation.

By 1845 the total number of kilometres of railway track in use in Germany was already slightly greater than in France. In 1850 there were 2,996 kilometres in use in France and 5,822 in Germany. The rate of addition to the railway network remained high after 1850 only dropping to a lower level after 1880 so that by 1875 Germany had a total kilometrage of track far greater than any other mainland European country and almost as great as that in Britain and in density of railroad per square kilometre was probably exceeded on the mainland only by Belgium. Not only did the length of line continue to increase but the volume of goods carried increased relatively to the extent of track. Between 1850 and 1860 the weight of goods carried on the Prussian railway system increased almost six times while the total kilometrage increased by 46 per cent. In 1913 prices railways accounted for about 3 per cent of the total capital stock in 1850–4 and over 11 per cent by 1880–4.

Table 28. *Additions to the railway system in Germany 1835-80* (*kilometres*)

Year	Length of system	% addition
1835	6	—
1840	549	—
1845	2,131	—
1850	5,822	—
1855	7,781	34
1860	11,026	41
1865	13,821	25
1870	18,560	34
1875	27,795	55
1880	33,865	21

Source: W. Sombart, *Die deutsche Volkswirtschaft im neunzehnten Jahrhundert* (1913), p. 393.

The greater speed with which the railway system was built in Germany than France was not at all due to the governments' attitudes. Most German states had the same military, economic and social fears of the railway as the French government. The drive to build the railways came from industrial speculators, particularly those with coal mines or iron works and this drive was allied to the economic and national hopes which this invention aroused in their breasts. Politically their incentive was greater than that motivating French railway builders. But the political opposition on the part of governments fearful of social and economic change was also greater. Out of such fears the Prussian government turned down early demands for a railway from Breslau (Wroclaw) to the Upper Silesian coalfield and frontiers and also Friedrich Harkort's first schemes for a Rhine–Weser line. King Ludwig of Bavaria was strongly against all railway building at first and, indeed, the railway was generally seen as a threat to the political structure and independence of most of the states. The first German passenger line, from Nuremberg to Fürth, was really built because of the energy and determination of the Nuremberg merchants. It was completed in 1835 and in its first years of operation showed a profit of 16 per cent on the capital invested. Its success increased the pressures from the Rhineland bourgeoisie for a railway linking them to the coast at Antwerp. The early construction of the Belgian network dictated that the new rail transit trade with western Germany would pass through that country rather than through Holland. These pressures were combined with demands for a line linking the Rhineland to the eastern areas of Prussia. Concessions for a line from Cologne to Minden on the Weser were granted by the Prussian government in 1836 and it was designed to link up with a projected route to the Belgian system.

In other states the same combination of interests pressed for lines linking the capital with nearby towns. The result was a series of lines radiating from important centres rather than the vague network which the geographical peculiarities of Prussia had called into being. Even in Prussia there emerged a series of unconnected lines fanning outwards from Berlin. But basically Prussian railway building policy like her earlier road building policy necessarily had also to imply a German transport system as well as a merely Prussian one. It was only after 1844 that junctions were effected between the many state systems and it became possible to make through journeys across German territory. In 1843 the Saxon government put forward plans for its own railway network. The Bavarian railways were planned from the outset as a purely Bavarian enterprise. After the first junctions between the state systems had been effected the various railway administrations began to collaborate for the through-running of certain trains. But even in 1847 when the Hamburg conference created the Union of German Railway Administrations to make such through-running easier the southern states refused to join.

The disadvantage of such disunity was that certain areas of Germany, particularly the smaller states, were neglected by railway builders. In spite of its nearness to the main centres of economic development Stuttgart saw little railway-building activity until the 1850s. By contrast in Prussia those areas where the mercantile interest was not strong enough were neglected. The line eastwards from Berlin to Danzig (Gdansk) and Königsberg (Kaliningrad) was only finished in 1862 after its financing had become the centre of a bitter political struggle. The forces of parliamentary liberalism were not prepared to subsidise a railway to the less-developed areas to help the landowners there without getting substantial constitutional gains in return. There were other initial disadvantages too; the Baden railways were built on a wider gauge and had to be converted after 1853. The junctions with countries outside the Zollverein were effected very late indeed, again in contrast to the Belgian network which had been expressly designed to link up with those of other countries. The links between the Saxon and Austrian systems were not completed until 1859 and between the Bavarian and Austrian systems not until one year later. No proper railway route along the Rhine from Rotterdam to Basel was operating until 1856, nine years after it had been possible with changes to make a similar north-south journey from Stettin (Szczecin) via Berlin to Vienna.

This haphazard combination of private business interests and deliberate state policy did, in spite of all the disadvantages, achieve the main thing – to build railway lines quickly. One reason was the element of competition between the various states. Another was the cheapness with which they were built; the speed of travel was slow and the equipment inferior to that in France. But the number of different arrangements made by the different authorities did introduce a kind of flexibility lacking elsewhere and this flexibility was maintained in the curious compromises which continued to operate in German railway building. The depression of 1848 caused the Saxon government to purchase those lines which had originally been privately financed. The railway from the River Main to the River Neckar was put out to private tender and when no private company would undertake it the governments of Württemberg, Hesse and Bavaria together put up the necessary capital. In Bavaria the main line from Munich to Augsburg was built by private capital and then bought by the state. By 1850 about one half of the total investment in German railways had probably come from the states.

This synthesis between private and public financing was built into Prussian legislation by the Railway Law of 1842 which proved to be the most flexible and successful of all the legal instruments controlling railway construction in nineteenth-century Europe, a remarkable tribute to the professionalism and ingenuity of the Prussian civil service. The law clearly established that the Prussian lines would continue to be the result of private business speculations but that these speculations would be supported by a foundation of government help. The state provided one-seventh of the capital while retaining shareholders' rights equivalent to one-sixth of the capital. Where the profit from the line was over 5 per cent on the capital invested one-third of this profit had either to go a fund guaranteeing a future interest of 3·5 per cent or to buying back the original shares. The law thus created a perpetual railway fund which the state could use to encourage new building in those areas which private speculation might neglect and at the same time gave the state an interest even in those areas such as the Rhineland where private speculation was very active. The law established a method of railway financing which was much copied in other countries afterwards, even in France. As the more profitable lines were completed and those with less potential profit begun the role of the state became bigger until by 1860 the Prussian government was itself operating about 55 per cent of the total network.

The effect of these rapid improvements in marketing possibilities will be apparent all the time in the early development of the iron and coal industries. But it stands out even more clearly if we look briefly at the development of Berlin as one of Europe's great industrial centres for its development was directly contingent on the process of political and economic unification and simplification. Although the city had the advantages of being a capital city in the eighteenth century and thus a seat of 'manufactures' and a centre of military contracting it was remote from the developed parts of Europe and from coalfields and ironfields. A series of improvements to its waterways beginning in 1771 made it over the course of the next hundred years into the second biggest inland harbour in Germany. But its nineteenth-century development would have been impossible without the Zollverein and the railway.

The first line from Berlin, completed in 1838, was to the nearby military garrison of Potsdam. By 1842 the city was joined to Frankfurt an der Oder and to Stettin (Szczecin) one year later. By 1848 it had become the centre of a major network and this in itself meant that the early engineering enterprises there developed into important constructors of locomotives and rolling-stock. The engineering industry did not depend on the transport system only for its markets but for its fuel and its raw materials also for there was neither coal nor easily-used water power available. As industry developed the market for fuel and raw materials also grew; coal, lignite and coke were only 9 per cent of total fuel consumption in Berlin in 1840, by 1870 they accounted for 66 per cent. Until the 1860s the greater part of the coal consumed in Berlin came from Britain and only after the adjustment of the rail tariff in 1863 could Silesian coal compete effectively on the market there. The iron used in machine building came from Silesia, the Ruhr, Scotland and Sweden.

The other important source of industrial employment in Berlin, textile manufacture and trade, was just as much the product of the sudden improvements in transport and marketing possibilities. Brandenburg had been a centre of the woollen manufacture in the eighteenth century but between 1825 and 1834 there were never more than 450 looms active in Berlin. The employment there was mostly in the cutting and finishing trades, for one reason because the city dictated fashions of military and court uniforms. The development of such businesses into manufactures of ready-made clothing coincided exactly with the building of the railways and the extension of marketing possibilities. This extension was both social and geographical. The evolution of a bourgeois market for ready-made articles such as shawls, frock-coats and men's night clothes did depend on the growth of the bourgeoisie itself but the increasing homogeneity of taste which made such ready-made goods acceptable was very much the result of local preferences and tastes becoming less strong as the railway made travel easier and opened great opportunities for cost-reduction and larger scale marketing. The bigger firms such as H. Gerson, R. Herzog or D. Lewin were all founded in 1839 and 1840 and by the 1850s they were successfully retailing Berlin fashions in the southern and western states where previously French goods had dominated the middle-class clothing market. After that the Berlin firms began to compete with the French in foreign markets but only in those where rail transport allowed them to penetrate such as the Netherlands, Poland and Denmark. Even where the creation of a homogenous market might be thought easier transport and unification still played a vital part. Mass-produced bed linen was made only in Berlin among Prussian towns in the early nineteenth century because it was the only town with a sufficiently large number of temporary residents. Linen merchants took advantage of the railway to open factories for making bed linen, collars, cuffs and other linen wares in the 1840s and to distribute them by rail throughout Germany. By the early 1850s such factories used American sewing machines operated by miserably-paid female labour and by 1860 Berlin had itself become a centre of the sewing machine industry. In such ways a remote city with very few natural advantages became as industrialised as the Rhineland cities.

THE COMPLETION OF ECONOMIC UNIFICATION

There was one other aspect of this unification of the market which had considerable importance, the gradual reduction and standardisation of the currencies used. Before the great extension of the Zollverein in 1834 the larger coins of six different currencies were widely accepted as a means of exchange. The extension of the Zollverein demanded some simplification of this situation. In 1837 the southern states agreed on a standard florin as the basic unit of their coinage and Frankfurt-am-Main and the Duchy of Hesse joined the agreement. In 1838 the Prussian taler became the standard unit of all the northern states and the relation between the northern and southern units of currency was fixed. By the 1850s Prussian banknotes had become a method of payment preferred over the whole Zollverein even in Bavaria, The German Monetary Convention of 1857 agreed on three monetary zones, with the coinages having a fixed relationship to each other. Austrian coinage was, however, less and less used even in Bavaria and when, in 1859, the Prussian government refused to accept payments in Austrian currency, it almost ceased to circulate in the Zollverein.

As in the case of road building these monetary decisions were influenced as much by political as economic factors. It was only with the development of a banking system in the 1850s which ignored as far as possible the surviving national frontiers that economic factors really played a large part. The unification of the market acquired an irresistible momentum of its own in the case of large institutions such as railways, iron works and investment banks whose directors thought always of a national market and a national codified commercial law rather than a bewildering set of state laws and customs. These entrepreneurial forces were harnessed behind the Zollverein since it was the only legal and constitutional framework within which a national market could exist. Hanover joined the Zollverein in 1851, in order to raise more revenue without having to summon the diet of Oldenburg, its possession, and when its accession was ratified in 1854 the Zollverein's coastline was greatly

N

increased. From 1852 onwards the Habsburg government tried to get the German areas of the Empire also included in the Zollverein or, alternatively, to form a customs union between the Austrian provinces proper and Bavaria. Although sentiment in favour of Austria was widespread in southern Germany, economic motives dictated remaining in the Zollverein rather than deserting it for a smaller and poorer market. The issue remained undecided in the 1850s as the Austrian government offered increasingly favourable terms including a larger measure of protection for the southern German states than they could ever receive in the Zollverein. These favourable proposals were always outweighed by the fact that any tariff which also included Austria would have to permit very low duties on agricultural produce in order to appease Hungarian wheat farmers whose sole market at that time was Austria. Furthermore it was precisely in the 1850s that the Zollverein became a considerable industrial power in its own right and this rapid industrial development had little counterpart in Austria which remained an agricultural land. Finally Prussia settled the frontiers of Germany by force by inflicting a crushing military defeat on Austria and with that defeat the question of the extension of the Zollverein to a greater German area ended for the time. The Franco-Prussian trade treaty of 1862 contained a most-favoured-nation clause which meant the end of any preferences for Austrian goods in the Zollverein tariffs. The southern states objected strongly to the Zollverein signing a treaty with France on the same terms, but to no avail. The Austrian government proposed that both it and the Prussian government should jointly negotiate similar trade treaties with both Britain and France on behalf of the Zollverein, the resulting tariff revenue would be allocated in the proportion of three-eighths to Austria and five-eighths to the Zollverein. The difference was a measure of the difference in consumption of imports of the two areas. Public opinion everywhere in Germany supported the Zollverein as a matter of economic life or death and Prussia had her way and the Zollverein was reconstituted under new terms which eliminated the continual threat of secessions and dissolution. Majority decisions of the states were to be binding and their voting on a proportional basis in relation to the size of their population. In 1865 the trade treaty between the Zollverein and Austria was negotiated as between two sovereign powers and the definitive bounds of the customs union were now laid down. The Prussian victory over France in 1870 only confirmed these boundaries and the area of the Zollverein became more or less the area of the German Empire with the addition of the annexed Alsace and Lorraine. The victory also confirmed that the work of the Diet of the North German Confederation in the previous five years would form the basis of the German Empire. The standard regulations on weights and measures of 1868 and the Commercial Code of 1869 were accepted after 1870 by the southern states. Yet it was to take some time before the different legacies of so many governments could be obliterated. When Duke Adolph of Nassau fled from the Prussian troops in 1866 he left to Prussia a province still with scarcely any modern industry other than an artificial fertiliser factory. In 1860, the year in which the Duke had tried to reintroduce the right, which he had been forced to give up in 1848, to hunt over his subjects' crops, there were still only 2 gasworks in the whole state out of about 250 in Germany.

AGRICULTURAL DEVELOPMENT

Whereas the creation and unification of the German market was the prime force in overcoming the obstacles to economic development in Germany some of these obstacles were removed by direct legislation for this purpose. Most importantly this was true of the dissolution of the social order of the old régime and the consequent restructuring of rural society. This of course could be said of any European society after the French Revolution and in some respects the problem was easier to solve in Germany, or, to put it another way, there already existed in 1815 some areas of Germany where the social structure placed relatively few hindrances in the path of development. The pattern over the whole country was, however, as might be expected, a very complicated one. Rural society was not re-shaped in Germany in one basic national pattern as it was in France or Russia; each state and each area had shown great differences in the eighteenth century and the lack of political unification until 1870 meant that great differences also persisted because the separate states tackled the problem in their own ways. In spite of these differences it remains true that without the dissolution of old régime society the German market would never have developed and the extraordinarily rapid industrialisation of the 1850s and 1860s would never have taken place.

– Changes in Land Management

All these changes in the framework of German economic life on which so much emphasis is laid here might have been less overwhelming in their impact had there not at the same time been taking place a gradual but steady dissolution of the legal arrangements of old régime society. For this dissolution the main force was not government but the events of the French Revolution. It has already been shown how even the government of so rigid an old régime state as Prussia was forced to reconstruct itself through its total defeat by the revolutionary armies. As part of that reconstruction the Edict of Emancipation of 9 October 1807 had pronounced the end of serfdom. It is certainly true that where serfdom survived in Europe economic development of the kind that took place in Germany even before 1850 was not possible. But the history of Prussia affords an excellent example of the general tendency of historians to simplify the rural economic arrangements of the old régime. Where agriculture had been the whole base of the economy, to reconstruct those rural economic arrangements was effectively to reconstruct the whole society. Such a task was vastly more complicated and required much more time than the issuance of an Edict of Emancipation. Everywhere in Europe in the nineteenth century the abolition of the institution of serfdom can be seen as an important milestone marking the path of economic change, but it is no more than a milestone.

In fact the Prussian Edict proved very difficult to interpret. Although it drew on a line of reform proposals from 1799 onwards its principal architect, Stein, gave it a distinctively conservative slant for the most humane of reasons. He wished to remove the worst personal injustices of serfdom while avoiding a rapid dissolution of the ties which bound rural society together by which the injustices of serfdom would be merely replaced by the injustices of the labour market. The Edict permitted freedom of movement and abolished those dues which appertained to the person of the serf. But for the non-servile peasantry everything still depended on the extent to which their tenures had developed in the eighteenth century. Where policies of peasant protection had not established the equivalent of hereditary tenures even those heavy dues which derived from a former servile status had still to be paid. The peasant not covered by *Meierrecht* (see p. 54), still paid dues to acknowledge the right of his wife to share in his property, or the right of his child to leave the land or his own right to bequeath his property. Such dues were abolished by administrative action on crown estates but on private estates remained untouched until Hardenberg's regulations in 1816. Nor did the abolition of serfdom provide any new legal framework governing land tenures.

The decrees of September 1811 established those conditions under which the peasant could become a legal 'owner'. In all cases

⅓ - ½ 12 → lord r peasant

this involved the surrender to the lord of a substantial part of the peasant holding, usually between one-third and one-half. The weaker the tenure, the larger the surrender of land required. In the midst of a bitter war these decrees remained more or less unenforced but they served to establish the legal principles on which the new rural society would be reconstructed. In one very important respect, however, they were changed. Hardenberg had hoped to create both an active land market and an active labour market by this policy of land-surrender. The decrees were less protective of the peasant than the Edict of 1807 and although they confirmed the loss of the nobles' supply of free labour they also envisaged a situation where the peasant would still have to sell much of his labour on the market. By 1816 this had become too bold a policy for the Prussian government. The right to secure ownership by means of a partial surrender of land was confined in that year to those who were *spannfähig*, that is to say whose holding was capable of supporting a plough-team. In that category only those who paid the 'contribution' to the central exchequer could apply and only those whose tenure went back to 1763, when the ravages of the Seven Years War had reduced tenures to their lowest level. Such arrangements it should be noted completely excluded all whose tenancy rested on labour alone.

The Prussian reforms are not only interesting because Prussia was larger than the other states and preceded most of them in her plans. They are interesting also because in no other area of Germany did the dissolution of the old régime lead to such radical changes in economic relationships on the land. The surrender of land meant that in some cases peasants were left with holdings too small to allow them to survive, a result not unwelcome to the small group of nobles who had influenced the reform policy. The total amount of land surrendered by the peasants in the east to release themselves from labour dues has been estimated at 420,000 hectares. In addition the nobles seized other peasant farms, some of which would have been economically viable undertakings. Somewhere between 300,000 and 500,000 hectares were gained by the great estates in this way. Measurements of land ownership between 1837 and 1851 in fact show a substantial loss of 'noble' land in the eastern provinces but by that time the land transfers associated with the dissolutions of the dues had taken place and of course the noble was forced into the same competitive land market as the peasant. In fact the number of farms in the largest category increased from 12,200 to *# Farms* ↑ 33,300 between 1816 and 1858. In some ways the dissolution actually created differences between the eastern and western regions.

In western parts of Prussia there was a much smaller proportion of peasants performing labour dues and thus only able to cancel them by surrenders of land. A higher proportion paid these dues in cash rather than labour and were able to cancel them out by a cash payment. The Prussian decrees of 1829 on the dissolution of feudal dues in those territories which Prussia had gained in 1814 stipulated that the peasant must keep at least two-thirds of his land and even more if it was necessary to feed his family. The Hanoverian decrees of 1831 forbade the peasant to sacrifice more than one-sixth of his land. In the eastern provinces no such care was taken, although it is no doubt true that for many peasants in these provinces a cash payment would have been more difficult to make than a surrender of land.

None of these changes coincided initially with any noticeable increase in the demand for labour elsewhere in the economy, certainly no increase sufficient to balance the high rate of natural increase of the population. Prussian rural society remained in a curious intermediate stage between the old régime and the ideal of the new until the middle of the nineteenth century when the revolution of 1848 combined with the effects of economic development and of emigration in providing alternative labour markets to complete the transformation. It has already been noted how rural practices of the old régime, *vaine pâture* for example, survived in France after 1815 because they were the best economic arrangement. In Germany such survivals were more common. The bondsmen (*Insten*) who performed domestic service on the great estates east of the Elbe were scarcely to be distinguished in their economic lot from the earlier serfs. They voluntarily entered into tenancy agreements requiring from them similar services to those required before 1807 by law and custom. The development in the 1850s of active labour markets in the Ruhr and the United States had a far greater effect on the lives of these unhappy people than any government legislation and in a wholly agricultural state like Mecklenburg it was not until that decade that change became a social rather than a legal fact. In one respect, however, change was unavoidable. The high rate of increase of the population meant an increase in the number of small farms. To some extent this was nullified by the increase in the numbers of all farms, from less than one million in 1816 to over two million in 1858.

The precise legal arrangements governing the transition varied widely in each state just as the legal status of the peasantry had differed in the previous century. In the areas west of the Rhine 'personal' serfdom (*Leibeigenschaft*) had been abolished by the French. In 1803 a start had been made with removing it in Bavaria. In Saxony and Hanover changes had to wait until the revolutions of 1830. In 1834 a new land bank took over the payment of the Saxon peasants' dues and the peasants themselves were established in freehold tenure. There, and in Hanover where the decrees and regulations of 1831 and 1833 operated on what was already a favourable tenure position for the peasants, the dissolution of serfdom led to much less disturbance than in Prussia and to the establishment of larger and securer peasant farms. The 1848 revolutions completed the process, sometimes, as in the south-west, under the direct pressure of peasant revolts. The remaining money payments were usually funded through the establishment of land banks often based on the Saxon model.

In Prussia in 1850 all servile dues were abolished and all other charges and dues made redeemable in the form of a money rent. Peasant holdings were declared freehold without compensation to the landlord. The peasant's fees were paid into an agricultural bank, the Rentenbank, specially constituted for the purpose and through the same bank the government paid the landowner previously entitled to servile dues four-fifths of the sum established as the total money rent and funded the remaining one-fifth. If the peasant were rich enough he could act without recourse to the Rentenbank by paying the lord eighteen times the previously established annual rental. These arrangements foreshadowed the arrangements which the Russian government would have recourse to in the next decade to deal with the same problem. But in Prussia they came into force in a rural economy already much changed after 1807 and in a rapidly industrialising country. As Germany became more and more a unified market the differences in the structure of rural society came to matter less from a legal point of view. Only in Württemberg after 1848 were there attempts to physically restrain the poorer population from moving elsewhere to sell their labour. But the differences in the structure of landholding survived unchanged. The south-west remained a land of small peasant farms, the north-east a land of great agricultural estates and landless labourers. The process of rearrangement of the strips in the fields lasted throughout the century. In Baden in 1856 general legislation provided for a redrawing of the village map. In 1842 in Hanover came the first act providing for the division of commons and rearrangement of the fields. But in many areas the strips remained and even today are still being painstakingly reconstituted into contiguous landholdings by the government of the Federal Republic.

– Changes in Agricultural Practice

The failure to complete the redistribution of landholding and to enclose the farms constituted an obstacle to improving agricultural productivity. The cause of the failure in Prussia is to be found in the difficult period at which the reforms were introduced. Although the war against France had brought very high food prices these were to last but a short time. The harvests of 1819, 1822 and 1824 were very good, that of 1823 a record. The glut of grain brought prices down by about one-half in some places to below their levels of 1780. The introduction of tariffs in Britain and the Low Countries reduced Prussian grain exports. In such circumstances the exhausting war against France, which had been particularly severe in some grain-growing areas such as East Prussia, finally took its toll and the decade of the 1820s was one of agricultural depression throughout Germany. The capital necessary to redistribute the farm land and erect new buildings was not forthcoming and the costs of having the Commissioners-General redraw the village map and re-allocate the land were quite high.

Yet it is interesting to note how well the old system of land distribution was able to respond to the demands of the new century. Total agricultural production increased in Germany as a whole by between three and three and a half times between 1815 and 1914, the population increased by less than two and a half times. Only the increasing consumption of the population turned Germany from a food exporter to a food importer about 1860. The increase in agricultural production may seem insignificant by the side of the twenty-six-fold increase in non-agricultural output or the forty-five-fold increase in industrial output over the same period. But until 1870 most measurements, which are of course very crude and general, indicate that the productivity of labour in agriculture increased at least as fast as, and perhaps faster than, that in some growing industries. Between 1801–10 and 1846–50 Helling's index gives a 60–65 per cent increase in labour productivity in agriculture.[2] Over the same period Kuczynski calculates the increase in labour productivity in Prussian coal mines (excluding lignite mines) at 32 per cent.[3] If the comparison is prolonged to the period 1866–70 the overall increase for coal mining is 110 per cent, for agriculture 141–152 per cent. Of course were the comparison made with an industry like cotton spinning it would be overwhelmingly to the disadvantage of agriculture. Nor was the level of productivity of a worker in German agriculture as high as that of a worker in French or Belgian agriculture. Nevertheless, in spite of the depression of

[2] G. Helling, 'Zur Entwicklung der Produktivität in der deutschen Land-wirtschaft im neunzehnten Jahrhundert' *Jahrbuch für Wirtschaftsgeschichte*, vol. 1, 1966.

[3] J. Kuczynski, *Die Geschichte der Lage der Arbeiter in Deutschland von 1800 bis in der Gegenwart*, vol. 1, 1800–1932 (Berlin, 1949), pp. 112–14.

the 1820s, the main characteristics of German agriculture between 1815 and 1870 were increasing output and increasing productivity.

The increasing productivity was not necessarily the prime cause of the increasing output. The total area of land farmed grew markedly in this period; in Prussia from 12,542,000 hectares in 1816 to 15,683,000 hectares in 1870. The increase in cultivated land was greatest in East Prussia and in Pomerania. In Pomerania heathland declined from 51·9 per cent of the total in 1816 to 7·9 per cent in 1870; in Westphalia it fell only from 14·5 to 10·9 per cent. The gain in arable land was a direct consequence of the land reforms because it had previously been non-arable common land which disappeared under the plough with the concept of private ownership. The output of all grains rose in the same period, so did the output of animal products and of vegetables, especially potatoes. The only crop to decline in Prussia was green fodder. Potatoes which had accounted for about 0·5 per cent of the arable area of East Prussia in 1815, accounted for 8 per cent in 1883, in Silesia and Pomerania the increase was greater. In spite of the development of vegetable production and the increase in animal products German agriculture remained very much a grain-growing agriculture. Between 1816 and 1861 the proportion of arable land devoted to bread grains (including barley) in Prussia fell only from 49·3 to 41 per cent. The stock of horses increased by 51 per cent in the same period, of cattle by 108 per cent, of sheep by 190 per cent and of pigs by 380 per cent.

Table 29. *Grain production in Prussia (pre-1866 area) (tons)*

	Wheat	Rye	Barley	Oats
1816	392,000	1,798,000	895,000	1,541,000
1831	527,000	2,437,000	1,056,000	1,916,000
1852	818,000	3,017,000	1,040,000	1,832,000
1870	847,000	4,353,000	1,335,000	2,371,000

Source: H. W. Graf Finck von Finckenstein, *Die Entwicklung der Landwirtschaft in Preussen und Deutschland* (Munich, 1960), p. 313.

The increase in draught animals, it should be noted, was by no means sufficient to keep pace with the increase in the number of farms or the increase in the total cultivated area. This, in its turn, was a consequence of the re-drawing of the village maps and the gradual disappearance of the commons. Many of the smaller farmers must have had to use cows as draught animals and such a development is testimony to the difficulties which underlay German agriculture in this period of adjustment. It also makes the apparent increase in productivity all the more difficult to explain.

It is certainly not to be explained by any substantial mechanisation. Steam ploughs, reaping machines and cream-separators were only just beginning to be seen by 1870. Of course the gradual replacement of the older three-field system of leaving the land fallow one year in every three by crop rotations permitting a harvest every year was a great productivity gain. But Conrad's calculations, although their basis is not wholly reliable, reveal a remarkably steady gain in productivity which suggests that it cannot be attributed to any one particular innovation unless that innovation were spread over an equally long time.[4] The only period when his calculations show a noticeable acceleration in productivity gains is between 1860 and 1865 and the calculations are too rough and ready to attribute too much to that. The answer seems to be in the continual diffusion of knowledge and of improved techniques amongst German farmers. One incentive for this may have been the relatively greater increase in the price of agricultural labour between 1791 to 1800 and 1873 (264 per cent) than in the price of grain (158 per cent). But too much reliance ought not to be placed on evidence of this kind for peasant farmers could easily substitute the labour of their own families for wage labour. Indeed as the mechanisation of the textile industries led to a fall in the profitability of many rural domestic handicrafts it is quite probable that more family labour was available for the peasant farm. There must have been a constant improvement in the methods of farming the traditional crops and possibly in the crops themselves. The weight of animals does not seem to have increased very strikingly before 1870 but the length of time taken to get them to that weight may have decreased. It seems likely that the effect of elementary scientific knowledge was quite widely felt for illiteracy was far less common among the German peasantry than amongst the French. Germany was in the forefront of the study of agricultural chemistry and the first great organiser of empirical education in chemistry, Justus von Liebig, was himself an agricultural chemist. His work *Chemistry and its Bearing on Agriculture and Physiology* was published in 1840. There was also a considerable improvement in the quality of farm implements, particularly in ploughs.

Some of the crops which were increasingly being grown, such as potatoes and sugarbeet, had an inherently high yield per hectare. But until the 1840s the capacity of the beet sugar industry in

[4] J. Conrad's index of output which reduces it to hypothetical grain values is in *Jahrbuch für Nationalökonomie und Statistik*, vol. 34, 1879.

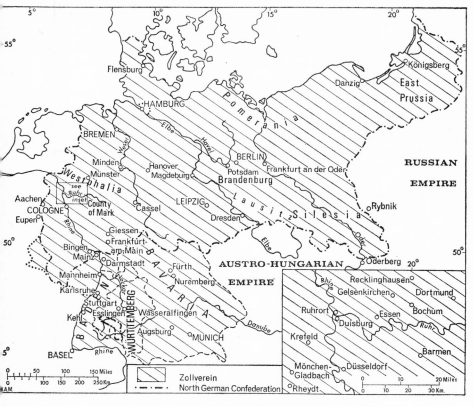

Map 6.   Germany on the eve of the Franco-Prussian War

Germany was too small and the competition from sugar cane too stiff for the production of sugar to be rationalised. There were two big increases in production, the first in the harvest year 1837–8 and the second in 1839–40. But trade treaties with the Netherlands which lowered the price of imported cane sugar in Germany then stopped any further significant growth until 1845–6 although in the same period the sugar consumption per head of the population increased by about one pound. After that date a protective tax on cane sugar began to take its effect and the output of beet sugar increased more than fivefold by 1852–3. Subsequently improvements in the distillation process continued to encourage its output which had increased by a further 150 per cent by 1870–1. Domestic consumption of sugar had scarcely doubled since 1845–6 and Germany had become practically self-sufficient in sugar. Many of the refineries, however, remained very old fashioned in their methods, in 1874 only one-third of them used the diffusion process.

INDUSTRIAL DEVELOPMENT

Having looked in this way at the underlying causes of the German industrial revolution it is important to look next at the developments in particular industries. For the German industrial revolution was significantly different from previous ones in that the mechanisation of textile production and the increase in textile output was of much less significance in the development of the economy. The leading sectors in the development of the Germany economy in its most rapid period of growth were the mining and metallurgical industries. Although textile manufacture played an important role its development into an industry comparable with that in France did not take place until after 1850, when the whole economy was being transformed by the pace of change in the coal and iron industries. To some extent this can be explained by the especially important role of the railway in Germany but such an explanation is obviously incomplete. Railway building not only produced a great demand for coal, it also reduced its price to the textile industries. The problem is a wider one which can only be examined by considering first the history of the German textile industry in the period when that industry in Britain and France was transforming not only those countries but the world.

Dieterici's calculations of earlier estimates made in 1780, in spite of what must be their many inaccuracies, nevertheless enable us to get some idea of how little the use of cotton fabrics had developed in Germany by that time compared to the traditional fabrics.[5] He estimated that linen cloths accounted for 30·8 per cent of the value of non-agricultural output in Prussia and woollen cloths 27·4 per cent. Cottons, by contrast amounted to only 4·2 per cent of the total value, much less even than silk. Whatever the margin of error in these figures it is certain that linen remained the basic manufacture of Germany and the only commodity produced on a large scale in which Germany had a big place in European markets. In spite of the development of the Saxon cotton industry this was still the situation in 1815. By the time of the census of employment of 1875 the textile industries as a whole employed 20·7 per cent of the total labour force. The total employment in mining and metallurgy was slightly greater, but in all other industrial sectors much smaller. Unfortunately we do not know the distribution of this employment as between the various sectors of the textile industry. The figure for the textile industry as a whole is high but it must have grown very rapidly in the 1850s when, in the general investment boom of those years, the mechanisation of the textile industries also proceeded very rapidly. Before that decade the mechanisation of the textile industries was much less marked than in France.

– *The Linen Industry*

One aspect of this slow mechanisation is explained by the initial size and importance of the linen industry which everywhere became mechanised more slowly than the other sectors of textile production. Some part of that is to be explained by the technical difficulties in building efficient flax-spinning machinery. But much the biggest part of the explanation is to be found in the diffuse organisation of the linen industry itself and in the nature of its markets. Most of the output was for immediate local household consumption and only a small part of it, the luxury cloths which came particularly from Silesia, was for export. These exports failed to increase because of the competition from foreign goods and on the domestic market lower income consumers also increasingly preferred cotton cloth. This was made worse by the general failure of the whole economy to develop as fast as those of neighbouring lands so that by the mid-1830s the first linens imperfectly made by mechanised means in other lands began to undercut those still made by domestic

[5] C. F. W. Dieterici, *Statistische Übersicht der wichtigsten Gegenstände des Verkehrs und Verbrauchs im preussischen Staate und im Zollverband in dem Zeitraum von 1831 bis 1836* (Berlin, 1837).

producers in Germany. The peak year for imports of linen into the Zollverein was 1843 and after that the German industry began to hold its own on the domestic market although exports continued to fall. Mechanisation of spinning did develop, especially when the American Civil War put up cotton prices, but even in the 1860s the German linen industry had not lost the essentially local and domestic character which had stamped it in the eighteenth century and about one-third of the yarn consumed was still hand-spun. The story therefore is one of the gradual mechanisation of the industry but a mechanisation too slow to prevent long periods of stagnation and to sustain any effective competition to foreign textile producers.

It is very difficult to make any worthwhile statement about the changes in the volume of linen production in the Zollverein as a whole. It appears from rather imperfect indices that the output in Prussia did not increase between 1834 and 1843 and may even have declined but that between 1843 and 1852 it increased by about one-third. Prussian output was about 43 per cent of Zollverein output. In spite of this recovery linen exports, which had accounted for 28 per cent of the value of all Zollverein cloth exports in 1837 accounted for only 9 per cent in 1864. In 1861 there were only 136,500 mechanical flax spindles in the Zollverein compared to over 2,200,000 in the cotton industry and 1,300,000 in the woollen and worsted industries.

This decline was the subject of many attempts by the various governments to reverse it. With encouragement from the Prussian government the brothers Alberti improved Swiss spinning machinery and installed it in Prussia in the same year as flax-spinning machinery was introduced in Britain. But there was no overcoming the fact that the organisation of the industry in the eighteenth century had not been in the hands of putters-out but in the hands of small part-time producers working on a casual basis and lacking capital. Until the 1840s every mechanical spinning works in Prussia required state help. Only in the 1840s did the linen merchants begin to put out the yarn themselves and collect the finished product from the weavers, a stage of organisation reached a century earlier in the French cotton industry. As for mechanical linen weaving it was not significant until the 1860s when firms like K. G. Grossmann in Dresden and the Bielefelder A/G imported mechanical looms from Britain.

– The Woollen Industry

The history of the woollen industry provides an almost complete contrast. Like linens coarse woollen cloths were produced in almost every part of eighteenth-century Germany but unlike linens woollens not only retained their importance but became a major industry in the nineteenth century. At the start of the nineteenth century Germany was an exporter of raw wool; by 1850 she was an importer supplying by herself only about one-tenth of her total consumption. The industry had been organised on a less narrow and local basis in the eighteenth century mainly because a greater proportion of its cloths had been exported by merchants who had injected capital into production. In the early nineteenth century the woollen and worsted industries gained export markets at the moment when the linen industry was losing them. In 1837 woollen cloths came second to linen cloths as the Zollverein's most important export. In the subsequent period production showed a steady rise as that of linens fell. The total consumption of raw wool increased more than fourfold between 1834 and 1870. The influence of the export market on this rise in output was vitally important.

In fact in the 1820s there is a good deal of evidence that the woollen industry was losing markets through tariffs and through British and French competition. The main export markets were by then confined to Poland and Russia. From the time when the Zollverein was extended the picture changed and in the period 1834–8 there was a decisive upward movement in exports. Such exports were more vital than to the linen industry for the per capita domestic consumption of woollen cloths was much lower than of either linens or cottons. One reason for the sudden upward movement may lie in the extension of the Zollverein itself because the number of operations needed to produce a finished woollen cloth and the fact that they were often carried out in widely-separated places meant that the removal of internal tariffs and dues had a greater cost-reducing effect than it did on linen production. In the late 1830s one-fifth of the total production was being exported. It is interesting to observe that in the same period British woollens exports were stagnating. German goods captured some British markets in the United States and opened new markets in Italy. In some areas, Aachen and the Lausitz for example, exports were two-thirds of output.

In the next decade the growth in exports was much less noticeable except that a steady progress was still made in North American markets. This re-assertion of the domestic market was only a temporary stage. The curious thing is that with the extraordinarily rapid development of other industries after 1850 and the growth in income and employment the woollen industry came to depend more on exports. Between 1847 and 1857 its exports increased more rapidly than those of its foreign rivals and even in 1850 when only the first signs of recovery from the 1848 slump were to be seen woollen exports surpassed their previous record level. Exports grew more rapidly than domestic sales in the 1850s. The United States by now had become easily the biggest market with eastern Europe second in importance. The role of the domestic market was important throughout and woollen cloth consumption there rose from about 2 metres per head in 1834 to at least 5 metres by 1870. Nevertheless the woollen industry in Germany repeated many of the aspects of the development of the cotton industry in France, escaping from the suffocation of foreign rivals by successful exporting. After 1840 woollens were always the most important textile export of the Zollverein and by 1864 were over half the value of all textile exports.

The beginnings of mechanisation in the woollen industry were very early. The firm of Hoppe and Tappert was building spinning machines with thirty spindles in Berlin before 1800 and before 1810 sixty spindle machines were in use in Brandenburg and Saxony. The main builder and supplier in the early years however was the Cockerill works in Belgium. The machines were usually water-driven. Mechanical worsted spinning also began during the 'continental system' at Langensalza in Thuringia but was abandoned afterwards. It really owed its beginnings in Germany to Johann Weiss who had worked in the English worsted industry for some time and began to use mechanical spinning machinery in Germany in 1819. He was followed by the firm of B. G. Scheibler in Eupen on the Belgian border in 1820 using English machines. Mechanised worsted spinning spread more slowly than wool spinning because it demanded a higher initial investment. The machines had to be installed in a factory, and a greater initial quantity of wool was necessary than in woollen spinning in order to keep the different machines operating in series. The first worsted spinning machinery was not used in Saxony until 1825. The first steam-driven wool-spinning machinery was used in 1818 in Aachen, steam power was not applied to worsted spinning until Weiss used it in 1827 in his Glucksbrunn works.

All these were in the nature of experiments rather than radical changes in the industry as a whole. The real development of centrally-driven wool spinning mills came in the 1840s with the large-scale adaptation of the mule-jenny. The next step was the introduction of the self-actor which came from Britain in 1859 and spread rapidly in the 1860s. The worsted industry not only required more initial investment and consequently a higher output to justify mechanisation, it also had no tradition of manufacture on a smaller scale. The smallest Saxon worsted works in 1834 had 340 spindles and no hand spinning. The big technical problem was the amount

of casual labour needed for the combing process which still had
to be done by hand. The firm of Opelt and Wieck in Saxony was
the first to solve this problem and their solution was adopted
elsewhere in Europe together with Heilmann's wool-combing
machines. Hand-combing died out in Saxony by 1865.

As far as the weaving side was concerned in 1850 the flying
shuttle was still not used in many places. The first mechanical
looms appeared in both woollens and worsted between 1835 and
1837 but were still not very widespread even in the 1850s. The real
elimination of the hand-loom weaver did not begin in wool until the
1860s. There were plenty of weavers, their pay was low, the material
was less adaptable to mechanical weaving than cotton, the cost of
a loom was falling (from about 450 talers in the 1830s to 280 talers
in the 1850s) and the cost of power for a mechanical loom was
relatively high. Even where steam engines were installed before 1850
they were often used to regulate the flow of water power. After 1850
as the price of coal fell this changed; by 1875 steam power accounted
for over 70 per cent of the horse-power used in woollen and worsted
weaving.

This process took place in wool without any marked regional
shifts in production. In worsted the old centre of Eichsfeld became
insignificant as a powerful new industry developed outside its
bounds. Until 1875 Brandenburg, the most important producer of
coarse woollens in the eighteenth century, was responsible for about
one-third of total output of woollens and also had the largest
percentage of its work force in firms with over five employees. It is
interesting to note that when Alsace and Lorraine were annexed
from France the percentage of the work force in such enterprises
there was much higher than elsewhere in Germany. In the Rhineland
both woollen and worsted production grew steadily to make that
area as important a seat of the industry as Brandenburg. In the
south the development of these industries was on a less substantial

Table 30. *Production indexes of the German wool industry,*
1834–68

Period	Worsted Spinning	Worsted Weaving	Wool Spinning	Wool Weaving
1834–8	100	100	100	100
1839–48	170	170	120	120
1849–59	340	510	192	174
1860–8	575	969	307	261

Source: H. Blumberg, *Die deutsche Textilindustrie*, (Berlin, 1965)
p. 406.

base and was more erratic. Bavarian woollens output actually declined from 1840 to 1847 although in the 1850s it grew extremely rapidly again.

– Other Textiles

Neither the manufacture of cotton nor silk cloths was a peasant handicraft in the eighteenth century. Cotton had never penetrated into the German market as it had in France and silk, as everywhere, was a luxury article. Cotton, being an imported raw material, soon gave rise wherever it was spun or woven to a more capitalistic form of organisation than the native fibres but the total consumption remained too small for this to have the same overall effects on the economy that it had in France. In 1835 the total consumption of raw cotton in the Zollverein was only about 4,500 tons. By 1846–50 the total consumption in Germany was perhaps about 15,800 tons, about one-quarter of the French consumption. Until the 1840s in fact the German cotton industry remained little larger than that of Russia or the Habsburg Empire and only under the influence of rapid development in other industrial sectors did it grow in size and go over completely to the modern techniques of the more westerly lands. It depended on the domestic market where other textiles still retained a strong influence. The domestic production of yarn never reached the level it did in France; in 1849 over 60 per cent of the yarn used by German weavers was imported.

The origins of the industry were very much like its beginnings elsewhere. In the late eighteenth century putters-out in the Mönchen–Gladbach and Rheydt areas began to distribute cotton yarn to linen weavers. But the first steam-powered spinning mills were not built in that area until the 1840s and many of those went out of business in 1848. Only in the next decade with the establishment of big firms like the Gladbacher Spinnerei und Weberei which had 15,000 spindles and 250 looms did mechanical spinning replace hand spinning in the area. In the southern states the story was very similar. The first mechanical spinning mill in Augsburg was built by von Schaezler in 1837 to supply the weavers with local rather than Saxon yarn. With 750 workers it was the biggest firm in Bavaria. The skilled workmen were imported from Alsace and Switzerland to train the local labour force. Three years later a tobacco manufacturer from Baden, Ludwig Sander, joined with the Alsatian engineer, Dollfuss, to build the first textile machine shop in the town. The works was taken over in 1844 by Carl Reichenbach and became the nucleus of the famous M.A.N. engineering works.

It was not until the 1850s that mechanised cotton spinning became really established in Bavaria. When it did so it played a role in the industrialisation of that state very like the role it had played previously in France and Britain and domestic spinning and weaving there were quickly eliminated as an important force by the construction of factories more modern than those developed elsewhere in Germany. In 1861 in Bavaria only about 2 per cent of the cotton looms at work were hand looms; in Prussia the proportion was 35 per cent and in Saxony over 50 per cent. Nevertheless, until the 1850s Saxony remained the most important centre of production. There were 361,200 cotton spindles there in 1830.

The silk industry like the woollen industry thrived on exports. But it was a much smaller affair altogether and very local, a large part of it being in the town and neighbourhood of Krefeld. The number of looms there roughly doubled between 1815 and 1835, a lower rate of increase than in Lyons or the Swiss silk manufacturing centres. Yet the industry retained its hold on foreign markets, especially the London market. One explanation seems to be its nearness to the Dutch ports which brought its transport costs below those of its rivals. The total consumption of raw silk approximately doubled in Germany between 1840 and 1870 but by that time it was less than one-seventh of French consumption. Krefeld remained very dependent on Lyons for technical developments and for innovations in styles and a lot of the success of the manufacturers there depended on the speed with which they copied the ideas of their French rivals.

The textile industry was the vehicle by which the capitalist mode of production which lay at the heart of the industrial revolution was introduced into Germany in the first half of the nineteenth century and it was the basis for the subsequent development of the economy in other fields. But the volume of production was less than in France and the pace of mechanisation much slower. As far as economic growth is concerned the textile industry seems less important than the metallurgical and chemical industries which developed later. But it was in the textile industries that new forms of organisation, new methods of capital management and a new scale of production were first introduced. The most rapid rate of growth of production for both spun and woven goods of all kinds was in the period 1849–59. But the growth of production in spinning was less even showing the influence of more suddenly applied innovations. The actual total of capital invested in the texile industry was low compared to railways or iron, yet its growth was remarkable, it increased sixfold between 1846 and 1875. The cotton industry was the most capitalised branch of the industry and the linen industry the least capitalised, reflecting the extreme development of the capitalist mode of production in cotton, particularly in cotton spinning where the machinery was so large, and the survival of domestic production in linen. In 1875 the ratio of fixed capital to total capital in the cotton industry was 52 per cent, in the linen industry only 26 per cent.

The effect of these changes in the textile industries on the rest of the economy was all the greater because textile manufacture was so widespread. In the early stages the areas which had taken the lead in textile manufacture in the eighteenth century retained that lead because the workmen were familiar with the peculiarities of the raw material and local merchants with the peculiarities of the markets. In this way the Saxon cotton spinning industry remained the most important despite the high cost of coal. In the investment boom of the 1850s Bavaria, especially the town of Augsburg, became the seat of a much more modern cotton-spinning industry than Saxony or the Rhineland, an interesting example of how a very backward region could be developed by importing techniques long in use in neighbouring regions. By 1875 Bavaria still had the only cotton-spinning mills in Germany as modern and as highly-mechanised as those in the annexed French provinces of Alsace and Lorraine. By that date Saxony had only 23 per cent of the spindles in Germany for all fibres. The impulse to development of the cotton industry in southern Germany also made it by 1875 a bigger employer than the woollen industry. It can also be argued that it was more mechanised. The number of employees per firm was twice as great in cotton as wool. But there were also more very small firms surviving in cotton because there was still scope for the older forms of enter- prise whereas in wool the number of operations involved and the fierce competition for international markets eliminated the really small producers.

The main advantage which Germany had over France and Britain was that of lower wages. This was offset by the high price of raw cotton although the relative prices of raw wool were more equal. By gradually recapturing the domestic market and by inserting itself into some foreign markets the textile industry was able to initiate the German economic recovery from the desperate years after 1815. It was only able to do so by great specialisation and by remaining relatively less developed on the international scale. The average number of spindles in a British mill in 1856 was over 12,000 and in France about 6,000. The average for Saxony in 1854 was 4,170 and for Prussia 2,400.

– Coal Mining and Iron Manufacture

The gradual changes in the textile industry before 1850 had little counterpart in the iron industry. It remained very outmoded and cautious until the late 1840s when it developed with quite extraordinary rapidity into a powerful modern industry to become the dynamic force in the period of most rapid economic growth. Even here a word of caution is necessary. The German iron industry was still very small in 1870 by the side of its British rival both in terms of output and in terms of the size of its plant. It also remained very much an iron industry. In spite of the development of cheap steel-making techniques after 1856 steel was less than 15 per cent of the finished product in 1870. As a mass-producer of iron, however, Germany had caught France up by that date.

The underlying cause of this remarkable transformation was the rapidity of the change from charcoal-smelting techniques to coke-smelting techniques. The basis of the change was the discovery of a large supply of good coking coal, a commodity still relatively expensive in France. The discovery was the result of a burst of exploration stimulated by the sudden increase in demand from railways and the iron industry. In the two decades after 1850 Germany became not only as great a pig-iron producer as France but a greater coal producer. Total output of coal (excluding lignite) in Germany rose from approximately 4,200,000 tons in 1850 to 24,000,000 tons in 1871. French output in 1871 was only 13,000,000 tons. Between 1850 and 1870 the installed steam-power capacity in Germany also surpassed that of France. How great a force for economic development the discovery of the Ruhr coking coals was can be realised when it is remembered that these increases in output were not based on new techniques but on techniques already established in France for a long time. Deep coal mining and the coke smelting process had been established there since the 1780s while for sixty years they had made but little progress in Germany. At the same time the rapid construction of the railway system produced a great demand for both iron and coal and encouraged investment in prospecting.

The major part of the increase in German coal output came from the Ruhr coalfield. Its output had increased only very slowly from 1815 to 1850 when it stood at 1,961,000 tons about equivalent to that of Silesia in the 1830s. Geologically speaking it was only a deeper extension of the coalfield of Belgium and northern France but its depth had already been a deterrent in the Ruhr valley itself. The main body of the coalfield as it stretched northwards and eastwards from the Ruhr got progressively deeper. The best reserves of coking coal were in these deeper sections and the path of exploitation led further and further away from the older areas of the valley itself, as methods of drainage and transport improved, towards Dortmund and even beyond. With each successive stage of exploitation a minor industrial boom hit each small country town on the way and in twenty years a peaceful rural area (the population of Essen, for example, was barely 4,000 in 1850 and its main activity the weekly market), developed rapidly towards becoming the most concentrated industrial area of the whole continent. The great wave of development after 1850 carried mining from the Rhine area to east of Bochum and northwards to Recklinghausen.

By 1870 this development was still far from complete, Gelsenkirchen, to become by 1914 the biggest colliery town in Europe, still had only 8,000 inhabitants. However, Ruhr coal output more than doubled between 1850 and 1860 when it stood at 4,276,000 tons, doubled again by 1865 when it reached 8,526,000 tons and by 1870 stood at 11,571,000 tons. By this date Silesian output was roughly 6,000,000 tons. Employment in the Silesian coalmines increased from 4,600 in 1850 to 14,700 in 1865. Production of coke in the Ruhr trebled between 1850 and 1855, to reach 224,000 tons but then stagnated on a lower level until contact was made with larger veins of rich coking coals after 1865. By 1870 it stood at 341,000 tons. This great increase in coal output was accompanied by a great increase in labour productivity. Output per man had more or less remained the same between 1815 and 1845. By 1870 it had almost doubled due to the greater richness of the seams, the greater size of the mines which permitted economies of scale, and a more rational organisation of work at the coal face.

This rapid industrialisation, colonisation and urbanisation of a hitherto unimportant rural area, seemed to contemporaries to resemble the kind of development taking place in America. It should not blind us to the development taking place at the same time in other coalfields because their growth in the same period, if less spectacular, was sufficient to show that what underlay the development of the Ruhr was not a lucky strike of raw material resources but a rising demand for coal throughout the economy. Deep mining began in the Saarland in 1820 under the influence of Leopold Sello, who had developed such techniques in Silesia. The first steam engines were used in 1825. The building of the Saarland railway in the 1850s created a wave of new mining activity for the coal was particularly suitable for railway locomotives. In 1866 the Saar canal was built to facilitate coal transport to France. Even in Silesia, where the connection of mining with large-scale landownership limited the intrusion of outside capital, to the extent that Silesia was less affected in the financial crashes of 1857 and 1873 than the western mining areas, big mining companies were developed in the 1850s. The Hedwigswunsch mines were opened in 1854 and Borsig founded his integrated coal and iron company there in 1857.

At the beginning of this rapid expansion of coal output the techniques of iron production in Germany were still circumscribed by the almost universal use of charcoal for smelting. Although there were blast-furnaces in Silesia using coke and although since the early nineteenth century there had been occasional successful smelts with coke in the Saarland, Rhineland industry remained local and highly specialised. In the valleys of the Siegerland and the Sauerland handicraft workers continued to produce nails, tools, pots, pans and agricultural implements much as the population of the areas around Liége had done in the eighteenth century. Before the coming of the railway the market for mass-produced pig iron was even less buoyant in Germany than in France. By contrast there was a reliable market for charcoal-smelted pig of particular specification. The total pig iron output of the Zollverein in 1834 is estimated at 110,000 tons, mainly produced in Prussia and Hesse. This covered about 90 per cent of domestic consumption. The first railway boom depended on rail imported from Britain. By 1845 total pig iron output in Germany was about 184,000 tons, sufficient to cover less than half the domestic consumption. Between 1850 and 1870 output increased from 211,600 tons to 1,391,100 tons and by that date once again covered almost all domestic consumption. That consumption itself had changed remarkably, increasing from 4·44 kilograms per head in 1833 for the Zollverein as it was then constituted to 46·9 kilograms per head for the German Empire in 1874. Between 1840 and 1850 there was a decade when the Zollverein was dependent on imports to meet the growing demand for iron and in the period 1842–6 imports of iron were three times their level of 1837–41. It was the switch to the coke-smelting process after this date which restored the balance.

The use of the puddling furnace developed soon after the end of the war and it proved the origin of what were later to become some of the biggest German metallurgical firms. Eberhard Hoesch bought the Lendesdorf blast-furnaces in 1817 and after a visit to South Wales to recruit puddlers installed puddling ovens. The English engineer who installed them, Dobbs, subsequently built the Eschweiler rolling-mills in 1822 for Friedrich Thyssen. The first puddling ovens in Silesia were installed at Rybnik in 1818. Two acquaintances of John Cockerill, the Rémy brothers, bought the iron works at Rosselstein near Neuwied in 1835 expressly to manufacture rail for the Nuremberg–Fürth railway. Two years later

Hoesch began to manufacture rail also but only after he had brought in another set of English and Belgian workers.

But there was no real possibility of competing with coke-smelted iron in the production of rail and from the start both the Rémy and Hoesch works conducted numerous, mostly unsuccessful, experiments with the newer smelting techniques. After 1840 the Geislautern blast-furnaces belonging to the Dillinger works in the Saarland operated permanently with coke but there was no successful commercial use of Westphalian coal for the same purpose. Only in a long series of trials between 1846 and 1852 by Julius Rönhold was success achieved. The moment of success meant a sudden burst of company foundation to exploit the enormous possibilities. In that year, 1852, Rönhold himself built the blast furnaces of the Niederrheinischen Hütte at Duisburg and the Vulkan works in the same town, the Belgian entrepreneur Charles Détillieux built the nearby Borbeck blast-furnaces, and the Hochdahl works of the Bergischer Gruben–und Hüttenverein was opened in the same area. The success of another Ruhr company, the Hoerder Bergwerks–und Hüttenverein, begun as a joint-stock company in 1852 set the seal on these developments. In its previous existence as a private company it had had no blast furnaces and their provision would never have been financed by Cologne banking circles had the firm not discovered iron reserves of its own. Between 1854 and 1857 its dividends were never less than 10 per cent. These new firms were large. The Hoerder Verein employed 1,700 workers in 1852. The new works were all on the coalfield. Capital, entrepreneurs and workers all migrated northwards from the upland valleys which had sheltered the old German iron industry. The only obstacle was now a reliable supply of good coking coal. By 1854 the deep-mining explorations of Franz Haniel and W. T. Mulvaney had demonstrated that this was in fact available. There was no mistaking the decisiveness of these events for the German iron industry. Yet it is also interesting to note that the output of puddled iron continued to increase until 1870.

Whereas in France the new iron technology had struggled along for decades before the railway had finally provided a large and dynamic market for its products, in Germany it was the existence of the market that called the new technology into being. In 1850 less than one-tenth of the total output of pig iron in the Zollverein was smelted by coke; by 1858 imports of coke-smelted iron rail had become insignificant. The virtual elimination of the charcoal smelters took scarcely more than a decade from 1850. In Prussia by 1862 only 12 per cent of the total make was charcoal smelted. By comparison with other major producers Germany remained in

1870 a country of small furnaces and her output less diversified. But the rate of increase of output of iron between 1850 and 1870 was far more rapid than in other lands.

So rapid, indeed, that the local supplies of good quality iron ore found in conjunction with the new coal measures were becoming exhausted in the 1860s and Germany was already developing into an iron ore importer from other areas of Europe, in this period from Spain and the isle of Elba. The first blackband ores were discovered near Dortmund in 1849 but their use on a large scale really began in 1854. Iron ore production in the Ruhr rose from 20,000 tons in 1852 to about 300,000 tons in 1862. The total extraction in the whole of Prussia was 1,288,000 tons in 1857; in the Zollverein in 1864 it was 2,130,000 tons. After that date it ceased to provide a satisfactory basis for the powerful industry which had grown up on it and German iron producers came to depend on iron ore imports as their French competitors on coal imports. The ultimate consequences for Europe were very far-reaching, the immediate consequences for Germany a sense of profound malaise in the iron industry which was to play a big part in the catastrophic slump of 1873.

– Engineering

Such developments had direct repercussions on the machine-building industry. The ready supply of coal and of iron castings led to a great increase in the output and use of steam engines while the demand for railway locomotives produced another powerful branch of the machine-building industry. In the following table the great increase in the use of steam engines other than locomotives in Prussia between 1855 and 1861 is most apparent. A similar phenomenon can be observed in Saxony where the number of steam engines including railway locomotives rose from 697 with a total horse power of 16,332 in 1856 to 1,206 with a total horse power of 45,930. For purposes of comparison, in Belgium in 1860 there were 4,997 steam engines including locomotives and steamships with a total horse power of 161,909. In France in 1850 there were 6,832 steam engines at work including locomotives and steamships with a total horse power of 186,363. By 1860 the figures had increased to 18,718 with a total of 527,344 horse power. Although, therefore, the increase in the use of steam power in France in these years was also a remarkable phenomenon and in 1860 France was still by this measurement a much more developed industrial power, Prussia alone, leaving out of account the other German states, was already closing the gap between her own installed steam engine capacity and that of Belgium.

Table 31. *The employment of steam engines in Prussia*

Year	Steam Engines in Industry and Agriculture		Locomotives		Steamships		Total	
	No.	h.p.	No.	h.p.	No.	h.p.	No.	h.p.
1840	615	11,712	13	340	6	226	634	12,278
1846	1,139	21,716	275	14,676	77	4,737	1,491	41,129
1852	2,124	43,049	607	40,194	102	9,232	2,833	92,475
1855	3,049	61,945	913	88,922	123	10,907	4,085	161,774
1861	7,000	142,658	1,449	106,350	198	16,368	8,647	365,376

Source: E. Engel, *Das Zeitalter des Dampfes* (Berlin, 1880), p. 151.

The first locomotive to be built entirely in Germany from German materials was the *Saxonia* constructed as early as 1839 for the Dresden–Leipzig main line. In 1841 Borsig delivered his first locomotive to the Berlin–Anhalt railway. By 1846 there were thirty-three machine-building shops in Berlin employing 2,821 workers. Their number was drastically reduced by the crash of 1848 but the foundations of a widely-diversified industry had been laid. There were sixty-seven such firms in the city in 1861 employing 5,313. Between 1854 and 1858 the Borsig locomotive works, the biggest Berlin factory, doubled its output of locomotives, from 500 to 1,000. By 1873 it had produced 3,000 locomotives. The biggest rolling-stock firm in the city, F. A. Pflug, built 400 wagons between 1839 and 1846; in the 1860s about 15,000 wagons were manufactured in the city. Before 1857 1,730 locomotives were manufactured in Germany, about one half of them by Borsig. In fact even in the 1840s many German machine shops did not have the machine-tools which had been available in Britain in the 1790s but they drew on a great tradition of mechanical skills in handicrafts. The first firm to make a real success of manufacturing metal-working machines was A. Hamann which began to make such machines in 1832. In the 1840s makers such as Hirtz or Voigt began to specialize in lathes or boring machines. Their market was the local Berlin market but similar developments took place in other German capital cities, especially those where locomotive workshops were developed. Locomotive builders like Maffei in Munich, Kessler in Karlsruhe, Henschel in Cassel, Egestorff in Hanover and Hartman in Chemnitz (Karl Marx Stadt)

were all well established before 1850 and after that date few locomotives were imported. The other big market was for steam engines
and pumps in the newly-opened coal mines. The Egells works was
the greatest supplier in this field. Yet it was the establishment of
the sewing-machine industry in the 1860s that first brought German
machine makers to make precise single-purpose accurate tools. In
1864 the firm of Frister and Rossmann began to make sewing
machines by what could fairly be described as serial production
and the engineering firm of L. Loewe followed suit in 1869. In its
early days the electrical industry was an offshoot of these developments. Werner von Siemens, whose inventions dominated the
beginnings of the industry went into partnership with a Berlin
machine builder, J. G. Halske, in the 1840s. In 1848 they won the
contract for the first big European underground telegraphic cable
from Berlin to Frankfurt-am-Main. By 1851 they had so many
foreign contracts they needed a new works. By 1870 the firm still
employed only 400 workers but it functioned as a European
monopoly because of its pool of skilled workers; the future size
of this industry in Germany and its concentration in Berlin were
clearly foreshadowed.

– Changes in Economic Organisation

Such a rapid development in so many fields of industrial production
could hardly have taken place without equally rapid changes in the
methods of industrial organisation. In fact the period saw remarkable
changes in the methods of company foundation and in the methods
of manipulating capital, changes which altered almost beyond
recognition the framework in which production had previously
taken place. It was of course possible in late eighteenth-century
Germany to find examples of firms which operated in the same
capitalist mode of production as French firms. But more communal
forms of industrial production and quite different concepts of
industrial capital survived until the late 1840s in Germany. Their
supersession by the newer concepts of industrial capitalism which
the new technologies demanded was astonishingly rapid. The
replacement of domestic spinning and weaving by factory processes
is not really to be compared to the replacement of the communal
forges in Germany by modern iron works because this replacement
not only took a longer time in the textile industries but where it
was successful it was often so because the domestic workers had
already been taken out of the more communal modes of production
by the capitalists who controlled their operations. In the textile

industries the concentration of labour into the factory was only the last stage in the introduction of capitalist methods of production; in the iron industry in Germany the transformation often took place in one giant bound of investment.

Journeying through the Duchy of Nassau in 1847, an English traveller, T. C. Banfield, excellently caught the spirit of the older form of organisation at the very moment when it was doomed to disappear.

'The furnace of Eiserfeld stands about a mile up the valley, on a site to which water has been led to drive the blast. The wheel is 24 feet high, and the furnace itself not much higher; but the latter stands in the centre of a large casting-house, which affords shelter in the inclement season to the numerous smelters and their gossiping neighbours. We have mentioned that each furnace is limited to a number of days. It is common for every man to manage his smelting during his own days in person. He has therefore two sheds, one for his ore, and another for his charcoal; . . . Here, then, through the long winter, unless frozen out by the intense cold of the season, the villagers sit breaking up their ore with hand-hammers, the never-failing pipe in their mouths, to light which frequent trips to the furnace below are necessary, and give an opportunity of relieving the tedium of their task with gossip. As each man's turn comes, he wheels his ore to the furnace-mouth under the superintendence of the "Hüttenmeister", an official elected by the shareholders, of whom the majority are usually villagers. The whole establishment becomes in some measure a portion of the village property; and the labourers, women, and all required beyond the actual shareholders, are taken from the inhabitants.'[6]

The analogy between such a blast-furnace and the older forms of coal-mining organisation is very strong. In mining enterprises the 'shares' were frequently held by each miner and did actually represent a physical share in the mine to the extent that it was mined for different periods of time by different groups of miners, the time varying with the size of their stake. In such a case the number of people amongst whom capital could be raised for further expansion was limited to those immediately concerned. In any case the ethos of such an operation was not an expansionist one, the operation was carried on to sustain a certain number of people with a modest income at no great risk. The Prussian mining administration, a highly qualified service, which was ultimately in charge of all mines

6 T. C. Banfield, *Industry of the Rhine*, series 2 (London, 1848), pp. 98-9.

in that country recognised no firms, but only the names of individual lessees of mining rights until the changes in mining law in the 1840s. The mining captain who directed operations in the mine was also a state official with loyalties both to the lessees and the state. Banfield estimated the output per man in German iron ore mines in 1842 at about 4 tons per year whereas in Britain it was 47 tons.

Such methods of organisation were unable to provide the capital required for new techniques. The puddling oven, the coke-smelting process, and deep mining demanded not only more capital but a new concept of capital. One further example of this fundamental change was in the organisation of shipping. Most German ships in the late eighteenth century were owned in the form of 'shares' in the cargo by a small group of shipping financiers. Often the captain was the biggest 'shareholder'. In the Baltic trade this form of organisation survived until the 1840s. At that time in Rostock a profit of 1 per cent per year, after the ship's mortgage debts had been paid, sufficed. No real risk was possible within such a framework, nor was any economic rationalisation likely. In fact it was precisely the growth of more rational, specialised shipping functions which caused the system to change. When the overseas, and particularly the transatlantic, trade of North Sea ports like Bremen and Hamburg began to develop it emerged as a much more specialised and strictly run affair than the general cargo carrying of the coastal or Baltic trades. The first liner service between Bremen and America began in 1826. By the 1840s such liners were making three regular transatlantic voyages a year. This strained the older forms of organisation beyond what they would bear. The final blow was delivered by the need to replace sailing boats with steamers on such runs.

In the 1850s a steamer had about twice the capacity of a transatlantic sailing boat and usually could make one more voyage in the year. It cost, however, the equivalent of about five first class sailing ships. On such routes competition was so keen that the shipowners of Bremen and Hamburg had to take the plunge and equip steamers although the economics of the decision scarcely suggested any clear advantage for the steamboat. In the Baltic trade where such factors did not apply the number of sailing boats continued to increase. Faced with so massive an investment decision the merchants of the Hanse towns had to combine in a new way. The Hamburg–America Line was founded in 1854 to begin steamer services and the Norddeutscher Lloyd founded for the same purpose in Bremen three years later. Such companies had little resemblance to earlier methods of shipping operation. The company raised its much larger capital by public subscription throughout the whole town and neighbourhood. The captain became merely an executive official running the ship. In Hamburg, where there were more foreign ships than Bremen, the companies even became coordinators and organisers of general shipping and trade movements rather than shipowners. In 1840 in Bremen a ship would be fitted out for 125,000 talers divided into twenty-five 5,000 taler shares which were traded only among a minority of the town's merchant group. The Norddeutscher Lloyd issued 30,000 100 taler shares to a much wider public on the capital market.

GOVERNMENT AND INDUSTRY

The capacity of industries to adapt to the new investment demands was also determined by changes in the law. One of the main rallying cries of the Prussian liberal reform movement had been the concept of *Gewerbefreiheit*, liberty of occupation. This was legally accorded in 1808 but only for textile and food industries and the fiscal regulations still often required a permit to produce and sell. The status of the guilds and corporations in Germany thenceforward was the subject of continual bitter argument until the great upsurge of industrial production outside their control in the 1850s made the argument less relevant. Of course where direct French rule had been in force before 1814 the closed corporations had been swept away, but in other states, Saxony and Pomerania for example, the peace treaties brought a more tightly restricted industrial governance than in the previous century. In Prussia the legislation of 1811 retained the corporations as autonomous institutions but the subsequent reaction tended once again to strengthen their organic connection with the state along eighteenth-century lines and to turn them at times into instruments of industrial control. The Bavarian law of 1825 permitted freedom of entry into all occupations but only after the entrepreneurs had satisfied the state and the police and had passed a means test. These restrictions were increased by the 1834 law limiting the number and type of new artisanal enterprises. The unwelcome increase of population in the Palatinate was attributed by the Bavarian government to the greater job opportunities which the earlier law had created.

In fact the greatest force behind these restrictive laws was invariably the artisans themselves. Threatened by new modes of production in foreign countries and threatened domestically by the rapid increase of population and the dismantling of the rigid social structure of the old régime, their reaction was to use every means to restrict entry into handicraft occupations. This they could do with great effect as in many states they had not been weakened by early events nor destroyed by the French Revolution like the French and Belgian guilds. In alliance with the deeply conservative absolute rulers of most states they were able to put up very substantial barriers to the spread of the new methods of industrial production into Germany. The liberal reformers, in whose ranks the major entrepreneurs were usually to be found, therefore concentrated their political energies on curbing the power of the guilds and creating both a less-supervised and controlled method of business foundation and a freer labour market. Generally speaking, for more than two decades after 1815 they had little success. Although the Württemberg laws of 1828 removed some of the more blatant restrictions on entry into trades and handicrafts they retained the corporations with great powers and, in answer to the complaints of the artisans, these powers were much increased by the law of 1836. There was no effective reduction of guild powers in Saxony until 1840 when the legal distinctions between rural and urban dwellers were removed. Means tests and certificates of good conduct were still required for all founders of enterprises. The General Industrial Ordinance of 1845 in Prussia abolished many special corporation privileges and did not make membership of guilds compulsory, but it did lay down very stringent tests for admission to a handicraft and it also retained the usual means test for the entrepreneur.

The liberal revolutions of 1848 saw earnest attempts in all the states to sweep away these restrictions. A large part of the time of the all-German parliament at Frankfurt-am-Main was taken up with preparing an all-German code of commercial law, with standardising weights and measures and with removing limitations on company foundation. At the same time the Artisans' Congress meeting in the same city was demanding exactly the opposite. In reality the revolutions had been made by artisans and peasants. The absolute governments had only to resign themselves to the final abolition of serfdom and they could return to power offering with one hand a programme of agricultural reform designed to pacify the peasantry and regain their loyalty and with the other hand a programme of restrictions on industry designed to meet the complaints of the artisans. The great economic changes of the 1850s in Germany were not in the least preceded by any liberal break-through in thought or legislation. On the contrary, they took place in a climate of opinion and under governments more repressive and restrictive than those which had been reinstated in 1815. Membership of some guilds in Prussia became compulsory. The Bavarian law of

1853 was more restrictive than that of 1834 and even stipulated minimum capital requirements for entry into trade and business. Almost everywhere state shops to purvey artisans' wares were developed and apprenticeships to trades became compulsory. The irony is that in a decade when governments interested in their own preservation tried to restrict industrial development and impose limitations on the pace of economic change the economy was completely altered from within by the fierce development in industries which were almost completely outside the control of the older corporations; a development which the governments concerned scarcely understood nor were prepared to cope with. So rapid was the change, in spite of the conservatism of government, that by the 1860s the debate over *Gewerbefreiheit* had more or less resolved itself. In 1860 Nassau reverted to the relatively liberal laws of 1819, Saxon regulations were relaxed in 1861, Württemberg established *Gewerbefreiheit* in 1862, Prussia laws were amended in the same direction in 1868 and 1869. These changes in the states' laws opened the way for legal concepts of business foundation such as joint-stock companies and limited liability which were only permissible by grant of the ruler in the first half of the century, where they existed at all. In this case it was certainly the pace of economic change which altered governmental attitudes, there was little direct encouragement from government for such economic development and much discouragement.

Some forms of state encouragement of industry did, however, persist from the previous century. The Saar coalmines which had been the pet 'manufacture' of the Dukes of Nassau-Saarbrücken passed under French control in the Napoleonic period and when the territory passed to Prussia they remained the property of the Prussian state. Similarly the blast-furnaces of Königshütte which Frederick II of Prussia had caused to be constructed on the remote Silesian border remained state property as did the nearby Malapane smelting works. Gun foundries like the Royal Berlin Foundry also were state property. Not only were the first Prussian blast-furnaces state property but so were the first puddling ovens used in Silesia, those at Rybnik. The basis of the states' interest in metallurgy was of course a military one. But since each state needed guns the foundries provided a firm basis for later private metallurgical developments. Bavaria, for example, owned the St Ingbert mines and foundries in the Palatinate, a works which was often in the forefront of technological change. Württemberg had eight metallurgical works and at one of them, Wasseralfingen, the famous metallurgist Faber du Faur conducted his experiments. Hanover owned six blast-furnaces. It is also interesting to note in the 1850s how many state officials appear among the founders of great enterprises. Often this was necessary to get the concession in the first place but an equally strong reason was the capacity to raise capital which such people had. In the earlier period the state even provided capital. In 1834 the government of Württemberg lent 10,000 talers free of interest to the firm of Merkel and Wolff to introduce the weaving of merino wool. Such methods were still not uncommon in Prussia in the 1830s.

The impact of classical liberal economic theory on Germany was by no means to destroy the mercantilistic attitudes of eighteenth-century governments. In less developed countries 'The Wealth of Nations' appeared to have a message very different from the message it had for Britain or France. It suggested a different path to economic development but did not weaken the prime importance of encouraging such development as a desirable goal. Mercantilist policy therefore changed in Germany from the rather unsophisticated policy of direct subsidisation of desirable 'manufactures' to a policy where the governments' role was seen as providing the necessary basis for development, the social overhead capital, as creating the right atmosphere and then as withdrawing from the arena. In early nineteenth-century Germany both the older and newer strains of mercantilist thought survived side by side in different states and even within the frontiers of the same state. When a Prussian state official like Peter Beuth encouraged the descendants of William Cockerill to leave Belgium and build spinning machinery in Prussia he was acting in the direct tradition of eighteenth-century German statesmen. When Stein began his reforms of the mining laws of the County of Mark and when von Vincke used government money to encourage the construction of roads in the Ruhr after 1815 they were the harbingers of a changed mercantilism, changed by the impact of liberal economic theory as it had evolved elsewhere. In fact von Vincke read Smith's work daily and he and his collaborators believed it to be the duty of the state to intervene in the economy not so much to promote development as to remove obstacles to development. The establishment of the Prussian tariff of 1818 by von Maassen and the first faltering steps towards the Zollverein also exemplified these newer modes of economic thought. This curious coexistence of different periods produced a situation in which the state governments were always more ready to help with capital, with equipment or with privileges than the government of France. Industrialists who did not rock the ship of state too-much expected help from the state and it was provided in many devious and complicated ways. For all the long triumphant history of entrepreneurial activity in Germany the beginnings of the industrial

O

revolution there also sounded the death knell for the concept of European industrialisation as an unaided breakthrough by the bourgeoisie. To successive industrialising countries the attitude taken by early nineteenth-century German governments seemed much more nearly in touch with economic realities than the rather idealised and frequently simplified model of what had happened in Britain or France which economists presented to them.

THE DEVELOPMENT OF FINANCIAL INSTITUTIONS

It is against this background that the development of the German banking system has to be seen, not as the sudden escape of bourgeois capitalism from the control of reactionary governments leading to a tremendous onward leap in the process of economic development, but as a perfectly normal evolution of a mode of thought and practice already created in the first decade of the century. What changed was not the supply of capital but the demand for it as the availability of resources and the scale of technology both changed.

There were throughout the period a much greater number of important enterprises under direct government control than in France or Belgium. The economic development of the Silesian coal and ore fields remained for a long time as tied to military considerations as it had been in the eighteenth century. Vast forest reserves remained the preserve of the Prussian state. Even coal reserves could be so allocated. The Saarbrücken railway, completed in 1852, was the first Prussian state railway. Indeed the ease with which the government of Prussia resumed control over railway construction in the 1860s is symptomatic of how different relations were. Even in 1866 the Prussian government rejected a plan to sell the Saar mines to a newly formed joint-stock company for a large sum of revenue.

Apart from providing capital directly in this way governments frequently participated in institutions whose aim was to facilitate development. When former Duke Frederick of Württemberg went into partnership with the court banker Kaulla in 1802, reserving half the capital to himself in the newly founded Königlicher Hofbank he was merely modernising the traditional court bank which looked after the private interest of the ruler. But as economic thought changed so did the activities of the bank. After 1835 it provided loans to cotton manufacturers and to a chemical works and in 1846 was represented in the founding of the Esslinger Maschinen-fabrik. The first example of a modern bank of issue in Germany was the Bayerische Hypotheken- und Wechselbank founded in Munich in 1835. Although a private company it was founded only under the strictest conditions imposed by the king, who, like his queen, was a substantial shareholder. It was the first private bank in Germany to issue shares and although its contacts with industry were negligible it served as the model for all subsequent German mortgage banks. Mortgages of this kind were in fact a frequent source of industrial capital in these early days. The Preussische Bank was created as a joint-stock company in 1846 out of the old Royal Bank of Prussia to serve as a bank of issue. Like its predecessor it was empowered to issue secured mortgages on very favourable terms (*Pfandbriefe*) to landowners. The original intention had been to preserve the nobility as the basic organisational unit of Prussian society but in the nineteenth century the issuing of such mortgages permitted many large landowners to play a very active part in industrial investment. In an area like Silesia, where the mercantile bourgeoisie was less developed than in the Rhineland, landowners like Count Andreas Renard, builder of a large rolling-mill, developing their own resources were often the driving force behind regional development. When peasants were freed from the old régime the landlords were also freed. In the Rhineland the bonds issued by the land bank to redeem feudal dues were sometimes invested directly in railway shares.

In addition to the existing banks and the numerous other sources of capital available there was also the possibility of financing extensions to the firm out of profits. In this respect the history of most German textile firms is like that of French firms. As in France textile firms were usually financed with as little as possible recourse to borrowing on the money market. However it was only in the very early stages of either the wool or the cotton industry that the weaving master could himself become an entrepreneur. J. A. Oberempt, who owned a cotton mill with 7,200 spindles at Rauendahl near Münster in 1843 had started life as a handworker. As the machinery increased in complexity and cost this became impossible. The more usual thing was for the putter-out, in those parts of Germany where he had existed, to become the manufacturer. Sometimes the traders themselves used their capital to control the manufacturing end. This was the history of the cotton spinning firm of Schmölder at Rheydt, whose founder was originally an importer of British yarn. Some entrepreneurs came from families which had been in the finishing trades for a long time, as, for instance, the founders of the firm of Ermen and Engels which began business in Barmen and Manchester in 1837.

To some extent this sort of process was also possible in the metallurgical industries. Many of the famous Berlin machine shops were started by men who had been handworkers, A. Borsig, F. A. Egells, J. F. L. Wöhlert and A. Hamann all started in this way. J. Freund had worked in the Berlin mint as a mechanic, C. J. Heckmann had been a coppersmith. This is one reason why these firms for so long often had a semi-handwork character. Most machine building at the start consisted of one-off jobs. Borsig had worked in Egells's shops and invested his savings in his own business. They were, however, less than one-eighth of the investment required, the rest came from a rentier and a court uniform maker. In these cases, too, in the earlier years, the entrepreneurs were not entirely unfriended. Hamann got a cheap loan from the Prussian government in 1845 to buy foreign machines which were indispensable. Hoppe was given two foreign machines by the government provided he used them to produce for five years after 1846. Siemens, who had been an army officer received a great deal of indirect help because his early electrical experiments were of military value. But the Berlin firms, although their early history is in some ways paralleled by the rise of the Rhineland steel firm of Krupp, were not the typical firm of the 1850s. That was rather the large bank of blast furnaces erected from scratch or the railway company or deep coal mine. All such investments were both sudden and heavy, making the gradual path of family and local capital accumulation out of the question.

Although changes in the law due to the activities of liberal reforms, or the direct desire of conservative governments to strengthen their economic position could each at times enable a firm to meet this situation most firms had to solve it without help of this kind. The agitation in the 1840s for note-issuing banks which could provide capital raised by their operations to firms, particularly railway companies, which needed it was sternly opposed by the Prussian government. The government was fearful of the loss of revenue from any infringement of its own minting rights, was afraid of the effect which financial speculation might have on the state finances and anxious lest investment in railways should divert investment from the land and drive down the value of estate mortgage bonds (*Pfandbriefe*). In 1846 the Royal Bank was converted into the Preussische Bank, a joint-stock company with private capital and the exclusive right of note issue but under strict government supervision demanding a most conservative policy. Until 1856 there was quite a low maximum limit on the permitted note issue. This was certainly in consonance with minting policy before 1846 for there had never been sufficient coinage and foreign monies of various kinds had circulated freely. Between 1850 and 1865 the total note circulation rose from 18,000,000 to 120,000,000 taler.

It cannot, however, be argued, on the other side, that this conservatism before 1856 was a real impediment to development. It is true that the bank's metal reserve which backed up the currency to one-half its value was higher than that of other note-issuing banks and that its loan policy was extremely cautious. It is also true that in an unsophisticated economy like Prussia industrial investment was more dependent on a note-issuing bank than in a country like France with a more developed money market. But Prussian industrialists got support from note-issuing banks in other states whose bank notes began to circulate in Prussia after 1850, and were in some years equal to the amount of Prussian banknotes in circulation, until they were banned in 1857. More importantly there sprang up outside the frontiers of Prussia after 1850 a network of large joint-stock banks, inspired by the boom and by the example of the Crédit Mobilier, who were directly and immediately interested in railway construction, mining and metallurgy. In addition the older private banks widened their range of interests beyond foreign exchange and government paper and also participated in the industrial boom. Where the boom took place in a rural area like the newer parts of the Ruhr coalfield local traders and merchants readily provided credit where banking institutions were lacking. By 1865 bank credits of this type were three times the value of the total note circulation. It may be said, therefore, that government policy made little difference either way to these events.

It is an exaggeration to claim that the rapid development of the German economy after 1850 could not have taken place without the growth of joint-stock banks. The history of many important and successful enterprises shows that such banks often served to provide capital only when no other of the available sources could be tapped. Such arguments put too much weight on what was after all only a mechanism. It is similarly an exaggeration to suggest that Germany was dependent on foreign capital in these years. There were numerous examples of important foreign investments in Germany between 1850 and 1870, some of them on a massive scale, and foreign capitalists and entrepreneurs were very ready to join in so great an investment boom. Important though their role often was it was less important than in the development of more backward lands, Norway, Russia or south-eastern Europe, for example, where they sometimes represented the only possible sources of capital and entrepreneurial knowledge. Nevertheless for two decades there was a very close connection between foreign capital, joint-stock investment banks and the industrial sectors, iron-manufacture and coal-mining, which were growing most rapidly. In part this represented the interest of businessmen in neighbouring areas in the discovery of new resources. French and Belgian coal companies followed the coal seams over the frontier to the Ruhr. French iron makers found better quality coking coal just across the German borders and railway prospectors and speculators from all western lands were obliged to plot the great European through routes over German soil. But the more important aspect was the sudden shift from a technology in which investment could be a matter of gradual accumulation to one in which this was impossible. In order to effect the vital technological changes some alteration in the method of making capital available was essential because in Germany these changes required a much more sudden input of large amounts of capital.

The development of the textile industries imposed very few demands on the German money market but that does not mean that until the 1850s there were no financial institutions capable of providing industrial credit. There were sufficient to meet the demand for such credit. Indeed it is an unfortunate tendency of much recent writing to suppose that the enormous increase in the rate of foundation of large industrial enterprises after 1852 was in some way a *result* of the development of new banking institutions in Germany. It would be much truer to consider these developments in banking as a *consequence* of changes in the demand for capital. The importance of the banking practices introduced by these banks has also been exaggerated. Essentially the so-called 'credit' or 'investment' banks did nothing new in the way of banking other than to take advantage of investment opportunities which had seldom existed for an earlier generation of banks. The difference lay in their organisational form, they were not private banks but banks constituted with some form of limited liability, and in the sources of their profit of which a much higher proportion was derived from company investment. In this way the changes in the organisation of banks simply mirrored the changes in the organisation of the firm. They took place at the same time and just as quickly. What can be said is that the response of the banks to this new demand was a very successful one.

As in France, private bankers before 1850 derived profits from handling government remittances and transfers of money and from foreign exchange transactions based on international trade. Frankfurt-am-Main was the greatest centre of such private banking activities, but every court city had facilities of this kind. Berlin, in particular, was well provided with bankers who from time to time before the 1840s were the source of working capital for the earlier Berlin industrialists. Mendelssohn and Co., Bleichröder, and Robert Warschauer all made occasional loans for such purposes. The origins of such banks were far removed from the world of nineteenth-century industry with which they struck up only a chance acquaintance before 1850. As the demand for capital shifted sharply upwards with the heavy investment requirements of the new iron works and coal mines of the 1850s a different type of banking institution emerged. The investment boom of that decade produced nationwide banks operating successfully on a large scale where previously only small and restricted banks had existed. The original ideas and techniques of such banks came from the example of the Crédit Mobilier in France. But the German banks, far from meeting the sad end of the Crédit Mobilier, soon developed into a powerful and coherent system. Their success can only be understood against the background of the economic and political unification of the country. The climate of investment changed in these years from a fearful concern with small local economies to a powerful and optimistic belief in the future of a great and rich country.

Although the private banks were mainly concerned with governmental and international transactions they were by no means hostile to industrial investment, often in the kind of highly-speculative enterprises which bankers in older developed lands shunned like the plague. The risky nature of such enterprises made the bank even more concerned with their management especially in the early stages of company foundation. The German banking system was in some ways a product of the less developed nature of the country and came into being to overcome certain structural problems in the economy which were less noticeable in France. It was a system suited to a different society and a different stage of technology, revealing the way in which essential differences in underdeveloped economies still persist and influence their structures even when development has taken place.

The share-issuing company with some form of limited liability appealing to a much wider range of capital holders became the basic organisational form of coal and iron companies and of banks only after 1850. Between 1850 and 1859 107 joint-stock companies were founded in Prussia, sixty-six of these were in the iron industry or in mining and fifteen in the chemical industry, mostly gasworks. Only ten were in the textile industries. In Saxony eighty-seven were founded in the same period, fifty-one were mining companies and twelve were gasworks. In spite of permitting so great an increase in the rate of foundation of such joint-stock companies (only thirty-seven had been founded between 1815 and 1850) the Prussian government set its face firmly against joint-stock banks which were both banks of issue and of credit. The most that could be permitted to banks wishing to issue shares to the public was the form of organisation known as *Kommanditgesellschaft*, the equivalent of the French *société en commandite* which had been partly responsible for Lafitte's downfall. Six such banks were founded in Prussia by 1857. The most important, the Diskontogesellschaft had some industrial enterprises of its own but foreign exchange was still responsible for 40 per cent of its annual turnover.

The joint-stock banks of this decade clustered near but outside the Prussian frontier. The Darmstädter Bank, founded in 1853, took its name from that small town because it could not be constituted in Prussia nor would the private bankers of Frankfurt-am-Main allow it to be founded in their city. Its founders, like those of the Crédit Mobilier, on which it was modelled and which provided the largest portion of the original capital, had been early railway promoters impressed with the enormous capacity of the railway for changing man's economic existence and also with the difficulty of raising the necessary capital to effect these changes. Abraham Oppenheim had been the main projector of the Cologne to Aachen railway in 1835, Gustav von Mevissen the co-founder of the bank, the first president of that railway. In his subsequent career von Mevissen resembled both in his ideas and activities a more cautious Isaac Péreire. His bank remained for several years a subsidiary of Péreire's bank with little independent existence. Other joint-stock credit banks of the same kind were sooner emancipated. The Schaffhausenscher Bankverein, reconstituted from an older bank in 1848, never quite had the scope of the Darmstädter Bank but the two together served as the inspirers of a large number of others founded before the close of 1856. The private bankers of Berlin combined to found the Berliner Handelsgesellschaft. One of their number, Bleichröder, helped to found the Waren Kredit Gesellschaft in the remote city of Königsberg (Kaliningrad). In Breslau (Wroclaw) the Schlesischer Bankverein was created, in Magdeburg the Handels Gesellschaft, in Leipzig the Allgemeine Kredit Anstalt. Only in Bavaria and Württemberg did royal governments refuse to amend either the law or administrative practice to permit such institutions. In Bavaria permission had to wait until the law on freedom of occupation in 1868.

It would be a mistake to suppose that all, or even a majority, of the joint-stock enterprises founded between 1850 and 1859 were dependent on credit banks of this kind. Nevertheless, even in a city like Berlin where the great firms like Borsig remained for the most part private companies a distinct change in financing was noticeable in this decade. The Diskontogesellschaft, known as a 'railway bank', financed extensions to Schwartzkopf's engineering works; the Berliner Handelsgesellschaft became involved in the early struggles of the electrical industry. Over the country as a whole the railways were the great attraction. The Schaffhausenscher Bankverein and the Darmstädter Bank jointly financed the Cologne–Bingen and the Cologne–Giessen lines. The Darmstädter Bank financed almost all the railways in Hesse and Thuringia. In 1856 15 per cent of the capital of the Diskontogesellschaft was in the line from Cassel to Oderberg. In the Rhineland and in Silesia coal mines were the biggest attraction. The deeper and larger mines of the 1850s, without which the Ruhr coalfield would not have been opened up, were heavily supported by the Rhineland branches of these banks.

Subsequently company law in Germany recognised the kind of connections that had grown up. The process of company foundation known legally as *simultane Gründung* involved the bank putting capital into the enterprise and then selling the shares off to the public over its counter when the enterprise was safely off the ground. Essentially this was what the 'investment banks' of the 1850s had introduced and what the Crédit Mobilier had been unable to introduce permanently into France. Legislation in Germany accepted the *fait accompli* and incorporated it into the legal system giving the banking system and company foundation there a different legal and institutional framework. It became common practice for members of the bank to sit on the *Aufsichtsrat*, the higher of the two boards of directors with which German companies were equipped, and, particularly in time of financial crisis, to influence the running policy of the firm. Not that the big firms were necessarily in the grip of the bankers, but that the day to day links between the world of bank capital and the world of industry, so difficult to forge in France, remained very strong in Germany. To some extent this was a consequence of 'backwardness', the banks having to fill the institutional gap which was filled in a more complicated way in the more developed economy of France. But it was even more a consequence of the particular industries and their technology which were the dynamic sectors in the German industrial revolution.

The extent to which banks of this kind drew upon foreign capital cannot be distinguished from the influx of foreign capital into Germany in these years through other channels. The proportion of foreign capital to total capital was greater in the leading sectors of the economy than in other sectors because it was precisely in these sectors that more gradual forms of capital accumulation were impossible. The first joint-stock mining company in the Ruhr was formed as early as 1838 by a group of French coal-owners from Valenciennes and Anzin whose rate of return was diminishing because of the increasingly difficult seams there. The Anglo–Belgian Düsseldorf Mining Company founded in 1847 was to become one of the biggest coal companies of the next decade. Belgian capital built the Eschweiler rolling-mills in 1841 and the first rolling-mills in Düsseldorf in 1842, in each case staffing the works with Belgian and French supervisors and managers and using the local population only as labour. One of the first firms to use Ruhr coke for smelting iron ore was the Borbeck works of the Belgian ironmaster Charles Détillieux. The first of the integrated coal and iron concerns, the Phoenix works at Ruhrort in 1852, was owned by Belgian and French capital. The greatest name in the development of deep coal mining in the Ruhr field in the 1850s was that of the Irish capitalist W. T. Mulvaney, later president of the Ruhr Coal Owners' Association. His two biggest mines, the Erin and the Shamrock, changed the whole scope of technical possibility by the speed with which they were dug. Germans were at first employed by him only as miners.

It is interesting to note that the supposition in most writing that foreign capital meant non-German capital has tended to cover up differences in capital availability between German states. In Prussia, on whose territory so many of the more important developments took place, capital for large investments was more difficult to get because the laws controlling the formation of joint-stock companies were stricter and relatively few of the banks of the 1850s had their headquarters in Prussia. But this may well not have been the only reason for the high volume of non-Prussian capital in Prussian companies, the fact that the state was less rich than some of the smaller states and that in many of its regions the bourgeoisie was less developed may also have played its part. More than one-third of the capital in Prussian joint-stock companies in the 1850s came from outside Prussia, the proportion being even higher in the iron industry. But in the textile industry, which had less recourse to the banking system, the proportion of non-Prussian capital in joint-stock companies was still one-quarter.

LABOUR SUPPLY

The origins of the labour force are partly discussed in the chapter on population. Internal migration, most usually over short distances combined with the high rate of natural increase seems to have prevented the scarcity of labour which was sometimes apparent in the early stages of the French industrial revolution. Although only a small part of the working population of the Ruhr came from any great distance those that did were crossing what were still formidable barriers of custom. In 1870 about 80 per cent of the population of the big towns now growing up on the coalfield had originated in the Rhineland or in Westphalia; only 2 per cent came from east of the Elbe. They came from handicraft industries and from the 'surplus' agricultural population but there is considerable evidence to show that for employment in factories workers who had previously been in an industrial situation were preferred to peasants. The number of coal miners employed in the Saarland increased from 2,489 in 1840 to 12,159 in 1860; the employers there always sought to attract miners from other areas rather than to take on untrained labour. Their efforts were not too successful and a very high proportion of the miners came from the nearby agricultural areas of the Hunsrück and the Eifel. Similarly in Silesia the main source of labour in the mines was the peasantry perhaps encouraged by the large surrenders of land which some of them were obliged to make by Prussian law. In Berlin the numbers of workmen from greater distances was higher. Even there however the biggest part of the migration into the city was from the poorest members of the rural community of Brandenburg. Few migrants came to Berlin from the western areas.

In one respect there was a shortage of labour, in those few industries where labour skills needed to be quite high. This applied above all to the electrical industry which in its early days almost solely recruited skilled labour. The industry employed only 400 in 1870 and was still completely dominated by the Siemens–Halske cable and dynamo works, but it existed only in Berlin and the first twenty years' history of the firm were a constant struggle to get an adequate labour force. Something of the same problem existed in machine-building. In the Berlin machine-building shops in 1850 82 per cent of the labour force had formerly been handicraftsmen. The trade from which they were mainly recruited was that of locksmith. The one firm's records which have survived from the 1840s indicate that one-half of its workers had previously been locksmiths. In the chemical industry the skilled workers came mostly from textile dyeing shops.

CONCLUSION

There were obvious weaknesses in Germany's economic position in 1870. The major industries were less sophisticated and less diversified than those of the other industrialised countries. Their sources of supply were more unsure for Germany did not have the world empire of her European rivals and the domestic raw material base was already inadequate to sustain the developments which had taken place. In the late 1860s German ironmasters began to run into serious difficulties as domestic ore proved inadequate and British pig iron was increasingly imported and production costs for iron manufactures became significantly higher than in Britain. Absence of empire also meant absence of international trading connections. German industrialisation had been more dependent on the domestic market than the industrialisation of France or Britain and such development had its own inherent limitations which were to be made very clear in the catastrophic slump of 1873. Raw materials accounted for 62·5 per cent of all imports in 1869 and raw materials for the textile industries alone accounted for 31 per cent. Finished textile goods accounted for 35 per cent of all exports. After 1853 Germany became a net iron exporter and coal exports also began in the 1850s. But for iron and coal the domestic market still retained a decisive importance. Observers elsewhere saw the speed of economic development in Germany and drew from it optimistic conclusions for other economies with similar disadvantages. And yet, for the more observant, the German experience contained some quite different, and certainly less optimistic lessons.

The proportion of registered handicraft workers in Prussia according to official tables, increased from 11·6 per cent of the population in 1816 to 14·9 per cent in 1861 – their total number by about 130 per cent. There were great differences between trades but the pressure to get such employment was high and the standard of living of the workers in it low. As population grew agriculture did not provide sufficient new employment. The movement from the land, particularly from the increasingly sub-divided farms of the south-west, into handicraft occupations gave a hungry urgency, far more cogent than the philosophical attitudes of legislators, to the battle for *Gewerbefreiheit* before 1840. In the ensuing period of rapid industrial growth the guild members carried on a bitter agitation against the same concept of liberty of occupation. Employment in handicrafts continued to grow in Germany as it dwindled away in France and even in those handicraft occupations which were least well equipped to compete with the new technology. Hand-loom weavers and even hand-spinners still clung tenaciously to their existence in 1870. Two-thirds of the cotton weavers in 1875 were still hand-loom weavers. Rural domestic industries such as clock making, wood carving and toy manufacture continued to grow until 1870 as a source of employment. Even in 1900 20,000 people were still employed in the Erzgebirge in making wooden toys. It only remains to consider what might have happened had Germans not been able to emigrate in such massive numbers throughout the century to the United States. Like the battle of Waterloo the industrialisation of Germany was in many ways 'a damned close-run thing'.

One further remark may be made about the social system thus produced. The opposition to the forces of liberal capitalism retained great strength in Germany because those older forms of opposition which died out in Britain, France and Belgium, were still very strong in Germany when workmens' movements with a distinct socialist philosophy first began to show some strength. A landed nobility, who in some eastern regions retained the economic power they had had in the eighteenth century, a guild organisation backed by large numbers of craftsmen, a numerous and well-established peasantry, all were still powerful forces in German society in 1870. Their survival after that date was to create a distinctly different society in Germany, one which politically and economically constantly sought for compromises with the forces of capitalist development in order to preserve itself. It survived only by a series of social and economic balancing acts and although it achieved the material prosperity of other industrialised societies and in technological development surpassed them, the complicated social problems which were the result of so rapid an industrialisation were not to be resolved for another seventy-five years after two ghastly wars and several revolutions.

SUGGESTED READING

Very little work has been published in English on the economic history of Germany in this period. There is an excellent, but very short, summary in K. BORCHARDT, *The Industrial Revolution in Germany 1700–1914*, Fontana Economic History of Europe, vol. 4, section 4 (London, 1972). D. S. LANDES, *The Unbound Prometheus* (Cambridge, 1969) has a good account of technological change. W. O. HENDERSON, *The State and the Industrial Revolution in Prussia 1740–1870* (Liverpool, 1958) contains a lot of useful factual information, and there is some more in the same author's, *The Industrial Revolution in Europe* (London, 1961). T. S. HAMEROW, *Restoration, Revolution, Reaction, Economics and Politics in*

Germany 1815-71 (Princeton, 1958) is a lively essay on the political and social changes of the period in relation to economic development but does not venture very far into economic history.

On more specialised topics there are also a few works in English. R. TILLY, *Financial Institutions and Industrialisation in the Rhineland 1815-1870* (Madison, 1966) is scholarly but not very wide-ranging. There are two rather old-fashioned studies of the Zollverein both of which are confined to the history of its formation and do not really deal with the economic questions involved. They are W. O. HENDERSON, *The Zollverein* (Cambridge, 1939) and A. H. PRICE, *The Evolution of the Zollverein* (Ann Arbor, 1949). To supplement them there is an article by W. FISCHER, 'The German Zollverein: a case study in customs union' in *Kyklos*, vol. 13, 1960. A work on geography, N. J. G. POUNDS, *The Ruhr: a Study in Rural and Economic Geography* (London, 1952), contains some information on the economic development of that region. Two articles discuss rather wider issues. They are, R. CAMERON, 'Some French contributions to the industrial development of Germany' in the *Journal of Economic History*, vol. 16, 1956 and N. J. G. POUNDS, 'Economic growth in Germany' in H. G. J. AITKEN (ed.), *The State and Economic Growth* (New York, 1959).

The available literature in English will not adequately take the discussion beyond our chapter itself although it does occasionally present a different point of view or some more factual information. To progress beyond our own analysis here there is no alternative to the literature in German, which is far more rewarding. A fairly recent bibliography of it may be found in W. TREUE, 'Wirtschafts- und Sozialgeschichte Deutschlands im neunzehnten Jahrhundert' which is a section of B. GEBHARDT, *Handbuch der deutschen Geschichte*, vol. 3, eighth edition (Stuttgart, 1962). It is very difficult, and also a bit unfair, to single out any particular items. Much the best general economic history of Germany for the period is H. MOTTEK, *Wirtschaftsgeschichte Deutschlands. Ein Grundriss*, vol. 2, *Von der Zeit der französischen Revolution bis zur Zeit der Bismarckschen Reichsgründung* (Berlin, 1964). A work which, while not a general economic history, covers several important themes is H. MOTTEK, H. BLUMBERG, H. WUTZMER and W. BECKER, *Studien zur Geschichte der industriellen Revolution in Deutschland* (Berlin, 1960). H. BLUMBERG, *Die deutsche Textilindustrie in der industriellen Revolution* (Berlin, 1965) is an important contribution to the role of textile industries in industrialisation in general. The relationship of government to economic development is better handled in W. FISCHER, *Der Staat und die Anfänge der Industrialisierung in Baden 1800-50*, vol. 1, *Die staatliche Gewerbepolitik* (Berlin, 1962) than in the literature in English. An older work in another language, P. BENAERTS, *Les Origines de la grande industrie allemande* (Paris, 1933) shows how long a good book of fine scholarship can be useful, important and pleasing. Most research on German economic history appears in a number of specialised journals which also carry book reviews and guides to the available literature. The more important of them are, *Vierteljahrschrift für Sozial- und Wirtschaftsgeschichte, Jahrbücher für Nationalökonomie und Statistik,*

Jahrbuch für Wirtschaftsgeschichte, Kyklos and *Tradition.* There are occasional and haphazard surveys of some of the latest books on the subject in *Economic History Review* and from time to time research appears in other journals.

Chapter 7

The Economic Development of Belgium and Switzerland in the Early Nineteenth Century

THE SIMILARITIES IN THEIR DEVELOPMENT

In Chapter 3 we discussed the great importance for western European industrialisation of the French Revolution and the Empire which succeeded it. This reconstruction of the continent and the changes which it brought about both in political boundaries and the structure of society did not only have important economic effects on France itself but also on France's neighbours. In two of these especially it was a period of intense economic development which was based on the protection of the European market from British competition. The Austrian Netherlands, after 1830 to emerge as the kingdom of Belgium, were actually incorporated into the French Empire and given access free of tariffs to the French market itself. In Chapter 3 we discussed the consequences of this. The availability of so large a market brought about an industrial revolution in those provinces of very much the same kind as that which occurred in France. In Switzerland it was the effects of protection which were more important than sudden access to a larger market and the 'continental

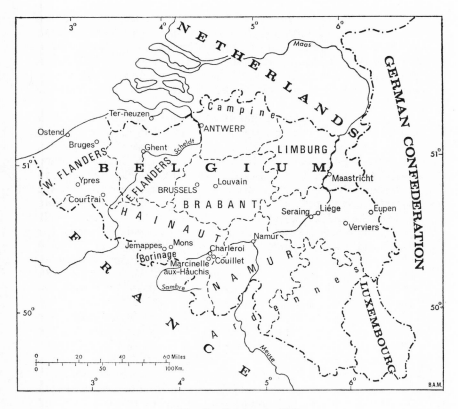

Map 7.   Belgium in 1848

system' provided the framework for a similar industrial revolution based on the mechanisation of cotton spinning. To fully understand the economic development of western Europe it is useful to follow the history of what happened to these two areas after 1814 when the French Empire collapsed and they were again subjected to a far more vigorous and massive British competition than that of the eighteenth century.

This question is the more important because it reveals the peculiar problems of economic development in such small economies. Once divorced from France and French policy they were to discover that the market on which they had relied was to be closed to them irrespective of political sympathy, for France was well enough endowed with natural resources and had a large enough domestic market to rely on protection as a defence against British competition. By 1818 she had already erected a formidable tariff barrier not only against the renewed flood of British goods but against those of her neighbours also. A comprehensively prohibitive tariff of this kind offered few possibilities to countries like Belgium or Switzerland. The association of nationalist sentiment with the idea of a well-defined national frontier and a protectionist tariff, an association very much strengthened by the growth of British economic and political power, threatened the very existence of countries like Belgium and Switzerland. Neither could lay claim to the kind of cultural and linguistic unity on which most European nationalist movements were based and as a consequence the concept of a national frontier marking the bounds of 'a national economy' in the sense in which an economist like List used the phrase in relation to German national aspirations had no great relevance to them. Furthermore, the economy of both depended very much on the fact that they both lay across major international trade routes between the greater European economies. Belgium lay across the trade route between Britain and the mainland and Switzerland across that between Germany and Italy and between the Rhineland and south-eastern Europe. The free flow of this international transit trade was so important to them as to add greatly to the other obstacles to raising a tariff on the frontier. In addition their own resource endowment was so small as to offer them no real hope of development in a Europe consisting of competing 'national economies'. The reorganisation of Europe in 1815, the definition of national frontiers and the movement towards nationalism and protection raised the question, not merely of whether the development of the Belgian and Swiss economies which had taken place under the continental system would continue, but even of whether it would survive.

Their development was completely dominated by their size, which gave them both opportunities and disadvantages which did not apply to the larger powers. They were the first of the small European economies to develop and their development was directly contingent on the same process in the larger economies with which they were in contact. Their history throws a rather different light on the development problems we have been considering so far and is of great relevance to an understanding of the industrialisation of western Europe as an area.

Unfortunately, because their development was so early there is an almost complete lack of the statistical information which with other economies allows us to erect a good chronological framework of the timing and dimensions of economic growth. This difficulty is made worse by the relative lack of historical research into their economies, particularly into that of Switzerland. The economic history of both countries raises a lot of interesting questions to which the only fair answer at the moment is 'we do not know'. Some of these questions are also brought into the open by the economic development of Scandinavia which took place much later and about which rather more precise information is available. What follows should therefore be seen as an attempt to meet as far as possible the reader's curiosity and perhaps to stimulate it further.

There are other factors which both economies had in common apart from their smallness, the timing of economic development there and their international situation. But these factors also point up the way in which, more than any other European countries, their development was inescapably bound up with the overall problem of the organisation of Europe as a continent. Problems of frontiers and tariffs lay at the heart of their existence as independent political units. Their geographical situation was such that when they embarked on programmes of railway building, their railways were just as important for the international connections which they made as for the domestic routes which they took. A second point, which is obviously related, is the extreme importance of foreign trade in their economies. In the early stages of economic development export possibilities, whether seized by the initiative of Swiss or Belgian entrepreneurs or presented by the process of development elsewhere, had an extraordinary influence on the nature and timing of that development.

None of this should be taken as playing down the singularities of the national economic history of these countries or the domestic forces which made for development. Another factor which applied to both economies points this up. The nexus of feudal social arrangements in the agricultural sector was of much less importance than in most other economies and this meant not only that there were less barriers to social mobility and to occupational change but also that agriculture was able to adapt itself very quickly to the changes that had to take place if the economy was to seize the few international opportunities it had. A highly-specialised agriculture developed in both economies at an early stage and in spite of increasing population, or urbanisation, and of industrialisation, the agricultural sector made a substantial contribution to feeding the population and also managed to seize certain limited export opportunities. Although we have no information on the trade balances in this period it is clear that these small agricultural exports were of great significance in permitting larger imports of raw materials.

In Switzerland the feudal ties had decayed very early, partly because of the very small amount of arable farming that had gone on there and partly because of the curious nature of the body politic. The very sparse population of the mountain cantons had always lived as much by trade and by hiring themselves out as soldiery as by agriculture. In the cantons where there was more arable land the countryside had tended to be dominated by the nearest powerful town and its governing bodies. The governance of the city fathers of a community like Zürich, Basel, Bern, or Schaffhausen replaced the rule of a feudal superior. This combination of political and geographical factors left the Swiss rural dwellers in a relatively freer situation than in most other parts of Europe. In Belgium the work of demolishing the feudal ties was a more violent affair completed by the invasion and occupation by the French revolutionary armies. As in France the peasants had already in many cases acquired a virtual title to their land and the eruption of the Revolution gave them that title unencumbered by feudal dues and payments. But, unlike their French cousins, the Belgian peasants had not fought for this outcome and this very fact had an important bearing on their subsequent attitudes. Yet it should also be borne in mind that in each country the rural classes were poor, divided amongst themselves and ignorant and there was no attempt to change this (as there was for example in Denmark). The disappearance of the feudal nexus only provided the possibility of response to particular opportunities; in itself it achieved nothing further. Most of the agricultural changes in these countries were induced subsequently by changes in industry and trade.

BELGIUM

– The General Problem of its Development

In one respect it is much easier to understand the domestic development of the Belgian economy than that of Switzerland for Belgium
was endowed with certain resources which were particularly useful
for early nineteenth-century industrial technology. There were *Coal*
extensive and easily-mined coal reserves and coal was cheaper at
the Belgian pit-head than anywhere else on the mainland until the *iron*
middle of the nineteenth century. In addition there were reserves of
iron ore, which, though not very extensive, were of the right quality
for use in the newer iron manufacturing processes. Industrial
manufacturing costs therefore were often lower in Belgium than
elsewhere on the mainland. But in so small an economy with so
restricted a domestic market this factor was of much more limited
importance than it would have been in an economy like that of
France. In order for Belgium to reap full advantage from her
favourable resource endowment there had to be important changes
in her international situation and significant economic development
elsewhere. Until this occurred the main importance of Belgium's
cheap coal was that it provided a raw material export being sent in
increasing quantities to France and to the United Netherlands. And
until 1815 the main thrust to industrialisation was provided by water-
powered textile industries, using in some cases imported raw materials.

   The connections between France and the former Austrian Netherlands had become so strong that the great powers refused to create
an independent state of Belgium after Napoleon's defeat lest it
should be merely a French puppet state. They therefore created a
joint monarchy out of the United Provinces of the Netherlands in
the north and the former Austrian provinces and Liége in the south.
Had that union been a true union many of the problems we are
considering here might never have arisen. But in fact it was a
failure in the political, economic and social dimensions. The two
societies had separate economic interests and a separate political
tradition. There was not even a satisfactory monetary union between
the two halves of the country and in 1830 the southern provinces
asserted their independence and were formed by the great powers
into the neutral monarchy of Belgium. Although the division between
the two areas had its origins only in the military frontier against
the Spanish created during the Dutch wars of independence in the
sixteenth century the course of history since then had driven them
far apart.

Nothing had done more to create this gap than the completely different economic experience of the two areas after their separation. The independent Dutch provinces, the United Netherlands, had become one of the world's richest mercantile societies. The events of their long struggle for independence and the facts of their geographical situation eroded the economic and social structure of the old régime more completely than anywhere else in Europe. It remains one of the unexplained mysteries of economic history why this society, blessed with practically every advantage which modern scholars have considered either necessary or useful for economic development, with the exception of a supply of cheap coal, developed more and more slowly in the eighteenth century. Some scholars have argued that this was merely a function of its size and that the greater resources of states like France and Britain were bound to outdistance the Netherlands. But when all is said and done the imperfect measurements of development which can be made do indicate that the general impression of economic stagnation there in the eighteenth century is not a false one. What most confirms this is that the United Provinces, which became after 1830 the Kingdom of the Netherlands, remained for a long time a small unindustrialised island in the midst of the most industrialised areas of the world, while the southern provinces, whose economic experience had been very discouraging before the late eighteenth century, experienced the full force of rapid industrialisation and economic development.

When the northern provinces of the Netherlands had grown richer the southern provinces had fallen into deep decay, their mediaeval splendour quite forgotten, their trade and industry insignificant. But in the late eighteenth century, as the dynamic colonial and maritime expansion of the northern provinces slowed, the spread of manufacturing into the countryside became a noticeable feature of the economy of the southern provinces. The early industrial changes which led directly to the industrial revolution occurred not in the developed north but in the less developed south. One difference from the eighteenth century developments in France or Britain was that rural domestic industry in Belgium showed a greater disposition towards metal working although rural textile manufacture was also growing in importance. The relatively greater employment in metal working is probably to be explained by the accessibility of cheap coal and ores.

The speeding-up of these developments during the period of the French Empire coincided with a deepening economic depression in the northern Netherlands whose enmity with Britain cut them off from their empire and their world commerce. It was therefore a country embarked on an industrial revolution which was torn from the French Empire and coupled with a state in which none of these changes had taken place, and a country whose economic development had been stimulated by the opening of a wide European market which was coupled with a declining colonial and imperial power. The effects on the expanding Belgian textile industries were very severe.

The cotton spinners of Ghent who had reached high levels of prosperity during the French period were selling their machines at knock-down prices by 1817 to equip spinning mills in northern France and closing down their own operations. After 1815 the leading sector of Belgian industry ceased to be the textile industry. Access to the Dutch colonial market did permit a partial recovery but further mechanisation never had the dynamic urgency it had had before 1815. Eventually the leading sector of Belgian industry became the iron and metallurgical industries. The widespread development of armaments manufacture and of nail-making around Charleroi and Liége provided the basis and the coal-mining boom induced by the Empire and the continental system gave Belgian ironmasters a plentiful supply of cheap coking coal. But the domestic market for the industry's product was necessarily very restricted and by their very nature iron products were more costly and more difficult to sell abroad than textiles. There are unfortunately no reliable general economic statistics for Belgium in this period but the metallurgical industries seem to have been the biggest source of industrial employment after 1820 and were clearly so by the time the first census of industrial employment was taken.

One immediate consequence of this shift from textiles was that Belgium's exports were confined to those countries which were immediately adjacent. Coal and iron goods could not economically be transported very far and apart from the Dutch colonial trade, which fell to a very low level with independence in 1830, textile manufacturers were never able to compete on foreign markets with British goods. Belgium had practically no mercantile marine nor consular services and complaints were rife all through the nineteenth century that her exports were carried by her rivals. Only 1·6 per cent by value of Belgian exports went to the United States in 1841–5. The attempt to open a regular transatlantic liner service in 1841 with two second-hand British ships was a miserable failure. In the 1840s the countries bordering on Belgium took nine-tenths of her exports and provided two-thirds of her imports. The later acquisition of an African empire and the growth of exports to the United States to the level of about 4 per cent of the total did not substantially alter the fact that Belgium's only chance of breaking the bounds of her very small domestic market depended on exporting to the immediately surrounding areas of Europe. Her industrialisation was in many ways an aspect of the industrialisation of northern France and the Rhineland. The development of these areas provided her with two important export trades, the export of coal to northern France and the export of metals, and metal-manufactures and machinery to western Europe in general.

The coal export to France had become so vital to northern French manufacturers that Belgian coals were allowed in tariff free to some and at low tariffs to other frontier zones. But in all other respects the French market was protected against Belgium. Fortunately the Prussian tariffs were relatively low and they and the later Zollverein tariffs allowed scope for Belgian exports to the Rhineland. King William I tried to remedy the Belgian manufacturers' situation after 1815 by every known mercantilist device short of a protective tariff, which would have been against the interest of his Dutch subjects and which might have been of only temporary benefit to Belgian textile interests. Instead the Ghent cotton manufacturers were given subsidies and special export facilities and privileges in the Dutch Empire. This wholesale mercantilism was applied to all other Belgian industries by a set of regulations reminiscent of small German states in the eighteenth century and whose purpose was to force domestic consumers in the new country to consume Belgian products as far as possible. Major iron works such as that of Cockerill at Seraing near Liége had extensive defence contracts, and state employees and organisations had to use domestically-produced shirts.

All these efforts again collapsed with independence and after 1830 Belgian industry once more suffered a catastrophic slump as it had after 1814. Between 1831 and 1835 the number of cotton spindles in Ghent fell by a third. The iron works and machine shops at Seraing, the greatest on the European mainland, were practically closed in 1831 and 1832, their labour force dispersed throughout the countryside. It was the recovery of the now much smaller domestic market inspired by the government's decision in 1834 to build a railway network which restored the economy. But this very decision again called into question Belgium's international status. Negotiations for a customs union with France were begun in 1836 but as Belgian rail-making capacity became a greater threat to French manufacturers they ran into opposition in France. Negotiations were finally broken off in 1842 when the British government declared that such a union would be an infringement of Belgian neutrality. In the meantime business interests in Belgium had come to see their economic future as more closely tied to the Rhineland.

The Zollverein had a lower tariff than France and the Belgian railway system had been deliberately constructed to capture the transit trade between the Rhineland and the coast for the Belgian port of Antwerp and to divert it from the river itself and Dutch control. The Duchy of Luxembourg joined the Zollverein in 1842 but the French forbade Belgium to join in 1844. As compensation Belgium signed a trade treaty with the Zollverein which gave tariff reductions on Belgian iron exports. This treaty was subsequently elaborated into agreements with Britain, France and the Zollverein. Until the construction of a European railway network and the lowering of tariffs in the 1860s Belgium's trade problems were always critical. Had the Zollverein tariffs been as high as the French Belgium's development might have been even more erratic than it was.

– Development of Belgian Industry

Trade difficulties were alleviated by her geographical position which assured her of some of the growing trade between Britain and Germany. From the time when the French occupation freed the mouth of the river Scheldt and liberated the seaway into Antwerp from Dutch control the port began to take trade destined for Germany away from Rotterdam and Amsterdam. The Dutch levied tolls on the river until 1863 but the Belgian government refunded them to all but the Dutch. A determined policy of road and canal building strengthened the natural geographical links with the developing parts of Europe. The turnpike gates which had been abolished by the French were re-established in 1814 and the funds were used to extend the road network by a quarter by 1830. By 1850 it had again doubled in length. The canal from Charleroi to Brussels, which would bring Charleroi coals to the capital, was begun in 1827 as part of William I's grand designs. In the same year the new canal from Ghent to the sea at Terneuzen was completed. By 1830 there were already 1600 kilometres of navigable waterway of which 450 kilometres were canals. After 1843 a canal which traversed the whole country from Maastricht to Antwerp, linking the Meuse to the Scheldt and opening up the sterile lands of the Campine was constructed. It was completed in 1856. By this time Liége had been linked to Maastricht by the Meuse lateral canal. The dense population, the relative nearness to each other of the towns, and the heavy coal and iron traffic made such canal construction a profitable venture. In ratio to its surface area Belgium had proportionately about three times the length of road and navigable waterway of Britain in 1850 and about four times that of France.

But the readiness of investors to form turnpike and canal companies was not mirrored by their readiness to invest in railways, for these hinged more on international politics. Indeed the significant thing about the construction of railways in Belgium was not their national routes but their international connections, because it was the latter which had to determine the former. In no other European country did railway building have such specific and such well thought out aims before 1850. The construction of the Belgian railway system was a deliberate attempt to give Belgian manufacturers easier access, after the revolution of 1830, to a neighbouring European market to compensate them for exclusion from the Dutch empire and also to give the iron industry a bigger domestic market. At the same time it was also conditioned by the race to construct the first railway from the low countries to the Rhine and by connecting Antwerp directly to Cologne to take more trade away from Rotterdam and the Netherlands. The government was forced in 1834 to accept the logic of its own decisions and itself to bear the cost of constructing a line from Antwerp to the German frontier through Brussels and Liége and another north–south line to intersect it. The early start to main line railway building on a large scale and its planned nature therefore owed everything to political decisions. By 1840 Belgium had 334 kilometres of railway open. By 1860 when 1,730 kilometres were open to traffic the system was comparable in total length to that of Russia or Spain and it continued to grow until 1880 when it stabilised itself at a length of just over 4 million kilometres. By this time it was the densest national railway network in the world and every part of the country was served by a nearby railway line. After 1880 there took place a most remarkable proliferation of 'light' railways, sub-standard lines built cheaply for the carriage of workmen and agricultural produce. Such lines were encouraged by legislation in 1884 and 1885 which allowed generous terms to private companies constructing them. In 1907 there was just under one kilometre of railway in Belgium for every 3 square kilometres of territory. The comparable ratio for Britain was less than 1:4, for Germany 1:6 and for France only 1:8. In a country where the difficulties of internal transport were already rather less than in France or Germany such a development was very remarkable. By the 1840s it was reflecting the profitability of construction rather than government decisions because in that decade private entrepreneurs promoted and completed most of the companies and the government's role became smaller. Coal, as everywhere, was a very profitable freight, but whatever the reasons for the success of railway construction in Belgium, its effects on the iron industry, and thus on the industrial economy of the whole country, were immediate. Indeed, without the courageous decision to build a railway network, however politically inspired, Belgium may have continued in the relative stagnation of the post-1815 period.

Where French and German iron masters had good reasons for persevering with the older technologies, in Belgium there was every reason to convert to the new iron technology as soon as possible. Iron rail was the basic product of most of the big new Belgian forges after 1834. Coking coal was available and the sudden surge of internal demand meant that Belgium developed a modern iron industry whose products were cheaper than those of the French ironmasters even though the French had begun their experiments with puddling and coke-smelting much earlier. It is hardly likely that such an industry could have developed purely for export. Bairoch's calculations indicate that *per capita* production of pig iron in Belgium in 1840 was twice as high as in France and was exceeded on the continent only in Sweden. It was over four times as great as in Germany. By 1860 it was greater than in Sweden. *Per capita* coal consumption after 1840 was also higher than in any other economy on the continent.[1]

The introduction of both puddling and coke-smelting in fact preceded railway building. Paul Huart-Chapel set up a puddling furnace at Charleroi in 1821 and in the next year at Marcinelle-aux-Hauchis there were several in operation. Coke-smelting was used in the Charleroi area as early as 1823 but does not seem to have been really successful there until 1828. If that is so it makes the history of the Cockerill works at Seraing in the 1820s even more important. John and James Cockerill, sons of William Cockerill who had done so much to establish the woollen industry in Verviers, were provided with a government loan in 1821 to set up a modern iron works in the former bishop's palace at Seraing near Liége. This was not the only example of the property of the dispossessed church providing useful factory buildings. In its origins it was no more than a small part of William I's general determination to encourage Belgian industry. But the first coke-smelting blast furnaces were built there in 1823 and by 1825 the works already employed 2,000 people. The whole complex of ironworks, rolling and slitting mills, machine factories and a steamship building yard quickly became the industrial wonder of Europe. This degree of integration was not unique in the 1820s. The Couvin iron works built by

[1] P. Bairoch, 'Niveaux du développement économique', *Annales*, vol. 20. pp. 1104, 1107.

Hanonnet-Gendarme in 1826 was also subsidised initially to use the coke-smelting process and the works at Marcinelle had almost as complete a range of activities as Seraing.

Concerns of this kind did not aim to satisfy domestic iron demand completely but used British iron even for their own products when higher grades were required. In fact there seems to have been, in contrast to France, no increase in the output of charcoal-smelted iron after 1815, the output remaining stable at about 55,000 tons. By 1830 there were in addition about 10 coke blast-furnaces with a production capacity of about 20,000 tons. Whether this capacity was fully utilised is doubtful. Certainly the same difficulties which beset the more adventurous French ironmasters were also present in Belgium and were made far more acute by the political crisis. The Marcinelle works was taken over by the Paris banker Jacques Lafitte and the Belgian financier Fontaine-Spitaëls in 1828. Like the Seraing works it was practically closed down by the end of 1830. Part of the Cockerill works was mortgaged to the government as an additional subsidy in 1829 and under the terms of another arrangement with the royal government half its capacity was to be used for defence contracts.

The confirmation of these difficulties may lie in the relative absence of further technological change until 1835. In that year the Seraing works made the first railway locomotive in Belgium, the Providence ironworks in Charleroi was built with new coke-smelting furnaces, new and much larger rolling mills were constructed at Couillet by a British engineer, and the Marcinelle works was converted into a joint-stock company to increase its capacity. In the following two years the entrepreneurs who had founded the iron works of the 1820s were driven into the capital market for the same reason. By 1841 the amalgamated iron works at Marcinelle and Couillet was probably the biggest iron works on the mainland. In 1845 its output of rail reached 30,000 tons. In 1842 the Seraing works signed a contract to export 7,000 tons of rail to Bavaria. Charcoal smelting had disappeared for all practical purposes by 1851.

The growth of the iron industry is reflected also in the development of machine manufacture. Between 1830 and 1838 there was a sharp rise of imports of machines into Belgium but after that date Belgium's machine exports began to gain until by 1850 they were twelve times the value of her machine imports. Steam engine building developed early; Cockerill built his first steam engine at Seraing in 1818; by 1830 he had built a further 201, which was roughly the equivalent of the number employed in all Belgian coal mines at the same date. In the 1830s the growth of important textile machinery manufacturers like the Phoenix works at Ghent, and the firm of

Houget and Teston, which supplied the best woollen machinery in Europe, was also helped by government subsidies and other encouragements. As far as can be established the price of iron to machine builders was much lower in Belgium than in France after 1835 and certainly the price of iron rail was much lower.

The textile industries by contrast never had the same potentiality for rapid expansion. The foundation of the Société de Commerce des Pays-Bas in 1824 was intended to provide government capital and trading privileges to the Ghent cotton manufacturers so that they might revive their industry by exporting to the Dutch East Indies. They also received government subsidies from the customs revenue as a substitute for a higher tariff. Some estimates suggest that about 60 per cent of the cottons made in Ghent were exported in the 1820s. Yet it is clear that this attempt to reorientate Belgian cotton exports was only a very limited success. The production of cotton yarn had been 693,000 kilograms in 1810. In 1817 it had fallen to 374,134 kilograms, by 1826 it was 1,719,600 kilograms and in 1833 2,700,000. The number of mechanised spindles rose from 128,658 in 1810 to 300,000 in 1829. Comparison with the rate of increase of output of French and British cotton goods shows to what extent Belgium suffered from her exclusion from European markets and that the Java market did not provide the same potential for export growth. It was equally important that the type of cloth manufactured had to be quite different. The colonial market demanded the coarser cottons and concentrating on it so exclusively deprived the Ghent manufacturers of any possibility of manufacturing the finer grades which were responsible for the lasting success over the same period of the cotton manufacturers of Alsace or Switzerland. And after their concentration on Java they were again excluded from that market with the Belgian revolution and confined to their own domestic market, already thoroughly permeated by British competition. Nor did the monopoly privileges of the Java trade even prove properly effective against British competition because the trading system itself, shipping out goods in single large convoys, was too inflexible and rather reminiscent of the failing colonial trading system of eighteenth-century Spain. Imports of British cotton yarn into Belgium grew more rapidly than Belgian yarn output. At 200,000 kilograms in 1817 they were lower than Belgian output, at 3,100,000 kilograms in 1829 they had become much greater. The expansion of the Belgian cotton industry after 1830 was determined by the expansion of the domestic market and reflects the growth of incomes in that market brought about by economic development. In 1832 87 per cent of Belgian cotton cloth production was consumed internally, in 1840 96 per cent. After 1850 the general proportion of exports was between 15 and 25 per cent. By 1861 there were 612,000 cotton spindles in Belgium, about one third the number in the comparatively undeveloped Habsburg Empire.

The woollen industry succeeded rather better in coping with these problems. The Verviers region continued to export its special lines to Germany and to the United States. But production was small and the industry which had begun the mechanisation of European woollen production lost its leading role and by the mid-nineteenth century had shown the way to the whole Belgian economy by coming to specialise in the finishing of semi-manufactured goods produced elsewhere. The Cockerill works in Liége which turned out 2,600 machines mainly for woollen spinning works in 1812 manufactured only 26 in 1825 and the failure of the Verviers woollen industry to maintain its previous high rate of growth was responsible for Cockerill's investments in machinery for wool spinning in Prussia. But the evidence is only impressionistic for there are no reasonable statistics of Belgian woollen production in this period. Trade figures show that between 1831 and 1840 Belgium had an import surplus of woollen cloth which was only reversed in 1841 after which date the export surplus became steadily larger. That these impressions are correct ones however seems to be shown by the history of the linen industry, a history which more than anything else indicates how painful economic development can be even when it is successful.

Although the preparation of flax and the making of linen cloth were as widespread in the Belgian countryside as in north Germany, they were particularly concentrated in the area of Europe's densest rural population and the home of the 'agricultural revolution', Flanders. In these lowlands, by the intense cultivation of a basically infertile area, by an extreme subdivision of the land, and by conducting a highly labour-intensive agriculture, a population which in some areas reached a density of 350 per square kilometre survived. The average size of land holdings there was about 3 hectares and in 1846 only 16 per cent of the holdings were larger than 5 hectares. No matter how skilled the agriculture the population could not have survived without the wide variety of employment associated with the transformation of flax into linen cloth. The seasonal routine of agriculture coincided with the seasonal routines of heckling, scutching, retting, spinning, weaving, washing, bleaching and dyeing, performed by the whole family. About one worker in every three in Flanders depended more on linen than on farming for his bread. And where linen production was highest, there the population was also at its densest, in the districts of Courtrai and Oudenarde.

Competition from mechanical spinning in other countries first began to be felt in the mid-1830s. In 1837 the first joint-stock companies to establish mechanical spinning mills in Belgium were founded. The following year the Linière Gantoise with 10,000 spindles and La Lys with 8,000 were erected in Ghent and by 1841 there were 47,000 mechanical linen spindles in Belgium. None of these new firms, however, was in West Flanders, the region where domestic spinning was most important, and their general effect was only to intensify the local effect of foreign competition. There was no hope that the domestic process could compete; the new machinery gave yarn of a more consistent quality than the variable finenesses of hand-spun yarn and it gave it much more quickly. A whole regional economy and a pattern of human existence which had survived for over two centuries was thus rendered unviable in a few years. Faced with the same narrow market as the other textile industries entrepreneurs in west Flanders could either not find or not risk the capital to be invested on such a scale quickly enough to mechanise. Even a fairly rapid measure of adjustment through the price mechanism could not avoid a severe crisis. There is no doubt that such adjustments did begin at once; the area devoted to the cultivation of flax in Flanders dropped by 20 per cent between 1840 and 1846. But at the same time powerful pressure groups arose to defend the interests of the domestic linen industry and postpone mechanisation.

The most powerful of these groups was the National Society for the Protection of the Linen Industry. Its president, E. Desmet, wrote in 1841

'Some people have been looking for new methods of making yarn without following those which the spinners use exclusively with so much skill and intelligence. It was thought they had been found with the help of machines and believed that cylinders and spindles, moved all at the same time by a single engine, could replace the fingers and that human saliva could be easily imitated by artificially prepared water. It was so thought because the inventors of machinery ignored the essential points of hand-spinning and because they did not know that the adhesive strength of saliva which forms a kind of glue, could not be imitated.'[2]

In the following year the government began to subsidise the domestic industry and in the same year negotiated a reduction in the French tariff on Belgian linens for four years. Nine-tenths of linen exports

[2] G. Jacquemyns, *Histoire de la crise économique des Flandres 1845–50* (Louvain, 1929), p. 110.

went to France in the whole period but the tariff agreement, although in its first two years of operation it led to a recovery of Belgian exports, could not mitigate the hard fact that exporters were competing by the oldest methods against the new methods rapidly being adopted in northern France.

Belgium exported 800,000 kilograms of linen yarn to France in 1829 when British exports to France were quite insignificant. In 1839 Belgian exports to France were only 400,000 kilograms and in their turn insignificant by the side of British exports of mechanically-spun yarn. Between 1832 and 1838 imports of British yarn into Belgium itself increased threefold. In the 1840s France also began to export yarn to Belgium. The 97,000 linen spindles in Belgium in 1846 may be compared to the 280,000 in Northern Ireland alone or the 235,000 in France. Within two decades an industry of European pre-eminence and the basis of the Flanders economy had come to the edge of disaster. The terrible harvests of the next two years and the potato blight produced scenes of poverty and hunger in Flanders which were exceeded only in Ireland and the Belgian government had to embark on a programme of re-settling some of the population on the heathlands of the Campine.

Yet it was the crisis itself which speeded up the process of change. In 1854 there were only 67,000 domestic linen spinners left. The industry shrank and mechanised at the same time as a response to these disasters. But the mechanisation was also very local for the new factories had to be located near to coal supplies. By the end of the 1850s yarn exports again began to exceed imports and the new mechanical industry had achieved the same balance as the old domestic industry before 1834. But in 1914 Flanders remained a purely agricultural area where one of the most illiterate and most neglected of Europe's peasant groups eked out a living from some of Europe's smallest peasant farms and a substantial part of the male population had to sell its labour seasonally on the larger farms of northern France. One of the richest and most developed areas of western Europe became one of the poorest and most backward.

– *Capital and Finance*

The delay in investment in the mechanisation of the linen industry does not mean that capital was difficult to come by in Belgium. The noble and clerical wealth of the eighteenth century provinces was disseminated into bourgeois hands by political events and this compensated for the lack of old-established mercantile wealth.

Continuity with the eighteenth century was not entirely lacking however. The textile manufacturer Simonis had been a cloth merchant in the eighteenth century and the Peltzer family, the first to use self-actors in the woollen industry, had been tanners in the Verviers area. But the typical source of capital and entrepreneurial talent was more modern. Mosselmann, founder of the Vieille Montagne zinc works, the biggest in Europe, was a speculator in the confiscated church lands and so was the Liége arms manufacturer Gosuin. Michel-Joseph Orban, founder of a dynasty of iron masters and statesmen, was a speculator in *assignats* during the French Revolution. The government provided a lot of direct capital help to firms like Cockerill, several times staving off their threatened bankruptcies. Also there was foreign capital; by 1873 about one half of the capital in joint-stock companies in mining and metallurgy was French.

But the bias of the industrial structure of the country after 1815 towards metal-based industries and machine building meant that most industrial developments required much heavier single investments than in the textile industries. After 1815 Belgium frequently pioneered a new path in capital management and the history of Belgian banking reveals the origins of many of the banking practices which became established in Germany, for many of the same reasons, in the 1850s. From the mid 1830s there was an intimate, often an embarrassingly intimate, relationship between the major financial institutions and the large new iron works.

Of course, the previous period between 1815 and 1830 established an atmosphere conducive to such links. The whole basis of William I's mercantilist policies was the public finances and the royal domain. At the start of his reign the king tried to use the large public debt of the northern provinces as a source of further bank credit to support the new industries in his southern provinces. But the old-established Nederlandsche Bank preferred its responsibilities to Dutch rentiers and merchants. The consequence of its refusal to co-operate was the founding of the Société Générale in 1822. This bank has often been considered as the first of the nineteenth century investment banks but in reality it had more in common with the financial institutions of mercantilist states in late eighteenth-century Germany. The original proposals for a bank by the Brussels merchants envisaged one with only one-twelfth of the capital with which the Société Générale was ultimately endowed. The increase in capital came from the addition of the royal domains which formed two-fifths of the bank's initial capital and through the fact that the king himself took one half of the shares which were offered. The tensions between the royal wish to use the bank for the development of the country and the Brussels merchants' desire for a safe discount

P

house were unresolved and unresolvable. The bank had to be dragooned into the financing of public works of which, in any case, the biggest part was the construction of fortresses. But it was also used to finance canal building. Certain other funds existed for industrial loans and subsidies. Of the total provided in this way before 1830 over three-quarters went to the Belgian provinces, but about one-third of the overall total went on shipbuilding and fisheries and subsidisation of the type that Cockerill received at Seraing could not have been very common.

After 1830 the Société Générale which had managed the money supply in the southern provinces was regarded as politically suspect. But the concept of a huge bank which would develop Belgian resources remained. The project which Charles de Brouckère laid before the Assembly in 1835 for a new bank of issue, the Banque de Belgique, was for a bank with a capital of 20,000,000 francs. Such an institution was on a far greater scale than anything Lafitte had conceived in France; in fact the three largest French banks, excluding the Bank of France, had a joint capital of about 8,000,000 francs. The Banque de Belgique and the Société Générale, which came much nearer to playing the role originally intended for it, played a key part in the economic revival of the 1830s. But they did so only by demonstrating the inherent instability of a banking system so closely connected with long-term industrial investment. When French private bankers, for example, were able to get out of railway investment in the 1838 downturn Belgian bankers could not get out of metallurgy. The Banque de Belgique had too large a part of its capital in industrial shares. The sudden transformation of the scale of production in the iron industry after 1834 had only been achieved by private firms forming themselves into joint-stock companies and drawing on the fund-raising resources of the Banque de Belgique and the Société Générale. The capital of the big iron firms and that of the banks became so tied as to be inseparable. The branch of the Banque de Belgique in Liége covered almost the whole of the share capital of the principal firms in the area, it provided their working capital and its directors were also directors of the major iron works. It was forced to close its doors in December. The Société Générale survived but only by cashing half its banknotes. A year later the government paid off its debts with the help of the Rothschild bank which still had important railway interests in Belgium. But no recovery was really possible for the Banque de Belgique and a new version of the bank again collapsed in 1842. Central banking matters, such as they were, once more reverted to the suspect Société Générale until the creation of a more orthodox central bank, the National Bank of Belgium, in 1850.

There were important differences between these institutions and the joint-stock banks of the 1850s in Germany or a bank like the Crédit Mobilier. But in the evolution of the Société Générale and in the development of the Banque de Belgique as a challenge to it can be seen the first examples of large financial institutions playing the dominant role in investment in a leading sector of a nation's industry. Of course, given Belgium's political situation it is not particularly surprising that it should have been there that the 'captain of industry' should have been first replaced as a dynamic force by the bank. But the development is equally attributable to the difference in industrial structure between Belgium on the one hand and France and Britain on the other. The dominant role of the iron industry meant that the slow accumulation of family capital, the typical process in the textile industries, was much less noticeable in Belgian industry. The fierce burst of development after 1834 required a wholly new investment apparatus and started a new period of banking development in the whole continent. The Belgian railways were the first example of foreign bankers interesting themselves in the profits to be made from the economic development of a new country rather than in safer operations on public debts and as such they are the start of a long story.

The Advantages of Smallness

The history of the Belgian banks illustrates the advantages and the possibilities of development which do exist in small economies. To solve the industrial problems of larger economies more credit institutions with a wider range of activity were necessary and the possibility of government involvement with the credit mechanism in so purposive but so simple a way was only possible in a small economy with so long a mercantilist tradition. The advantages of smallness are also revealed by the development of agriculture.

Belgium shared with Russia in the nineteenth century the ignominy of having no compulsory public education. It is universally agreed that illiteracy there was at a very high level and that this was a particular feature of the countryside. In addition Belgian farms were very small, smaller than the peasant holdings of France and western Germany. Not only this but the holdings themselves were often broken up into ten or twelve separate patches of land. Yet this combination of circumstances does not seem to have played the same role in holding back development as it did in France. One reason may be that a high and growing proportion of the holdings were rented. The effect of the French Revolution on Belgian land-

how were they speculators if they rented out?

holding was only very indirect. The lands confiscated from the church passed mostly to bourgeois land speculators who rented them out in small parcels to farmers. Secondly the absence of genuine agricultural tariff protection forced Belgian farmers to specialise. But above all the small size, dense population, and good transport network meant that Belgian farmers possessed comparative advantages to a more noticeable extent than French farmers. The urban market, except in the Ardennes, was near and accessible. Commons survived on a substantial scale only in the less populated and less urban regions of the Ardennes, elsewhere they disappeared early. The nearness of the urban market produced a greater sensitivity to change than greater literacy would have done. Market gardening became the particular speciality of Belgian agriculture from an early period. The density of population and the nearness of towns to each other produced a great demand for land which put its price per hectare higher than in France or Germany. *4.5 ha farm* To survive, even on their 4·5-hectare smallholding, the Belgian farm family had to keep pace with the rising demand for particular foodstuffs by changing their their crops and by improving their farming methods.

The area under bread grains declined. Sheep farming similarly declined in place of animals which could be better kept on small units. The area under flax began to increase again in the 1850s but then to decline in the next decade in the face of imports from Russia. The most important new crop, as everywhere in north-west Europe, was sugar beet, but the small size of farm units and the openness of Belgian agriculture to foreign competition kept its importance down. With only a low protective sugar duty after 1830 only a small area was under beet in 1846. There are no estimates of the output of market gardening but new crops became noticeable. Early vegetables, tobacco and grapes could all be produced by intensive methods and after 1846 chicory became a profitable export to France. By 1840 Belgium had become a cereal importer and after 1850 these imports grew quickly. She was also a net importer of potatoes and sugar. In return for such important staple crops she exported vegetables and fruit.

The structure of farming contributed as much as the lack of protection to breaking down the rigidities which handicapped France. So small were the farms that the same labour force was frequently shared between agricultural and industrial employment. *farmer-worker* The factory worker returned to the smallholding after his day's work often at a considerable distance. This was no transient stage in the development of a proletariat but a permanent feature of the Belgian economy. It seems to have developed from a long tradition of labour migration within Belgium and it was one reason for the relatively lower industrial wages in Belgium than France, for the entrepreneur did not need to entice his labour force permanently away from the land. This was recognised by the Belgian government which pioneered the use of workmens' cheap tickets on the trains, a device copied in many other countries.

The widespread impression that Belgium was an extremely *laissez-faire* economy is true only after the 1850s when most of her international political problems had been solved and her balance of payments looked healthier. The investment boom and the high rate of economic growth in France and Germany after 1852 changed Belgium's international situation and in these changed circumstances the government was able to adopt a very liberal stance and commit the country to what was very close to being free trade. Before that period Belgium's economic situation was a very uneasy one and there is much evidence that the slumps after 1814 and 1830 were of far greater severity and their depressing effect on economic development much more widely felt than the cyclical movements in other west European lands. After 1852 the textile industries increasingly became finishing industries treating semi-manufactured cloths from elsewhere, particularly Germany and Britain. As reserves of iron ore and other ores were depleted the metal industries came to depend on imported raw materials. The 10,000 tons of zinc made entirely from Belgian ore in 1845 may be compared with the 200,000 tons of 1913 made almost entirely from foreign ores. But the road to this particular solution had been a long and difficult one.

SWITZERLAND

– The general problem of its development

The population of Switzerland was smaller than that of Belgium and its density much less. There were 3,100,000 inhabitants in the territorial area of Belgium in 1800 and less than 2,000,000 in Switzerland. But whatever advantage this may have brought to the Swiss was wholly annulled by the nature of the terrain and the lack of resources. Half of Switzerland consisted of high Alpine valleys and barren mountains where a sparse population had little scope for developing improved farming methods. In striking contrast to Belgium, Switzerland has no worthwhile coal resources and hardly any iron ore. Furthermore it is a completely landlocked country.

The Rhine is navigable as far as the northwest boundary, but in the early nineteenth century the navigation was extremely difficult and not of any great importance.

The rapid economic development of Switzerland in the early nineteenth century shows that for an economy of a sufficiently small size it was not in fact necessary to have good raw material resources. And thereby it is a useful warning against accepting the simple explanation that the reason why Belgium became an industrial economy in the same period was that there were coal and iron ore resources there. The history of development shows that a much wider range of factors than this must be taken into account in considering development possibilities in small economies.

Swiss economic historians sometimes claim that the industrial revolution in Switzerland preceded that in France and Belgium and that Switzerland was in the forefront of mechanisation and industrial innovation on the continent. Whereas such a view is not necessarily wrong, it leaves so much unsaid as to be very misleading. It seems to be based on the high level of industrialisation in the Swiss country-side in the eighteenth century and the relatively high proportion of the labour force whose income was more derived from industrial than agricultural employment. When these facts are connected to the obvious success of the cotton industry in the nineteenth century, Swiss development seems much like that in France or Britain. But in reality the progression was much less smooth and involved important shifts in the final product of the Swiss cotton industry such that its scope and structure were very different from that of its French and British rivals.

The development of rural domestic industry in eighteenth-century Switzerland was conditioned by three forces, the nature of political society, the specialised nature of agriculture and the existence of the French market. Switzerland had completely escaped the process of integration and subordination to a central government which had characterised other west European states. Law and custom varied widely from canton to canton. The ancient guilds of Zürich or Bern could exercise no control in the more rural cantons. Above all there was a much lower level of taxation, and since feudal payments scarcely existed the cultivator could retain a large part of his income. In one way this only compensated him for the difficulty of his task. But the combination of poor land, a shortage of arable land in particular, and comparative freedom of occupation, led to a great variety of occupations being pursued in the country-side from an early date. The carriage and transport of people and goods, the manufacture of textiles and the assembling of watches all supplemented agricultural incomes in the harsh winter season.

Once again the curious paradox emerges that it was often the worse-endowed areas of Europe that were most able to industrialise in the eighteenth century because more labour was released for non-agricultural tasks and agricultural profits were lower. But the total volume of industrial output was small and directed almost entirely towards the French market. In Chapter 3 we discussed the way in which industrial techniques in cotton printing spread from Switzerland into France and began the growth of the cotton industry in Alsace. Although relatively small in quantity Swiss exports were high in value. They already consisted of sophisticated manufactures at the period when Belgium was just beginning to develop raw material exports to the same market.

The continental system provided the same protection for Swiss industry as for Belgian but for Switzerland it also had inherent dangers. The continued rapid development of the French cotton industry deprived Switzerland of her technological advantage in cotton printing and by 1815 the lead had shifted decisively to the larger market, France. Printing by cylinders was adopted much more slowly in Switzerland than in Alsace. Given the nature of the Swiss economy there was no point in copying France's protectionist policies. Nor was there any possibility of relying on central government action to overcome the difficulties. Switzerland was an extremely loose federation of cantons with scarcely any machinery of central government. There was discussion of a common policy to implement reprisals against the French agricultural tariffs of 1822 but it came to nothing. Until the 1848 revolution and the formation of the Swiss Bund each canton settled its own economic affairs. Although this resulted in a great variety of internal economic policies external policy tended in the circumstances, even if only by default, to remain very liberal. The absence of a national tariff was the lowest common denominator of agreement between the cantons. After the revolution and civil war free trade subsequently became established in the 1850s as a deliberate act of intellectual and political conviction.

– *Development of Swiss Industry*

Between one-third and one-half of the cotton yarn woven in Switzerland in 1822 was imported from Britain. Yet by 1835 imports of British yarn had almost ceased. There were 300,000 cotton spindles in Switzerland in 1825, by 1850 there were about one million. The Swiss cotton industry successfully avoided the fate of that of Belgium. Only in Britain was the number of spindles in relation to the population and the per capita output of cotton higher than in Switzerland. Since Switzerland had a far narrower range of industrial activities than Britain it can quite reasonably be argued that the cotton industry was more important to its economic development than to that of any other European economy. The peak level of employment in the cotton industry was the period 1868–70. At that time between 15,000 and 20,000 were employed in spinning, 57,000 in weaving, 12,000 in finishing and 20,000 in embroidery. About 45,000 of the weavers were still hand-loom weavers. Even by 1892 textiles still accounted for 44 per cent of the total industrial employment and 57 per cent by value of the total exports. How did this come about?

Table 32. *The relative importance and mechanisation of the cotton industry in western Europe, 1834–61*

Country	Date	Approx. number of spindles	No. of inhabitants per spindle	No. of workers in cotton industry for each 1000 spindles
U.K.	1834	10,000,000	1·70[a]	n.a.
	1852	21,000,000	1·22[a]	9·6
	1861	30,387,000	0·76[a]	n.a.
Switzerland	1844	660,000	3·56	15·0
	1852	1,000,000	2·40	14·0
	1861	1,350,000	1·86	n.a.
France	1846	4,300,000	8·45	14·0
Belgium	1852	400,000	11·00	n.a.
Zollverein	1846	800,000	37·50	21·25

Source: W. Bodmer, *Die Entwicklung der schweizerischen Textilwirtschaft im Rahmen der übrigen Industrien und Wirtschaftszweige* (Zürich, 1960); C. Fohlen, *L'Industrie textile au temps du Second Empire* (Paris, 1956); J. Lewinski *L'Évolution industrielle de la Belgique* (Brussels, 1911); B. R. Mitchell and P. Deane, *Abstract of British Historical Statistics* (Cambridge, 1962); W. Rappard, *La Révolution industrielle et les origines de la protection légale du travail en Suisse* (Bern, 1914).

[a] Population of Ireland not included in the calculation.

It can be seen from Table 32 that although cotton spinning, when allowance is made for the difference in size of the population, was as important to that population in Switzerland as in Britain, the overall level of mechanisation in the industry was less than in France. In fact, as far as the spinning side of the operations was concerned Switzerland never developed cotton spinning mills on the same scale as those of Alsace, much less those in Britain. One reason for this was the absence of coal. No better example can be found of the substitutability of one resource for another and also of the technological differences which such substitution involves. Water power was plentiful and cheap in Switzerland and had certainly been an important factor in the development of rural textile industries there in the eighteenth century. Swiss spinning mills used all the available improvements to water wheels and hydraulic machinery in the nineteenth century and often, towards the close of the century, passed directly to other sources of power. Steam engines were costly to use and functioned mainly as supplementary sources of power. This imposed certain size limits on the mill. Nevertheless British visitors to Switzerland after 1830 indicate that in level of technical expertise and quality of product the Swiss industry was in no way behind that of Britain and this is confirmed by the success of Swiss cotton exports in those years.

There seem to be two explanations of this success. One is in the technical ingenuity and readiness to innovate on the weaving side of the industry. The other is in the determination with which Swiss exporters opened up quite new markets in the early nineteenth century. For a small population with a high level of engagement in industry and accustomed to skilled work such possibilities did exist. The fact that British cotton manufacturers like those in Normandy concentrated on the cheaper quality goods left a niche available for producers of better quality more expensive goods. But even here the Swiss were faced with Alsatian competition and it was necessary to develop distinctive and particular Swiss export lines. In both cottons and watches the identification of the product as Swiss came to be a mark of quality and also distinctiveness of style. The structure of Swiss industry came to reflect very directly the country's foreign trading position. Whereas the mechanisation of cotton spinning had been entirely a matter of borrowing, as far as it was suitable, the latest technology from Britain, in weaving a distinctive Swiss technology emerged based on the types of Swiss cloth exported.

The use of the fly shuttle for weaving does not seem to have become general in Switzerland until the Napoleonic period. Hand loom weavers used the most traditional of methods. The first significant change was the adaptation of the Jacquard loom to cotton weaving. This innovation came by way of the silk industry. Many Swiss worked in Lyons and studied the new silk techniques there and tried to apply them to cotton weaving, achieving success in St Gallen canton in 1821. The Jacquard loom could weave coloured designs in the cloth much more cheaply. Its use enabled Swiss manufacturers to produce the first of those specialities which allowed them to escape from the grasp of the British cotton industry. The cloths produced by the Jacquard looms became the biggest part of Swiss exports to the Levant market. The introduction of the Jacquard loom led directly to the invention of the broad-stitch loom (*Plattstichstuhl*) by Johann-Conrad Altherr which permitted simple embroidery designs to be imitated by the weaver. Embroidery had always been another Swiss speciality and reducing its cost in this way increased its export potential. Its success was sealed by the chain-stitch loom (*Kettenstichstuhl*) which increased the range of the weaver's embroidery techniques. After 1830 exports of embroideries to the Levant, to the United States, and even to Britain, mounted rapidly. Power looms at first were only applied to weaving the plainer cloths. They were introduced at an early date but their spread was not very rapid. They seem to have been first used by Egli-Wagner of Flawil in 1825 but their establishment as a going concern dates rather from the weaving factory built by Neuhaus and Huber at Wil in 1830. The application of power to the finer weaving did not really develop until the 1850s. Jakob Oberholzer then introduced power looms successfully in the Zürich Oberland with the consequence that the regional centre of patterned weaving began to shift to there from St Gallen and Appenzell which had led the Swiss export trade in the earlier period. In 1844 there were still only about 1,000 mechanical looms in the whole country and about 90,000 hand-looms. The distinctive technological contribution of the Swiss was therefore in the refinement of the hand loom, but it was sufficient to provide a basis for the continued increase of output of mechanically-spun yarn and, more important, it sustained a high level of exports from what had become, by European standards, a small total output.

The only other textile industry of importance was the old-established silk industry. There were about 1,800 silk looms in Zürich canton in the late eighteenth century; by 1848 there were 12,400. The number employed in the silk industry increased from about 20,000 between 1820 and 1830 to 48,000 in 1855. As with cotton it is impossible to say exactly what the ratio of exports to production actually was but the industry produced in fact mainly for export. In the eighteenth century it had exported to Italy and south Germany; by the 1840s about one-half of the exports went to the United States. Silk had the same export advantages as high grade cottons. It did not demand huge factories and coal resources and laid a premium on the weavers' skills in producing a better product. Over the same period of time textiles without these advantages almost died out in Switzerland. The first mechanical linen-spinning mill built in Thurgau in 1828 still stood in lonely splendour in 1836 with its mere 300 spindles. In the 1840s there were three such mills but they represented a last attempt and no more were constructed. The triumph of cotton over the other textiles was more complete in Switzerland than elsewhere perhaps because the domestic market was too small to sustain sales of woollen and linen goods.

It is even more difficult to be precise about the success of Swiss watch-making in the nineteenth century than about cotton but it also depended on technical ingenuity and marketing determination. It had been started in Geneva in the seventeenth century by refugees from south Germany and, together with Paris and London, Geneva was still a great centre of production for more expensive and traditional items. The Neuenburg and the Bernese Jura, where it was the main source of employment and income for many rural dwellers, produced the more standardised items. The industry consisted of a very large number of separate operations controlled by the entrepreneur and although a distinct tendency can be observed to collect the work force together into workshops, there was no application of power to the workshop which could turn it into a factory in the true sense of the word before 1870. Nevertheless, the increased division of labour was as marked there as in the textile industries. It took an average of 54 separate workmen carrying out distinct operations to make a watch in Neuenburg in 1830; in 1870 it took 100. Part of this increased division of labour was the result of the standardisation of interchangeable watch parts by the development of new precision machine tools for the industry after 1839 by Georges Leschot. The new processes were taken up in the 1840s by Vacherin and Constantin and then by the Geneva firm of Patek, Philippe and Co. in 1847.

They marked the beginning of a shift from the export of expensive gold and silver watches to a much more standardised and cheaper product. This shift was no doubt dictated by differences in the consumer market with the decay of the old régime and the slow spread of incomes downwards into other social groups. It also reflected the greater need of people to have a watch in the 1840s with the introduction of railway timetables and the spread of more regular working hours. In this kind of international competition Switzerland had the enormous advantage of a pool of skilled labour and a long tradition of watch making. Machine tools had not yet developed to such a point as to eliminate the large number of skilled and semi-skilled manual operations, knowledge of which was transmitted through successive generations of the family. Watches were Switzerland's third most valuable export after cottons and silks. Production in 1848 was between 200,000 and 230,000 watches a year. The change in markets was carried through in the same period as that of the textile industries and after 1835 the United States was always the most important market. In 1872 366,000 watches and watch-movements were exported to the United States alone.

In the first decades of the nineteenth century Swiss industrialists were able to open up distant markets much more easily than those of Belgium. The element of transport costs in the final price of her main exports was of course lower than in the case of Belgian exports. But the history of these developments is still not written and there seems no special advantage other than the nature of her products which Switzerland enjoyed in extending her trade beyond Europe, unless familiarity with foreign trade and foreign investment from an early period was such an advantage. In the late eighteenth century one-tenth of the wealth of the Alpine canton of Glarus was invested in trade and one-fourteenth invested abroad. A network of wealthy private bankers in the bigger Swiss towns provided insurance and exchange facilities for exporters. In the 1850s special export houses developed such as that of Heinrich Fierz which opened agencies throughout the Levant. One aspect may be the improvement in transport facilities in the early nineteenth century which reflected more the interests of a society accustomed to live by trading than deliberate government action as they did in Belgium.

Napoleon caused a road for wheeled traffic to be built over the Simplon pass in 1805. In the 1820s roads were built over the Saint Bernard and the Splügen passes and in 1830 the St Gotthard road was opened. One of the first actions of the Bund in 1848 was to order the construction of new roads in order to recapture the trade from France to Italy which had begun to flow directly through the Mont Cenis pass rather than through Switzerland. The use of steamships for water transport developed very quickly and they provided the main market for Swiss steam engine manufactures. The 'Guillaume Tell' made its first voyage on the lake of Geneva in 1823 and in the next year steamship services developed on all the bigger lakes. In 1832 the first Rhine steamship to reach Basel stimulated a programme of improving the navigation between that town and Strasbourg. The Basel city council inaugurated a regular service between the two towns in 1838.

This improvement of the Rhine navigation was only temporary, for already interest was turning to the railway. Swiss railways were constructed very late and very slowly. There was nothing to compare with the profitable coal and iron traffic of Belgium. Nor was there any possibility of central government help, nor even of central

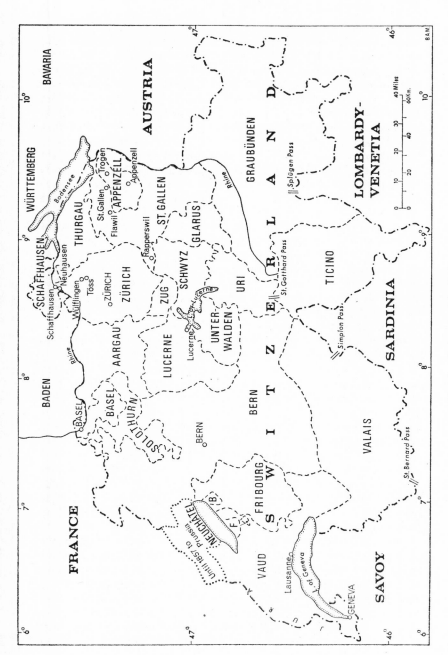

Map 8. Switzerland in 1850

government agreement on the direction of the lines. The first line was a French line which arrived from Strasbourg in 1844. The entrepreneurs of Zürich made repeated strenuous efforts to get the government to aid railway building after 1830 but they were left to their own resources. After 1848 the situation changed and the new federal government commissioned a plan for a network from two British engineers, both of whom advised against any possibility of an Alpine crossing and suggested a network of only 650 kilometres. The Zürich entrepreneurs rejected the proposed line to Basel and built their own line northwards to Baden, a line which reached the Rhine only in 1859. Disputes of this kind meant that effective railway building in Switzerland did not begin before the 1850s in which decade over 1,000 kilometres were built, a rate of building which was only again achieved in the 1870s. The initial boom was due to the ready provision of capital by French banking interests. But the piercing of the Alpine passes had to wait until much later. It can hardly be argued that railway building was very important in the Swiss industrial revolution. Indeed in the very period when railway building developed the native Swiss iron industry began to decline. It was quite incapable of competing against the cheaper products of coke blast-furnaces and coal forges. None of the rail used in Switzerland was domestically produced.

In this respect again, however, the Swiss economy seems to have gained from its openness to international competition. In spite of the decay of the native iron industry, from an early stage Switzerland developed its own machine-making industry. The tradition of skilled labour played its part here and also the high premium which circumstances placed on innovation in the export industries. By 1848 the firm of Escher Wyss had 1,000 workers and produced spinning machines, hydraulic machines and steam engines for steamships. The firm of J. J. Rieter produced a similar range of products and exported two-thirds of them. After 1842 Kaspar Honegger began to supply weaving machinery to the factories around Zürich. The first rolling-stock works was at Neuhausen in 1853. Several iron manufacturers developed machine building shops using scrap iron and imported iron to replace their own product.

There must also have been other factors at work to explain the success of Swiss competition. There is a lot of evidence to show that two of them were the cheapness of capital and the cheapness of labour, a combination sufficient to overcome the high cost of raw materials. The comparatively high level of *per capita* incomes in the eighteenth century made capital in small sums fairly easy to raise and meant that the self-financing of the textile enterprises met few difficulties. A low interest rate and a high savings rate prevailed in the early nineteenth century. The structure of industry meant that there was no need for investment banks of the Belgian kind until the railway building of the 1850s. The Banque Générale de Crédit Foncier et Mobilier founded in 1853 and the Schweizerische Kreditanstalt of 1856 were basically banks of the Crédit Mobilier type whose investments were in transport and public works. Before that time manufacturers had access to sufficient capital in the local capital networks that had existed since the eighteenth century.

Industrial wages seem in the early nineteenth century to have been lower and to have risen less rapidly than in France or Britain. The apparently high level of income in the eighteenth century reflected the large addition to agricultural incomes coming from industrial employment. With the development of factory industry the wages paid by the entrepreneurs did not have to increase as much as in France to bridge this change because of the nature of Swiss industrialisation. The rural setting of the cotton industry to take advantage of water power and the smaller size of the factories enabled the labour force to keep a connection with the land. This combined with the prevalence of family farms to retain both the habit of investment in land and the custom of combining industrial and agricultural incomes in the same family. Swiss economic historians tend to pride themselves on the absence of a proletariat there but measures of the real wages of industrial workers show that there was no improvement and perhaps a decline between 1810 and 1850. As in Belgium the entrepreneur was often able to count on low industrial wages being supplemented by income from the land. This made the international market even more important to Switzerland after 1815. The amount of a working-class budget available for clothing stayed at about 12 per cent of total income in the first half of the nineteenth century and increased domestic cloth consumption depended on the price-reducing effects of technological innovation.

CONCLUSION

As a proportion of the total value of world trade the trade of Belgium and Switzerland was not especially significant. Swiss trade was about 2 per cent of world trade between 1810 and 1870. Belgian trade, because of the connection with the Netherlands, is more difficult to estimate but it could not have been much greater than 3 per cent. Over the same period French trade was about 11 per cent of world trade. All such figures are very rough, yet this limited corner of world trade was more significant for the economic development of these small states than was France's much larger share for France. Belgium's trade depended on providing raw materials and manufactured products directly used in the growing industries and in the transport networks of her European neighbours. Switzerland's depended more on the marginal increases in consumer's incomes resulting from economic development. In each case we are concerned only with a small volume of production. And in the case of Belgium in particular the growth of the economy appears to have pursued a very erratic path.

By 1850 both economies were amongst the most industrialised in Europe; indeed, better figures might reveal that by most conventional methods of measuring development they were the most developed areas of the mainland. The limitations of such a statement must be borne in mind. By that date Switzerland had practically no railways and in Belgium the Flanders linen industry was in its worst agonies. Both economies revealed the conventional advantages and disadvantages of an open economy, although in fact neither had much choice in the matter. For a variety of reasons they were able to take limited international trading opportunities. They would not have been able to do so without powerful domestic forces also making for development. Despite these forces it was the development of larger economies which provided the significant opportunities and the export sector which gave a renewed impetus to development, in Switzerland in the 1820s and in Belgium in the 1830s.

Obviously the acceptance of so internationalist an economic stance was easier for countries which were deliberately created to function as neutral buffer states. But it did affect their economies in ways which have not yet been properly explored. One example of this is the development of the tourist trade in Switzerland about which very little is known, surprisingly enough when tourism is now often seen by developing countries as a key to development. Switzerland was the first economy to be influenced to this extent by tourism. The concept of a 'tourist industry' appears in Swiss writing as early as 1850. Twenty years before that the building of 'guest houses' was already waking many Swiss villages from a long repose. Thomas Cook's first 'accompanied voyages' to Switzerland began in 1864. As important numerically as the tourists were the foreigners resident in Switzerland of whom a large proportion must have been foreign workers. The census of 1870 gave 5·7 per cent of the population as foreigners and the percentage rose very steadily after that date. French, Italian and south German workers all came to Switzerland in significant numbers from the mid-nineteenth century since when the economy has always depended on immigrant labour. Another example is the early specialisation of agriculture in both countries. Although both countries were increasingly dependent on food imports both developed profitable export lines based on a specialised agriculture at an early period. Condensed milk and children's foods were first exported from Switzerland in 1866. In 1883 Julius Maggi began to make the first dehydrated soups. In fact agriculture still accounted for the income of about half the population of both countries in 1850 and the changes in it before that date must have been far-reaching.

By the mid-nineteenth century each economy had come to have a significant stake in trade liberalisation. Although the tariff reductions of the 1860s and the movement back to protection after 1873 had profound effects on their economies, these effects are another story. The fact that after 1815 the Zollverein's tariffs were much lower than those of France, the development of the American market, the shift to free trade in Britain, were all vital developments for these small economies. So was the building of a European railway system, in particular the construction of the German railways. But, of course, all these depended on being able to take advantage of such opportunities and for that the changes which took place in these societies during the eighteenth century and the French Revolution once again show their true importance.

SUGGESTED READING

There is virtually no work in English on the economic history of Belgium and Switzerland. J. CRAEYBECKX, 'The Beginnings of the Industrial Revolution in Belgium' is a good article translated in R. CAMERON (ed.), *Essays in French Economic History* (Homewood, Ill., 1970). There is a chapter by the editor himself about Belgium in R. CAMERON (ed.) *Banking in the Early Stages of Industrialisation* (New York, 1967). B. S. ROWNTREE, *Land and Labour; Lessons from Belgium* (London, 1910) is a rather opinionated study of Belgian agriculture in the late nineteenth century. J. DHONDT, 'The cotton industry in Ghent during the French Occupation' in F. CROUZET ET AL. (eds.) *Essays in European Economic History*, published for the Economic History Society (London, 1969) discusses the period of the French Empire. J. DHONDT and M. BRUWIER, *The Industrial Revolution in Belgium and Holland*, Fontana Economic History of Europe, Volume 4, Section 1 (London, 1970), does not add very much to that article. The work on Belgium in other languages is certainly better than that on Switzerland but it is still very sparse. There are two general economic histories of Belgium, J. A. VAN HOUTTE, *Esquisse d'une histoire économique de la Belgique* (Louvain, 1943) and L. DECHESNE, *Histoire économique et sociale de la Belgique* (Paris, Liége, 1932). R. DEMOULIN, *Guillaume Ier et la transformation économique des provinces belges (1815–1830)* (Paris, Liége, 1938) is a rather eclectic study of an interesting theme. R. S. CHLEPNER, *La Banque en Belgique* (Brussels, 1926) is only an approach to the interesting problem of the early history of Belgian banking.

For Switzerland, A. HAUSER, *Schweizerische Wirtschafts- und Sozial Geschichte* (Erlenbach-Zürich, 1961) has only a small number of pages on modern Switzerland but is one of the few attempts to get beyond the confines of the individual canton. W. BODMER, *Schweizerische Industriegeschichte (Die Entwicklung der schweizerischen Textilwirtschaft im Rahmen der übrigen Industrien und Wirtschaftszweige)* (Zürich, 1960) is an unanalytical but encyclopedic study with a detailed bibliography. W. RAPPARD, *La révolution industrielle et les origines de la protection légale du travail en Suisse* (Bern, 1914) is still to be surpassed and is of wider interest than its title suggests. Switzerland is fortunate in having a massively detailed work on labour history, E. GRUNER, *Die Arbeiter in der Schweiz im neunzehnten Jahrhundert* (Bern, 1968), while R. BRAUN, *Sozialer und kultureller Wandel in einem ländlichen Industriegebiet (Züricher Oberland) unter der Einwirkung des Maschinen- und Fabrikwesens im neunzehnten und zwanzigsten Jahrhundert* (Erlenbach-Zürich, 1965) is an interesting book in its own right.

The historical journals published in Belgium and Switzerland usually contain economic history research only of a very local kind. Although research on and discussion of Belgian economic history sometimes appears in *Annales* and other French journals there is really at the moment no periodical in either Belgium or Switzerland which can be used for reference or bibliographical purposes. But there is a good bibliography for modern historical research on Belgian history which includes economic history in J. A. VAN HOUTTE (ed.), *Un quart de siècle de recherche historique en Belgique 1944–68*, Comité National Belge des Sciences Historiques (Louvain and Paris, 1970).

Chapter 8

The Economic Development of Scandinavia

In this chapter we have undertaken a comparative study of the development of three neighbouring countries, Denmark, Norway and Sweden. We shall not make any attempt to go into the kind of detailed treatment that was devoted to France and Germany. The aim is more to pick out the essential features of the growth of three small countries, depending very heavily on exporting to the industrialising countries of Europe which were geographically proximate to them. Yet despite this basic similarity, we shall be concerned also to mark out the important and substantial differences in the nature, timing and extent of economic change in all three.

In 1800 the total population of these countries was only a little more than 4m – Sweden 2·35m: Denmark 0·93m: Norway 0·88m.

1	ÄLVSBORG
2	BLEKINGE
3	GÄVLEBORG
4	GÖTEBORG och BOHUS
5	-HALLAND
6	JÄMTLAND
7	JÖNKÖPING
8	KALMAR
9	KOPPARBERG
10	KRISTIANSTAD
11	KRONOBERG
12	MALMÖHUS
13	NORRBOTTEN
14	ÖREBRO
15	ÖSTERGÖTLAND
16	SKARABORG
17	SÖDERMANLAND
18	STOCKHOLM
19	UPPSALA
20	VÄRMLAND
21	VÄSTERBOTTEN
22	VÄSTERNORRLAND
23	VÄSTMANLAND

Map 9.   Sweden and Norway in the nineteenth century

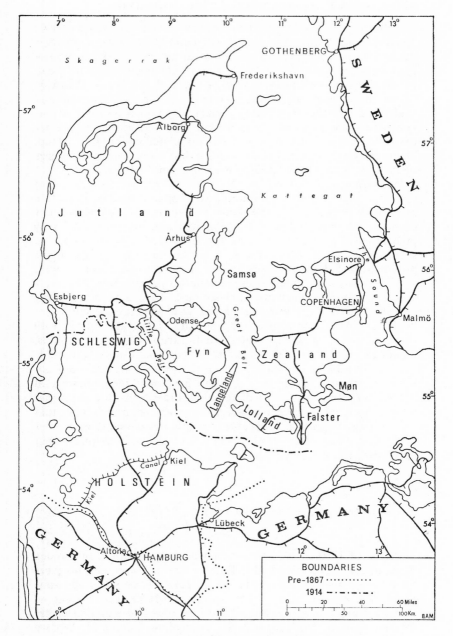

Map 10.   Denmark in the nineteenth century

In 1910 it was less than 11m – Sweden 5·5m: Denmark 2·8m: Norway 2·4m. Furthermore, in Sweden and Norway the population density was remarkably low. Sweden was approximately the size of France but in 1910 its population was only one-seventh as great. Its density was one-twentieth that of England and Wales; Norway, two-thirds as large, had a density one-thirtieth that of England and Wales and was the most thinly populated political unit in Europe. Only the three small counties around Oslo had a density greater than Westmorland, the most sparsely populated county in England. Denmark was a much smaller country, less than one-tenth the size of Sweden, with a population density five times as great.

In Sweden beyond the 61st parallel lay Norrland, 60 per cent of the total area, a huge virgin arctic wilderness, a land of mountain and forest populated in 1800 only by nomadic Lapps and a few hunters. The central lowland region was also heavily forested by pine forests on thin, rocky soil, the land broken by hundreds of small lakes. The finest arable land lay in the southern tip, in the province of Skåne. In Norway the mountains and slopes were particularly steep: much of the country was a plateau severely eroded by ancient glaciation and streams. This, and its northerly location, made three quarters of the area barren. The cultivated lands lay in narrow strips along streams, lakes and fjords with communication between them difficult except in coastal regions. Denmark enjoyed a more temperate climate and a more favourable location in relation to world trade routes, but nature had been unkind to her in another way, for the land contained no mineral deposits of commercial value of any kind. Indeed, the three countries were almost unique in the nineteenth-century environment in that they produced almost no coal at all, thouth it is as well to remember that Switzerland had neither coal nor mineral resources but developed industrially earlier than Scandinavia.

THE EIGHTEENTH-CENTURY SCENE

A survey of 1760 showed 85 per cent of the population of Sweden living in the countryside and only 7 per cent in the towns, no more than the number of soldiers in the strikingly large standing army. Stockholm was the only town of significance. It had been the capital of a great empire; now it was an excellent port and a market centre for the Gulf of Bothnia and the immediate hinterland. With a population over 70,000 it was a significant city by European standards. Smaller than London, Paris, Vienna, Berlin, smaller than Copenhagen which had nearer 100,000, it lay in the second rank along with Brussels, Warsaw and Rotterdam and rather larger than the second tier of German towns such as Munich, Dresden, Frankfurt and Cologne. The size of the next largest town, Gothenberg with 7,500 inhabitants in 1760 is indicative of the generally backward state of the economy. Then there were a number of small towns, marketing centres for agricultural products and containing small concentrations of manufacturing activities – tobacco-processing, sugar-refining, soap-making, wool and silk textile manufacture. Upon them the government looked benignly and hopefully, limiting overseas competition, encouraging the work of guilds, but all to little purpose. The factory wool textile industry, concentrated in Stockholm and also in Norrköping to the south, could never match the quality of imported cloths. Neither did it have any technological advantage over the domestic producers and it survived only on the basis of very local urban demand.

Mining and metal-making were the chief non-agricultural pursuits. By the end of the eighteenth century the great copper mine at Stora Kopparberg, the largest in the world in the previous century, was becoming exhausted and copper gradually yielded place to fish and tar in the list of exports. But it was the making of iron that dominated Sweden's foreign trade. Though employing only 3 per cent of the population in 1760, its importance was out of all proportion to that figure. The industry was scattered in an area known as Bergslagen, a belt of forest and lakes, 150 km, long and 80 km. wide, lying to the north-west of Stockholm. Iron making was carried on wherever ore and wood for charcoal were available together. Individual peasants mined the ore, made the charcoal and smelted in their small blast furnaces: middle men bought the pig iron and sold it to the refiners who used expensive water-driven tilt hammers to convert the pig into bar iron in ironworks employing usually thirty to forty men. Increasingly the refiners were integrating backwards to replace the peasant smelters until by 1850 hardly any such were left. The final link in the chain was provided by the merchant houses of Stockholm and Gothenberg which provided both the long-term capital and, more important, in a relatively unsophisticated technical age, the working capital required by the industry. The merchant bankers in turn borrowed this working capital in Amsterdam, London and Hamburg where it was cheaply available, using their own money for that longer term investment which foreigners eschewed because of legal disabilities. It was a reasonable division of labour and as a result of their wealth, their contacts and the complexity of their operations, these houses provided one of the dynamic elements in the Swedish economy until well into the second half of the next century.

The importance of the iron industry can be gauged from the fact that in the mid-eighteenth century it was turning out roughly half of all the iron produced in Europe. Normally, half of the exports went to Britain, and 20–25 per cent to Baltic ports – only a little was consumed in Sweden. Yet Sweden's share of Britain's imports fell from 90 per cent around 1700 to only one-third in the 1780s. The reason was that from the middle of the century the Swedish ironmasters agreed to a rigid limitation of output, partly in the hope of maintaining a semi-monopoly price and also to conserve the forest resources. The former aim might have failed entirely in view of the technical stagnation of the industry and the very rapid growth of competition from the Russian iron industry in the Urals, to such an extent that in the 1780s two-thirds of Britain's imports came from there. Nevertheless prices rose and the Swedes enjoyed high prosperity simply on account of the rapid growth of total demand. Partly Sweden gained too from the emphasis given to quality production, something which probably owed much to the Swedish mercantilist tradition of interference in economic life and which certainly was to have long-run advantages for the industry in the next century.

Though iron making played such a vital role in the Swedish economy, some of its secondary effects had been disappointingly slight, for no significant engineering or metal manufacturing trade had developed out of it. All the same it provided a background of technological know-how and of commercial and entrepreneurial experience which was to be of great help in the transition to a more advanced stage of manufacturing in the next century.

Apart from their use for charcoal, the exploitation of Sweden's timber resources was limited. So long as the Norwegian forests along the Atlantic coast remained undepleted, the Swedish lumber industry was at a serious disadvantage geographically, while the favourable location gave the Norwegian industry a stimulus to technical progress in sawmilling techniques that was lacking in Sweden. The large areas of pine forest in Central Sweden which were distant from iron ore were used commercially largely for the manufacture of tar and pitch and eventually in the 1770s these became by value the second largest export, though in fact a considerable amount of Swedish tar originated in Finland.

But despite its unique features, foreign trade affected only a tiny minority of Swedes. Just as in every other country, the internal economy was dominated by agricultural production for home consumption. The land was farmed mostly in small units by peasants: some of it was peasant owned too – perhaps one-third of *land ownership* the cultivated area in 1700 and over one-half by 1800. Tenant farmers performed the usual services for their lords – work on his land, forced labour on road making – and they were forced to defer to him over the usual hunting and other similar privileges. The non-noble land was subject to taxes from which the nobles themselves were largely exempt and tithes had to be paid to the church. Below the peasants in the social scale were the sub-tenants, crofters and cottagers who helped out on the peasant holdings, or acted as substitute for the peasant's labour service obligations to eke out their own meagre subsistence. The open-field system was well-nigh universal – either a two-field system with one fallow and the other under crops, or the more sophisticated three-field system found in the southern counties which were already beginning to show the response to technical advances which were eventually to lead them to their role as Sweden's granary in the next century. In Sweden and Norway the most widespread crop was barley which grew in the far north: in the southern plains rye was more common but the growing of oats was becoming more widespread. Animal husbandry was in a rudimentary state: farm techniques generally were crude but, as we saw in chapter 2 except for short periods of particularly severe winters, the land provided a rude plenty and a standard of living which matched that of all but the most advanced agricultural areas in Europe.

However slight the actual signs of economic development during the first three-quarters of the century, there were two vital aspects of Swedish life at this time which were to have important consequences in the long run. The first we have already discussed – the steadily rising population. As for the second, the years of relative peace after 1720 ushered in an era of intense interest in social and economic problems known as the enlightenment, an era too of real social change. Traditional estate society was eroded by the entry of non-nobles into fields previously closed to them. At the beginning *nobles* of the century there were rather more than 1,000 noble families, but between 1719 and 1792 624 more families were ennobled – military men, civil servants, industrialists, men of learning in both science and the arts. Commoners bought noble land: in 1718 some 7 per cent of noble land was in their hands: by 1772 it was over 16 per cent. Nobles put their money into iron works. Merchants and ironmasters constituted a new upper class of formidable intellectual as well as economic power. In an important way Sweden became socially a more mobile society. Precisely why all this happened is hard to say. Eli Heckscher saw it as the result of the lifting of the heavy burden of continuous wars. He put it this way: 'A new spirit descended upon the country. To an astonishing degree, even by modern standards, all eyes were upon "utility"; all minds concerned with material improvements. The utilitarian craze undeniably created a narrow minded petty bourgeois atmosphere: yet it was by no means incompatible with a genuine enthusiasm for the arts and sciences.'[1] A number of scientific societies were formed which, among other activities, sent observers to England and elsewhere to spy out what was happening in the industrial field. Many countries in the eighteenth century, influenced by mercantilist theories gave grants for new technological ideas: it was particularly the case in Sweden but was to be found in even very backward areas like Scotland. Even so it was some time before the opportunity arose for radical change and the abandonment of an economic policy geared more to preserving the past than creating the future.

Matters were very different in Denmark. Here was a land without copper or iron, with no great forests and no wide expanses of fertile land. The distribution of population was not unlike that in Sweden, for in 1770 about 80 per cent of the people lived in villages in the countryside. But the capital, Copenhagen, played a more dominant role. With 93,000 inhabitants it contained 12 per cent of the population. Its importance derived from its role in the country's overseas trade and as a Baltic shipbuilding and repair centre. The sea was Denmark's chief natural asset. It is a land of islands and creeks and local shipping was of necessity a major industry. Denmark commanded the great commercial route of the Sound between Elsinore and southern Sweden and this strategic geographical location made her well able to play an active part in the growth of Europe's grain trade from the seventeenth century onwards. The crown was able to give Danish ships preferential treatment in the Norwegian carrying trade, for that country was a vassal state to Denmark until 1814 and from this developed a profitable grain export trade to Norway too. Danish ships also took some part in the carrying of Norwegian timber to England and to other parts of Europe. The Arctic empire – Iceland, Greenland, the Faroes – demanded contact by long distance shipping. Above all shipping was vital for trade with the tropical empire in the East Indies, West Indies and Africa, and the Danes were able to expand their European and Asiatic carrying trades particularly effectively when Britain and France were at war between 1776 and 1783 and after 1793.

Agriculture was organised in the usual open field pattern, following commonly a simple three-field rotation of winter rye, spring oats and fallow. Animal husbandry was on the decline except in north-

[1] E. Heckscher, *An Economic History of Sweden* (Cambridge, Mass, 1963), p. 131.

west Jutland where it was successfully practised on the Flanders model but to the peasant dairying was of little significance. There were some eighty great landowners and perhaps 2,000 lesser gentry who together owned about three-quarters of the land. As little as one-eighth was in the hands of peasants – crown and church owning the rest. The biggest estates were very large and covered several villages but the demesne farm which the owner cultivated for himself was nowhere as extensive and was limited by statute from further expansion. Some 75,000 peasants held farms of 10 to 60 hectares, mostly as tenants: as such they enjoyed life tenancy and the right to convey this on their deaths. However, many surrendered their leases through inability to pay their dues and there was therefore some movement up and down the social scale between these less fortunate peasants and men inheriting only very small landholdings. These were the cottars with farms of up to 5 hectares. They were less than a third as numerous as the peasants in 1780. Finally there were 50,000 or so labourers and servants, many the sons of peasants and cottars who would some day inherit: only a few thousand were genuine landless labourers who had no prospects of becoming owners in their own right.

What distinguished Denmark from its neighbours was the existence of serfdom. There had been serfdom in the islands from medieval times and as elsewhere in the west, leaseholders were already subject to heavy labour service requirements and to corporal punishment if they did not perform them in the seventeenth century. But serfdom was reimposed on the country as a whole by a series of decrees which, by 1733, had attached them to the soil. In part it was brought in to secure a ready supply of conscripts for the army as well as to provide an easy source of taxation. More significantly, grain prices declined in the first half of the eighteenth century. More grain was being traded within Europe at a time when population was growing only slowly. The peasant found it hard to pay his taxes and tended to abandon his land. Not only did the lord lose his source of labour but in return for tax exemption he was responsible for collecting local tax payments and consequently found himself paying taxes for the absent peasants. The answer was to force peasants to stay. The agricultural crisis was most pronounced between 1720 and 1746, with very bad years in 1730–4. Prices of rye and barley collapsed and in 1724 came a high Dutch tariff on livestock imports. In 1730 the conscription laws were loosened, and this resulted in an immediate exodus of peasants. Consequently the law of 1733 reimposed conscription much more strictly; no one was to leave his birth place without permission from the landlord between the ages of 14 and 36. It soon became clear that there were more than enough soldiers but serfdom was then maintained because it effectively lowered labour costs at a time of crisis when it was hard otherwise to keep down costs and ensured a supply of tenants with none of the empty holdings that had been threatened. But along with serfdom had gone a freezing of the existing pattern of land ownership and cultivation: the landowners could not increase their demesne farms nor the peasant take in more land. The tenants' rights were preserved too, as we have seen. The result was to preserve a society of peasant equals. There was a strong feeling that a landless proletariat was undesirable in itself, for a yeoman with his own farm fights best because he has something to fight for, and the Danish authorities went out of their way consciously to avoid such a development. In practice it did not always work out in this way as many peasants were able to buy exemption from military service or run off to Schleswig Holstein and Holland. In critical years there were many conveyances of tenancies to sons and sons-in-law, and marriages of young men to widows so as to avoid service, and it was the cottars and labourers who were conscripted in the main.

What were the consequences of all this? As elsewhere in the west, labour services interfered badly with the peasants' own operations, though gradually more and more were commuted for money payments. The reformers later in the century reckoned that above all it was the combination of these services and serfdom which degraded the peasant and also lowered his productivity. State taxes and tithes were onerous burdens but this form of serfdom was nothing like the oppressive systems of the east, where the peasant had all too often entirely inadequate land, was more heavily taxed and was subjected to more arbitrary and vicious forms of manorial justice. Revolts were uncommon in Denmark: by the standards of the time the peasants enjoyed the kind of simple sufficiency of their Swedish counterparts. If their legal status was unfavourable, they were not cowed and the state gave them considerable protection. Contrary to common generalisations about the process of economic development, it was not necessary to destroy the pattern of equal access to land and let the freeplay of the market reshape the pattern of cultivation in order to bring about a sharp rise in agricultural productivity. In the long run the eighteenth-century Danish rural structure, under-pinned by the strong tradition of peasant village consultation over open field farming, produced a form of co-operative farming which fitted well into the changing economic circumstances of the late nineteenth century. But this was a long way ahead. In the short run, any landowner, large or small, wishing to increase his income had to do it by improving his operations rather than by getting more land, though considerable reclamation of forest and heath land was going ahead too. More significantly, the uniform conditions of settlement, far more so than in Sweden, made it possible to carry through in one generation a complete reform of the open field system and of owner–tenant relationships with a minimum of internal discontent.

RURAL REFORM

The modernisation of the structure of Swedish farming came about through a series of reforms stretching over the century from 1750. The social structure was not shattered by any drastic revolutionary changes or by economic disasters. The rising population was probably the most powerful economic factor lying behind what took place. It helped to bring about a rise in corn prices and this encouraged some nobles to take the initiative in commuting services and changing the organisational pattern of farming. Well aware of the potential perils of rising numbers of landless labourers, the state put through the necessary legislation to allow these private experiments to be made. Nevertheless it is important to note the contrast between this action and the infinitely more repressive response to agricultural difficulties in Russia at much the same time. As we have pointed out, the eighteenth century brought new elements to the fore in Swedish society and the cultural trends of the age played their part too. Science, the supreme authority of the enlightenment, was brought to the aid of agriculture, with the British and Dutch experience to show the way. With technical reform went economic reform too with, for example, the establishment of internal free trade in agricultural products between 1775 and 1780. The crown, in need of finance, played its part by allowing crown tenants to buy their freeholds but not until prices began moving upwards towards the end of the century did it seem profitable to exchange tenancy for a taxable freehold, encumbered by labour dues and services.

Though the population of Sweden rose by three-quarters from 1720 to 1815 there was no serious fall in standards of nourishment and only a marginal reduction of grain exports. The drainage of marshes, clearing of woods, cultivation of former meadow land may have added in the region of 15 per cent to the cultivated area, but given the much greater rise in numbers it is obvious that land productivity rose considerably. In part those very climatic changes which played a part in bringing about the growth of population assisted the response, for it was now found that crops such as oats could be grown successfully in places where it had earlier been impossible. The growing of potatoes spread rapidly after 1800 too.[2] But enclosure of the open fields and the distribution of the commons and waste to individuals were as critical for the raising of the standards of cultivation and experimentation with new crops and greater adherence to the market as everywhere else in the west.

These organisational changes began slowly. An act of 1757 allowed owners to ask for official surveyors to organise the consolidation of strips into larger parcels of land. The two- and three-field systems remained and peasants usually got more than one parcel in each field as well as a separate area of meadowland. Individual experimentation was still difficult but this first consolidation (*Stårskifte*), by saving time and labour, may have permitted more intensive and careful cultivation of the existing crops. Some larger owners then began to urge for greater consolidation and this was made possible in 1783. Individuals could now consolidate their farms altogether but leave the village system intact for those that remained. In 1803 the law moved towards that complete division into single farms which started in Denmark forty years earlier. This ultimate form of enclosure (*Enskifte*) was typically followed in Skåne, the most fertile grain area in the south. It was not necessarily suitable further north where the cultivable land was often broken by marshes and rocky outcrops and where the pressure of the market was less intense anyway. The compromise, widely adopted after a law of 1827, was to abandon communal activity altogether but to have strips consolidated into two or three parcels of land. The authorities acted with much tenderness towards the peasant, urging change, offering financial assistance, but being sparing of mandatory action. But the gradual nature of these organisational reforms was paralleled by even slower modification of the labour services, and though commutation gathered speed as time went on, still by mid-century services remained common and though the peasant kept day labourers to do the work for him, the cost and injustice rankled. Not until 1878 was the posting obligation ended, later than in Norway or Denmark. This was a common feature of eighteenth-century Europe by which peasants along highways were forced to haul goods and passengers at a fixed fee for private individuals and free for government officials. Tithes went in 1869 but equal taxation of land had to wait still longer, despite the long political pressure applied by the peasants for such a reform.

[2] The ratio of land under potatoes to that under grain was 1 : 100 in 1800 and 1 : 15 by 1830.

To a marked degree the changes in the pattern of farming activity were pre-industrial, deriving from rural pressures not from the demand of urban markets. The peasant had little inducement to leave the land: farming remained peasant-based but more effectively prepared to meet the demands that industrialisation and other switches in the economy were to bring. The problem of the growing cottager class, living off the land but with little of it, remained basically unresolved. Their numbers doubled between 1750 and 1815 and then expanded even more rapidly with the great population increase of the 1820s. Emigration and the rise of alternative occupations outside agriculture were to be the answer but not before the second half of the century. Change was largely a response to rural pressures, then, but even so, it remains likely that Baltic corn prices of the eighteenth century were to a degree affected by what happened in England and Holland. When these countries were producing enough for themselves and when England was exporting significant quantities, this affected Scandinavia and the whole Baltic by acting as a kind of damper on change. Areas such as Skåne were more likely to stay at subsistence farming because it was hard to sell corn outside in the face of a European surplus and English dumping – in Norway, for example. When population began to expand more rapidly in Britain and exports of grain were turned into growing, if irregular, imports in the last few decades of the eighteenth century, the pressure came off and corn prices started to lift everywhere. Perhaps in Sweden with the much larger internal population these trends were of marginal importance, but in Denmark the recovery of agriculture in the 1750s and 1760s, its setback in the 1770s and its revival in the 1780s does seem to be linked with what happened in the west rather than with population growth locally. Population growth came late to Denmark and was at least as much a consequence of agricultural development as a causal factor. As markets revived for both grain and animals the reformers' arguments about replacing services by free labour began to be attended to. In some measure at least, the cost vice which was behind the imposition of serfdom was unscrewed by the opportunity for higher profits.

However that may be, in Denmark rural reform was certainly carried through with a success which equalled that of Sweden and without pressure from internal urbanisation. It was fortunate that economic events and political intentions allowed the process to take time and avoid all possibility of the expropriation endured elsewhere. The pressures for change then, were not unlike those found in Sweden. They arose out of liberal political and economic ideas: they came from landowners who knew what was being done elsewhere, and what their opportunities were. There was, too, a feeling that serfdom was out of date now that the military justifications for it had largely disappeared. More directly, reform gained full impetus when in 1784 Count Reventlow, one of the leading advocates of change, came to hold powerful office in the Department of Internal and Agricultural Affairs. For more than a decade permissive legislation had allowed consolidation for single individuals and even, by an Act of 1781, for whole villages but the 1770s were not prosperous years and little constructive progress was accomplished. When in 1786 the Great Rural Commission was set up with Reventlow as its most powerful member, to study agrarian conditions throughout the country, it did so against the background of hard times. On the basis of the Commission's recommendations, extensive changes in the pattern and institutions of Danish farming were quickly set in train and yet brought about with a sympathy towards the peasant and cottar which had some affinity with the spirit of reform in Sweden. In 1788 serfdom was abolished, labour services were regulated and then, as prices rose during the 1790s, came to be widely commuted. In 1788, over 100,000 hectares of land were subject to compulsory services: by 1807 this had fallen to 45,000 hectares and by 1861 to 6,000 hectares. This rationalisation spread southwards to the Duchies of Schleswig and Holstein. There the pressure for reform came from the peasants. In 1771 a Land Commission was established and in 1805 serfdom was abolished. Consolidation of strips in Denmark under the 1781 Act went forward rapidly. Here and there star-shaped consolidation was attempted to allow the peasant to stay on his farm in the village but eventually complete dispersion was inevitable. By 1802 half the land had been enclosed and the end of the 1830s saw only 1 per cent still left in joint tenure. Financial assistance was given to tenants to buy their holdings, though the high grain prices of the war years helped much more. Landowners were encouraged to sell by an act of 1807 which allowed them to preserve the manorial rights of tax exemption if they sold off tenant farms. Leases were set at a minimum of fifty years and rent increases supervised and in addition the old restriction against merging of holdings was preserved. The upshot was that by 1860 five-sixths of the peasants were no longer tenants but freeholders. A law of 1861 allowed a landowner who sold land to his tenants to absorb into the demesne farm from the rest of his peasant land as leases expired, an area equivalent to one-ninth of that sold. It increased the size of the big estates slightly but virtually completed the process of creation of a peasant ownership. The cottar was scrupulously granted 4 to 6 acres of land in lieu of common rights but the freezing of the pattern of landholding meant that this class inevitably grew with the rise of population. It was one problem the Great Commission failed to cope with. The rise of population was a recent phenomenon and a big demand for labour during the prosperous last years of the century concealed the real nature of the problem. In any case, apart from the break up of the large estates it is hard to see what else could have been done in the absence of significant alternative occupations away from the land.

The fall of prices after 1815 caused some readjustment. Some who had bought freeholds could not service their debts: small men might buy up these farms and make money growing potatoes for the market but the essential pattern created by the reforms was not shaken. Final accomplishment of equal rights for peasants waited some time as in Sweden, however, the insistent demand for equal taxation being realised only in 1850.

THE SWEDISH ECONOMY IN THE MIDDLE YEARS OF THE NINETEENTH CENTURY

In both Sweden and Denmark, therefore, rural reform evolved gradually and peacefully, but compared with most parts of Continental Europe, it was remarkably complete. What was the nature of the economic developments which followed upon this structural transformation of the countries' basic industry?

Agriculture

In Sweden a still rapidly-rising population continued to be fed entirely from home resources and in addition an export trade in grain was developed, to such an extent that after mid-century it came to rival iron for second place – behind timber – in total exports. After the repeal of the Corn Laws in Britain in 1846 there was a huge expansion of British demand for oats to feed to the growing number of horses employed for pulling buses, cabs and other forms of transport, in London in particular, a demand that Sweden was well placed to help satisfy. Not only had her agriculture become more flexible and commercial but the poor quality land being reclaimed proved to be highly suited to growing oats and, as we have seen, the move to that crop had been under way for at least a century before. It is possible, too, that the increase in potato output released grain for export. In the area of large estates in the east crofts were annexed to take advantage of the profits of this

Q

grain export trade and their owners reduced to farm labourers. In 1870 perhaps 40 per cent of the crop was exported and over the 1860s grain exports made up one-fifth of all Sweden's exports and she was supplying more than one-third of Britain's imports of oats. In some degree it was a one-sided growth, for the development of animal husbandry, as well as the growing of root crops, was neglected, but a niche in European trade was there to be filled and the beneficial effects were striking. Through their impact on the balance of payments these new exports helped to enhance the eventual possibility of raising foreign loans on favourable terms. Perhaps most important of all, the profits from the trade offered ready funds for investment in other sectors of the economy. The augmentation of farmers' incomes and the income-generating effects of reclamation itself helped boost demand for consumer goods at home. Early in the century a peasant home typically contained home-made furniture and implements and the family made its own clothing: after the middle of the century more and more of these articles were being purchased from outside. The concentration on grain production showed some element of caution and some element of rational response to the market. Which was the more powerful would be shown when another and more difficult market situation arose for agriculture during the 1880s.

– Iron

Meantime, other sectors of the economy were changing yet more radically. The successful introduction of new techniques for the manufacture of wrought iron in Britain during the 1780s faced the Swedish iron industry with a most serious crisis. Not only were British ironmasters able to dispense with imports to a growing extent, but more and more they began to enter the export market. Russian iron exports were virtually eliminated. This collapse of a competitor helped Swedish ironmasters to ride the storm, but the industry only survived in the long run because the very high quality charcoal-iron produced from certain ores in Bergslagen, proved to be indispensable for the making of crucible steel, though total exports were for a time much reduced. Recovery set in after 1825 as a result of three factors. One was a growth in demand for this kind of bar iron for steel-making in Britain and elsewhere in Europe. A second was the successful invasion of the American market, where local iron production was expanding only slowly. As stiffer British and local competition built up there, Swedish exporters concentrated on supplying the needs of the nail factories of the north-east and the trade survived reasonably well until the Civil War. Finally, the search for a cheaper way of making high-quality charcoal-iron was resolved by the adoption in the 1840s of an English refining process known as the Lancashire process, after puddling and rolling had been tried with very little success.

Even in 1830 the industry consisted of several hundred production units, each by its little waterfall, the pig and bars being transported long distances. But this pattern, which had been based on the need to preserve a supply of wood for charcoal, began to break down and more and more ironmasters were allowed to expand their productive units to reap the economies of scale. Despite the advances made in finding new markets and in developing new techniques the industry had a hard time struggling to match the 30 per cent fall in iron prices brought about by technological developments in Britain between 1815 and 1840. Still, output of pig iron rose from 80,000 tons in the 1820s to 270,000 in the late 1860s. An industry formerly so strictly regulated and inflexible had shown striking resilience in the face of considerable difficulties. The adjustment to new technologies and new market conditions came only just in time though, for the arrival of cheap steel in the 1860s presented yet another major problem.

– Timber

The most spectacular element in the growth of the economy in mid-century was the boom in exports of timber and, through it, the opening up of the great virgin forests to the north in Norrland. As late as the 1830s Sweden's timber exports were only one-fifth of those from Norway. Both supplied the same cheap woods but in this bulk trade transport costs were critical. Norway was nearer the big consuming markets, her ports were less ice-bound, she still had readily accessible forests and these factors, together with a superior saw-milling technology in Norway, kept Sweden at the fringe of the market. Potentially, urbanisation in Britain offered a massive market: France, Germany, Belgium, The Netherlands, Denmark were increasing their imports too until during the 1860s the volume of world trade in timber was rising at 5–6 per cent annually. Certain factors now began to operate to transform the trade pattern. The tariff preference given to Canadian timber, which had effectively held back European exports to Britain, was removed in the 1850s, but both Norway and Western Sweden began to suffer from exhaustion of supplies and could not readily respond to the increase in demand. So though from the 1860s sawn softwoods from all Northern Europe made a comeback in world markets, it was Norrland above all that profited most; later Finland too came heavily into the market.

With over 20m hectares of productive forest, Sweden possessed the largest such area in Europe after Russia, and no country was so well placed for floating logs to the coast for processing and transport. Rivers in the forest area provided 18,600 miles of suitable waterway. In 1914 an armada of 85m logs was floated to the sea. Because of this cheap transport even timbers of the smallest dimension could be economically taken away for charcoal making, pulping and so forth. The growing class of underemployed cottars provided an ample supply of seasonal labour and in the early days, with working capital more important than fixed capital, credit was supplied from overseas after the pattern already established by the iron industry. Gradually, moreover, experts brought in new technologies from Norway, especially the use of steam engines and fine bladed saws at the mills. There remained the problem of distance. In the 1850s the freight rate for a standard of timber from Norrland to England was about £3·50–£4 or about the cost of the wood itself: from Canada it was much the same. From Gothenberg the freight was only £1·75–£2·25 and from Narvik even less. But in the last two decades of the century the Norrland rate rarely exceeded £1·50. The absolute and relative advantages of competing areas were much reduced and, by lowering the delivery price of wood, demand was boosted. The reason lay partly in improvements of shipping technology, both steam and sail, but also because steam came to monopolise the most lucrative routes and forced sailing ships to compete fiercely for the bulk cargo that was left for them. In addition, as Sweden's own industrialisation gathered pace, the necessary imports of coal and cotton provided excellent inward freights and so lowered the outward.

During the early part of the nineteenth century the State had transferred most of its forest rights (almost all of them valueless at that time) into private hands. A farm of 10 hectares might have 6,000 hectares of woodland with it. The law forbade the acquisition of one without the other and so, when the timber men came along, they bought timber-cutting rights for, say, fifty years, often at a very low price – maybe a sack of flour, barrel of salt, case of tobacco – for the peasant could hardly cut himself and there was plenty on offer. It was a situation conducive to very rapid exploitation of the forest and the industry attracted many ruthless entrepreneurs whose methods aroused much resentment and whose regard for reforestation and conservation was negligible but the consequence was a very sharp boom in the short run. After 1875 the State reversed its policy and began to acquire forests in the northern regions and about this time the timber companies began to purchase whole farms too, often with unfortunate consequences for the tenants on the farmland who became entirely dependent on the whims and requirements of these companies. By 1900 the timber industry owned around 2m hectares in the six northern provinces: of the land in private ownership their share ranged from 24 per cent in Västerbotten to 43 per cent in Gävleborg and Jämtland. Thirteen joint stock companies owned nearly 1m hectares – the largest was a British-owned firm, the Bergvik Ala Nija Aktiebolag, with 100,000 hectares. In the long run the existence of large holdings in the hands of wood-using companies was beneficial for output and exports, for with some prodding from the State, their estates were scientifically managed, in sharp contrast to the reckless cutting that was usually to be found on peasant-owned land both in Norway and in Sweden.

Exports of softwood from Sweden rose from 450m cubic metres in 1850 to 2,000 in 1870 and 4,800 in 1900, and by the 1860s provided 40 per cent of all Sweden's exports, a proportion that was held for the next two decades. Developments in ocean transport and the supply situations of her competitors favoured Norrland. She already possessed in her merchant houses the basic source of enterprise and capital for the industry. The old association with the European market through exports of iron was most valuable as well. The growth of the sawmill industry was to be the strongest element in Swedish economic expansion as a whole before 1870. Mechanisation of the industry gave the first significant boost to the engineering industry through demand for steam engines and saws. More important was the general impetus given to internal growth while at the same time keeping the balance of payments in a healthy condition. Sweden could therefore pay for the imports of manufactures and materials induced by this expansion and yet keep the kroner strong so that when the time came to borrow overseas, loans could be arranged easily on favourable terms, the element of risk being so low.

It is hardly surprising that exports should have been the focus of growth, for the low level of urbanisation and poor internal communications contrasted sharply with the opportunities offered by seaborne trade to higher income countries, to Britain above all. Nevertheless the contrast between home and export growth should not be exaggerated: here was no dual economy with advanced export and backward home sectors. Partly this was due to the fact that the general improvement in agricultural techniques had raised the consumption of the mass of peasants, especially after mid-century.

Partly also, through the merchant houses there was a sufficient reservoir of finance and enterprise to make sure that the expansionary effects of the growing export sector would not be devoted simply to increasing imports. In addition other important internal developments came at this time too.

– Railways

Railways came relatively late to Sweden. Not until 1853–4 was even a preliminary decision made as to the extent and financing of the first lines. A network was planned in which the main lines were to be built and administered by the state, with private investors financing the subsidiary lines. The idea was deliberately to stimulate internal development by pushing lines into relatively thinly-populated areas, by-passing, even, some of the older centres. One result of this was that unusually heavy investment was needed to create the new communities that developed around the railway centres. The income-generating effects of railway construction were therefore greater than they would otherwise have been and there may also have been considerable benefits derived from the relocation of population from areas of relatively low production to more productive regions.

The length of railway was 527 km in 1860. During the next decade 1,200 km were added, 4,150 km in the 1870s, 2,140 in the 1880s and nearly 3,300 in the 1890s. Not only were the actual increases greatest during the 1870s, but with the economy then less developed, the relative role of railways was even more significant. Over that decade 3 per cent of the national income was devoted to the railways: in 1876 such investment reached as high a level as 6·3 per cent. The expansionary effects can be gauged partly, too, from the fact that in the middle of the decade over a quarter of a million men – well over one-tenth of the total male population – found employment on the railways. Mechanical engineering gained most of all from this investment. Swedish economists have calculated that from 1868 to 1880 17 per cent of the industry's output was destined for this market and for two years it was as high as 30 per cent. Given the future role of engineering in Sweden's growth, this ability to dispense with imported supplies so early, and without the help of a high tariff, was extremely significant. In large part it was based on the earlier growth of the industry under the impetus of demands from the sawmilling industry, for almost all the work was done by existing firms. After 1877 all coaches and wagons were made in Sweden: they were easy to build and there was a lot of joinery work in them but all the same, the numbers required were large. From 1868 to 1880 304 locomotives were imported, 145 were built in Sweden and in 1880 the first locomotive was exported. In complete contrast, the iron and steel industry gained very little: railway requirements were under 1 per cent of production in the 1870s, simply because all rails were imported from Britain and Germany, for the Swedish industry could not hope to compete in the supply of such bulk products. The impact of lower transport costs is less well documented: some trades such as timber that depended on waterways so heavily, were not greatly affected and it is as well to remember that the economy had made considerable strides through the development of grain exports and realignment of the iron industry before the railways arrived. But with a country of such broken terrain and hostile climate, it is reasonable to assume that the direct impact was eventually very substantial. Certainly, despite the late start, by 1914 Sweden had 25 km of railway for every inhabitant, twice that of any other European country. This reflects in part the low density of population but it reflects too a real determination to overcome the disadvantages of such sparseness.

– Commercial Policy

The middle decades of the century saw Sweden following the general European trend towards trade liberalisation under very similar philosophical and economic pressures. In 1846 the guilds were dissolved and virtually complete internal free trade brought about. The severe navigation laws had been whittled down by international treaties earlier: protectionist duties lasted longer but they too were much reduced by the mid-1860s. The attitude of the State towards the formation of joint stock companies also became less restrictive in that decade too. There emerged a new type of joint stock bank, willing to undertake the kind of deposit banking that the central bank – the Riksbank – and the private note-issuing banks founded in the 1830s, had eschewed altogether. 1857 saw the founding of Stockholms Enskilda Bank, which was later to build close contacts with industry and also with overseas financiers. In 1863 it was followed by Skandinaviska Kreditaktiebolaget. Their development followed that of similar institutions in France and Germany: the merchants who had formerly fed money into industry turned to these new institutions, as their own private resources became too limited to satisfy the growing needs of the time.

In their various ways these institutional changes reflected the pressures of a growing economy and in turn led to further development. It would be wrong, however, to suggest that they were all that important for Swedish growth *at this time*. Industrialisation was very limited in 1870, industry and handicrafts employing only 15 per cent of the population. Of 80,000 men in manufacturing and mining, 26,000 were employed in the iron industry and 15,000 in sawmills. There were some 12,400 in textiles and 6,400 in engineering. Industry had been growing steadily over the previous two decades: imports of cotton were 563 tons in 1836–40 and 8,000 in 1871–5: imports of coal rose from 13,000 tons to 600,000 tons but these were very low absolute levels and industrialisation in any real sense had not yet begun. Norrköping, the textile centre, was still a small place of 24,000 inhabitants in 1870 and Stockholm, the chief industrial centre, was still losing its share of the country's total population. Even the iron districts comprised small separate communities. There was nothing comparable to the coal and iron centres of Britain, Belgium and the Ruhr.

THE SWEDISH ECONOMY 1870–1914

Table 33 shows how the economy developed over the next half century. For the whole period national income rose 2·8 per cent per annum in current prices, compared with 4·4 per cent for industrial production, and just over 3 per cent for exports. This table shows that national income grew most rapidly during the early 1870s when it was boosted by very favourable terms of trade,

Table 33. *Percentage rates of growth of the Swedish economy 1869–1912*

	National income (fixed prices)	Industrial production (fixed prices)
1869–78	30·7	17·4
1874–83	10·0	22·5
1879–88	8·4	17·7
1884–93	12·7	24·1
1889–98	16·2	37·8
1894–1903	18·6	25·9
1899–1908	16·0	20·0
1904–1912	15·6	15·7

Source: L. Jorberg, *Growth and Fluctuations of Swedish Industry, 1869–1912* (Stockholm, 1961), pp. 19 and 23.

brought about by the high demand for timber, which arose during the worldwide boom ending in 1873. Industrial production grew relatively slowly during the 1880s after enjoying an expansion which must have been influenced directly and indirectly to a considerable degree by railway building. The 1890s saw industrial production growing most quickly but a high rate was maintained until just before 1914, by which time industry may have been suffering from some degree of over-capacity. The same may also have been true of the 1880s. It is interesting to note that investment in machinery rose 29 per cent in real terms from 1874 to 1883, and only 4 per cent from 1883 to 1888. Similarly it rose 16·4 per cent from 1894 to 1903, and only 9·6 over the next ten years.

The overall effect was that the national product per head in Sweden rose in real terms faster than in any other country except Japan, and, by a small margin, the United States. It grew by 26·2 per cent per decade: within Europe next came Germany at 21·6 per cent, Denmark at 19·3 per cent, France 16·3 per cent and Russia at 10·4 per cent. The share of agriculture and forestry in Gross Domestic Product fell from 38 per cent in 1873 to 24·5 per cent in 1913, though the absolute numbers engaged in agriculture only began to fall after the 1880s. The share of mining and manufacture rose from 13·2 per cent to 29·7 per cent over these same years, though a considerable amount of manufacturing was derived from timber production of course. The distribution of industrial workers is shown in Table 34.

This is the statistical skeleton of the industrial revolution in Sweden. One striking feature is the minor degree to which Swedish growth was set back by cyclical fluctuations. One may explain this

Table 34. *Percentage share of industrial workers by industrial groups in Sweden, 1869–1908*

	1869–78	1879–88	1889–98	1899–1908
Total workers (000)	100	126	208	306
Value of production (m Kr)	345	415	716	1,372
Food, drink, tobacco	5·8	6·0	7·4	9·2
Textiles	14·8	12·9	12·9	12·8
Wood	17·4	19·9	20·8	17·5
Pulp, paper, printing	4·0	4·5	7·7	8·4
Chemicals	4·5	4·9	4·2	3·6
Engineering	11·7	13·5	15·8	18·9
Mines, Iron and Steel	27·2	23·0	14·5	10·1

Source: L. Jorberg, *Growth and Fluctuations of Swedish Industry, 1869–1912* (Stockholm, 1961), p. 51.

partly by special circumstances. As we have seen, the powerful upsurge of growth in the 1870s was led by a boom in overseas demand for Swedish exports and intensified by a great rise in railway construction. The crisis of 1873 passed relatively easily, though prices fell back, largely because Britain, which was Sweden's biggest market, enjoyed a strong rise of home investment immediately after the termination of the burst of overseas investment. Furthermore, the British boom in house building in the 1870s brought particularly heavy requirements for Swedish timber. To some degree her agricultural exports were counter-cyclical and in this way Sweden gained from her balanced growth. But also her ability to surmount fluctuations was a function of her astonishing rate of growth and how do we explain that? She benefited from being able to tap the technology and the capital resources of other countries – in terms of foreign loans per head she was the biggest borrower in Europe. Her wage levels in the 1870s, at least, were below those in Britain and probably below those in comparable German industries. For most of the period she benefited from improving terms of trade, for her raw materials were of a kind that were in highly elastic demand in a Europe of rising incomes and rapid industrialisation. But explanations such as these seem to fit the experience of most under-developed areas in Europe. Two other factors apply particularly to Sweden, however. First of all, as we saw earlier, Sweden came to enjoy a much greater degree of social mobility in the eighteenth century and with the government carefully encouraging structural changes in agriculture too, the country was particularly receptive to economic opportunities when the time for radical change came. Then, by no means divorced from that first point, there was the atonishing ability of Swedish entrepreneurs to exploit the potentially very bountiful gifts of nature, to move from one area to another, to adjust technology in accordance with the shifting pressures of European demand. Unfortunately historians have not been particularly successful in explaining why this was so. It may be that it owed something to the quality of education in Sweden. Gymnasia, on the German model, teaching modern subjects, went back to the seventeenth century and although education was not made compulsory until 1882 the evidence seems to be that literacy was high and certainly the fact that in 1882 school was required up to the age of 14 suggests that the importance of education was already widely recognised. However that may be, the general pattern was that if the boom of the 1870s was dominated by the building of railways, that of the 1890s was dominated by the exploitation of new technologies; both periods saw high exports for part of the time, leading to high profits and a direct stimulus to home investment. It is with all these points in mind that we can now look at the post-1870 period in more detail.

– Agriculture in Crisis

As industrialisation went forward agriculture naturally lost some of its relative importance in the economy but this trend was intensified by the peculiar difficulties facing the rural population. The share of agriculture in gross domestic capital formation fell from one-third in 1873 to one-twelfth in 1913. Agriculture's share of the labour force was 49 per cent in 1913 compared with 72 per cent in 1873. The absolute numbers fell for the first time in 1880 and declined by 4 per cent over that decade and continued with a loss of 5 per cent in each of the two succeeding decades. All the same it is important to realise that these losses were sustained above all by the subsistence agricultural sector. The large estates and peasant farms of high productivity competed strongly with industry for labour from the underemployed sector of the agricultural economy. The crisis that faced all European farmers as a consequence of the fall in grain prices during the 1880s was met by the imposition of protective duties in 1888 and 1892. The results were complicated. In the late 1880s only a half of consumption of wheat was grown at home. By 1906–10 home output had risen by three-quarters with the help of protection but this was still only a half of total consumption. The rise in population and a shift away from rye bread explain why this was so. Rye output also rose slowly but from being five times that of wheat, fell to little over three times as large over the same period. Perhaps more revealing are the figures for international trade in cereals. In 1871–5 exports were about twice imports (36·8m Kr compared with 19·2m). Only a decade later imports were considerably above exports (41·2m Kr as against 29m) and by 1910 imports, though held back by the tariff, had risen to 58m Kr and exports were negligible. In Sweden as in every country in Western Europe, trends of this kind were inevitable and only modified by varying degrees by protection. The export of oats reached its peak in the late 1870s and then declined rapidly. There were two reasons for this: growing competition developed from Russian oats and American maize but more important, the divergent movement of the prices of oats and of animal produce made it more profitable to feed the oats to cattle at home to produce milk for butter making. By the turn of the century butter exports were as high as oats exports had ever been, but thereafter they stagnated, as producers concentrated on satisfying the home market. The adjustment towards animal products was not nearly so complete in Sweden as in Denmark, if only because of the tariff on grains. In the north, too, the long winter made rearing and fattening costly. The area under fodder roots for example was five times as great in Denmark as in Sweden in 1911–15. At the outbreak of war Swedish butter exports were only a quarter of the Danish. Nevertheless there was much progress in rotations, in the use of fertilisers and, after 1900 in mechanisation. The Holstein form of twin cultivation with about half the land under corn and the rest under artificial grasses was very widely used. Natural meadows were largely ploughed up: the area under crops rose from 2·5 to 3·6m hectares from 1870 to 1910 while that under grass fell from 2·0 to 1·3m. Subsidies for beet sugar refining brought a new crop into the rotations as well as eliminating imports of sugar which had been worth some 18m Kr in the late 1870s. Tariffs and subsidies for agriculture distorted the allocation of resources and raised prices to the consumer but all the same a notable increase in labour productivity was gained while the framework of peasant society was preserved largely unaltered. Just before 1914 the larger gentry farms, comprising 2–3 per cent of the freeholds, covered a quarter of the cultivated land though only 10 per cent of this land was directly cultivated by them. A quarter of the farms and half the cultivated land comprised the peasant estates of 10–50 hectares though it should be borne in mind that only one-ninth of the land area was cultivated. In general, the total number of landowners did not greatly change over the second half of the nineteenth century: the great break up of estates of the second half of the eighteenth century was now halted. Emigration and industrialisation mitigated the difficulties of the less well off by offering alternative opportunities. Between 1870 and 1910 the numbers of cottars and their children fell from 134,000 to 91,000 and there was an even sharper drop in numbers of farm servants from 241,000 to 93,000. Agriculture ceased to be a leading force in growth but it did not stagnate. There was some distortion of trade patterns but also more adjustment than is sometimes allowed. The overall effect on the balance of payments was not great: in 1871–5 trade in animals, meat, butter, cereals and sugar gave an export surplus of 7m Kr: in 1906–10 there was an import surplus of 17m Kr. Over these same years the total import surplus grew from 36 to 123m Kr so that the turnaround in agriculture was hardly critical. The tensions of economic development were lessened by the fact that agriculture had been transformed before significant industrialisation and foreign competition came about. Industrial growth arrived when the problems of feeding an urban proletariat had largely been resolved and the difficulties of international competition did not markedly modify this situation.

– Timber and its Products

The sawmill industry continued to give the greatest single impetus
to the economy right to 1900 and though the rate of growth of
output slackened in the eighties, in the next decade it was almost as
high as before and the absolute gains were naturally much greater,
a development only made possible by the rapid spread and improvement of steam sawing techniques, which permitted the sawmills to
operate near the coast instead of up the rivers near water-wheels.
After 1900, when the industry came to face greater competition,
mechanisation went forward very rapidly. The number of workers
fell by one-fifth between 1900 and 1912, whereas horse power per
worker rose by three-quarters: it was one of the most important
contributions that industrial technology made to economic growth
in Sweden. In 1900 Sweden enjoyed 43 per cent of the European
timber trade and such exports provided 40 per cent of her own
total exports. But then came a decline in the rate of growth and
output and an absolute fall in exports. They still made up over a
quarter of the total in 1914 but timber had ceased to be the driving
force in the economy. The stagnation derived partly from depletion
of home resources, partly from the competition of pulp manufacturers and, externally, from Russian and Finnish competition.

The first pulp mill was set up in Sweden in 1857, though it was a
primitive form of production: the wood was ground into fibres but
the lignin, which causes its disintegration, was not removed. The
paper produced by this mechanical method was poor and the
industry grew slowly. Then came the introduction of chemical
processes to dissolve out the lignin, leaving a pure cellulose from
which strong and durable paper could be made. The first chemical
pulp factory in the world was established at Bergvik in northern
Sweden in 1872. A further impetus to growth came after 1890 when
a new process, based on sodium sulphate, was developed for the
manufacture of coarse paper. The timber men looked upon pulp as
a competitor and did all they could to hinder its growth and
abstained from any significant investment until the sulphate techniques made possible the utilisation of sawdust in pulp manufacture.
Much of the capital for the pulp industry tended to come from firms
looking for a substitute for their own activities: above all it came
from the small iron and steel makers, in danger of being put out of
business by technological and organisational changes in that industry.
Growth of output was astonishingly rapid – 17 per cent per annum
from 1870 to 1895 and 11 per cent from 1896 to 1913, though the
value of output grew more slowly to 1910 as the cost-reducing
innovations brought pulp prices down and gave added impetus **to**

demand. This was a period of great growth in newspapers throughout the world, a growth which encouraged pulp production and which was itself stimulated in part by falling costs as well as by rising incomes and literacy. The price of mechanical pulp fell from 400 Kr/ton in the 1870s to 50 Kr in the 1890s: chemical pulp was roughly twice as expensive at each decade. Exports by 1904–12 were 70 cer cent of production: only timber was more dependent on foreign trade than that.

Along with the rise of the pulp industry went the manufacture of paper, above all newsprint, coarse wrapping paper and paper board, most of these mills being fully integrated with their pulp factories. They were concentrated in central and southern Sweden, above all in the Norrköping region. Again Sweden was fortunate that her resource pattern fitted in with the astonishing rise in demand for paper among the high income countries of the world. It was fortunate too that demand for paper was far less subject to cyclical fluctuations than that for timber and steel, for example. But the growth of the industry owed much to Swedish initiative, both through the invention of the new technologies and also through their later improvement – to such an extent that from 1890–1910 output per worker in paper mills went up by 218 per cent and in pulp mills by 160 per cent. Certainly after 1900 these two industries replaced timber as driving forces in the economy.

Swedish technology also played an important role in the growth of the match industry, though quantitatively this was a much less important aspect of the timber product industry. In 1855 Johann Edvard Lundstrom of Jönköping took up the production of a safety match invented some years before by Professor Pasch of the Swedish Royal Academy of Science. This match had replaced the horribly poisonous yellow phosphorus previously used, by the non-toxic red phosphorus and transferred it from the match head to the striking surface. Then in 1872 Alexander Lagermann invented a machine to eliminate much of the labour in the manufacturing process. By 1913 54 per cent of the matches used in the U.K. were imported, over one-half of them from Sweden, though by this time the supply of aspen wood was rapidly being exhausted and more and more had to be imported from Russia and Finland. The Jönköping factory had amalgamated with six others in 1903 and in 1913 Ivan Kreuger grouped another nine factories to form United Swedish Match Factories; four years later the two groups amalgamated. Already by 1900 there were extensive international market sharing agreements between the Swedish makers and the American Diamond Match Company: from its earliest days Jönköping had had close links with Bryant and May in Britain and as a result of

Kreuger's intervention the stage was set for one of the most spectacular international cartel movements of the twentieth century.

– Iron and Steel

The iron and steel industry, by contrast, grew much more slowly, production rising by 3·2 per cent per annum from 1867–9 to 1892–5 and 2·2 per cent from 1896 to 1918, and achieved this only as a result of very extensive structural and technical changes. The 1870s saw the last great boom for iron but then the readjustment problems became severe indeed. In 1856 Bessemer discovered his revolutionary new method for making steel and though Swedish writers stress that the process was first used in Sweden, the point is of only antiquarian interest, as the enterprise was entirely unprofitable and short-lived. The fundamental point was that it now became possible for the main industrial countries to make steel cheaply without utilising Swedish charcoal iron. In the event demand for Lancashire iron did not fall drastically until after 1900. The Swedes continued to make pig iron exclusively by charcoal – uniquely in Europe. Exports of this pig and Lancashire iron were supplemented by a new trade in very high grade steel made from charcoal pig. The danger always was that advances in metallurgy would undermine these very specialised exports. Like Britain, Sweden continued to concentrate on acid steel. The basic steel made from phosphoric ores now being exploited in the north, was mainly for internal use. The industry continued to rely mainly on the ores in the central field and after 1900 considerable progress was made in treating the huge dumps of low grade ore – less than 40 per cent iron content – to be found near all the mines in that area. Such a change in the pattern of output was accompanied by big structural changes: smaller works closed, production was concentrated, furnaces grew in size. The increased output after 1870 was achieved with an almost stationary labour force but the new technologies were even more capital-saving and the capital/output ratio fell from 2·6 in the 1880s to 1·8 in 1900. But the Swedish scale of production remained very small in comparison with that elsewhere: in 1913 her blast-furnaces were only one-tenth the size of the best in Europe. The industry survived by dominating the world market for the highest quality iron and steel – in 1912–13 70 per cent of the output was exported – whilst retaining the home market for the lower quality metal with the help of tariff protection. After 1900 some initial efforts were made to produce high quality steel in electric furnaces, using cheap hydroelectric power, making a metal fitting Sweden's traditional specialism and employing a technology where scale economies were slight. Before 1914, however, progress was not great, though the Stora Kopparberg plant at Domnarfvet was at that time the largest producer of electric pig iron in the world. The share of iron and steel in total exports fell from 26 per cent in the early 1870s to 9 per cent in 1906–10 and in addition there was a gradual increase in imports of low quality pig and steel.

– Iron Ore

Yet once again stagnation in one sector was offset by developments elsewhere, trends which were to supply one of the most dynamic elements in the twentieth-century Swedish economy – the exploitation of the northern ores. Not until 1857 was the export of iron ore allowed at all: the obvious customer, Britain, began to increase imports of non-phosphoric ore after 1870 but such ores in central Sweden were poorly placed to compete with the better located supplies from Spain. It was the Gilchrist–Thomas process of 1878 which focussed interest upon the prospect of mining phosphoric ores, and it was to Germany, not to Britain, that the trade was eventually to be geared. Such ores were to be found in vast quantities in Norrbotten in the iron mountains at Gällivare and Kirunavare. From the former it was 170 miles to the Norwegian port of Narvik – ice-free all the year round. A railway to Luleå on the Baltic from the ore field was completed in 1886, though that port was open for only five months of the year. The line to Narvik in Norway was opened in 1903. The iron content of the ore was high, more than 60 per cent. Output grew by over 9 per cent per annum from 1896 to 1913 and by the latter date provided 8 per cent of all exports and was contributing far more strikingly to the expansion of steel making in the Ruhr than in Sweden itself, the small size of the home market giving Sweden no basis upon which to compete internationally in the routine bulk products made by the basic process with these phosphoric ores.

– Manufacturing Industry

The level to which Sweden succeeded in restructuring her exports in these various ways is indicated by the fact that the three leading commodities, timber products, grain and iron and steel accounted for 68 per cent of all exports in 1881–5 and only 36 per cent in 1911–13 and yet exports had risen to be 22·1 per cent of national income in 1913 compared with less than 18 per cent in 1870: of the major European countries only Denmark could show a higher proportion in 1913 with 29 per cent. Despite all this, such was the pace of internal development that Sweden ran an ever-growing trade deficit, rising from over 36m Kr on average from 1871–5 (18 per cent of exports) to 123m Kr in 1906–10 (24 per cent of exports), though in the last four years before 1914 the situation was transformed by the boom in exports of pulp, paper and iron ore.

We shall examine the financing of these deficits later: looking simply at the most important imports related to industrial growth, in 1913 coal imports were valued at 103m Kr, chemicals for a whole range of industries such as pulp, glass, fertilisers, soap, surprisingly enough about the same. Imports of oils were 55m Kr, textile raw materials and hides and skins 78m Kr, steel 28m, copper 19m, engineering goods 40m. It was imports of foodstuffs and of textiles that lost their relative importance, being over a half of imports in 1870 and only a little over a quarter at the end of the period. Only to a minor extent can these new industrial imports be regarded as import content of exports. They were basically required by Swedish manufacturing industry, which was growing after 1890 at a faster pace then exports.

It would be tedious to go through this industrial development in any detail, not because it was unimportant but because much of it calls for no special comment. Based on a small local market though much encouraged by the improvement of internal transport, protected by moderate tariffs, the consumer goods industries concentrated on eliminating imports as far as possible, without producing goods of a type, price or quality that would make an impact on world markets. The expansion of consumer goods production went forward at 3·3 per cent per annum from 1867–9 to 1892–5 compared with 5·2 per cent for capital goods which were geared more towards the demands of the export sectors and which were much stimulated by railway construction. From 1896 to 1912, however, both grew at a rate just in excess of 6 per cent per annum. This acceleration of growth and above all the much faster rate of growth of consumer goods output points to an important change in the nature of the Swedish economy.[3] Expansion now began to reflect more the call of the home market: Swedish industry was becoming self-generating. New industries such as sugar refining, ready-to-wear clothing, and furniture began to expand rapidly just as did the older trades such as brewing and textiles. With the exception of engineering, the main export industries were still rural based but not in the same highly

[3] The absolute annual levels of output 1904/12 were 791m. Kr. for consumer goods and 864 m. for capital goods.

dispersed way as before. Now sizeable communities were growing up in each centre of production, whether it be steel, or sawmilling, pulp or paper-making, matches or iron ore. Whereas in 1870 13 per cent of the population lived in towns, in 1910 it was almost one quarter. Stockholm, so long stagnant, rose from 136,000 inhabitants to 342,000: Gothenberg from 56,000 to 168,000. There was no other town above 100,000 inhabitants, but it is well to remember that Sweden was still a very thinly populated land and, compared with what was taking place in France, Germany, Austria, Russia, her growth, though striking by proportions, was small in absolute terms. But this small size was an advantage in a very real sense, especially to the mature engineering industry, for with output so small it was not difficult to find specialist niches in world trade. If Britain were to compete with Germany in electrical engineering on such a scale as to restructure her industrial economy significantly, for example, she had no alternative but to compete in all the main fields of generating equipment, motors, vehicles and so forth. For Sweden it was enough to establish particular specialities.

Mechanical engineering grew up initially on the basis of home orders for threshing machines, wood-working machinery and steam engines. Typically they were very small businesses started up by men who had learned their trades as foremen in similar kinds of undertakings. The railway boom of the 1870s added a powerful boost to industry and a continuing flow of orders thereafter. The industry's most spectacular success originated in de Laval's patent for an improved cream separator and turbine taken out in 1878. His company began manufacturing in 1883 and after 1900, as the patents ran out, more companies came in to manufacture other models in Sweden. In 1912 exports of dairy machines provided a quarter of all engineering exports. Turbines, oil engines, pumps, ball bearings, wood-working machinery, gas accumulators were other major exports. Perhaps a quarter of total engineering output was exported, mainly by a group of large specialist firms. But the bulk of the industry was less specialised, smaller in scale, catering for regional and local markets and imports of engineering products were only slightly smaller than exports. Danish engineering was very similar and so was that of several other semi-industrial countries – Bohemia, Holland, Hungary, Italy for example. The small sector of export specialities marked out each from the others but its relative importance was everywhere limited. The electrical industry got an early start in Sweden, for the first central station was set up there in 1885 only two years after the first in Europe at Milan. The degree of concentration of production was very high – two firms providing 84 per cent of total output in 1912. One, L. M. Ericssons, produced telephone and telegraph equipment mainly for export: the other, Allmänna Svenska Elektriska AB (Asea) produced electrical machinery and power equipment for the home market, though the company played a big part in the development of hydroelectric power in Norway just prior to 1914. By international standards, however, neither firm was very large, employing about 1,500 workers each in 1912.

Nevertheless here was an important break from the traditional Swedish reliance on exports of primary products and semi-manufactures. Especially after 1900 exports of manufactures expanded quickly to reach over 10 per cent of all exports in 1912. It was an expansion deriving little from import substitution, but generated by the adoption of new technologies, most of which originated outside Sweden in the last quarter of the nineteenth century. Insofar as several were concerned with non-coal power technologies, the link with Sweden's resource pattern is obvious. Cheap hydroelectric power not only allowed Sweden to overcome earlier disadvantages in fuel supply but also offered positive cost advantages in some industrial sectors. Exports benefited too from the support offered by the deposit banks of the Enskilda type. That organisation gave support to de Laval, to the development of telephone manufacture, to diesel production, helped provide the kind of bulk capital a firm such as Asea required and through investment in Norway's electro-chemical and electro-metallurgical industries helped provide orders. All this in addition to investment in the northern ore fields and the sawmills in Norrbotten. All the same it is important to keep the overall scene in perspective and to remember that all the workers involved in Swedish engineering exports in 1912 were no more than those to be found in one large German railway works.

– *Factors in Swedish Economic Growth*

We have already suggested a variety of reasons to explain the pace of Swedish growth in particular sectors. It was of basic importance that the agricultural sector had been modernised and a significant *(1)* export trade built up before the process of industralisation came about. In a low income country such as Sweden was in the mid-*(2)* nineteenth century, it was easier for the export sector to grow than the home market. Yet the existence of a substantial reservoir of *(3)* surplus agricultural labour meant that for several decades workers could be drawn from that sector both for industry and for the commercial agricultural sector at a low supply price, thereby boosting profits and encouraging further investment. Sweden was fortunate in that her markets were the highest income countries in Europe. Britain dominated but when Germany began to grow quickly at the end of the nineteenth century her need for iron ore enabled Sweden to begin to exploit that market effectively too. The range of her exports and her small size made it less difficult to adjust to the changing patterns of world trade and made her less susceptible to cyclical swings in activity. The very rapid expansion during the 1890s was, as it was elsewhere, a second wave of the first surge of growth in the 1870s but Sweden, being so strongly export oriented, gained an extra boost from those other economies, Germany in particular, which were growing under the same time pattern. Her timber trade gained from the massive rise in house building in Britain at that time too. She was able to benefit from imported technology but her wide trading networks made the diffusion process all that faster. The profits from exports passing onto the capital market also helped maintain low rates of interest.

The balance of payments situation was helped by two factors above all. In the first place the terms of trade – the relationship between import and export prices – were extremely favourable, improving by almost 50 per cent from 1872 to 1913. The switch away from exports of oats meant that Sweden avoided most of the unfavourable effects of falling grain prices that plagued many of Europe's agricultural exporters to 1900 but remarkably enough the European boom after 1896 maintained the prices for Sweden's exports well enough to keep the terms of trade improving after 1900 when they were falling for every other country in Western Europe except Italy. In the second place, in *per capita* terms, Sweden was the biggest overseas borrower in Europe. Given the degree of development of the economy prior to 1870, it was not surprising that capital was ready to move into Sweden on relatively favourable terms: to him that hath shall be given. Mortgage banks were the largest single borrowers abroad before 1860, selling bonds on somewhat onerous terms in Hamburg. In the 1870s and 1880s much larger amounts of foreign money moved into these mortgage institutions, much of it for investment in agriculture, through the medium of Sveriges Allmänna Hypoteksbank, established in 1861 as part of a move to improve the capital market. The state and local authorities borrowed heavily too. After 1890 foreign banking consortia began to place money in Swedish industry, usually through the medium of one or other of the deposit banks. One estimate suggests that of foreign capital placed in Sweden by 1908, 38 per cent comprised National Debt holdings, 16·5 per cent Municipal Bonds, 11·5 per cent had gone to banks, 11 per cent to the mortgage banks and 8 per cent into industrial and mining companies. The

[margin note: 90% held abroad]

State debt in 1913 stood at 683m Kr the greatest part arising from investment in railway construction. Of this, 90 per cent was held abroad, mostly in France. So large was foreign investment that in the 1880s it had provided 45 per cent of Gross Domestic Capital Formation, a level not far exceeded in any other country in the world and certainly unique in Europe. From 1900 to 1910 it averaged about 16 per cent. In this way foreign money financed the building of much of the infrastructure of the economy, boosted its major raw material and industrial export sectors and gave substantial help to agriculture too. At the same time, the balance of payments problems that might be expected to arise from the growth of an urban economy with a relatively high import propensity, were set aside. The tariff on individual imports was modest by European standards as Table 35 shows. Being subject to competition either in the export market or from imports, a relatively high rate of growth of productivity was not surprising. From 1911 Sweden became a small net capital exporter. The trade balance improved dramatically from a deficit of 142m Kr in 1909 to only 50m Kr in 1913 largely because of increased exports of iron ore, and shipping income rose too from 59m Kr to 98m Kr partly as a result of this growth of trade.

[margin note: net cap. xp.]

Table 35. *Index of the level of tariff on fifty industrial products, 1913*

Sweden	100	Germany	110	France	201
Denmark	51	Austria/Hungary	139	Italy	182
Norway	88	Switzerland	46	Russia	372

Source: Swedish Tariff Commission Report 1913, quoted in E. Jensen, *Danish Agriculture* (Copenhagen, 1937), p. 151.

According to Phelps-Brown, on average from 1905 to 1911 the National Domestic Product per occupied person in Sweden averaged £65 per annum, the same as in Germany but compared with £96 in Britain. The figures are only broad estimates but the higher level of income in Britain was largely due to the much smaller share of the occupied population engaged in agriculture – 12 per cent compared with 50 per cent in Sweden. Industrial output per head in Sweden must have been much closer to the British level and possibly above the German, given the fact that 35 per cent of the working population in Germany were engaged in agriculture. We can perhaps get some indication of this from Phelps-Brown's calculation that around 1905–9 the average annual industrial wage in Sweden was £47 compared with £42 in Germany and £36·50 in France.[4] It was £56 in

[margin note: income]
[margin note: wages]

[4] E. H. Phelps-Brown, *A Century of Pay* (London, 1968), p. 46.

Britain but the evidence is that a big rise in relative wages took the Swedish near to the British in 1914. It is possible that with the slowing down of the rate of growth of population and the apparent limitation to the supply of surplus agricultural labour as shown by the rapid decline in emigration after 1900, the share of wages in national income was higher in Sweden than in many other places on the Continent.

DENMARK IN THE NINETEENTH CENTURY

– Agricultural Change

In Denmark, as in Sweden, the development of the economy was given a major impetus by changes in agriculture. The great rural reforms of the turn of the century placed the farming community in a situation in which it was able to respond vigorously to the challenges and opportunities offered by economic growth in Europe. In general, once the difficulties occasioned by the fall of prices after the Napoleonic Wars had been overcome, Danish agriculture enjoyed a half century of relatively untroubled expansion, and this growth brought some development of the provincial towns whose population expanded three times as fast as that of the capital down to 1850. Traditionally Denmark had relied on the export of two commodities, grain and cattle. Live animals continued to be sent south but the trade in rye to Norway was severely handicapped by the effects of the separation of the two countries in 1814 and the export of wheat to Britain was also restricted by the Corn Laws. It is doubtful how important these laws were in keeping grain out of Britain and as the population was growing fast and a sliding scale of duties substituted in 1828, Danish exports were already moving upwards before complete repeal came in 1846. By the end of the 1860s grain exports were twice what they had been thirty years before, and already about a third of total farm output was exported. Rising prices from the 1840s onwards encouraged new investment in marling, draining (helped by a lowering of the duty on British drain pipes in 1857), and reclamation. The idea of reclaiming the moors of Central and West Jutland was a century old but in the thirty years after 1850 half of it was accomplished. In part it was a patriotic response to the call for action after the loss of Schleswig Holstein. 'What we have lost without we will gain within.' Indeed much of Danish history in the middle and later nineteenth century was marked by this kind of emotion and in this instance the long run economic benefits were highly satisfactory, though not surprisingly the short run effect of reclamation was to reduce overall agricultural productivity quite markedly.

Denmark had never relied exclusively on grain, however: there had always been a pastoral tradition, strongest in Jutland but present in most other areas too. From the eighteenth century, on enclosed lands, Danish farmers had begun to adopt more and more a system of rotations copied from the Holstein convertible husbandry pattern – one of putting the land under corn for four years and then putting it down to grass for the next five to seven years. It was a system suited to a country where there was little permanent meadow land, no large home market for cereals and a climate not ideal for wheat. It was geared to corn and cattle exports in a ratio roughly of 3 : 2. In 1861, taking the country as a whole, half the land was under corn and pulses (rye output was four times that of wheat), 39 per cent under grass and green fodder, 9 per cent fallow, the rest under potatoes and roots. The great advantage of the Holstein system was that the proportions could be altered in response to changes in the relative prices of farm products. To the 1860s there was a gradual shift towards livestock and some significant experiments in large scale dairying on the large scale estates in the south. Possibly the farming community was somewhat conservative in its attitude to new technologies but the real price changes warranted no substantial acceleration of the process to this time.

Nevertheless, though the pattern of farming was technically easy to adjust, the crisis which followed the collapse of world grain prices in the 1870s was not easily surmounted. Techniques were poor in many areas, for there was still much fallow and inadequate use of fertiliser and among the peasants in general dairying was very backward. Exports of grain dropped sharply and more and more was imported for fodder and after 1882 imports were always in excess of exports. The area under grains actually rose by 10 per cent from 1870 to 1900, but this represented an increase in the output of rye and oats and other crops for animal feeding. The area under wheat was halved; it remained as a major crop on the rich loam land of the islands, but more and more the varieties grown at home were those giving high yields and suitable for animal feeding. Roots were brought into the Holstein rotation in imitation of practice on the best Scottish farms, and to supplement these feeds there were considerable imports of oil cake. There was also a jump in the import of fertiliser, though this came most markedly after 1900.

These modifications in cropping practice were directed towards raising the animal population. Table 36 shows that the numbers of

Table 36. *Output of Danish agriculture, 1871–1914*

		1871	1893	1914
Dairy cows	(000)	808	1,011	1,310
Other cattle	,,	431	685	1,153
Pigs	,,	442	829	2,497
Sheep	,,	1,842	1,247	515
Poultry	,,	n.a.	5,856	15,140
Butter	(Million kg)	36	75	143
Milk	,,	1,024	1,945	3,574
Eggs	,,	8	15	48
Pork, bacon	,,	39	72	217
Beef	,,	50	68	123

Source: E. Jensen, *Danish Agriculture* (Copenhagen, 1937), pp. 393 and 397.

sheep fell as world wool prices declined and the Jutland sheep runs were reclaimed. The number of dairy cattle rose sharply but the yield of milk per cow almost tripled. The increase shown for 'other cattle' was entirely due to a quadrupling of the number of calves, not a surprising development as efficient dairy farming saw the weeding out of semi-barren or middle-aged cows. The general increase in the cattle population, however, inevitably provided for increased sales of live cattle or beef. Butter and beef were produced jointly in variable proportions and on the whole changes in relative prices were reflected in changes in relative output. Thus between 1900 and 1913 the butter/beef price ratio declined by 10 per cent and the butter/beef output ratio fell by 20 per cent. These exports went mainly to Germany and though together they amounted to only one-sixth of the value of the butter exports, in 1913 only Holland and Argentina exported more live cattle than Denmark. On the basis of this rise in the cattle population, butter exports soared from 4,000 tons in 1865–9 to 83,000 in 1906–10. The price of butter was extremely buoyant, rising from 140 Kr per 100 kg in 1866–70 to 190 Kr in 1896–1900 and 204 Kr in 1906–10. Already by the middle of the nineteenth century there was a considerable market for butter imported into Britain in bulk. The Dutch were at that time the chief suppliers. The agents of firms such as Jurgens and Van den Berghs travelled to markets as far away as Munich, Passau and Linz, to Switzerland and Northern Italy to collect it for shipment to London. As late as 1880, one-third of Britain's butter imports still came through Holland and both France and the United States were sending more than Denmark. But then came the Danish flood until between 1900 and 1914 she exported 80 per cent of her output and all but 2 or 3 per cent of these exports went to Britain. She was not without competition however. After 1900 imports into Britain from Australia and New Zealand and from Russia rose much faster than those from Denmark, and even in absolute terms, imports from those two areas rose half as fast again as those from Denmark. All the same in 1914 she still held 40 per cent of the market and much of the investment in the hundreds of cooperatives on the route of the Trans-Siberian railway was Danish. Surprisingly enough the Danes also produced and even imported large quantities of margarine for home consumption. The peasant found it profitable to sell butter and buy margarine.[5] So much so that in 1913 Danish consumption of margarine was easily the highest in Europe at 15 kg per head per annum; in Norway it was 11 kg and next was Sweden with 4·5 kg. In Holland, the centre of the margarine industry and a butter exporter in her own right now, consumption was only 3 kg. Certainly the process was aided in Denmark by the existence in rural centres of a number of small margarine factories – forty-two in 1913 – which delivered their product fresh to the shops without going through a middleman. The big European producers made no headway there.

The Danish switch to exporting bacon to Britain was yet more radical, for just prior to the change there had been a big increase in the number of pigs exported live to Germany through Hamburg. In 1883 350,000 went there compared with 37,000 in 1865–8. But prices were low and on grounds of checking swine fever the trade was sharply cut back by the German government during the 1880s. Another swift adjustment was called for and so successfully was this carried out that the numbers of pigs on Danish farms tripled between 1891 and 1914 and the export of pigmeat rose from 8,000 tons in 1881–5 to 95,000 tons in 1906–10. In 1890–1, butter provided 39 per cent of Danish exports and bacon, pork and pigs 18 per cent: by 1912–13 the figures were 31 per cent and 25 per cent respectively. In a very short space of time butter and bacon replaced the older exports, and Britain came to dominate all Denmark's trade.

Like Sweden she was fortunate to be able to enjoy a market where incomes were rising fast and which remained unprotected throughout the crisis period. In areas near the great urban centres and away from the traditional grain areas of the east, the British farmer's response was not dissimilar, though faced by this Danish competition he sought his comparative advantage in the production of high quality beef and of liquid milk for sale as such. The Danish

[5] In 1914 Danish butter production was 117m. kg. and consumption 23m. kg. Margarine consumption was 45m. kg.

farmer succeeded where high standards of processing and of marketing were essential. He supplied a butter of uniformly good quality,
working through the large retail chains of organisations such as the
Co-operative Wholesale Society and Maypole Dairies. These two
groups in 1913 took about 60 per cent of the Danish butter entering
Britain. But the net benefit to the balance of payments was only
slowly achieved, for the decline of grain exports and rise of imports
of human and animal foods and of fertilisers preceded the growth
of new exports. In 1874–6 net agricultural exports were 105m Kr:
a decade later they were only 64m Kr. By 1894–6 they were back
to 104m Kr and by 1903–4 had surged on to 173m Kr. The timing
is important, however, as we shall see shortly.

This is the skeleton of the story: exactly how was the change
brought about? The unique feature of the Danish response was the
formation of agricultural co-operatives for buying, processing and
Coops selling the product, first for butter, then for bacon and finally for
eggs. Similar organisations were also used to purchase bulk feeding
stuffs and fertilisers. The co-operatives were not unpolitical: they
were anti-landlord and a high level of education made the peasants
unusually vocal and literate on the subject: but their fundamental
rationale was technical and economic. The idea first expressed
itself through local agricultural credit associations of the Raiffeissen
type and an investigation made in 1909 showed how important
these and other credit sources had become in helping to bring about
the modernisation of Danish agriculture. In that year the value of
all farms was put at £184m and total indebtedness was £79m or
43 per cent of their value. One half of the loans were held by the
local associations. In an important sense the co-operative dairies
derived from the technical requirements of the cream separator. The
volume of milk produced by the average farm was too small to get
enough cream for churning within a reasonable time to get good
quality butter. On the large estates this was not a problem and
already very excellent butter was produced there. Before 1880
peasants co-operated to operate dairies like those in the manors
getting milk from surrounding farms but they were short of capital
and milk shaken when cold yielded much less butter. It was here
that the separator, invented by L. C. Neilsen in 1878, was decisive,
for it operated perfectly well with milk that had been so transported.
The peasant now had a cheap, labour-saving way of making butter
to a standard hitherto only achieved on the highly capitalised farms
of the nobility. But it too could only be operated economically
with a constant supply of milk, more than the cows of one peasant
could provide. It was first used by the estate dairies, supplementing
their own supplies of milk by buying from local farms. Then in

1882 the peasants at Hjedding banded together to run a co-operative separator. In the next three years 84 more co-operatives were founded and 595 between 1886 and 1890: by 1914 there were 1503.[6] In that year of all the holdings with cows, 86 per cent were selling milk to peasant co-operatives. There were examples of such dairies recouping the cost of the machine in three years even though members received the normal market price for their milk. Of course, there were problems. In early days enthusiasm led to overproduction. The mixing of milk from herds meant that there was a real danger of passing disease from tuberculous cows through the skim milk fed to calves and pigs – a problem rapidly solved in the 1890s by pasteurisation. In general, however, success was achieved with remarkable ease.

Around 1880 Danish pig farmers found themselves trying to supply the needs of three different markets. The Germans wanted a heavy, very fat pig: the British a lighter, longer and leaner pig, and the home market something in between. Their problem was complicated by the relative prices of these three varying considerably. The difficulty was largely resolved through Danish dissatisfaction over their lack of control of the grading and valuation of pigs in the German trade, by the arbitrary imposition of health regulations which were beginning to threaten the very existence of the trade and by the doubling of the German pig tariff in 1885. In 1887, largely through the initiative of a high school principal, 1,200 farmers agreed to supply 10,000 pigs annually to a co-operative bacon factory for seven years with the intention of exporting to Britain. It was a huge success. The whole operation was more ambitious than the dairies: more capital was required and much wider sources of supply tapped. But not only had they the model of the butter co-operatives to encourage them, but the surplus skim milk from the separators proved to be excellent for feeding to the pigs. By 1914 53 per cent of the holdings with pigs were supplying them to the co-operatives. Co-operatives also took over egg marketing which had formerly been in the hands of the middlemen. Their buyers had gone around farms collecting eggs and the producers suffered from the fact that the eggs were not fresh when they reached the consumer. Egg co-operatives did not become nearly so widespread as the butter and bacon types, largely because the competition they offered forced the existing private buyers to reorganise their trade.

Co-operatives succeeded, therefore, partly because they satisfied

[6] It is important to note that this was not a purely Danish phenomenon and therefore must not be attributed too inflexibly to Danish institutional and educational systems. In Schleswig Holstein in 1891 there were 372 co-operative dairies and 126 others, all but 65 of them using separators.

the technical requirements so admirably. But it was more than that. Co-operation works most easily among equals and here the social homogeneity of the peasantry, so carefully fostered over the period of rural reform, was a great asset. This of course is not to ignore the fact that there was a great rift in Danish rural society between peasants and cottars. In 1894 more than half the holdings were in the cottar category though as in Sweden after 1880 the cottars more and more tended to leave the land to emigrate or go to the towns. But the point holds for those peasants typically joining the co-operatives. Their farms were big enough to make a co-operative feasible but not large enough to make the owner feel he could go it alone. But it was unusual for peasants rather than landowners to take so much of the initiative: their enthusiasm for new ideas was most striking. The reasons for this are not entirely clear but some writers stress considerably the role of the Danish Folk High Schools.

_ed._ The source of inspiration for these schools was Bishop Grundvig (1783–1872), poet and student of history as well as churchman. Grundvig was brought up under the influence of the humiliations Denmark suffered during the Napoleonic Wars, the wide yearning for liberty that characterised those years, and the economic changes going on in Britain. He believed that if democracy was to be more than a sham it must be based on broad cultural foundations. He made up his mind that the only solution to the problem of putting Denmark on the road to material and spiritual advance was education, not education of the narrow traditional Prussian pattern, but education of a broad liberal and democratic nature. He was attracted by Pestalozzi's view of the importance of adapting education to the pupil and to the development of his natural abilities. Inspiration and understanding were to be the keynotes, not factual knowledge. He urged the formation of schools where the main subjects would be Danish history, language and literature. There were to be no examinations and the singing of songs before and after a class would be an excellent form of participation. The first such school was started in Schleswig in 1844. The idea was slow to catch on but then the 1860s saw more dark days for Denmark. The southern duchies with two-fifths of the land area and one-third of the population were lost to Prussia and in the gloom that followed, many of the democratic features of the Constitution of 1849 were abandoned, and control was again handed back to the big landowners. One effect was to encourage men of energy and courage to begin a fight for better ideals and many high schools were formed under the influence of just such people. By the early twentieth century there were eighty schools with 7,000 students. Directed mainly to the peasant, they made him the equal, if not the superior, of other classes intellectually.

They helped break down his conservatism and hostility to new ideas and stimulated a democratic approach to both political and economic problems.

Such is the argument. The influence of education on growth is widely recognised to be important but in precisely what ways is not always clear. There is always a danger that ideas of liberal education which seem intellectually sound, will be assumed inevitably to be economically valuable. The High Schools, by their very timing could only be partially responsible for the mental and material well-being that came to characterise Danish agriculture and which must be traced back, at least in part, to the determination of the crown to preserve the peasant as an independent force in Danish Society. Excessive concentration on the Folk High Schools may so easily lead us to forget other aspects of Danish education. As early as 1814, education was made compulsory for children of 7–14: by the 1820s there were evening schools in towns and villages and in the 1840s and 1850s efforts were being made to provide further education by giving teachers more pay if they took on the sons of farmers, this at the request of farmers themselves. Schools of agriculture date from 1867, and while they were influenced by Folk High School ideals they were much more vocational. Later in the nineteenth century there arose too an important body of 'continuation schools'. The Folk High Schools were almost exclusively for farmers, not for cottars nor for town workers, but they were regarded by the peasants as substitutes for other secondary schools, and farmers who had been to the latter often went to the schools of agriculture but seldom to High Schools. When in the late nineteenth century there was a survey of the educational backgrounds of chairmen and managers of co-operative dairies, it was found that 47 per cent had attended a Folk High School, 34 per cent an agricultural school and 62 per cent a dairy school. But for all this it is likely that the co-operatives would have been less vigorous than they were had young people not received in the High Schools the incentive to personal effort for a common as well as a private good that they did. The last word should go to one who was a pupil in such a school in the 1870s,

'We did not talk much of what we had heard but all the more of the great things which we would still have time to do in this life . . . As those who had been to High School grew older, and got families of their own, it was from their homes that progress got into its stride. It was these families that set up co-operative societies, co-operative stores, dairies and bacon factories. . . .'[7]

[7] T. Rørdam, *The Danish Folk High Schools*, (Copenhagen, 1965), p. 152.

- Agriculture and the Economy

These changes in agriculture were accompanied by, and indeed required major changes in the infrastructure. Railways and ferries were constructed after 1860, and after the war with Prussia, a positive decision was made to emphasise east–west communications rather than those to Germany. Out of such political and economic considerations came the founding of the port of Esbjerg as a terminus for the trade with Britain. Building began in 1867 and a hamlet with a population of 30 in 1860 was a thriving town of 13,000 inhabitants forty years later. The tonnage of Danish shipping doubled between 1870 and 1914, partly because of the British trade, partly because of the emigrant traffic. Just as the structural shifts in agriculture derived from the enterprise of the peasants, so these consequent developments in services owed much to the investment of the merchants of Copenhagen whose roots reached back well before the nineteenth century as we have already seen.

One major consequence of these changes in agriculture was that the absolute numbers employed on the land declined for only a few years of the 1880s and by 1914 stood at 1·1m compared with 938,000 in 1870. As in every other developing country the share of agriculture in the occupied population fell, in this case, from 51 per cent to 36 per cent between 1880 and 1911. Danish national income accounts show that total output and productivity in agriculture rose very slowly during the 1870s and 1880s, at a time when productivity in other sectors was increasing much more quickly. Furthermore the evidence seems to be that Danish farms suffered a deterioration of their internal terms of trade at this time too. The returns began to come home during the 1890s. Eventually from 1900 to 1914 total agricultural production rose by 60 per cent and net production (excluding imports of feeding stuffs) by 57 per cent. Prices received rose more than prices paid and net farm income more than doubled. With the returns from current and earlier investment in buildings and machinery coming home, labour productivity was rising as fast as productivity in the whole economy. It was during the earlier decades that productivity in agriculture fell so markedly compared with that in other sectors. The initial stages of modern Danish industrial growth therefore seem to have owed less than is sometimes argued to the effects of agricultural change. It may be that this was why sustained and rapid growth of Danish industry did not come until later, though the steady growth of exports helped maintain the exchange rate and made overseas borrowing that much easier. From the 1890s onwards, however, the further expansion of industry was encouraged to a greater extent by rising incomes and investment from the agricultural sector. Money wages in Danish agriculture rose 11 per cent in real terms between 1875–6 and 1890–1 and then more than doubled over the next twenty years. Higher productivity not only allowed farmers to pay high wages but they were compelled to do so by the alternative opportunities offered elsewhere in the economy.

– Industrialisation in Denmark

There has been much discussion among Danish historians about the timing of industrialisation. Some argue that the critical developments came in the 1850s with the beginning of railway construction: others plump for the investment boom of the early 1870s: yet others for the similar boom after 1882 and some are reluctant to write of rapid industrialisation for any period prior to 1900. The argument shows more than anything else that industrialisation was a more gradual process than in most countries. The annual growth rate of industrial output at fixed prices was 4–5 per cent for the whole period from 1855 to 1905 except for 1890–7 when it rose to over 7 per cent. From 1905 to 1913 the rate was 5·4 per cent. Certainly there were no leading sectors to give a particularly strong boost to any one time comparable to cotton in Britain steel in Germany or the forest-based industries in Sweden. Instead the pattern is one of a range of industries advancing more or less together on a broad front, from the big firms in brewing and ship-building to crafts such as furniture making. The first industries to grow were in fact those with a strong craft element: they were then followed by such typical home market industries as cement and brick manufacture, the production of fertilisers, sugar-refining and brewing. In 1913 only 6 per cent of industrial output was exported compared with 63 per cent of agricultural output, With such a small home market and a resolutely free-trade tariff policy the development of major industries facing international competition was unlikely to proceed far. Denmark possessed neither the natural resources nor the deep rooted industrial traditions that Sweden enjoyed. In all countries there was a mass of non-agricultural activities never affected by international competition at all. Construction trades, the processing of locally produced foods and drinks, clothing, repair and jobbing shops for metal and engineering products and the local industries for which demand was as much a product of the cultural pattern of the Danes as of anything else. But small countries were also able to build up modern, if small scale, industrial sectors, given certain conditions. In all three Scandinavian countries, for example, the shoe industry was completely modernised by the introduction of American machinery in the 1880s and the craft makers quickly disappeared. But the scale of production remained small – there were thirty-eight factories in Denmark alone in 1913 – and the operatives were much less specialised than in the United States, and the upper stitching might still be put out to hand workers. Danish firms could not compete against German supplies of ordinary lathes with a total demand of only some 200 a year but a firm such as Nielsen & Winther of Copenhagen could build up a significant export trade by specialising in series production of new big turret lathes, selling them even to such firms as Skoda and Panhard. Atlas, the very high quality high speed steam engine makers, imported many parts such as gears and special forgings from Germany and to some degree acted as assemblers. In this way they could build a reputation high enough to put their engines in some of the best factories in Europe.

Inevitably the links with agriculture were strong. Brewing was one of the largest and oldest of Denmark's industries. It came to be concentrated into a relatively small number of large firms early in the process of industrial change, partly for technical reasons and partly because the monopoly of the brewers' guild was broken as early as 1805, whereas general industrial freedom did not come until 1857. There were 100 independent brewers in Copenhagen in 1805, 28 in 1847 and 16 in the much enlarged city of 1891. Agriculture generated direct demands for various types of machinery – separators (though many of them came from Sweden), refrigeration equipment, rakes, hoes, plows, simple reapers. Then there were the effects on demand for consumption goods of rising farm incomes, though it must be noted that labour productivity was twice as high outside agriculture and the numbers employed in agriculture were stable and their share in total employment always falling. Industrialisation in Denmark inevitably was in part a function of the level of income in agriculture and the high level of farm produce marketed even in the 1850s gave a continuous spur to this and other sectors of the economy. There is, however, evidence that agricultural incomes were not rising fast in the 1870s and 1880s but after 1890 these incomes undoubtedly did much to sustain the level of industrial growth.

Industrialisation in Denmark was to a considerable degree self-generating as it was in Sweden. The construction of railways and ports was a powerful expansionary force: even more the building of houses and local public utilities. The four main provincial towns (Odense, Århus, Alborg and Esbjerg) increased their populations from 36,000 in 1860 to 160,000 in 1911. Above all there was Copenhagen. Before the loss of Schleswig Holstein much of Danish trade was carried on through Hamburg, and the profits made by German merchants were much less likely to have provided funds for Danish development generally than did those of the merchants of Gothenberg and Stockholm for Sweden. But after the Prussian war a different situation arose. The pattern of trade changed. The population of Copenhagen rose from 130,000 in 1858 to 462,000 in 1910. 40 per cent of all workers in establishments of more than six people were to be found there in 1914. Above all it was the centre for financial and trading services of all kinds. In 1911 service activities accounted for 36 per cent of the occupied population in Denmark compared with 32 per cent in Norway and 19 per cent in Sweden. Trade in turn not only provided finance for industry but also initiative and management. In some measure the growth of such a city perpetuated its own self-reinforcing impetus, creating incomes and creating industries to satisfy the demands of those incomes.

The number of workers in Danish factories was small, only 108,000 compared with three times that number in Sweden, for example. There are technical difficulties in comparing the structure of industry in the two countries. Denmark had proportionately a much larger food, drink and tobacco sector, the Swedes the big timber and pulp sector which was very small in Denmark. The Swedish cotton industry employed 12,460 workers in 1912 compared with only 3,282 in the Danish. This latter was equivalent to only one big mill in Lancashire and suggests how little import substitution really was achieved in that sector. Mechanical engineering, foundries and shipyards took a comparable share of total employment in both countries, but this gave the Swedes 41,500 employees compared with 20,000 in Denmark. Manufacturing output per head in Denmark was 12 per cent below that in Sweden in 1913, probably due to the ability of the Swedes to develop a number of relatively large, highly competitive firms in some export sectors, and also due to scale effects.

But industrialisation of the Danish kind, would, in the absence of other circumstances, soon come up against balance of payments constraints. Rails and railway equipment, all structural iron and steel, most machine tools and machinery in general, all fuel had to be imported as well as the rising tide of mass-produced consumer goods. It was here that agriculture played its most vital role in the economy through its booming exports, particularly taking into account the sharp improvement in the terms of trade which such exports enjoyed after 1890 compared with the sharp deterioration experienced during the 1880s. In 1872 Denmark was actually a net overseas investor to the extent of about 157m Kr, mostly to Sweden

R

and Germany.[8] Over the next two decades this net creditor position was eliminated, thereby easing the pressures brought about by a current deficit as grain prices fell and avoiding the necessity for any serious rise in interest rates. Imports of capital became significant for the first time in the 1880s, coinciding with a burst of railway construction, the 1,400km of line open in 1880 more than doubling over the next two decades. The inflow reached its peak just before the first world war and by 1912 Danish net overseas borrowing stood at almost 900m Kr. In the 1880s foreign investment provided over 18 per cent of gross domestic capital formation and over the whole period from 1880 to 1909 more like 16 per cent. It was a significant contribution but far less than in Sweden, smaller too than in Norway. Possibly the shift to overseas sources of finance in the 1880s can in part be attributed to the fact that increased demands for capital for agricultural investment cut off a traditional source of supply to other sectors. But in Denmark as elsewhere it was also due to institutional factors: the great banking houses of Europe were anxious to lend to such reliable borrowers.

Earnings from shipping freights and from emigrants' remittances helped to moderate the need for capital imports. Shipbuilding was one of Denmark's most successful industries which had long historical roots, as we have seen. Copenhagen was an old and renowned ship repair centre and her ships had a well-established carrying trade. Further stimulus was derived from the expansion of the export and emigrant trades. The firm of Burmeister and Wain was founded in 1846 to specialise in marine engineering, though it only took its modern name in 1865 when William Wain, an English engineer, joined one of the original partners. Before 1914 at peak they employed 3,000 men. They built engines as well as ships but were also general engineers: in 1881 for example, they obtained the rights to manufacture Nielsen's cream separator, though an American observer in 1909 thought their progress in this sector had been limited largely because they undertook too many different kinds of activity. Their outstanding achievement was the early realisation of the potential of Diesel's new type of oil engine for ship propulsion and in 1912 launched the first ocean-going motor ship, the *Selandia*. In this they were greatly helped by the vision of the owners of the *Selandia* – the Danish East Asiatic Company. Three years later that company had ten motor ships at sea and were leading the world in this new development. By 1914 Burmeisters had already bought

[8] In 1850 she had been a debtor nation but this was reversed over the next two decades. In addition she was granted 63m Kr on the abolition of the Sound Tolls and 46m Kr from Prussia in compensation for assuming Schleswig Holstein's share of the joint national debt of Denmark.

a yard to develop the building of such ships on the Clyde, the very centre of the British shipbuilding. Output of ships in Denmark was very small in a world context – about 41,000 gross tons of merchant ships in 1913 or 1·2 per cent of the world total – but since 1900 it had increased more than three times and undoubtedly the industry was in the van of technological progress.

An important factor in the growth of industry was the rise of deposit banks after the German model. The most remarkable of these was the Privatbank, founded in 1857. Its first director, at the age of 28, was a remarkable financier, C. F. Tietgen. It was he who was responsible for a great deal of company formation over the next twenty years. In 1866 he founded the United Steamship Company, the biggest Danish shipping line, in 1869 the Great Scandinavian Telegraph Company and, three years later turned Burmeisters into a joint-stock company. These were the spectacular coups but possibly more important was the large number of mergers of small firms he arranged in a variety of different industries. But even in the Tietgen enterprises only a small part of the investment was in industry – one-sixth in 1886 – and the bulk went into transport. In the 1890s other banks continued the work of company promotion and amalgamation, more particularly Landmansbanken and Handelsbanken, which unlike Privatbanken, had branches outside Copenhagen and helped to widen the impact of the boom. But Denmark benefited, as Sweden did, from its earlier mercantile traditions. The great commercial houses of Copenhagen could provide the know-how and finance essential for the development of trade connections and it was partly from them that the new banking institutions developed when the needs of the economy came to change. Then there was technology. The cream separator we have already mentioned but the coming of oil engines and of electric power was certainly of great benefit to the small industrial concerns which made up all but a very small part of Danish industry, and offered great potential gains to a country devoid of coal resources. The success and relative importance of small firms, operating through craft traditions and depending on a fastidious consumer taste was remarkable. It is striking that the share of handicrafts in Gross Domestic Product was higher in 1890 than in 1855 and only thereafter began to decline. The guilds died late and even in the 1880s and 1890s there were serious proposals to resurrect them as a means of controlling quality. Also the craft tradition derived strength from an educated labour force able enough and involved enough in their work to achieve superior quality. In a very real sense this was a small country's specialised niche. The comparison between the Danish and Swedish industrial structure is most reveal-

R*

ing, for the Swedes found their niche in a different way. In 1914 84 per cent of Danish workers were in establishments employing up to five people: in 1912 only 24 per cent of Swedish workers were in establishments employing up to ten people.

Danish growth was therefore less widely based than that of Sweden, heavily dependent on foreign trade, precariously placed in view of the overwhelming importance of two export commodities and one market. But from this base the economy had so extended itself that the proportion of workers engaged in agriculture was lower than in all but the most industrialised of European countries. No country in the nineteenth century could absorb the rise in population completely in the agricultural sector without great loss of income per head. In Denmark urbanisation and emigration saved the day as in so many other places. The consequences where this did not happen on anything like the required scale will be seen when we come to look at Russia. But the ability of the Danish economy to expand and grow as it did derived above all from the circumstances, the timing and the completeness of the policy of agrarian reform carried out so smoothly during the turn of the century. This success could not have been consummated without the prospects held out by the British market but without it these possibilities would never have been seized as they were.

NORWAY IN THE EIGHTEENTH CENTURY

Norway's closest links with Sweden and Denmark were political. Until 1814 Norway was part of the Kingdom of Denmark and, indeed, her economy suffered under Britain's pre-emptive attacks on Denmark during the Napoleonic Wars. In 1814 the king of Sweden was elected king of Norway and, though Norway acted as an autonomous state, the economic, as well as the political, ties were strong until that union ended in 1905. The most striking contrast in the process of development between the two countries, however, was that in Norway it was not preceded by, nor even accompanied by, modernisation of agriculture. Indeed, development of any kind in Norway was very limited throughout the nineteenth century. Where it did come about – in shipping and fishing for example – it represented a widening of existing forms of activity and had little spill-over effect for the economy as a whole.

The difficult climate, generally poor soils, extremely poor land communications all combined to cut off the Norwegian peasant from knowledge and first-hand experience of the experiments in crops and techniques going forward elsewhere in Western Europe. Until late into the century he remained attached to the primitive methods employed in the mountains and fjord valleys for generations. Many employed no rotation at all but planted the same crop year after year until the yield fell so far that it was necessary to work new land. The feeding of the growing population of Norway in the eighteenth century was only possible because of this ready availability of new land, poor though the soil might be. Drainage systems were little known, and in some areas the peasant still worked the soil with spade and hoe rather than with plough and harrow. The open field pattern of cultivation was widespread with oats the main crop. Sometimes there was periodic redistribution of strips and there were varying degrees of common ownership of woods, meadows and lakes. But the kind of far-reaching social reform, required in Denmark for example, was unnecessary here. Norway was a striking exception to the general pattern of eighteenth-century European society whereby the nobility stood at the top of the social pyramid. In Norway there was no such powerful landed group and consequently the breaking down of estate society by the entry of non-nobles into fields previously closed to them – something very relevant in Sweden for example – was not necessary: merchants and gentlemen farmers formed the top layer of society. Serfdom was rare: there were some big noble estates around Oslo fjord but the sale of crown lands to existing tenants and the willingness of landlords to sell out so as to invest in mines, timber, trade and avoid the rigorous obligations to tenants set down by the Crown at the end of the seventeenth century resulted in a marked rise in the number of peasant proprietors. At the same time the labour obligations of tenants were falling away too. Certain privileges dating back to earlier centuries still persisted. Such were the rights of guilds, the reservation of trade to town burghers, monopolies of cutting timber for sale. But in a curious way the absence of crying social injustice, while doing little in itself to promote development, also deprived Norway of an opportunity for radical social change which might have brought economic reform along with it too.

Social injustice is always a relative matter. Half the rural population in 1800 consisted of cottars and labourers and the economic situation of both was precarious. The cottar enjoyed a secure lease over the land he worked but he owed labour service to his superior for his land. Five days a week of service was not unknown. The system of primogeniture required a peasant's eldest son to provide for his younger brothers and sisters and generally they would be granted a cottar's plot or act as servants. In this way subdivision was limited, although it became severe enough as Norway had less land easily available to offset the population rise than Sweden for example. These limitations on land ownership led eventually to a huge burst of emigration in the second half of the nineteenth century, a problem based less on actual want than on the difficulty of gaining access to land or obtaining alternative employment in an under-developed economy at home. From 1801 to 1855 the numbers of landowners rose 27 per cent but the cottars doubled and labourers tripled in numbers. They grew partly because, although the cultivated area increased, this occurred largely within existing farms so that relatively few new holdings came available: rather there was an increase in demand for labour on the existing farms. One new development which was taken up quickly and contributed to the increase of these poorer groups was the growing of potatoes, though it is sometimes argued that potato growing was stimulated by the disappearance of the spring herring from Norway's coasts around 1800. In 1835 the crop was enough to feed one-fifth of the population and by 1865 had doubled again. Since a considerable proportion of the harvest was distilled, it became a cash crop of some significance. The spirits produced were probably in large measure exchanged for fish when that trade revived some years later.

In the seventeenth century Norway had built up two important centres of mining, silver at Kongsberg and copper at Røros. There was also a small iron industry which benefited from the protection enjoyed in the Danish market, though it was to wither when sub-jected to open competition from Sweden after 1814. The major industry of the eighteenth century was sawmilling, carried out by seasonal labour where water power was available, under privileges granted by the Crown. Norway supplied much the largest proportion of British timber imports at that time – most of it as deals. In the seventeenth century this timber was collected by the Dutch, sawn in Holland before being exported, but now it was an all Norwegian activity. The wars of the second half of the century greatly swelled the demand for this wood and for the Norwegian ships to carry it. In the last twenty-five years to 1780 the tonnage of Norwegian shipping increased 250 per cent partly for this reason and also because of the growth of the Norwegian carrying trade especially during these same wars when the shipping trade of the belligerents was much disrupted. Nevertheless, there was a considerable increase of competitive exports of sawnwoods from the Baltic towards the end of the eighteenth century, though they did not reach the Norwegian level. After 1800 Norwegian production capacity was further increased under pressure of demand and Baltic deals met a rebuff which was intensified by the British preference given to

Canadian timber. But the wider benefits of the timber trade for the Norwegian economy were not very apparent. The timber farmers were said to have converted their profits into silver plate and other imported luxuries for want of alternative outlets and travellers frequently commented on the quality of the houses and furnishings of merchants and shipbuilders.

The other major activity was fishing. For many farmers both fishing and forestry were complements to their basic subsistence economy. It has been suggested that only some 10–15 per cent of the Norwegian people lived in the money economy in 1801. This would not mean that the other 85–90 per cent bought and sold nothing in money but that such market activities were essentially marginal. Most of the trading in fish was carried on between peasants themselves often on a barter basis: coastal farmers exchanged fish for the spirits, forest and animal products of their inland brethren. Norwegian fish had a bad reputation in overseas markets, for Bergen had a monopoly of salting and much of the fish was caught far from the port. However, the last three decades of the century saw an upsurge of liberal thinking on economic questions, possibly under the influence of The Wealth of Nations which was produced in a Danish translation in 1779 but more likely as a result of the movement for rural reform then gathering force in Denmark itself. In 1785 all the salt monopolies were abolished and in 1797 import and export duties were lowered including those on the import of salt and export of herring. However, their effect was partly, if temporarily, nullified by the spring herring leaving the coast for two decades after 1784.

This then was the simple eighteenth-century economy, yet it was one, as we have seen, where population was growing quickly after the middle of the century so far as can be determined because of the elimination of the frightful calamities that had decimated population from time to time and last struck in the 1740s. But a disaster of another kind struck Norway after a few golden years of booming timber exports, following the resumption of war in Europe in 1803. Denmark was forced to join Napoleon against Britain and Norway had to follow suit. The British blockade was imposed with full rigour, exports were cut back, the sea route to Denmark was interrupted and Norway was unable to import grain. Finally invasion was threatened from Sweden. If this was not enough the dissolution of the Union with Denmark closed the market there for iron, the British preference in favour of Canadian timber disrupted that trade and the post-1815 problems were hardly eased by an ill-conceived export duty, large enough to provide one third of all government revenues.

NORWAY IN THE NINETEENTH CENTURY

Agriculture

Unlike Denmark and Sweden, Norway was to receive little boost to the economy in the nineteenth century as a result of agricultural improvement. Techniques changed only slowly: consolidation of strips began to come about very gradually after 1850 when the process was well nigh over in Sweden and Denmark.

Table 37. *Farm holdings in Norway, 1929*

Size of holding holding (hectares)	Number of farms	% of total farms	% of land area
Below 0·5	89,810	30·1	1·7
0·5– 2	75,920	25·5	9·1
2·0– 10	111,630	37·4	47·8
10·0– 30	19,214	6·4	32·8
30·0– 50	1,392	0·47	6·0
50·0–100	292	0·1	2·1
Over 100	32	0·01	0·5

Source: A. Milward, *The Fascist Economy in Norway* (Oxford, 1972), p. 43.

Norway was dominated by small peasant farms – many of them very small indeed to a degree paralleled elsewhere in Europe perhaps only in Belgium and Bulgaria. We do not have useful figures for our period but Table 37 shows the distribution of the land area by size of farm in 1929 and there is no reason to think that this was very different from the situation before the war. There were only thirty-two farms over 100 hectares and 80 per cent of the farmed area was given over to farms of 2–30 hectares with over a half in farms under 10 hectares. Only a few of the peasants were exclusively farmers: the majority had some woodland and many also were engaged in fishing. These activities together formed the basis of the agricultural economy but because of this small scale and often part time character, the fishing and forestry industries could not compare in technology with those of many other countries. These joint operations by peasant families made Norwegian agriculture fundamentally different from that of Denmark and Sweden. They made it possible to adjust the balance of activity as the relative profitability of these forms of production changed but made it far more difficult to bring about a radical change in the structure of agriculture. Most farmers were still content to stay outside the market, not seeking to sell any surplus for themselves, unable to enjoy or unable to compete with imports of foodstuffs which affected only those near the coastal towns. In his book, *Prospector in Siberia*, Jonas Lie wrote of his father trading in a rural area in southern Norway where as late as 1878 his business was still largely of the barter kind. In return for the textiles and other merchandise he brought in his father shipped back to his wholesaler tar, timber, smoked and salted fish, cheese, cranberries, whortleberries, wool, hides, and anything he could lay his hands on. The rising number of cottars and labourers gave no stimulus to internal purchasing power. After 1850 there was gradual improvement and a shift to dairy farming but Norwegian agriculture was unable to adapt itself successfully to the new pattern of world specialisation in foodstuffs that came about after 1870. In 1911 her butter exports were worth 3·3m Kr, whereas her imports of grain totalled 67m Kr and of animal foodstuffs 16m Kr. She had no other food exports of importance, apart from fish.

– The Staple Trades: fish, timber, shipping

The impetus to recovery after 1815 came from the old staples, timber, fish and shipping, as Table 38 shows. By happy chance the spring

Table 38. *Exports from Norway, 1815–45*

	Timber	Fish	000 specie Dalers Iron and copper	Shipping
1815–20 (av.)	1178	953	200	1050
1835	1685	2480	246	1595
1845	2300	3400	1000	2300

Source: S. Lieberman, *The Industrialisation of Norway* (Oslo, 1970), p. 93.

herring returned to Norway around 1808 and left the Swedish west coast for good. The biggest competitor had now gone and, helped by the effects of the Union, Sweden now became Norway's best customer. A revival of free-trade sentiment lowered the export duties on herrings and there followed a rapid expansion of the trade. In 1840, not an outstanding year, the spring herring catch was 800,000 barrels, four times the best year of the previous century. During 1861–5 on average 600,000 barrels were exported compared with an eighteenth-century maximum of 80,000 and now 40,000 fishermen were involved. Townsmen went into salting and exporting: local industries for making barrel staves and hoops and weaving nets sprang up. If Bergen remained the chief centre of the trade it was Stavanger above all that got a new lease of life. Some peasants sold off their farms to join the boom but more frequently farms were mortgaged to supply younger sons with the cash to go fishing.

The herring moved away again in the 1870s until the end of the century but this time the consequences were far less serious. The economy of western Norway had achieved an impetus of its own and the peasantry adjusted to the new circumstances more easily. There was a considerable reversion to farming and indeed the disappearance of herring stimulated agricultural improvement. To some degree the fishermen turned to other, more distant, fishing but even so, the Norwegian fishing industry, large and more resilient though it was, suffered from certain basic weaknesses. Almost all of it was coastal. Cod was caught early in the year at the Lofoten and Finnmark fisheries and the bulk of it was exported dried and salted, the chief markets being low income countries such as Spain, Portugal, West Africa, South America. Norway played no part in the really profitable and growing demand from the high income countries for fresh, frozen cod caught on the Dogger Bank or off Newfoundland. Lack of capital prevented the Norwegians from building the much bigger boats required for that trade or the quick freezing plants. Similarly with herring the best prospects lay in exports of fresh fish but in 1912 such exports to Germany and Britain were valued at only half the exports of the less profitable salt herring. Two important developments occurred before 1914. One was the growth of fish canning centred around Stavanger, supplying smoked brisling to Britain and the United States in particular: exports in 1912 were 14·8m Kr or about 10 per cent of the value of all fish exports. Just off the coast at certain times of the year the sea was full of this type of migratory fish which were caught in almost any kind of boat with extremely low capital expenditure once there was a market for them. The second was the rapid development of whaling first in the Arctic and, after the turn of the century, in the South Seas and undoubtedly here the Norwegians showed immense entrepreneurial and innovative skills. In general, however, the fishing industry reflected the weaknesses of the Norwegian economy as a whole and in particular the fact that it remained very much a part of a capital starved agricultural system.

Timber exports recovered more slowly: for one thing the British duties tended to discriminate in favour of the large size Swedish timber. Eventually Britain abandoned the Canadian preference and duties were lowered throughout Europe and Norway's exports boomed from 285,000 lasts in 1850 to about 600,000 in 1872–3. In an economy biased towards foreign trade, Norway rationally adopted a free trade outlook and among the privileges that disappeared after 1839 were those of the sawmills. With this the industry moved towards the coast, the export of logs fell away and sawing and planing reached a peak in the 1870s. But over these same years Swedish exports rose much faster with the explosive breakthrough derived from opening up the forests of Norrland. Norway's most accessible forests had been cut and she simply did not possess the same reserves. But there was more to it than that. The management of Norwegian forests was much poorer than that of Sweden and the yield correspondingly lower. Nowhere else in Europe was such a large share of the forests in the hands of smallholders and with descendants able to force any new owner to sell land back at a price determined by the authorities, buyers were severely inhibited. Unlike Sweden too, few sawmills were located on holdings with enough timber to keep them fully occupied: the forests were recklessly and unintelligently cut and with these unsatisfactory conditions, the mills were generally small and poorly equipped. In this way the Norwegian industry surrendered its earlier technological lead. The degree of over-felling can be measured from the fact that in 1914 an estimate put the cut at 442m cubic feet and the annual increment of wood at only 343m. For all these reasons exports of timber stagnated from the 1870s to the turn of the century and then fell off sharply. The first wood pulp was made in Norway in 1863 and the first chemical pulp was manufactured, using the sulphite method, twenty years later. Some large enterprises were developed, partly with the backing of British capital, so much so that by 1900 pulp exports were as large as those of timber and by 1913 twice their size. In that year Norwegian exports, at 465,000 tons, were the second largest in the world and compared with 847,000 tons from Sweden. Between them they provided some 65 per cent of world trade in pulp. The average value of Norwegian pulp was lower, however, for there was a higher proportion of mechanical pulp, and the Norwegians made little progress in paper making before 1914. The economy had therefore adjusted itself in some measure to the pressures of world demand but without enjoying the kind of boost which came to Sweden from the much greater rise of timber exports and the greater level of processing of wood products.

From mid-century the pressure of British and Swedish competition virtually eliminated the iron industry whose ores were poor in quality and difficult of access anyway. The old copper mines received a considerable boost from the discovery of the method of making sulphuric acid from pyrites and at almost 15m Kr in 1912 pyrites had become one of Norway's major exports. The major growth sector now was shipping. Developed during the eighteenth century as a subsidiary to the timber trade, it expanded along broader and independent lines. Again British commercial policy was important because the repeal of the Navigation Acts in 1849 opened wide areas of world trade to outside shipping. The Netherlands liberalised her navigation policy in 1850 to be followed by many others: seven years later the Sound tolls were abolished and Norway was also helped by winning the right to carry Swedish goods to and from Britain after the union in 1814. Norwegian ships carried Swedish timber to Britain, moved into the coal trade and then ferried grain to Britain from the Black Sea and across the Atlantic. In the 1850s ships began to carry emigrants to Quebec and timber back to Britain and more and more ships then began to specialise on the emigrant trade. But grain, timber and coal were the mainstays and it was a development entirely independent of Norway's own transport needs. Rather it was based on historical experience of shipbuilding techniques, on the availability of local timber and on the growth and liberalisation of world, above all, British, trade. Norwegian ships were tramps, common carriers, quite independent of any old connections formed by Norwegian merchants. Norwegians were said to be skilled sailors but often it was the only way of supplementing low farm incomes. It was at once a form of cottage industry and of emigration, only less final. So it was always easy to get a cheap crew, ships were cheap too, their own mutual insurance societies made insurance inexpensive, and the lack of alternative outlets possibly made owners happy with a moderate return on their investment. Whatever the reasons, the fleet rose from 300,000 tons in 1850 to 1,500,000 tons in 1880 when it was the third largest in the world, greater than that of France, Germany or The Netherlands and the earnings came to an astonishing 45 per cent of all exports (visible and invisible) though this in part reflected the low level of all other exports. Not until 1890 did the number of men employed in industry exceed those crewing Norwegian ships. But even shipping was to lose some of its impetus: in 1905 it provided only 32·5 per cent of total exports. For one thing freight rates fell markedly and, even ignoring the unusually high freights prevailing in the early

1870s, the terms of trade moved against shipping though, as Table 39 shows, Norway, like Sweden, enjoyed favourable terms of trade for her commodity exports throughout the half century to 1914. There was, however, one decadal period from 1895 to 1904 when the terms of trade were favourable on all counts and it is significant that these years saw considerable progress in Norway as they did to a much greater degree in Sweden.

Table 39. *Norwegian foreign trade prices, 1865–1914*

1938=100

	Commodity exports	Shipping earnings	Imports
1865–74	65	140	90
1875–84	71	120	80
1885–94	61	93	66
1895–1904	71	114	67
1905–1914	85	88	78

Source: Norway, Statistisk Sentralbyrå, *Trends in Norwegian Economy, 1865–1960*, (Oslo, 1966).

The second problem was the transition to steam which came about slowly in Norway for a variety of reasons. Norway was only moderately interested in the regular routes which first employed steamships and consequently she was ill-prepared for the change when these vessels began to compete on the bulk tramp trades too. The Norwegian shipbuilding industry was not well endowed for building iron and steel vessels, the problem being one of capital shortage rather than steel supplies which were cheaply available from Germany, and for a time Norwegian shipowners made short term profits through buying up cheap second hand sailing ships from those who were changing over. Most sailing ships in any case were owned by small men who could not raise the money required for steamships which had to be bought abroad from builders who usually wanted cash on delivery. In 1896 only 2 per cent of the world's steamships had been constructed in Norway. As Table 40 shows, the average size of ship was very small. Although an important shipbuilder in terms of total tonnage – eighth in the world in 1913 – Sweden, The Netherlands, Italy, Denmark had the capacity to build larger and more sophisticated ships. The size of Norway's output must not be allowed to conceal the weakness of her technology. Right until 1914 many Norwegian shipowners acquired second-hand tonnage which could operate at a profit because of

Table 40. *Output of steamships and motor ships, 1913*

	No.	Tonnage	Average tonnage
Norway	74	50,637	685
Sweden	18	18,524	1,030
Denmark	31	40,932	1,300
Italy	38	50,356	1,325
Netherland	95	104,296	1,100

Source: Lloyd's Register of Shipping.

low total costs and because of the type of trades in which they were used. Some of these ships were used as floating boilers for the whaling trade in the South Seas, for example. The general pattern of Norwegian shipping can be determined from an examination of the immediate pre-war years. From 1911 to 1913 she bought an equal tonnage of new steamships from foreign makers and of foreign second hand ships. In those years only 20 per cent of her requirements were obtained from home builders. Thus, although the industry had built up a considerable tonnage it was not a modern industry and still contained a high proportion of sail. After 1914 the industry was forced to undergo a very radical transformation. Even in its old speciality, the bulk cargoes, it had missed out in the new trade in oil tankers and by 1913 had only 3 per cent of the world's tanker fleet. This was probably because the Norwegians were organised for tramp shipping with maximum flexibility and minimum cost, which was not what the oil companies wanted. It was a remarkable achievement for a country such as Norway to have in 1914 the world's fifth largest fleet – after Britain, the United States, Germany and Japan. Of this there can be no doubt. But in the last two decades before the War there were clear signs that this extra-ordinary drive was not being sustained either through lack of capital or obsession with short run as opposed to long run objectives.

In several ways, therefore, the economy was showing a lack of impetus. Exports were noticeably failing to have powerful linkage effects on the rest of the economy. For the most part they were converted directly into imports of consumption goods for the burghers in the coastal towns. The town economies were very much enclaves. The slow, disorganised development of railways did little to break down the isolation of rural areas and create anything like a coherent internal market. By 1871 only 359 km were in operation: some 750 km were added in the next decade but then 350 km in the 1880s and only 400 km in the 1890s. It took twenty-nine years from 1851 to 1880 to complete the line from Oslo to

Trondheim and then only after political pressures had forced a diversion to feed the copper mine at Røros and by making it narrow gauge. A Commission of 1875 reported in favour of big artery lines to open up the country rather than the existing tendency to link the coast and existing inland waterways. But the response was slow. The first tiny stretch of the Bergen–Oslo line was opened in 1874 but the full line was opened only in 1907. Even in 1914 there was no line from Stavanger to Oslo, though the southern line from Stavanger to Egersund was extended to Flekkefjord in 1904 to cut out the worst part of the sea route from Oslo. It is possible that given the nature of the terrain, coastal transport was in fact the cheapest method even allowing for the longer time taken. But the poor state of internal transport and the absence of a powerful boost to the economy as a result of a railway building were serious disadvantages.

– New Developments

Except for the boom years of the early 1870s the rise of Gross G N P
Domestic Product was very slow from 1865 – the first date for which we have estimates – until 1885 and indeed, from 1877 to 1886 when emigration was very high and freight rates dropping rapidly, it actually fell by 0·3 per cent per annum per head. But this was a turning point and except for a slump at the turn of the century, which was a European-wide phenomenon, gross domestic product rose from the late 1880s to 1914 at 2–3 per cent *per capita* per annum. It seems likely that, despite the unfavourable short term effects of emigration, by eliminating rural underemployment it helped to boost output per head considerably. The ratio of Gross Domestic Product per head in manufacturing to that in agriculture actually fell from 2·7 in 1865 to 1·68 in 1900, rising again to 1910. Despite the distinct if belated modernisation of agriculture it is hard to believe that such a unique, almost perverse development, could have come about from that source alone.

Outside the pulp mills and the development of fish canning at Stavanger from the 1870s onwards, industrial growth was very modest even if showing some large percentage gains over very small beginnings. The full customs union with Sweden, established in 1873, helped the textile and clothing industries, especially when Sweden returned to protection in 1883 and Norway continued to enjoy free entry. But the preferences were terminated in 1897 and Norway responded with a mildly protective tariff which may have given assistance to some local industries. But they remained minute in size. In 1909, for example, the whole textile and clothing industry employed only 11,000 workers. But to some extent Norway was able to enjoy a kind of autonomous industrial growth similar to that experienced in Denmark, as a result of the urban expansion in the 1890s in particular. But the most vital industrial changes were yet to come. As we shall see, they depended heavily on foreign capital. From 1894 onwards the Norwegian government began to borrow almost annually in Paris to finance construction projects such as the costly Oslo–Bergen line. Private capital entered to provide money for the establishment of a central bank in 1899 but above all it went into direct industrial investment. For the two decades before 1914 capital imports were 5 per cent of Gross Domestic Product and just over one third of Gross Domestic Capital Formation, a high figure for such an extended period of time.

One spectacular new development was the whaling industry of the Antarctic. The foundations were laid in 1865 when Svend Foyn invented a new method of harpooning, but for long growth was inhibited by a lack of demand for whale oil. Soon after 1900, however, whale oil, along with vegetable oils, began more and more to replace animal fats in the manufacture of soap and to a lesser extent, so far as whale oil was concerned, in the making of margarine. This development derived partly from a desire by the users to free themselves from dependence on supplies from the Chicago meat packers and also from the development of a process to turn liquid oils into solid fats on a commercial basis. The production of whale oil rose from 75,000 barrels in 1906 to 600,000 in 1911 and sixty Norwegian companies produced two-thirds of the world's output.

But infinitely more significant was the break-through arising out of the development of hydroelectric power. Once the basic technology had been established in Europe and the United States, her abundant water resources and high falls allowed Norway to produce power at remarkably low cost. Two water turbine power stations had been constructed by British and German firms by 1900 but the full utilisation of Norway's power possibilities came through the development of electro-chemical and electro-metallurgical processes for which cheap power was absolutely vital. The first big electrolytic works was the Kellner Partington Paper Company which started making sodium hydrochloride for bleaching paper in 1896. More important, in the last decade of the nineteenth century widespread fear arose that the Chilean saltpetre deposits, the world's main source of artificial fertiliser, would become exhausted within a relatively short time especially as consumption was bounding upwards. The current price was not rising for output was expanding steadily, but the long term prospects were gloomy. So scientists and engineers began to look for alternative sources of nitrogen. The first process by which the nitrogen of the air was converted into useful compounds on a large scale was the direct combination of nitrogen and oxygen in the electric arc. The reaction had been demonstrated by Cavendish as long ago as 1784 but it only became a realistic commercial prospect with the coming of cheap hydro-electric power. Experiments were first made at Niagara but it was the combination of the experimental work and the engineering skills of two Norwegians, Professor Birkeland and Sam Eyde that produced the world's first successful electric arc plant. At the high temperature of the arc nitrogen in the air was burnt by oxygen to form nitric oxide and from this diluted nitric acid was produced. The acid was then run into granite tanks filled with broken limestone and calcium nitrate produced – known as Norge Saltpetre. Such a process was ideally suited to Norwegian conditions; it required huge power supplies and only two raw materials – limestone and water – which were readily available in Norway.

Eyde began work in 1903 and in the next year Stockholms Enskilda Bank, supported later by an international group led by the French Banque des Pays-Bas, provided the necessary finance and this led to the formation of Norsk Hydro in 1905. There were fears in Norway of foreign control over the waterfalls and a law was passed to prevent further alienation but Eyde persuaded the government to make an exception for Norsk Hydro and further money came from Paris and from the Bavarian chemical firm, Badische-Anilin-und-Soda-Fabrik. However, B.A.S.F. left the group in 1911 to develop an alternative process and put Norsk Hydro in serious financial straits.

Nevertheless though spectacular in conception, the arc process was never really very economical. Meantime, cheap electric power was already being used for the production of calcium carbide, employed initially in the manufacture of acetylene gas, through a process, discovered by the French chemist Henri Moissan in 1892, involving heating a mass of line and coke at a temperature of 3,000 °C. The first Norwegian carbide plant started operations in 1899, but with the development of electric lighting, demand for the gas and so for carbide began to fall off. However, a number of German firms were already experimenting with processes whereby calcium carbide took up nitrogen at high temperatures to form calcium cyanamide. The first commercial plant was opened in Germany in 1904 and in 1908 manufacture commenced at Odda in Norway with the help of another international financing operation involving Stockholm's Enskilda Bank. The technology was simple and the investment low compared with the arc process and to 1914 it was the main source of synthetic nitrogen. By 1910

Norway was producing 20 per cent of the world's demand for carbide. Calcium cyanamide could be used as a fertiliser directly or to give ammonia fixed as ammonium sulphate. Cyanamide from Odda was also used at Norsk Hydro to produce ammonium nitrate (instead of calcium nitrate) which was used for fertilisers and explosives.

The only significant imported raw material for all these processes was the coke imported for the carbide manufacture. The same was not true of the next major development, the manufacture of aluminium. In 1906 the British Aluminium Company began to produce the metal by the use of an electrolytic process on the basis of imported ore and further plants were opened in the next few years. An electric steel smelting plant was set up in 1909 and small scale production of pure zinc in an electro-thermal plant began using imported spelter, but to 1914 these were relatively minor activities.

All these new industries were highly capital intensive: according to the 1908 census the electro-chemical and metallurgical industries employed 1,830 workers and used 100,000 h.p.: the relatively well-developed pulp industry employed 8,000 workers and 135,000 h.p.: the paper industry employed 3,500 workers and 19,000 h.p. In all these advanced industries the proportion of foreign capital employed was very high. In 1909 it was 80 per cent in mining and in chemicals 85 per cent; in paper manufacture it was 44 per cent, in electric lamps, 47 per cent and in metals 32·5 per cent. These were technically the most advanced and the largest concerns in the country by a considerable margin.

The attraction to foreign capital was simply cheap power: almost all of the output was disposed of outside of Norway and much of it without further processing. This was entirely the case with aluminium and also with the pyrites: much of the calcium carbide was exported for processing overseas – in Germany and Britain above all. Very little of the fertiliser produced was used by Norwegian farmers. In 1913, for example, 32,214 tons of Norges Saltpeter was produced and only 5,500 tons consumed at home. In this sense the exploitation of her major resource, power, to produce raw materials which were mainly processed and used elsewhere, though giving a highly desirable boost to the Norwegian economy, also demonstrated its undeveloped state.

Until this leap forward Norway's growth had been strikingly retarded compared with that in Sweden and Denmark. The absence of any major agricultural change, either in techniques or organisation, until near the end of the century, the failure to break down rural isolation, the inability to respond effectively to changes in world supply and demand patterns for foodstuffs after 1870 were all serious weaknesses. Foreign trade played an extremely vital part in the economy: in the period from 1905–14 exports (including freight earnings) comprised about one-third of Gross Domestic product and again, unlike Sweden and Denmark, over the previous half-century foreign trade had steadily grown faster than production. Yet the staple exports, such as timber and shipping, were by the end of the century hardly booming. The failure of shipping to respond quickly and effectively to technological change was representative of the essential weaknesses of the economy, short of capital, relying on the advantages of cheap labour, moving to the fringes of world trade with old and second-hand equipment. But after 1900 this industry at last began to come to terms with reality, a change which coincided with the first real taste of modernisation that the economy enjoyed over our whole period.

COMPARATIVE GROWTH PATTERNS OF THE SCANDINAVIAN ECONOMIES

From 1870 to the First World War output per head in Norway grew in real terms by 14·2 per cent per decade compared with 24·9 per cent in Sweden and 23·2 per cent in Denmark. The process was not an even one, however. Denmark moved ahead of Sweden between 1885 and 1895 but from then until 1906 the Swedish economy expanded at a rate exceeding that of any of the economies over a decadal period. Output per worker in Danish agriculture rose 76 per cent between 1880–4 and 1900–4 compared with a rise for Swedish agriculture of only 24 per cent. The Swedish lead derived from the much more rapid rise in the proportion of her workers engaged in industry. But when we turn from rates of growth to actual levels of income we are on much more dangerous ground. Gross Domestic Product per head in Denmark in 1911–15 has been calculated to have been almost 10 per cent above that in Sweden, presumably because of the higher productivity of agriculture in Denmark and the fact that this relatively low productivity sector employed only 36 per cent of the workforce compared with 49 per cent in Sweden, thus more than offsetting the fact that Swedish industrial output per head of total population was some 10 per cent higher than in Denmark. Given these figures and the rates of growth over the previous half-century, Danish *per capita* income must have been even more ahead of the Swedish in 1870. It must be emphasised that such comparisons are subject to much error; they say nothing about the distribution of income and ignore the possibility that price levels within each country might vary. More difficult is the measurement of income in Norway. National Income calculations suggest that income per head was as high as that of Sweden in 1911–15 and therefore given the rates of change, higher than that of either Denmark or Sweden in 1870. All that we know of the Norwegian economy in a qualitative sense indicates that this cannot possibly be true. The figures may be complicated by the extremely important role of shipping but it will probably be wiser to ignore the Norwegian comparison in the present state of our knowledge.[10]

All three economies were very dependent on foreign trade: all benefited from the rapid growth of world trade in the late nineteenth century and above all from the rise of income and the liberal free trade policy in Britain. Sweden and Denmark gained an impetus from agrarian reform which transcended its direct impact on agricultural output. From it derived an environment of change and experimentation that meant so much to subsequent growth. Possibly it was this dynamic environment that Norway missed most of all. Norway being the most backward of the three, needed the most positive thrust to induce change and such a thrust failed to materialise until foreign initiative, foreign capital and foreign control over that capital brought the first major technological breakthroughs after 1900. In that sense Norway was not dissimilar to the 'enclave' type of economy found today in Africa and elsewhere. But the importance of foreign trade in all three economies must not be stressed to the neglect of the powerful domestic forces making for growth both on the demand and the supply side. Such forces include the influence of a growing population on urban growth, and the building of railways, which were by no means always geared to encouraging exports. Apart from those industries linked with the exploitation of natural resources, industrial development in all three was unspectacular by European standards. By this is meant not its relative importance to each economy but the significance of each industry in an international context. By that measure only Burmeisters could compare with other European firms. The Swedish electrical industry had nothing as significant as Brown Boveri or Oerlikon in Switzerland. The Swedish locomotive makers were not exporters as those in Austria and Belgium and

---

[10] See generally Ö Johansson, *The Gross Domestic Product of Sweden* (Stockholm, 1967), especially Tables 58 and 60; K. Bjerke, 'The National Product of Denmark, 1870–1952' in *Income and Wealth*, series V (1955), and Statistisk Sentralbyrå, *Trends in Norwegian Economy, 1865–1960* (1966).

Italy were, there were no textile specialities for export, no firm had the reputation for supreme workmanship like Carel in Belgium or Tosi in Italy. This is not to minimise what did take place, but to place it in its context.

Growth was much assisted by the ease with which all were able to borrow overseas – Sweden over 9,000 Kr after 1860, Denmark about 900m Kr mainly after 1880 and Norway 1,100m Kr in the last two decades to 1914. There were no political strings. The excellent record of financial rectitude of all countries enabled them to borrow at favourable rates and of course for private investment there were the usual attractions of mining and the hydroelectric developments.

Norway and Sweden above all were small, sparsely population countries: Denmark small but less sparsely peopled. Does their history bear out the view that population density and size go far to explain the division of a country's exports between manufactured and other goods? Small countries may have comparative disadvantages in world trade because of scale effects in both production and marketing and also through the lack of external economies, that is to say the benefits one industry enjoys from the simultaneous existence of others nearby. Or it may be that the comparative disadvantage of small, sparsely populated countries in manufacturing is just the reverse side of their superior *per capita* natural resources. The argument fits well the pattern of Norwegian growth and that of Sweden too, but within this framework one must note that there were clear differences in the ability of different sectors to carve out specialised areas of manufacture and of processing. Small size itself had advantages: it was easier for Sweden to insert herself into limited areas of world engineering than it was for Britain to transform whole sectors of the same industry. What would Denmark have done had she been twice as big? Already by 1914 she had taken half of the only market for butter that tariffs left available to her. She would have had to search out other opportunities but it is not clear that in these circumstances bigger size would have been an advantage to her.

It has also been argued that small nations because of their greater homogeneity and closer ties may find it easier to make the social adjustments necessary to take advantage of the potentialities offered by new technologies. It is not always so as the case of the linen industry in Flanders shows (see p. 448). Some such nations are sometimes deeply split, but for Denmark and Sweden the point may have some relevance. The ability of Denmark to face the grave problems of the second half of the nineteenth century after the surrender of Schleswig Holstein is surely a positive example.

SUGGESTED READING

The literature on Scandinavian economic history is, in general, very limited. Above all, the student should work through the issues of the *Scandinavian Economic History Review*, and also, if possible, those of a less well known but high quality journal, *Economy and History*. As for general works the most famous – and deservedly so – is ELI HECKSCHER *An Economic History of Sweden* (Cambridge, Mass., 1956). The original Swedish work, in three volumes, can be used by those without a knowledge of the language for its excellent tables and diagrams. A short but excellent book is L. JORBERG, *The Industrial Revolution in Scandinavia*, Fontana Economic History of Europe, vol. 4 (London, 1970). The bibliography gives some indication of the most important works in the Scandinavian languages and in German. In his book *The Possibilities of Economic Progress* (Cambridge, 1954) A. J. YOUNGSON has two excellent chapters on Sweden and Denmark in the nineteenth century. On Norway there is S. LIEBERMAN, *The Industrialization of Norway 1800–1920* (Oslo, 1970). In the proceedings of the *First International Economic History Conference* (Stockholm, 1958), there are papers of a general nature on Scandinavian economic history: E. BULL, 'Industrialisation as a factor in economic growth' on Norway; K. GLÅMANN, 'Industrialisation as a factor in economic growth in Denmark since 1700', and K. HILDEBRAND, 'Sweden'. Some points of interest will be found in P. DRACHMANN, *The Industrial Development and Commercial Policies in the Three Scandinavian Countries* (Oxford, 1915).

On Danish agricultural development there is F. SKRUBBELTRANG, *Agricultural Development and Rural Reform in Denmark*, Agricultural Studies, No. 22, FAO (Rome, 1953) E. JENSEN, *Danish Agriculture. Its Economic Development* (Copenhagen, 1937), H. FABER, *Co-operation in Danish Agriculture* (London, 1931), and P. DOSSING, *Population Changes in Danish Agriculture 1870–1953*, U.N. World Population Conference, vol. V (New York, 1954). The Danish Folk High Schools are discussed in two books with just that title by F. SKRUBBELTRANG (Copenhagen, 1947) and T. RØRDAM (Copenhagen, 1965). For Danish industrial development the only book is S. A. HANSEN, *Early Industrialisation in Denmark* (Copenhagen, 1970). The growth of output is measured by K. BJERKE, 'National Product of Denmark, 1870–1952' in *Income and Wealth*, series V (London, 1955) edited by S. KUZNETS, though with N. USSING he published in 1958 *Studier over Danmarks Nationalprodukt 1870–1950* (Copenhagen, 1958). There is an interesting study of the Danish terms of trade by A. ØLGAARD in Chapter 12 of his *Growth, Productivity and Relative Prices* (Copenhagen, 1966).

Outside the journals there is little on Swedish agriculture other than the book by G. FRIDLIZIUS, *Swedish Corn Exports in the Free Trade Era* (Lund, 1957). E. SÖDERLUND's splendid book *Swedish Timber Exports 1850–1950* (Stockholm, 1952) says much that is relevant to many different aspects of development. As for industry there is A. MONTGOMERY, *The*

Rise of Modern Industry in Sweden (Stockholm, 1939) and L. JORBERG, *Growth and Fluctuations in Swedish Industry 1869–1912* (Lund, 1961). O. J. GASSLANDER'S *History of Stockholms Enskilda Bank* (Stockholm, 1962) shows the contribution of the bank to industrial development as well as many other interesting aspects, such as international investment, which is dealt with in more general terms in E. E. FLEETWOOD, *Sweden's Capital Imports and Exports* (Geneva, 1947). Growth overall is measured in Ö. JOHANSSON, *The Gross Domestic Product of Sweden and its Composition 1861–1955* (Stockholm, 1967).

As for Norway there is very little that can be added. M. DRAKE, *Population and Society in Norway 1735–1865* (Cambridge, 1967) contributes much that is new on rural society for English readers. A popular description of industry will be found in O. J. ADAMSON, *Industries of Norway* (Oslo, 1952), and the growth of national income is measured in the Norwegian Central Bureau of Statistics publication *Trends in Norwegian Economy 1865–1960* (Oslo, 1966).

A great deal can be learned from the extensive literature on population growth and emigration which has already been reviewed in Chapter 2.

Index